ZAGAT
2015

New York City
Restaurants

D0169886

EDITORS
Curt Gathje and Carol Diuguid

COORDINATOR
Larry Cohn

Published and distributed by
Zagat Survey, LLC
76 Ninth Avenue
New York, NY 10011
feedback@zagat.com
www.zagat.com

ACKNOWLEDGMENTS

First and foremost, we thank the thousands of people who participated in this survey – they are the real authors of this guide.

We also thank Bernard Onken and Karen Hudes, as well as the following members of our staff: Aynsley Karps (editor), Bill Corsello (editor), Brian Albert, Maryanne Bertollo, Danielle Borovoy, Reni Chin, John Deiner, Kelly Dobkin, Michael Endelman, Brian Farnham, Jeff Freier, Michelle Golden, Randi Gollin, Justin Hartung, Marc Henson, Alex Horowitz, Anna Hyclak, Ryutaro Ishikane, Cynthia Kilian, Michele Laudig, Mike Liao, Caitlin Miehl, Molly Moker, James Mulcahy, Polina Paley, Josh Rogers, Emil Ross, Emily Rothschild, Rebecca Salois, Albry Smither, Amanda Spurlock, Chris Walsh, Art Yagci, Yoji Yamaguchi, Sharon Yates, Anna Zappia and Kyle Zolner.

ABOUT ZAGAT

In 1979, we asked friends to rate and review restaurants purely for fun. The term "user-generated content" had yet to be coined. That hobby grew into Zagat Survey; 36 years later, we have loyal surveyors around the globe and have covered restaurants, hotels, nightlife and more. Along the way, we evolved from being a print publisher to a digital content provider. You can find us on zagat.com and across the Google products you use every day.

The reviews in this guide are based on public opinion surveys. The ratings reflect the average scores given by the survey participants who voted on each establishment, while the text is based on quotes from, or paraphrasings of, the surveyors' comments. Ratings and reviews have been updated throughout this edition based on our most recent survey results. Phone numbers, addresses and other factual data were correct to the best of our knowledge when published in this guide.

JOIN IN

To improve our guides, we solicit your comments – positive or negative; it's vital that we hear your opinions. Just contact us at **nina-tim@zagat.com**

CONTENTS

WINNERS & TRENDS

TOP FOOD & TOP SERVICE

Le Bernardin: For the sixth year running, chef Eric Ripert's Midtown mecca for French-accented seafood ranks No. 1 for Food, and it also nabs the top spot for Service.

TOP DECOR

Daniel: The elegant neo-classical interior of Daniel Boulud's Upper East Side French refuge places first for Decor.

TOP NEWCOMER

Sushi Nakazawa: Daisuke Nakazawa, protégé of the renowned Jiro Ono, wins top newcomer honors for his West Village sushi destination.

MOST POPULAR

Gramercy Tavern: Danny Meyer's American institution in the Flatiron is voted NYC's favorite restaurant, a ranking it has won six times since it opened in 1994.

TOPS BY SPECIALTY

Top BBQ | **Mighty Quinn's**
Top Coffee | **La Colombe**
Top Dim Sum | **RedFarm**
Top Ice Cream | **Ample Hills**
Top Lobster Roll | **Pearl Oyster Bar**
Top Pizza | **Paulie Gee's**
Top Ramen | **Chuko**
Top Sandwich | **Il Bambino**

OUTER-BOROUGH CHAMPS

Brooklyn | **St. Anselm**
Queens | **Sripraphai**
Bronx | **Roberto**
Staten Island | **Denino's Pizzeria**

Top three most-searched-for food items on Google:
Pizza | Chicken | Cake

WINNERS & TRENDS

On plates all over town these days: **Duck,** from David Waltuck's mixed grill at **Élan** to the sausage with pickled ramps and cherries at the **NoMad Bar,** not to mention the debut of **RedFarm** spin-off **Decoy,** solely serving prix fixe Peking duck feasts . . . **Pricey Roast Chicken for Two,** from **Rotisserie Georgette**'s $72 *poule de luxe*, **Dover**'s $65 version (with legs confited in, yes, duck fat) and **M. Wells Steakhouse**'s $70 showstopper . . . **Sea Urchin,** from the Bucatini with Smoked Uni at **All'onda** to the Uni Butter Toast at **Navy** . . . **Fancy Toasts,** including the Peekytoe Crab and Avocado at **East Pole** and Burrata-Tuna at **Bergen Hill** . . . **Funky Butters,** like the Smoked Sardines and Dulse Butter at **French Louie** and the Porgy with Bonito Butter at **The Gorbals.**

Almanac: Galen Zamarra's replacement for Mas (La Grillade)
Amada: Battery Park City outpost of Jose Garces' Philly Spaniard
Beekman Hotel: Eateries by Tom Colicchio and Keith McNally
Cosme: Flatiron Mexican from Enrique Olvera, his first NYC foray
Dirt Candy: The veggie champ reopens in roomy, new LES digs
Maritime Hotel: Eateries by Mario Batali and Joe Bastianich
Mission Chinese: Danny Bowien's LES hit finally reopens
Tijuana Picnic: Mexican–SE Asian hybrid from Acme team
Via Carota: Village Italian from the Buvette and I Sodi chefs

For Zagat's first-ever burger survey, we rated NYC's patties on their Flavor, Value and Ingredients. Here are the top 10, based on Overall score.

	Overall	Flavor	Value	Ingredients
Peter Luger | *Luger-Burger*	24	26	18	26
Burger Joint | *Cheeseburger*	23	24	23	22
Minetta Tavern | *Black Label*	22	26	15	26
B&B Winepub | *Bash Style*	22	24	17	24
Spotted Pig | *Roquefort Burger*	22	24	16	25
Umami Burger | *Original*	22	24	17	23
DuMont Burger | *DuMont Burger*	21	23	18	23
Shake Shack | *ShackBurger*	21	22	20	21
Keens | *Hamburger*	21	23	16	23
J.G. Melon | *Cheeseburger*	20	22	19	20

KEY NEWCOMERS

Our editors' picks among this year's arrivals (see map at the back of this book; full newcomers list on p. 321).

(see map at the back of this book; full newcomers list on p. 321)

CHELSEA / HELL'S KITCHEN

Barchetta | David Pasternack's refined Italian seafood in Chelsea
Bodega Negra | Hopping Mexican in the Dream Downtown Hotel
Empire Diner | Iconic diner reimagined by Amanda Freitag
Gotham West Market | Food hall with name-brand purveyors
Monarch Room | Swanky retro-style American with a busy bar
Toro | Big, sceney offshoot of Boston's Barcelona-style tapas fave

EAST VILLAGE / LES

Bar Primi | Bowery pasta specialist from Andrew Carmellini
Contra | Sophisticated New American tasting menus at bargain rates
Dirty French | France's classic cuisine gets the Torrisi treatment
Ivan Ramen | Ramen legend Ivan Orkin hits the Lower East Side
Mission Cantina | Mexican from Mission Chinese's Danny Bowien
Narcissa | John Fraser's stylish, veggie-centric standout
Root & Bone | Upscale Southern eats and cocktails
Russ & Daughters Cafe | The LES's queen of lox spawns a cafe
Somtum Der | Vibrant Bangkok import cooking Isan Thai dishes

FLATIRON / UNION SQUARE

Élan | David Waltuck's American follow-up to Chanterelle
The Gander | Jesse Schenker's innovative American Recette sequel
Marta | Pizzeria/family-style Italian from Danny Meyer & Nick Anderer
NoMad Bar | Offshoot of The NoMad with haute cocktails & bar bites
Park Avenue | More casual reboot of the erstwhile Uptown hit
The Pavilion | Open-air American in the middle of Union Square

GREENWICH VILLAGE / WEST VILLAGE

All'onda | Japanese-accented Venetian with interesting wines
Bar Bolonat | Chef Einat Admony's upscale modern Israeli
The Clam | Upscale shore fare from the Market Table chef
Claudette | Sceney Provençal near Washington Square
Decoy | Ed Schoenfeld's Peking duck specialist below RedFarm
Han Dynasty | Seriously spicy Sichuan, imported from Philly
Margaux | All-day Parisian scene in the Marlton Hotel
Piora | Snug boîte for ambitious American cuisine
Sushi Nakazawa | Masterful sushi from a Jiro Ono protégé

KEY NEWCOMERS

SOHO / NOHO / NOLITA / LITTLE ITALY

Bacchanal | Bowery American with a massive wine list

Cherche Midi | Keith McNally French bistro on the Bowery

Gato | Bobby Flay supplies Spanish-Mediterranean in NoHo

Ladurée | Luxe French patisserie/eatery from Paris' macaron icon

Navy | Hip SoHo nook for cocktails and seafood

TRIBECA / BATTERY PARK CITY

American Cut | Marc Forgione steakhouse in the heart of TriBeCa

Bâtard | Prix fixe New American dining from Drew Nieporent

El Vez | Stephen Starr's over-the-top Mexican in Battery Park City

Hudson Eats | Sprawling, high-end food hall in Brookfield Place

Racines | Paris wine bar import specializing in natural vintages

Telepan Local | Locavore chef Bill Telepan sets up in TriBeCa

UPTOWN / MIDTOWN

Beautique | Glitzy underground American near The Plaza

East Pole | British-accented American from the Fat Radish team

Kingside | Midtown hotel American with a bustling bar scene

Ristorante Morini | Buttoned-up UES Italian from Michael White

Rotisserie Georgette | French-style spit-roasting for refined UESers

Tavern on the Green | A Central Park American legend reborn

Writing Room | Bookish American in the old Elaine's space

BROOKLYN / QUEENS

Bergen Hill | Small-plate seafood in tiny Carroll Gardens digs

Berg'n | Crown Heights food hall from the Smorgasburg folks

Cherry Izakaya | Williamsburg sibling of swanky Chelsea Japanese

Dover | Carroll Gardens American spun off from Battersby

French Louie | Boerum Hill French via Buttermilk Channel vets

The Gorbals | Ilan Hall's LA-born Scottish-Jewish concept

Humboldt & Jackson | All-American food & drink in Williamsburg

Marco's | Italian fine-dining offspring of nearby Franny's

M. Wells Steakhouse | Elevated surf 'n' turf in an LIC ex-body shop

The Runner | Rustic Americana and craft pours in Clinton Hill

Saul | Saul Bolton's flagship relocated to the Brooklyn Museum

Shalom Japan | Jewish-Japanese mash-up in Williamsburg

MOST POPULAR

This list is plotted on the map at the back of this book.

1. **Gramercy Tavern** | *American*
2. **Le Bernardin** | *French/Seafood*
3. **5 Napkin Burger** | *Burgers*
4. **Shake Shack** | *Burgers*
5. **Peter Luger** | *Steak*
6. **Union Square Cafe** | *American*
7. **ABC Kitchen** | *American*
8. **Gotham Bar & Grill** | *American*
9. **Jean-Georges** | *French*
10. **Bouley** | *French*
11. **Daniel** | *French*
12. **Rosa Mexicano** | *Mexican*
13. **21 Club** | *American*
14. **2nd Ave Deli** | *Deli/Kosher*
15. **Atlantic Grill** | *Seafood*
16. **Marea** | *Italian/Seafood*
17. **Babbo** | *Italian*
18. **Katz's Deli** | *Deli*
19. **Capital Grille** | *Steak*
20. **The Palm** | *Steak*
21. **La Grenouille** | *French*
22. **Balthazar** | *French*
23. **Eleven Madison Park** | *Amer.*
24. **Del Posto** | *Italian*
25. **Becco** | *Italian*
26. **Carmine's** | *Italian*
27. **Del Frisco's** | *Steak*
28. **Per Se** | *American/French*
29. **Jean-Georges' Nougatine** | *Fr.*
30. **Telepan** | *American*
31. **BareBurger** | *Burgers*
32. **Eataly** | *Food Market/Italian*
33. **Four Seasons** | *American*
34. **The Modern*** | *Amer./French*
35. **Blue Water Grill** | *Seafood*
36. **Café Boulud** | *French*
37. **Nobu** | *Japanese*
38. **Aquagrill** | *Seafood*
39. **Bar Boulud*** | *French*
40. **Il Mulino** | *Italian*
41. **A Voce** | *Italian*
42. **Boulud Sud** | *Mediterranean*
43. **Ai Fiori** | *Italian*
44. **Fig & Olive** | *Mediterranean*
45. **Carnegie Deli** | *Deli*
46. **Keens** | *Steak*
47. **Wolfgang's** | *Steak*
48. **Bobby Van's** | *Steak*
49. **Lincoln** | *Italian*
50. **Dinosaur** | *BBQ*

* Indicates a tie with restaurant above

TOP FOOD

WINNERS

29	**Le Bernardin** | *French/Seafood*	27	**Little Owl** | *American/Med.*
29	**Bouley** | *French*	27	**Pearl Oyster Bar** | *Seafood*
28	**Jean-Georges** | *French*	27	**Milos** | *Greek/Seafood*
28	**Gotham Bar & Grill** | *American*	27	**Dovetail** | *American*
28	**Eleven Madison Park** | *Amer.*	27	**Aquagrill** | *Seafood*
28	**Daniel** | *French*	26	**Trattoria L'incontro** | *Ital.*
28	**Sushi Yasuda** | *Japanese*	26	**Café Boulud** | *French*
28	**Gramercy Tavern** | *American*	26	**Tamarind** | *Indian*
28	**Peter Luger** | *Steak*	26	**Del Posto** | *Italian*
28	**La Grenouille** | *French*	26	**Taverna Kyclades** | *Greek*
28	**Annisa** | *American*	26	**Barbuto** | *Italian*
28	**Sea Fire Grill** | *Seafood*	26	**Blue Hill** | *American*
27	**Per Se** | *American/French*	26	**Scalini Fedeli** | *Italian*
27	**Marea** | *Italian/Seafood*	26	**Keens** | *Steak*
27	**Benjamin Steak House** | *Steak*	26	**Colicchio & Sons** | *Amer.*
27	**Tocqueville** | *Amer./French*	26	**Craft** | *American*
27	**Nobu** | *Japanese*	26	**Telepan** | *American*
27	**Union Square Cafe** | *American*	26	**River Café** | *American*
27	**Mas (Farmhouse)** | *American*	26	**Four Seasons** | *American*
27	**Jean-Georges' Nougatine** | *Fr.*	26	**Morimoto** | *Japanese*

TOPS BY CUISINE

AMERICAN

28	**Gotham Bar & Grill**
28	**Eleven Madison Park**
28	**Gramercy Tavern**
28	**St. Anselm**
28	**Annisa**
27	**Per Se**
27	**The Grocery**
27	**Momofuku Ko**
27	**Juni**
27	**Tocqueville**
27	**Battersby**
27	**Union Square Cafe**

ASIAN

26	**Asiate**
25	**Talde**
25	**Buddakan**
24	**Pig and Khao**
24	**Spice Market**
23	**Tao**
23	**China Grill**
22	**Wild Ginger**

AUSTRIAN/SWISS/GERMAN

25	**Wallsé**
24	**Seäsonal**
23	**Zum Stammtisch**
22	**Café Sabarsky/Fledermaus**
22	**Zum Schneider**
22	**Blaue Gans**
21	**Heidelberg**
21	**Mont Blanc**

Ratings are based on a 30-point scale, rounded to the nearest whole number; rankings are determined using the full non-rounded scores. These lists exclude coffee and dessert specialists, and places with low votes, unless otherwise indicated.

TOPS BY CUISINE

CARIBBEAN

24 **Ali's Roti**
24 **Sofrito**
24 **Victor's**
24 **Cuba**
23 **Negril**
23 **Sazon**
23 **Amor Cubano**
22 **Havana Alma de Cuba**

CHINESE

25 **RedFarm**
25 **Wu Liang Ye**
24 **Pacificana**
24 **Wa Jeal**
24 **Shun Lee Palace**
24 **Excellent Dumpling House**
23 **Peking Duck House**
23 **Szechuan Gourmet**

FRENCH

29 **Le Bernardin**
29 **Bouley**
28 **Jean-Georges**
28 **Daniel**
28 **Chef's Table at Brooklyn Fare**
28 **La Grenouille**
26 **Café Boulud**
25 **The Elm**

FRENCH BISTRO

24 **Jeanne & Gaston**
24 **Le Gigot**
24 **db Bistro Moderne**
24 **Raoul's**
24 **Buvette**
24 **JoJo**
24 **Bar Boulud**
23 **Le Parisien**

GREEK

27 **Milos**
26 **Taverna Kyclades**

26 **Elias Corner**
26 **Pylos**
25 **Avra**
24 **MP Taverna**
24 **Periyali**
24 **Thalassa**

INDIAN

26 **Tamarind**
25 **Amma**
24 **Junoon**
24 **Dhaba**
24 **Tulsi**
23 **Dawat**
23 **Chola**
23 **Indus Valley**

ITALIAN

27 **Marea**
27 **Roberto**
26 **Trattoria L'incontro**
26 **Del Posto**
26 **Barbuto**
26 **Scalini Fedeli**
26 **Al Di La**
26 **Ristorante Morini**
26 **Babbo**
26 **Ai Fiori**
26 **L'Artusi**
26 **Gennaro**

JAPANESE/SUSHI

28 **Sushi Yasuda**
27 **Takashi**
27 **Ushiwakamaru**
27 **Nobu**
27 **Zenkichi**
27 **Sushi Nakazawa**
27 **Kyo Ya**
26 **Soto**
26 **Morimoto**
26 **Brushstroke**

TOP FOOD

TOP FOOD

TOPS BY CUISINE

25 **El Quinto Pino**
25 **Toro**
25 **Beso**
24 **Sevilla**
24 **Casa Mono**
24 **Tertulia**

STEAKHOUSES

28 **Peter Luger**
27 **Benjamin Steak House**
26 **Keens**
26 **Porter House NY**
26 **Quality Meats**
25 **Maloney & Porcelli**
25 **Sparks**
25 **BLT Prime**
25 **Old Homestead**
25 **Wolfgang's**
25 **Smith & Wollensky**
25 **Del Frisco's**

THAI

27 **Sripraphai**
26 **Pure Thai Cookhouse**
25 **Uncle Boons**

25 **Ayada**
24 **Pok Pok Ny**
24 **Joya**
23 **Topaz**
23 **Thai Market**

TURKISH

24 **Uskudar**
24 **Taci's Beyti**
23 **Sahara**
23 **Turkish Cuisine**
23 **Turkish Kitchen**
22 **Sip Sak**
22 **Akdeniz**
22 **Beyoglu**

VIETNAMESE

24 **Nha Trang**
23 **Nightingale 9** ▽
23 **Le Colonial**
22 **Omai**
21 **Pho Bang**
21 **Indochine**
21 **Bo-Ky**
21 **Hanco's**

TOPS BY SPECIALTY

BAKERIES

24 **Ladurée**
24 **Balthazar**
23 **ChikaLicious Dessert Club**
23 **Bouchon Bakery**
23 **Ferrara**
22 **Maison Kayser**
22 **Runner & Stone** ▽
22 **City Bakery**

BARBECUE

26 **Mighty Quinn's**
26 **Fette Sau**
24 **BrisketTown**

23 **Hill Country**
23 **Smoke Joint**
23 **Dinosaur BBQ**
22 **Daisy May's**
21 **Blue Smoke**

BURGER JOINTS

23 **Burger Joint**
23 **Black Iron Burger**
23 **Umami Burger**
22 **Corner Bistro**
22 **67 Burger**
22 **Bonnie's Grill**
21 **Burger Bistro**
21 **BareBurger**

TOP FOOD

CHICKEN

22 Pio Pio
21 Coco Roco
21 Flor de Mayo
21 BonChon
20 Malecon
20 Hill Country Chicken
20 Kyochon
19 Blue Ribbon Fried Chicken

COFFEE

24 La Colombe
23 Blue Bottle
23 Stumptown
22 Toby's Estate ▽
21 Queens Kickshaw
21 Joe
21 Fika
21 Café Grumpy

DELIS

25 Katz's Delicatessen
24 Mill Basin Deli
24 Ben's Best
24 B & H Dairy
24 Barney Greengrass
23 Carnegie Deli
23 2nd Ave Deli
23 Sarge's

DESSERT
(see also Bakeries, Ice Cream)

24 Chocolate Room
23 ChikaLicious Dessert Bar
22 Café Sabarsky/Fledermaus
22 Sweet Revenge ▽
22 Omonia Cafe
20 Cafe Lalo
19 Junior's
19 Serendipity 3

DIM SUM

25 RedFarm
22 Golden Unicorn
22 Cafe Evergreen
22 Buddha Bodai
21 Oriental Garden
21 Nom Wah Tea Parlor
21 Jing Fong
21 Dim Sum Go Go

DUMPLINGS

24 Excellent Dumpling
23 Prosperity Dumpling
23 Mandoo Bar
22 456 Shanghai
22 Joe's Shanghai
22 Nice Green Bo
19 Vanessa's Dumpling
-- Mimi Cheng's

GLUTEN-FREE OPTIONS

26 Del Posto
26 Caracas
25 Alta
25 Rubirosa
24 Amali
24 Candle 79
23 Rosa Mexicano
22 Bistango

ICE CREAM

27 Ample Hills Creamery
25 The Lemon Ice King
25 Il Laboratorio
25 Amorino
25 Grom
24 Ralph's Famous
24 Eddie's Sweet Shop
24 Cones

KOSHER

25 Azuri Cafe
24 Mill Basin Deli

TOP FOOD

24 **Ben's Best**
24 **Prime Grill**
23 **Peacefood Café**
23 **Abigael's**
23 **2nd Ave Deli**
22 **Pastrami Queen**

LOBSTER ROLLS

27 **Pearl Oyster Bar**
25 **Mary's Fish Camp**
24 **Red Hook Lobster Pound**
24 **Luke's Lobster**
24 **Cull & Pistol**
24 **Ed's Lobster Bar**
22 **Mermaid Inn**
21 **John Dory**

LOCAVORE

27 **Union Square Cafe**
27 **Narcissa**
26 **Blue Hill**
26 **Roberta's**
25 **Riverpark**
24 **Marco's**
23 **Telepan Local**
21 **Smorgas Chef**

NEWCOMERS

27 **Sushi Nakazawa**
27 **Narcissa**
27 **Dover**
26 **Piora**
26 **Ristorante Morini**
25 **Gotham West Market**
25 **Toro**
24 **Ladurée**

PIZZA

27 **Paulie Gee's**
27 **Lucali**
26 **Juliana's**
26 **Totonno's***
26 **Roberta's**
26 **Denino's**
25 **Franny's**
25 **Di Fara**

QUICK BITES

26 **Caracas To Go**
25 **Azuri Cafe**
25 **Taïm**
24 **Pommes Frites**
24 **Empanada Mama**
23 **Mamoun's**
23 **Crif Dogs**
22 **Kati Roll Co.**

RAW BARS

27 **Pearl Oyster Bar**
27 **Aquagrill**
25 **Esca**
25 **BLT Fish**
25 **Oceana**
24 **Blue Ribbon**
24 **Lure Fishbar**
24 **Cull & Pistol**

SANDWICHES
(see also Delis)

25 **Il Bambino**
25 **Banh Mi Saigon**
24 **Parm**
24 **Defonte's**
24 **Taboonette**
23 **Brennan & Carr**
23 **Num Pang**
23 **Press 195**

SMALL PLATES
(see also Spanish/Tapas)

28 **Graffiti** *(Eclectic)*
27 **Zenkichi** *(Japanese)*
26 **Degustation** *(Fr./Spanish)*
26 **Mehtaphor** *(Eclectic)*
26 **Traif** *(Eclectic)*
25 **Neta** *(Japanese)*

TOP FOOD

TOPS BY SPECIALTY

25 **Danji** *(Korean)*
25 **Estela** *(Med.)*

TACO JOINTS

25 **Tacombi at Fonda Nolita** ▽
23 **Toloache Taqueria**
23 **La Esquina**
22 **Otto's Tacos** ▽
22 **Calexico**
22 **Tres Carnes**
21 **Oaxaca**

20 **Dos Toros**

VEGETARIAN

26 **Hangawi**
25 **Taïm**
24 **Pure Food & Wine**
24 **Candle 79**
23 **Peacefood Café**
23 **Angelica Kitchen**
23 **Candle Cafe**
23 **V-Note**

TOPS BY LOCATION: MANHATTAN

CHELSEA

26 **Del Posto**
26 **Colicchio & Sons**
26 **Morimoto**
26 **Txikito**
25 **Scarpetta**
25 **El Quinto Pino**
25 **Old Homestead**
25 **Toro**

CHINATOWN

24 **Nha Trang**
24 **Excellent Dumpling House**
23 **Peking Duck House**
23 **Xi'an Famous Foods**
23 **Great NY Noodle Town**
22 **Golden Unicorn**
22 **456 Shanghai Cuisine**
22 **Joe's Shanghai**

EAST 40s

28 **Sushi Yasuda**
28 **Sea Fire Grill**
27 **Benjamin Steak House**
25 **Pietro's**
25 **Sparks**
25 **Avra**

25 **Smith & Wollensky**
25 **Hatsuhana**

EAST 50s

28 **La Grenouille**
26 **Four Seasons**
26 **Aquavit**
25 **Amma**
25 **Maloney & Porcelli**
25 **Felidia**
25 **Wolfgang's Steakhouse**
25 **DeGrezia**

EAST 60s

28 **Daniel**
25 **Tiella**
25 **Il Mulino Uptown**
25 **Sushi Seki**
24 **Rotisserie Georgette**
24 **Amali**
24 **David Burke Fishtail**
24 **Scalinatella**

EAST 70s

26 **Café Boulud**
26 **Sushi of Gari**
26 **Tanoshi Sushi/Bento**

TOP FOOD

25 **Sasabune**
25 **Lusardi's**
25 **Caravaggio**
25 **Sojourn**
24 **Il Ristorante Rosi**

EAST 80s

26 **Ristorante Morini**
24 **Elio's**
24 **Sandro's**
24 **Wa Jeal**
24 **Luke's Lobster**
24 **Flex Mussels**
23 **Toloache**
23 **Crown**

EAST 90s / EAST HARLEM

25 **Sfoglia**
23 **Nick's**
23 **Table d'Hôte**
23 **Paola's**
23 **Amor Cubano**
22 **Pio Pio**
22 **El Paso**
22 **Moustache**

EAST VILLAGE

28 **Graffiti**
27 **Momofuku Ko**
27 **Narcissa**
26 **Kyo Ya**
26 **Taverna Kyclades**
26 **Degustation**
26 **Mighty Quinn's Barbecue**
26 **Pylos**

FINANCIAL DISTRICT

24 **Morton's**
24 **Luke's Lobster**
24 **Capital Grille**
24 **Adrienne's Pizzabar**
23 **Toloache Taqueria**
23 **Delmonico's**

23 **Bobby Van's**
22 **Harry's Cafe & Steak**

FLATIRON / UNION SQ.

28 **Eleven Madison Park**
28 **Gramercy Tavern**
27 **Tocqueville**
27 **Union Square Cafe**
26 **Craft**
26 **Ilili**
26 **NoMad**
26 **15 East**

GRAMERCY PARK

25 **Maialino**
25 **BLT Prime**
24 **Pure Food & Wine**
24 **Casa Mono**
24 **Yama**
24 **Novitá**
24 **Ponty Bistro**
23 **Posto**

GREENWICH VILLAGE

28 **Gotham Bar & Grill**
27 **Ushiwakamaru**
26 **Blue Hill**
26 **Babbo**
25 **Kotobuki**
25 **Neta**
25 **Il Mulino**
25 **Alta**

HARLEM

24 **Lido**
24 **Melba's**
23 **The Cecil**
22 **Amy Ruth's**
22 **Red Rooster**
21 **Miss Mamie's/Miss Maude's**
21 **Chez Lucienne**
21 **5 & Diamond**

TOP FOOD

TOPS BY LOCATION: MANHATTAN

HELL'S KITCHEN
(West of Ninth Ave.)

25 **Gotham West Market**
25 **Azuri Cafe**
25 **Totto Ramen**
25 **Casellula**
25 **Print**
25 **Esca**
24 **Taboon**
24 **Empanada Mama**

KIPS BAY

25 **Marcony**
25 **Riverpark**
24 **Dhaba**
23 **Le Parisien**
23 **Vezzo**
23 **Saravanaa Bhavan**
23 **Turkish Kitchen**
23 **I Trulli**

LITTLE ITALY

25 **Banh Mi Saigon**
23 **Angelo's of Mulberry St.**
23 **Ferrara**
23 **Nyonya**
22 **Wild Ginger**
22 **Il Cortile**
21 **La Mela**
21 **Pho Bang***

LOWER EAST SIDE

25 **Katz's Delicatessen**
24 **Clinton St. Baking Co.**
24 **Stanton Social**
24 **Pig and Khao**
23 **Rayuela**
23 **Ápizz**
23 **Beauty & Essex**
23 **Freemans**
23 **Prosperity Dumpling***

MEATPACKING

24 **Macelleria**

24 **Valbella**
24 **Spice Market**
23 **Catch**
23 **STK**
22 **Fatty Crab**
22 **Standard Grill**
21 **Fig & Olive**

MURRAY HILL

25 **Villa Berulia**
23 **Num Pang**
23 **El Pote**
23 **Phoenix Garden**
23 **Sarge's**
22 **El Parador Cafe**
22 **Rossini's**
22 **Cibo**

NOHO

26 **Il Buco**
25 **Bond St**
24 **Il Buco Alimentari**
24 **Gato**
24 **Saxon & Parole**
23 **Siggy's**
23 **Le Philosophe**
23 **Great Jones Cafe**
23 **Hecho en Dumbo***

NOLITA

26 **Musket Room**
25 **Uncle Boons**
25 **Estela**
25 **Peasant**
25 **Taïm**
25 **Rubirosa**
25 **Public**
25 **Torrisi Italian Specialties**

SOHO

27 **Aquagrill**
25 **Charlie Bird**
25 **Osteria Morini**
25 **David Burke Kitchen**

TOP FOOD

25 **Blue Ribbon Sushi**
25 **Costata**
24 **Ladurée**
24 **Blue Ribbon**

TRIBECA

29 **Bouley**
27 **Nobu**
27 **Jungsik**
26 **Tamarind**
26 **Scalini Fedeli**
26 **Mehtaphor**
26 **Atera**
26 **Brushstroke**

WEST 40s
(Fifth to Ninth Aves.)

26 **Gari**
26 **Aureole**
25 **Wu Liang Ye**
25 **Wolfgang's Steakhouse**
25 **Del Frisco's**
25 **Oceana**
25 **Strip House**
25 **Sushi Zen**

WEST 50s
(Fifth to Ninth Aves.)

29 **Le Bernardin**
27 **Per Se**
27 **Marea**
27 **Nobu 57**
27 **Milos**
26 **Porter House NY**
26 **Asiate**
26 **The Modern**

WEST 60s

28 **Jean-Georges**
26 **Telepan**
26 **Picholine**
25 **Boulud Sud**
25 **Lincoln**

24 **Bar Boulud**
23 **Rosa Mexicano**
22 **Atlantic Grill**

WEST 70s

27 **Dovetail**
26 **Gari**
25 **RedFarm**
24 **'Cesca**
24 **Salumeria Rosi Parmacotto**
23 **Piccolo Cafe**
23 **Fishtag**
23 **Ocean Grill**

WEST 80s

24 **Luke's Lobster**
24 **Celeste**
24 **Barney Greengrass**
23 **Peacefood Cafe**
23 **Machiavelli**
23 **Kefi**
23 **Candle Cafe West**
22 **Mermaid Inn**

WEST 90s & UP

26 **Gennaro**
23 **Pisticci**
23 **Szechuan Gourmet**
23 **Dinosaur Bar-B-Que**
23 **Xi'an Famous Foods**
23 **Thai Market**
23 **Indus Valley**
23 **Numero 28**

WEST VILLAGE

28 **Annisa**
27 **Takashi**
27 **Sushi Nakazawa**
27 **Mas (Farmhouse)**
27 **Little Owl**
27 **Pearl Oyster Bar**
26 **Louro**
26 **Piora**
26 **Soto***

BAY RIDGE

- 27 **Tanoreen**
- 25 **Tuscany Grill**
- 24 **Areo**
- 23 **Fushimi**
- 23 **Chadwick's**
- 23 **Arirang Hibachi Steakhouse**
- 23 **Gino's**
- 22 **Pearl Room**

BOERUM HILL/ COBBLE HILL

- 27 **Battersby**
- 26 **La Vara**
- 25 **Rucola**
- 25 **Hibino**
- 24 **Joya**
- 24 **Chocolate Room**
- 22 **Cafe Luluc**
- 22 **Wild Ginger**

BROOKLYN HEIGHTS/ DUMBO

- 26 **River Café**
- 26 **Juliana's**
- 24 **Henry's End**
- 24 **Luke's Lobster**
- 24 **Colonie**
- 23 **Noodle Pudding**
- 23 **Queen**
- 23 **Siggy's**
- 23 **Fornino**

CARROLL GARDENS

- 27 **The Grocery**
- 27 **Lucali**
- 27 **Dover**
- 25 **Buttermilk Channel**
- 24 **Prime Meats**
- 23 **Frankies Spuntino**
- 22 **Brooklyn Farmacy**
- 22 **Fragole**

CROWN HEIGHTS/ PROSPECT HEIGHTS

- 27 **Chuko**
- 24 **Bar Corvo**
- 24 **Ali's Roti**
- 24 **Marco's**
- 24 **Chavela's**
- 24 **Mayfield**
- 23 **James**
- 23 **606 R&D**

FORT GREENE/ CLINTON HILL

- 25 **Locanda Vini & Olii**
- 24 **Roman's** ▽
- 24 **Madiba** ▽
- 23 **Smoke Joint**
- 22 **Walter's** ▽
- 22 **67 Burger**
- 21 **No. 7**
- 21 **Zaytoons**

GREENPOINT

- 27 **Paulie Gee's**
- 24 **Five Leaves**
- 23 **Luksus** ▽
- 23 **Fornino**
- 23 **Littleneck Outpost**
- 22 **Calexico**
- 22 **Lobster Joint**
- 21 **No. 7 North**

PARK SLOPE

- 26 **Al Di La**
- 26 **Convivium Osteria**
- 25 **Rose Water**
- 25 **Talde**
- 25 **Franny's**
- 24 **Blue Ribbon Brooklyn**
- 24 **Applewood**
- 24 **Stone Park Café**

TOP FOOD

TOPS BY LOCATION: BROOKLYN

WILLIAMSBURG

28 **St. Anselm**
28 **Peter Luger**
27 **Zenkichi**
26 **Traif**
26 **Fette Sau**
26 **Caracas Brooklyn**
25 **The Elm**
25 **Mesa Coyoacan**

BROOKLYN: OTHER AREAS

28 **Chef's Table** *(Downtown)*
26 **Totonno's** *(Coney Island)*
26 **Roberta's** *(Bushwick)*
25 **Di Fara** *(Midwood)*
24 **Mill Basin Deli** *(Flatlands)*
24 **Defonte's** *(Red Hook)*
24 **Pacificana** *(Sunset Park)*
24 **Pok Pok Ny** *(Columbia St.)*

TOPS BY LOCATION: OTHER BOROUGHS

BRONX

27 **Roberto**
25 **Patricia's**
25 **Enzo's**
24 **Beccofino**
24 **Ali's Roti**
23 **Zero Otto Nove**
23 **F & J Pine Restaurant**
23 **Jake's Steakhouse**

QUEENS: LONG ISLAND CITY

25 **LIC Market**
25 **Hibino**
24 **M. Wells Dinette**
23 **Tournesol**
22 **Corner Bistro**
22 **Manducatis**
22 **M. Wells Steakhouse**
22 **Water's Edge**

QUEENS: ASTORIA

26 **Trattoria L'incontro**
26 **Taverna Kyclades**
26 **Elias Corner**
25 **Il Bambino**
25 **Piccola Venezia**
24 **MP Taverna**
24 **Sanford's**
24 **Stamatis**

QUEENS: OTHER AREAS

27 **Sripraphai** *(Woodside)*
26 **Danny Brown** *(Forest Hills)*
25 **Don Peppe** *(S. Ozone Park)*
25 **Alberto** *(Forest Hills)*
25 **Ayada** *(Elmhurst)*
25 **Park Side** *(Corona)*
25 **Salt & Fat** *(Sunnyside)*
24 **Ben's Best** *(Rego Park)*

QUEENS: FLUSHING

25 **Biang!**
23 **Szechuan Gourmet**
23 **Xi'an Famous Foods**
22 **Joe's Shanghai**
21 **Pho Bang**
21 **Kum Gang San**
20 **Kyochon Chicken**
— **Little Lamb**

STATEN ISLAND

26 **Denino's Pizzeria**
25 **Da Noi**
25 **Bocelli**
25 **Beso**
25 **Joe & Pat's**
24 **Bayou**
24 **Trattoria Romana**
23 **Fushimi**

TOP DECOR

WINNERS

28 Daniel	27 River Café
28 Asiate	27 Del Posto
28 Le Bernardin	27 Buddakan
28 La Grenouille	27 Robert
28 Eleven Madison Park	27 Gotham Bar & Grill
28 Bouley	27 Spice Market
28 Per Se	26 One if by Land
28 Four Seasons	26 Tocqueville
28 Jean-Georges	26 Boathouse
27 Tao	26 Lincoln

STELLAR SPACES / ATMOSPHERE

DESIGN STANDOUTS

Atera
Four Seasons
Jungsik
Lafayette
Lincoln
Musket Room
NoMad
Perry St.
Per Se
Tao

OLD NY VIBE

Bamonte's
Ferrara
John's of 12th St.
Katz's Delicatessen
Keens
Landmark Tavern
Oyster Bar
Peter Luger
Rao's
21 Club

BIG & SPLASHY

Beauty & Essex
Buddakan
Hakkasan
Megu
Qi (Midtown)
Russian Tea Room
Spice Market
Tao
Tavern on the Green
Urbo

VIEWS

Alma
Asiate
Gaonnuri
The Modern
Porter House NY
Riverpark
Robert
Rock Center Café
Shi
The View

PATIOS & GARDENS

Barbetta
Bottega
French Louie
Ladurée
M. Wells Steakhouse
New Leaf
The Pavilion
Pure Food & Wine
Salinas
Tavern on the Green

WATERSIDE

Battery Gardens
Boathouse
Brooklyn Crab
Hudson Eats
P.J. Clarke's on the Hudson
Randazzo's
River Café
Shi
Water Club
Water's Edge

TOPS BY SPECIAL FEATURE

BEER STANDOUTS

Birreria
Café d'Alsace
DBGB
Eleven Madison Park
Gramercy Tavern
John Brown Smokehouse
Luksus
Pickle Shack
Queens Kickshaw
Resto

HAPPY HOURS

Costata
FishTag
John Dory
Keens
Maialino
Millesime
Monarch Room
Red Rooster
Rye
Upstate

BIG BAR SCENE

Arlington Club
Bodega Negra
East Pole
El Toro Blanco
Gato
Harlow
Kingside
Margaux
Salvation Taco
The Smith

WINE BARS

Bacaro
Bar Boulud
Casellula
Corkbuzz
Danny Brown
El Quinto Pino
Il Buco Alimentari
I Trulli
Peasant
SD26

BYO

A Cafe & Wine Room
Kaz an Nou
Kuma Inn
Lucali
Nook
Petite Crevette
Queens Comfort
Sauce
Taci's Beyti
Tartine

WINE: CONNOISSEUR PICKS

Babbo
Bâtard
Charlie Bird
Daniel
Eleven Madison Park
Gramercy Tavern
Jean-Georges
Le Bernardin
Pearl & Ash
Per Se

COCKTAIL STANDOUTS

Alder
Atera
Beatrice Inn
Betony
Crif Dogs (East Village)
Distilled
Eleven Madison Park
The Elm
The NoMad Bar
Saxon & Parole

WINE: UNUSUAL LISTS

All'onda
Casa Mono
Estela
Marco's
Musket Room
M. Wells Steakhouse
Racines
Reynard
Rouge et Blanc
Seäsonal

TOPS BY SPECIAL FEATURE

DESTINATIONS

BARCLAYS CENTER

Alchemy
Bark
Chick P
Habana Outpost
Miriam
Morgans BBQ
No. 7
Prospect
67 Burger
Stonehome

BROOKLYN BRIDGE PARK
(North)

Brooklyn Ice Cream
Gran Electrica
Jack the Horse
Juliana's
Luke's Lobster
Noodle Pudding
No. 7 Sub
Shake Shack
Siggy's
Smorgasburg

BROOKLYN BRIDGE PARK
(South)

Ample Hills
Bocca Lupo
ChipShop
Fornino
Hanco's
Hibino
Luzzo's
No. 7 Sub
Pok Pok Ny
Red Gravy

GRAND CENTRAL

Cafe Centro
Café Grumpy
Joe
Junior's
La Fonda del Sol
Michael Jordan's
Naples 45
Oyster Bar

Shake Shack
Two Boots

HIGH LINE
(Gansevoort St. Exit)

Bagatelle
Bubby's
Catch
The Chester
Dos Caminos
Fig & Olive
Paradou
Serafina
Spice Market
Standard Grill

HIGH LINE *(23rd St. Exit)*

Artichoke Basille's
Bottino
Co.
Cookshop
Empire Diner
La Lunchonette
Red Cat
Tía Pol
Trestle on Tenth
Txikito

MADISON SQUARE GARDEN

Arno
Brother Jimmy's
David Burke Fabrick
Delmonico's Kitchen
Frankie & Johnnie's
Keens
Lazzara's
Nick & Stef's
Uncle Jack's
Uncle Nick's

METROPOLITAN MUSEUM

Café Boulud
Café Sabarsky/Fledermaus
Caravaggio
E.A.T.
Giovanni Venticinque
Le Pain Quotidien

TOPS BY SPECIAL FEATURE

DESTINATIONS

The Mark
Ristorante Morini
Sant Ambroeus
Serafina

MoMA

Benoit
China Grill
Circo
Fogo de Chão
Il Gattopardo
La Bonne Soupe
Michael's
The Modern
PizzArte
Soba Nippon

MUSEUM OF NATURAL HISTORY

Cafe Con Leche
Caffe Storico
Calle Ocho
Dovetail
Gazala's
Isabella's
Luke's Lobster
Nice Matin
Ocean Grill
Shake Shack

9/11 MEMORIAL

BLT Bar & Grill
Blue Smoke
El Vez
Harry's Italian
Hudson Eats
Les Halles
Morton's
North End Grill
P.J. Clarke's
Shake Shack

ROCKEFELLER CENTER

Bouchon Bakery
Brasserie Ruhlmann
Del Frisco's Grille
Empire Steakhouse
Fogo de Chão
Oceana
Rock Center Café
Sea Grill
'Wichcraft
Wu Liang Ye

THEATER DISTRICT DELUXE

Aureole
db Bistro Moderne
Esca
Hakkasan
Lambs Club
Oceana
STK
Strip House
Triomphe
Wolfgang's

THEATER DISTRICT FAMILY-FRIENDLY

Carmine's
5 Napkin Burger
John's Pizzeria
Junior's
Ruby Foo's
Schnipper's
Shake Shack
Thalia
Tony's Di Napoli
Virgil's Real Barbecue

THEATER DISTRICT OLD-SCHOOL

Barbetta
Chez Josephine
Chez Napoléon
Frankie & Johnnie's
Joe Allen
Landmark Tavern
Le Rivage
Orso
Patsy's
Sardi's

ANNIVERSARY-WORTHY

Del Posto
The House
Il Buco
La Lanterna
Lambs Club
One if by Land
The Place
River Café
Water's Edge
Waverly Inn

BREAKFAST

Balthazar
Barney Greengrass
Egg
Jean-Georges
Ladurée
Maialino
Maison Kayser
Norma's
Okonomi
Veselka

BRIDAL/BABY SHOWERS

Alice's Tea Cup
Anassa
Beauty & Essex
Bobo
Il Buco Alimentari e Vineria
Kings' Carriage House
Lady Mendl's
Ladurée
Mari Vanna
Palm Court

BRUNCH (Downtown)

Back Forty
Bubby's
Cafe Cluny
Clinton St. Baking Co.
Fat Radish
Locanda Verde
Miss Lily's
Narcissa
Prune
Rosemary's

BRUNCH (Midtown)

Artisanal
Bar Americain
db Bistro Moderne
44 & X
Lavo
Lexington Brass
Má Pêche
The Marshal
Palm Court
Penelope

BRUNCH (Uptown)

Café d'Alsace
Cafe Luxembourg
East Pole
Isabella's
Lido
Nice Matin
Ouest
Ristorante Morini
Telepan
Writing Room

BUSINESS DINING
(Financial District)

Bobby Van's
Capital Grille
Cipriani Club 55
Delmonico's
Harry's Cafe
Les Halles
MarkJoseph Steak
Morton's
North End Grill
P.J. Clarke's on the Hudson

BUSINESS DINING
(Midtown)

Casa Lever
Del Frisco's
Four Seasons

TOPS BY SPECIAL FEATURE

OCCASIONS & SITUATIONS

Lambs Club
Le Bernardin
Marea
Michael's
Milos
Smith & Wollensky
21 Club

CHILD-FRIENDLY

Alice's Tea Cup
Brooklyn Farmacy
Bubby's
Cowgirl
Hamilton's Soda Fountain
L&B Spumoni
Ninja
Otto
Peanut Butter & Co.
Serendipity 3

CHILDREN'S MENU

Blue Ribbon Brooklyn
Blue Smoke
Buttermilk
DBGB
Dinosaur BBQ
Farm/Adderley
L'Albero Dei Gelati
Landmarc
Rosa Mexicano
Schiller's

GROUP DINING

Beauty & Essex
DBGB
Decoy
Fette Sau
Fogo de Chão
Ilili
Momofuku Ssäm Bar
The NoMad Bar
Stella 34
Tavern on the Green

HOT DATES

All'onda
Bond St
Charlie Bird
Cherry
Gemma
Margaux
Monarch Room
Recette
Reynard
Zenkichi

JURY DUTY (Manhattan)

Blaue Gans
Buddha Bodai
Excellent Dumpling
Great NY Noodle Town
Kitchenette
Lotus Blue
Nha Trang
Peking Duck House
Pongsri Thai
Xi'an Famous Foods

JURY DUTY (Brooklyn)

Blue Marble
Ganso
Hanco's
Hill Country
Joya
Junior's
Mile End
Queen
Shake Shack
Siggy's

LATE-NIGHT SCENES

Artichoke Basille's
Blue Ribbon
Coppelia
Crif Dogs
La Esquina
Macao Trading
Minetta Tavern
Spotted Pig

TOPS BY SPECIAL FEATURE

OCCASIONS & SITUATIONS

Veselka
Wo Hop

NEW YEAR'S EVE

Bagatelle
Balthazar
Beauty & Essex
Bodega Negra
Buddakan
Catch
Lavo
Narcissa
Spice Market
Tao

SOCIETY WATCH

Amaranth
Beautique
Elio's
Harlow
Le Bilboquet
Ristorante Morini
Sant Ambroeus
Sirio
Swifty's
Ze Café

THANKSGIVING

Blue Hill
Breslin
Cookshop
Fraunces Tavern
Gramercy Tavern
Hearth
One If By Land
Telepan
21 Club
Waverly Inn

24/7

BCD Tofu House
Bubby's
Coppelia
Empanada Mama
Gahm Mi Oak
Kunjip
New WonJo
Sanford's
Sarge's
Veselka

TOP SERVICE

WINNERS

29 Le Bernardin	27 Tocqueville
28 Bouley	27 Del Posto
28 Eleven Madison Park	27 Four Seasons
28 Daniel	27 Annisa
28 Jean-Georges	26 Brushstroke
28 La Grenouille	26 Benjamin Steak House
28 Per Se	26 Union Square Cafe
27 Gramercy Tavern	26 River Café
27 Gotham Bar & Grill	26 Blue Hill
27 Sea Fire Grill	26 Marea

BEST $40 & UNDER

WINNERS

27 Chuko	26 Elias Corner
27 Sripraphai	26 Pure Thai Cookhouse
27 Paulie Gee's	26 Fette Sau
27 Lucali	26 Caracas Arepa Bar
26 Taverna Kyclades	25 Kotobuki
26 Juliana's	25 LIC Market
26 Totonno's*	25 Gotham West Market
26 Roberta's	25 Azuri Cafe
26 Denino's Pizzeria	25 Patricia's
26 Mighty Quinn's	25 Totto Ramen

BY NEIGHBORHOOD: MANHATTAN

CHELSEA

23 Num Pang
23 Westville
22 Artichoke Basille's Pizza
22 Co.
22 Grey Dog

CHINATOWN

24 Nha Trang
24 Excellent Dumpling House
23 Xi'an Famous Foods
23 Great NY Noodle Town
22 Golden Unicorn

EAST VILLAGE

26 Taverna Kyclades
26 Mighty Quinn's Barbeque
26 Caracas Arepa Bar
25 Luzzo's
24 Motorino

FINANCIAL DISTRICT

24 Luke's Lobster
24 Adrienne's Pizzabar
22 Tres Carnes
21 Shorty's
21 BonChon

FLATIRON

23 Num Pang
23 Hill Country
23 Ootoya
22 Maison Kayser
22 Grimaldi's

GREENWICH VILLAGE

25 Kotobuki
25 Ippudo
24 Joe's Pizza
23 Han Dynasty
23 Mamoun's

HELL'S KITCHEN
(West of Ninth Ave.)

25 Gotham West Market
25 Azuri Cafe
25 Totto Ramen
24 Empanada Mama
23 Turkish Cuisine

KIPS BAY/MURRAY HILL

24 Dhaba
24 Vezzo
23 Num Pang
23 Phoenix Garden
23 Saravanaa Bhavan

LOWER EAST SIDE

- 25 Katz's Delicatessen
- 24 Clinton St. Baking Co.
- 23 Prosperity Dumpling
- 22 Calexico
- 22 Lobster Joint

MIDTOWN

- 26 Pure Thai Cookhouse
- 25 Totto Ramen
- 25 Wu Liang Ye
- 25 Ippudo
- 24 Cho Dang Gol

TRIBECA

- 20 Terroir
- 20 Sarabeth's
- 20 Petite Abeille
- 20 Kitchenette
- 20 Baluchi's

UPPER EAST SIDE

- 24 Wa Jeal
- 24 Luke's Lobster
- 24 Uskudar
- 23 Szechuan Gourmet
- 23 Nick's

UPPER WEST SIDE

- 24 Luke's Lobster
- 24 Celeste
- 24 Barney Greengrass
- 23 Peacefood Cafe
- 23 Saravanaa Bhavan

WEST VILLAGE

- 25 Taïm
- 24 Joe's Pizza
- 23 Murray's Cheese Bar
- 23 Keste Pizza & Vino
- 23 Westville

BOERUM HILL/COBBLE HILL/DOWNTOWN

- 24 Joya
- 23 Hill Country
- 22 Cafe Luluc
- 22 Wild Ginger
- 22 Mile End

BROOKLYN HEIGHTS/DUMBO

- 26 Juliana's
- 24 Luke's Lobster
- 23 Siggy's
- 23 Fornino
- 22 Grimaldi's

CROWN HEIGHTS/PROSPECT HEIGHTS

- 27 Chuko
- 24 Ali's Roti
- 24 Chavela's
- 24 Mayfield
- 21 Zaytoons

PARK SLOPE

- 24 Bogota Latin Bistro
- 22 La Villa
- 22 67 Burger
- 22 Calexico
- 22 Scottadito Osteria Toscana

WILLIAMSBURG

- 26 Fette Sau
- 26 Caracas Arepa Bar
- 25 Mesa Coyoacan
- 24 Motorino
- 24 BrisketTown

RESTAURANT
DIRECTORY

	FOOD	DECOR	SERVICE	COST

Abboccato *Italian*

20 | 18 | 20 | $57

Midtown | Blakely Hotel | 136 W. 55th St. (bet. 6th & 7th Aves.) | 212-265-4000 | www.abboccato.com

It boasts "convenient" coordinates – near both City Center and Carnegie Hall – and this Midtown Italian "sleeper" follows through with "dependably good" eats, "prompt" service and "intimate" environs; the $38 dinner prix fixe is a "bargain" vis-à-vis the otherwise "higher-end" tabs.

ABC Cocina *Pan-Latin*

24 | 24 | 22 | $58

Flatiron | ABC Carpet & Home | 38 E. 19th St. (bet. B'way & Park Ave. S.) | 212-677-2233 | www.abccocinanyc.com

Jean-Georges Vongerichten has "done it again" at this "energetic" Pan-Latin in ABC Carpet & Home, where a "vibrant crowd" shares "stellar" "farm-to-table" bites (think "tacos as an art form") chased with "killer margaritas"; the edgy-but-"chic" space fills up one-two-three, so "be sure to reserve" ahead – and "bring your wallet."

ABC Kitchen *American*

25 | 24 | 23 | $63

Flatiron | ABC Carpet & Home | 35 E. 18th St. (bet. B'way & Park Ave. S.) | 212-475-5829 | www.abckitchennyc.com

"From A to Z", Jean-Georges Vongerichten's "happening" Flatiron "charmer" in ABC Carpet & Home "gets it right", showcasing "tantalizing", "farm-to-fork" American cooking composed from "top-notch" seasonal and organic ingredients; given the "genial" team manning the "chic, minimalist" setting, it's a "huge hit" with "fashionable folks" and "still a tough reservation."

Abigael's *Eclectic/Kosher*

23 | 19 | 22 | $52

Midtown | 1407 Broadway (bet. 38th & 39th Sts.) | 212-575-1407 | www.abigaels.com

A menu spanning "short ribs to sushi" gives kosher cuisine an "upscale" gloss at this double-decker Midtown Eclectic overseen by "creative" chef Jeff Nathan; "bland" atmospherics detract, but it remains a "staple" for observant folks.

Abraço Espresso *Coffee*

▽ 26 | 14 | 23 | $8

East Village | 86 E. Seventh St. (bet. 1st & 2nd Aves.) | no phone | www.abraconyc.com

Java junkies heap "hugs" on this "teeny" East Village coffee counter, dispenser of "premium-quality espresso" and drip brews plus "delicious" treats like the "must-try" olive oil cake; just be prepared to "get in line" and do your sipping at a "stand-up bar."

Aburiya Kinnosuke *Japanese*

24 | 18 | 21 | $66

East Midtown | 213 E. 45th St. (bet. 2nd & 3rd Aves.) | 212-867-5454 | www.aburiyakinnosuke.com

The "real deal" in East Midtown, this "classic izakaya" transports you to Japan with a "top-notch", sushi-free lineup featuring grilled robata bites and housemade tofu; since course after course can do some "damage to your wallet", bargain-hunters opt for lunch.

A Cafe & Wine Room *Caribbean/French*

▽ 24 | 18 | 22 | $36

West 100s | 973 Columbus Ave. (bet. 107th & 108th Sts.) | 212-222-2033 | www.acafeny.com

"Bring your own wine" to this UWS "hideaway" purveying "delicious"

French-Caribbean chow that's great for "impressing that special some-one"; what's "cozy" to some is "tiny" to others, but all agree the early-bird prix fixe is a "deal."

Acappella *Italian*
22 | 21 | 22 | $83

TriBeCa | 1 Hudson St. (Chambers St.) | 212-240-0163 | www.acappella-restaurant.com

Dining is "an event" at this "old-world" TriBeCa Northern Italian renowned for "excellent" food, "over-the-top" service and *"Godfather opulent"* decor; "try not to faint when you get the check" or you'll miss out on the complimentary grappa.

A Casa Fox *Pan-Latin*
∇ 24 | 21 | 21 | $43

Lower East Side | 173 Orchard St. (Stanton St.) | 212-253-1900 | www.acasafox.com

What this "little" LES Pan-Latin joint lacks in legroom is made up for in "homey", "candlelit" ambiance and a "fab assortment" of tapas and clay pots; given the "friendly" hospitality, modest tabs and "cozy fireplace", it's sure to "warm your soul."

Acme *American*
21 | 20 | 19 | $61

NoHo | 9 Great Jones St. (Lafayette St.) | 212-203-2121 | www.acmenyc.com

A "hot" ticket in NoHo, this "former down-home roadhouse" draws crowds with "inventive" New American fare featuring chef/"vegetable wizard" Mads Refslund's Nordic twists; it's a "buzzing scene" with "noise" and "tight quarters", but trendsetters dig the "hip vibe" and happening downstairs lounge.

Acqua at Peck Slip *Italian*
21 | 19 | 20 | $44

South Street Seaport | 21 Peck Slip (Water St.) | 212-349-4433 | www.acquarestaurantnyc.com

"Away from the touristy Seaport places", this "simple", rustic Italian is praised for its "homemade" pastas and "interesting" selection of bou-tique wines; despite "reasonable" prices, "attentive" service and "lovely" outdoor seating on a cobblestone street, there's "never a long wait" here.

Acqua Santa *Italian*
∇ 22 | 21 | 22 | $54

Williamsburg | 556 Driggs Ave. (7th St.) | Brooklyn | 718-384-9695 | www.acquasanta.com

A "find" for fans of "rustic Italian" eats, this Williamsburg storefront spins "wonderful" pizzas and pastas into a "satisfying experience"; an additional plus is a "whimsical", year-round courtyard fit for a "European small town."

Adrienne's Pizzabar *Pizza*
24 | 15 | 16 | $27

Financial District | 87 Pearl St. (Hanover Sq.) | 212-248-3838

Brace yourself for "lunchtime madness" when "Wall Street suits" and "casual passersby" descend on this FiDi pizzeria for its "outstanding" thin-crust pies; "adequate" service and "nonexistent decor" are part of the package, making it best enjoyed at an alfresco seat on "pictur-esque Stone Street."

	FOOD	DECOR	SERVICE	COST

Afghan Kebab House *Afghan*

20 | **13** | **18** | **$29**

East 70s | 1345 Second Ave. (71st St.) | 212-517-2776
Midtown | 764 Ninth Ave. (bet. 51st & 52nd Sts.) | 212-307-1612
"Mouthwatering" kebabs get skewered at these "authentic" Afghans
hailed for "flavorful", "substantial" grub for "bargain-basement" dough;
"no-frills" service and "dark", "nothing-to-write-home-about" settings
are the downsides.

Agnanti *Greek*

23 | **15** | **19** | **$37**

Astoria | 19-06 Ditmars Blvd. (19th St.) | Queens | 718-545-4554 |
www.agnantimeze.com
A "notch above the typical Astorian", this "tried-and-true" Hellenic taverna rolls out "delicious", "reasonably priced" meals that conjure up the
"Greek isles"; the decor is on the "forgettable" side, so regulars request
seats on the "wonderful" patio facing Astoria Park and the East River.

Ai Fiori *Italian*

26 | **25** | **25** | **$93**

Midtown | Langham Place Fifth Avenue Hotel | 400 Fifth Ave. (bet. 36th &
37th Sts.) | 212-613-8660 | www.aifiorinyc.com
"High standards" are a given at Michael White's "swanky" showcase
in the Langham Place Fifth Avenue Hotel, where "discreet" servers set
down "swoon-worthy", Riviera-inspired cuisine led by "exceptional pastas" in a sanctum of "ultrasleek" luxury made for "celebrating something
special"; the prices are predictably "splurge"-worthy, yet its "upscale"
clientele has "no complaints."

Aita *Italian*

▽ **25** | **23** | **25** | **$42**

Clinton Hill | 132 Greene Ave. (Waverly Ave.) | Brooklyn |
718-576-3584 | www.aitarestaurant.com
"Nestled away" in Clinton Hill, this "quaint, cozy" trattoria turns on the
"rustic charm" as "accommodating" servers deliver handmade pastas
and other "delicious" Italian dishes from a locavore-leaning menu; fortu-
nately, it's a "neighborhood joint", so "you can almost always get a table."

Aji Sushi *Japanese*

21 | **17** | **19** | **$41**

Murray Hill | 519 Third Ave. (bet. 34th & 35th Sts.) | 212-686-2055 |
www.ajisushinyc.com
Maybe it's "just a standard sushi spot", but Murray Hill locals swear
by this "reliable" Japanese "staple" for its "good variety" and "value"
tabs; "swift delivery" seems the preferred way to go, what with
the "bland" atmosphere.

Akdeniz *Turkish*

22 | **13** | **19** | **$34**

Midtown | 19 W. 46th St. (bet. 5th & 6th Aves.) | 212-575-2307 |
www.akdenizturkishusa.com
It's all about "value" at this Midtown Turk offering a "can't-be-beat" $27
dinner prix fixe that's a showstopper for theatergoers; the "tiny", "un-
memorable" setting can feel a bit "claustrophobic", but the grub's "tasty"
and the service "accommodating."

A La Turka *Turkish*

20 | **15** | **18** | **$39**

East 70s | 1417 Second Ave. (74th St.) | 212-744-2424 |
www.alaturkarestaurant.com
"Surprisingly good" Turkish food is yours at this "reliable" Upper Eastsider

where the prices are "affordable" and the noise level "manageable"; those who shrug "nothing exceptional" cite "drab" decor and "spotty" service.

Alberto *Italian*   25 | 19 | 24 | $47

Forest Hills | 98-31 Metropolitan Ave. (bet. 69th & 70th Aves.) | Queens | 718-268-7860 | www.albertorestaurant.com

A "Forest Hills find", this "marvelously old-fashioned" Italian remains a "steady" neighborhood "institution" (since '73) thanks to "well-prepared classics" and a "staff and owners who greet you like family"; indeed, the "high prices" and "romantic", fireplace-equipped room suggest "special occasion."

Al Bustan *Lebanese*   21 | 18 | 20 | $54

East Midtown | 319 E. 53rd St. (bet. 1st & 2nd Aves.) | 212-759-5933 | www.albustanny.com

"Hidden" on an East Midtown side street, this upscale double-decker delivers "succulent" Lebanese classics in a "modern", chandeliered room; although the "big space" is "rarely busy" at the dinner hour, at least it's "comfortable" and you can "hear yourself speak."

Alchemy *American*   ∇ 20 | 19 | 20 | $22

Park Slope | 56 Fifth Ave. (bet. Bergen St. & St. Marks Pl.) | Brooklyn | 718-636-4385 | www.alchemybrooklyn.com

Both "kid-friendly" (with a special children's menu) and "very adult" (thanks to a "terrific" beer list), this all-day Park Slope American gastropub appeals to everyone with its "delicious takes on pub classics" and moderate prices; the service is solid, ditto the "lovely" backyard and "pleasant" urban-rustic dining room.

Aldea *Mediterranean*   24 | 21 | 23 | $75

Flatiron | 31 W. 17th St. (bet. 5th & 6th Aves.) | 212-675-7223 | www.aldearestaurant.com

"Calm, cool and classy", this Flatiron "winner" matches the "wonderful" coastal Iberian dishes on George Mendes' "standout" modern Med menu with "refined" surroundings and "impeccable" service – understandably at an "expensive" cost; for "added enjoyment", grab a seat at the chef's counter "to ooh and aah."

Alder *American*   22 | 19 | 21 | $63

East Village | 157 Second Ave. (bet. 9th & 10th Sts.) | 212-539-1900 | www.aldernyc.com

Culinary wiz Wylie Dufresne's rep for "innovation" carries over to this "more accessible" East Village sequel to WD-50 that furnishes "well-executed" spins on American pub classics conceived with his signature "playful" flair; the design is "minimalistic" and the mood "jovial", but costs can "add up quickly" here.

Al Di La *Italian*   26 | 19 | 23 | $53

Park Slope | 248 Fifth Ave. (Carroll St.) | Brooklyn | 718-783-4565 | www.aldilatrattoria.com

This "rustic" Park Slope "star" draws a "devoted clientele" with its "brilliant" Venetian dishes and "20th-century prices"; blame the no-reservations policy for al di "long lines", though the nearby wine bar "helps pass the time" and "you can avoid waiting" altogether at lunch.

	FOOD	DECOR	SERVICE	COST

NEW Alfredo 100 *Italian*   − − − M

Midtown | 7 E. 54th St. (bet. 5th & 6th Aves.) | 212-688-1999 |
www.alfredo100.com

Transplanted from Rockefeller Center, this Midtown descendant
of the original in Italy (with the "100" added to honor its parent's
1914 founding) serves upscale Roman classics, including the famed
fettuccine, now with modern accompaniments like truffles and caviar;
its white-tablecloth setting is crisp, business-ready and adorned with
Al Hirschfeld drawings.

Ali Baba *Turkish*   21 16 19 $38

East Midtown | 862 Second Ave. (46th St.) | 212-888-8622 |
www.alibabasterrace.com
Kips Bay | 212 E. 34th St. (bet. 2nd & 3rd Aves.) | 212-683-9206 |
www.alibabaturkishcuisine.com

Ottoman expats say these "convivial" Turks "taste like home", then
up the ante with "generous portions" at real-"value" tabs; proponents
praise Second Avenue's "lovely roof deck", though the "neon sign" and
"nothing-fancy" decor are another story.

Alice's Tea Cup *Teahouse*   20 22 20 $27

East 60s | 156 E. 64th St. (Lexington Ave.) | 212-486-9200
East 80s | 220 E. 81st St. (bet. 2nd & 3rd Aves.) | 212-734-4832
West 70s | 102 W. 73rd St. (bet. Amsterdam & Columbus Aves.) |
212-799-3006
www.alicesteacup.com

"Cute" options for a "girls' day out", these "simply adorable" tearooms
offer "yummy" scones and a "mind-blowing selection" of potted brews in
settings "decked out in *Alice in Wonderland* style"; spendy tabs, "spotty"
service and "inevitable waits" don't dampen the "fairy-tale ambiance."

Ali's Roti *Trinidadian*   24 12 18 $15

Wakefield | 4220 White Plains Rd. (E. 233rd St.) | Bronx | 718-655-2178
Bedford-Stuyvesant | 1267 Fulton St. (Arlington Pl.) | Brooklyn |
718-783-0316
Crown Heights | 337 Utica Ave. (Carroll St.) | Brooklyn | 718-778-7329
Prospect Lefferts Gardens | 589 Flatbush Ave. (bet. Midwood St. &
Rutland Rd.) | Brooklyn | 718-462-1730

"Mouthwatering" rotis with "fresh dough" and meaty fillings ("ask
for them spicy") bring the "Trini flavor" to NYC at these low-cost
Trinidadians; despite "no-frills" setups and sparse seating, expect a
"line of loyal customers" at prime times.

NEW All'onda *Italian*   23 21 22 $71

Greenwich Village | 22 E. 13th St. (bet. 5th Ave. & University Pl.) |
212-231-2236 | www.allondanyc.com

Chef Chris Jaeckle's "delicious" roster of Japanese-influenced Venetian
cuisine – especially the signature sea urchin pasta – is paired with an
"excellent Italian wine list" at this "top-flight" Village duplex from restaurateur Chris Cannon; the "knowledgeable" service and "inviting" backdrop
(with a bar downstairs and the dining room above) are equally "all'uring."

	FOOD	DECOR	SERVICE	COST

Alloro *Italian*

23 | 18 | 23 | $58

East 70s | 307 E. 77th St. (bet. 1st & 2nd Aves.) | 212-535-2866 | www.alloronyc.com

"Original" is the consensus on this "small" UES Italian "sleeper" where "imaginative", "ambitious" dishes from a "skilled" chef are conveyed by an "eager-to-please" crew; loyalists are so grateful it's "not just another red-sauce joint" that they overlook the "bland" setting.

Allswell *American*

22 | 19 | 19 | $39

Williamsburg | 124 Bedford Ave. (10th St.) | Brooklyn | 347-799-2743 | www.allswellnyc.tumblr.com

"Just like the name says", this Williamsburg pub fields a "fresh, inventive" American menu that showcases "local ingredients" and "changes daily"; a "small", old-timey setting equipped with a communal table makes its "hipster" following feel at home, despite a few gripes about the pricing.

Alma *Mexican*

20 | 21 | 20 | $39

Columbia Street Waterfront District | 187 Columbia St., 2nd fl. (Degraw St.) | Brooklyn | 718-643-5400 | www.almarestaurant.com

"Mind-altering" Manhattan skyline views from a "year-round" rooftop are the bait at this Columbia Street Waterfront District Mexican where the chow is as "solid" as the margaritas are "strong"; an "off-the-beaten-path" address "not close to public transportation" makes "walking shoes" the footwear of choice.

Almayass *Armenian/Lebanese*

23 | 24 | 22 | $52

Flatiron | 24 E. 21st St. (bet. B'way & Park Ave. S.) | 212-473-3100 | www.almayassnyc.com

For a "delicious" introduction to Lebanese-Armenian cooking, this "lovely" Flatiron branch of a Beirut-based chain offers a share-worthy menu offering an "amazing range" of cold and hot meze; the "enjoyable" scene includes a room "spacious" enough to "go with a few people so you can try more", plus there's an adjacent bar/lounge for grabbing a drink.

Almond *French*

21 | 20 | 19 | $49

Flatiron | 12 E. 22nd St. (bet. B'way & Park Ave. S.) | 212-228-7557 | www.almondnyc.com

"Comforting" French fare meets "rustic charm" at this "buzzing" Flatiron bistro, a Bridgehampton spin-off where the tabs are "reasonable" and the crowd "young"; it's an "easy choice" for "big groups", so expect "noisy" decibels and a "happening" brunch.

Alobar *American*

∇ 22 | 21 | 20 | $38

Long Island City | 46-42 Vernon Blvd. (47th Ave.) | Queens | 718-752-6000 | www.alobarnyc.com

An "intelligent" take on "farm-to-table" cuisine showcased in rustic-chic accommodations sets this LIC American abuzz with local foodies; the "quality" offerings can make for spendy tabs, but the consensus is it's a "desperately needed" addition to the nabe.

Alta *Mediterranean*

25 | 23 | 20 | $62

Greenwich Village | 64 W. 10th St. (bet. 5th & 6th Aves.) | 212-505-7777 | www.altarestaurant.com

An "inventive" array of "delectable" Med small plates ("two words: Brussels sprouts") chased with "wonderful sangria" keeps this duplex Village boîte hopping with "discerning" sorts who know that "sharing is key"; be ready for "big prices", including a $490 option to "order the whole menu."

Amali *Mediterranean*

FOOD	DECOR	SERVICE	COST
24	22	23	$57

East 60s | 115 E. 60th St. (Park Ave.) | 212-339-8363 | www.amalinyc.com

"Classic Mediterranean flavors" with "farm-to-table" sensibilities are a "tempting" mix at this Periyali sib tucked away near Bloomie's, which also "surprises" Midtowners with a "biodynamic wine list"; "pleasant" service and rustically "stylish" decor help justify the "high" price tag.

Amaranth *Mediterranean*

21	19	21	$70

East 60s | 21 E. 62nd St. (bet. 5th & Madison Aves.) | 212-980-6700 | www.amaranthrestaurant.com

Aka "air-kissing central", this "buzzy" Madison Avenue–area Med is the kind of place where the "better-than-average" food is incidental to the "social scene"; service is "diffident" if you've got a "European title", "inattentive" if you don't, but the "expensive" pricing applies to all.

NEW American Cut *Steak*

24	23	24	$92

TriBeCa | 363 Greenwich St. (bet. Franklin & Harrison Sts.) | 212-226-4736 | www.americancutsteakhouse.com

With "outstanding" chops and crafty preparations framed as "homages to NYC", chef Marc Forgione updates the "old steakhouse formula" at this TriBeCa followup to his erstwhile Atlantic City original; given the "grand", "modern" setting and servers who go "above and beyond", there's no surprise "it will cost you."

Amma *Indian*

25	19	23	$46

East Midtown | 246 E. 51st St. (bet. 2nd & 3rd Aves.) | 212-644-8330 | www.ammanyc.com

"Breaking away from the clichés", this East Midtown "contender" provides a "tantalizing array" of "refined" Northern Indian fare served by a "calm" crew in a setting that falls somewhere between "intimate" and "cramped"; tabs skew a bit "high", though there is a $12 lunch deal.

Ammos *Greek/Seafood*

21	20	19	$57

Midtown | 52 Vanderbilt Ave. (bet. 44th & 45th Sts.) | 212-922-9999 | www.ammosnewyork.com

The "only thing missing is the plate-breaking" at this "authentic" Grand Central–area Greek that offers a "hustle-bustle" lunch for "expense account"–wielding "suits" as well as a more "quiet" dinner hour; tabs are a bit on the "high" side, but expect serious "sticker shock" if you order whole fish, priced by the pound.

Amor Cubano *Cuban*

23	19	23	$47

East Harlem | 2018 Third Ave. (111th St.) | 212-996-1220 | www.amorcubanonyc.com

Giving "Miami" a run for its money, this "hopping" East Harlem Cuban doles out "tasty, traditional" chow right out of "pre-Castro Havana", paired with "amazing" mojitos; "live music" via a "loud band" adds "authenticity" and distracts from the just "ok" ambiance.

	FOOD	DECOR	SERVICE	COST

Amorina *Italian/Pizza*
▽ 23 | 15 | 21 | $26

Prospect Heights | 624 Vanderbilt Ave. (Prospect Pl.) | Brooklyn |
718-230-3030 | www.amorinapizza.com

When in the mood for "delicious" Roman-style pizzas and pastas, all at
"low, low prices", locals turn to this Prospect Heights Italian; the "small",
red-checkered-tablecloth setting exudes a "homey" vibe and is overseen
by a "hard-working" staff.

Amorino *Ice Cream*
25 | 19 | 20 | $12

NEW **Chelsea** | 162 Eighth Ave. (18th St.) | no phone
Greenwich Village | 60 University Pl. (bet. 10th & 11th Sts.) | 212-253-5599
www.amorino.com

"Awesome gelatos" are the draw at these "efficient" gelaterias, part of a
"direct-from-Europe" chain; known for its roster of "rich, delicate flavors"
and unique presentation "in the shape of flowers", it's "not cheap" but
provides a "real" taste of "Roma."

Ample Hills Creamery *Ice Cream*
27 | 18 | 24 | $7

NEW **Brooklyn Heights** | 334 Furman St. (Joralemon St.) | Brooklyn |
347-240-3926
NEW **Gowanus** | 305 Nevins St. (Union St.) | Brooklyn | 347-725-4061
Prospect Heights | 623 Vanderbilt Ave. (St. Marks Ave.) | Brooklyn |
347-240-3926
www.amplehills.com

"Glorious" housemade ice cream flaunting "fresh, local ingredients" and
"fun, funky" flavors (e.g. "addictive-as-it-sounds" Salted Crack Caramel)
keeps these Brooklyn parlors "mad busy", but "the line moves" thanks
to "quick", "smiling" scoopers; the triple-decker new Gowanus flagship
boasts a "lovely" rooftop deck.

Am Thai Bistro *Thai*
▽ 23 | 15 | 21 | $23

Ditmas Park | 1003 Church Ave. (bet. E. 10th & 11th Sts.) | Brooklyn |
718-287-8888 | www.amthaibistro.com

Am-Thai Kitchen *Thai*

Kensington | 359 McDonald Ave. (Albemarle Rd.) | Brooklyn |
718-871-9115 | www.amthaikitchen.com

With "generous" portions of "wonderful" Thai staples, these "local"
Brooklyn standouts appease Siamese cravings at "reasonable" rates;
the Ditmas Park branch offsets "tiny" dimensions with "welcoming
service", while the seatless, cash-only Kensington outlet dispenses
"absolutely great takeout."

Amy Ruth's *Soul Food*
22 | 14 | 18 | $29

Harlem | 113 W. 116th St. (bet. Lenox & 7th Aves.) | 212-280-8779 |
www.amyruthsharlem.com

Those jonesing for a taste of "classic Harlem" head to this low-budget
soul-food "stalwart" for "hearty" cooking highlighted by "amazing"
chicken and waffles; regulars "ignore the decor" and "spotty" service,
and get there early "before the tourist buses arrive."

Anassa Taverna *Greek*
21 | 19 | 19 | $58

East 60s | 200 E. 60th St (3rd Ave.) | 212-371-5200 |
www.anassataverna.com

A "lively" Avra sibling "convenient to Bloomie's", this UES Greek "hits the
spot" with a lineup of seafood and other staples that's "pretty solid" if "a

little pricey"; the "attractive", split-level setting emits "feel-good vibes", though at peak hours it can be "quite noisy."

Andanada 141 *Spanish*　20 | 21 | 19 | $53

West 60s | 141 W. 69th St. (bet. B'way & Columbus Ave.) | 646-692-8762 | www.andanada141.com

This "lovely" Upper Westsider serves tapas and other Spanish classics "done with modern flair" in sleek, graffiti-mural-adorned digs; the vibe is "lively but allows for conversation", and "high prices" notwithstanding, it's tailor-made for the "pre-Lincoln Center" set.

Angelica Kitchen *Vegan/Vegetarian*　23 | 17 | 19 | $27

East Village | 300 E. 12th St. (2nd Ave.) | 212-228-2909 | www.angelicakitchen.com

A longtime East Village vegan "standard-bearer", this "go-with-the-flow" BYO is a "wholesome" destination for "your-body-as-a-temple" dining at a "reasonable", cash-only cost; though the decor is "spartan" and the service "loose", there's "always a line for a table."

Angelina's *Italian*　23 | 25 | 21 | $71

Tottenville | 399 Ellis St. (Arthur Kill Rd.) | Staten Island | 718-227-2900 | www.angelinasristorante.com

"Fine dining" comes to Tottenville at this "highly recommended" Italian offering "fabulous" food and "professional" service in a "stunning" tri-level mansion on the water; sure, it's "expensive" for SI and the crowd can be a bit "Jersey Shore", but to most it's a bona fide "special-occasion" hub.

Angelo's of Mulberry Street *Italian*　23 | 15 | 19 | $49

Little Italy | 146 Mulberry St. (bet. Grand & Hester Sts.) | 212-966-1277 | www.angelosofmulberryst.com

It doesn't get more "old-school" than this circa-1902 Little Italy "favorite" that stays popular thanks to "good, old-fashioned" Neapolitan cooking and "attentive" service; maybe the "stereotypical" decor could use "a little touching up", but otherwise fans "feel the love" – "maybe the tourists know something" after all.

Angelo's Pizzeria *Pizza*　20 | 13 | 17 | $26

East Midtown | 1043 Second Ave. (55th St.) | 212-521-3600 | www.angelospizzany.com
Midtown | 1697 Broadway (bet. 53rd & 54th Sts.) | 212-245-8811 | www.angelosnyc.com
Midtown | 117 W. 57th St. (bet. 6th & 7th Aves.) | 212-333-4333 | www.angelospizzany.com

These "family-friendly" Midtown pizzerias turn out "worthy" brick-oven pies with "generous" toppings for "economical" dough; ok, "ambiance is not their strong point", ditto the "hit-or-miss" service, but regulars say a "glass of wine always helps."

Ann & Tony's *Italian*　21 | 15 | 20 | $39

Arthur Avenue/Belmont | 2407 Arthur Ave. (bet. 187th & 188th Sts.) | Bronx | 718-933-1469 | www.annandtonysonline.com

Talk about "classic" – this circa-1927 "Arthur Avenue mainstay" remains a steady "favorite" thanks to its "healthy portions" of "old-fashioned"

Italiana served by a "treat-you-like-family" crew; "great prices" mean most don't notice the "decor from the '70s."

Annisa *American* `28` `23` `27` `$94`

West Village | 13 Barrow St. (bet. 7th Ave. S. & W. 4th St.) | 212-741-6699 | www.annisarestaurant.com

"Culinary mastermind" Anita Lo's "endlessly inventive" West Village "treasure" continues to "wow" fans with "spectacular" Asian-accented American cuisine delivered by servers who "take great care of you"; tucked into an "intimate" room that's "grown-up but not stuffy", it's a "charming escape" that's "worth every cent."

Antica Pesa *Italian* `23` `23` `24` `$69`

Williamsburg | 115 Berry St. (bet. 7th & 8th Sts.) | Brooklyn | 347-763-2635 | www.anticapesa.com

"One of the posher" options in Williamsburg, this American branch of a Rome stalwart puts forth "cooked-to-perfection pastas" and other Italian classics delivered by a "welcoming" staff; the space breaks from the nabe's shabby-chic norm, offering instead an "elegant" fine-dining vibe and a salonlike, fireplace-equipped lounge.

NEW Antonioni's *Italian* `–` `–` `–` `M`

Lower East Side | 177 Chrystie St. (Rivington St.) | 646-998-3407 | www.antonionis.com

Decidedly cooler than your usual trattoria, this LES newcomer from the Cafe Gitane team is a neighborhood fallback for reasonably priced Italian food (largely pizza and pasta); decorated in a retro style, it stays open late into *la notte*.

Antonucci Cafe *Italian* `23` `17` `21` `$58`

East 80s | 170 E. 81st St. (bet. Lexington & 3rd Aves.) | 212-570-5100 | www.antonuccicafe.com

In a "neighborhood filled with Italian restaurants", this "nice and easy" UES trattoria holds its own with "authentic" fare highlighted by especially "excellent pastas"; seating is "tight" and tabs "pricey for everyday", but "warm" vibes and "unhurried" service help compensate.

A.O.C. Bistro *French* `20` `17` `18` `$46`

Park Slope | 259 Fifth Ave. (Garfield Pl.) | Brooklyn | 718-788-1515 | www.aocbistro.com

A.O.C. L'aile ou la Cuisse *French*

West Village | 314 Bleecker St. (Grove St.) | 212-675-9463 | www.aocnyc.com

"Genuinely French", these "straightforward" West Village–Park Slope bistros roll out "better-than-expected" Gallic menus for A-ok tabs; service may skew "indifferent" and the decor's "pleasant" but "nothing special", though all is forgiven in Bleecker Street's "lovely" back garden "escape."

Aperitivo Pizza Bar *Pizza* ∇ `22` `16` `17` `$29`

East Midtown | 780 Third Ave. (bet. 48th & 49th Sts.) | 212-758-9402 | www.aperitivonyc.com

This East Midtown pizzeria specializes in "flavorful" brick-oven pies bolstered by standard Italian plates, all priced for "value"; the lofty, bi-level digs are "convenient" for "U.N. and media" types who make it a "popular business lunch" nexus.

	FOOD	DECOR	SERVICE	COST

Ápizz *Italian*

23 | 21 | 21 | $54

Lower East Side | 217 Eldridge St. (bet. Rivington & Stanton Sts.) | 212-253-9199 | www.apizz.com

One of the "coziest" joints in town, this "sexy" LES Italian purveys "excellent" pizza and other "melt-in-your-mouth" dishes straight from a "wood-burning oven"; despite "quality" service, "accessible" rates and "intimate", "rustic" digs, it remains something of a "hidden gem" – maybe because of the "tucked-away" location.

Applewood *American*

24 | 21 | 23 | $55

Park Slope | 501 11th St. (bet. 7th & 8th Aves.) | Brooklyn | 718-788-1014 | www.applewoodny.com

"Inventively prepared farm-fresh ingredients" lure "locals and foodies" to this "charming" New American that's "like going to the country without leaving Park Slope"; sure, it's "a tad pricey", but "welcoming" service, "cozy" atmospherics and a "fabulous brunch" compensate.

Aquagrill *Seafood*

27 | 20 | 23 | $65

SoHo | 210 Spring St. (6th Ave.) | 212-274-0505 | www.aquagrill.com

Fin fans have "nothing but love" for this "ever-popular" SoHo seafooder, where a "polished" crew ferries the "briny best" in fresh catch along with "phenomenal oysters" from the raw bar's "superb shuckers"; its long-running rep for "piscatorial excellence" keeps the "snug" quarters "boisterous" and "congested."

Aquavit *Scandinavian*

26 | 25 | 26 | $86

Midtown | 65 E. 55th St. (bet. Madison & Park Aves.) | 212-307-7311 | www.aquavit.org

"Quintessential" Scandinavian dining is alive and well at this "high-end" Midtown "oasis" providing "sublime" Nordic dishes (and a "second-to-none" aquavit list), all dispatched by an "exceptional" staff in "subdued" "contemporary" surrounds; *ja*, "it'll cost you a fistful of krona", but the experience is "special in every way."

Areo *Italian*

24 | 19 | 21 | $52

Bay Ridge | 8424 Third Ave. (bet. 84th & 85th Sts.) | Brooklyn | 718-238-0079

"Fuhgeddaboudit" – this "busy" Bay Ridge "staple" continues to "stand the test of time" as a supplier of "wonderful" Italiana and "old-world" service; assuming "you can handle the noise", its "lively scene" and "local color" are an all-around "hoot."

Arepas Café *Venezuelan*

23 | 14 | 18 | $22

Astoria | 33-07 36th Ave. (bet. 33rd & 34th Sts.) | Queens | 718-937-3835

Arepas Grill *Venezuelan*

Astoria | 21-19 Broadway (bet. 21st & 23rd Sts.) | Queens | 718-355-9686 www.arepascafe.com

"Flavors straight out of Caracas" are stuffed into "fluffy", affordable arepas at these "something-different" Astoria Venezuelans; the bite-size Cafe original sports a "diner atmosphere" that suggests "takeout", but the Grill offshoot is roomier, with a broader menu that includes Caribbean and Med dishes.

Aretsky's Patroon American

FOOD	DECOR	SERVICE	COST
25	23	24	$80

East Midtown | 160 E. 46th St. (bet. Lexington & 3rd Aves.) |
212-883-7373 | www.aretskyspatroon.com

Ken Aretsky's "polished" East Midtown "business" "oasis" remains a
place to "impress clients" with "solid" American fare and "first-class service" in "men's club" digs done up with "classic photos"; "especially nice"
are the private rooms and roof bar, but just "watch out for those prices."

Arirang Hibachi Steakhouse Japanese

23	20	22	$43

Bay Ridge | 8814 Fourth Ave. (bet. 88th & 89th Sts.) | Brooklyn |
718-238-9880
Great Kills | 23 Nelson Ave. (Locust Pl.) | Staten Island | 718-966-9600
www.partyonthegrill.com

"Interactive" is the philosophy of these cross-borough "Benihana wannabes", where the Japanese steaks and sides arrive "projectile-style"
from "amusing" hibachi chefs "swinging their implements around"; "kids
can't get enough of it", but adults sigh "hokey" even though the pricing's
pretty "reasonable for dinner and a show."

Arirang Korean Korean/Noodle Shop

22	12	16	$30

Midtown | 32 W. 32nd St. (bet. B'way & 5th Ave.) | 212-967-5088 |
www.koreanrestaurantnyc.org

"Delicious" Korean soups that showcase "handmade noodles" and are
ladled out in "generous" portions deliver "comfort-food" satisfaction
at this third-floor K-town slurp house; quite "decent" prices, "no-fuss"
service and "minimal" decor complete the "neat little" picture.

Arlington Club Steak

21	22	20	$82

East 70s | 1032 Lexington Ave. (bet. 73rd & 74th Sts.) | 212-249-5700 |
www.arlingtonclubny.com

A "winner" for "serious carnivores", Laurent Tourondel's "upscale"
UES steakhouse supplies "pricey" chops in a "busy" setting sporting a
"vaulted ceiling" and "hardwood" aplenty; the "over-the-top" scene is
popular with locals "of a certain age" who've "removed their wedding
rings" at the "cougarville" bar.

Armani Ristorante Italian

24	25	23	$74

Midtown | Armani/5th Avenue Bldg. | 717 Fifth Ave., 3rd fl. (56th St.) |
212-207-1902 | www.armaniristorante.com

"Serious shoppers" in Giorgio Armani's Fifth Avenue flagship unwind
at this "hidden" third-floor Italian whose "chic", "beautiful" setting is
populated with equally "pretty people"; it's a "favorite for lunch", but the
food's just as "delectable" at dinner (the pricing less so).

Arno Italian

21	16	21	$61

Midtown | 141 W. 38th St. (B'way) | 212-944-7420 |
www.arnoristorante.com

A "go-to place" in Midtown's Garment District, this "old-fashioned"
Northern Italian is targeted to the "garmento" business-lunch trade;
the "down-to-earth" cooking is "fine" though "not exotic", but the decor
seems a bit "tired" given the tabs.

	FOOD	DECOR	SERVICE	COST

Aroma Kitchen & Winebar *Italian*   ▽ 23 | 19 | 21 | $63

NoHo | 36 E. Fourth St. (bet. Bowery & Lafayette St.) | 212-375-0100 |
www.aromanyc.com

For a "big surprise" in a "tight" but "delightful" space, sniff out this
NoHo "hideaway" where "wonderful" Italian flavors are matched with
"nicely picked" wines and delivered by "friendly" staffers; it's convenient
to the Public Theater, and its private party rooms are perfect for an
"intimate get-together."

Artichoke Basille's Pizza *Pizza*   22 | 9 | 15 | $15

Chelsea | 114 10th Ave. (17th St.) | 212-792-9200
East Village | 328 E. 14th St. (bet. 1st & 2nd Aves.) | 212-228-2004
Greenwich Village | 111 MacDougal St. (bet. Bleecker & 3rd Sts.) |
646-278-6100
www.artichokepizza.com

This "no-frills" mini-chain "will change the way you see pizza" with
its "goopy", "super-filling" slices slathered with "deliciously creamy"
artichoke dip that leaves fans "yearning for more"; although not much on
looks, it's a "beacon" for bar-crawlers given its "late-night" hours.

Artie's *Seafood/Steak*   22 | 15 | 20 | $48

City Island | 394 City Island Ave. (Ditmars St.) | Bronx | 718-885-9885 |
www.artiesofcityisland.com

"Actual City Island residents" eat at this "been-there-forever" surf 'n'
turfer offering a "retro" Italian-accented menu; true, it's "not on the
water" and the decor is "generic seafooder", yet "unhurried" service and
fair pricing keep locals "happy as clams."

Artisanal *French*   23 | 21 | 21 | $56

Midtown | 2 Park Ave. (bet. 32nd & 33rd Sts.) | 212-725-8585 |
www.artisanalbistro.com

An "unparalleled" cheese selection is the "main attraction" at Terrance
Brennan's "inviting" Midtown "simulation of a Parisian brasserie", also
home to "wonderful" French comfort food and "killer" fondues; the "cavernous" quarters are "always humming" and filled with "din", evidence
that it's "still as good as ever."

Arturo's Pizzeria *Pizza*   23 | 16 | 19 | $29

Greenwich Village | 106 W. Houston St. (Thompson St.) |
212-677-3820 | www.arturoscoaloven.com

"Old Greenwich Village" endures at this 1957-vintage pizzeria where a
"slice of the past" comes via "delicious, no-nonsense" pies "straight out
of the coal oven"; a live jazz combo and an "unpretentious" mood compensate for decor that's somewhere between "faded" and "dingy."

A Salt & Battery *British*   22 | 13 | 19 | $18

West Village | 112 Greenwich Ave. (bet. 12th & 13th Sts.) |
212-691-2713 | www.asaltandbattery.com

Fish 'n' chips fanciers say this "cleverly named" West Village "hole-in-
the-wall" does a "jolly good" rendition of the British staple for an "affordable" sum; "anti-health food" treats like "deep-fried candy bars" fill out
the "greasy" bill, but since there's "no decor" and seating's just a "few
stools", most get the goods to go.

	FOOD	DECOR	SERVICE	COST

Asellina Italian
20 | 22 | 18 | $54

Flatiron | Gansevoort Park Avenue Hotel | 420 Park Ave. S. (29th St.) | 212-317-2908 | www.togrp.com

Designed with "the Kardashians" in mind, this "big", "dimly lit" Flatiron Italian is "more about atmosphere than food", leading some to declare the "bar scene's the thing" here; fans praise the "stylish" setting, but the "spotty service", "noisy" acoustics and "pricey-for-the-quality" tabs are another matter.

Asiate American/Asian
26 | 28 | 26 | $96

Midtown | Mandarin Oriental Hotel | 80 Columbus Circle, 35th fl. (B'way) | 212-805-8881 | www.mandarinoriental.com

Dine "on top of the world" at the Mandarin Oriental's "transcending" Asian-New American aerie, where "magnificent" Central Park views and "totally elegant" surroundings set a "serene" scene for "exquisite" prix fixe menus served by a "polished" team; all this "indulgence" comes at "astronomical prices", but "if you're going to splurge, this is the place to do it."

Astor Room American
20 | 20 | 21 | $47

Astoria | Kaufman Astoria Studios | 34-12 36th St. (bet. 35th & 36th Aves.) | Queens | 718-255-1947 | www.astorroom.com

It "feels like the 1920s" at this "throwback" spot inside Kaufman Astoria Studios, supplying American eats to "TV and movie" industry types; "speakeasy" looks, a "great bar" mixing "vintage" drinks and frequent "live jazz" complete the "old-school" vibe.

Atera American
26 | 24 | 26 | $228

TriBeCa | 77 Worth St. (bet. B'way & Church St.) | 212-226-1444 | www.aleranyc.com

"Always an experience", this TriBeCa 18-seater features chef Matthew Lightner guiding an "avant adventure" as "foraged, artisanal" ingredients are "creatively transformed" into "inspiring" American tasting menus; front-row spots at the chef's counter "contribute to the magic" and distract from the "skyrocketing" $195 set price.

Atlantic Grill Seafood
22 | 19 | 21 | $58

East 70s | 1341 Third Ave. (bet. 76th & 77th Sts.) | 212-988-9200
West 60s | 49 W. 64th St. (bet. B'way & CPW) | 212-787-4663
www.atlanticgrill.com

"Tried-and-true", these "big", "bustling" seafooders can be counted on for "something-for-everyone" menus, including "first-rate" fish, "dependable" turf and a "go-to" brunch; manned by a "smart staff", they're "not cheap" and can be "awfully noisy" but remain "perennial favorites" for a reason.

Atrium Dumbo American
∇ 23 | 25 | 22 | $49

Dumbo | 15 Main St. (bet. Plymouth & Water Sts.) | Brooklyn | 718-858-1095 | www.atriumdumbo.com

Hailed by locals as a "keeper", this roomy Dumbo New American furnishes a "select" but "excellent" menu of market-driven dishes with "no pretentiousness"; a "lovely", split-level setup with a "living plant wall" and "wonderful" vibrations is more reason to be "impressed."

	FOOD	DECOR	SERVICE	COST

Aureole *American*
26 | 25 | 25 | $88

Midtown | Bank of America Tower | 135 W. 42nd St. (bet. B'way & 6th Ave.) | 212-319-1660 | www.charliepalmer.com

"Charlie Palmer does it right" at this Times Square–area benchmark for "truly fine dining" that "lives up to its billing" with "superior" New American fare, "wonderful wines" and "expert service"; while the "elegant" main room offers "phenomenal", prix fixe–only menus at "steep" tabs, the "lively" front bar offers less expensive à la carte options.

Aurora *Italian*
24 | 20 | 21 | $55

SoHo | 510 Broome St. (bet. Thompson St. & W. B'way) | 212-334-9020
Williamsburg | 70 Grand St. (Wythe Ave.) | Brooklyn | 718-388-5100 | www.aurorabk.com

At these "quaint" Williamsburg and SoHo Italians, the "delectable" rustic cooking is a match for the "Tuscan countryside" settings, complete with a "lovely garden" at the Brooklyn original; "hip" crowds, midrange prices and "helpful" service ensure "enjoyable" repasts.

A Voce *Italian*
23 | 23 | 22 | $70

Flatiron | 41 Madison Ave. (26th St.) | 212-545-8555
Midtown | Time Warner Ctr. | 10 Columbus Circle (bet. 58th & 60th Sts.) | 212-823-2523
www.avocerestaurant.com

An "attractive crowd" voices approval for these "high-end" contemporary Italians, where "spot-on" staffers supply an "impressive", pasta-centric menu that's "complex" but "not over the top"; the Flatiron original is a "civilized" "oasis" off Madison Square, while the "more lively" Columbus Circle sequel boasts a "sweeping view of Central Park."

Avra *Greek/Seafood*
25 | 22 | 21 | $67

East Midtown | 141 E. 48th St. (bet. Lexington & 3rd Aves.) | 212-759-8550 | www.avrany.com

A "mainstay" for East Midtown "suits", this "buzzing" "upscale taverna" beckons with "unforgettable" grilled fish and other "terrific Greek seafood" items dispatched by a "helpful" team; the by-the-pound selections can be quite "expensive", though the "tight", "loud" quarters can be sidestepped by snagging a "great" outdoor table.

Awash *Ethiopian*
21 | 12 | 16 | $25

East Village | 338 E. Sixth St. (bet. 1st & 2nd Aves.) | 212-982-9589
West 100s | 947 Amsterdam Ave. (bet. 106th & 107th Sts.) | 212-961-1416
Cobble Hill | 242 Court St. (bet. Baltic & Kane Sts.) | Brooklyn | 718-243-2151
www.awashny.com

"Different experience" seekers tout these "unsung", utensil-free Ethiopians where "delectable" stews are scooped up with injera flatbread; "decidedly relaxed" service and settings that "need sprucing up" come with the territory, but at least you'll walk out awash with cash.

Ayada *Thai*
25 | 14 | 20 | $25

Elmhurst | 77-08 Woodside Ave. (bet. 77th & 78th Sts.) | Queens | 718-424-0844

"Behind a nondescript storefront", this "authentic" Elmhurst Thai supplies "exceptional" takes on all the favorites "without breaking the bank" – just "don't order 'spicy' unless you mean it"; service is "efficient", but "crowds" form in the "smallish" space now that "the secret is out."

	FOOD	DECOR	SERVICE	COST

Azuri Cafe *Israeli/Kosher* — 25 | 7 | 15 | $17

Hell's Kitchen | 465 W. 51st St. (bet. 9th & 10th Aves.) | 212-262-2920 | www.azuricafe.com

Falafel "from heaven" and other "cheap", "delicious" Israeli eats offset the "dumpy" decor at this Hell's Kitchen "hole-in-the-wall"; just "don't expect a warm welcome" – the "short-tempered" owner is the neighborhood's "favorite curmudgeon."

Babbo *Italian* — 26 | 23 | 24 | $94

Greenwich Village | 110 Waverly Pl. (bet. MacDougal St. & 6th Ave.) | 212-777-0303 | www.babbonyc.com

Still "in a class by itself", this "special" Village destination from the Batali-Bastianich team draws capacity crowds to revel in "sinful" pastas and other "alchemical" Italian cuisine in a "wonderful" carriage house overseen by an "engaging" crew; despite the "cacophony", "challenging" tabs and reservations "drama" ("like winning the lottery"), it's a "necessary pilgrimage."

Bacaro *Italian* ∇ 24 | 26 | 20 | $44

Lower East Side | 136 Division St. (bet. Ludlow & Orchard Sts.) | 212-941-5060 | www.bacaronyc.com

There's a "sultry", "wine-cellar vibe" in play at this "candlelit" LES basement offering "delicious" Venetian small plates (and particularly "wonderful" pastas) to a crowd of "hipsters, artists and the Uptowners who love them"; a "great" all-Italian vino list and "attentive" service are added bonuses.

NEW Bacchanal *American* — | — | — | M

Little Italy | Sohotel | 146 Bowery (Broome St.) | 646-355-1840 | www.bacchanalnyc.com

This New American arrival in the Bowery's Sohotel offers a Mediterranean-influenced menu that draws from Italy, France and Spain; like the name suggests, there's a massive wine selection and the vaguely retro room is dominated by a copper-topped U-shaped bar.

Bacchus *French* — 21 | 20 | 21 | $47

Downtown Brooklyn | 409 Atlantic Ave. (bet. Bond & Nevins Sts.) | Brooklyn | 718-852-1572 | www.bacchusbistro.com

Francophiles tout the "classic French bistro" fare at this "charming little" Downtown Brooklyn wine bar/eatery; "reasonable" rates, "no pretension" and a "beautiful" back garden lend "lazy-day" appeal, even if a few Francophobes feel it has "no particular distinction."

Back Forty *American* — 22 | 19 | 21 | $44

East Village | 190 Ave. B (12th St.) | 212-388-1990
Back Forty West *American*
SoHo | 70 Prince St. (Crosby St.) | 212-219-8570
www.backfortynyc.com

Early "farm-to-table proponent" Peter Hoffman is the mind behind these "easygoing" eateries offering "comforting", "everyday" New American cooking with notably "terrific burgers" and an "outstanding brunch"; the East Village original boasts a "bucolic" back patio, while the SoHo follow-up has all-day hours.

	FOOD	DECOR	SERVICE	COST

Bagatelle *French*

21 | 24 | 22 | $87

Meatpacking District | 1 Little W. 12th St. (9th Ave.) | 212-488-2110 | www.bagatellenyc.com/contact

"Hot and cool at the same time", this Meatpacking jet-setter central bolsters its splurgy but "better-than-average" French fare with an exuberant "funday mentality"; its infamous "party brunch" featuring "expensive champagne", "throbbing Euro house" sounds and "dancing on the tables" is "not for the faint of heart" (or wallet).

Bahari Estiatorio *Greek*

∇ 26 | 18 | 22 | $37

Astoria | 31-14 Broadway (32nd St.) | Queens | 718-204-8968 | www.bahariestiatorio.com

"Excellent" Hellenic "home cooking" served "with a smile" explains why this Astoria "neighborhood" joint is usually "packed"; the spare storefront space may be "a little tight", but given the "authentic" eats and "bargain prices", no one minds.

Bakehouse Bistro & Bar *French*

∇ 21 | 21 | 19 | $38

Meatpacking District | 113 Horatio St. (West St.) | 646-559-9871 | www.bakehousenyc.com

From the creators of Bonsignour comes this all-day Meatpacking French bistro where the home-baked breads, rolls and pastries are the "real stars" of the show; "rustic" looks with a "warehouse feel" and "welcoming" service enhance the overall "charming" picture.

Balaboosta *Mediterranean/Mideastern*

23 | 18 | 21 | $48

NoLita | 214 Mulberry St. (Spring St.) | 212-966-7366 | www.balaboostanyc.com

Med-Mideastern "comfort food" gets an "imaginative" and "delicious" boost at this "homey" NoLita "favorite" from the Taïm team; the "understated" space may seem "cramped", but the "welcoming" staff and relatively "affordable prices" help keep it a "player."

Balade *Lebanese*

24 | 20 | 23 | $36

East Village | 208 First Ave. (bet. 12th & 13th Sts.) | 212-529-6868 | www.baladerestaurants.com

"Authentic across the board", this "affordable" East Village "discovery" supplies "fantastic" Lebanese eats including grilled platters, pita pizzas and a "dynamite" meze lineup; a casually "upbeat" setup overseen by a "hospitable" team, it "deserves repeat visits."

Balkanika *Mediterranean*

∇ 21 | 16 | 20 | $31

Hell's Kitchen | 691 Ninth Ave. (bet. 47th & 48th Sts.) | 212-974-0300 | www.balkanikarestaurantnyc.com

"Something different" in Hell's Kitchen, this "well-priced" Mediterranean wine bar offers a "tasty" "tour of the Balkans" encompassing meze, grilled meats and vinos to match; with "super-friendly" service and a "cozy hangout vibe", it's a welcome "alternative" for pre-theater types.

Balthazar *French*

24 | 24 | 21 | $61

SoHo | 80 Spring St. (Crosby St.) | 212-965-1414 | www.balthazarny.com

"Keith McNally has a perennial winner" in this "splashy" SoHo brasserie, supplying "delectable" French fare (including "delish breakfasts" and a "fabulous" bread basket) in a "Left Bank"–style space perpetually "abuzz" with "tourists, natives" and "famous" folks; despite "shoe-horned" seating and "challenging" acoustics, it "has an electricity of its own" that "never gets old."

Baluchi's *Indian*

| 20 | 15 | 18 | $32 |

East 80s | 1724 Second Ave. (bet. 89th & 90th Sts.) | 212-996-2600
Kips Bay | 329 Third Ave. (25th St.) | 212-679-3434
TriBeCa | 275 Greenwich St. (bet. Murray & Warren Sts.) | 212-571-5343
Park Slope | 310 Fifth Ave. (2nd St.) | Brooklyn | 718-832-5555
Forest Hills | 113-30 Queens Blvd. (76th Ave.) | Queens | 718-520-8600
www.baluchis.com

This "Americanized" Indian chain is popular for its "serviceable" food and "economical" tabs (lunch is a particular "bargain"); but critics citing "conventional" cooking, "mundane" settings and "dull-witted" service say "don't expect nirvana."

Bamonte's *Italian*

| 23 | 16 | 22 | $51 |

Williamsburg | 32 Withers St. (bet. Lorimer St. & Union Ave.) | Brooklyn | 718-384-8831

"Auld Brooklyn" lives on at this circa-1900 Williamsburg Italian, a "throwback" for "real" red-sauce fare and "lots of it" (the "only things locally sourced are the waiters"); ok, it may be "short on decor", but the tabs are "reasonable" and the ambiance "right out of *The Godfather*."

B&B Winepub *Pub Food*

| 21 | 20 | 20 | $42 |

SoHo | 25 W. Houston St. (bet. Greene & Mercer Sts.) | 212-334-7320 | www.burgerandbarrel.com

"Trendy" burgers, "barrel beers" and "wine on tap" collide in a "high-energy" setting at this "happy" SoHo gastropub from the Lure Fishbar folks; sure, it's "loud", with "lighting so low you can barely see your food", but its "cool", cost-conscious crowd doesn't care.

B & H Dairy *Deli/Vegetarian*

| 24 | 9 | 20 | $16 |

East Village | 127 Second Ave. (bet. 7th St. & St. Marks Pl.) | 212-505-8065

This "hole-in-the-wall" East Village "patch of history" has been filling bellies with veggie borscht-and-blintz fare (aka "Jewish soul food") since the 1940s; talk about kickin' it "old school" – the "diner" ambiance "hasn't changed since your grandpa ate there" way back when.

Banh Mi Saigon *Sandwiches/Vietnamese*

| 25 | 7 | 15 | $9 |

Little Italy | 198 Grand St. (bet. Mott & Mulberry Sts.) | 212-941-1541 | www.banhmisaigonnyc.com

"Super-delicious" Vietnamese sandwiches with "crusty" French bread and "flavorful" pork are the eponymous specialty at this cash-only Little Italy storefront; "dirt-cheap prices" make it "popular with the lunch crowd", though spare seating at "countertops with stools" encourages takeout.

Bann *Korean*

| 24 | 22 | 21 | $56 |

Midtown | Worldwide Plaza | 350 W. 50th St. (bet. 8th & 9th Aves.) | 212-582-4446 | www.bannrestaurant.com

"Classy" Korean barbecue is no oxymoron at this Theater District "change of pace" where the smokeless tabletop grills impress do-it-yourselfers and the "modern" setting thrills aesthetes; maybe the tabs skew "upscale", but the food's "exciting", the service "caring" and the overall experience "satisfying."

BaoHaus *Taiwanese*　　20 | 11 | 15 | $14

East Village | 238 E. 14th St. (bet. 2nd & 3rd Aves.) | 646-669-8889 | www.baohausnyc.com

The "savory" Taiwanese steamed buns are "seriously delicious" at Eddie Huang's East Villager, whose "fast-food vibe" gets a boost from "blaring hip-hop music"; despite "teenage" service and "no decor to speak of", "cheap" checks keep its "college" crowd content.

Bar Americain *American*　　23 | 22 | 23 | $66

Midtown | 152 W. 52nd St. (bet. 6th & 7th Aves.) | 212-265-9700 | www.baramericain.com

A "big, bold" Bobby Flay "hit", this Midtown brasserie stands out with "top-notch" New American plates served in a "dramatic, soaring" space by a "diligent" team; a "boisterous" bar lures the after-work set, and it's also "popular" with pre-theater types despite the "expense-account" price tags.

NEW Barawine Harlem *American*　　20 | 23 | 19 | $42

Harlem | 200 Lenox Ave. (120th St.) | 646-756-4154 | www.barawine.com

Hosting a "convivial" scene kindled by an "extensive" list of by-the-glass vinos (plus 200 more by the bottle), this "well-appointed" Harlem wine bar also supplies a "surprisingly good" New American menu; a "bright" space with a "subtle Parisian feel", it's a favored nexus for "upbeat" locals.

NEW BarBacon *American*　　∇ 22 | 18 | 22 | $41

Midtown | 836 Ninth Ave. (bet. 54th & 55th Sts.) | 646-362-0622 | www.barbacon.com

"Life is better with bacon in it", and this Midtown American gastropub is a "popular" place to "pig out" on "quality" cured swine "in all forms", "spectacular" bacon flights included; "willing" staffers also decant a lengthy whiskey list in the "simple", "loud" setting.

Barbès *French/Moroccan*　　21 | 17 | 20 | $45

Midtown | 21 E. 36th St. (bet. 5th & Madison Aves.) | 212-684-0215 | www.barbesrestaurantnyc.com

An "exotic escape from *la vie ordinaire*", this Midtown "sure thing" purveys "toothsome" French-Moroccan vittles in a setting akin to an "Algerian bistro in Marseilles"; it may be "cramped" and "noisy", but "pleasant" service and "value" pricing help to distract.

Barbetta *Italian*　　22 | 22 | 23 | $67

Midtown | 321 W. 46th St. (bet. 8th & 9th Aves.) | 212-246-9171 | www.barbettarestaurant.com

Dating to 1906, this Theater District "grande dame" turns back the clock with "polite waiters" setting down "marvelous" Northern Italian dishes in a "lovely old" setting that includes a "beautiful", "vacation"-like back garden; just be aware that this "throwback to a different time" has distinctly up-to-date pricing.

	FOOD	DECOR	SERVICE	COST

NEW **Bar Bolonat** *Israeli/Mideastern* — | — | — | M

West Village | 611 Hudson St. (W. 12th St.) | 212-390-1545 |
www.barbolonatny.com

Chef Einat Admony (Balaboosta, Taim) is behind this West Village newcomer turning out modern takes on Israeli–Middle Eastern fare, paired
with creative cocktails; the minimalist space features banquette seating
on one side, tables on the other and a bar in the middle, plus there's a
downstairs room for private parties.

Barbone *Italian*   ∇ 24 | 17 | 23 | $58

East Village | 186 Ave. B (bet. 11th & 12th Sts.) | 212-254-6047 |
www.barbonenyc.com

"Hidden away in the East Village", this "no-tourists" Italian sleeper earns
raves for "well-prepared" classic dishes ferried by "friendly" folks overseen by a "charismatic" chef-owner; "good overall value" and a "great
backyard patio" keep the locals coming.

Bar Boulud *French*   24 | 20 | 22 | $64

West 60s | 1900 Broadway (bet. 63rd & 64th Sts.) | 212-595-0303 |
www.barboulud.com

A "more relaxed" showcase for Daniel Boulud's "artistry", this "vibrant"
French bistro/wine bar in a "hard-to-beat" address opposite Lincoln Center serves "magic" charcuterie and other "sophisticated dishes" at "fair"
prices; if the "sleek", "narrow" quarters seem "too close", there's always
fun alfresco "people-watching" from the sidewalk tables.

Barbounia *Mediterranean*   23 | 23 | 20 | $51

Flatiron | 250 Park Ave. S. (20th St.) | 212-995-0242 |
www.barbounia.com

"Stylish" and "upbeat", this "cacophonous" Flatiron Med lures "see-and-
be-seen" "Gen-X" types with a "tasty", "something-for-everyone" menu
(and one "crazy brunch"); still, it's the "beautiful", "airy" setting – replete
with vaulted ceilings – that's the star of the show here.

Barbuto *Italian*   26 | 19 | 22 | $55

West Village | 775 Washington St. (bet. Jane & W. 12th Sts.) |
212-924-9700 | www.barbutonyc.com

A "repurposed garage" is the "cool" backdrop for Jonathan Waxman's
"sophisticated" yet "approachable" Italian menu (notably that "astonish-
ing" roast chicken) at this "inviting" West Villager; though the "lively"
crowd can kick up "deafening" decibels, warmer months are mellower
when the doors "open to the street."

NEW **Barchetta** *Italian/Seafood*   — | — | — | E

Chelsea | 461 W. 23rd St. (bet. 9th & 10th Aves.) | 212-255-7400 |
www.barchettanyc.com

Seasonal Italian seafood lands in Chelsea at this new venture from
Esca chef David Pasternack that features an array of crudos (flights
are available) along with stylish pastas; the airy space is decked out in
handsome, wood-lined style with an aptly nautical drift.

NEW **Bar Chuko** *Japanese*   — | — | — | I

Prospect Heights | 565 Vanderbilt Ave. (Pacific St.) | Brooklyn |
347-425-9570 | www.barchuko.com

Those who line up at the Prospect Heights ramen favorite Chuko welcome this roomier nearby spin-off, a Japanese izakaya specializing in small plates from skewers to crispy sweetbreads; the wood-lined space features an open kitchen and a mix of communal tables and two-tops, plus a front bar offering a wide range of sakes, whiskeys and shochu cocktails.

Bar Corvo *Italian*

24 | 20 | 22 | $48

Prospect Heights | 791 Washington Ave. (bet. Lincoln & St Johns Pls.) | Brooklyn | 718-230-0940 | www.barcorvo.com
Hailed as a "boon to the area", this Prospect Heights "Al Di La offspring" fields a "well-curated menu" of "delicious" Italian dishes in "cozy" quarters run by an "attentive" team; "real-steal" prices ensure it "does fill up", though a patio helps stretch the space.

BareBurger *Burgers*

21 | 16 | 19 | $23

Chelsea | 153 Eighth Ave. (bet. 17th & 18th Sts.) | 212-414-2273
East 70s | 1370 First Ave. (73rd St.) | 212-510-8559
East Village | 85 Second Ave. (5th St.) | 212-510-8610
Greenwich Village | 535 Laguardia Pl. (bet. 3rd St. & Washington Square Vill.) | 212-477-8125
Murray Hill | 514 Third Ave. (bet. 34th & 35th Sts.) | 212-679-2273
Park Slope | 170 Seventh Ave. (bet. 1st St. & Garfield Pl.) | Brooklyn | 718-768-2273
Astoria | 23-01 31st St. (23rd Ave.) | Queens | 718-204-7167
Astoria | 33-21 31st Ave. (34th St.) | Queens | 718-777-7011 |
Bayside | 42-38 Bell Blvd. (bet. 42nd & 43rd Aves.) | Queens | 718-279-2273
Forest Hills | 71-49 Austin St. (bet. 71st Rd. & 72nd Ave.) | Queens | 718-275-2273
www.bareburger.com
Additional locations throughout the NY area
"Branching out beyond the conventional", this "eco-conscious" burger chain flips "fab" organic patties with beef, "exotic meats" and veggie options that are all "super-customizable" with a "mind-blowing" array of toppings; if the "price is a bit much" for "bare-bones" dining, many feel "less guilty" dining here.

Bar Eolo *Italian*

∇ 23 | 17 | 20 | $49

Chelsea | 190 Seventh Ave. (bet. 21st & 22nd Sts.) | 646-225-6606 | www.eolonewyork.com
There's "intelligent life in the kitchen" of this Sicilian "contender" offering "off-the-beaten-recipe-path" dishes paired with "exceptional wines"; the "nondescript" trattoria setting may be at odds with the "Chelsea prices", perhaps why there are "no struggles to get a table."

Bar Italia *Italian*

23 | 22 | 22 | $66

East 60s | 768 Madison Ave. (66th St.) | 917-546-6676 | www.baritaliamadison.com
"Wanna-be-seen" Euros flock to this "fashion-forward" Madison Avenue Italian where the "better-than-expected" cooking takes a backseat to the "sleek" white setting and "*Real Housewives*" people-watching; expect serious tabs and "lots of attitude."

	FOOD	DECOR	SERVICE	COST

Bar Jamón *Spanish*
22 | 18 | 18 | $45

Gramercy Park | 125 E. 17th St. (Irving Pl.) | 212-253-2773 |
www.casamononyc.com

Mario Batali's "convivial" Gramercy tapas bar–cum–"holding pen" for his
'round-the-corner Casa Mono puts out "top-of-the-line" Spanish small
plates paired with an "extensive" wine list; it's a "tight squeeze" and the
tabs are "not cheap", but most don't mind given the "sexy-time" mood.

Bark *Hot Dogs*
20 | 16 | 16 | $17

Park Slope | 474 Bergen St. (bet. 5th & Flatbush Aves.) | Brooklyn |
718-789-1939 | www.barkhotdogs.com

The "dogs are hot and the crowd cool" at this Park Sloper where the
"artisanal" dawgs with "great snap" are made from "locally sourced",
"pedigreed ingredients" and paired with "outstanding" sides and Brooklyn craft beers; "hip-minimalist" digs where "everything's recycled" help
justify prices kinda "high-end" for wieners.

Barney Greengrass *Deli*
24 | 10 | 17 | $33

West 80s | 541 Amsterdam Ave. (bet. 86th & 87th Sts.) | 212-724-4707 |
www.barneygreengrass.com

A circa-1908 "throwback", this "renowned" Upper Westsider "brings
back memories" with "classic Jewish" deli fare and "unsurpassed smoked
fish" slung by a "gruff but efficient" staff; "cash-only" tabs and "functional" decor don't deter the perpetual "crowds on the weekend."

Barosa *Italian*
23 | 18 | 21 | $44

Rego Park | 62-29 Woodhaven Blvd. (62nd Rd.) | Queens |
718-424-1455 | www.barosas.com

"Tasty" red-sauce fare "like mom used to make" is available for a "good
price" at this "neighborhood favorite" Rego Park Italian; its "upscale"
ambitions are apparent in the "polite" service, while "fantastic specials"
seal the deal.

Bar Pitti *Italian*
23 | 15 | 18 | $44

Greenwich Village | 268 Sixth Ave. (bet. Bleecker & Houston Sts.) |
212-982-3300

Home to "many a celeb sighting", this "jet-set" Village Italian is best known
for its "excellent people-watching", even if the "easygoing" fare is pretty
"delicious" as well; no reservations, no plastic, "no discernible decor" and
"far-from-friendly" service don't faze its "paparazzi"-ready patrons.

NEW Bar Primi *Italian*
— | — | — | M

East Village | 325 Bowery (2nd St.) | 212-220-9100 | www.barprimi.com
Set in the former Peels digs, this casual new Bowery Italian from Andrew
Carmellini (The Dutch, Locanda Verde) offers a pasta- and small plates-
centric menu along with snacks, antipasti and Amaro-based cocktails;
the double-decker setting exudes rustic, relaxing vibes, but expect a lot
of commotion as it's an instant hit.

Barraca *Spanish*
▽ 21 | 19 | 18 | $49

West Village | 81 Greenwich Ave. (Bank St.) | 212-462-0080 |
www.barracanyc.com

This West Village "neighborhood" Spaniard skews "traditional" with an
"enjoyable" lineup of paellas bolstered by a "good variety" of tapas; add

"strong" sangrias and "comfortable" quarters with outdoor tables, and it's a natural for "group outings."

Barrio Chino *Mexican*

▽ 22 | 17 | 18 | $36

Lower East Side | 253 Broome St. (bet. Ludlow & Orchard Sts.) | 212-228-6710 | www.barriochinonyc.com

A "total hipster joint", this LES cantina serves a "tasty", "authentic" Mexican menu in a "microscopic" setting; it's still "something of a scene" after more than a decade, maybe because of its "highly affordable" price point and "lay-you-out-flat" tequila list.

Bar Tabac *French*

20 | 18 | 19 | $33

Cobble Hill | 128 Smith St. (Dean St.) | Brooklyn | 718-923-0918 | www.bartabacny.com

A "Parisian bistro transplanted" to Cobble Hill, this "hip" Gallic eatery has plenty of "good energy", especially during its "tasty" brunch; "tight" seating and occasionally "lackadaisical" service aside, it's a neighborhood "favorite" and late-night "staple."

Bar Toto *Italian*

▽ 21 | 20 | 21 | $34

Park Slope | 411 11th St. (6th Ave.) | Brooklyn | 718-768-4698 | www.bartoto.com

A Park Slope "hangout" for everyone from "families to singles", this "comfortable" Italian sibling of Bar Tano and Provini fields "moderately priced" panini, pasta and pizza in a "relatively quiet" setting; space may be "tight", but service is "nice" and the vibe "relaxed."

NEW Bassanova

▽ 21 | 11 | 16 | $23

Ramen *Japanese/Noodle Shop*

Chinatown | 76 Mott St. (bet. Bayard & Canal Sts.) | 212-334-2100 | www.bassanovanyc.com

Noodle bowls via Tokyo are the "tasty" stock in trade at this subterranean Chinatown niche, known for dispensing pork-based "twists" on ramen like the "superior" green curry specialty; slurpers say the "portions aren't huge" but still "pretty filling" all the same.

Basso56 *Italian*

24 | 19 | 24 | $58

Midtown | 234 W. 56th St. (bet. B'way & 8th Ave.) | 212-265-2610 | www.basso56.com

An "excellent Carnegie Hall resource", this Midtown Italian features a "nicely-put-together menu" with "modern flair" ferried by an "accommodating" team; some sniff at the "narrow", "nothing-fancy" setting, but admit the prices are "reasonable for the quality."

Basta Pasta *Italian*

24 | 17 | 20 | $50

Flatiron | 37 W. 17th St. (bet. 5th & 6th Aves.) | 212-366-0888 | www.bastapastanyc.com

"Japanese-style Italian food" begs the question "where else but NY?" – and this "unusual" Flatiron "change of pace" comes through with "interesting" vittles led by a signature "pasta tossed in a Parmesan wheel"; if the decor's getting "dated", the "hospitable" service and "reasonable" rates are fine as is.

	FOOD	DECOR	SERVICE	COST

🆕 **Bâtard** *American/European* — | — | — | E

TriBeCa | 239 W. Broadway (bet. Walker & White Sts.) | 212-219-2777

In the TriBeCa space once home to Corton and Montrachet, restaurateur Drew Nieporent has opened a more casual fine-dining venture, this time offering a European-leaning New American menu in a variety of prix fixe formats; tablecloths and carpeting have been banished in the redo, and the coolly minimal result features hardwood floors, embossed plasterwork and soft lighting.

Battersby *American* 27 | 18 | 25 | $75

Boerum Hill | 255 Smith St. (bet. Degraw & Douglass Sts.) | Brooklyn | 718-852-8321 | www.battersbybrooklyn.com

"One of Brooklyn's finest", this "really special" Smith Street New American merges "masterful" cuisine with a "warm, down-to-earth" style and "engaged" service; the "tiny venue" is "always full" and the no-reservations rule makes for "interminable" waits, though rezzies are accepted for the "sublime", "well-priced" tasting menu.

Battery Gardens *American/Continental* 19 | 23 | 20 | $55

Battery Park City | SW corner of Battery Park (State St.) | 212-809-5508 | www.batterygardens.com

The "harbor is at your feet" at this "shoreline" Battery Park bastion where the "peerless" views of the harbor and Lady Liberty are matched with "better-than-expected" American-Continental fare; for the most "priceless" experience, go for "outdoor cocktails at sunset."

Bayou *Cajun* 24 | 22 | 23 | $45

Rosebank | 1072 Bay St. (bet. Chestnut & St. Marys Aves.) | Staten Island | 718-273-4383 | www.bayounyc.com

"Ragin' Cajun" cooking and "real Southern hospitality" come to Staten Island via this Rosebank "favorite" where the "tasty" cooking is as "true" to N'Awlins as the "Big Easy" decor; "affordable" tabs and "designated-driver-recommended" drinks ratchet up the "festive" vibrations.

🆕 **Baz Bagel** *Bakery/Jewish* — | — | — | I

Little Italy | 181 Grand St. (bet. Baxter & Mulberry Sts.) | 212-335-0609 | www.bazbagel.com

Hand-rolled bagels, smoked fish platters and other Jewish breakfast and lunch classics are the focus of this new Little Italy bakery/cafe opened by alums from Rubirosa and the legendary Barney Greengrass; the decor recalls an old-school coffee shop with tile floors, retro dinnerware and a long lunch counter.

B. Café *Belgian* 21 | 16 | 18 | $42

East 70s | 240 E. 75th St. (bet. 2nd & 3rd Aves.) | 212-249-3300
West 80s | 566 Amsterdam Ave. (bet. 87th & 88th Sts.) | 212-873-0003
www.bcafe.com

"Belgian pub grub" is yours at these "satisfying" crosstown "reliables" offering "consistently fine" mussels and frites washed down with "high-test" brews; ok, the "railroad" settings are a bit "drab" and "squashed", but the staff "tries its best" and you do get "lots for your money."

	FOOD	DECOR	SERVICE	COST

BCD Tofu House *Korean*
22 | 17 | 16 | $29

Midtown | 5 W. 32nd St. (bet. B'way & 5th Ave.) | 212-967-1900 | www.bcdtofu.com

Reopened in a new K-town location, this 24/7 Korean "go-to" from an LA-based chain is a "no-brainer" for "bubbling pots" of "tasty" tofu stew that can be custom-spiced from tame to "the hottest"; "reasonable" tabs trump "spotty" service and decor that's "nothing to write home about."

Beatrice Inn *American*
∇ 20 | 22 | 22 | $84

West Village | 285 W. 12th St. (bet. 4th & Hudson Sts.) | 917-566-7400 | www.thebeatriceinn.com

This "grown-up" destination from editor Graydon Carter (Monkey Bar, Waverly Inn) inhabits a storied West Village basement, where the New American fare is considered "good" enough, but it's the cocktails and clubby "mystique" that people "love"; it's equally suited "for a group of friends or date night", though plan on "upscale" pricing.

NEW Beautique *American/French*
- | - | - | E

Midtown | 8 W. 58th St. (bet. 5th & 6th Aves.) | 212-753-1200 | www.beautiquedining.com

Nestled next to the Paris Theatre, this glitzy Midtowner serves seasonal American dishes prepared with French techniques, plus craft cocktails and a wine list emphasizing the Burgundy region; the hidden, subterranean setting features swanky touches like a grand piano, gilded ceilings and an over-the-top chandelier that's catnip for its fashionable, free-spending following.

Beauty & Essex *American*
23 | 26 | 20 | $66

Lower East Side | 146 Essex St. (bet. Rivington & Stanton Sts.) | 212-614-0146 | www.beautyandessex.com

"Trendy" types duck through a "cheeky" pawn-shop entrance to access this double-decker LES "extravaganza" where it's "easy to feel swank" nibbling "creative" New American bites amid AvroKO's "gorgeous" decor; "exciting buzz" offsets "expensive" tabs and "hit-or-miss" service, and that complimentary "champagne in the ladies' room is a kick."

Becco *Italian*
23 | 18 | 21 | $49

Midtown | 355 W. 46th St. (bet. 8th & 9th Aves.) | 212-397-7597 | www.becco-nyc.com

Continuing its "hit run" on Restaurant Row, this Joe and Lidia Bastianich "phenomenon" provides "super" "homestyle Italian" meals via a $23 "unlimited pasta deal" and a "tough-to-beat" $25 wine list; it sure "packs them in", but "punctual" servers get you "out the door in plenty of time" to make the curtain.

Beccofino *Italian*
24 | 18 | 22 | $42

Riverdale | 5704 Mosholu Ave. (bet. Fieldston Rd. & Spencer Ave.) | Bronx | 718-432-2604 | www.beccofinorestaurant.com

Pretty "happening" for Riverdale, this "traditional" Italian offers "Manhattan-quality" red-sauce cooking at Bronx prices; its "neighborly atmosphere" draws huzzahs, but "no reservations" and "small" dimensions mean you must "come early or be prepared to wait."

	FOOD	DECOR	SERVICE	COST

Beecher's Cellar *American*
▽ 21 | 19 | 17 | $49

Flatiron | 900 Broadway (20th St.) | 212-466-3340 |
www.beechershandmadecheese.com

Downstairs from Beecher's cheese factory (which makes artisanal fromage "right in front of your eyes"), this "secret" lounge/eatery in the Flatiron features a "limited" American menu highlighted by a "magical mac 'n'
cheese"; the "candlelit" setting possesses a "low-key", "romantic" vibe.

Bella Blu *Italian*
22 | 19 | 19 | $59

East 70s | 967 Lexington Ave. (bet. 70th & 71st Sts.) | 212-988-4624 |
www.baraondany.com

"Well-to-do" Upper Eastsiders "get happy" at this "popular" Italian serving a "high-quality" menu led by "fantastic" pizzas; granted, it's "pricey",
the seating's "cheek-by-jowl" and service depends on "how familiar you
look", but "superior people-watching" saves the day.

Bella Via *Italian*
▽ 22 | 18 | 21 | $37

Long Island City | 47-46 Vernon Blvd. (48th Ave.) | Queens |
718-361-7510 | www.bellaviarestaurant.com

"Funky Long Island City" is home to this "reliable" Italian known for its
"fresh" pastas and coal-fired pizzas at prices that "won't break the bank";
set in a big-windowed storefront, it features "simple" decor that contributes to its "pleasant", "friendly" mien.

Bell Book & Candle *American*
▽ 23 | 20 | 21 | $50

West Village | 141 W. 10th St., downstairs (bet. Greenwich Ave. &
Waverly Pl.) | 212-414-2355 | www.bbandcnyc.com

Best known for an aeroponic roof garden that supplies most of its
produce, this "cozy-chic" West Villager is appreciated for its "delicious"
"seasonal" American menu; the "dark" basement setting has "great
date" potential, and it's also "worth checking out" for its "awesome
happy-hour" deals.

Ben & Jack's Steak House *Steak*
24 | 20 | 22 | $80

Flatiron | 255 Fifth Ave. (bet. 28th & 29th Sts.) | 212-532-7600 |
www.benandjackssteakhouse.com

Among the "best of the Luger's imitators", this Flatiron carnivorium features "cooked-to-perfection" steaks and "man-size" sides; "boys'-club"
looks and "friendly" staffers offset the typically "expensive" tabs.

Benares *Indian*
▽ 21 | 17 | 19 | $42

Midtown | 240 W. 56th St. (bet. B'way & 8th Ave.) | 212-397-0707
TriBeCa | 45 Murray St. (bet. B'way & Church St.) | 212-766-4900
www.benaresnyc.com

The "flavorful" Indian menu includes dishes "not often found" at
these "upscale" venues where the wide-ranging choices ("veggie-
friendly" options are a focus) are presented in "comfortable", modern
surrounds; the Midtown branch's buffet lunch "steal" is matched by prix
fixe deals in TriBeCa.

Benchmark *American/Steak*
21 | 19 | 20 | $53

Park Slope | 339 Second St. (bet. 4th & 5th Aves.) | Brooklyn |
718-965-7040 | www.benchmarkrestaurant.com

Nestled in an "intimate" carriage house, this "somewhat overlooked"
Park Slope steakhouse offers "terrific" chops as well as "quite good"

American accompaniments; fans admire its "calm" mood and midrange tabs, while a "lovely patio" allows it to "double in size" in good weather.

Benjamin Steak House *Steak*   27 | 25 | 26 | $88

Midtown | Dylan Hotel | 52 E. 41st St. (bet. Madison & Park Aves.) | 212-297-9177 | www.benjaminsteakhouse.com

"Eat like a man" at this "first-class" chop shop in the Dylan Hotel, supplying "perfectly prepared" beef and "top-shelf" service in "clubby" quarters with a "soaring ceiling" and "massive fireplace"; it's certainly "not cheap", but then again this "sublime experience" is always "memorable."

Benoit Bistro *French*   23 | 22 | 21 | $66

Midtown | 60 W. 55th St. (bet. 5th & 6th Aves.) | 646-943-7373 | www.benoitny.com

"As French as could be", this durable Midtown bistro from Alain Ducasse turns out "well-done" traditional dishes (e.g. "killer roast chicken") in "bright, lively" digs that channel the City of Light; ever the "worthy destination", it's on the "expensive" side but certainly "worth the cost."

Ben's Best *Deli/Kosher*   24 | 10 | 19 | $25

Rego Park | 96-40 Queens Blvd. (bet. 63rd Dr. & 64th Rd.) | Queens | 718-897-1700 | www.bensbest.com

For an "authentic artery-clogging experience", look no further than this circa-1945 Rego Park Jewish deli known for "old-time" kosher fare "and lots of it"; the "oy!" decor is "just what you'd expect", but "Queens prices" and "ok service" compensate.

Ben's Kosher Deli *Deli/Kosher*   20 | 13 | 17 | $27

Midtown | 209 W. 38th St. (bet. 7th & 8th Aves.) | 212-398-2367
Bayside | 211-37 26th Ave. (Bell Blvd.) | Queens | 718-229-2367
www.bensdeli.net

These "retro" delis cater to the "masses" with "colossal" sandwiches and other kosher staples; purists protest the "pedestrian" eats, "so-so" service and "run-down" "Miami Beach decor", but they're "accessible" enough in a pinch.

NEW Bergen Hill *Seafood*   – | – | – | M

Carroll Gardens | 387 Court St. (1st Pl.) | Brooklyn | 718-858-5483 | www.bergenhill.com

Tiny but ambitious, this Carroll Gardens seafood specialist via a pair of Le Cirque alums offers a concise menu of share-worthy plates; the crowd is hip Brooklynites, crammed into an old-school setting featuring a butcher-block counter and a few tables.

NEW Berg'n *Food Market*   – | – | – | M

Crown Heights | 899 Bergen St. (bet. Classon & Franklin Aves.) | Brooklyn | 718-857-2337 | www.bergn.com

The crew behind Brooklyn Flea and Smorgasburg goes brick-and-mortar with this all-day Crown Heights beer hall offering a well-curated brew list along with small-batch vendors offering BBQ, pizza, hot dogs and ramen burgers; carved out of a former garage, the wide-open space channels an industrial-chic mess hall with a long bar, communal tables and roll-up glass doors.

	FOOD	DECOR	SERVICE	COST

Berlyn *German* ▽ 22 | 20 | 21 | $52

Fort Greene | 25 Lafayette Ave. (Ashland Pl.) | Brooklyn | 718-222-5800 |
www.berlynrestaurant.com
"Handy for BAM" given its right-across-the-street location, this Fort
Greene German takes a "refined" approach with a "well-prepared",
meat-centric menu; the "laid-back", banquette-lined space and all-
seasons garden area add incentive pre- or post-performance.

Beso *Spanish* 25 | 22 | 22 | $42

St. George | 11 Schuyler St. (Richmond Terr.) | Staten Island |
718-816-8162 | www.besonyc.com
A "short walk from the ferry", this St. George Spaniard rolls out "outstanding" tapas and sangria in a "relaxed" setting that "feels very far
away from Staten Island"; admirers "wish it were bigger", though the
"reasonable" rates and staff that "never misses a beat" are fine as is.

Best Pizza *Pizza* ▽ 24 | 13 | 17 | $13

Williamsburg | 33 Havemeyer St. (bet. 7th & 8th Sts.) | Brooklyn |
718-599-2210 | www.best.piz.za.com
"They picked a ballsy name", but this Williamsburg pizza joint "does
itself proud" with a succinct lineup of "excellent" brick-oven pies, slices
and sandwiches; paper plate–adorned digs that "leave a lot to be desired" encourage takeout or delivery.

Betony *American* 25 | 24 | 24 | $92

Midtown | 41 W. 57th St. (bet. 5th & 6th Aves.) | 212-465-2400 |
www.betony-nyc.com
A "feast for all the senses", this "stylish" Midtown New American
delivers with "much fanfare" thanks to a "crazy creative" menu served
in "gorgeous" digs with "refined dining" upstairs and a downstairs bar
mixing "interesting cocktails"; the "stiff bill" doesn't faze its "pampered"
fan base who deem it a "worthwhile splurge."

Beyoglu *Turkish* 22 | 16 | 17 | $38

East 80s | 1431 Third Ave. (81st St.) | 212-650-0850
A "lively crowd" descends on this UES Turkish "standby" to graze on
"irresistible meze" at an "oh-so-reasonable" cost; it can be "rushed",
"cramped" and "loud", but the upstairs room is "quieter" and come summer the sidewalk seats are a "big draw."

Bianca *Italian* 21 | 16 | 18 | $35

NoHo | 5 Bleecker St. (Bowery) | 212-260-4666 | www.biancanyc.com
The "hearty" Emilia-Romagna dishes are "clearly made with love" and
a "fabulous bargain" to boot, making this cash-only NoHo Italian "gem"
well worth the "tight squeeze"; no reservations means there's "definitely
a wait", which those in the know spend "next door at the wine bar."

Biang! *Chinese/Noodle Shop* 25 | 18 | 17 | $21

Flushing | 41-10 Main St. (bet. 41st Ave. & 41st Rd.) | Queens |
718-888-7713 | www.biang-nyc.com
"Tease your taste buds" with "spicy goodness" at this Flushing "table-
service" site spun off from the Western Chinese staple Xi'an Famous
Foods, a biang-up source of "amazing" hand-ripped noodles and "excel-

lent skewers" at "reasonable", cash-only rates; seekers of the "authentic" say it's "worth the schlep."

Big Gay Ice Cream Shop *Ice Cream*
23 | 15 | 20 | $9

East Village | 125 E. Seventh St. (bet. Ave. A & 1st Ave.) | 212-533-9333
West Village | 61 Grove St. (7th Ave. S.) | no phone
www.biggayicecream.com

The name's as "hard to resist" as the "swell licks" at these soft-serve ice cream parlors, famed for creating "cool" cones with "campy" handles (e.g. the "life-changing" Salty Pimp); most agree the "long lines" are a "small price to pay" for the "sweet finish."

Big Wong *Chinese*
21 | 7 | 14 | $16

Chinatown | 67 Mott St. (bet. Bayard & Canal Sts.) | 212-964-0540 |
www.bigwongking.com

"Genuine, moan-provoking" Cantonese fare ("amazing congee", "outstanding roast meats") explains the "mob scene" at this cash-only C-towner; given the "insanely inexpensive" checks, it's easy to overlook the "nonexistent" decor, "rushed" service and unfortunate name.

Bill's Food & Drink *American/Steak*
18 | 19 | 20 | $50

Midtown | 57 E. 54th St. (bet. Madison & Park Aves.) | 212-518-2727 |
www.bills54.com

Prohibition-era speakeasy Bill's Gay Nineties reboots as this Midtown American grill, where chef John DeLucie (Crown, The Lion) focuses on "juicy" steaks; a townhouse setting replete with vintage artwork and a "great piano bar" recalls '20s Gotham, though some wonder if retro chic is "too cool" for this turf.

Birreria *Italian*
20 | 21 | 18 | $47

Flatiron | Eataly | 200 Fifth Ave. (bet. 23rd & 24th Sts.) | 212-937-8910 |
www.eataly.com

"Hard to beat on a nice summer" day, this "beer-lover's garden" atop Eataly is an all-seasons, retractable-roofed "experience" dispensing an "excellent" selection of cask ales soaked up with "light" Italian bites (mostly cheeses and salumi); the place is "hopping" from lunch till late, so "to actually gain access, go early."

Bistango *Italian*
22 | 16 | 21 | $42

NEW **East Midtown** | 145 E. 50th St. (bet. Lexington & 3rd Aves.) |
212-888-4121
Kips Bay | 415 Third Ave. (29th St.) | 212-725-8484
www.bistangonyc.com

While the Italian offerings at this "old-school" Kips Bay perennial (and its new East Midtown sibling) are certainly "tasty", it's the "wonderful gluten-free" options – "even beer" – that earn the most praise; "reasonable" pricing and "accommodating" service led by an "engaging host" seal the deal.

Bistro Cassis *French*
20 | 17 | 18 | $50

West 70s | 225 Columbus Ave. (bet. 70th & 71st Sts.) | 212-579-3966 |
www.bistrocassis.com

For a serving of "old Paris on the UWS", this French bistro can be counted on for "traditional", "satisfying" dishes at a relatively "reasonable price";

| | FOOD | DECOR | SERVICE | COST |

the "intimate" atmosphere and "expeditious" service make it "good pre–Lincoln Center", an "easy walk" away.

Bistro Chat Noir *French*

20 | 19 | 21 | $62

East 60s | 22 E. 66th St. (bet. 5th & Madison Aves.) | 212-794-2428 | www.bistrochatnoir.com

A "low-key fave" in a "chic" address off Madison Avenue, this Gallic Eastsider caters to "fashionable" folk with "Parisian intimacy" and "quite good" French bistro fare dispensed in a "snug" setting; tabs are "expensive", but a "fantastic" owner and "convivial staff" keep customers satisfied.

Bistro Les Amis *French*

20 | 18 | 22 | $50

SoHo | 180 Spring St. (Thompson St.) | 212-226-8645 | www.bistrolesamis.com

Bringing a soupçon of the "Left Bank" to SoHo, this seasoned French bistro lures fans with its "comforting" cooking vs. cost ratio; ok, there's "no scene" going on, but sidewalk seats provide prime people-watching and the "*charmant*" staff lives up to the promise of its name.

Bistro Milano *Italian*

∇ 20 | 17 | 19 | $56

Midtown | 1350 Sixth Ave. (bet. 54th & 55th Sts.) | 212-757-2600 | www.bistromilanonyc.com

"Fresh pastas", "excellent pizzas" and a "spacious" outdoor terrace combine to make this Midtown Northern Italian a "reliable" drop-in; given its "convenience to City Center" and "Fifth Avenue shopping", it's a natural for theatergoers and "tourists" alike.

Bistro Vendôme *French*

22 | 18 | 21 | $57

East Midtown | 405 E. 58th St. (1st Ave.) | 212-935-9100 | www.bistrovendomenyc.com

"Sutton seniors" gather at this "upscale bistro" for French fare dispatched by "Gallic-accented staffers" who are as "charming" as the tri-level townhouse setting; the less-impressed shrug "nothing special", but those who love the "particularly pretty" terrace call it a "neighborhood jewel."

NEW Black Ant *Mexican*

– | – | – | M

East Village | 60 Second Ave. (bet. 3rd & 4th Sts.) | 212-598-0300 | www.blackantnyc.com

The Ofrenda team is behind this modern East Village Mexican where of-the-moment ingredients (chia seeds, cod cheeks, braised rabbit) and not-so-of-the-moment items (ants, grasshoppers) make for completely original dishes; a long list of tequilas and mezcals helps make the dark, noir-ish setting feel all the more exotic.

Black Iron Burger *Burgers*

23 | 15 | 20 | $23

East Village | 540 E. Fifth St. (Ave. B) | 212-677-6067 | www.blackironburger.com

"Pretty damn good" "no-frills" burgers paired with draft pints "go down easy" at this East Village "hole-in-the-wall"; though the "earthy" setting's on the "small" side, the staff is "fun", the tabs "reasonable" and the late-night hours a bonus.

Black Whale *American*

23 | 20 | 21 | $33

City Island | 279 City Island Ave. (Hawkins St.) | Bronx | 718-885-3657 | www.theblackwhalefb.wix.com

The "offbeat" nautical decor conjures up "Cape Cod in the Bronx" at this "cute" City Island vet where the "inexpensive" New American menu includes some notably "decadent desserts"; fans find the "terrific" Sunday brunch and "lovely" back patio equally "memorable."

Blanca *American*

∇ 24 | 21 | 26 | $223

Bushwick | 261 Moore St. (Bogart St.) | Brooklyn | 347-799-2807 | www.blancanyc.com

An "epic food adventure" awaits at this loft annex of the Bushwick phenom Roberta's, which presents chef Carlo Mirarchi's "unbelievable" New American tasting menu at a 12-seat counter fronting a pristine kitchen; the $195 set price may mean "dumping out your whole wallet", but the payoff is a "one-of-a-kind" dining experience.

Blaue Gans *Austrian/German*

22 | 18 | 20 | $55

TriBeCa | 139 Duane St. (B'way) | 212-571-8880 | www.kg-ny.com

"First-rate" Wiener schnitzel heads the list of "hearty" Austro-German dishes at Kurt Gutenbrunner's "down-to-earth" "neighborhood" TriBeCan, abetted by "wonderful" Teutonic brews; the "artsy poster-clad" room is "simple" but "cool", while "fair prices" and "pleasant" staffers add to the "gemütlich" mood.

Blossom *Vegan/Vegetarian*

22 | 16 | 20 | $32

Chelsea | 187 Ninth Ave. (bet. 21st & 22nd Sts.) | 212-627-1144
West Village | 41 Carmine St. (bet. Bedford & Bleecker Sts.) | 646-438-9939
www.blossomnyc.com

Blossom du Jour *Vegan/Vegetarian*

Hell's Kitchen | 617 Ninth Ave. (bet. 43rd & 44th Sts.) | 646-998-3535
Chelsea | 259 W. 23rd St. (bet. 7th & 8th Aves.) | 212-229-2595
West 60s | 165 Amsterdam Ave. (bet. 67th & 68th Sts.) | 212-799-9010
www.blossomdujour.com

The food's "completely vegan" but "you wouldn't know" at these "earthy" organic "havens", whose "satisfying" fare makes healthy almost seem "hedonistic"; "efficient" service and "relaxed" surroundings add to the overall "solid" feel, while the du Jour outlets offer a "quick" fix to go.

BLT Bar & Grill *American*

22 | 19 | 20 | $49

Financial District | W Hotel Downtown | 123 Washington St. (bet. Albany & Carlisle Sts.) | 646-826-8666 | www.bltbarandgrill.com

A "classier" option in the "barren Financial District", this all-day American tavern in the W Downtown serves "upscale" standards to "expense-account" wielders and "9/11 Memorial" visitors; the high ceilings in this duplex add some airiness to the "lively" after-work scene.

BLT Fish *Seafood*

25 | 21 | 23 | M

Flatiron | 21 W. 17th St. (bet. 5th & 6th Aves.) | 212-691-8888 | www.bltfish.com

"Straight-out-of-the-water" seafood is the bait at this Flatiron fishmonger famed for its "expertly prepared" catch and "exceptional" service; the swanky upstairs rooms are now reserved for private parties only, but the "funky" ground-floor Fish Shack remains open to all comers, with its lower prices and "loud" acoustics intact.

BLT Prime   *Steak*

FOOD	DECOR	SERVICE	COST
25	22	24	$91

Gramercy Park | 111 E. 22nd St. (bet. Lexington Ave. & Park Ave. S.) | 212-995-8500 | www.bltprime.com

"They know their way around a cow" at this "chic" Gramercy steakhouse touted for "perfectly cooked" chops and "light-as-a-feather" popovers; "stellar" wines, "solicitous" service and "sleek" decor add to the overall "special experience" and help explain tabs that may "leave your credit card smoking."

BLT Steak   *Steak*

FOOD	DECOR	SERVICE	COST
24	21	22	$82

East Midtown | 106 E. 57th St. (bet. Lexington & Park Aves.) | 212-752-7470 | www.bltsteak.com

East Midtown "power brokers" mix "business and pleasure" at this "classy" cow palace featuring "spot-on" "quality" via its famed "melt-in-your-mouth" popovers and "beautifully prepared" steaks; a "stylish", "modern" enclave tended by a "professional" team, "it ain't cheap" but "you get what you pay for."

Blue Bottle Coffee   *Coffee*

FOOD	DECOR	SERVICE	COST
23	18	20	$8

Chelsea | 450 W. 15th St. (10th Ave.) | 510-653-3394
Hell's Kitchen | Gotham West Mkt. | 600 11th Ave. (bet. 44th & 45th Sts.) | 212-582-7945
Midtown | 1 Rockefeller Plaza (bet. 48th & 49th Sts.) | 510-653-3394
NEW **Boerum Hill** | 85 Dean St. (bet. Hoyt & Smith Sts.) | Brooklyn | 510-653-3394
Williamsburg | 160 Berry St. (bet. 4th & 5th Sts.) | Brooklyn | 718-387-4160
www.bluebottlecoffee.com

Every hipster's "favorite way to start the day", these imports from the Bay Area are known for their "marvelous" slow-drip coffee and "intense", freshly roasted blends; "knowledgeable baristas" do the honors, but "the line's often long" – "and deservedly so."

Blue Fin   *Seafood*

FOOD	DECOR	SERVICE	COST
23	21	20	$59

Midtown | W Hotel Times Sq. | 1567 Broadway (47th St.) | 212-918-1400 | www.bluefinnyc.com

Broadway "buzz" is in full swing at this Times Square seafood "staple" supplying "excellent fish" via "aim-to-please" servers in "slick, modern" surrounds with "hustle and bustle" downstairs and a "mellower" mezzanine; "high prices" are the catch, but it's always a "best bet on a theater evening."

Blue Hill   *American*

FOOD	DECOR	SERVICE	COST
26	23	26	$94

Greenwich Village | 75 Washington Pl. (bet. MacDougal St. & 6th Ave.) | 212-539-1776 | www.bluehillfarm.com

Experience the "essence" of Dan Barber's farm-to-table "vision" at this "transporting" Village American, a "top destination" for "exceptional food" that melds the "freshest" local sourcing with "inspired" preparations; "responsive service", "quiet" decibels and "soothing decor" make for "flawless" dining that's "definitely expensive" but worth "saving up for" – "it doesn't get much better than this."

Blue Marble Ice Cream *Ice Cream*   ▽ 21 | 13 | 16 | $7

Prospect Heights | 186 Underhill Ave. (bet. Sterling & St. Johns Pls.) | Brooklyn | 718-399-6926
Cobble Hill | 196 Court St. (Wyckoff St.) | Brooklyn | 718-858-5551
www.bluemarbleicecream.com

Dispensing some of the "dreamiest scoops" around, these "do-good" parlors ply "heavenly" organic ice cream that's produced with a local focus and served with a "sprinkled smile"; the "premium" treats may run on the "expensive" side, but they're "popular for good reason."

Blue 9 Burger *Burgers*   20 | 8 | 15 | $12

East 70s | 1415 Second Ave. (bet. 73rd & 74th Sts.) | 212-988-8171
Greenwich Village | 92 Third Ave. (bet. 12th & 13th Sts.) | 212-979-0053
Though the mood's "fast food" and there's "no ambiance to speak of", the burgers are "quite delectable" at these "quick, cheap" patty places; the Village original is an "after-hours" magnet for the "student" set, though some turn to it only for "delivery" given the "indifferent service" and "unexciting" digs.

Blue Ribbon *American*   24 | 18 | 22 | $61

SoHo | 97 Sullivan St. (bet. Prince & Spring Sts.) | 212-274-0404
Blue Ribbon Brooklyn *American*
Park Slope | 280 Fifth Ave. (bet. 1st St. & Garfield Pl.) | Brooklyn | 718-840-0404
www.blueribbonrestaurants.com

A certified winner, the Bromberg brothers' "loud, lively" SoHo "fixture" (and its "family-friendly" Park Slope sibling) concocts "diverse" New American eats "with heart and soul"; thanks to a "wonderful staff", the "bonhomie" carries into the "wee hours", even though the pricing is "up there" and the no-reservations policy has a "downside: the wait."

Blue Ribbon Bakery *American*   23 | 18 | 21 | $49

West Village | 35 Downing St. (Bedford St.) | 212-337-0404 | www.blueribbonrestaurants.com

The "wonderful smell" of bread perfumes the air at the Bromberg brothers' "crusty" West Village American bistro that supplies the "epitome of comfort food", plus "enthusiastic" service and a particularly "standout" brunch; both its "shoebox"-size ground floor and bigger "wine-cellar"-esque basement are "long on charm."

Blue Ribbon Fried Chicken *Chicken*   19 | 13 | 16 | $19

East Village | 28 E. First St. (2nd Ave.) | 212-228-0404 | www.blueribbonfriedchicken.com

Offering over-the-counter access to the "super-tasty", Southern-style fried chicken served at the Bromberg brothers' other restaurants, this "functional" East Villager vends its "well-seasoned" poultry by the piece; even so, penny-pinchers cluck it's "a little pricey for fast food."

Blue Ribbon Sushi *Japanese*   25 | 19 | 22 | $73

NEW **Battery Park City** | Hudson Eats | 200 Vesey St. (West St.) | 212-417-7000
SoHo | 119 Sullivan St. (bet. Prince & Spring Sts.) | 212-343-0404
www.blueribbonrestaurants.com

Long a "standard-bearer of cool" in SoHo, this Bromberg brothers Japanese (with a counter-service sequel in Hudson Eats) slices "top-flight", "work-of-art" sushi along with a "wonderful array" of cooked items; "proactive service" and "cozy", "denlike" digs offset "pretty-penny" price tags and that "frustrating" no-rez thing.

Blue Ribbon Sushi Bar & Grill *Japanese*   25 | 21 | 22 | $74

Midtown | 6 Columbus Hotel | 308 W. 58th St. (bet. 8th & 9th Aves.) | 212-397-0404 | www.blueribbonrestaurants.com
Somewhat "swankier" than its "bohemian kin", this "inviting" Japanese "tucked away" in a Columbus Circle hotel is touted for its "fresh-off-the-boat" sushi and "impeccable" grilled fare; it shares the "mellow" vibe, late-night hours and "steep tabs" of its Downtown siblings.

Blue Ribbon Sushi Izakaya *Japanese*   22 | 21 | 22 | $60

Lower East Side | Sixty LES Hotel | 187 Orchard St. (bet. Houston & Stanton Sts.) | 212-466-0404 | www.blueribbonrestaurants.com
The Bromberg brothers' take on the traditional izakaya, this all-day Sixty LES Hotel Japanese offers an extensive menu that "ain't cheap" but includes a "terrific" signature fried chicken plus "delish sushi"; still, many "go more for the location" and the "cool" feel of its loungey, dimly lit digs.

Blue Smoke *BBQ*   21 | 18 | 20 | $44

Battery Park City | 255 Vesey St. (bet. North End Ave. & West St.) | 212-889-2363
Kips Bay | 116 E. 27th St. (bet. Lexington Ave. & Park Ave. S.) | 212-447-7733
www.bluesmoke.com
"Meat fiends" have a "grand time" at Danny Meyer's "smokin'", "family-friendly" BBQ joints, where "up-tempo" staffers supply "fall-off-the-bone ribs" and other "honest" staples; a "fine selection of bourbons" (and "cool" sounds at the Kips Bay flagship's downstairs Jazz Standard) should cure any "pseudo-Texas atmosphere" blues.

Blue Water Grill *Seafood*   24 | 22 | 22 | $60

Union Square | 31 Union Sq. W. (16th St.) | 212-675-9500 | www.bluewatergrillnyc.com
Expect a "class operation" at this "upbeat" Union Square "favorite" that owes its "staying power" to "superb" seafood, "smart" service and an "expansive" former bank setting with a "lovely" marbled interior and "delightful" wraparound terrace; add a "jazz room downstairs", and its "good-looking" clientele doesn't mind the "high sticker price."

Boathouse *American*   17 | 26 | 17 | $57

Central Park | Central Park Lake, enter on E. 72nd St. (Park Dr. N.) | 212-517-2233 | www.thecentralparkboathouse.com
It's all about the "unbeatable location" at this lakeside American, where "the decor is Central Park" and watching the rowboats drift by "feels like being on vacation"; the menu's "not overly exciting" and the service just "so-so", but for tourists and natives alike, this "must-have" NYC experience truly "sells itself."

Bobby Van's Grill *Steak*   23 | 19 | 22 | $73

Midtown | 135 W. 50th St. (bet. 6th & 7th Aves.) | 212-957-5050
Midtown | 120 W. 45th St. (bet. 6th & 7th Aves.) | 212-575-5623

continued

Bobby Van's Steakhouse *Steak*

East Midtown | 131 E. 54th St. (bet. Lexington & Park Aves.) | 212-207-8050
East Midtown | 230 Park Ave. (46th St.) | 212-867-5490
Financial District | 25 Broad St. (Exchange Pl.) | 212-344-8463
JFK Airport | Terminal 8, Across from Gate 14 | JFK Access Rd. | Queens | 718-553-2100
www.bobbyvans.com

A "safe bet" for "suits" entertaining clients over lunch, these "straightforward" chop shops feature career waiters ferrying "well-executed" slabs of beef in "masculine", "clubby" environs (including a "really cool" bank-vault setting at the FiDi branch); expect "no surprises", right down to the "hefty" check.

Bobo *French*   24 | 24 | 22 | $64

West Village | 181 W. 10th St. (7th Ave. S.) | 212-488-2626 | www.bobonyc.com

The "ambiance is the selling point" at this "low-lit" West Village townhouse serving "well-prepared" French fare to a "Euro"-heavy following either in an "ornate dining room", outdoor terrace or "more youthful" downstairs bar; it may be a tad "expensive", but service is "friendly" and the vibe "charming."

Bocca *Italian*   22 | 18 | 21 | $48

Flatiron | 39 E. 19th St. (bet. B'way & Park Ave. S.) | 212-387-1200 | www.boccanyc.com

It "feels like Rome" at this "enjoyable" Cacio e Pepe sibling in the Flatiron known for its "expert" Italian cooking, "appealing" modern look and "reasonable" rates; regulars say "pasta is the thing to eat" here, notably its "cool" signature dish tossed tableside in a wheel of pecorino.

Bocca di Bacco *Italian*   20 | 19 | 19 | $49

NEW **Chelsea** | 191 Seventh Ave. (bet. 21st. & 22nd Sts.) | 212-675-5980
Chelsea | 169 Ninth Ave. (20th St.) | 212-989-8400
Midtown | 828 Ninth Ave. (bet. 54th & 55th Sts.) | 212-265-8828
Hell's Kitchen | 635 Ninth Ave. (bet. 44th & 45th Sts.) | 212-262-2525
www.boccadibacconyc.com

"Old-world Italy" comes to Manhattan via these Italians vending "jazzedup" standards bolstered by "sure-hit" wines by the glass and "rustic", brick-walled settings; "up-and-down" service strikes off-notes, but given the "decent prices" and "positive energy", most "go home happy."

Bocca Lupo *Italian*   ∇ 22 | 20 | 20 | $46

Cobble Hill | 391 Henry St. (Warren St.) | Brooklyn | 718-243-2522 | www.boccalupo-brooklyn.com

Cobble Hill denizens tout this "terrific local" enoteca for "seductive" Italian small plates paired with a "great wine list", also via The Boot; the "cozy" quarters are "super kid-friendly" during the first wave but transition to a "busy late-night" scene for singletons.

	FOOD	DECOR	SERVICE	COST

Bocelli *Italian/Seafood*
25 | 21 | 23 | $57

Old Town | 1250 Hylan Blvd. (Parkinson Ave.) | Staten Island | 718-420-6150 | www.bocellirest.com

With "delicious" seafood specialties, "professional" service and "pretty elegant" Tuscan decor, this Old Town Italian "definitely stands out" among its Staten Island peers; despite Manhattan-style pricing, "reservations are a must" on weekends.

NEW Bodega Negra *Mexican*
∇ 23 | 23 | 21 | $63

Chelsea | Dream Downtown Hotel | 355 W. 16th St. (bet. 8th & 9th Aves.) | 212-229-2336 | www.bodeganegranyc.com

"High expectations" set by the London original are met at Serge Becker's "over-the-top" hacienda in Chelsea's Dream Downtown Hotel that matches "fabulous" Mexican fare and primo mezcals with "cool vibes"; the main room is "filled with artifacts" from guitars to tequila casks, while a front cafe is a bit more casual.

Bodrum *Mediterranean/Turkish*
20 | 15 | 19 | $38

West 80s | 584 Amsterdam Ave. (bet. 88th & 89th Sts.) | 212-799-2806 | www.bodrumnyc.com

"Small and cozy", this UWS "neighborhood" Med is the "real deal" for "inexpensive" dining on "stellar" Turkish meze and "tasty thin-crust pizza"; though service is "speedy", it's often "crowded and cramped", so insiders flee to the "outside tables."

Bogota Latin Bistro *Pan-Latin*
24 | 19 | 21 | $36

Park Slope | 141 Fifth Ave. (St. Johns Pl.) | Brooklyn | 718-230-3805 | www.bogotabistro.com

"It's always a party" at this "hyper-popular" Park Slope Pan-Latin, where the "awesome", "Colombian-style" eats and "exotic drinks" whisk you to "Bogotá"; "decent prices" and an "incredible staff" help keep the "good times" and "noise level" going strong.

Bohemian *Japanese*
∇ 25 | 24 | 24 | $87

NoHo | 57 Great Jones St. (bet. Bowery & Lafayette St.) | no phone

"You'll need a reservation" and a referral (there's "no listed phone number") to access this "exclusive" NoHo Japanese hidden "behind a butcher shop", where the "exceptional" food and cocktails are presented by "truly wonderful people"; an "intimate", denlike room furnished with "low couches" is perfect for conversation, and while prices run "steep", it will leave a "lasting memory."

The Boil *Seafood*
∇ 23 | 14 | 18 | $56

Lower East Side | 139 Chrystie St. (bet. Broome & Delancey Sts.) | 212-925-8815 | www.theboilny.com

"Be ready to get messy" at this LES New Orleans–style seafooder where "peel 'n' eat shellfish" and more are offered with a variety of "spiced-crazed sauces"; "decent pricing", no reservations and somewhat "cramped", brick-lined digs make for a "very casual" vibe.

Bo-Ky *Noodle Shop*
21 | 6 | 14 | $14

Chinatown | 80 Bayard St. (bet. Mott & Mulberry Sts.) | 212-406-2292 | www.bokynyc.com
Little Italy | 216 Grand St. (Elizabeth St.) | 212-219-9228

One of the few "good things about jury duty" is the chance to lunch at these Chinatown–Little Italy noodle shops churning out "authentic" Chinese and Vietnamese soups for ultra-"cheap" coin; "dreary" decor, "busy" atmospherics and "poor" (albeit "quick") service come with the territory.

Bombay Palace *Indian* 21 | 18 | 19 | $46

Midtown | 30 W. 52nd St. (bet. 5th & 6th Aves.) | 212-541-7777 | www.bombaypalacenyc.com

On the Midtown scene since 1979, this "spacious" Indian remains a "solid standby" for all the "standards"; maybe the once-"sumptuous" surroundings are getting "a little tired", but no one's weary of its "good-value" $18 lunch buffet.

BonChon *Chicken* 21 | 12 | 15 | $21

Financial District | 104 John St. (Cliff St.) | 646-692-4660
Midtown | 207 W. 38th St. (bet. 7th & 8th Aves.) | 212-221-3339
Midtown | 325 Fifth Ave. (bet. 32nd & 33rd Sts.) | 212-686-8282
Bayside | 45-37 Bell Blvd. (bet. 45th Dr. & 45th Rd.) | Queens | 718-225-1010
www.bonchon.com

"Habit-forming" is the verdict on the "out-of-sight" Korean fried chicken with "crispy, parchmentlike skin" sold at this international chain; since the birds are cooked to order, expect "forever" waits, not to mention "slipshod" service, "no decor" and just-"decent" prices.

Bond 45 *Italian/Steak* 19 | 18 | 19 | $55

Midtown | 154 W. 45th St. (bet. 6th & 7th Aves.) | 212-869-4545 | www.bond45.com

Shelly Fireman's "cavernous", "vibrant" trattoria in Times Square's old Bond clothing store presents a "straight-up", "something-for-everybody" Italian steakhouse menu in a "well-decorated barn" of a setting; "service with alacrity" suits theatergoers, though "loud" acoustics and kinda "high" prices are less well received.

Bond St *Japanese* 25 | 22 | 21 | $79

NoHo | 6 Bond St. (bet. B'way & Lafayette St.) | 212-777-2500 | www.bondstrestaurant.com

"They've still got it" at this NoHo Japanese "knockout", where the "work-of-art" sushi and "swanky" space with a "cool" downstairs lounge deliver both "style and substance"; "beautiful" people out "to see and be seen" readily bond with the "trendy vibe", less so with the "expensive" tabs.

Bonnie's Grill *Burgers* 22 | 13 | 20 | $28

Park Slope | 278 Fifth Ave. (bet. 1st St. & Garfield Pl.) | Brooklyn | 718-369-9527 | www.bonniesgrill.com

Park Slopers refuel at this "short-order joint" slinging "damn good burgers" and other basics in "classic diner" digs; it's "fun sitting at the counter" and the grub's "well priced", but since the dimensions are "slim", "good luck getting a seat on the weekend."

Boqueria *Spanish* 23 | 19 | 20 | $49

Flatiron | 53 W. 19th St. (bet. 5th & 6th Aves.) | 212-255-4160
SoHo | 171 Spring St. (bet. B'way & Thompson St.) | 212-343-4255
www.boquerianyc.com

"Graze your way" through "top-class tapas" at these "happening" Spaniards bringing a "transported-to-Barcelona" feel to the Flatiron and

SoHo; a "competent" crew navigates the "no-room-to-spare" settings and "well-priced" wines offset tabs that "add up pretty quickly", but the no-rez rule results in "discouraging" waits.

NEW Bo's *Creole/Southern*

∇ 20 | 24 | 20 | $47

Flatiron | 6 W. 24th St. (bet. B'way & 6th Ave.) | 212-234-2373 | www.bosrestaurant.com

This "easygoing" "find" brings New Orleans–inspired "excitement" to the Flatiron with its "appetizing" twists on Southern cuisine ("gator, anyone?"); a snazzy backdrop turns on the "Creole charm", and the specialty drinks are "a must" since it's always "Mardi Gras at the bar."

Bosie Tea Parlor *Teahouse*

∇ 23 | 18 | 20 | $29

West Village | 10 Morton St. (bet. Bleecker St. & 7th Ave. S.) | 212-352-9900 | www.bosienyc.com

This "quiet" West Village teahouse offers "exotic" brews and "delicate" nibbles (including "delish" French macarons) in a "quaint" cafe setting; fans say this "delightful oasis" makes for a "truly relaxing" dining experience.

NEW Botequim *Brazilian*

– | – | – | E

Greenwich Village | Hyatt Union Square | 132 Fourth Ave. (13th St.) | 212-432-1324 | www.onefivehospitality.com

São Paulo–born chef Marco Moreira (Tocqueville) produces modern takes on Brazilian classics – including lots of hearth-roasted meats – at this arrival below The Fourth in the Hyatt Union Square; its warmly lit, subterranean space features communal seating as well as small tables, with an open kitchen providing glimpses of the culinary action.

Bottega *Italian*

∇ 20 | 20 | 20 | $58

East 70s | 1331 Second Ave. (bet. 70th & 71st Sts.) | 212-288-5282 | www.bottegany.com

A "nice neighborhood place", this UES trattoria turns out "accessible" Italian staples in a "pleasant" atmosphere; other pluses include a "large, comfortable" setting with a "busy bar" and "terrific outdoor" seating, as well as "personable" service.

Bottega Del Vino *Italian*

22 | 18 | 18 | $66

Midtown | 7 E. 59th St. (bet. 5th & Madison Aves.) | 212-223-2724 | www.bottegadelvinonyc.com

"Situated near everything" – or at least Bergdorf's, the Plaza and the Apple Store – this "relaxed" Midtown "replica of the Venice original" dispenses "tasty" Italiana backed by an "immense" wine list; buoyant staffers maintain the "happy mood", at least until the bill arrives.

Bottino *Italian*

21 | 18 | 18 | $48

Chelsea | 246 10th Ave. (bet. 24th & 25th Sts.) | 212-206-6766 | www.bottinonyc.com

Convenient to West Chelsea's gallery district and the High Line, this "all-around pleasant" Tuscan "pioneer" delivers "solid" meals at "moderate-to-a-bit-expensive" prices; the "unhurried" pace suits its "arty" constituents, though the "charming", "spacious" garden is bound to please everyone.

	FOOD	DECOR	SERVICE	COST

Bouchon Bakery *American/French* 23 | 15 | 18 | $30

Midtown | Rockefeller Ctr. | 1 Rockefeller Plaza (bet. 48th & 49th Sts.) | 212-782-3890
Midtown | Time Warner Ctr. | 10 Columbus Circle, 3rd fl. (60th St. at B'way) | 212-823-9363
www.bouchonbakery.com

Thomas Keller's "exceptional" Time Warner Center bakery/take-out counter (and its Rock Center sidekick) serves "addictive goodies" with a "French accent" – think "must-have" macarons, "lovely pastries" and "terrific" sandwiches and breads – that make for a "perpetual queue"; though it's "mall-like" and "not inexpensive", the "splendid view over Columbus Circle" "lifts the spirits."

Bouley *French* 29 | 28 | 28 | $132

TriBeCa | 163 Duane St. (bet. Hudson St. & W. B'way) | 212-964-2525 | www.davidbouley.com

"You'll be swept off your feet" at David Bouley's "enchanting" TriBeCa "shrine" to "first-class" French dining – rated No. 2 for Food in NYC – where "unmatched" "attention to detail" informs the "meticulously" crafted cuisine, "masterful service" and "posh", jackets-required milieu; since such "crème de la crème" dining comes with "a bill to remember", the $55 prix fixe lunch is "a steal."

Boulton & Watt *American* ∇ 22 | 21 | 20 | $36

East Village | 5 Ave. A (1st St.) | 646-490-6004 | www.boultonandwattnyc.com

This "big" East Village American is named for the inventors of the steam engine, and its "cool-looking" industrial decor takes a page from steampunk design; the "better-than-expected" American gastropub menu consists of updated comfort classics – with a "banging" pickle selection – and is accompanied by an innovative cocktail list.

Boulud Sud *Mediterranean* 25 | 23 | 24 | $76

West 60s | 20 W. 64th St. (bet. B'way & CPW) | 212-595-1313 | www.bouludsud.com

"Lincoln Center–goers never had it so good" thanks to Daniel Boulud's "grown-up" Mediterranean "treat" alongside Bar Boulud, where "engaging" staffers serve "glorious" cuisine in "spacious", "comfortable-chic" surroundings; it's simultaneously "expensive" and right "on the money", but its "high-end" fan base can handle the rates.

Braai *S African* ∇ 20 | 17 | 17 | $42

Midtown | 329 W. 51st St. (bet. 8th & 9th Aves.) | 212-315-3315 | www.braainyc.com

Diners with a "taste for adventure" mingle with "homesick expats" at this "different" Midtown outpost specializing in South African barbecue; the "flavorful", "unique" eats (think ostrich and venison) arrive in a "hut"-like, "thatched-roof" setting that adds to the "novelty."

Brasserie *French* 21 | 21 | 21 | $55

East Midtown | Seagram Bldg. | 100 E. 53rd St. (bet. Lexington & Park Aves.) | 212-751-4840 | www.patinagroup.com

A "tried-and-true" "crowd-pleaser", this sunken brasserie in the Seagram Building remains a "go-to" for "delicious" French bites and "unpretentious" service in a "stylish", "futuristic space"; steadfast supporters keep it "happening" (and "noisy") despite the "steep-ish prices."

Brasserie Cognac *French*   19 | 18 | 18 | $52

Midtown | 1740 Broadway (55th St.) | 212-757-3600 |
www.cognacrestaurant.com

Brasserie Cognac East *French*

East 70s | 963 Lexington Ave. (70th St.) | 212-249-5100 |
www.cognaceast.com

"Homesick Parisians" feel at home at these "debonair" brasseries where "simple, tasty" standards come at "reasonable" prices; the West 50s original is "convenient to Carnegie Hall" and City Center, but both locations are deemed "attractive" enough for a "romantic" tête-à-tête.

Brasserie 8½ *French*   22 | 23 | 22 | $65

Midtown | 9 W. 57th St. (bet. 5th & 6th Aves.) | 212-829-0812 |
www.patinagroup.com

Make an "entrance" down a "sweeping stairway" at this subterranean Midtown brasserie that provides "delicious" French fare and "cordial" service in "charming" environs with "fine art on display"; it's a "decorous" nexus for "conversational dining", albeit with a "busy" post-work bar scene.

Brasserie Ruhlmann *French*   19 | 19 | 18 | $61

Midtown | Rockefeller Ctr. | 45 Rockefeller Plaza (bet. 50th & 51st Sts.) |
212-974-2020 | www.brasserieruhlmann.com

"Hobnob with the NBC crowd" and others "happily expensing their meals" at Laurent Tourondel's "heart-of-Rock-Center" brasserie providing a "sumptuous art deco" setting for "good" (if "not spectacular") French cooking; the "fascinating people-watching" from its "amazing" patio supplies added "fun."

Bread *Italian/Sandwiches*   ∇ 20 | 16 | 18 | $36

NoLita | 20 Spring St. (bet. Elizabeth & Mott Sts.) | 212-334-1015

Bread To Go *Italian/Sandwiches*

West Village | 450 Hudson St. (bet. Barrow & Morton Sts.) | 212-929-1015

There's "much more than bread" on offer at this "low-key" NoLita nook dishing up "affordable" Italiana highlighted by "satisfying" panini and "wonderful tomato soup"; service and "elbow room" may be in short supply, but its "cool hipster" fan base doesn't seem to mind; P.S. there's also a West Village take-out adjunct.

Breeze *French/Thai*   ∇ 21 | 12 | 18 | $33

Hell's Kitchen | 661 Ninth Ave. (bet. 45th & 46th Sts.) | 212-262-7777 |
www.breezenyc.com

"Bright-orange decor" draws attention to this "unique" Hell's Kitchen venue that plies "serious" Thai-French fusion vittles backed by "fruity drinks" in "long, narrow" digs; "rapid" service and "too-good-to-be-true" pricing make it a "great first act" pre-theater.

Brennan & Carr *Sandwiches*   23 | 11 | 18 | $19

Sheepshead Bay | 3432 Nostrand Ave. (Ave. U) | Brooklyn | 718-646-9559

More than 75 years old, this cash-only Sheepshead Bay "tradition" still "rocks" thanks to "outrageous" double-dipped roast beef sandwiches "drowned in au jus"; it's something of a "dive" with "table-mat menus", but enthusiasts of "old-fashioned goodness" keep returning "with the new generation in tow."

The Breslin *British*   24 | 22 | 18 | $53

Flatiron | Ace Hotel | 16 W. 29th St. (bet. B'way & 5th Ave.) | 212-679-1939 | www.thebreslin.com

"Haute comfort food" reigns at April Bloomfield and Ken Friedman's "NY version of an English pub" in the Ace Hotel, dishing up "elevated", "unapologetically hearty" fare to the "über-hip throngs"; despite no reservations (except for hotel guests) and surplus "attitude", most find it "worth" the "steep" bill.

Brgr *Burgers*   20 | 13 | 16 | $20

Chelsea | 287 Seventh Ave. (bet. 26th & 27th Sts.) | 212-488-7500
East 60s | 1026 Third Ave. (bet. 60th & 61st Sts.) | 212-588-0080
NEW West 70s | 2233 Broadway (bet. 79th & 80th Sts.) | 212-875-1800
www.brgr.com

"Brgr lvrs" plug these "highbrow fast-food" places for their "solid" grass-fed beef patties "made to order" with "neat toppings" and augmented with "excellent" shakes; however, critics find "only average" goods that "can be pricey" for their "abbreviated" size.

Bricco *Italian*   20 | 18 | 20 | $48

Midtown | 304 W. 56th St. (bet. 8th & 9th Aves.) | 212-245-7160 | www.bricconyc.com

This Midtown Italian hideaway is a "steady" source of "well-prepared" pasta and wood-oven pizza delivered by the "nicest staff"; "reasonable rates" and "warm" atmospherics (check out the lipsticked kisses on the ceiling) buttress its "reliable" rep.

Brick Lane Curry House *Indian*   21 | 15 | 18 | $30

East Midtown | 235 E. 53rd St. (bet. 2nd & 3rd Aves.) | 212-339-8353 | www.bricklanetoo.com
East 90s | 1664 Third Ave. (bet. 93rd & 94th Sts.) | 646-998-4440 | www.bricklane93rd.com
East Village | 99 Second Ave. (bet. 5th & 6th Sts.) | 212-979-2900 | www.bricklanecurryhouse.com

There's "no need to go to London – let alone India" – thanks to this curry-savvy East Side mini-chain purveying "real-deal" dishes with heat levels ranging from "mild to crazy hot" (the "fiery phaal" requires "extra napkins to wipe away the sweat and tears"); like the decor, the tabs are distinctly "low budget."

Brindle Room *American*   20 | 15 | 18 | $36

East Village | 277 E. 10th St. (Ave. A) | 212-529-9702 | www.brindleroom.com

It's all about the "worth-a-trip" burger – an off-the-menu item at din-nertime – at this compact but "cozy" East Villager that also features a "small" menu of American dishes; some complain about "sitting on high stools", but at least the service and pricing are "accommodating."

BrisketTown *BBQ*   24 | 13 | 19 | $29

Williamsburg | 359 Bedford Ave. (bet. 4th & 5th Sts.) | Brooklyn | 718-701-8909 | www.delaneybbq.com

Pitmaster Daniel Delaney is the mind behind this "destination" Williamsburg joint smoking "melt-in-your-mouth" BBQ – notably "unequaled" brisket – at "great prices"; a "friendly" counter crew and "rustic, old-wood" decor are also part of the package – just know it "can be crazy" at prime times, and when they run out of meat, it's closing time.

Brooklyn Crab *Seafood*   20 | 19 | 18 | $43

Red Hook | 24 Reed St. (bet. Conover & Van Brunt Sts.) | Brooklyn | 718-643-2722 | www.brooklyncrab.com

From the owners of Alma, this "casual" Red Hook triplex fields a "solid" menu of fish-shack classics and raw bar snacks that taste even better given its "to-die-for" views of the harbor; additional perks like "fun" mini-golf and plenty of "outdoor seats" offset the "ridiculous" waits and "slow" service.

Brooklyn Farmacy *Ice Cream*   22 | 23 | 21 | $20

Carroll Gardens | 513 Henry St. (Sackett St.) | Brooklyn | 718-522-6260 | www.brooklynfarmacy.blogspot.com

"Nostalgia" and seasonal, locally sourced ice cream add up to "a lot of fun" at this Carroll Gardens homage to "old-school soda shops", where the sundaes, egg creams and such – plus "simple, satisfying" diner staples – are "expertly" dispensed by "friendly" staffers; housed in a "beautiful" restored pharmacy, it's "retro" to the core.

Brooklyn Ice Cream Factory *Ice Cream*   24 | 14 | 17 | $8

Dumbo | 1 Water St. (Old Fulton St.) | Brooklyn | 718-246-3963
Greenpoint | 97 Commercial St. (Manhattan Ave.) | Brooklyn | 718-349-2506
www.brooklynicecreamfactory.com

"Super-creamy" scoops served by "friendly" folks fill the "old-fashioned" bill at these popular Brooklyn ice cream parlors; the Dumbo waterfront flagship boasts an "unbeatable" skyline view, so "huge lines in good weather" come with the "touristy" territory.

The Brooklyn Star *Southern*   ▽ 24 | 17 | 18 | $41

Williamsburg | 593 Lorimer St. (Conselyea St.) | Brooklyn | 718-599-9899 | www.thebrooklynstar.com

"Loosen the belt a couple notches" before hitting this Williamsburg standout whose "fun takes on Southern comfort" classics include a few "twists" ("love the pig tails"); a "solid" drinks list, "fair" prices and a "spacious" setting "away from the Bedford Avenue crowds" seal the deal.

Brother Jimmy's BBQ *BBQ*   17 | 13 | 15 | $30

East 70s | 1485 Second Ave. (bet. 77th & 78th Sts.) | 212-426-2020
Gramercy Park | 116 E. 16th St. (bet. Irving Pl. & Union Sq. E.) | 212-673-6465
Kips Bay | 181 Lexington Ave. (31st St.) | 212-779-7427
Midtown | 416 Eighth Ave. (31st St.) | 212-967-7603
West 80s | 428 Amsterdam Ave. (bet. 80th & 81st Sts.) | 212-501-7515
www.brotherjimmys.com

This "popular chain" is a no-brainer for "raucous", "beer-swilling" "bros" scarfing down "sloppy" BBQ in "low-end" digs with "indifferent service" and "all the panache of a local frat house"; that said, you can get "a ton of food" here "without breaking the bank."

	FOOD	DECOR	SERVICE	COST

Brucie *Italian*   ▽ 20 | 16 | 19 | $49

Cobble Hill | 234 Court St. (Baltic St.) | Brooklyn | 347-987-4961 |
www.brucienyc.com

Local foodies laud this Cobble Hill Italian "keeper" for its "always-changing" menu of "inventive" fare, served in "informal", rustic environs; talk
about taking the "neighborhood restaurant" concept to the next level –
drop off a pan and they'll bake you a take-home lasagna.

Brushstroke *Japanese*   26 | 25 | 26 | $161

TriBeCa | 30 Hudson St. (Duane St.) | 212-791-3771
Ichimura at Brushstroke *Japanese*
TriBeCa | 30 Hudson St. (Duane St.) | 212-791-3771
www.davidbouley.com

David Bouley and Osaka's Tsuji Culinary Institute team up to "pamper
your taste buds" at this "lovely" TriBeCa Japanese, where "transcendent"
kaiseki menus and sushi paired with "polite" service dazzle diners, as do
the price tags; meanwhile, chef Eiji Ichimura's 12-seat omakase "temple"
renders "sublime" spreads starting at $180.

Bryant Park Grill/Cafe *American*   18 | 22 | 18 | $49

Midtown | 25 W. 40th St. (bet. 5th & 6th Aves.) | 212-840-6500 |
www.bryantparkgrillnyc.com

"Primo" Bryant Park scenery is the main "selling point" of these American
eateries, where "location, location, location" trumps the "pricey" tabs
and rather "average" food and service; the Grill's the more "handsome"
of the pair with both indoor and outdoor seats, while the alfresco-only
Cafe is more of a "tourist magnet."

Bubby's *American*   19 | 15 | 18 | $36

TriBeCa | 120 Hudson St. (Moore St.) | 212-219-0666
NEW Bubby's High Line *American*
Meatpacking District | 71 Gansevoort St. (bet. Greenwich & Washington
Sts.) | 212-206-6200
www.bubbys.com

A local "favorite" that fills your "breakfast needs" 24/7, this "diner-
type" TriBeCa American fields "warm-hug" cooking that attracts "crazy
crowds" on weekends; the soda fountain–equipped Meatpacking sequel
is similarly upbeat, and now offers a midnight-to-4 AM brunch.

Buddakan *Asian*   25 | 27 | 23 | $78

Chelsea | 75 Ninth Ave. (bet. 15th & 16th Sts.) | 212-989-6699 |
www.buddakannyc.com

The "jaw-dropping" theatrical setting sets a "splashy" tone at Stephen
Starr's "cavernous" Chelsea showpiece where "beautiful people" nibble
on "fabulous" Asian plates delivered by a "personable" team; predictably,
"prices are high", the noise level "thunderous" and the excess "glorious."

Buddha Bodai *Chinese/Kosher*   ▽ 22 | 9 | 18 | $20

Chinatown | 5 Mott St. (Worth St.) | 212-566-8388 |
www.chinatownvegetarian.com

"It may be fake meat", but the "sheer variety" and "excellent quality"
of the "inventive" kosher vegetarian options "blow your mind" at this
Chinatown dim sum dojo; an "eclectic" following also feels blessed that
it's so "reasonably priced."

	FOOD	DECOR	SERVICE	COST

Buenos Aires *Argentinean/Steak*

22 | 18 | 22 | $45

East Village | 513 E. Sixth St. (bet. Aves. A & B) | 212-228-2775 | www.buenosairesnyc.com

Beef eaters convene at this East Village Argentine steakhouse for "mouthwatering", chimichurri-slathered chops that you can "cut with a fork" and wash down with a "great selection of Malbecs"; forget the "don't-judge-a-book-by-its-cover" decor: "super" service and "gentle" tabs make this often-crowded spot a "keeper."

Bukhara Grill *Indian*

▽ 25 | 17 | 21 | $41

East Midtown | 217 E. 49th St. (bet. 2nd & 3rd Aves.) | 212-888-2839 | www.bukharany.com

They "spice it up" at this "authentic" North Indian near the U.N., where the cooking's "tasty" and the service "courteous"; if it seems a bit "pricey" given the "nothing-to-write-home-about" digs, at least the $17 lunch buffet is a "terrific bargain."

Bull & Bear *Steak*

23 | 21 | 22 | $91

East Midtown | Waldorf-Astoria | 540 Lexington Ave. (bet. 49th & 50th Sts.) | 212-872-1275 | www.bullandbearsteakhouse.com

"Time travel" to *Mad Men* days at this circa-1960 Waldorf-Astoria steakhouse where "professional" servers ply *Wall Street Journal* subscribers with "superb" cuts ("strong" cocktails gratify those on a "liquid diet"); it's a NYC "tradition", assuming one can "bear what they charge" for those bulls.

Bun-Ker Vietnamese *Vietnamese*

▽ 25 | 11 | 20 | $30

Ridgewood | 46-63 Metropolitan Ave. (bet. Onderdonk & Woodward Aves.) | Queens | 718-386-4282 | www.bunkervietnamese.com

A "little bit of Saigon" lands in Ridgewood's industrial fringe via this "middle-of-nowhere" Vietnamese offering a "heavenly" lineup of street-food favorites made from top-quality ingredients; the moderate pricing is more in line with the "unassuming" (verging on "funky") decor, while "sweet hipster" service ices the cake.

NEW Bunna Cafe *Ethiopian/Vegan*

— | — | — | M

Bushwick | 1084 Flushing Ave. (Porter Ave.) | Brooklyn | 347-295-2227 | www.bunnaethiopia.net

Following stints as a pop-up restaurant and a Smorgasburg vendor, this vegan Ethiopian now has a brick-and-mortar home in Bushwick; in addition to the "incredibly tasty" traditional menu, it also offers a signature coffee ceremony and occasional live music.

Burger Bistro *Burgers*

21 | 15 | 21 | $21

East 80s | 1663 First Ave. (bet. 86th & 87th Sts.) | 646-368-1134
Bay Ridge | 7217 Third Ave. (bet. 72nd & 73rd Sts.) | Brooklyn | 718-833-5833
Park Slope | 177 Fifth Ave. (bet. Berkeley & Lincoln Pls.) | Brooklyn | 718-398-9800

"So many options to choose from" is the hallmark of this born-in-Brooklyn "build-your-own-burger" chainlet offering "perfectly cooked" patties accessorized with "every topping imaginable"; "friendly" service and "cute", casual setups help keep 'em "busy."

	FOOD	DECOR	SERVICE	COST

Burger Joint *Burgers* — 23 | 13 | 15 | $19

Greenwich Village | 33 W. Eighth St. (bet. 5th & 6th Aves.) | 212-432-1400
Midtown | Le Parker Meridien | 119 W. 56th St. (bet. 6th & 7th Aves.) |
212-708-7414
www.burgerjointny.com

"Daunting" lines through the Parker Meridien's "gorgeous lobby" lead
to the "hidden" entry of this "down-and-dirty" dispensary of "superior
burgers", where the service is "no-nonsense" and "getting a table is a
contact sport"; the "quieter" Village offshoot features "plenty of seating"
and "awesome boozy milkshakes."

Bustan *Mediterranean* — ∇ 25 | 22 | 22 | $54

West 80s | 487 Amsterdam Ave. (bet. 83rd & 84th Sts.) | 212-595-5050 |
www.bustannyc.com

An emerging "neighborhood" favorite, this "welcoming" Upper Westsider is hailed as an "outstanding" source of "adventurous" Mediterranean
cooking, notably specialties fired in a wood oven; the "cool", colorful
quarters are usually "bustling", with the "accompanying high decibels."

Butcher Bar *BBQ* — ∇ 21 | 15 | 20 | $30

Astoria | 37-08 30th Ave. (bet. 37th & 38th Sts.) | Queens |
718-606-8140 | www.butcherbar.com

"When you crave some smoky meat", this Astoria BBQ outlet (and
organic butcher shop) ups the ante with "high-quality", "grass-fed" beef
that yields "damn good dry rub" coupled with down-home sides; an
"amazing backyard" adds to its folksy feel.

Butcher's Daughter *Vegan* — ∇ 22 | 19 | 14 | $30

NoLita | 19 Kenmare St. (Elizabeth St.) | 212-219-3434 |
www.thebutchersdaughter.com

Fans "feel healthier just entering" this all-day vegan cafe/juice bar, a
"hot spot" for "delicious" (if "pretty expensive") soups, sandwiches and
salads; the "rustic" bleached-wood, white-tiled space exudes a sunny
vibe, and there's a take-out shop next door.

Butter *American* — 22 | 22 | 20 | $71

Midtown | Cassa Hotel | 70 W. 45th St. (bet. 5th & 6th Aves.) |
212-253-2828 | www.butterrestaurant.com

The Lafayette Street original has shuttered, but this "hip" eatery has
been transplanted to a "nice new location" in the Theater District's Cassa
Hotel, where "class-act" chef Alex Guarnaschelli whips up "delicious"
New American food for breakfast, lunch and dinner; the "urban-rustic"
subterranean setting exudes "downtown vibes" and helps to offset
the "splurge" pricing.

NEW Butterfish *Japanese/Kosher* — – | – | – | E

Midtown | Sony Bldg. | 550 Madison Ave. (bet. 55th & 56th Sts.) |
212-729-1819 | www.butterfishny.com

A Midtown Japanese go-to from Hitoshi Fujita (ex Sushiden), this kosher
sushi specialist in the Sony Building spotlights an accessible list of omakase options; two nightly seatings at the chef's table provide exclusive access for a $95 set price (with reservations required 48 hours in advance),
though à la carte options are also available.

	FOOD	DECOR	SERVICE	COST

The Butterfly *American*
▽ **19** | **16** | **17** | **$52**

TriBeCa | 225 W. Broadway (bet. Franklin & White Sts.) | 646-692-4943 | www.thebutterflynyc.com

At this TriBeCa ode to the '50s, chef Michael White eschews pasta in favor of nostalgic American comfort fare (shrimp cocktail, patty melts) with "midcentury-modern decor to match"; still, to some it's the "ingenious" retro cocktails and happening "bar scene" that "are the focus here."

Buttermilk Channel *American*
25 | **20** | **22** | **$47**

Carroll Gardens | 524 Court St. (Huntington St.) | Brooklyn | 718-852-8490 | www.buttermilkchannelnyc.com

This "warm", "farmhouse-style" Carroll Gardens spot holds "rock steady", furnishing "creative" takes on "hearty homestyle cooking" from a "wonderful" New American menu; the no-reservations "hassle" leads to "crazy lines" (especially for the "awesome brunch"), but most agree it's "worth the wait."

Buvette *French*
24 | **21** | **20** | **$46**

West Village | 42 Grove St. (bet. Bedford & Bleecker Sts.) | 212-255-3590 | www.ilovebuvette.com

"Ooh-la-la!", this West Village "godsend" "oozes charm" thanks to chef-owner Jody Williams' "glorious" French small-plate fare served in "cute", "pint-size" quarters by an "easygoing" crew; the "upbeat" vibe includes "chairs bumping" at peak hours, but in warm weather there's always the "lovely" (but equally "tiny") back garden.

Cabana *Nuevo Latino*
22 | **18** | **20** | **$42**

East 60s | 1022 Third Ave. (bet. 60th & 61st Sts.) | 212-980-5678
Forest Hills | 107-10 70th Rd. (bet. Austin St. & Queens Blvd.) | Queens | 718-263-3600
www.cabanarestaurant.com

It "always feels like a party" at these "casual", "colorful" Nuevo Latinos where "nicely spiced" chow and "rocket-fuel" mojitos make for a "happening" vibe; the "noise factor" and "erratic" service may be sore points, but at least the tabs are "reasonable."

Cacio e Pepe *Italian*
20 | **15** | **19** | **$43**

East Village | 182 Second Ave. (bet. 11th & 12th Sts.) | 212-505-5931 | www.cacioepepe.com

The "titular" signature pasta served in a "massive round" of pecorino is the star of the "traditional Roman" menu at this "sweet" East Village Italian; "pleasant" service and "fair prices" keep things "bustling", so regulars take "respite" in the "pretty" back garden.

Cafe Asean *SE Asian*
▽ **22** | **16** | **20** | **$39**

West Village | 117 W. 10th St. (bet. Greenwich & 6th Aves.) | 212-633-0348 | www.cafeasean.com

"Modest" looks belie the "well-crafted" Southeast Asian lineup purveyed at this "tiny" West Villager where the "inexpensive", cash-only menu "takes you further East with every bite"; an "easy vibe", "accommodating" service and a "serene" garden round out this "offbeat find."

	FOOD	DECOR	SERVICE	COST

Café Boulud *French*

26 | 24 | 26 | $86

East 70s | Surrey Hotel | 20 E. 76th St. (bet. 5th & Madison Aves.) | 212-772-2600 | www.cafeboulud.com

"All class, all the way", Daniel Boulud's "cherished" Upper Eastsider lures "tony" types with "sumptuous" French cuisine served by an "unbeatable" team in "elegant, understated" surrounds; the "fancy prices" are "worth it and then some", though the lunch prix fixes are easier on the pocketbook; P.S. chef Gavin Kaysen's departure may put the Food rating into question.

🆕 Cafe Cambodge *Cambodian/French*

– | – | – | M

East Village | 111 Ave. C (bet. 7th & 8th Sts.) | 646-370-5158 | www.cafecambodge.com

Take a tour of Khmer cookery at this Alphabet City arrival, a rare chance to sample Cambodian specialties via an expat chef with a decidedly French penchant; cozy, crimson-walled digs with a thatched bar complement an inventive menu spanning seafood to pork belly.

Cafe Centro *French/Mediterranean*

21 | 19 | 22 | $51

East Midtown | MetLife Bldg. | 200 Park Ave. (45th St.) | 212-818-1222 | www.patinagroup.com

There's always a "big hubbub" at lunchtime at this "steady" Grand Central–area magnet for "networking" suits who dig the "satisfying" French-Med cooking, "prompt" service and "modern", patio-equipped setting; it's "quieter" at dinner, despite a weeknight $36 prix fixe "deal."

Cafe China *Chinese*

23 | 19 | 19 | $41

Midtown | 13 E. 37th St. (bet. 5th & Madison Aves.) | 212-213-2810 | www.cafechinanyc.com

Fans praise the "authentically spicy Sichuan" fare at this "inviting" Midtown Chinese that offers "outstanding" specialties in a setting recalling a "circa-1930 Shanghai teahouse"; "moderate" prices make some amends for sometimes "spotty service."

Cafe Cluny *American/French*

21 | 21 | 20 | $52

West Village | 284 W. 12th St. (4th St.) | 212-255-6900 | www.cafecluny.com

A "wonderful vibe" has evolved at this "cute" West Village bistro, a once-"trendy" joint that's now a bona fide "neighborhood favorite" thanks to "terrific" Franco-American cooking served in a "charming", "sun-filled" space; since the weekend brunch can be a "free-for-all", regulars say "arrive early."

Cafe Con Leche *Cuban/Dominican*

20 | 14 | 19 | $25

West 80s | 424 Amsterdam Ave. (bet. 80th & 81st Sts.) | 212-595-7000 | www.cafeconlechenyc.com

"Tasty" Cuban-Dominican vittles and some of the "best cafe con leche around" are slung in "lively" digs at this "funky" Upper Westsider where both the service and prices are "laid-back"; sure, it's "nothing fancy", but all-day hours and a "convivial" vibe keep it "always crowded."

Café d'Alsace *French*

22 | 17 | 19 | $48

East 80s | 1695 Second Ave. (88th St.) | 212-722-5133 | www.cafedalsace.com

This "unpretentious" Yorkville brasserie is a "bustling" standby for "stick-to-your-ribs" Alsatian fare paired with an epic beer menu that rates its own sommelier; given the "too-close" quarters and "high decibels", many opt to sit "outside", weather permitting.

NEW Cafe El Presidente *Mexican* — | — | — | M

Flatiron | 30 W. 24th St. (bet. 5th & 6th Aves.) | 212-242-3491 | www.cafeelpresidente.com

Spun off from Tacombi at Fonda NoLita, this all-day Flatiron outfit channels a Mexican market where a taqueria vending chef Jason DeBriere's street fare shares the big, bright layout with coffee, juice and cocktail bars and a station producing fresh tortillas; cafe seating awaits the Eataly-like throngs.

Cafe Espanol *Spanish* 21 | 15 | 20 | $41

Greenwich Village | 172 Bleecker St. (Sullivan St.) | 212-505-0657 | www.cafeespanol.com
West Village | 78 Carmine St. (7th Ave. S.) | 212-675-3312 | www.cafeespanolny.com

When you "don't want to spend much" on "traditional" Spanish fare, these separately owned, "been-there-forever" Villagers provide "satisfying" basics doled out in "generous", "paella-for-days" portions; sure, the space is "tight" and "hokey", but the sangria "always calls you back."

Cafe Evergreen *Chinese* 22 | 15 | 19 | $34

East 70s | 1367 First Ave. (bet. 73rd & 74th Sts.) | 212-744-3266 | www.cafeevergreenchinese.com

Upper Eastsiders who "don't want to schlep to Chinatown" depend on this "reliable" vet for "terrific" dim sum and other "quality" Chinese classics dished up by "pleasant" servers; despite a relocation, the decor gets mixed responses, but there's always "speedy delivery."

Cafe Fiorello *Italian* 20 | 17 | 19 | $54

West 60s | 1900 Broadway (63rd St.) | 212-595-5330 | www.cafefiorello.com

"Convenience to Lincoln Center" makes this Italian vet a "swift"-paced "default" for "satisfying" staples like its "fresh antipasti bar" and "super pizza"; the interior gets "ridiculously crowded" and "chaotic" pre-performance, so "don't forget the outdoor seating."

Cafe Gitane *French/Moroccan* 23 | 19 | 18 | $38

NoLita | 242 Mott St. (Prince St.) | 212-334-9552
West Village | Jane Hotel | 113 Jane St. (bet. Washington & West Sts.) | 212-255-4113 |
www.cafegitanenyc.com

The food's a match for the "trendy vibe" at these "fashionable" French-Moroccan lairs where "affordable" bites like "fabulous" couscous are dispensed by a "gorgeous" staff; the NoLita original is on the "tight" side, but the more spread-out Jane Hotel spin-off is just as "energetic."

Café Grumpy *Coffee* 21 | 17 | 19 | $10

Chelsea | 224 W. 20th St. (bet. 7th & 8th Aves.) | 212-255-5511
NEW East Midtown | Grand Central | 89 E. 42nd St. (Lexington Ave.) | 212-661-2198
Lower East Side | 13 Essex St. (Hester St.) | 212-260-3454
Midtown | 200 W. 39th St. (bet. 7th & 8th Aves.) | 646-449-8747

continued

Greenpoint | 193 Meserole Ave. (Diamond St.) | Brooklyn |
718-349-7623
Park Slope | 383 Seventh Ave. (bet. 11th & 12th Sts.) | Brooklyn |
718-499-4404
www.cafegrumpy.com

"Coffee connoisseurs" arrive grumpy and "walk out all caffeinated and smiley" from these local "custom-drip" whizzes, where the single-origin roasts "blow minds" and the baristas "know what they're doing with a pour-over"; most overlook any "hipsterish" attitude given the "very fine cups."

Café Habana *Cuban/Mexican*

21 | 15 | 16 | $25

NoLita | 17 Prince St. (Elizabeth St.) | 212-625-2001 |
www.cafehabana.com

Habana Outpost *Cuban/Mexican*

Fort Greene | 757 Fulton St. (Portland Ave.) | Brooklyn | 718-858-9500 |
www.habanaoutpost.com

Don't miss the "killer grilled corn" and other "delicious" Mexican-Cuban bites at these "lovable" "hipster paradises"; "happening" hordes endure "long waits" for a table at the "funky" NoLita original and its "environmentally friendly" Fort Greene sibling, while "economic" tabs and "amazing" libations keep them *"muy caliente."*

Café Henri *French*

▽ 22 | 18 | 20 | $31

Long Island City | 10-10 50th Ave. (Vernon Blvd.) | Queens |
718-383-9315 | www.henrinyc.com

"Quaint" and "always inviting", this all-day "slice of Paris" in LIC supplies "delicious" crêpes and other "simple" French bites at an agreeable "quality-to-price ratio"; it's "relaxed" *jour et nuit* "if you need a place to chat."

Cafe Katja *Austrian*

▽ 25 | 22 | 25 | $36

Lower East Side | 79 Orchard St. (bet. Broome & Grand Sts.) |
212-219-9545 | www.cafekatja.com

"Sure to please any meat eater", this compact LES "find" is the "real thing" for "delicious" Austrian specialties (and "refreshing" imported quaffs) served in "rustic" neighborhood" digs by "happy" staffers; for those in the know, the wurst news is "the secret's out."

Cafe Lalo *Coffee/Dessert*

20 | 21 | 17 | $24

West 80s | 201 W. 83rd St. (Amsterdam Ave.) | 212-496-6031 |
www.cafelalo.com

Famously "featured in *You've Got Mail*", this veteran UWS "sweetery" is ever a "tempting" rendezvous for "decadent desserts"; despite "wall-to-wall" tourists and "can't-be-bothered" service, it still makes fans "fall in love with NYC all over again."

Cafe Loup *French*

19 | 19 | 21 | $47

West Village | 105 W. 13th St. (6th Ave.) | 212-255-4746 |
www.cafeloupnyc.com

Long a West Village "neighborhood standby", this "timeless" bistro is a "grown-up" nexus for "fairly priced" French fare "like *grand-mère* used to make" dispatched by a "personable" crew; the room may need "updating", but loyalists attest it's "worth repeating", especially for "Sunday jazz brunch."

	FOOD	DECOR	SERVICE	COST

Cafe Luluc *French*
22 | 16 | 18 | $29

Cobble Hill | 214 Smith St. (bet. Baltic & Butler Sts.) | Brooklyn | 718-625-3815

An "easy way to feel Parisian", this "cash-only" Cobble Hill French bistro offers "satisfying" food served "sans attitude" at "Brooklyn prices"; just "be ready to wait" on weekends – it's a renowned "brunch destination", flipping some of the "world's best pancakes."

Cafe Luxembourg *French*
21 | 19 | 20 | $56

West 70s | 200 W. 70th St. (bet. Amsterdam & West End Aves.) | 212-873-7411 | www.cafeluxembourg.com

By "now a neighborhood landmark", this "perennial favorite" brings a "touch of glamour" to the UWS with its "arty", "adult" crowd, Parisian atmosphere and "jolly" mood (think "Balthazar West"); the "simple" French cooking is "delicious" enough, but the "stargazing" and "eaves-dropping" are even better.

Café Mogador *Moroccan*
24 | 18 | 18 | $30

East Village | 101 St. Marks Pl. (bet. Ave. A & 1st Ave.) | 212-677-2226
Williamsburg | 133 Wythe Ave. (bet. 7th & 8th Sts.) | Brooklyn | 718-486-9222
www.cafemogador.com

Popular with the "tattooed, leathered" set, this "go-to" East Village Moroccan and its newer garden-equipped Williamsburg sibling "have it down to a science", providing "memorable" tagines for "super-afford-able" dough; to avoid "long waits" for the "delicious" brunch, go for "early dinner."

Cafe Noir *African/Mediterranean*
– | – | – | M

TriBeCa | 35 Lispenard St. (bet. B'way & Church St.) | 212-431-7910 | www.cafenoirny.com

Following a 19-year run in SoHo, this Downtown staple has relocated to TriBeCa and updated its Med–North African menu with locally sourced small plates, cheese and charcuterie boards; the somewhat larger setting still channels Casablanca with its bistro-style mirrors and colorful floor tiles.

NEW Café Paulette *French*
– | – | – | M

Fort Greene | 136 Dekalb Ave. (S. Elliott Pl.) | Brooklyn | 718-694-2044 | www.cafepaulette.com

With its red leather banquettes and walls lined with French movie posters, this all-day bistro brings a touch of Paris to Fort Greene; the traditional Gallic menu is modestly priced, and sidewalk tables overlook-ing Fort Greene Park complete the charming picture.

Café Sabarsky *Austrian*
22 | 24 | 19 | $43

East 80s | Neue Galerie | 1048 Fifth Ave. (86th St.) | 212-288-0665

Café Fledermaus *Austrian*

East 80s | Neue Galerie | 1048 Fifth Ave., downstairs (86th St.) | 212-288-0665
www.kg-ny.com

Kurt Gutenbrunner's "civilized" Neue Galerie cafes transport you to "fin de siècle Vienna", with "exquisite pastries" and "vonderful" Austrian savories dispensed in "glorious", "old-worldy" settings; Sabarsky is the "prettier" of the pair while Fledermaus is "easier to get into", but both are "pretty expensive."

NEW Cafe Standard *American* ▽ 20 | 20 | 14 | $29

East Village | Standard East Village Hotel | 25 Cooper Sq. (bet. 5th & 6th Sts.) | 212-475-5700 | www.standardhotels.com

"Small but adorable", this casual cafe off the Standard East Village Hotel lobby serves a "nice" American menu via chef John Fraser throughout the day and into the wee hours; a "great location" and fun outdoor seating overlooking Cooper Square help distract from the "unamazing" service.

Cafeteria *American* 20 | 18 | 18 | $37

Chelsea | 119 Seventh Ave. (17th St.) | 212-414-1717 | www.cafeteriagroup.com

With a 24/7 open-door policy, this longtime Chelsea "after-the-clubs" spot serves "dressed-up" American comfort classics to a crowd that "clearly expects to be watched"; though it's lost the "allure of years past", it's reassuring to know that it's there when you feel like "meatloaf and a Cosmopolitan at 3 AM."

Caffe e Vino *Italian* ▽ 22 | 15 | 21 | $43

Fort Greene | 112 DeKalb Ave. (bet. Ashland Pl. & St. Felix St.) | Brooklyn | 718-855-6222 | www.caffeevino.com

"Delightful", "rustic" Italian food is the thing at this "tiny but terrific" Fort Greene trattoria near BAM; the "unpretentious" setting (complete with "requisite brick wall") can be "cramped", but the "attentive" servers will "get you out well-fed" before curtain time.

Caffe Storico *Italian* 22 | 20 | 20 | $56

West 70s | NY Historical Society | 170 CPW (77th St.) | 212-485-9211 | www.caffestorico.com

From restaurateur Stephen Starr, this Upper Westsider "hits all the right marks" with an "innovative", Venetian-influenced Italian menu featuring "delicious" cicchetti (small plates); set in the New-York Historical Society, the "airy", white-on-white room is lined with "antique dishes from the museum's collection."

NEW Cagen *Japanese* — | — | — | E

East Village | 414 E. Ninth St. (bet. Ave. A & 1st Ave.) | 212-358-8800 | www.cagenrestaurant.com

Former Nobu chef Toshio Tomita composes high-end tasting menus at this East Village Japanese where the fish is overnighted from Tokyo, the soba is made in-house, and sushi and sashimi are offered as supplements; the small subterranean setting (formerly Kajitsu) may be unassuming, but the premium pricing is anything but.

Calexico *Mexican* 22 | 16 | 18 | $21

Lower East Side | 153 Rivington St. (bet. Clinton & Suffolk Sts.) | 646-590-4172
Columbia Street Waterfront District | 122 Union St. (bet. Columbia & Hicks Sts.) | Brooklyn | 718-488-8226
Greenpoint | 645 Manhattan Ave. (Bedford Ave.) | Brooklyn | 347-763-2129

| | FOOD | DECOR | SERVICE | COST |

continued

NEW **Park Slope** | 278 Fifth Ave. (1st St.) | Brooklyn | 347-254-7644
www.calexiconyc.com

Mexican mavens "all abuzz" over these "rough-and-ready" street-cart spin-offs call out their "outstanding", "Cali-inspired" tacos, tortas and burritos; "fabulous prices" and "fast service" offset the "simple" "hole-in-the-wall" settings; P.S. "make sure to get the 'crack' sauce on anything you order."

Calle Ocho *Nuevo Latino*

20 | 19 | 19 | $49

West 80s | Excelsior Hotel | 45 W. 81st St. (bet. Columbus Ave. & CPW) | 212-873-5025 | www.calleochonyc.com

The "gourmet aspirations" are still "interesting" and the "fabulous mojitos" still flowing at this Upper West Side Nuevo Latino vet, now firmly settled in its "attractive" Excelsior Hotel digs; weekends the "party" picks up during the "unlimited sangria brunch" (just "bring a designated driver").

Camaje *American/French*

∇ 20 | 16 | 21 | $43

Greenwich Village | 85 MacDougal St. (bet. Bleecker & Houston Sts.) | 212-673-8184 | www.camaje.com

A "sweet place in the heart of the Village", Abigail Hitchcock's "small, funky" bistro matches "homey yet sophisticated" Franco-American meals with "mellow" vibes; it also hosts "cooking lessons" and 'dark dining' events ("you're blindfolded before you enter") that are "a blast."

Campagnola *Italian*

23 | 18 | 21 | $79

East 70s | 1382 First Ave. (74th St.) | 212-861-1102

All eyes are on the "floor show" at this "old-school" UES veteran where the stellar people-watching is on par with the "excellent", "garlicky" Italian cooking and "all-business" service; for best results, "go with somebody they know" – it's much "better if you're a regular" – and better yet if you bring "someone else's expense account."

Candle Cafe *Vegan/Vegetarian*

23 | 17 | 21 | $40

East 70s | 1307 Third Ave. (bet. 74th & 75th Sts.) | 212-472-0970

Candle Cafe West *Vegan/Vegetarian*

West 80s | 2427 Broadway (bet. 89th & 90th Sts.) | 212-769-8900
www.candlecafe.com

Candle 79's "cheaper", "more utilitarian" cousins, these crosstown spots feature "intriguing" vegan eats "prepared with love" in "cramped", "unpretentious" environs; though they're "often crowded" with "Gwyneth Paltrow wannabes", the "right-on" cooking is "worth the wait."

Candle 79 *Vegan/Vegetarian*

24 | 19 | 23 | $52

East 70s | 154 E. 79th St. (bet. Lexington & 3rd Aves.) | 212-537-7179 | www.candle79.com

"Tasting is believing" at this UES vegan "fine-dining" "phenom" that "sets the standard" with "quality-sourced", "distinctive" organic dishes and wines delivered by "enthusiastic" servers in "intimate", "classic" digs; a "pleasant departure from meaty fare", it's "so worth" the "premium price."

	FOOD	DECOR	SERVICE	COST

The Cannibal Belgian
21 | 18 | 19 | $44

NEW **Hell's Kitchen** | Gotham West Mkt. | 600 11th Ave. (bet. 44th & 45th Sts.) | 212-582-7947

Kips Bay | 113 E. 29th St. (bet. Lexington & Park Aves.) | 212-686-5480
www.thecannibalnyc.com

A spin-off of Kips Bay's Resto, this next-door butcher shop–cum–Belgian gastropub plies a "meat-heavy" menu of "superlative" small plates backed up by an "amazing" selection of brews; maybe the snug, communal table–equipped setting is "not comfortable", but few "headhunters" mind given the "swoon"-inducing chow; P.S. a new satellite has landed in Gotham West Market.

The Capital Grille Steak
24 | 22 | 24 | $74

East Midtown | Chrysler Ctr. | 155 E. 42nd St. (bet. Lexington & 3rd Aves.) | 212-953-2000

Financial District | 120 Broadway (Pine St.) | 212-374-1811

Midtown | Time-Life Bldg. | 120 W. 51st St. (bet. 6th & 7th Aves.) | 212-246-0154
www.thecapitalgrille.com

"Power brokers seal deals" while others mark "special occasions" at these steakhouses known for "top-notch" beef "prepared with care" and "impressive" wines delivered by "pro" staffers in "refined", "contemporary" rooms; the Chrysler Center locale is particularly "splendid", but they're all a "splurge."

Caracas Arepa Bar Venezuelan
26 | 17 | 20 | $21

East Village | 93½ E. Seventh St. (bet. Ave. A & 1st Ave.) | 212-529-2314

Caracas Brooklyn Venezuelan

Williamsburg | 291 Grand St. (bet. Havemeyer & Roebling Sts.) | Brooklyn | 718-218-6050

Caracas to Go Venezuelan

East Village | 91 E. Seventh St. (1st Ave.) | 212-228-5062

Caracas Rockaway Venezuelan

Rockaway Park | 106-01 Shore Front Pkwy. (Beach 106th St.) | Queens | 718-474-1709
www.caracasarepabar.com

An "amazingly delicious" "change of pace", these "authentic" Venezuelans churn out "crisp arepas" loaded with "flavorful" fillings "on the cheap"; to bypass "insane" waits at the "chaotic" East Village "hole-in-the-wall", try the "funky" Williamsburg branch (complete "with a cute backyard") or hang "at the beach" in Rockaway.

Cara Mia Italian
20 | 16 | 20 | $39

Midtown | 654 Ninth Ave. (bet. 45th & 46th Sts.) | 212-262-6767 | www.nycrg.com

"Not fancy but plenty comfortable", this "red-sauce" Italian is a Theater District "standby" for "homemade pasta" and "spot-on" service; granted, it's "space-challenged" and "crazy busy" pre-curtain, but at least you can mangia "without paying an arm and a leg."

Caravaggio Italian
25 | 24 | 25 | $92

East 70s | 23 E. 74th St. (bet. 5th & Madison Aves.) | 212-288-1004 | www.caravaggioristorante.com

More than "just dining out", this "refined" UES Italian is a "special-occasion" nexus owing to its "sophisticated" cooking, "flawless" service and "exquisite" modern setting; "money is no object" for most of its "mature" fan base, though frugal folks find the $30 prix fixe lunch quite "enticing."

Caravan of Dreams   Kosher/Vegan   ▽ 23 | 16 | 19 | $32

East Village | 405 E. Sixth St. (1st Ave.) | 212-254-1613 | www.caravanofdreams.net

A dream come true for "healthy food" fanatics, this East Village vet offers "transformative" kosher vegan fare in "mellow", "bohemian" quarters; fair prices and occasional "live music" enhance its "aura of peace and satisfaction", making followers "feel good inside and out."

Carbone   Italian   24 | 22 | 23 | $106

Greenwich Village | 181 Thompson St. (bet. Bleecker & Houston Sts.) | 212-254-3000 | www.carbonenewyork.com

An "homage" to "traditional Italian-American cuisine", this "lively" Village "hit" from the Torrisi team turns out "huge portions" of "outstanding" dishes (including a "divine veal parm") for a beyond-"hefty" price; the mood is "Rat Pack", the soundtrack classic "Motown" and the "maroon-tuxedoed waiters" recall the days when "service came first" – no wonder it's "nearly impossible" to get reservations, but "so worth trying."

Carlyle Restaurant   French   23 | 26 | 25 | $95

East 70s | Carlyle Hotel | 35 E. 76th St. (Madison Ave.) | 212-570-7192 | www.thecarlyle.com

"Synonymous with class", this "old-world" room in the Carlyle Hotel holds "fond memories" for a "blue-blood" fan base in thrall to its "refined" New French fare, "royal-treatment" service and "Dorothy Draper"-esque digs; plan to wear your "finest baubles" (jackets required for dinner) and be prepared for "super-premium prices."

Carmine's   Italian   21 | 17 | 19 | $46

Midtown | 200 W. 44th St. (bet. 7th & 8th Aves.) | 212-221-3800
West 90s | 2450 Broadway (bet. 90th & 91st Sts.) | 212-362-2200
www.carminesnyc.com

Built for "group feasting", these "boisterous", "fast-paced" Italians offer "whirlwind experiences in family-style dining" via "large platters" of "red-sauce" cooking with a "punch of garlic"; granted, the Times Square outlet may be too "touristy" for some, but overall "you can't beat it for taste and value."

Carnegie Deli   Deli   23 | 12 | 16 | $31

Midtown | 854 Seventh Ave. (55th St.) | 212-757-2245 | www.carnegiedeli.com

"Sandwiches large enough to fill Carnegie Hall" set the "oversized" mood at this "iconic" all-day Midtowner that's been dishing out "scrumptious" deli (and "lots of leftovers") to "loud" crowds since 1937; despite "plain" looks, "famously surly" service and "elbow-to-elbow" seating, the experience is "always entertaining", starting with the "starry-eyed tourists" looking for "Woody Allen"; news flash: it now takes credit cards.

Carol's Cafe   Eclectic   ▽ 24 | 19 | 21 | $60

Todt Hill | 1571 Richmond Rd. (bet. 4 Corners Rd. & Garretson Ave.) | Staten Island | 718-979-5600 | www.carolscafe.com

"Thoughtful", "Manhattan-quality" cooking via chef Carol Frazzetta is yours at this "pretty" Eclectic standby in Staten Island's Todt Hill; maybe the tabs run "a little high" for these parts, but "perfect-ending" desserts and weekly "cooking lessons" sweeten the pot.

Casa Enrique *Mexican*

∇ 24 | 15 | 20 | $36

Long Island City | 5-48 49th Ave. (bet. 5th St. & Vernon Blvd.) | Queens | 347-448-6040 | www.henrinyc.com

The Cafe Henri crew goes south of the border at this "cozy, comfortable" LIC Mexican where "expertly prepared", "aesthetically presented" fare inspired by the cuisine of the Chiapas region comes in "comfortable", "no-pretenses" environs; "fantastic" service and moderate tabs are two more reasons locals declare they've "died and gone to heaven."

Casa Lever *Italian*

23 | 25 | 22 | $83

Midtown | Lever House | 390 Park Ave. (53rd St.) | 212-888-2700 | www.casalever.com

Luring Park Avenue "power" players, this Midtown Milanese from the Sant Ambroeus team offers "delicious" chow delivered by an "attentive" crew; set in the "historic" Lever House, the "modernist" room lined with "wall-to-wall Warhols" is so "fashionable" that many say you're "paying for the style" here.

Casa Mono *Spanish*

24 | 18 | 20 | $58

Gramercy Park | 52 Irving Pl. (17th St.) | 212-253-2773 | www.casamononyc.com

"Inspired" tapas and an "encyclopedic" selection of Spanish vintages pack the house nightly at this "standout" Gramercy tapas bar from Mario Batali; sure, it's "like eating in a phone booth", and tabs "can mount up", but "who cares when the grub's this good?"

Casa Nonna *Italian*

22 | 21 | 21 | $52

Midtown | 310 W. 38th St. (bet. 8th & 9th Aves.) | 212-736-3000 | www.casanonna.com

A "perfect place to unwind" near the Javits Center, this Italian has its "act together" offering "creative glosses" on Roman-Tuscan standards served with "quick" "professionalism"; it's a "relaxing" option in a "lacking" dining zone, with well-spaced tables allowing for "private conversations."

Cascabel Taqueria *Mexican*

19 | 15 | 16 | $29

NEW **East 80s** | 1556 Second Ave. (81st St.) | 212-717-8226
West 100s | 2799 Broadway (108th St.) | 212-665-1500
www.nyctacos.com

"Ay caramba", these "popular" taquerias are about as "legitimate" as you'll find in these parts, slinging "above-average" tacos in "funky" quarters; "bargain" tabs and "downtown" vibes keep them "overwhelmingly busy", so expect service that's "cheerful" but "not very polished."

Casellula *American*

25 | 18 | 22 | $43

Hell's Kitchen | 401 W. 52nd St. (bet. 9th & 10th Aves.) | 212-247-8137 | www.casellula.com

"First-date" places don't get much more "cute" than this rustic Hell's Kitchen cheese specialist where the "never-ending" wine and fromage list is available nightly till 2 AM; the "little sliver" of a setting is "cozy" to some, "tight" to others, but the "bustling" mood speaks for itself.

	FOOD	DECOR	SERVICE	COST

Cata *Spanish*
▽ 22 | 20 | 22 | $51

Lower East Side | 245 Bowery (bet. Rivington & Stanton Sts.) |
212-505-2282 | www.catarestaurant.com

"Taking tapas to the next level", this "low-key" Bowery Spaniard from
the Alta crew offers both "creative and traditional" small plates in a
"relaxed", brick-lined room outfitted with a dining counter and communal
tables; regulars recommend "working your way" through its "extensive
gin-and-tonic selection", 23 versions at last count.

Catch *Seafood*
23 | 22 | 20 | $73

Meatpacking District | 21 Ninth Ave. (bet. Little W. 12th & 13th Sts.) |
212-392-5978 | www.emmgrp.com

"Beautiful people" and random "Kardashians" populate this "trendy"
Meatpacking "scene" where "outstanding" seafood via *Top Chef* winner
Hung Huynh is dispensed by "Abercrombie model"-like staffers in a
sprawling, "pumping" duplex; reservations can be hard to catch despite
the "expensive" tabs.

Ça Va *French*
22 | 20 | 20 | $59

Midtown | InterContinental Hotel Times Sq. | 310 W. 44th St. (bet. 8th &
9th Aves.) | 212-803-4545 | www.cavatoddenglish.com

Todd English assumes a "straightforward French" accent at this pleasing
Theater District brasserie; though the "nondescript", "hotel-lobby" decor
may be at odds with the "high-end" prices, "thoughtful" service and a
"convenient" address make it a natural "pre-theater."

Caviar Russe *American*
▽ 21 | 19 | 19 | $103

Midtown | 538 Madison Ave., 2nd fl. (bet. 54th & 55th Sts.) |
212-980-5908 | www.caviarrusse.com

The "decadent experience" at this Midtown New American "conjures up
tsars" as patrons are "pampered" with "exquisite caviar" and crudo from
"knowledgeable" staffers in "deluxe" digs suitable for an "illicit affair";
prices are predictably "astronomical", but big spenders urge "indulge in
this when you can."

Cávo *Greek*
22 | 23 | 18 | $60

Astoria | 42-18 31st Ave. (bet. 42nd & 43rd Sts.) | Queens |
718-721-1001 | www.cavoastoria.com

A "cool-looking", "spacious" setting is the lure at this "upscale" Astoria
Greek offering "solid" Hellenic fare that's upstaged by its "spectacular",
waterfall-equipped garden; just be aware it "can get pricey" and "loud" –
as the evening progresses, it becomes "more of a nightclub."

Cebu *Continental*
20 | 17 | 18 | $44

Bay Ridge | 8801 Third Ave. (88th St.) | Brooklyn | 718-492-5095 |
www.cebubrooklyn.com

"Large" and "busy", this "reasonably priced" Continental brings a bit of
"Manhattan chic" to Bay Ridge via an "enjoyable" menu, "on-the-ball"
service and night-owl noshing "till 3 AM"; "younger" folks with "fake
tans" keep the bar scene "buzzing."

NEW The Cecil *American/Eclectic*
23 | 22 | 21 | $55

Harlem | 210 W. 118th St. (St. Nicholas Ave.) | 212-866-1262 |
www.thececilharlem.com

"Go, Harlem!" cheer fans who "love everything about" this "hopping addition" to the neighborhood, from chef Alexander Smalls' "refreshingly different" 'Afro-Asian-American' fare to the "exuberant" staff and "chic" atmosphere that feels like "one big party"; somewhat "pricey" tabs don't seem to bother its "happening" crowd.

Celeste *Italian*
24 | 11 | 18 | $36

West 80s | 502 Amsterdam Ave. (bet. 84th & 85th Sts.) | 212-874-4559 | www.celestenewyork.com

"Celestial" Neapolitan cooking, "wonderful" cheese plates and "tough-to-beat" tabs make for "crammed" conditions at this UWS "winner" whose engaging owner is "part of the experience"; despite "no rezzies", "no credit cards" and "little ambiance", "long lines" are the norm here.

Cellini *Italian*
22 | 18 | 21 | $66

Midtown | 65 E. 54th St. (bet. Madison & Park Aves.) | 212-751-1555 | www.cellinirestaurant.com

A "staple" for "entertaining clients", this "expense-account" Midtowner draws a "chatty lunch crowd" with "authentic", "sure-bet" Italian standards served in a "not-so-fancy" setting; it's more subdued come suppertime, but you can expect "comfortable, grown-up" dining at any hour.

NEW Cerveceria Havemeyer *Mexican*
– | – | – | I

Williamsburg | 149 Havemeyer St. (bet. S. 1st & 2nd Sts.) | Brooklyn | 718-599-5799 | www.cerveceriahavemeyer.com

Spun off from nearby standby La Superior, this casual new Williamsburg cantina serves inexpensive chow (including aguachiles, similar to ceviche) in a convivial space outfitted with picnic tables and a small front patio; margaritas and Mexican beers are the lubricants of choice here.

'Cesca *Italian*
24 | 21 | 22 | $65

West 70s | 164 W. 75th St. (Amsterdam Ave.) | 212-787-6300 | www.cescanyc.com

"Fine-dining" fanciers frequent this UWS "standout" for its "delectable" Italian fare, "stellar" wine list and "warm", "no-rush" service; although it's "as expensive as it is sophisticated", payoffs include a "relaxing" rustic setting, acoustics perfect for "normal conversation" and an open kitchen that's catnip for "armchair chefs."

Cha An *Japanese/Teahouse*
∇ 22 | 19 | 20 | $26

East Village | 230 E. Ninth St. (bet. 2nd & 3rd Aves.) | 212-228-8030 | www.chaanteahouse.com

A refuge from East Village craziness, this "tranquil" second-story "sanctuary" offers "quality" Japanese teas and "delicate bites" served in "traditional" environs; just know that attempting to pay with plastic might disrupt your "serenity" – it's cash only.

Chadwick's *American*
23 | 20 | 22 | $53

Bay Ridge | 8822 Third Ave. (89th St.) | Brooklyn | 718-833-9855 | www.chadwicksny.com

On the Bay Ridge scene since '87, this American "stroll down memory lane" bats out a "solid" menu dispatched by "old-time waiters" who "treat you right"; the decor may "need a little uplift", but the "value" is intact, notably its "early-bird specials" Monday–Thursday.

	FOOD	DECOR	SERVICE	COST

Chai Home Kitchen *Thai* ▽ 22 | 18 | 19 | $21

Midtown | 930 Eighth Ave. (55th St.) | 212-707-8778
Williamsburg | 124 N. Sixth St. (Berry St.) | Brooklyn | 718-599-5889
www.chai-restaurants.com

"Incredibly reasonable prices" keep the trade brisk at these Siamese twins in Midtown and Williamsburg vending "spot-on" Thai food ferried by a "prompt" crew; the seating's strictly "sardine"-style in Manhattan, with more room at the Brooklyn original.

NEW Chalk Point Kitchen *American* — | — | — | M

SoHo | 527 Broome St. (Thompson St.) | 212-390-0327

It's all about market-to-table fare at this new SoHo American where the menu sources many of its ingredients from local purveyors; look for a farmhouselike setting heavy on exposed brick, reclaimed wood and checkered napkins, with a separate cocktail lounge (the Handy Liquor Bar) downstairs.

Charlie Bird *American* 25 | 22 | 23 | $71

SoHo | 5 King St. (6th Ave.) | 212-235-7133 | www.charliebirdnyc.com

The "inventive" cooking tastes even better thanks to the "hip downtown vibe" at this "super-trendy" SoHo scene where the Italian-accented Americana arrives in a "fun" room decorated with microphones, boombox artwork and "beautiful people" galore; a "knowledgeable" sommelier offers guidance on the "exceptional" wine list, while "solicitous" staffers compensate for the "noisy" acoustics.

NEW Charlie Palmer Steak *Steak* — | — | — | E

Midtown | 3 E. 54th St. (5th Ave.) | 646-559-8440 |
www.charliepalmer.com

Charlie Palmer's steakhouse franchise comes to NYC via this slick arrival in the revamped former Rothmann's space in Midtown; the predictably pricey offerings are mostly standard surf 'n' turf, but with a locavore focus, backed by a 400-label wine list and a roster of craft cocktails.

Char No. 4 *Southern* ▽ 22 | 21 | 21 | $44

Cobble Hill | 196 Smith St. (bet. Baltic & Warren Sts.) | Brooklyn | 718-643-2106 | www.charno4.com

"Brooklyn edge" is everything at this Cobble Hill "pork-and-bourbon paradise" that matches "memorable" Southern eats with a "world-class selection" of brown liquids; "knowledgeable", professional service and "one heck of a weekend brunch" draw flocks of "young, trendy" folk.

Chavela's *Mexican* 24 | 22 | 21 | $26

Crown Heights | 736 Franklin Ave. (Sterling Pl.) | Brooklyn | 718-622-3100 | www.chavelasnyc.com

Crown Heights Mexican that "shines" with "fantastic" cuisine, a "quick" staff and prices that "don't hurt"; sure, "there's always a wait" to get in, but the reward – at least according to margarita mavens – is a "permanent smile on your face."

Chef Ho's Peking Duck Grill *Chinese* 22 | 14 | 20 | $35

East 80s | 1720 Second Ave. (bet. 89th & 90th Sts.) | 212-348-9444 | www.chefho.com

De-ho-tees say you "won't find better Peking duck" than at this "old-school" Yorkville Chinese, a "neighborhood favorite" also lauded for its "above-average" cooking, "below-average" tabs and "efficient" service; fans say it's so good that there's "no need to go to Chinatown."

Chef's Table at Brooklyn Fare *French* | 28 | 22 | 27 | $321 |

Downtown Brooklyn | Brooklyn Fare | 200 Schermerhorn St. (bet. Bond & Hoyt Sts.) | Brooklyn | 718-243-0050 | www.brooklynfare.com

"Dinner as theater" comes alive at this "king of all chef's tables", an 18-seat counter in a Downtown Brooklyn prep kitchen, where "inventive" chef Cesar Ramirez unveils a 20-course tasting menu of "sophisticated", Japanese-influenced French plates; it makes for "unique" communal dining, and while it's "impossible to get in" – and priced at $255 per person – word is this "amazing experience" is "absolutely" worth it; P.S. an outpost inside Hell's Kitchen's Brooklyn Fare-Manhattan is in the works.

NEW Cherche Midi *French* | – | – | – | M |

NoLita | 282 Bowery (Houston St.) | 212-226-1966 | www.cherchemidiny.com

Keith McNally's remake of the former Pulino's space, this new Bowery French bistro reprises many of the restaurateur's greatest hits, starting with its menu of tried-and-true Gallic classics (think foie gras, frogs' legs, steak frites); the straight-out-of-Paris room similarly resurrects his trademark design elements, with distressed mirrors, bottle-lined shelves, a faux nicotine-stain paint job and some of the rosiest lighting in town.

NEW Cheri *French* | – | – | – | M |

Harlem | 231 Lenox Ave. (bet. 121st & 122nd Sts.) | 212-662-4374 | www.cheriharlem.com

Styled to mimic a dinner party in a private home – complete with a fireplace and piano – this Harlem newcomer offers a French table d'hôte menu, along with a few specials; brunch and early-evening charcuterie are also served, and the space expands in warm weather with sidewalk tables and a back garden.

Cherry *Japanese* | ▽ 22 | 22 | 19 | $78 |

Chelsea | Dream Downtown Hotel | 355 W. 16th St. (bet. 8th & 9th Aves.) | 212-929-5800 | www.cherrynyc.com

Set in Chelsea's Dream Hotel, this swanky subterranean lair supplies "flavorful", French-inspired Japanese fare (including sushi) and a "dimly lit", nightlife-friendly vibe courtesy of the team behind Bond Street; appointed with "sexy" red-velvet banquettes, it draws "young and prosperous" types ready to head out to one of the area's many clubs post-meal.

NEW Cherry Izakaya *Japanese* | – | – | – | M |

Williamsburg | 138 N. Eighth St. (Berry St.) | Brooklyn | 347-889-6300

From the team behind Bond St and Cherry in Manhattan comes this hip new Williamsburg Japanese offering sharable, izakaya-style plates (think skewers, sushi, sashimi and more) washed down with a variety of whiskeys, sakes and shochus; the bi-level, wood-lined space is meant to evoke 1970s Tokyo, with a vintage Pachinko game, a handmade tile bar and artwork inspired by ukiyo-e paintings.

	FOOD	DECOR	SERVICE	COST

Cheryl's Global Soul *Soul Food*
▽ 23 | 18 | 22 | $24

Prospect Heights | 236 Underhill Ave. (bet. Eastern Pkwy. & Lincoln Pl.) | Brooklyn | 347-529-2855 | www.cherylsglobalsoul.com

"Friendly" Prospect Heights retreat where Food Network star Cheryl Smith dispenses "delicious", "global-inspired" soul food and "excellent baked goodies"; though its dimensions are "small", a "charming garden" allows room to spread out in clement weather.

NEW The Chester *American*
– | – | – | M

Meatpacking District | Gansevoort Meatpacking | 18 Ninth Ave. (bet. Little W. 12th & 13th Sts.) | 646-253-2284 | www.thechesternyc.com

Just off the lobby of the Meatpacking's Gansevoort Hotel sits this all-day American bistro offering elevated comfort fare in a stylish, sprawling space with a large bar area and back dining room; there's also an L-shaped atrium with walls of windows and an upstairs lounge.

Chez Jacqueline *French*
20 | 18 | 19 | $52

Greenwich Village | 72 MacDougal St. (bet. Bleecker & Houston Sts.) | 212-505-0727 | www.chezjacquelinerestaurant.com

"Unassuming", "been-there-forever" Village bistro that has a "winning way" thanks to "satisfying" traditional French fare served by a "charming" staff that "keeps the vin rouge flowing"; maybe you "won't be surprised by any of the dishes", but most report "pleasant times" here.

Chez Josephine *French*
21 | 22 | 22 | $55

Hell's Kitchen | 414 W. 42nd St. (bet. Dyer & 9th Aves.) | 212-594-1925 | www.chezjosephine.com

"Eat and be entertained" at this longtime Theater District "favorite", a "shrine" to Josephine Baker overseen by her "hand-kissing", "lays-on-the-charm" son, Jean-Claude; the kitchen's got its "French bistro standards down pat", while live piano music lends a *"la vie en rose"* mood.

Chez Lucienne *French*
21 | 18 | 20 | $40

Harlem | 308 Lenox Ave. (bet. 125th & 126th Sts.) | 212-289-5555 | www.chezlucienne.com

"Parisian soul" is the thing at this French bistro on a happening stretch of Harlem's Lenox Avenue, where the midpriced Gallic grub is as "genuine" as the "accommodating" service; it's a "great alternative" to Red Rooster next door, and sidewalk seats supply people-watching galore.

Chez Napoléon *French*
22 | 14 | 20 | $55

Midtown | 365 W. 50th St. (bet. 8th & 9th Aves.) | 212-265-6980 | www.cheznapoleon.com

"Vérité" could be the motto of this circa-1960 Theater District "relic" where an "old-school" crew dispatches "time-stood-still" French bistro classics à la escargot, frogs' legs and calf's brains; the "tiny" setting exudes "faded elegance", but prices are "moderate" and you're "there to eat, not sight-see."

Chick P *Israeli/Sandwiches*
– | – | – | I

Prospect Heights | 490 Bergen St. (6th Ave.) | Brooklyn | 718-783-1525 | www.chick-p.com

This Prospect Heights vegetarian Israeli specializes in falafel sandwiches and platters, along with classic salads and sides; the pricing is as modest as its no-frills, counter-service space, with just a handful of seats.

	FOOD	DECOR	SERVICE	COST

Chikalicious *Dessert*   `23` `15` `20` `$23`

East Village | 203 E. 10th St. (bet. 1st & 2nd Aves.) | 212-475-0929 |
www.chikalicious.com
East Village | 204 E. 10th St. (bet. 1st & 2nd Aves.) | 212-475-0929 |
www.dessertclubnyc.com

"Sophisticated sweet tooths" applaud this "blink-and-you-missed-it" East
Village "dessert nirvana" for its "scrumptious", three-course prix fixes
paired with "perfect" wines; those sour on the "postage stamp"–size digs
get takeout from the counter-service bakery across the street.

Chimichurri Grill *Argentinean/Steak*   `21` `17` `20` `$50`

Hell's Kitchen | 609 Ninth Ave. (bet. 43rd & 44th Sts.) | 212-586-8655 |
www.chimichurrigrill.com

"Well-cooked" Argentine steaks topped with the namesake sauce thrill
carnivores at this "tiny" Hell's Kitchen hideout; "efficient" staffers and
"reasonable" pricing make it a natural for the "pre-theater" crowd, who
only "wishes it had more tables."

NEW China Blue *Chinese*   ∇ `18` `18` `19` `$51`

TriBeCa | 135 Watts St. (Washington St.) | 212-431-0111 |
www.chinabluenewyork.com

Upscale dim sum and "unique" Shanghainese seafood are the draws
at this TriBeCa newcomer, a sibling of Midtown's Cafe China set in a
"quiet", lofty room (formerly Capsuoto Frères) with a vague 1930s
Shanghai vibe; some find the overall result "only fair", but optimists say
the service is "steadily improving."

China Grill *Asian*   `23` `22` `21` `$58`

Midtown | 60 W. 53rd St. (bet. 5th & 6th Aves.) | 212-333-7788 |
www.chinagrillmgt.com

Long a bastion of "upmarket chic", this Midtown "powerhouse" offers
"fancy takes" on Asian cuisine served in "dark", airy digs with an "'80s
James Bond" vibe; it's "deafeningly loud" and "definitely not a bargain",
but "business" types still belly up for its "fun bar scene."

Chinatown Ice Cream Factory *Ice Cream*   `24` `8` `17` `$8`

Chinatown | 65 Bayard St. (bet. Elizabeth & Mott Sts.) | 212-608-4170 |
www.chinatownicecreamfactory.com

"Hard-to-find" flavors – from "fragrant" litchi to "sesame and taro galore"
– along with standard American varieties make for "sumptuous" scoops
at this Chinatown ice cream shop; service can be "rushed" and the space
could use a "revamp", but it's "always busy" for a reason.

Chin Chin *Chinese*   `22` `17` `20` `$53`

East Midtown | 216 E. 49th St. (bet. 2nd & 3rd Aves.) | 212-888-4555 |
www.chinchinny.com

On the scene since 1987, this "fancy" East Midtowner is a nexus for "im-
pressive" haute Chinese cuisine (don't miss the "off-the-menu" Grand
Marnier shrimp) served by a "crisp" crew led by owner Jimmy "Energizer
Bunny" Chin; despite rather "expensive" tabs, the "crowds keep coming."

ChipShop *British*   `20` `16` `19` `$25`

Brooklyn Heights | 129 Atlantic Ave. (bet. Clinton & Henry Sts.) |
Brooklyn | 718-855-7775

More on zagat.com

continued

Park Slope | 383 Fifth Ave. (6th St.) | Brooklyn | 718-832-7701
www.chipshopnyc.com

Get your "British soul food" fix at these Brooklyn "go-tos" for "standard chip shop" fare, including "cardiologist-disapproved" favorites like "killer fish 'n' chips" and "seriously deep-fried" candy bars; they're "small" and kinda "divey", but the "'80s punk memorabilia" helps boost the "fun" mood.

Chocolate Room *Dessert*   24 | 19 | 20 | $19

Cobble Hill | 269 Court St. (bet. Butler & Douglass Sts.) | Brooklyn | 718-246-2600 | www.thechocolateroombrooklyn.com

Dedicated to "all things chocolate", this "brilliant" Cobble Hill dessert specialist vends "sinful" desserts and chocolates best paired with a glass of vino to cut the "sugar rush"; the Park Slope location vacated its original quarters but is expected to reopen soon at 51 Fifth Avenue.

Cho Dang Gol *Korean*   24 | 14 | 19 | $36

Midtown | 55 W. 35th St. (bet. 5th & 6th Aves.) | 212-695-8222 | www.chodanggolny.com

"Real-deal" Korean cooking is offered at this "step-above" K-town joint that's famous for its "luscious homemade tofu"; "low prices", "utilitarian" decor and "typical" service are all part of the package, along with a "full house" at prime times.

Chola *Indian*   23 | 16 | 19 | $39

East Midtown | 232 E. 58th St. (bet. 2nd & 3rd Aves.) | 212-688-4619 | www.cholamidtowneast.com

"Spices abound" at this "delectable" Indian on East 58th Street's subcontinental strip, supplying a "wide-ranging" roster of "complex" dishes; tariffs are generally "moderate", but for "quality and selection" the $14 buffet lunch provides true "value for the money."

Christos Steak House *Steak*   ▽ 22 | 16 | 20 | $62

Astoria | 41-08 23rd Ave. (41st St.) | Queens | 718-777-8400 | www.christossteakhouse.com

"Fabulous" cuts of meat plus apps and sides with a "Greek twist" are "cheerfully served" at this Astoria "neighborhood steakhouse"; it's "not cheap" for these parts and the space "could be fixed up", but hey, the valet parking's a "real winner."

Chuko *Japanese/Noodle Shop*   27 | 19 | 22 | $26

Prospect Heights | 552 Vanderbilt Ave. (Dean St.) | Brooklyn | 718-576-6701 | www.barchuko.com

Some of the "best ramen" in the city turns up at this small, cash-only Prospect Heights Japanese where the "magnificent" pork and vegetarian bowls showcase "flavorful" broths and "springy noodles", backed up by a short list of "interesting" sides; since it's "impossibly popular" and accepts no reservations, "long lines" are the norm.

Churrascaria Plataforma *Brazilian/Steak*   24 | 19 | 23 | $70

Midtown | 316 W. 49th St. (bet. 8th & 9th Aves.) | 212-245-0505 | www.churrascariaplataforma.com

Brace yourself for a "food coma" after dining at this Brazilian rodizio all-you-can-eat "extravaganza" in the Theater District, where "skewer-bearing" waiters bring on a "nonstop" barrage of "cooked-to-perfection" meats; since it's "kinda expensive", gluttons "try not to fill up" at the "bountiful" salad bar.

Cibo *American/Italian*

22 | 20 | 23 | $50

Murray Hill | 767 Second Ave. (41st St.) | 212-681-1616 | www.cibonyc.com

A "grown-up" favorite in the land of "limited" options around Tudor City, this "comfortable" Tuscan–New American plies "fresh seasonal" fare in a "spacious", "white-tablecloth" milieu; "excellent value" (e.g. the $39 dinner prix fixe) makes it "worth coming back to."

Ciccio *Italian*

– | – | – | M

SoHo | 190 Sixth Ave. (bet. Spring & Vandam Sts.) | 646-476-9498 | www.ciccionyc.com

Tucked into a small, simple SoHo space with whitewashed brick walls, this moderately priced Tuscan offers lunchtime panini (as well as meatballs made from a secret family recipe), then rolls out housemade pastas at the dinner hour; inventive cocktails and a well-curated wine list seal the deal.

Cipriani Club 55 *Italian*

∇ 23 | 24 | 23 | $64

Financial District | 55 Wall St., 2nd fl. (William St.) | 212-699-4096 | www.cipriani.com

"One-percenters" who relish the "high life" "feed their egos" at this FiDi branch of the Cipriani empire, where "excellent" Italiana is dispensed in "posh" environs that include a jaw-dropping columned terrace; "prestige"-wise, it's a "solid" investment "when you have money to burn."

Cipriani Downtown *Italian*

24 | 22 | 22 | $74

SoHo | 376 W. Broadway (bet. Broome & Spring Sts.) | 212-343-0999 | www.cipriani.com

The only thing missing is "Fellini" at this SoHo slice of "la dolce vita", a "ritzy" nexus where "international" types "park their Lamborghinis" out front, then tuck into "molto bene" Italian food and "delicious" Bellinis; "astronomical" price tags and "attitude" galore come with the territory.

Circo *Italian*

23 | 24 | 22 | $65

Midtown | 120 W. 55th St. (bet. 6th & 7th Aves.) | 212-265-3636 | www.circonyc.com

Exhibiting its "Le Cirque DNA", this "big-top" Midtowner from the Maccioni family purveys "wonderful Tuscan fare" in a "playful" room festooned with "circus-themed decor"; given the "high-end" price tags, the "prix fixe deals" draw bargain-hunters, especially "pre- or post–City Center."

Circus *Brazilian/Steak*

21 | 20 | 21 | $55

East 60s | 132 E. 61st St. (bet. Lexington & Park Aves.) | 212-223-2965 | www.circusrestaurante.com

There's "no clowning around" in the kitchen at this Brazilian "sleeper" near Bloomie's where a "marvelous", meat-centric menu is served by a "jolly staff" that keeps the "knockout" caipirinhas flowing; "intimate" digs with a "circus motif" add to the "pleasant" vibe.

	FOOD	DECOR	SERVICE	COST

Citrus Bar & Grill *Asian/Nuevo Latino* | 20 | 18 | 17 | $45 |

West 70s | 320 Amsterdam Ave. (75th St.) | 212-595-0500 |
www.citrusnyc.com

"Festive" is putting it mildly at this UWS Latin-Asian fusion specialist where the "interesting" chow takes a backseat to the "awesome"
specialty tipples shaken at the "lively bar"; bargain-hunters drawn by
"decent-value" pricing "go early" to avoid the "loud" decibels later on.

City Bakery *Bakery* | 22 | 13 | 15 | $19 |

Flatiron | 3 W. 18th St. (bet. 5th & 6th Aves.) | 212-366-1414 |
www.thecitybakery.com

It's beloved for its "ever-so-rich" hot chocolate, "one-of-a-kind" pretzel
croissants and "scrumptious" sweets, but this Flatiron bakery also wins
favor with its "wholesome" salad and juice bars; maybe prices are "out
of whack" given the "mess-hall" decor and "unhelpful service", but that
doesn't faze the "crazed" lunch crowds.

City Hall *Seafood/Steak* | 22 | 22 | 21 | $55 |

TriBeCa | 131 Duane St. (bet. Church St. & W. B'way) | 212-227-7777 |
www.cityhallnyc.com

"Politicos" and "power" players rub elbows at Henry Meer's TriBeCa
"mainstay" where "attentive" staffers ferry "superb" surf 'n' turf in a
"lofty", "sophisticated" setting that feels like "old NY"; bonuses include
"space between tables" and "lovely private rooms" downstairs.

City Island Lobster House *Seafood* | 22 | 17 | 20 | $57 |

City Island | 691 Bridge St. (City Island Ave.) | Bronx | 718-885-1459 |
www.cilobsterhouse.com

Crustacean cravers commend this "basic" City Island "throwback" as a
"fine and dandy" option for "abundant", satisfying seafood; aesthetes
note it offers "not much decor", but "budget" pricing and alfresco dining
"overlooking Long Island Sound" give it "staycation" status.

City Lobster & Steak *Seafood/Steak* | 21 | 19 | 21 | $59 |

Midtown | 121 W. 49th St. (6th Ave.) | 212-354-1717 |
www.citylobster.com

For "standard" surf 'n' turf with "no surprises", this "convenient" harbor
is a "good all-around" performer in the "touristy" turf around Rock Center; foes crab about shelling out for "nothing special", but then again
the pre-theater prix fixes are a "best buy."

NEW The Clam *Seafood* | 23 | 22 | 24 | $62 |

West Village | 420 Hudson St. (St. Lukes Pl.) | 212-242-7420 |
www.theclamnyc.com

From the chef behind Market Table, this "wonderful", instantly "packed"
new West Village seafooder "pays homage" to the "humble clam" and
other shore staples on its "standout" menu; a "pretty room" and "fun"
staffers who "anticipate your every want" help justify the upscale tab.

NEW Claudette *French* | – | – | – | E |

Greenwich Village | 24 Fifth Ave. (9th St.) | 212-868-2424 |
www.claudettenyc.com

From the team behind Bobo and Rosemary's comes this new French
bistro offering a Provençal menu in a cozy corner space (fka Cru) just
north of Washington Square Park; whitewashed walls, cornflower-blue

tiles and glass doors that open to the sidewalk lend a country-cottage vibe, though the pricing is strictly big-city.

The Cleveland *American* ▽ 22 | 19 | 19 | $53

NoLita | 25 Cleveland Pl. (bet. Kenmare & Spring Sts.) | 212-274-0900 | www.theclevelandnyc.com

The "reliable", straightforward seasonal American fare with Mediterranean touches "matches the simple decor" at this small, whitewashed NoLitan that opens up to a garden "oasis"; with a "welcoming" vibe, it works for a "date" or "splitting a few things among friends."

Clinton St. Baking Company *American* 24 | 15 | 17 | $28

Lower East Side | 4 Clinton St. (bet. Houston & Stanton Sts.) | 646-602-6263 | www.clintonstreetbaking.com

"Bring *War and Peace*" to pass the time in the "brunch line" at this "tiny" LES bakery/cafe where the "ridiculous" waits pay off when homespun Americana "made with love" (especially those "divine pancakes") arrives; insiders hint "dinner is just as good" – and "you can get in."

Club A Steak House *Steak* 23 | 21 | 23 | $75

East Midtown | 240 E. 58th St. (bet. 2nd & 3rd Aves.) | 212-688-4190 | www.clubasteak.com

Set in the "lesser known" area near the Queensboro Bridge, this bi-level steakhouse draws "older" locals with "A-1" chops, "top-notch" service and a "sexy", "bordello"-hued, fireplace-equipped setting; sure, it's on the "pricey" side, but "live music" and a "relaxed" mood compensate.

Co. *Pizza* 22 | 16 | 17 | $35

Chelsea | 230 Ninth Ave. (24th St.) | 212-243-1105 | www.co-pane.com

It's all about the "love of dough" at this Chelsea pizzeria where "bread guru" Jim Lahey serves "gourmet" pies flaunting "innovative toppings" and crust that "hits the magic spot between crispy and pillowy"; just don't expect much "elbow room" – this baby is "always busy."

Coco Roco *Peruvian* 21 | 13 | 18 | $30

Boerum Hill | 139 Smith St. (bet. Bergen & Dean Sts.) | Brooklyn | 718-254-9933

Park Slope | 392 Fifth Ave. (bet. 6th & 7th Sts.) | Brooklyn | 718-965-3376 www.cocorocorestaurant.com

"Juicy-crisp" rotisserie chicken is the signature of these Park Slope–Boerum Hill Peruvians known for their "substantial portions" of "hearty", well-marinated grub that "won't empty your wallet"; "no atmosphere" leads aesthetes to fly the coop via takeout or delivery.

Cocotte *French* ▽ 23 | 22 | 22 | $56

SoHo | 110 Thompson St. (bet. Prince & Spring Sts.) | 212-965-9100 | www.cocotte-ny.com

"Dark" and moody, this tiny, wine-focused French boîte in SoHo offers up a "refined" small-plates menu with Basque accents, all spelled out on the chalkboard walls; though the "portions are tapas size" and the prices "main-course size", "cozy" atmospherics and "solicitous" service more than compensate.

	FOOD	DECOR	SERVICE	COST

Colbeh *Kosher/Persian*

▽ | 21 | 17 | 19 | $48

Midtown | 32 W. 39th St. (bet. 5th & 6th Aves.) | 212-354-8181 | www.colbeh.com

"Authentic Persian" cooking augmented with sushi is the "pleasant" scenario at this kosher Midtown sleeper where the portions are as "generous" as the flavors are "intense"; however, the "glitzy" decor divides voters – it's "stylish" or "tacky Miami" depending on whom you ask.

Cole's Dock Side *Seafood*

▽ | 23 | 20 | 22 | $50

Great Kills | 369 Cleveland Ave. (Hylan Blvd.) | Staten Island | 718-948-5588 | www.colesdockside.com

For "ample portions" of "tasty", "affordable" seafood (and nonfish options too), Staten Islanders sail into this "friendly", "casual" spot overlooking Great Kills Harbor, where the "bright" interior is augmented by a deck where you can "watch the boats glide by"; the weekday prix fixe dinner with a complimentary bottle of vino is a "steal."

Colicchio & Sons *American*

26 | 26 | 26 | $78

Chelsea | 85 10th Ave. (bet. 15th & 16th Sts.) | 212-400-6699 | www.craftrestaurantsinc.com

"Another triumph" from *Top Chef*'s Tom Colicchio, this Chelsea "winner" hits all the marks with its "spectacular" American fare, "serious" wine selection and "gorgeous", "grown-up" setting overseen by a "polished" team; ok, it's "not cheap by any means", but the "more casual" Tap Room offers the "same quality and service" at a gentler price.

NEW Colonia Verde *Latin American*

– | – | – | M

Fort Greene | 219 Dekalb Ave. (bet. Adelphi St. & Clermont Ave.) | Brooklyn | 347-689-4287 | www.coloniaverdenyc.com

Bringing fire-grilled Latin American cooking to Fort Greene, this newcomer from the Cómodo team plays on tradition with dishes like Mexican-style Scotch eggs and burgers on Brazilian cheese bread; flaunting reclaimed-brick floors, rustic tables and a greenhouselike back room, it's ready for everything from romantic dinners to festive brunching.

Colonie *American*

24 | 22 | 21 | $53

Brooklyn Heights | 127 Atlantic Ave. (bet. Clinton & Henry Sts.) | Brooklyn | 718-855-7500 | www.colonienyc.com

"Vibrant atmosphere meets inspired menu" at this Brooklyn Heights New American, where a seasonal lineup of "exceptional locavore" dishes pairs with "top-notch" service in a space sporting a "lush garden" wall; it's an acknowledged "keeper", though the "lively" crowds and no-reservations rule can make it "hard to snag a table."

Commerce *American*

23 | 20 | 19 | $65

West Village | 50 Commerce St. (Barrow St.) | 212-524-2301 | www.commercerestaurant.com

The "good surprises" include a "delicious bread basket" preceding the "fabulous" New American plates at this "hidden" West Villager, which draws an "attractive crowd" with "charming", retro-chic looks and a "scene at the bar"; just be ready for "noisy" acoustics and that "funky" "credit-cards-only" policy.

	FOOD	DECOR	SERVICE	COST

Community Food & Juice *American*
21 | 17 | 17 | $34

Morningside Heights | 2893 Broadway (bet. 112th & 113th Sts.) |
212-665-2800 | www.communityrestaurant.com

"Beloved by its own community", this "buzzy" Morningside Heights New
American is a "healthy" haven in "Columbialand" for "nourishing" eats
with "locavore-ish" leanings; exuding "good vibes" for three meals a day,
it's "wildly popular" for brunch, thus there's "always a line."

Cómodo *Latin American*
∇ 25 | 21 | 23 | $45

SoHo | 58 MacDougal St. (bet. Houston & King Sts.) | 646-580-3866 |
www.comodonyc.com

It's "always a pleasure" dining at this candlelit, brick-lined SoHo "date
spot" where a "gracious" staff serves "unique" Latin dishes drawn
from Mexican, Spanish and South American recipes; despite the "tiny"
dimensions, fans dig the "romantic", "relaxing" atmosphere, as well as
the "great value."

Cones Ice Cream Artisans *Ice Cream*
24 | 10 | 18 | $8

West Village | 272 Bleecker St. (Morton St.) | 212-414-1795

"World-class" Argentine-style ice creams and sorbets await at this
"exceptional" gelateria set in an "unassuming" West Village storefront;
along with the "classics", there are "creative flavors" galore (including
the "famous" sweet corn), all of which "never fail to please."

Congee Bowery *Chinese*
20 | 12 | 13 | $25

Lower East Side | 207 Bowery (bet. Rivington & Spring Sts.) |
212-766-2828

Congee Village *Chinese*

Lower East Side | 100 Allen St. (bet. Broome & Delancey Sts.) |
212-941-1818
www.congeevillagerestaurants.com

The namesake porridge is "fantastic" at these kinda "tacky" Lower
Eastsiders, which also ply a laundry list of "pleasing" Cantonese plates;
"major miscommunication" with staffers isn't uncommon, but the "con-
geenial" (read: "oh-so-cheap") pricing draws plenty of bargain-hunters.

NEW Contra *American*
∇ 25 | 19 | 20 | $89

Lower East Side | 138 Orchard St. (bet. Delancey & Rivington Sts.) |
212-466-4633 | www.contranyc.com

It's all about "experimentation" at this "innovative" Lower Eastsider offering a "brilliant", five-course American tasting menu for the "bargain" sum
of $55; the "narrow", "railroad" apartment-style room may not look like
much, but no one notices what with the feeling of "adventure" in the air.

Convivium Osteria *Mediterranean*
26 | 24 | 23 | $61

Park Slope | 68 Fifth Ave. (bet. Bergen St. & St. Marks Ave.) | Brooklyn |
718-857-1833 | www.convivium-osteria.com

"Superb cooking" and "ambiance to burn" define this Park Slope Mediterranean "date-night" nexus that's a "favorite of Mayor Bill" (among
others) thanks to an "intimate" mood and service that "shines"; a
"quality" wine list, "fantastic garden" and "particularly romantic" cellar
are additional bonuses, and if that's not enough, it's an "easy walk
to Barclays Center."

	FOOD	DECOR	SERVICE	COST

Cookshop *American*
23 19 20 $51

Chelsea | 156 10th Ave. (20th St.) | 212-924-4440 |
www.cookshopny.com

"Reasonably priced", "fresh-from-the-farm" fare served by an "informed" crew in a "gallery-chic" setting makes for an "energetic" scene at this all-day American near the High Line; since the "airy" dining room is usually "full" and "loud", insiders opt for the "great outdoor seating" or perhaps a "quiet midweek breakfast."

The Copenhagen *Danish/Sandwiches*
∇ **19 17 18 $47**

TriBeCa | Tribeca Film Bldg. | 13 Laight St. (bet. 6th Ave. & Varick St.) |
212-925-1313 | www.thecopenhagennyc.com

"Delicious" smørrebrød (an open-faced sandwich on "thick" rye bread), "superbly done" herring and "creative" Danish dishes meet "flavored aquavits" at this TriBeCa offshoot of a Copenhagen eatery; it's an "interesting concept" in an "airy" setting.

Coppelia *Diner/Pan-Latin*
20 16 19 $27

Chelsea | 207 W. 14th St. (bet. 7th & 8th Aves.) | 212-858-5001 |
www.coppelianyc.com

An "interesting" spin on a Cuban diner, this "friendly" Chelsea luncheonette slings "accomplished" Pan-Latin comfort chow in "casual", "colorful" confines; the "low tabs", "no-rush atmosphere" and 24/7 open-door policy make it a hit with early-risers and "all-nighters" alike.

Coppola's *Italian*
21 17 20 $44

Kips Bay | 378 Third Ave. (bet. 27th & 28th Sts.) | 212-679-0070
West 70s | 206 W. 79th St. (bet. Amsterdam Ave. & B'way) | 212-877-3840
www.coppolas-nyc.com

"Like an old friend", these longtime Upper West Side–Kips Bay Southern Italians are "relaxing", "reliable" fallbacks for "comfort" chow heavy on the "red sauce"; maybe the "homey" settings are becoming "outdated", but "plentiful" portions, "courteous" service and "moderate" prices compensate.

Corkbuzz *Eclectic*
21 21 22 $48

NEW **Chelsea** | Chelsea Mkt. | 75 Ninth Ave. (bet. 15th & 16th Sts.) |
646-237-4847
Greenwich Village | 13 E. 13th St. (bet. 5th Ave. & University Pl.) |
646-873-6071
www.corkbuzz.com

Its Eclectic shared plates are "tasty", but it's really "all about wine" at this Village boîte (and its new Chelsea Market sequel) where "lovely" pairings are culled from a "vast" list of vintages, including an "extensive" by-the-glass selection; the "modern", narrow space with communal tables in the rear is overseen by a "super-knowledgeable" staff.

Cornelia Street Cafe *American/French*
20 17 19 $42

West Village | 29 Cornelia St. (bet. Bleecker & W. 4th Sts.) |
212-989-9319 | www.corneliastreetcafe.com

"Old-school West Village" dining thrives at this circa-1977 "charmer" with a "yoga vibe", offering "perfectly acceptable" Franco-American fare and a "cheap and cheerful" brunch; although "starting to show its age", it gets "bonus" points for the "cool" performance space downstairs.

	FOOD	DECOR	SERVICE	COST

Corner Bistro *Burgers*
22 | 11 | 15 | $22

West Village | 331 W. Fourth St. (Jane St.) | 212-242-9502
Long Island City | 47-18 Vernon Blvd. (47th Rd.) | Queens | 718-606-6500
www.cornerbistrony.com

"Memorable", "messy" burgers dished out on paper plates in "sticky booths" make for classic "slumming" at this "dingy" Village perennial (with a slightly "nicer" LIC spin-off); "cheap beer", "long waits" and "student crowds" are all part of the timelessly "cool" experience.

Corsino *Italian*
21 | 19 | 19 | $40

Meatpacking District | 637 Hudson St. (Horatio St.) | 212-242-3093 | www.corsinocantina.com

They "get simplicity right" at this "stylish" Meatpacking Italian where "delectable" small plates are paired with a "vast, affordable" wine list; patronized by "beautiful, thin" types and patrolled by a "thoughtful" team, it's a "vibrant" – verging on "boisterous" – scene.

Costata *Italian/Steak*
25 | 22 | 24 | $93

SoHo | 206 Spring St. (bet. 6th Ave. & Sullivan St.) | 212-334-3320 | www.costatanyc.com

"Hitting on all cylinders", Michael White's Italian steakhouse features "sensational" chops, "steal-the-show" pastas and "perfect" seafood crudos in a SoHo triplex setting; even if the decor earns mixed marks ("wonderful" vs. "hotel lobby"), there's agreement on the "hospitable" service, "killer wine list" and "crazy expensive" tabs.

Cotta *Italian*
22 | 18 | 18 | $44

West 80s | 513 Columbus Ave. (bet. 84th & 85th Sts.) | 212-873-8500 | www.cottanyc.com

"Busy and lively", this "rustic" UWS "neighborhood" Italian puts forth "delicious" pizza and "tapas-type" plates in a ground-floor wine bar or "cozy upstairs" (watch out for those "candles on the stairs"); it's "perfect for a casual date", with equally casual tabs to match.

The Counter *Burgers*
21 | 14 | 17 | $23

Midtown | 1451 Broadway (41st St.) | 212-997-6801 | www.thecounterburger.com

"Near-infinite" burger options are the lure at this Times Square link of the "build-it-yourself" national chain, where diners customize their orders "from bun to patty to toppings"; some shrug "nothing stellar", but most agree it's an "easy, cheap pre-theater bite."

Covo *Italian*
▽ 23 | 18 | 21 | $33

Hamilton Heights | 701 W. 135th St. (12th Ave.) | 212-234-9573 | www.covony.com

"Solid" is the word on this "tucked-away" Hamilton Heights Italian supplying "tasty" pizza and pastas for "bang-for-the-buck" tabs in a "spread-out", brick-walled setting; "caring" servers distract from the "ear-ringing" noise, but night owls tout the "upstairs lounge."

Cowgirl *Southwestern*
18 | 18 | 19 | $33

West Village | 519 Hudson St. (W. 10th St.) | 212-633-1133 | www.cowgirlnyc.com

continued

Cowgirl Sea-Horse *Southwestern*

South Street Seaport | 259 Front St. (Dover St.) | 212-608-7873 |
www.cowgirlseahorse.com

"Down-to-earth" says it all about this West Village Southwesterner slinging "decent" chow in a "kitschy", "retro rodeo" setting that's "kid-friendly" by day and a "high-octane" margaritaville after dark; the Seaport
satellite gets a "fishy spin" with a seafood focus.

Craft *American*
26 | 24 | 26 | $87

Flatiron | 43 E. 19th St. (bet. B'way & Park Ave. S.) | 212-780-0880 |
www.craftrestaurant.com

"Still inventive, still exciting, still amazing", this "grown-up" Flatiron
American from *Top Chef* star Tom Colicchio offers "simply yet expertly
prepared" food that's "perfect for group sharing", served in "warm,
modern" digs by a "terrific" team; though the "one-percenter" pricing
suggests "special occasions", it's a "worthy splurge" at any time.

Craftbar *American*
23 | 19 | 22 | $57

Flatiron | 900 Broadway (20th St.) | 212-461-4300 |
www.craftrestaurantsinc.com

"More affordable" and thus "more accessible" than Tom Colicchio's
Craft, this "casually elegant" Flatiron American is "just as tasty as its
big brother", with a "dark", "relaxed" setting patrolled by an "attentive"
team; its "young, noisy" crowd labels it a "go-to for weekend brunch."

Crave Fishbar *Seafood*
24 | 20 | 22 | $53

East Midtown | 945 Second Ave. (bet. 50th & 51st Sts.) | 646-895-9585 |
www.cravefishbar.com

Bringing some "much needed" "cool" to Midtown East, this "fun",
"friendly" seafood specialist delivers "delicious" ocean fare in a "casual",
coastal-rustic setting; relatively "reasonable" rates and "$1 oysters dur-
ing happy hour" are further lures.

Crema *Mexican*
22 | 16 | 20 | $48

Flatiron | 111 W. 17th St. (bet. 6th & 7th Aves.) | 212-691-4477 |
www.cremarestaurante.com

"French techniques" give an "innovative" lift to the modern Mexican
cooking at chef Julieta Ballesteros' "tucked-away" Flatiron "sleeper"; it's
a "relaxed" enclave for "elevated" eating and "energetic" service – and
"affordable" enough for *fanáticos* to "go back again and again."

Creperie *French*
∇ 21 | 10 | 17 | $17

Greenwich Village | 112 MacDougal St. (bet. Bleecker & Houston Sts.) |
212-253-6705
Lower East Side | 135 Ludlow St. (bet. Rivington & Stanton Sts.) |
212-979-5521
www.creperienyc.com

"Savory or sweet", the "comprehensive" roster of "custom-made"
crêpes "hits the spot" at these counter-service standbys that are a
no-brainer for folks "on a budget"; it's one of the "only games in town"
for "late-night" noshing, though "tiny", "hole-in-the-wall" settings
encourage ordering "to go."

	FOOD	DECOR	SERVICE	COST

Crif Dogs *Hot Dogs*   23 | 14 | 17 | $12

East Village | 113 St. Marks Pl. (bet. Ave. A & 1st Ave.) | 212-614-2728
NEW **Greenwich Village** | 120 MacDougal St. (bet. Bleecker & W. 3rd Sts.) | 212-539-0100
Williamsburg | 555 Driggs Ave. (7th St.) | Brooklyn | 718-302-3200
www.crifdogs.com

"Spunky", "deep-fried" hot dogs are a "guilty pleasure" at these "gritty" tubesteak venues famed for their "fun toppings" (like bacon, avocado and cream cheese); they're a natural for "cheap", "late-night munchies", and the East Village original houses the famed "speakeasy" bar PDT, accessed through a "phone booth."

Crispo *Italian*   24 | 19 | 22 | $54

West Village | 240 W. 14th St. (bet. 7th & 8th Aves.) | 212-229-1818 | www.crisporestaurant.com

Pastaphiles are "blown away" by this "favorite" West Village trattoria purveying "gratifying" Northern Italiana led by a signature spaghetti carbonara that "has no rivals"; its "increasing popularity" results in "loud, cramped" conditions, so insiders head for the "all-seasons garden."

Crosby Bar *Eclectic*   ▽ 22 | 23 | 20 | $48

SoHo | Crosby Street Hotel | 79 Crosby St. (bet. Prince & Spring Sts.) | 212-226-6400

Eclectic describes the menu and decor of this "chic", "gallerylike" spot in SoHo's Crosby Street Hotel, which also boasts "lots of light", a "lovely garden" and "spacious seating"; the food's just as "wonderful", though the service lies somewhere between "great" and "indifferent."

Crown *American*   23 | 26 | 21 | $94

East 80s | 24 E. 81st St. (bet. 5th & Madison Aves.) | 646-559-4880 | www.crown81.com

"Luxurious" is the mind-set at this "stately" spot from chef John DeLucie (Bill's, The Lion), luring "UES billionaires" and "plastic-surgery" practitioners with its "gorgeous" townhouse setting, "upper-class–club" mood and "glass-walled" garden room; "excellent" American fare and "courteous" service round out this "royal treat", best savored when "someone else is paying."

Cuba *Cuban*   24 | 19 | 21 | $44

Greenwich Village | 222 Thompson St. (bet. Bleecker & 3rd Sts.) | 212-420-7878 | www.cubanyc.com

Everyone's "Havana great time" at this "high-energy" Village supplier of "authentic" Cuban standards and "heavenly" mojitos "charmingly" served in "funky" Latin digs; "live bands", "relatively affordable" tabs and a "cigar-rolling man" lend a "vacation" vibe to the proceedings.

Cull & Pistol *Seafood*   24 | 19 | 21 | $48

Chelsea | Chelsea Mkt. | 75 Ninth Ave. (bet. 15th & 16th Sts.) | 646-568-1223 | www.cullandpistol.com

Brought to you by the folks behind Chelsea Market's Lobster Place, this "bustling" next-door adjunct is a "sit-down" affair offering "so-fresh" seafood and raw-bar items in "tiny" but "friendly" digs; bargain-hunters report the "best bet" here is the "one-dollar-oyster" weekday happy hour.

	FOOD	DECOR	SERVICE	COST

Da Andrea *Italian*
23 | 18 | 21 | $41

Greenwich Village | 35 W. 13th St. (bet. 5th & 6th Aves.) | 212-367-1979 | www.daandreanyc.com

"Delicious" housemade pastas and other Emilia-Romagna standards are a "steal" at this "cozy", "unpretentious" Villager; with "warm", "friendly" staffers keeping the vibe copacetic, it's no wonder "neighborhood" denizens come back "time after time."

Daisy May's BBQ USA *BBQ*
22 | 8 | 13 | $28

Hell's Kitchen | 623 11th Ave. (46th St.) | 212-977-1500 | www.daisymaysbbq.com

"Fall-off-the-bone" ribs and other "darn-good" BBQ allow patrons to "get in touch with the caveman within" at Adam Perry Lang's Hell's Kitchen 'cue hut; despite "cafeteria-style" service, decor "best left undescribed" and a "nearly-in-the–Hudson River" address, fans feel "lucky to have it."

Da Nico *Italian*
21 | 17 | 20 | $41

Little Italy | 164 Mulberry St. (bet. Broome & Grand Sts.) | 212-343-1212
NEW **Tottenville** | 7324 Amboy Rd. (bet. Sleight & Sprague Aves.) | Staten Island | 718-227-7200
www.danicoristorante.com

A "Mulberry Street staple" for more than 20 years, this "traditional" Italian rolls out "gargantuan" portions of "tasty" vittles that are "a cut above the local" norm; "attentive" service, "nominal" prices and a large back garden complete the overall "comfortable" picture; P.S. there's also a new Staten Island outpost.

Daniel *French*
28 | 28 | 28 | $167

East 60s | 60 E. 65th St. (bet. Madison & Park Aves.) | 212-288-0033 | www.danielnyc.com

"Everything's exquisite" – from the "breathtaking" New French cuisine to the "above-and-beyond" service – at Daniel Boulud's UES "class-act" flagship, where the "aristocratic" dining room is voted No. 1 for Decor in NYC; the prix fixe-only menu is ideal "when you want to be lavished", though some do "love eating in the barroom", where you can order à la carte; wherever you land, bear in mind that "jackets (and money belts) are required."

Danji *Korean*
25 | 18 | 20 | $49

Midtown | 346 W. 52nd St. (bet. 8th & 9th Aves.) | 212-586-2880 | www.danjinyc.com

"Fantastic, elegant" cooking and a "lively, energetic" vibe mean this "upscale" Midtown Korean tapas specialist remains a "tough table to get" (brace for an "interminable wait"); a pleasant "pared-down" setting and capable – if slightly "indifferent" – service help ensure it's a "fun place to be."

Danny Brown Wine Bar & Kitchen *European*
26 | 20 | 25 | $57

Forest Hills | 104-02 Metropolitan Ave. (71st Dr.) | Queens | 718-261-2144 | www.dannybrownwinekitchen.com

"Rivaling any place in Manhattan", this Forest Hills "gem" is a "low-key" neighborhood retreat with "excellent" European food, a "fabulous" wine list and "on-the-mark" service, all for "Queens prices"; if that's not enough, try the "can't-be-beat" $30 prix fixe on Tuesday and Wednesday nights.

	FOOD	DECOR	SERVICE	COST

Da Noi *Italian*
25 | 21 | 23 | $52

East Midtown | 214 E. 49th St. (bet. 2nd & 3rd Aves.) | 212-754-5710
Shore Acres | 138 Fingerboard Rd. (Tompkins Ave.) | Staten Island | 718-720-1650
Travis-Chelsea | 4358 Victory Blvd. (Crabbs Ln.) | Staten Island | 718-982-5040
www.danoinyc.com

"Old-world" "red-sauce" cooking "like nonna's" draws fans to these "congenial" Italians where "generous portions" turn "pricey" tabs into "money well spent"; the crowd's right out of a "scene from *The Godfather*", while the sound level's a bit on "da noisy" side.

Darbar *Indian*
23 | 17 | 19 | $37

East Midtown | 152 E. 46th St. (bet. Lexington & 3rd Aves.) | 212-681-4500 | www.darbarny.com

Darbar Grill *Indian*

East Midtown | 157 E. 55th St. (bet. Lexington & 3rd Aves.) | 212-751-4600 | www.darbargrill.com

Aficionados of "high-quality Indian" cuisine patronize these East Midtowners for a "standard repertoire" of "solid", "well-prepared" dishes served by a "gracious" team in "comfortable" confines; even better, there's "no sticker shock", particularly at the "can't-be-beat" $14 lunch buffet.

Da Silvano *Italian*
21 | 16 | 19 | $64

Greenwich Village | 260 Sixth Ave. (bet. Bleecker & Houston Sts.) | 212-982-2343 | www.dasilvano.com

The "glitterati" draw the "paparazzi" to this ever-"trendy" Villager where "celeb-spotting" is the "main course", though the Tuscan eats are almost as "delicious"; it costs "wads of cash" and the staff can be "snooty" to outsiders, so for best results, bring "George Clooney" – and get him to pick up the check.

Da Tommaso *Italian*
21 | 16 | 21 | $49

Midtown | 903 Eighth Ave. (bet. 53rd & 54th Sts.) | 212-265-1890 | www.datommasony.com

The "quality never falters" at this veteran Midtown Italian purveying "lovely old-school" cooking with "waiters to match"; maybe da "dated" room "could use a face-lift", but "reasonable" rates and a "near-the–Theater District" address keep it "crowded" before a show.

Da Umberto *Italian*
25 | 20 | 24 | $76

Flatiron | 107 W. 17th St. (bet. 6th & 7th Aves.) | 212-989-0303 | www.daumbertonyc.com

"Still a classic", this longtime Flatiron "favorite" rolls out "serious" Northern Italian cuisine with "vibrant" flavors in a "simple" space where the white-tablecloth "elegance" is matched by "impeccable" service; "costly" tabs aside, it fits the bill for a "romantic" or otherwise "special" occasion.

David Burke at Bloomingdale's *American*
20 | 14 | 18 | $40

East Midtown | Bloomingdale's | 150 E. 59th St. (bet. Lexington & 3rd Aves.) | 212-705-3800 | www.burkeinthebox.com

Assuage a "shopping hangover" with "high-fashion" New American "quick bites" à la David Burke at this "fast-paced" cafe in Bloomie's (and its grab 'n' go counterpart); despite "uninspiring" surroundings and "sloppy service", it's "convenient" and thus "continuously crowded."

NEW David Burke Fabrick *American*   — | — | — | E

Midtown | Archer Hotel | 47 W. 38th St. (bet. 5th & 6th Aves.) | 212-302-3838 | www.davidburkefabrick.com

The name's a nod to its Garment District address, and this all-day dining room in Midtown's Archer Hotel serves David Burke's modern American menu with an emphasis on small plates and sharing; its high-ceilinged, modern-rustic setting (including an open kitchen equipped with a wood-burning oven) is a match for the chef's sophisticated yet playful cooking.

David Burke Fishtail *Seafood*   24 | 23 | 22 | $67

East 60s | 135 E. 62nd St. (bet. Lexington & Park Aves.) | 212-754-1300 | www.fishtaildb.com

"Fish so fresh you can smell the sea" earns kudos at David Burke's "class act" UES seafooder, where the "creative" preparations are dispensed by an "informative" crew; its "beautiful" townhouse setting includes a "busy" downstairs bar and a "quieter", "more formal" upper dining room, but no matter where you sit, the dining's "delicious."

David Burke Kitchen *American*   25 | 23 | 23 | $69

SoHo | James Hotel | 23 Grand St., downstairs (6th Ave.) | 212-201-9119 | www.davidburkekitchen.com

"Creative" but "casual", this far-from-cheap "farm-to-fork" option from David Burke matches "delightful" New Americana with "on-point" service and a "semi-subterranean" setting in SoHo's James Hotel; the Treehouse Bar upstairs adds an extra dimension to the "inviting" package.

Dawat *Indian*   23 | 18 | 22 | $49

East Midtown | 210 E. 58th St. (bet. 2nd & 3rd Aves.) | 212-355-7555 | www.dawatrestaurant.com

East Midtown's Indian "pioneer" (since 1986) "still pleases", thanks to actress/chef Madhur Jaffrey's "sophisticated" cooking, "graciously served" in a "quiet", "contemporary" room that's "conducive to conversation"; it may look "a little worn", but loyalists avow the tabs are "worth the extra cost."

db Bistro Moderne *French*   24 | 21 | 23 | $70

Midtown | City Club Hotel | 55 W. 44th St. (6th Ave.) | 212-391-2400 | www.dbbistro.com

"Elevated bistro fare" (i.e. that "decadent" burger stuffed with foie gras) is dispatched by a "swift" team at Daniel Boulud's "bustling" Theater District French that's a natural for high-end pre-curtain dining; following a recent redo, the "refreshed" room exudes "New York cool" and now sports an "actual sit-down bar", which may be needed when you see the bill.

DBGB *French*   22 | 22 | 21 | $57

East Village | 299 Bowery (bet. 1st & Houston Sts.) | 212-933-5300 | www.dbgb.com

Daniel Boulud "bridges the gap between champagne tastes and beer budgets" at this more "affordable" Bowery French serving "upscale pub food" like housemade sausages, burgers and other "delicacies for carnivores"; "incredible" suds and "inventive" cocktails help blot out the "high noise level" at prime times.

NEW Decoy Chinese — — — E

West Village | 529½ Hudson St., downstairs (bet. Charles & W. 10th Sts.) | 212-691-9700 | www.decoynyc.com

Parked just below RedFarm in the West Village, this petite spin-off is devoted to prix fixe Peking duck feasts, though small plates and sides are also available; designed with rough-hewn wood and vintage decoys, it's equipped with a big communal table, plus a bar for cocktails and snacks.

Dee's Mediterranean/Pizza 23 | 19 | 21 | $34

Forest Hills | 107-23 Metropolitan Ave. (74th Ave.) | Queens | 718-793-7553 | www.deesnyc.com

Dee-votees depend on this "homey" Forest Hills outlet for "wonderful" brick-oven pizzas, Mediterranean "comfort" classics and other grill items; "fair prices", a "huge" space and "ample seating" bolster the "amicable", "family-friendly" mood.

Defonte's Sandwiches 24 | 9 | 19 | $16

Red Hook | 379 Columbia St. (Luquer St.) | Brooklyn | 718-625-8052 | www.defontesinbrooklyn.com

"Don't eat for a week" before attacking the "two-handed" "Dagwood" sandwiches at this "lip-smacking" Italian sub shop in Red Hook; in business since the 1920s, it "used to feed the longshoremen" and still exudes a whiff of "old-fashioned Brooklyn."

DeGrezia Italian 25 | 23 | 25 | $74

East Midtown | 231 E. 50th St. (bet. 2nd & 3rd Aves.) | 212-750-5353 | www.degreziaristorante.com

A "real sleeper" hidden below street level, this East Midtowner is a model of "old-world elegance", offering "first-rate" Italian food, "expert" service and a "civilized" milieu where "one can actually talk"; though "expensive", it's "worth it for special occasions" and "business lunches."

Degustation French/Spanish 26 | 19 | 24 | $90

East Village | 239 E. Fifth St. (bet. 2nd & 3rd Aves.) | 212-979-1012 | www.degustation-nyc.com

"Anticipation" is in the air as chefs prepare "sublime" Franco-Spanish small plates with "meticulous attention to detail" at this "tiny" East Village tasting bar courtesy of Grace and Jack Lamb; even though the tabs may "pinch your wallet", the payoffs are "powerful flavors", "on-point" service and that "courtside" counter-seating experience.

Del Frisco's Steak 25 | 23 | 23 | $83

Midtown | 1221 Sixth Ave. (bet. 48th & 49th Sts.) | 212-575-5129 | www.delfriscos.com

Del Frisco's Grille Steak

Midtown | Rockefeller Ctr. | 50 Rockefeller Plaza (51st St.) | 212-767-0371 | www.delfriscosgrille.com

Carnivores "live it up" at this "sexy", "spacious" Midtown steakhouse (and its "less mobbed" Rock Center sibling), praised for "expertly prepared" cuts, "quality" sides and an "unforgettable" lemon cake; the "power-scene" mood extends to the "hopping bar", where "many a deal is made"; needless to say, the pricing is "recession proof."

	FOOD	DECOR	SERVICE	COST

Dell'anima *Italian*
| | 25 | 19 | 22 | $64 |

West Village | 38 Eighth Ave. (Jane St.) | 212-366-6633 |
www.dellanima.com

Ever "jam-packed" thanks to its "wonderful" rustic Italian fare (including "the best housemade pastas"), this "cozy" West Villager features a chef's counter where you can watch the "magic" happen; "reservations are a must", or be prepared for a "long wait" in its adjacent wine bar, Anfora.

Delmonico's *Steak*
| | 23 | 22 | 22 | $76 |

Financial District | 56 Beaver St. (William St.) | 212-509-1144 |
www.delmonicosny.com

Delmonico's Kitchen *Steak*

Midtown | 207 W. 36th St. (bet. 7th & 8th Aves.) | 212-695-5220 |
www.delmonicosrestaurantgroup.com

One of America's "most historic" restaurants, this FiDi steakhouse rolls out "gold-standard" chops along with "classic dishes" actually invented here (e.g. Baked Alaska, Lobster Newburg), all dispensed by a "top-notch" staff in "old-world" digs; its newer Midtown spin-off is a fine "oasis" near Penn Station and shares the "big bills" of the mother ship.

Del Posto *Italian*
| | 26 | 27 | 27 | $128 |

Chelsea | 85 10th Ave. (bet. 15th & 16th Sts.) | 212-497-8090 |
www.delposto.com

A "well-oiled machine" is putting it mildly at this "sumptuous" Chelsea destination from the Batali-Bastianich juggernaut offering "high-end Italian" cooking "without peer", abetted by "elegant" service, a "deep" wine list and a "majestic", balcony-lined setting; sure, the tabs are "extraordinarily expensive", but most agree it's the "total package for that special evening", and a relative bargain at lunch.

Delta Grill *Cajun/Creole*
| | 20 | 15 | 19 | $33 |

Midtown | 700 Ninth Ave. (48th St.) | 212-956-0934 |
www.thedeltagrill.com

"N'Awlins comes to Ninth Avenue" at this "funky" Hell's Kitchen roadhouse that channels the "Big Easy" with "reliable" Cajun-Creole grub that "somehow tastes better when a band is playing"; "cheery" vibes and "reasonable" tabs keep the "patrons marching in."

Denino's Pizzeria *Pizza*
| | 26 | 12 | 19 | $22 |

Elm Park | 524 Port Richmond Ave. (bet. Hooker Pl. & Walker St.) | Staten Island | 718-442-9401 | www.deninos.com

"Long established" for a reason, this 1937 Elm Park pizzeria turns out "delicious" pies with "crispy crusts" in a "plain", "no-frills" room; even though it's cash-only, "cheap" tabs keep it perennially packed.

Dévi *Indian*
| | 23 | 21 | 20 | $54 |

Flatiron | 8 E. 18th St. (bet. B'way & 5th Ave.) | 212-691-2100 |
www.devinyc.com

Among the first of NYC's "high-end Indians", this Flatiron eatery still comes across with "delicious" subcontinental cooking (including "veggies a carnivore could die for") served up in "exotic" environs; sure, it may be "a bit expensive" for the genre, but the prix fixe $20 lunch provides plenty of "bang for your rupee."

	FOOD	DECOR	SERVICE	COST

Dhaba *Indian*
24 | 16 | 18 | $31

Kips Bay | 108 Lexington Ave. (bet. 27th & 28th Sts.) | 212-679-1284 | www.dhabanyc.com

"Delicious and different", this "simple" Curry Hill Indian turns out "impressive", "pungently spiced" specialties – even "'regular' is hot, hot, hot" – at "terrific-value" tabs; there's "always a line" at the "sliver" of a space for the "bargain" $11 lunch buffet.

Di Fara *Pizza*
25 | 4 | 9 | $19

Midwood | 1424 Ave. J (15th St.) | Brooklyn | 718-258-1367 | www.difara.com

The "magical" pies prepared by octogenarian "pizza alchemist" Dom DeMarco at this 1964 Midwood "temple" will make you feel "all is good in the world"; "unnerving" waits, decidedly "nothing-fancy" digs and smile-free service are just part of the "total experience", but fans insist it's more than "worth the trouble" for a "slice of heaven."

Dim Sum Go Go *Chinese*
21 | 11 | 15 | $25

Chinatown | 5 E. Broadway (bet. Catherine St. & Chatham Sq.) | 212-732-0797 | www.dimsumgogo.com

"Cheap", "no-frills" dim sum ordered off a menu rather than snagged from a trolley makes this "utilitarian" Chinese "less chaotic" than the typical C-town outfits; however, traditionalists "miss the ladies schlepping the carts" and report "perfunctory service" and "run-of-the-mill" decor.

Diner *American*
∇ 23 | 17 | 20 | $41

Williamsburg | 85 Broadway (Berry St.) | Brooklyn | 718-486-3071 | www.dinernyc.com

The "daily changing", locally sourced New Americana – "far from diner fare" – is as "tops as the crowd" at this "cool, laid-back" Williamsburg pioneer; its "blast-from-the-past" 1927 dining car digs are a "snug fit", but the helpful staff ("don't be afraid to ask for direction") and "good wine/cocktail list" help keep the mood copacetic.

NEW Dinner on Ludlow *American*
∇ 21 | 21 | 19 | $48

Lower East Side | The DL | 95 Delancey St. (Ludlow St.) | 212-228-0909 | www.thedl-nyc.com

On the first floor of the DL, a "swanky" three-level LES club, this "chandelier-filled" stunner offers "solid" New American dinner and brunch fare plus "fresh" cocktails; to some it's more "impressive" for drinking than dining, but it's a "nice place to hang out" either way.

Dino *Italian*
20 | 19 | 20 | $37

Fort Greene | 222 Dekalb Ave. (Clermont Ave.) | Brooklyn | 718-222-1999 | www.dinorestaurantny.com

Fort Greene locals favor this "welcoming", well-priced standby for pastas and other Italian staples, plus "fantastic cocktails"; "small" and "relaxed", it's "noisy fun" at brunch but also a "great little date spot", with a "pleasant" back garden to seal the deal.

Dinosaur Bar-B-Que *BBQ*
23 | 18 | 19 | $34

Morningside Heights | 700 W. 125th St. (12th Ave.) | 212-694-1777
Gowanus | 604 Union St. (4th Ave.) | Brooklyn | 347-429-7030
www.dinosaurbarbque.com

"Funky" is the word on these "high-volume" Gowanus and Morningside

Heights smoke joints where the BBQ is "tender" and "juicy", and the settings "loud, crowded" and furnished with "wooden benches"; it's "welcoming to both bikers and families" alike, but be prepared for "hectic" atmospheres and "long lines."

NEW Dirty French *French*

FOOD	DECOR	SERVICE	COST
—	—	—	E

Lower East Side | The Ludlow Hotel | 180 Ludlow St.(bet. Houston & Stanton Sts.) | 212-254-3000 | www.dirtyfrench.com

Team Torrisi (Carbone, Parm) branches out at its first non-Italian venture, this new Lower Eastsider in the Ludlow Hotel where the pricey French fare is jazzed up with Moroccan and Cajun accents; the brasserie-like setting features the usual hip decor elements – subway tiles, red leather banquettes, wood-beamed ceilings, conversation-piece chandeliers – but what's on the plate and who are in the seats are far more interesting.

Distilled *American*

FOOD	DECOR	SERVICE	COST
23	20	22	$48

TriBeCa | 211 W. Broadway (bet. Franklin & White Sts.) | 212-601-9514 | www.distilledny.com

"Epic wings" are a menu standout at this "spacious" TriBeCan offering American public-house fare "taken to another level" and washed down with "delectable" cocktails and NY-made meads; it's a "welcome addition to the neighborhood" serviced by an "aim-to-please" staff.

Docks Oyster Bar *Seafood*

FOOD	DECOR	SERVICE	COST
20	19	19	$58

Murray Hill | 633 Third Ave. (40th St.) | 212-986-8080 | www.docksoysterbar.com

"Reliable" fish and bivalves galore reel in the masses at this "cavernous" seafood standby near Grand Central; "briskly professional" servers tend to schools of "biz lunchers" and "after-work" revelers who dive in for its "active" happy hour and high-octane "social" scene.

Do Hwa *Korean*

FOOD	DECOR	SERVICE	COST
∇ 22	18	19	$41

West Village | 55 Carmine St. (bet. Bedford St. & 7th Ave.) | 212-414-1224 | www.dohwanyc.com

"Authentic" eats packing "lots of spice" chased with "creative" cocktails fuel the "cool vibe" at this "hip" West Village Korean, a slightly "upscale" take on the "traditional" with grill-equipped tables on hand for hands-on types; sure, it may cost "a little more than K-town", but it's a much "sexier" experience.

Dominick's *Italian*

FOOD	DECOR	SERVICE	COST
23	10	18	$43

Arthur Avenue/Belmont | 2335 Arthur Ave. (bet. 184th & 187th Sts.) | Bronx | 718-733-2807

Patrons have been filling the communal tables of this "iconic" Arthur Avenue Italian since 1966, despite no decor, "no menus" ("you eat what they're cooking"), "no checks" ("trust the waiter") and no reservations or credit cards; "off-the-charts" food and "cost performance" make the "daunting waits" bearable, but to save time, go early.

Don Antonio *Pizza*

FOOD	DECOR	SERVICE	COST
22	14	17	$31

Midtown | 309 W. 50th St. (bet. 8th & 9th Aves.) | 646-719-1043 | www.donantoniopizza.com

Pizzaphiles ascend to "pie heaven" via the dozens of varieties built on "light, flaky" crusts (its flash-fried rendition is especially "scrumptious") at this "excellent" Midtown Neapolitan; the setting can be "cramped" and "hectic", yet in the end those "outstanding" wood-fired pies "overcome all."

Donovan's *American* | 21 | 20 | 20 | $28 |

Bayside | 214-16 41st Ave. (Bell Blvd.) | Queens | 718-423-5178 | www.donovansofbayside.com
Woodside | 57-24 Roosevelt Ave. (58th St.) | Queens | 718-429-9339 | www.donovansny.com

"Something-for-everyone" menus lure the "family" trade to these separately owned Queens vets lauded for "perfect" hamburgers along with "solid", "Irish-tinged" pub grub; "bargain" tabs and "pleasant" service come with the territory.

Don Peppe *Italian* | 25 | 11 | 19 | $52 |

South Ozone Park | 135-58 Lefferts Blvd. (149th Ave.) | Queens | 718-845-7587

An "old-school", cash-only red-sauce joint "unburdened by pretension", this circa-1968 South Ozone Park Italian is home to "marvelous" meals that end with "sacks of leftovers"; the house wines might have been "made yesterday" and the digs "could use redecorating", but it's hard to find a more authentic "NY experience."

Don's Bogam *Korean* ▽ | 24 | 20 | 17 | $49 |

Midtown | 17 E. 32nd St. (bet. 5th & Madison Aves.) | 212-683-2200 | www.donsbogam.com

"Deelish" meats draw diners to this K-Town Korean tabletop BBQ, with "decent prices" and decor that's "a little better" than the competition; the "quality of the food" trumps the sometimes "hurried" service.

Do or Dine *Eclectic* ▽ | 23 | 21 | 22 | $51 |

Bedford-Stuyvesant | 1108 Bedford Ave. (bet. Lexington Ave. & Quincy St.) | Brooklyn | 718-684-2290 | www.doordinebk.com

"Weird and wonderful", this Bed-Stuy Eclectic excels with "all kinds of crazy dishes and drinks" ("the foie gras donuts are a highlight") delivered by a "friendly staff"; the come-as-you-are space featuring a skull-and-bones mosaic, disco ball and "hip-hop" soundtrack can "get a little crowded", but most are too busy "having fun" to care.

NEW Dosa Royale *Indian* ▽ | 24 | 20 | 19 | $24 |

Carroll Gardens | 316 Court St. (bet. Degraw & Sackett Sts.) | Brooklyn | 718-576-3800 | www.dosaroyale.com

"Dosas meet hipsters" at this Carroll Gardens Indian (spun off from a Smorgasburg stand), where the signature item is offered in a multitude of vegetarian and gluten-free options; maybe the service could use some work, but the "reasonable" rates are fine as is.

Dos Caminos *Mexican* | 20 | 19 | 19 | $47 |

East Midtown | 825 Third Ave. (bet. 50th & 51st Sts.) | 212-336-5400
Kips Bay | 373 Park Ave. S. (bet. 26th & 27th Sts.) | 212-294-1000
Meatpacking District | 675 Hudson St. (bet. 13th & 14th Sts.) | 212-699-2400
SoHo | 475 W. Broadway (bet. Houston & Prince Sts.) | 212-277-4300
www.doscaminos.com

"Signature margaritas" and "delicious" tableside guacamole are menu standouts at these "lively" Mexicans fielding "standard fare done well"; "cheerful" service and stellar "people-watching" are other incentives, though some say the "party" atmospheres overshadow the food.

Dos Toros *Mexican*

FOOD	DECOR	SERVICE	COST
20	12	17	$13

NEW **Battery Park City** | Hudson Eats | 200 Vesey St. (West St.) | 212-786-0392
East 70s | 1111 Lexington Ave. (bet. 77th & 78th Sts.) | 212-535-4658
Greenwich Village | 137 Fourth Ave. (13th St.) | 212-677-7300
West Village | 11 Carmine St. (bet. Bleecker St. & 6th Ave.) | 212-627-2051
Williamsburg | 189 Bedford Ave. (bet. N. 6th & 7th Sts.) | Brooklyn | 718-384-8833
www.dostoros.com

"Legitimate" Mexican fare by way of the "Bay Area" is the specialty of these "cheap, fab" taquerias, "eco-friendly" stops luring both bullish burrito buffs and Cali transplants; there's "always a line and never a table", but "fast delivery" is an option at most outlets.

NEW Dover *American*

FOOD	DECOR	SERVICE	COST
27	19	25	$82

Carroll Gardens | 412 Court St. (bet. 1st & 2nd Pls.) | Brooklyn | 347-987-3545 | www.doverbrooklyn.com

"Culinary ambition" comes to Carroll Gardens via this "outstanding" American newcomer from the Battersby team, offering "delectable" dishes along with a "fantastic" tasting menu; fans like its "personable" service and "simple" blond-wood decor, but are more excited that "they take reservations", a "miracle in modern Brooklyn."

Dovetail *American*

FOOD	DECOR	SERVICE	COST
27	24	24	$93

West 70s | 103 W. 77th St. (Columbus Ave.) | 212-362-3800 | www.dovetailnyc.com

"Paying attention to every detail", John Fraser's "sophisticated" Upper Westsider offers "artful" New American cooking and "polite" service in a "formal but relaxed" bi-level room; such "memorable meals" naturally come at an "expensive" cost, though the $58 'Sunday suppa' is more of a "price performer."

Due *Italian*

FOOD	DECOR	SERVICE	COST
22	17	23	$56

East 70s | 1396 Third Ave. (bet. 79th & 80th Sts.) | 212-772-3331 | www.duenyc.com

Locals tout the "simple", "satisfying" Northern Italian cooking and "feel-at-home" atmosphere at this longtime "low-profile" Upper Eastsider; "rustic" looks and "warm" service enhance its "unpretentious" air, and fair prices seal the deal.

DuMont Burger *Burgers*

FOOD	DECOR	SERVICE	COST
21	14	16	$26

Williamsburg | 314 Bedford Ave. (bet. 1st & 2nd Sts.) | Brooklyn | 718-384-6127

Though the original DuMont has closed, its tiny offshoot is as "busy" as ever, serving "substantial" burgers, "crisp" onion rings and "slammin'" mac 'n' cheese; it's popular for takeout, but regulars "try to eat in", since most of the offerings "don't travel well."

	FOOD	DECOR	SERVICE	COST

The Dutch *American* — | 23 | 20 | 20 | $62 |

SoHo | 131 Sullivan St. (Prince St.) | 212-677-6200 |
www.thedutchnyc.com

Chef Andrew Carmellini's "delish" riffs on American dishes draw
"trendsetters" to this "fashionable" SoHo "winner"; critics cite "pricey"
tariffs, "scene over substance" and "construction-zone decibel levels",
but consensus says it's "well worth the investment" – "if only it were
easier to get in."

NEW Dutch Kills Centraal *American* — ∇ | 21 | 19 | 18 | $17 |

Long Island City | 3840 29th St. (39th Ave.) | Queens | 718-606-8651 |
www.dutchkillscentraal.com

At this "friendly" LIC "neighborhood" joint, locals consume American
gastropub grub sourced from farmer's markets, paired with craft
beers; the long communal table that splits the space in half makes
it easy to mingle.

Dylan Prime *American* — ∇ | 18 | 18 | 16 | $90 |

TriBeCa | 62 Laight St. (Greenwich St.) | 212-334-4783 |
www.dylanprime.com

Following a hiatus, this "upscale" TriBeCan is back with a retooled
American menu that still features "quality" steaks but now adds
seasonally focused fare and a build-your-own martini bar to the mix;
the digs now sport a more industrial look, though the "big-bucks"
pricing remains intact.

NEW East & West *American/Asian* — | – | – | – | M |

Hell's Kitchen | Yotel Hotel | 570 10th Ave. (bet. 41st & 42nd Sts.) |
646-449-7790 | www.yotelnewyork.com

Set in Hell's Kitchen's Yotel Hotel, this entry from Jeffrey Chodorow
(China Grill) offers a wide-ranging mash-up of Asian and American
dishes, everything from sushi rolls to short-rib sliders; the casual setting
is modeled after a business-class airport lounge, with counter seats,
communal tables and laptop-friendly tables.

East End Kitchen *American* — | 21 | 18 | 17 | $47 |

East 80s | 539 E. 81st St. (bet. East End & York Aves.) | 212-879-0450 |
www.eastendkitchennyc.com

"Finally", "sleepy" Yorkville has a "neighborhood" haunt all its own in this
"promising" place offering "homey" Americana, "casual" brunching and
even a grab-and-go espresso bar; the "Hamptons"-esque decor is "stylish", but critics wish the servers would "get their act together."

East Pacific *Asian* — ∇ | 24 | 19 | 20 | $34 |

Kips Bay | 120 E. 34th St. (bet. Lexington & Park Aves.) | 212-696-2818 |
www.34eastpacific.com
New Springville | Staten Island Mall | 2655 Richmond Ave. (Richmond
Hill Rd.) | Staten Island | 718-370-2225

These "surprisingly good" Pan-Asians in Kips Bay and the Staten Island
Mall offer menus running the gamut from sushi to dim sum and pad Thai,
all "bursting with flavor"; "strive-to-please" service and "won't-break-
the-bank" tabs complete the "palatable" picture.

	FOOD	DECOR	SERVICE	COST

NEW The East Pole American/British
22 | 20 | 19 | $65

East 60s | 133 E. 65th St. (bet. Lexington & Park Aves.) | 212-249-2222 | www.theeastpolenyc.com

"Downtown moves Uptown" via this Fat Radish offshoot that's "enchanting" Upper Eastsiders with its "farm-to-table-done-right", British-accented New American fare and "original" cocktails served in airy, "hip" quarters; despite "pricey" tabs, it's generally "crowded" – especially at the "fantastic brunch."

NEW East 12th Osteria Italian
∇ 25 | 22 | 23 | $61

East Village | 197 First Ave. (1st Ave.) | 212-432-1112 | www.east12osteria.com

A "great find" that's somehow "under the radar", this East Village Northern Italian offers "delectable" food (including "baked-on-premises" breads) served by an "exemplary" team in a "relaxed" setting; "lots of windows" providing excellent "people-watching" ice the cake.

E.A.T. American
20 | 10 | 14 | $43

East 80s | 1064 Madison Ave. (bet. 80th & 81st Sts.) | 212-772-0022 | www.elizabar.com

Before "Madison Avenue shopping" or hitting the "Museum Mile", "East Side ladies" and others drop by Eli Zabar's "high-style" American for "tastefully prepared" sandwiches and salads; despite "money-is-no-object" tabs, "rushed" service and "glamorized deli" digs, it's "always busy."

Eataly Food Market/Italian
23 | 18 | 17 | $41

Flatiron | 200 Fifth Ave. (bet. 23rd & 24th Sts.) | 212-229-2560 | www.eataly.com

An "experience like no other", this "mammoth" Flatiron food hall from the Batali-Bastianich team is a "foodie's dream come true", with its all-Italian array of counters selling cheese, coffee, fish, gelati, pasta, pizza, vegetables and wine, plus Manzo, a sit-down restaurant, and a new Nutella bar; despite "pricey" tariffs, "overwhelming" hordes and "limited seating" for noshers, this "mind-blowing" enterprise is "a definite must" for anyone who likes to eat.

Ecco Italian
21 | 18 | 20 | $70

TriBeCa | 124 Chambers St. (bet. B'way & Church St.) | 212-227-7074 | www.eccorestaurantny.com

"Still going strong", this "old-school" TriBeCan turns out "true-to-its-roots" Italian fare to the tune of a weekend "piano player"; "formal" staffers are also on key, leaving "Uptown prices" as the only off-notes.

Eddie's Sweet Shop Ice Cream
24 | 22 | 21 | $12

Forest Hills | 105-29 Metropolitan Ave. (72nd Rd.) | Queens | 718-520-8514

Around since "before they invented calories", this "throwback" Forest Hills soda shop still makes its own ice cream, toppings and fountain drinks to the "highest standards"; indeed, its "candy-store" decor and "old-fashioned service" recall a "kinder era of simple pleasures."

NEW The Eddy American
– | – | – | M

East Village | 342 E. Sixth St. (bet. 1st & 2nd Aves.) | 646-895-9884 | www.theeddynyc.com

Setting up shop on the East Village's curry row, this midpriced arrival presents a New American menu emphasizing seafood and market produce, matched with mostly French wines and creative cocktails; an arched mirror behind the bar lends extra shine to the petite space.

Edi & The Wolf *Austrian*   ▽ 19 | 21 | 19 | $52

East Village | 102 Ave. C (bet. 6th & 7th Sts.) | 212-598-1040 | www.ediandthewolf.com

"Unique" is the word on this "funky" East Village Austrian offering "rich", "authentic" fare paired with super suds and wines; the hipster "cozy-cottage" design seems straight out of a fractured fairy tale, while the "cute" garden is a quiet alternative to the "loud" goings-on inside.

Ed's Chowder House *Seafood*   20 | 20 | 20 | $58

West 60s | Empire Hotel | 44 W. 63rd St. (bet. B'way & Columbus Ave.) | 212-956-1288 | www.chinagrillmgt.com

"Civilized dining by Lincoln Center" is alive and well at this "sophisticated" seafooder in the Empire Hotel where the "skillfully prepared" catch is dispatched by a staff that "gets you out on time" for the show; "nicely spaced" tables and overall "convenience" make the rather "pricey" tabs more palatable.

Ed's Lobster Bar *Seafood*   24 | 16 | 20 | $43

SoHo | 222 Lafayette St. (bet. Broome & Spring Sts.) | 212-343-3236 | www.lobsterbarnyc.com

The "simple, whitewashed" setting gives this "upbeat" SoHo fish house a "New England" mood that goes well with its "pricey", "near-perfection" lobster rolls and bivalves; given the "cramped" table seating, regulars "eat at the bar" for "more attentive" service and added wiggle room.

Egg *Southern*   23 | 14 | 16 | $28

Williamsburg | 109 N. Third St. (bet. Berry St. & Wythe Ave.) | Brooklyn | 718-302-5151 | www.eggrestaurant.com

"Simple" yet "fulfilling" breakfast dishes have made a name for this daytime Williamsburg joint from George Weld, recently relocated to somewhat larger digs; expect the same "homey" vibes, "affordable" tabs and "super-long" weekend brunch lines, as well as something new: credit cards are now accepted.

Eisenberg's Sandwich Shop *Sandwiches*   17 | 10 | 17 | $16

Flatiron | 174 Fifth Ave. (22nd St.) | 212-675-5096 | www.eisenbergsnyc.com

A "bygone" ode to the "greasy spoon", this circa-1929 Flatiron luncheonette is known for "basics" like tuna sandwiches and "old-style" egg creams; modernists may moan about "shabby" decor and "rickety" service, but for many, this remains a "sentimental" favorite.

NEW Élan *American*   – | – | – | E

Flatiron | 43 E. 20th St. (bet. B'way & Park Ave. S.) | 646-682-7105

Five years after closing his fine-dining destination Chanterelle, chef-owner David Waltuck returns to the scene with this Flatiron American offering a contemporary menu prepared with French techniques, including signature favorites like his famed seafood sausages; the stripped-down, tablecloth-free dining room (the former Veritas digs) is a match for the modern, à la carte–only offerings.

| | FOOD | DECOR | SERVICE | COST |

El Centro *Mexican*
21 | 18 | 19 | $33

Midtown | 824 Ninth Ave. (54th St.) | 646-763-6585 |
www.elcentro-nyc.com

This "upbeat" Midtown Mexican throws a "hip", "loud" fiesta ramped up
by "awesome" margaritas and, oh yeah, "decently priced" south-of-the-
border bites; the "quirky", "kitschy" setting is "always packed", though
regulars wish the "music could be lowered a few decibels."

El Charro Espanol *Spanish*
▽ 23 | 14 | 20 | $50

West Village | 4 Charles St. (bet. Greenwich & 7th Aves.) |
212-243-5413 | www.el-charro-espanol.com

Tucked away in a West Village brownstone basement, this circa-1925
Spaniard fields "first-rate" tapas, large plates and deadly sangria; the
"generic decor" is "quaint" to some, "dated" to others, but everyone likes
the "reasonable" prices and "warm" service.

NEW El Colmado *Spanish*
– | – | – | M

Hell's Kitchen | Gotham West Mkt. | 600 11th Ave. (bet. 44th & 45th
Sts.) | 212-582-7948 | www.elcolmadonyc.com

Chef Seamus Mullen lands in Gotham West Market via this counter
concession that showcases some of the same Spanish tapas featured at
his Downtown hit, Tertulia; the cheeses, charcuterie and bite-size plates
on offer are fairly priced, and there's a wide selection of wines too.

Eleven Madison Park *American*
28 | 28 | 28 | $220

Flatiron | 11 Madison Ave. (24th St.) | 212-889-0905 |
www.elevenmadisonpark.com

"Gastronomic heaven awaits" at Daniel Humm's "unforgettable"
American dining room opposite Madison Square Park that "titillates
the imagination" with a "whimsical" tasting menu and "superb" wine
pairings ferried by "exceptional" staffers in "gorgeous" art deco quarters;
even given "luxury-car-payment" prices, admirers affirm this "once-in-a-
lifetime" experience "should not be missed."

Eliá *Greek*
▽ 26 | 21 | 22 | $53

Bay Ridge | 8611 Third Ave. (bet. 86th & 87th Sts.) | Brooklyn |
718-748-9891 | www.eliarestaurant.com

Bringing Bay Ridge an "exceptional" "taste of the Mediterranean", this
Greek "neighborhood" fixture produces "perfectly cooked" whole fish
and other "innovative" specials; sure, it's a "splurge", but the staff is
"hospitable" and there are bonus "outdoor seats" on the garden deck.

Elias Corner *Greek/Seafood*
26 | 11 | 18 | $40

Astoria | 24-02 31st St. (24th Ave.) | Queens | 718-932-1510 |
www.eliascorner.com

Grilled fish so fresh it tastes like it was "caught an hour ago" is the
specialty of this "no-frills" Astoria Greek with not much decor and "no
menus" (just check out the "cold case" and point); though it only accepts
cash and service is "so-so", the tabs are sure "hard to beat."

Elio's *Italian*
24 | 18 | 22 | $77

East 80s | 1621 Second Ave. (bet. 84th & 85th Sts.) | 212-772-2242

A magnet for "media" moguls, "Page Six regulars" and "monied" UES
types, this "old-school" Italian dispenses food "delectable" enough to

justify the "through-the-nose" tabs; expect the "cold shoulder" if you're not a "member of the club", but at least the "cheek-to-jowl" seating bolsters the chance of rubbing elbows with "Matt Lauer."

The Ellington *Pub Food*
▽ 16 | 16 | 18 | $32

West 100s | 936 Amsterdam Ave. (106th St.) | 212-222-4050 | www.theellingtonny.com

This "inviting" Upper UWS "find" serves elevated pub grub that's "fairly priced" and goes down well with drinks like the Sophisticated Lady, honoring onetime neighbor Duke Ellington; a "large", "lovely" sidewalk seating area is another reason it's a "great addition to the neighborhood."

The Elm *French*
25 | 23 | 24 | $91

Williamsburg | McCarren Hotel | 160 N. 12th St. (bet. Bedford Ave. & Berry St.) | Brooklyn | 718-218-7500 | www.theelmnyc.com

Chef Paul Liebrandt's "extraordinary", "absolutely beautiful" modern French dishes come in "sleek" subterranean quarters via a "pro" staff at this "haute" arrival to Williamsburg's McCarren Hotel; though "casual" by Liebrandt's standards, it'll "cost you", especially if you go for the "sublime" $135 tasting menu at Little Elm, the eight-seat chef's counter.

El Parador Cafe *Mexican*
22 | 18 | 22 | $51

Murray Hill | 325 E. 34th St. (bet. 1st & 2nd Aves.) | 212-679-6812 | www.elparadorcafe.com

A "devoted clientele" gets its "paella fix" at this '59-vintage Murray Hill vet that's known for "true-to-its-roots", "old-world" Mexican cooking; obscured by Midtown Tunnel traffic, it's a "hidden gem" – polished by "cordial" servers – that insiders want to keep "secret."

El Paso *Mexican*
22 | 14 | 18 | $32

East Harlem | 237 E. 116th St. (bet. 2nd & 3rd Aves.) | 212-860-4875
East Harlem | 1643 Lexington Ave. (104th St.) | 212-831-9831 | www.elpasony.com
East 90s | 64 E. 97th St. (bet. Madison & Park Aves.) | 212-996-1739

Eastsiders count on these "solid", unpretentious Uptown Mexicans for "terrific" tacos and other standards ("try the aguas frescas") made "fresh" with "quality ingredients"; "tight quarters" and "so-so" service are offset by "unbelievable-value" prices.

El Porrón *Spanish*
20 | 18 | 21 | $49

East 60s | 1123 First Ave. (bet. 61st & 62nd Sts.) | 212-207-8349 | www.elporronnyc.com

Tapas "like you'd find in Barcelona" make for "real-thing" dining at this UES Spaniard sporting a "something-for-everyone" menu; "winning wine" arrives in the namesake pitcher, and the crowd's a mix of "lively" types who "come hungry, thirsty and often."

El Pote *Spanish*
23 | 14 | 22 | $49

Murray Hill | 718 Second Ave. (bet. 38th & 39th Sts.) | 212-889-6680 | www.elpote.com

"Home away from home" for Murray Hill amigos since '77, this Spanish stalwart keeps business brisk with "fantastic paella" and other "first-rate" Iberian standards; maybe it's looking a bit "shabby", but locals count themselves "lucky" to have it.

	FOOD	DECOR	SERVICE	COST

El Quijote *Spanish* — 22 | 15 | 21 | $45

Chelsea | 226 W. 23rd St. (bet. 7th & 8th Aves.) | 212-929-1855 |
www.elquijoterestaurant.com

"Old-school to the hilt", this "colorful" Chelsea octogenarian may be
"faded" but is still "memorable" for Spanish food plated in "gut-buster
portions"; the decor lies somewhere between "tacky" and "kitschy", but
the prices are "decent" and that "lobster deal can't be beat."

El Quinto Pino *Spanish* — 25 | 21 | 23 | $46

Chelsea | 401 W. 24th St. (bet. 9th & 10th Aves.) | 212-206-6900 |
www.elquintopinonyc.com

Little plates "go a long way" at Alex Raij's "adorable", recently expanded
Chelsea tapas bar, where the "rich" Spanish bites – including that
"nothing-like-it-on-this-planet" uni panini – pair well with the "solid"
wines and "romantic" vibe; fans say the "super-chill" atmosphere alone
makes it a "come-back-to" kind of place.

El Toro Blanco *Mexican/Seafood* — 22 | 18 | 18 | $52

West Village | 257 Sixth Ave. (bet. Bedford & Downing Sts.) |
212-645-0193 | www.eltoroblanconyc.com

Elevating classic Mexican eats to "gourmet" levels, Josh Capon's slick
West Villager delivers dishes that "burst with flavor" amid a scene of
"trendy" "hustle and bustle"; though service can be "spotty", prices that
are relatively "reasonable" for the upscale milieu help make it a "zesty
addition to the 'hood."

NEW El Vez *Mexican* — — | — | — | M

Battery Park City | 259 Vesey St. (bet. North End Ave. & West St.) |
212-233-2500 | www.elveznyc.com

From restaurateur Stephen Starr (Buddakan, Morimoto) comes this
Battery Park City Mexican spin-off of his Philly original, serving upscale
takes on classic dishes washed down with an encyclopedic list of tequilas
and mezcals; the sprawling space is done up in kitschy, south-of-the-
border style and is quite the scene after work, though the crowds thin out
early once the commuters wind their way home.

Embers *Steak* — ∇ 23 | 15 | 19 | $58

Bay Ridge | 9519 Third Ave. (bet. 95th & 96th Sts.) | Brooklyn |
718-745-3700 | www.embersbayridge.com

A "working-class" Bay Ridge chophouse primed to "fill that steak craving", this circa-1985 area "institution" sears tender, "juicy" cuts at nearly
"half the price" of the Midtown big boys; it remains "reliable" under
"new ownership", but when it's "too crowded", there's always the "next-
door meat store."

Emilia's *Italian* — ∇ 23 | 15 | 20 | $34

Arthur Avenue/Belmont | 2331 Arthur Ave. (Crescent Ave.) | Bronx |
718-367-5915 | www.emiliasrestaurant.com

"In the heart of" Arthur Avenue's "food mecca", this longtime Italian
"mainstay" proffers "delicious" "red-sauce standards" in "generous
portions", including "wonderful daily specials"; happily there's "minimal
frenzy" within its "cozy", nothing-fancy digs, which are presided over
by a "friendly" staff.

| | | FOOD | DECOR | SERVICE | COST |

Emilio's Ballato *Italian* ▽ 24 | 19 | 21 | $65

NoLita | 55 E. Houston St. (Mott St.) | 212-274-8881
The "food sings" at this "back-in-the-day" "red-sauce" joint in NoLita
that "looks like an Italian farmhouse hallway" and is "one of the last of a
breed" (it's been around since 1956); owner Emilio is "always there", and
his presence "makes the evening complete."

NEW Emily *Pizza* – | – | – | M

Clinton Hill | 919 Fulton St. (bet. Clinton & Waverly Aves.) | Brooklyn |
347-844-9588 | www.pizzalovesemily.com
Credit a successful Kickstarter campaign for this new Clinton Hill
Neapolitan pizzeria offering both traditional and unusual pies (e.g.
cheese curds and truffle spread), along with some rustic Italian plates;
though table space is tight, the central open kitchen somehow makes
the dining room feel spacious.

NEW Emmett's *Pizza* ▽ 21 | 14 | 14 | $29

SoHo | 50 MacDougal St. (bet. Houston & Prince Sts.) | 917-639-3571
Chicago-style pizza arrives in SoHo at this "super-small" newcomer
offering "interesting" deep-dish versions that provoke mixed responses:
"greasy delicious" vs. "pretty good"; there's agreement, however, that
both the service and "uncomfortable" surroundings "need a little work."

Empanada Mama *S American* 24 | 11 | 16 | $19

Hell's Kitchen | 763 Ninth Ave. (bet. 51st & 52nd Sts.) | 212-698-9008 |
www.empmamanyc.com
Stuffing its "huge following" with "amazing" empanadas and arepas, this
24/7 Hell's Kitchen "hole-in-the-wall" is the mother of all "cheap" South
American "pocket"-food purveyors; undersized, "overcrowded" and at
times "disorganized", it "lends itself to takeout."

Empellón Cocina *Mexican* 23 | 19 | 20 | $55

East Village | 105 First Ave. (bet. 6th & 7th Sts.) | 212-780-0999
Empellón Taqueria *Mexican*
West Village | 230 W. Fourth St. (W. 10th St.) | 212-367-0999
www.empellon.com
Chef Alex Stupak's "bold" detour from desserts at WD-50 to "high-mind-
ed" Mexicana pays off at these "trendy" destinations; the original West
Village outlet "redefines the taco", while the "more upscale" East Village
spin-off aces "super-imaginative" small plates – between the "killer"
drinks and "fashionable" following, both enjoy crazy "buzz."

NEW Empire Diner *Diner* 21 | 18 | 19 | $37

Chelsea | 210 10th Ave. (bet. 22nd & 23rd Sts.) | 212-596-7523 |
www.empire-diner.com
The "Empire strikes back" with this reborn, circa-1946 Chelsea diner,
now helmed by Amanda Freitag, who's producing "elevated comfort
food" (a "stellar" patty melt, "must-have" mac 'n' cheese); the "historic"
setting's been "improved" in the "nice revamp", though "tight" conditions
and "hectic" atmospherics prevail at prime times.

	FOOD	DECOR	SERVICE	COST

NEW Empire Steak House *Steak*
22 | **19** | **23** | **$68**

Midtown | 237 W. 54th St. (bet. B'way & 8th Ave.) | 212-586-9700 | www.empiresteakhousenyc.com

Carnivores commend the "tender" steaks at this "busy" chophouse from the Ben & Jack's folks, "conveniently located" near Rock Center and the Theater District; "attentive" service contributes to the generally "pleasant" vibes, even if the decor doesn't rise above "standard Midtown."

Emporio *Italian*
▽ **24** | **19** | **17** | **$38**

NoLita | 231 Mott St. (bet. Prince & Spring Sts.) | 212-966-1234 | www.emporiony.com

Aurora alums are behind this "bellissimo" NoLita trattoria, a "sublime" option for "authentic" Neapolitan pizzas and "homemade pastas" served in a rustic-industrial setting; when the front room gets too "tight", regulars head for the "greenhouse"-like back room.

EN Japanese Brasserie *Japanese*
25 | **25** | **23** | **$80**

West Village | 435 Hudson St. (Leroy St.) | 212-647-9196 | www.enjb.com

"Excellent" Japanese cuisine – including "amazing" housemade tofu and "wow"-worthy kaiseki menus – served within "beautiful" digs have made a "favorite" of this "upscale" West Villager; a "tremendous sake list" and "earnest" service are other reasons it's spot on for "date night."

Enzo's *Italian*
25 | **19** | **22** | **$44**

Morris Park | 1998 Williamsbridge Rd. (Neill Ave.) | Bronx | 718-409-3828 | www.enzosbronxrestaurant.com

Enzo's of Arthur Avenue *Italian*

Arthur Avenue/Belmont | 2339 Arthur Ave. (bet. 184th & 187th Sts.) | Bronx | 718-733-4455

These "blue-ribbon" "red-sauce palaces" in the Bronx dish out "downhome" Italian standards in mammoth portions and toss in some "old-school charm" on the side; the "unpretentious" staff "treats you like family", so embrace the "time warp" – and "don't fill up on the bread."

Erawan *Thai*
▽ **22** | **19** | **20** | **$40**

Bayside | 42-31 Bell Blvd. (bet. 42nd & 43rd Aves.) | Queens | 718-428-2112 | www.erawanthaibayside.com

Bayside locals tout this "go-to Thai" for its "aromatic" offerings with "interesting modern twists", abetted by "gentle" service and a "Manhattan atmosphere"; though prices lie on the "premium" side for the genre, it's ever "crowded" at prime times.

Erminia *Italian*
23 | **22** | **23** | **$78**

East 80s | 250 E. 83rd St. (bet. 2nd & 3rd Aves.) | 212-879-4284 | www.erminiaristorante.com

If you're looking for "romance", try this "transporting" UES Roman boîte where a "cavelike", candlelit setting sets the mood for "knockout" cooking, while "attentive" service and a "leisurely" pace do the rest; sure, it's "expensive", but there are "only a few tables", lending exclusivity to this "special experience."

	FOOD	DECOR	SERVICE	COST

Esca *Italian/Seafood* | 25 | 20 | 22 | $83 |

Hell's Kitchen | 402 W. 43rd St. (bet. 9th & 10th Aves.) | 212-564-7272 | www.esca-nyc.com

"Like eating on the Positano coast", this "high-end" Hell's Kitchen fish specialist from the Batali-Bastianich-Pasternack team fields "impeccable" Italian seafood and pastas, paired with a "terrific" wine list; "knowledgeable" staffers, an "unpretentious" setting and a "hefty" check are all part of the "glorious" package.

Estela *American/Mediterranean* | 25 | 19 | 21 | $63 |

NoLita | 47 E. Houston St. (bet. Mott & Mulberry Sts.) | 212-219-7693 | www.estelanyc.com

"Paradise for adventurous eaters", this Med-influenced American from Isa alum Ignacio Mattos serves "clever but not overwrought" small plates and a "great wine selection" in a compact NoLita space; sure, it's "crowded and noisy", and seating is "cramped", but this doesn't seem to faze its "young, sophisticated" following one bit.

Etcetera Etcetera *Italian* | 23 | 20 | 23 | $56 |

Midtown | 352 W. 44th St. (bet. 8th & 9th Aves.) | 212-399-4141 | www.etcetcnyc.com

"Casual" but "lively", this Midtown Italian features a "modern" menu that's a match for its "contemporary" looks; "splendid", "get-you-to-the-theater-on-time" service makes up for "noisy" acoustics, though regulars say it's "quieter upstairs."

Ethos *Greek/Seafood* | 22 | 18 | 18 | $52 |

East Midtown | 905 First Ave. (51st St.) | 212-888-4060
Kips Bay | 495 Third Ave. (bet. 33rd & 34th Sts.) | 212-252-1972 | www.ethosrestaurants.com

"Generous" plates of "well-prepared" catch are the lure at these Greek seafooders, along with "polite" if "slow" service and "affordable" tabs; the Kips Bay branch is "dinerlike" but "comfortable", while the more "inviting" Sutton Place locale exudes a "laid-back beach vibe."

Excellent Dumpling House *Chinese* | 24 | 6 | 13 | $18 |

Chinatown | 111 Lafayette St. (bet. Canal & Walker Sts.) | 212-219-0212 | www.excellentdumplinghouse.com

There's "no false advertising" at this Chinatowner where the "name-says-it-all" dumplings are served with equally "excellent" Shanghainese plates; true, there's "no atmosphere" and service is of the "rush-you-out" variety, but "at these prices, who cares?"

Extra Virgin *Mediterranean* | 23 | 17 | 17 | $46 |

West Village | 259 W. Fourth St. (Perry St.) | 212-691-9359 | www.extravirginrestaurant.com

The "young" and "glamorous" hobnob at this "fashionable" West Villager over "seasonal" Med fare that "won't break the bank"; although the place is usually "crowded" and the no-rez policy leads to "waits", amusing "people-watching" helps pass the time.

F & J Pine Restaurant *Italian* | 23 | 20 | 20 | $45 |

Van Nest | 1913 Bronxdale Ave. (bet. Matthews & Muliner Aves.) | Bronx | 718-792-5956 | www.fjpine.com

"Gigantic portions" are the name of the game at this "doggy bag"–guaranteed Van Nest Italian ladling out "loads of red sauce" for fans of "old-time" carbo-loading; "checkered" tablecloths, "old Yankee" memorabilia and Bronx Bomber sightings are all part of the "colorful" package here.

Farm on Adderley *American* 23 | 20 | 21 | $34

Ditmas Park | 1108 Cortelyou Rd. (bet. Stratford & Westminster Rds.) | Brooklyn | 718-287-3101 | www.thefarmonadderley.com

Ditmas Park denizens feel "lucky" to have this "worthwhile" New American and its "ambitious" meals spotlighting "super-fresh" local ingredients; a harvest like this could "cost twice as much in Manhattan", and insiders hint the food tastes even better from a "garden" seat.

The Fat Radish *American* 21 | 20 | 18 | $54

Lower East Side | 17 Orchard St. (bet. Canal & Hester Sts.) | 212-300-4053 | www.thefatradishnyc.com

"Veggie fanatics" get the royal treatment at this "trendy" Lower Eastsider that "oozes cool" with its "creative", locavore-oriented New American cooking and "hiptastic" "art-crowd" following; regulars allow extra time, since the "slacker" servers are in no hurry to mete out the "pricey but princely" fare.

Fatty Crab *Malaysian* 22 | 14 | 18 | $45

Meatpacking District | 643 Hudson St. (bet. Gansevoort & Horatio Sts.) | 212-352-3592 | www.fattycrabnyc.com

"Sticky-salty-sweet" Malaysian street eats make for "delectable" dining at this "buzzy" Meatpacking joint that's a magnet for "adventurous" "heat"-seekers; still, it's "not for the faint of heart" given the "doing-you-a-favor" service, "pounding music" and "steadily climbing bills."

Fatty Fish *Asian* 21 | 15 | 20 | $43

East 60s | 406 E. 64th St. (bet. 1st & York Aves.) | 212-813-9338 | www.fattyfishnyc.com

Upper Eastsiders are hooked on this Asian-fusion practitioner boasting "surprisingly creative" cooking (and sushi) served by "solicitous" staffers who just "keep smiling"; a "Zen-like" mood and "beautiful" enclosed garden distract from the "small" dimensions.

Fedora *American/French* 22 | 20 | 21 | $63

West Village | 239 W. Fourth St., downstairs (bet. Charles & W. 10th Sts.) | 646-449-9336 | www.fedoranyc.com

Gabe Stulman's "low-key chic" relaunch of a longtime West Village basement earns a tip of the cap for its "interesting" Franco-American menu and "beautiful neon sign"; retaining the "speakeasy vibe" of the old haunt and tossing in some "Wisconsin hospitality", it's now "better than ever", except perhaps for the cost.

Felice *Italian* 21 | 21 | 20 | $46

East 60s | 1166 First Ave. (64th St.) | 212-593-2223 | www.felice64.com
East 80s | 1593 First Ave. (83rd St.) | 212-249-4080 | www.felice83.com
Financial District | 15 Gold St. (Platt St.) | 212-785-5950 | www.felice15goldstreet.com

These "moderately hip" wine bars spice up "date nights" with "affordable", "well-chosen" vinos paired with "tasty" Italian small plates; the "gracious" service and "sexy" ambiance "appeal to multiple generations", though they mainly draw "younger" folks.

	FOOD	DECOR	SERVICE	COST

Felidia *Italian*
25 | 21 | 23 | $84

East Midtown | 243 E. 58th St. (bet. 2nd & 3rd Aves.) | 212-758-1479 | www.felidia-nyc.com

A "classy gem" from cuisine queen Lidia Bastianich, this "memorable" East Midtown Italian is touted for its "silky" pastas and overall "stellar" fare "cooked to perfection" and complemented by "accommodating" service and a "lovely" (if "conservative") townhouse setting; while you'll "spend a bundle" for dinner, the $30 prix fixe lunch is a "bargain by any standard."

Ferrara *Bakery*
23 | 15 | 17 | $19

Little Italy | 195 Grand St. (bet. Mott & Mulberry Sts.) | 212-226-6150 | www.ferraracafe.com

Open 122 years "and counting", this Little Italy bakery is a "legend" famed for its "heaven-on-a-plate" cannoli and "pick-me-up" espresso; "crowds of tourists" and "expensive"-for-what-it-is tabs draw brickbats, yet most agree this NYC relic "still has charm."

Fette Sau *BBQ*
26 | 15 | 15 | $32

Williamsburg | 354 Metropolitan Ave. (bet. Havemeyer & Roebling Sts.) | Brooklyn | 718-963-3404 | www.fettesaubbq.com

It's the "quintessential Williamsburg experience" to "join the hipsters" at this "serious foodie" "heaven" for "awesome" dry-rub, by-the-pound BBQ paired with "artisan" beers and bourbons; no rezzies means "crazy lines" for "cafeteria-style" service in a "former garage" outfitted with "communal picnic tables" – but to most it's so "worth it."

15 East *Japanese*
26 | 22 | 24 | $102

Union Square | 15 E. 15th St. (5th Ave.) | 212-647-0015 | www.15eastrestaurant.com

At this Union Square Japanese, the "top-notch" sushi presented with "art and love" by chef Masato Shimizu might "ruin you for the everyday" stuff, likewise the "exquisite" small plates and "incredible sakes"; it's "elegant all the way down the line", from the "tactful" service to the "calming", "minimalist" decor – paired with a predictably "maximalist bill."

57 Napoli Pizza e Vino *Pizza*
21 | 16 | 18 | $30

East Midtown | 120 E. 57th St., upstairs (bet. Lexington & Park Aves.) | 212-750-4586 | www.57napoli.com

Ok, the obscure second-floor address may be "easy to miss", but this East Midtown pizzeria is worth seeking out for "tasty" Neapolitan pies fired in a "wood-burning oven"; there's not much decor save for a floor-to-ceiling window "with a good view of 57th Street", but service is "friendly" and the tabs "affordable."

Fig & Olive *Mediterranean*
21 | 21 | 19 | $54

East 60s | 808 Lexington Ave. (bet. 62nd & 63rd Sts.) | 212-207-4555
Meatpacking District | 420 W. 13th St. (bet. 9th Ave. & Washington St.) | 212-924-1200
Midtown | 10 E. 52nd St. (bet. 5th & Madison Aves.) | 212-319-2002
www.figandolive.com

"Small plates with big flavors" are the draw at these "upbeat" Mediterraneans that also roll out fun "olive oil flights"; the big Meatpacking branch has a "high-energy", "nightclub" atmosphere, while its East Side siblings are a natural for "client lunches" and the après-Bloomingdale's set.

	FOOD	DECOR	SERVICE	COST

Fika *Coffee*

21 | 16 | 17 | $12

East Midtown | 600 Lexington Ave. (52nd St.) | 917-475-1450
Financial District | 66 Pearl St. (Broad St.) | 646-837-6588
NEW Hell's Kitchen | 566 10th Ave. (bet. 41st & 42nd Sts.) |
212-239-0050
Kips Bay | 303 Park Ave. S. (bet. 23rd & 24th Sts.) | 917-262-0615
Kips Bay | 407 Park Ave. S. (28th St.) | 646-649-5133
Midtown | 41 W. 58th St. (bet. 5th & 6th Aves.) | 212-832-0022
NEW Midtown | 114 W. 41st St. (bet. B'way & 6th Ave.) |
212-840-0677
Murray Hill | 380 Lexington Ave. (bet. 41st & 42nd Sts.) | 212-867-3338
TriBeCa | 450 Washington St. (bet. Desbrosses & Watts St.) |
212-706-0565
West 70s | The Apthorp | 2211 Broadway (bet. 78th & 79th Sts.) |
212-873-1255
www.fikanyc.com

"Swedes take their coffee seriously", and it shows at these "high-end" espresso bars offering "fresh-pressed" java, "rich" chocolates and "reliable" bites in compact settings; since service and seating are "limited", most grab their goods to go.

Fiorentino's *Italian*

23 | 15 | 21 | $37

Gravesend | 311 Ave. U (bet. McDonald Ave. & West St.) | Brooklyn |
718-372-1445 | www.fiorentinosristorante.com

"Old-school Brooklyn" endures at this "bustling" Gravesend Italian best known for "grandma"-style Neapolitan food plated in "tremendous" portions; its "Goodfellas"-esque crowd doesn't mind the "no-frills" decor, "noisy" decibels and no-rez rule given the "astonishingly cheap" tabs.

Firenze *Italian*

23 | 20 | 23 | $54

East 80s | 1594 Second Ave. (bet. 82nd & 83rd Sts.) | 212-861-9368 |
www.firenzeny.com

"Candlelight and exposed-brick walls" set a "romantic" mood at this longtime UES Italian that evokes Florence with "solid" Tuscan cooking delivered by a "couldn't-be-nicer" crew; neighborly prices ice the cake.

Fish *Seafood*

23 | 14 | 20 | $42

West Village | 280 Bleecker St. (Jones St.) | 212-727-2879 |
www.fishrestaurantnyc.com

Like the "simpleton name" implies, there's "nothing fancy" going on at this West Village seafood shack, just "truly good" catch proffered with great shuck for your buck (check out the $8 oyster special); trade-offs include "funky" looks and "tight-squeeze" seating.

FishTag *Greek/Seafood*

23 | 18 | 22 | $52

West 70s | 222 W. 79th St. (bet. Amsterdam Ave. & B'way) |
212-362-7470 | www.fishtagrestaurant.com

Bringing a "Downtown" vibe to the UWS, Michael Psilakis' "relaxed" Greek is a "breath of fresh air" for "delectable" fish dispatched in "nice-looking" digs by "enthusiastic" staffers; "decoding the menu" may require repeat visits, if you can abide the "din" and the "pricey" check.

	FOOD	DECOR	SERVICE	COST

5 & Diamond *American*
21 | 19 | 18 | $41

Harlem | 2072 Frederick Douglass Blvd. (112th St.) | 917-860-4444 |
www.5anddiamondrestaurant.com

Exemplifying Harlem's "burgeoning" restaurant scene, this "intimate"
New American lures an "eclectic crowd" with "fine", moderately priced
takes on familiar classics, including a "luscious mac 'n' cheese."

Five Leaves *American*
24 | 20 | 16 | $43

Greenpoint | 18 Bedford Ave. (Lorimer St.) | Brooklyn | 718-383-5345 |
www.fiveleavesny.com

A "must-try" "signature burger" and "excellent pancakes" star on
the "fab" all-day New American menu at this "informal" Greenpoint
bistro; its "casual" quarters get "packed", especially during weekend
brunch, when the wait can be "tough" – though "friendly" service and
"fair" prices compensate.

5 Napkin Burger *Burgers*
20 | 16 | 17 | $29

Greenwich Village | 150 E. 14th St. (3rd Ave.) | 212-228-5500
Midtown | 630 Ninth Ave. (45th St.) | 212-757-2277
West 80s | 2315 Broadway (84th St.) | 212-333-4488
www.5napkinburger.com

"Good thing there isn't a five-napkin limit" given the "mammoth",
"messy" and "super-tasty" patties (and assortment of sushi, hurrah!)
proffered at this "family-oriented" burger chain; the faux "butcher"-
shop settings are often "congested", but it's still a "solid" standby – if
you "could only hear yourself eat."

Five Points *American/Mediterranean*
21 | 20 | 21 | $50

NoHo | 31 Great Jones St. (bet. Bowery & Lafayette St.) | 212-253-5700 |
www.fivepointsrestaurant.com

"Simple yet sophisticated" Mediterranean–New Americana draws
diners to this "off-the-beaten-track" NoHo "oasis of calm", where
"helpful" staffers and a "hypnotic" babbling brook supply the "feng
shui"; it's famed for an "out-of-this-world" brunch, when "reservations
are an absolute must."

Flatbush Farm *American*
21 | 19 | 18 | $40

Park Slope | 76 St. Marks Ave. (Flatbush Ave.) | Brooklyn |
718-622-3276 | www.flatbushfarm.com

"Farm-to-table" bounties are the draw at this affordable Park Slope
American where the "solid" menu is assembled from "wholesome" local
ingredients; the less-enthused cite "uneven" service, but it wins kudos
for a "super brunch" and a "little-piece-of-heaven" garden.

Fletcher's Brooklyn Barbecue *BBQ*
20 | 12 | 16 | $33

Gowanus | 433 Third Ave. (bet. 7th & 8th Sts.) | Brooklyn |
347-763-2680 | www.fletchersbklyn.com

There's "real BBQ" in store at this locavore-friendly Gowanus arrival
smoking the classics (St. Louis ribs, brisket) as well as more "unique
items"; the "super-casual" setup features "friendly" counter service,
by-the-pound pricing and communal seating.

Flex Mussels *Seafood*
24 | 18 | 20 | $49

East 80s | 174 E. 82nd St. (bet. Lexington & 3rd Aves.) | 212-717-7772

continued

West Village | 154 W. 13th St. (bet. 6th & 7th Aves.) | 212-229-0222
www.flexmussels.com

"Steamy pots of mussels" are served with "exotic sauces" and "crusty bread" at these "fast-moving" bivalve specialists also touted for their "standout" donuts and "won't-break-the-bank" tabs; not much decor and "noisy", "highly social" scenes come with the territory.

NEW Flinders Lane *Australian*   – | – | – | M

East Village | 162 Ave. A (bet. 10th & 11th Sts.) | 212-228-6900 |
www.flinderslane-nyc.com

A modern Australian menu reflecting the country's diverse cultures is on offer at this East Village newcomer set in the former Beagle space; a massive photo of the Melbourne street from which it takes its name is the most striking decor element in the otherwise bare-bones space.

Flor de Mayo *Chinese/Peruvian*   21 | 10 | 19 | $25

West 80s | 484 Amsterdam Ave. (bet. 83rd & 84th Sts.) | 212-787-3388
West 100s | 2651 Broadway (bet. 100th & 101st Sts.) | 212-663-5520
www.flordemayo.com

"Widen your belt a notch" before approaching these UWS Chinese-Peruvian "favorites" where "flavorful" rotisserie chicken and other "bracing" eats are slung in "huge" portions for "bargain" sums; "zero" decor, "minimal" service and "hectic" digs make a strong case for "takeout."

NEW Fogo de Chão *Brazilian*   24 | 23 | 25 | $76

Midtown | 40 W. 53rd St. (bet. 5th & 6th Aves.) | 212-969-9980 |
www.fogo.com

An "all-you-can-eat meat extravaganza" awaits at this big Brazilian churrascaria near Rock Center offering "positively delicious" skewers (along with a "vast" salad bar) in a "beautiful" triplex setting; true, the tabs are "not inexpensive", but it's "paradise" for those bent on "protein overload."

Fonda *Mexican*   24 | 18 | 20 | $44

NEW Chelsea | 189 Ninth Ave. (bet. 21st & 22nd Sts.) | 917-525-5252
East Village | 40 Ave. B (3rd St.) | 212-677-4096
Park Slope | 434 Seventh Ave. (bet. 14th & 15th Sts.) | Brooklyn |
718-369-3144
www.fondarestaurant.com

For "memorable Nuevo Mexican", these "festive" cantinas are "the place to go" for "upscale" (yet well-priced) cooking and "interesting cocktails"; the "small" Park Slope original can feel "cramped" ("go when the backyard is open"), but the East Villager and newest bi-level Chelsea addition are roomier – and boast "fantastic happy hours."

Forcella *Pizza*   21 | 15 | 18 | $29

Kips Bay | 377 Park Ave. S. (bet. 26th & 27th Sts.) | 212-448-1116
NoHo | 334 Bowery (bet. Bond & Great Jones Sts.) | 212-466-3300
Williamsburg | 485 Lorimer St. (bet. Grand & Powers Sts.) | Brooklyn |
718-388-8820
www.forcellaeatery.com

An "experience straight from Italy", these "real-deal" pizzerias feature "light-as-air" Neapolitan pies, many of which are "flash-fried", then oven-finished in brightly tiled stoves; the digs are plain and the service "could be more attentive", but at least they're "lively" and "affordable."

Fornino *Pizza* 23 | 16 | 19 | $26

Brooklyn Heights | Brooklyn Bridge Park Pier 6 (Joralemon St.) | Brooklyn | 718-422-1107

Greenpoint | 849 Manhattan Ave. (bet. Milton & Noble Sts.) | Brooklyn | 718-389-5300

Williamsburg | 187 Bedford Ave. (7th St.) | Brooklyn | 718-384-6004
www.forninopizza.com

In the eternal "NY pizza wars", these Brooklyn "favorites" are "strong players" thanks to "decadent" toppings and "perfectly done" wood-fired crusts; "price-is-right" tabs enhance their "can't-go-wrong" reputations.

Fort Defiance *American* ▽ 23 | 19 | 20 | $36

Red Hook | 365 Van Brunt St. (bet. Coffey & Dikeman Sts.) | Brooklyn | 347-453-6672 | www.fortdefiancebrooklyn.com

Named for a Revolutionary War fort that once stood nearby, this "funky" Red Hook haunt dishes up "solid" American food washed down with "terrific" classic cocktails; ok, the menu is "small" and the crowd "flannel-clad", but "excellent-value" pricing makes it a "home base" for locals.

Forty Four *American* ▽ 21 | 19 | 21 | $41

Midtown | Royalton Hotel | 44 W. 44th St. (bet. 5th & 6th Aves.) | 212-944-8844 | www.morganshotelgroup.com

This "swanky" New American has long been a favored "media" "power" player due to its "quiet" Theater District hotel location, "excellent cocktails" and "solid" cooking (especially at breakfast); sure, it'll "cost a lot" to hang with the "Condé Nast" folks, but playing like an "insider" could be worth the "indulgence."

44 & X *American* 22 | 20 | 21 | $49

Hell's Kitchen | 622 10th Ave. (bet. 44th & 45th Sts.) | 212-977-1170 | www.44andx.com

44½ *American*

Hell's Kitchen | 626 10th Ave. (bet. 44th & 45th Sts.) | 212-399-4450 | www.44andahalf.com

"Gaiety abounds" at these Hell's Kitchen "go-to" spots where "well-toned" waiters in "tight, witty" T-shirts serve "proficient" American fare with "theatrical flair"; "inviting" havens in an area with "limited" options, they host a "popular" brunch and "fit the bill" before or after a play at the nearby Signature Theatre complex.

456 Shanghai Cuisine *Chinese* 22 | 14 | 17 | $26

Chinatown | 69 Mott St. (bet. Bayard & Canal Sts.) | 212-964-0003 | www.456shanghaicuisine.com

"Wonderful" soup dumplings are the draw at this busy Chinatown "find" that's also a "reliable" source for "ample portions" of "authentic Shanghainese" chow; the "tight quarters" sport "minimal" decor, but prices are so "reasonable" that no one minds.

	FOOD	DECOR	SERVICE	COST

Four Seasons *American* | 26 | 28 | 27 | $114 |

East Midtown | Seagram Bldg. | 99 E. 52nd St. (bet. Lexington & Park Aves.) | 212-754-9494 | www.fourseasonsrestaurant.com

"Power, money, elegance – and Dover sole" – define this Midtown "restaurant for the ages" via owners Alex von Bidder and Julian Niccolini, where "remarkable" New American fare is served with "VIP" treatment to jacketed, well-heeled guests in "stunning", Philip Johnson–designed surrounds; at lunch, the Grill Room is for the "business" elite and the Pool Room is for "lovers" at dinner, but wherever you sit, it's "one of NYC's great" dining experiences.

The Fourth *American* | 20 | 20 | 18 | $64 |

Greenwich Village | Hyatt Union Sq. Hotel | 132 Fourth Ave. (13th St.) | 212-432-1324 | www.thefourthny.com

From the Tocqueville team, this all-day American brasserie in the Hyatt Union Square offers "quality" food in "upbeat", "high-ceilinged" environs (including a cafe and more formal dining room); it's "not inexpensive", but the "value is high" – especially at Sunday brunch when there's "live music."

Fragole *Italian* | 22 | 16 | 20 | $43 |

Carroll Gardens | 394 Court St. (bet. Carroll St. & 1st Pl.) | Brooklyn | 718-522-7133 | www.fragoleny.com

This veteran Carroll Gardens Italian remains a "neighborhood favorite" for its "solid" cooking "with an eye toward authenticity", "quality wine list" and overall "charm"; "affordable" tabs keep it filled with "happy" customers – but as it's "small", "be prepared to wait" for a table at prime times.

Franchia *Korean* | ∇ 25 | 20 | 21 | $31 |

Midtown | 12 Park Ave. (bet. 34th & 35th Sts.) | 212-213-1001 | www.franchia.com

"Innovative" vegan cuisine is the hallmark of this Midtown Korean "favorite" where the "wonderful, filling" offerings ("I didn't miss meat at all") are complemented by "friendly" service and a "Zen-like ambiance" that suffuses the "jewel-box" teahouse setting; thanks to "value" pricing, it's an "affordable oasis."

Francisco's Centro Vasco *Seafood/Spanish* | 23 | 13 | 19 | $50 |

Chelsea | 159 W. 23rd St. (bet. 6th & 7th Aves.) | 212-645-6224 | www.franciscoscentrovasco.com

"Monster-size" lobsters at "fair prices" are the highlight of this longtime Chelsea Spaniard that also offers "wonderful paella" and "potent sangria"; "dumpy" digs and "noisy, crowded" conditions don't deter fans who feel it's "cheaper to come here than to cook your own."

Frank *Italian* | ∇ 21 | 15 | 18 | $40 |

East Village | 88 Second Ave. (bet. 5th & 6th Sts.) | 212-420-0202 | www.frankrestaurant.com

This cash-only East Villager is a longtime standby for "da best" Italian "home cooking" at "solid-value" prices; it's a "jam-packed", no-frills joint with a "no-rez policy" that spells waits at prime times, but you can always pass the time at its next-door Vera Bar.

	FOOD	DECOR	SERVICE	COST

Frankie & Johnnie's *Steak* | 23 | 17 | 20 | $67 |

Midtown | 32 W. 37th St. (bet. 5th & 6th Aves.) | 212-947-8940
Midtown | 269 W. 45th St., 2nd fl. (8th Ave.) | 212-997-9494
www.frankieandjohnnies.com

To experience "days long past", try this circa-1926 Theater District
"throwback" accessed via "rickety stairs" and known for "delectable"
steaks, "career" waiters and "rough-around-the-edges" decor; its 37th
Street sibling (set in John Barrymore's former townhouse) is similarly
"old-fashioned", though prices are decidedly up to date.

Frankies Spuntino *Italian* | 23 | 18 | 20 | $44 |

West Village | 570 Hudson St. (11th St.) | 212-924-0818
Carroll Gardens | 457 Court St. (bet. 4th Pl. & Luquer St.) | Brooklyn |
718-403-0033
www.frankiesspuntino.com

"Terrific in all the ways that count", these "rustic Italians" with "pleasant
vibes" and "huge buzz" are touted for "impressive" Tuscan cooking and
"charming" settings; the Carroll Gardens original boasts a "beautiful
garden", but both share "decent" prices, "noise" and no-rez rules.

Franny's *Italian/Pizza* | 25 | 18 | 20 | $45 |

Park Slope | 348 Flatbush Ave. (bet. 8th Ave. & Sterling Pl.) | Brooklyn |
718-230-0221 | www.frannysbrooklyn.com

Sample "quintessential Brooklyn dining" at this longtime Park Slope favorite turning out "second-to-none" artisanal pizzas via two wood-burning ovens, along with "exquisite" appetizers, pastas and other "simple"-
yet-sophisticated Italian dishes; even though it's moved to larger digs,
there's "still a line to get in" owing to the no-reservations policy.

Fraunces Tavern *Pub Food* | 17 | 22 | 19 | $43 |

Financial District | 54 Pearl St. (Broad St.) | 212-968-1776 |
www.frauncestavern.com

Have a side of "history" with dinner at this FiDi "landmark" where George
Washington bid farewell to his troops in 1783; today, it's a "refurbished"
tavern serving "decent" pub grub and "diverse" beers in a "faux-Revolu-
tionary" setting; cynics snipe it's "all about the building - not the food."

Fred's at Barneys NY *American/Italian* | 22 | 19 | 21 | $53 |

East 60s | Barneys NY | 660 Madison Ave., 9th fl. (61st St.) |
212-833-2200 | www.barneys.com

"Shopping is hard work" and "sustenance is necessary", so "well-
Botoxed" types unwind and "pick at a salad" at this "chichi" department-
store canteen in Barneys; the "consistently good" Italian-American fare
may be "pricey for what it is", but no one cares - it's "fun to be chic" here.

Freemans *American* | 23 | 25 | 20 | $54 |

Lower East Side | Freeman Alley (off Rivington St., bet. Bowery &
Christie St.) | 212-420-0012 | www.freemansrestaurant.com

"Tucked away" down a Lower East Side alley, this "hipster" magnet feels
"miles from NY" given the "kooky" Colonial-tavern decor replete with
"taxidermy" and "creaky wooden floors"; "solid" American cuisine and
"great drinks too" offset the "hit-or-miss" service and "killer waits", but
mostly, it's about the "scene."

	FOOD	DECOR	SERVICE	COST

NEW French Louie *American/French* ▽ 26 | 25 | 26 | $60

Boerum Hill | 320 Atlantic Ave. (bet. Hoyt & Smith Sts.) | Brooklyn | 718-935-1200 | www.frenchlouienyc.com

From the Buttermilk Channel team comes this "hot" new Boerum Hill arrival on Atlantic Avenue, providing "inventive" French-American fare and "fantastic" drinks in a "lovely" bistro setting, along with "spot-on" service, a handsome patio and a "cool vibe"; tabs are at the "upper end of reasonable", but expect "waits" given the no-rezzie policy.

Fresco by Scotto *Italian* 22 | 18 | 20 | $63

Midtown | 34 E. 52nd St. (bet. Madison & Park Aves.) | 212-935-3434 | www.frescobyscotto.com

Fresco on the Go *Italian*

Midtown | 40 E. 52nd St. (bet. Madison & Park Aves.) | 212-754-2700 | www.frescoonthego.com

For "delicious", "dependable" Tuscan fare with "*Today Show*" people-watching on the side, try this "friendly" longtime Midtowner via the "dedicated" Scotto family; it's "pricey", and "always packed" for lunch, but there's "super-fast" takeout from the to-go outlet.

Friedman's Lunch *American* 21 | 15 | 18 | $24

Chelsea | Chelsea Mkt. | 75 Ninth Ave. (bet. 15th & 16th Sts.) | 212-929-7100

NEW Midtown | 132 W. 31st St. (bet. 6th & 7th Aves.) | 212-971-9400 | www.friedmanslunch.com

Name notwithstanding, they also whip up breakfast and brunch at this "pleasant" American in Chelsea Market – and dinner at the 31st Street outlet – though it's renowned for "hearty", "delicious" sandwiches and other "gourmet comfort" fare; "slow service" and "not much seating" explain the typical "waits" for a table.

Friend of a Farmer *American* 20 | 19 | 18 | $33

Gramercy Park | 77 Irving Pl. (bet. 18th & 19th Sts.) | 212-477-2188 | www.friendofafarmerny.com

Bringing a "Vermont" feel to Gramercy Park, this "quaint" American "country kitchen" has crowds crowing about its "farm-fresh" vittles and "hippie" air; citified pricing, "slow service" and weekend brunch "lines down the block" come with the territory.

NEW Fritzl's Lunch Box *American* – | – | – | I

Bushwick | 173 Irving Ave. (bet. Stanhope & Stockholm Sts.) | Brooklyn | 929-210-9531 | www.fritzlslunchbox.com

From a Roberta's alum, this self-described 'real simple neighborhood restaurant' in Bushwick proffers inventive, crowd-pleasing spins on classic American sandwiches, burgers and pastas; its "unassuming", banquette-equipped space exudes retro luncheonette vibes, and there's a back garden too.

NEW Fung Tu *American/Chinese* ▽ 23 | 22 | 23 | $52

Lower East Side | 22 Orchard St. (bet. Canal & Hester Sts.) | 212-219-8785 | www.fungtu.com

"Adventurous" eaters report it's "not your mama's eggroll" at this "artful" LES Chinese-American where the "unexpected" , "completely original" dishes are matched with "well-chosen" wines and "delicious" cocktails; "nicely timed" service and "understated-chic" decor complete the "upscale" picture.

Fushimi *Japanese*
23 | 24 | 21 | $43

Bay Ridge | 9316 Fourth Ave. (bet. 93rd & 94th Sts.) | Brooklyn | 718-833-7788
Williamsburg | 475 Driggs Ave. (bet. 10th & 11th Sts.) | Brooklyn | 718-963-2555
Grant City | 2110 Richmond Rd. (bet. Colfax & Lincoln Aves.) | Staten Island | 718-980-5300
www.fushimigroup.com

These "sexy" Japanese standouts are "an experience" complete with "sleek" settings, "fun atmospheres", "city-quality" sushi and "inventive" cocktails; maybe tabs are "not the cheapest", but then again these are "not your regular around-the-corner sushi" joints.

Gabriel's *Italian*
22 | 18 | 22 | $63

West 60s | 11 W. 60th St. (bet. B'way & Columbus Ave.) | 212-956-4600 | www.gabrielsbarandrest.com

"Polished service" overseen by "natural host" Gabriel Aiello sets the "classy" tone at this "even-keeled" Columbus Circle Italian known for "delicious" cooking, a "comfortable" setting and proximity to Lincoln Center; given the rather "hefty" tabs, "media" types from nearby CBS and CNN prefer it for lunch.

Gahm Mi Oak *Korean*
∇ 22 | 15 | 17 | $29

Midtown | 43 W. 32nd St. (bet. B'way & 5th Ave.) | 212-695-4113 | www.gahmmioak.com

Renowned for its "lifesaving" sollongtang beef soup – especially "good when hung over" – this K-town Korean is also commended for its "delectable" kimchi; "rushed" service and a "hectic" atmosphere are counterbalanced by "cheap" tabs and 24/7 availability.

Gallaghers *Steak*
22 | 19 | 21 | $74

Midtown | 228 W. 52nd St. (bet. B'way & 8th Ave.) | 212-586-5000 | www.gallaghersnysteakhouse.com

Longtime fans still find the "real deal" at this "premier" Theater District steakhouse that's been around since 1927 and recently "spiffed up" with "super" results; "succulent" chops, "amiable" service and "expensive" price tags are all part of this "old-style" experience.

NEW The Gander *American*
─ | ─ | ─ | M

Flatiron | 15 W. 18th St. (bet. 5th & 6th Aves.) | 212-229-9500 | www.thegandernyc.com

Recette chef Jesse Schenker is behind this Flatironer whose innovative New American offerings include housemade pastas and entrees alongside lighter bites (charcuterie, cheese boards), matched with cocktails and global wines; the airy setup features a big bar area and banquette-lined back room.

Ganso *Japanese/Noodle Shop*
∇ 23 | 17 | 18 | $22

Downtown Brooklyn | 25 Bond St. (Livingston St.) | Brooklyn | 718-403-0900 | www.gansonyc.com

A "welcome addition" to Downtown Brooklyn, this "priced-right" Japanese slurp shop ladles out "grade-A" bowls of ramen, featuring "rich", meticulously made broth and "delicious" noodles, alongside snacks like chicken wings and pork buns; it all arrives in "spare but comfortable" wood-lined digs.

Gaonnuri *Korean*   20 | 25 | 20 | $64

Midtown | 1250 Broadway, 39th fl. (32nd St.) | 212-971-9045 | www.gaonnurinyc.com

Its "biggest appeal" is the "stellar" panoramic Midtown vistas from its "chic", 39th-floor space, but this "upmarket" player on the K-town scene also "holds its own" with "stylishly prepared" Korean fare, including "traditional" tabletop BBQ; service is variable and you "pay for the view", but that "sunset over the Hudson" is more than "worth it."

Garden Café *American*   20 | 18 | 21 | $30

Inwood | 4961 Broadway (bet. Isham & 207th Sts.) | 212-544-9480 | www.gardencafeny.com

"Solid" New Americana turns up at this "cozy" Inwood spot near the Cloisters that "feels like downtown without the downtown prices"; some shrug "nothing special", but all agree on the "friendly" service and "cute" back garden.

Gargiulo's *Italian*   22 | 20 | 22 | $52

Coney Island | 2911 W. 15th St. (bet. Mermaid & Surf Aves.) | Brooklyn | 718-266-4891 | www.gargiulos.com

After a "swim at the beach", have a "swim in red sauce" at this circa-1907 Coney Island "time warp", a "catering hall"–size arena for good "old-fashioned" Neapolitan cooking ferried by "tuxedo-clad" waiters; the "colorful" crowd feels its "reputation is deserved", while a nightly raffle means "you could eat for free."

Gari *Japanese*   26 | 16 | 22 | $96

West 70s | 370 Columbus Ave. (bet. 77th & 78th Sts.) | 212-362-4816

Sushi of Gari *Japanese*

East 70s | 402 E. 78th St. (bet. 1st & York Aves.) | 212-517-5340
Midtown | 347 W. 46th St. (bet. 8th & 9th Aves.) | 212-957-0046
TriBeCa | 130 W. Broadway (Duane St.) | 212-285-0130
www.sushiofgari.com

"Omakase is a must" at these "exceptional" Japanese eateries from Gari Sugio, where avid fans "sit at the chef's bar" for a "thrilling" taste of "unique" sushi; though the settings are "tight", the decor "blah" and the price tags worthy of "two credit cards", the payoff is "memorable" dining that just might "blow your mind."

NEW Gato *Mediterranean*   24 | 24 | 24 | $78

NoHo | 324 Lafayette St. (bet. Bleecker & Houston Sts.) | 212-334-6400 | www.gatonyc.com

"See Bobby Flay in the kitchen – without a TV camera in sight" – at this NoHo newcomer offering "bold" Spanish-influenced Mediterranean dishes, an "interesting", "fairly priced" wine list and "spot-on" service; "busy" and "noisy", the "casual", cavernous setting has an industrial feel, with wooden beams, exposed ductwork and an open kitchen.

Gazala's *Mideastern*   22 | 14 | 19 | $34

Hell's Kitchen | 709 Ninth Ave. (bet. 48th & 49th Sts.) | 212-245-0709

continued

West 70s | 380 Columbus Ave. (78th St.) | 212-873-8880
www.gazalaplace.com
"Delectable" Druze dishes are delivered by these "casual" Mideasterns
where the "solid" cooking and "inexpensive" tabs offset "modest" decor
and "hit-or-miss" service; the UWS spin-off is "more spacious" than the
"cramped" Hell's Kitchen original (which features a BYO policy).

Gemma *Italian*　　　　　　　　　　　　　　23 | 23 | 21 | $45

East Village | Bowery Hotel | 335 Bowery (bet. 2nd & 3rd Sts.) |
212-505-7300 | www.theboweryhotel.com
Primo "people-watching" abounds at this "fun", all-day Bowery Hotel
Italian that lures "scenesters" with a "romantic", "country-chic" setting
festooned with "hundreds of candles"; "tasty" vittles, "attentive service"
and "fair prices" make the "no-rez" policy (except for hotel guests)
less of a drag.

The General *Asian*　　　　　　　　　　　　22 | 22 | 20 | $66

Lower East Side | 199 Bowery (Spring St.) | 212-271-7101 |
www.emmgrp.com
"Pretty people" are all over this "loungey" Bowery hot spot from the
EMM folks (Catch), whose "gorgeous", sprawling space is done up in
reclaimed wood and funky wallpaper; the "pricey" Asian shareable plates
via chef Hung Huynh are "delish", though in truth it's "really about the
scene" in the downstairs Jazz Room here.

The General Greene *American*　　　　　∇ 20 | 16 | 17 | $35

Fort Greene | 229 DeKalb Ave. (Clermont Ave.) | Brooklyn |
718-222-1510
"Small plates win big" at this "casual" Fort Greene "standby" where the
New American grub's "local", "seasonal" and "affordable"; it's a natural
for brunch or "before the Flea", and the "very Brooklyn" vibe extends to
the "simple" decor and pleasant "outdoor seating."

Gennaro *Italian*　　　　　　　　　　　　26 | 16 | 20 | $44

West 90s | 665 Amsterdam Ave. (bet. 92nd & 93rd Sts.) |
212-665-5348 | www.gennaronyc.com
Be ready for a "long line" at this "durable" UWS Italian that takes "no
reservations" and no plastic but does provide "wonderful", "hearty" fare
for "nongourmet prices"; even after a "third expansion", it's still "difficult
to get a table after 7 PM."

Gigino at Wagner Park *Italian*　　　　20 | 19 | 18 | $49

Battery Park City | 20 Battery Pl. (Little West St.) | 212-528-2228 |
www.gigino-wagnerpark.com
Gigino Trattoria *Italian*
TriBeCa | 323 Greenwich St. (Duane St.) | 212-431-1112 |
www.gigino-trattoria.com
It almost "feels like Florence" at this "affordable" TriBeCa Tuscan featuring "above-average" food, "friendly" service and a "high-ceilinged",
"farmhouselike" milieu; "outdoor dining" with a "one-of-a-kind view" of
the harbor and Statue of Liberty is the thing at its "off-the-beaten-path"
sibling in Battery Park.

	FOOD	DECOR	SERVICE	COST

Gimme Coffee *Coffee* ▽ 23 | 15 | 19 | $8

NoLita | 228 Mott St. (bet. Prince & Spring Sts.) | 212-226-4011
Williamsburg | 495 Lorimer St. (Powers St.) | Brooklyn | 718-388-7771
Williamsburg | 107 Roebling St. (bet. N. 5th & 6th Sts.) | Brooklyn | 718-388-4595
www.gimmecoffee.com

Providing java to the "hipster set", these "awesome" outposts of an Ithaca chain offer "micro-roasted, small-batch, single-origin beans", making for "carefully crafted" coffee with a "kick"; the stripped-down spaces don't offer a whole latte elbow room, so consider getting your "caffeine fix" on the fly.

Ginny's Supper Club *American* ▽ 21 | 24 | 21 | $49

Harlem | 310 Lenox Ave. (bet. 125th & 126th Sts.) | 212-421-3821 | www.ginnyssupperclub.com

A riff on legendary Harlem nightspots like the Cotton Club, this "relaxed" supper club in the basement of Marcus Samuelsson's Red Rooster serves New American fare with soul-food accents, along with updated classic cocktails; "great live jazz" and a "speakeasy" vibe add to the overall "fun scene."

Gino's *Italian* 23 | 17 | 20 | $38

Bay Ridge | 7414 Fifth Ave. (bet. Bay Ridge Pkwy. & 74th St.) | Brooklyn | 718-748-1698 | www.ginosbayridge.com

A "neighborhood" "staple" since 1964, this ever-"crowded" Bay Ridge Italian serves up "generous portions" of "fresh" classics "just like mom makes", in "casual" environs; "get ready to wait in line" at prime times, but the all-around "enjoyable" experience and "reasonable" tab ensure it's "well worth it."

Giorgione *Italian* ▽ 24 | 22 | 22 | $62

Hudson Square | 307 Spring St. (bet. Greenwich & Hudson Sts.) | 212-352-2269 | www.giorgionenyc.com

A "low-key neighborhood place", this Hudson Square trattoria caters to "sophisticated" types with "inventive Italian comfort food" abetted by an "appealing" wine list; the atmosphere is "chic without being trendy", and the "quality" team led by Giorgio DeLuca (of Dean & DeLuca) ensures "a lot of attention to detail."

Giorgio's of Gramercy *American/Italian* 23 | 19 | 22 | $51

Flatiron | 27 E. 21st St. (bet. B'way & Park Ave. S.) | 212-477-0007 | www.giorgiosofgramercy.com

The epitome of a "true sleeper", this longtime Italian-American "class act" in the Flatiron features "consistently good" cooking that suggests "unsung talent in the kitchen"; "reasonable" rates, "gracious" service and "early brothel" decor are other incentives.

Giovanni Venticinque *Italian* ▽ 22 | 19 | 21 | $72

East 80s | 25 E. 83rd St. (bet. 5th & Madison Aves.) | 212-988-7300 | www.giovanniventicinque.com

"Excellent" Tuscan fare and a "gracious" staff keep this UES Italian popular with a "neighborhood" crowd; "intimate" and "hushed" enough for "real conversation", it boasts "proximity to the Met" and a $25 lunch prix fixe that offsets otherwise "pricey" tabs.

	FOOD	DECOR	SERVICE	COST

NEW Glady's *Caribbean*

– | – | – | I

Crown Heights | 788 Franklin Ave. (Lincoln Pl.) | Brooklyn |
718-622-0249 | www.gladysnyc.com

A turquoise-heavy color scheme lends an island vibe to this new Crown Heights arrival, and the kitchen follows through with Caribbean fare like jerk chicken, curry goat and an array of sandwiches; as for drinks, expect rum flights and even a Dark 'n' Slushie with a ginger bite.

NEW Glasserie *Mediterranean*

▽ 24 | 22 | 22 | $53

Greenpoint | 95 Commercial St. (bet. Box St. & Manhattan Ave.) |
Brooklyn | 718-389-0640 | www.glasserienyc.com

Set in a "wonderful" former glass factory in Greenpoint, this "hidden gem" presents a "lovely" Mediterranean menu accompanied by a tightly curated cocktail, wine and beer list; its "hipster" fan base thinks it's "super-cool", though a much-publicized recent chef change may not be reflected in the Food score.

Glass House Tavern *American*

20 | 19 | 21 | $47

Midtown | 252 W. 47th St. (bet. B'way & 8th Ave.) | 212-730-4800 |
www.glasshousetavern.com

Something "calming" in the "hectic Theater District", this "solid performer" provides New Americana that tastes even better when Broadway "stars" are seated alongside you; "reasonable" rates and "cordial" service also draw applause, though conversationalists advise "eat upstairs."

Gnocco *Italian*

▽ 23 | 19 | 20 | $37

East Village | 337 E. 10th St. (bet. Aves. A & B) | 212-677-1913 |
www.gnocco.com

"Authentic Emilian fare" is the focus of this East Village Italian praised for its "tasty pizza", "lengthy wine list" and "excellent" namesake dish; the "most prized tables" are in its "lovely", all-seasons garden, though "modest" pricing and "helpful" service are available throughout.

Gobo *Vegan/Vegetarian*

22 | 18 | 19 | $37

West Village | 401 Sixth Ave. (bet. 8th St. & Waverly Pl.) | 212-255-3242
www.goborestaurant.com

Vegan food gets some "fancy" twists at this "nonpreachy" West Villager offering an "unusually varied" menu of Asian-accented vittles that are "wonderfully healthy"; overall, the vibe is "earthy" and the service correspondingly "down to earth."

Golden Unicorn *Chinese*

22 | 13 | 14 | $27

Chinatown | 18 E. Broadway (Catherine St.) | 212-941-0911 |
www.goldenunicornrestaurant.com

"Mobbed and noisy" is a given at this "huge" C-town Cantonese featuring "endless carts" stocked with "heavenly dim sum"; "hurried", English-challenged service and "basic Chinatown wedding-party decor" are forgiven, since it's a lot "cheaper than flying to Hong Kong."

Good *American*

22 | 16 | 21 | $47

West Village | 89 Greenwich Ave. (bet. Bank & W. 12th Sts.) |
212-691-8080 | www.goodrestaurantnyc.com

"Should be named 'great'" say die-hard supporters of this West Village American "respite" that's still something of a "hidden gem" despite "simple", "hearty" cooking and "kind service"; aesthetes may find the decor "boring", but there's always a "weekend line" for its "amazing brunch."

Good Enough to Eat *American*   20 | 15 | 16 | $29

West 80s | 520 Columbus Ave. (85th St.) | 212-496-0163 | www.goodenoughtoeat.com

This "great-value" UWS "favorite" offers all-day dining à la "Vermont" via a "simple" American "comfort-food" menu; the "no-frills" setting exudes farmhousey vibes and also offers outdoor seating, although "painful waits" are the norm at weekend brunch.

Good Fork *Eclectic*   23 | 17 | 21 | $49

Red Hook | 391 Van Brunt St. (bet. Coffey & Van Dyke Sts.) | Brooklyn | 718-643-6636 | www.goodfork.com

"Hidden away" in Red Hook, this Eclectic destination maintains a "loyal following" for its "excellent", "creative" Asian-accented cooking dispensed in "intimate", "funky" digs with an "amazing" back garden; "warm" service, a "small but fine" drinks list and "value" prices are other reasons reservations are a "must."

NEW The Gorbals *Eclectic*   – | – | – | M

Williamsburg | Space Ninety 8 | 98 N. Sixth St. (Wythe Ave.) | Brooklyn | 718-387-0195 | www.thegorbalsbk.com

Top Chef winner Ilan Hall exports his successful LA concept to NYC with this newcomer inside Williamsburg's Space Ninety 8, offering a bargain-priced Eclectic menu that throws some Scottish-Jewish curveballs; the eye-catching industrial space features wood-beam floors, a colorfully tiled bar and an expansive skylight, plus an outdoor deck.

Gordon Ramsay *French*   22 | 21 | 21 | $124

Midtown | London NYC Hotel | 151 W. 54th St. (bet. 6th & 7th Aves.) | 212-468-8888 | www.gordonramsay.com

Though he's just a consultant now, Gordon Ramsay's "spirit" lives on at his namesake Midtown hotel dining room where the "first-rate", prix fixe-only French menu is "expertly crafted" and delivered by a "charming" crew; the "modern" setting is "elegantly decorated", but some feel the "high tariffs" could use "fine tuning" absent the star of the show.

Gotham Bar & Grill *American*   28 | 27 | 27 | $86

Greenwich Village | 12 E. 12th St. (bet. 5th Ave. & University Pl.) | 212-620-4020 | www.gothambarandgrill.com

An "evergreen" NYC dining experience since 1984, this "glorious" Villager showcases chef Alfred Portale's "towering" New American "art on a plate" delivered by "finely orchestrated" staffers in a "sophisticated", "white-tablecloth" setting; sure, it's "costly", but "you get what you pay for" and the $34 greenmarket lunch is an "unbeatable" deal.

NEW Gotham West Market *Food Market*   25 | 24 | 23 | $26

Hell's Kitchen | 600 11th Ave. (bet. 44th & 45th Sts.) | 212-582-7940 | www.gothamwestmarket.com

Some of the city's best-regarded chefs – including Seamus Mullen and Ivan Orkin – whip up "everything from burgers to tapas to noodles" at this "industrial-chic" Hell's Kitchen food hall offering both counter and communal table seating; it's perfect for "grazing" and definitely "worth the trip to 11th Avenue."

	FOOD	DECOR	SERVICE	COST

Gradisca *Italian*
23 | 18 | 21 | $59

West Village | 126 W. 13th St. (bet. 6th & 7th Aves.) | 212-691-4886 |
www.gradiscanyc.com

"Superb pastas" hand-rolled by the owner's mama are the "main attraction" at this "low-key" West Village Italian, but other "savory" dishes and a "strong wine list" further secure its standing as an area "favorite"; some say it's a bit "pricey" considering the "small portions" and "casual ambiance", but "friendly" service adds value.

Graffiti *Eclectic*
28 | 23 | 25 | $48

East Village | 224 E. 10th St. (bet. 1st & 2nd Aves.) | 212-464-7743 |
www.graffitinyc.com

"Talented" chef Jehangir Mehta offers an "amazing", Indian-accented Eclectic menu at this "well-kept secret" in the East Village; granted, the space is "beyond tiny", with "shared tables" and plenty of "eavesdropping" potential, but "personal" service and "easy" price points (e.g. the $25 wine list) make it an "absolute bargain."

Gramercy Tavern *American*
28 | 26 | 27 | $96

Flatiron | 42 E. 20th St. (bet. B'way & Park Ave. S.) | 212-477-0777 |
www.gramercytavern.com

The epitome of "feel-good fine dining" – and winner of Most Popular honors in NYC – Danny Meyer's Flatiron "legend" showcases the "wizardry" of chef Michael Anthony, whose "delectable" New American fare is served by a "silky-smooth" staff in "rustic-elegant" environs festooned with "lush flower arrangements"; while the prix fixe–only main room is a "worthy splurge", the "convivial", nonreserving front tavern offers à la carte options to "keep the tab in check."

Grand Sichuan *Chinese*
19 | 9 | 14 | $29

Chelsea | 172 Eighth Ave. (bet. 18th & 19th Sts.) | 212-243-2267 |
www.grandsichuaneasternnyc.com
Chelsea | 229 Ninth Ave. (24th St.) | 212-620-5200 |
www.grandsichuan.com
East Midtown | 1049 Second Ave. (bet. 55th & 56th Sts.) |
212-355-5855 | www.grandsichuaneasternnyc.com
East Village | 19-23 St. Marks Pl. (bet. 2nd & 3rd Aves.) | 212-529-4800
Midtown | 368 W. 46th St. (bet. 8th & 9th Aves.) | 212-969-9001 |
www.grandsichuan.com
West 70s | 307 Amsterdam Ave. (bet. 74th & 75th Sts.) | 212-580-0277 |
www.grandsichuan74.com
West Village | 15 Seventh Ave. S. (bet. Carmine & Leroy Sts.) |
212-645-0222 | www.grandsichuannyc.com
Forest Hills | 98-108 Queens Blvd. (bet. 66th & 67th Aves.) | Queens |
718-268-8833

"Hot stuff" seekers tout the "mouth-numbing" Sichuan fare served at this all-over-town mini-chain where the "huge" plates are on par with the "extensive" menu; service is "perfunctory" and there's "no ambiance", but otherwise it's "fast", "reliable" and "doesn't hurt the wallet."

Gran Electrica *Mexican*
∇ 22 | 24 | 21 | $42

Dumbo | 5 Front St. (Old Fulton St.) | Brooklyn | 718-852-2700 |
www.granelectrica.com

"Simple but super-delicious", the midpriced Mexican eats at this "pleasant" Dumbo taqueria pair well with its extensive list of mescals, tequilas and specialty cocktails; "Day of the Dead–inspired wallpaper" adds to the "festive" vibrations, while the "fun patio" provides a "civilized respite from the noisy interior."

Gray's Papaya *Hot Dogs*
22 | 6 | 16 | $7

West 70s | 2090 Broadway (72nd St.) | 212-799-0243 | www.grayspapayanyc.com

This 24/7 UWS hot dog stand vends "surprisingly good" wieners washed down with "frothy" papaya drinks; "quick" turnaround and "chump-change" tabs offset the "gruff" service, "what-a-dump" decor and lack of seats at this "quintessential" NY "institution."

Great Jones Cafe *Cajun*
23 | 16 | 21 | $35

NoHo | 54 Great Jones St. (bet. Bowery & Lafayette St.) | 212-674-9304 | www.greatjones.com

"No-frills" says it all about this "friendly" NoHo Cajun where the "solid" vittles arrive in a "dumpy", verging on "campy" setting; 30-plus years on, the crowd's still "local", the vibe "downtown" and the jukebox as "great" as ever.

Great NY Noodle Town *Noodle Shop*
23 | 6 | 14 | $20

Chinatown | 28 Bowery (Bayard St.) | 212-349-0923 | www.greatnynoodletown.com

"Surrender to the crowd experience" and "sit with strangers" at this "chaotic" C-town noodle shop known for "dirt-cheap" Cantonese chow (and notable salt-baked seafood) served into the wee hours; not so great is "no decor", "no credit cards" and "difficult" service.

NEW The Greek *Greek*
∇ 21 | 22 | 21 | $43

TriBeCa | 458 Greenwich St. (bet. Desbrosses & Watts Sts.) | 646-476-3941 | www.thegreektribeca.com

This "friendly" TriBeCa 'gastrotaverna' is declared a "nice addition to the neighborhood" thanks to its "fresh" traditional dishes (plus free meze) matched with all-Greek wines; the space has an "awesome" rustic pub feel, down to the moose antlers hanging over one banquette.

Greek Kitchen *Greek*
21 | 13 | 18 | $31

Hell's Kitchen | 889 10th Ave. (58th St.) | 212-581-4300 | www.greekkitchennyc.com

"Tasty", "economical" eats make this "real Greek" a "staple" on the edge of Hell's Kitchen, a location "convenient to Lincoln Center"; there's "no decor" to speak of and service is "hit-or-miss", but the servings are "generous" and they "never rush you" out.

The Green Table *American*
∇ 24 | 16 | 22 | $40

Chelsea | Chelsea Mkt. | 75 Ninth Ave. (bet. 15th & 16th Sts.) | 212-741-6623 | www.cleaverco.com

"Farmalicious!" rave fans of the "fresh, well-prepared" American fare on offer at Mary Cleaver's Chelsea Market nook spotlighting "locally sourced everything" on an ever-changing seasonal menu; the "cozy" space is "no-frills", but most don't mind given the favorable "price-to-quality ratio."

| | FOOD | DECOR | SERVICE | COST |

NEW Greenpoint Fish & Lobster Co. *Seafood*

| | – | – | – | M |

Greenpoint | 114 Nassau Ave. (Eckford St.) | Brooklyn | 718-349-0400 | www.greenpointfish.com

Part raw bar, part seafood market, this Greenpoint multitasker offers an array of shore favorites like lobster rolls, clam chowder, crudo and oysters, plus beer and wine; it's all served in a white-tiled space with a marble bar, a few high-top tables and a retail area up front.

Grey Dog *American*

| | 22 | 17 | 18 | $19 |

Chelsea | 242 W. 16th St. (8th Ave.) | 212-229-2345
Greenwich Village | 90 University Pl. (E. 12th St.) | 212-414-4739
NoLita | 244 Mulberry St. (bet. Prince & Spring Sts.) | 212-966-1060
West Village | 49 Carmine St. (Bedford St.) | 212-462-0041
www.thegreydog.com

Folks find a "sweet throwback" to what neighborhood coffee stops "used to be" in these "comfortable" hangouts for "relaxing" and "people-watching" over "inexpensive", "above-average" java and American comfort fare; yes, "brunch lines" can be "over the top", but staffers "know how to work the crowd."

Grimaldi's *Pizza*

| | 22 | 12 | 16 | $23 |

Flatiron | Limelight Mktpl. | 656 Sixth Ave. (bet. 20th & 21st Sts.) | 646-484-5665
Coney Island | 1215 Surf Ave. (bet. Stillwell Ave. & 12th St.) | Brooklyn | 718-676-2630
Dumbo | 1 Front St. (bet. Dock & Old Fulton Sts.) | Brooklyn | 718-858-4300
Douglaston | Douglaston Plaza | 242-02 61st Ave. (Douglaston Pkwy.) | Queens | 718-819-2133
www.grimaldisnyc.com

Brace yourself for "endless crowds" at this Dumbo pizzeria–cum–"tourist" magnet where the payoff is "excellent" "thin-crust", coal-fired pies; the other branches can usually be accessed "without the wait", but they share the mother ship's no-plastic, no-reservations, no-slices rules.

NEW Grindhaus *American*

| | – | – | – | M |

Red Hook | 275 Van Brunt St. (bet. Pioneer St. & Visitation Pl.) | Brooklyn | 718-909-2881 | www.grindhausnyc.com

This freewheeling Red Hook eatery makes its own daily bread, "Parkerhaus" rolls and pastas, and sources local farmers and fishmongers for its short, ever-changing American menu, paired with a robust wine list; the tiny setting is simply furnished and equipped with an equally casual backyard.

The Grocery *American*

| | 27 | 18 | 25 | $86 |

Carroll Gardens | 288 Smith St. (bet. Sackett & Union Sts.) | Brooklyn | 718-596-3335 | www.thegroceryrestaurant.com

This longtime "beacon of deliciousness" on Smith Street continues to offer "top-notch" New American fare "made with love" and "best-of-the-season ingredients"; it's beloved for its "charming, family-owned" milieu with "welcoming" service and a "wonderful" garden, if not its "closet"-size room and portions a bit "scaled back" for the price.

	FOOD	DECOR	SERVICE	COST

Grom *Ice Cream*
| 25 | 13 | 16 | $10 |

Midtown | 1796 Broadway (58th St.) | 212-974-3444
West Village | 233 Bleecker St. (Carmine St.) | 212-206-1738
www.grom.it

"Some of the best gelato around" is found at these artisanal gelaterias whose "heavenly" product incorporates ingredients "imported from Italy", including the water for its sorbets; despite *molto* grumbling about "long lines", "small" portions and "exorbitant prices", most agree it's "worth the extra bucks."

Guantanamera *Cuban*
| 22 | 17 | 20 | $46 |

Midtown | 939 Eighth Ave. (bet. 55th & 56th Sts.) | 212-262-5354 | www.guantanamerany.com

"Jumping" is the word on this "fun" Midtown Cuban where the "tasty", "authentic" chow is nearly overwhelmed by the "amazing mojitos" and "ridiculously loud live music"; "reasonable" rates and hand-rolled cigars on weekend nights supply extra "oomph."

Gyu-Kaku *Japanese*
| 22 | 18 | 20 | $45 |

East Midtown | 805 Third Ave., 2nd fl. (bet. 49th & 50th Sts.) | 212-702-8816
Greenwich Village | 34 Cooper Sq. (bet. Astor Pl. & 4th St.) | 212-475-2989
Midtown | 321 W. 44th St. (bet. 8th & 9th Aves.) | 646-692-9115
www.gyu-kaku.com

"Novelty"-seekers hype this "delicious, do-it-yourself" Japanese yakiniku franchise where you "cook your own" BBQ on tabletop charcoal braziers; since the "small portions" can add up to "pricey" tabs, bargain-hunters show up for the "happy-hour specials."

Hakata Tonton *Japanese*
| ▽ 23 | 15 | 20 | $51 |

West Village | 61 Grove St. (7th Ave. S.) | 212-242-3699

You'll feel "instantly transported" at this West Village Japanese where the "refreshing" menu of "obscure" small plates is heavy on "fantastic" pork dishes ("try the pig's feet") that attract a "mostly Japanese clientele"; the "warm" staff is "eager to educate" first-timers, though, and "reasonable" tabs are a plus.

Hakkasan *Chinese*
| 23 | 25 | 21 | $77 |

Midtown | 311 W. 43rd St. (bet. 8th & 9th Aves.) | 212-776-1818 | www.hakkasan.com

"Beautiful" Shanghai-chic decor sets the "glitzy" mood at this "upscale" Theater District outpost of the London-based chain turning out "fancy" Cantonese-inspired dishes with Western accents; ornate latticework partitions make the "massive" space feel more intimate, but the super-"expensive" tabs are harder to disguise.

NEW Hamilton's Soda Fountain *Diner*
| – | – | – | I |

West Village | 51 Bank St. (4th St.) | 212-661-1515 | www.hamiltonsoda.com

A throwback to an earlier era, this all-day West Village diner boasts a reclaimed soda fountain offering old-timey concoctions like phosphates, fizzes, egg creams and rickeys, plus milkshakes, malts and sundaes; in addition, it dishes out classic comfort food at surprisingly affordable prices for this very upscale nabe.

Hanci Turkish Cuisine *Turkish* ▽ 21 | 12 | 21 | $32

Hell's Kitchen | 854 10th Ave. (56th St.) | 212-707-8144 | www.hanciturkishcuisine.com

"Worth the walk" to way west 10th Avenue, this "low-key" Turk proffers "simple", "nicely prepared" plates for a modest price; not much decor is offset by "good service" and convenience to "John Jay College and Lincoln Center."

Hanco's *Vietnamese* 21 | 9 | 15 | $14

Brooklyn Heights | 147 Montague St. (bet. Clinton & Henry Sts.) | Brooklyn | 347-529-5054
Cobble Hill | 134 Smith St. (bet. Bergen & Dean Sts.) | Brooklyn | 718-858-6818 | www.hancosny.com
Park Slope | 350 Seventh Ave. (10th St.) | Brooklyn | 718-499-8081 | www.hancosny.com

"Addictive", "drool"-inducing banh mi sandwiches washed down with "excellent" bubble teas (plus pho in Park Slope and Brooklyn Heights) ensure these Vietnamese storefronts are "always busy"; "no-frills" sums up both the decor and service, but few mind given the price.

NEW Han Dynasty *Chinese* 23 | 12 | 16 | $32

Greenwich Village | 90 Third Ave. (bet. 12th & 13th Sts.) | 212-390-8685 | www.handynasty.net

There's lots of "hype" about this Philly export in the Village where the "aromatic", "seriously spicy" Sichuan menu is "mouth-numbing in the best way" and the dan-dan noodles are a "must-order"; despite "basic" looks and "abrupt" service, the reasonable pricing makes for a "packed" house.

Hangawi *Korean/Vegetarian* 26 | 26 | 25 | $50

Midtown | 12 E. 32nd St. (bet. 5th & Madison Aves.) | 212-213-0077 | www.hangawirestaurant.com

A "wonderful respite" in "honky-tonk" K-town, this "transporting" Korean provides "exotic" vegetarian fare that tastes even better in its "calm atmosphere"; "impeccable" service is also part of the "relaxing" package, but be prepared to "check your shoes at the door" – it's a "requirement" here.

Hanjan *Korean* 23 | 19 | 19 | $49

Flatiron | 36 W. 26th St. (bet. B'way & 6th Ave.) | 212-206-7226 | www.hanjan26.com

On a "booming stretch" of the Flatiron lies this upscale gastropub (a Danji sibling), where "inspired" Korean small plates pair well with "awesome" rice beer and "exotic cocktails"; the "long waits" to get into its "simple", "minimalist" space speak for themselves, and night owls say its "late-night ramen hits the spot."

Harlem Shake *Burgers* 20 | 20 | 18 | $17

Harlem | 100 W. 124th St. (Lenox Ave.) | 646-396-3040 | www.harlemshakenyc.com

"Excellent smash-griddled burgers" are the signature of this all-day Harlem patty palace with "malt-shop-meets-*Jet*-magazine" decor and a neighborhood-centric "wall of fame"; "sidewalk seating" and "affordable" tabs add to its popularity.

Harlow *Seafood*

20 | 25 | 21 | $80

East Midtown | Lombardy Hotel | 111 E. 56th St. (bet. Lexington & Park Aves.) | 212-935-6600 | www.harlownyc.com

"Glamorous" is the word for this East Midtown seafooder from restaurateur Richie Notar (Nobu), where the "gorgeous" setting and "beautiful" crowd are in keeping with its "pricey", "high-quality" catch; service is equally "upscale", though some find the "bar scene better than the cuisine."

The Harrison *American*

22 | 21 | 22 | $64

TriBeCa | 355 Greenwich St. (Harrison St.) | 212-274-9310 | www.theharrison.com

By now a "TriBeCa standard", Jimmy Bradley's "time-honored favorite" keeps on keeping on with "excellent" New American cooking delivered by a "welcoming" crew; the "buzz of regulars" fills its "comfortable" quarters, which possess a "neighborhood-y" yet "upscale" vibe (with prices to match).

Harry Cipriani *Italian*

23 | 22 | 22 | $97

Midtown | Sherry-Netherland Hotel | 781 Fifth Ave. (bet. 59th & 60th Sts.) | 212-753-5566 | www.cipriani.com

"Billionaires" and "divorcées" nibble on "upscale" Venetian victuals at this Sherry-Netherland "one-percenter" refuge known for serving the "best Bellinis in town"; the "eye-popping" tabs may cause more of a stir than the food, but then again, "you're paying to see who's sitting next to you."

Harry's Cafe & Steak *Steak*

22 | 21 | 22 | $60

Financial District | 1 Hanover Sq. (bet. Pearl & Stone Sts.) | 212-785-9200 | www.harrysnyc.com

Long "Wall Street's go-to eatery", this FiDi "throwback" in the historic India House attracts "captains of industry" with "mouthwatering" steaks and more backed by one of the best wine cellars in the city; it's "busy" for lunch, quieter at dinner and "expense account"–worthy all the time.

Harry's Italian *Italian*

21 | 16 | 18 | $29

Battery Park City | 225 Murray St. (West St.) | 212-608-1007
Financial District | 2 Gold St. (Platt St.) | 212-747-0797
Midtown | 30 Rockefeller Plaza, Concourse Level (bet. 49th & 50th Sts.) | 212-218-1450
www.harrysitalian.com

"Sterling" pizzas are standouts on the menu of "standard Italian favorites" at these "welcoming" fallbacks from the Harry's Cafe folks; "ample portions" and "reasonable pricing" cement their "go-to" status for "less-than-formal lunches" at the Downtown locations or eats on the move from the "busy", takeout-only Rock Center outlet.

Haru *Japanese*

21 | 16 | 18 | $44

East 70s | 1327 Third Ave. (76th St.) | 212-452-1028
East 70s | 1329 Third Ave. (76th St.) | 212-452-2230
Financial District | 1 Wall Street Ct. (Pearl St.) | 212-785-6850
NEW **Midtown** | 229 W. 43rd St. (bet. 7th & 8th Aves.) | 212-398-9810

continued

Union Square | 220 Park Ave. S. (18th St.) | 646-428-0989
West 80s | 433 Amsterdam Ave. (bet. 80th & 81st Sts.) | 212-579-5655
www.harusushi.com

This "consistent" Japanese mini-chain is a "default" choice for many, thanks to "big pieces" of "solid" sushi for fairly "modest" sums; though "nothing special" in terms of service or ambiance, it perpetually draws "young, loud" types.

Hasaki *Japanese*   ▽ 23 | 15 | 19 | $50

East Village | 210 E. Ninth St. (Stuyvesant St.) | 212-473-3327 | www.hasakinyc.com

"Gourmet" sushi and "authentic" Japanese dishes are served for "reasonable" rates at this compact, '84-vintage East Villager; a no-rez rule makes for "long lines" at prime time, so regulars show up for the "can't-go-wrong" lunch specials.

Hatsuhana *Japanese*   25 | 18 | 22 | $58

Midtown | 17 E. 48th St. (bet. 5th & Madison Aves.) | 212-355-3345 | www.hatsuhana.com

"Serious", "old-school sushi" is the lure at this "long-established" Midtown Japanese where the "artful presentation" begins with "aim-to-please" service; "bland decor" that "needs refreshing" seems at odds with the rather "pricey" tabs, but you don't last this long without doing something right.

Havana Alma de Cuba *Cuban*   22 | 17 | 19 | $40

West Village | 94 Christopher St. (bet. Bedford & Bleecker Sts.) | 212-242-3800 | www.havananyc.com

"Good-humored" servers pass "pitchers of mojitos" and "substantial" portions of appealing Cuban comfort chow at this "festive" West Villager; "live music", "reasonable" rates and a "lovely rear garden" keep things "bustling" here, so be prepared for "noise" and "chair-bumping."

Havana Central *Cuban*   21 | 21 | 20 | $39

Midtown | 151 W. 46th St. (bet. 6th & 7th Aves.) | 212-398-7440 | www.havanacentral.com

A "festive" pick for "entertaining friends", this Midtown Cuban "escape" offers "affordable", "well-prepared" food and "delicious" drinks in a "tropical" setting where "Desi Arnaz" would feel at home; too bad the "enthusiastic" service and "spirited" live music can make for "jet-airplane" noise levels.

Haveli *Indian*   21 | 15 | 19 | $36

East Village | 100 Second Ave. (bet. 5th & 6th Sts.) | 212-982-0533
This "reliable" East Village Indian just around the corner from Sixth Street's Curry Row is among "the best of the bunch" thanks to "cut-above" cooking and "welcoming" service; its consistent "quality" helps justify tabs slightly "pricier" than others in the zone.

Hearth *American/Italian*   25 | 20 | 24 | $71

East Village | 403 E. 12th St. (1st Ave.) | 646-602-1300 | www.restauranthearth.com

Bringing "fine dining to the East Village", this Tuscan-American from chef Marco Canora offers "delectable" fare from a "farm-to-table menu", complemented by an "interesting" wine list; granted, such "locavore goodness doesn't come cheap", but "sincere" service and a "warm", "bustling" atmosphere help ensure it's "worth the splurge."

Hecho en Dumbo *Mexican* 23 | 19 | 21 | $51

NoHo | 354 Bowery (bet. 4th & Great Jones Sts.) | 212-937-4245 | www.hechoendumbo.com

"Inventive" Mexican small plates are "served with a side of hipster" at this "sceney", "sex-Mex" standout that's a prime example of the "Bowery renaissance"; sure, "service could be better", but tabs are "pretty reasonable" and insiders say the tasting menu–only "chef's table is the way to go" – and there's also a next-door bar/event space, Salón Hecho.

Heidelberg *German* 21 | 19 | 19 | $41

East 80s | 1648 Second Ave. (bet. 85th & 86th Sts.) | 212-628-2332 | www.heidelbergrestaurant.com

When it comes to "classic", "stick-to-your-ribs" Germanica, this vintage-1936 Yorkville "time capsule" fields a "heavy", "no-apologies" menu washed down with "boots of beer"; "costumed" staffers and a "kitschy", "oompah-pah" setting are part of the "fun" package.

Hell's Kitchen *Mexican* 20 | 15 | 18 | $52

Hell's Kitchen | 679 Ninth Ave. (bet. 46th & 47th Sts.) | 212-977-1588 | www.hellskitchen-nyc.com

"Tasty modern" Mexican food draws "big crowds" to this "high-concept" Hell's Kitchen cantina where the "margaritas keep flowing" as the "noise" levels rise; even "thoughtful service" can't ease the "pre-theater crush", yet the overall experience is "closer to heaven" than the name suggests.

Henry's End *American* 24 | 17 | 23 | $54

Brooklyn Heights | 44 Henry St. (bet. Cranberry & Middagh Sts.) | Brooklyn | 718-834-1776 | www.henrysend.com

"As good as the day it opened" in 1973, this "distinctive" Brooklyn Heights destination remains a "sentimental favorite" due to "inventive" New American cooking, including its seasonal wild-game festival bringing "exotic critters" to the table; a "small-town" atmosphere and "efficient" service make the "sardine seating" feel almost "cozy."

Hibino *Japanese* 25 | 16 | 22 | $43

Cobble Hill | 333 Henry St. (Pacific St.) | Brooklyn | 718-260-8052 | www.hibino-brooklyn.com

NEW **Long Island City** | 10-70 Jackson Ave. (bet. 49th & 50th Aves.) | Queens | 718-392-5190 | www.hibino-lic.com

"Fresh-as-one-can-get" sushi vies for the spotlight with the "daily changing" obanzai (small plates) and "compelling" housemade tofu at these "unusual", Kyoto-style Japanese eateries; "budget-friendly" tabs and "unobtrusive" service embellish the "subdued" ambiance.

Hide-Chan *Japanese/Noodle Shop* 23 | 15 | 18 | $24

East Midtown | 248 E. 52nd St., 2nd fl. (bet. 2nd & 3rd Aves.) | 212-813-1800 | www.hidechanramen.com

The sound of diners "noisily slurping" "cooked-to-perfection" noodles swimming in "flavorful" broth provides the background music at this "authentic" East Midtown Japanese ramen joint; alright, the service can be "a bit rushed" and the setting "cramped", but "low costs" keep the trade brisk.

Hill Country *BBQ*

| 23 | 16 | 16 | $35 |

Flatiron | 30 W. 26th St. (bet. B'way & 6th Ave.) | 212-255-4544
NEW **Downtown Brooklyn** | 345 Adams St. (bet. Fulton & Johnson Sts.) | Brooklyn | 718-885-4608
www.hillcountryny.com

"Hip BBQ" is yours at these "cafeteria-style" joints where patrons order the "messy", "smoky" 'cue from a counter, then find a "communal table" and dig in; "toe-tapping" live music, a "good bourbon selection" and "friendly" vibrations make it the "next best thing to being in Austin."

Hill Country Chicken *Southern*

| 20 | 12 | 15 | $21 |

Flatiron | 1123 Broadway (25th St.) | 212-257-6446
NEW **Downtown Brooklyn** | 345 Adams St. (bet. Fulton & Johnson Sts.) | Brooklyn | 718-885-4609
www.hillcountrychicken.com

"Crispy-crunchy" fried chicken (including a "fabulous" skinless version) and "decent sides" make it hard to "save room for pie" at these low-budget Southerners; regulars ignore the "service hiccups" and "groan-inducing", "rec-room" decor, since the desserts are "nothing short of spectacular."

Hillstone *American*

| 22 | 20 | 20 | $47 |

East Midtown | Citicorp Bldg. | 153 E. 53rd St. (enter on 3rd Ave. & 54th St.) | 212-888-3828
Flatiron | NY Life Bldg. | 378 Park Ave. S. (27th St.) | 212-689-1090
www.hillstone.com

"Corporate crowds" like these "busy" Americans serving "well-executed" food (including a "must-have" spinach-artichoke dip) in "dark", "modern" digs that work equally well for everything from "business lunches" to "date nights"; just be ready for "crowded", "noisy" bar scenes, particularly "after work."

NEW Hirohisa *Japanese*

| – | – | – | E |

SoHo | 73 Thompson St. (bet. Broome & Spring Sts.) | 212-925-1613 | www.hirohisa-nyc.com

Hidden behind a barely marked door in SoHo, this exotic, kappo-style Japanese offers both à la carte and omakase options, plus a serious sake list; the modern minimalist setting features an open kitchen, sushi bar and a handful of tables.

NEW Hometown BBQ *BBQ*

| – | – | – | M |

Red Hook | 454 Van Brunt St. (Reed St.) | Brooklyn | 347-294-4644 | www.hometownbarbque.com

Classic Texas-style BBQ with a Brooklyn edge awaits at this Red Hook "find", a mammoth affair with a walk-up counter offering "seriously good" 'cue, craft beers and an array of whiskeys; its "first-come, first-served" policy can make for "long lines", but service is "enthusiastic" and regulars report leaving "satiated."

	FOOD	DECOR	SERVICE	COST

Hope & Anchor *Diner*

▽ 21 | 17 | 20 | $40

Red Hook | 347 Van Brunt St. (Wolcott St.) | Brooklyn | 718-237-0276 | www.hopeandanchorredhook.com

A "little bit of everything for everyone" is what's on offer at this Red Hook diner with a "friendly, small-town vibe" and a "rockabilly sensibility"; the "great brunch" is a draw on weekends, while "good value" is a pull at all times.

Hop Kee *Chinese*

21 | 8 | 15 | $21

Chinatown | 21 Mott St., downstairs (bet. Chatham Sq. & Mosco St.) | 212-964-8365 | www.hopkeenyc.com

"Old-guard", cash-only Chinatown cellar that's been slinging "traditional" Cantonese food – "and plenty of it" – since 1968; "dank" decor and "zombie" service are offset by "late"-night hours, "rock-bottom" tabs and an "Anthony Bourdain" endorsement.

The House *American*

23 | 23 | 20 | $60

Gramercy Park | 121 E. 17th St. (bet. Irving Pl. & Park Ave. S.) | 212-353-2121 | www.thehousenyc.com

This tri-level Gramercy standout proffers "solid" New American cooking but "even better ambiance" given its "romantic", "candlelit" setting in a "gorgeous" 1854 carriage house; factor in "attentive" service, and you've got a "perfect" date place – though you'll pay to "impress" here.

Hudson Clearwater *American*

22 | 21 | 20 | $58

West Village | 447 Hudson St. (Morton St.) | 212-989-3255 | www.hudsonclearwater.com

A "hidden entrance" on Morton Street isn't deterring the crowds from this West Village "total scene", incidentally offering "first-rate" New American food backed up by "exceptional" cocktails; its "hip young" following doesn't seem to mind the "lively" acoustics and "tables on top of one another", though it's more manageable at breakfast and lunch.

NEW Hudson Eats *Food Market*

– | – | – | M

Battery Park City | Brookfield Pl. | 200 Vesey St. (West St.) | 212-417-7000 | www.brookfieldplaceny.com

Set in the massive Brookfield Place development, this shiny new food court brings of-the-moment favorites like Black Seed, Mighty Quinn's Barbecue, Num Pang and Umami Burger to Battery Park City's former World Financial Center; suits and locals alike order at the various counters and grab one of the 600 seats in the airy, modern space where Hudson River views complement the offerings at breakfast, lunch and dinner.

NEW Humboldt & Jackson *American*

– | – | – | M

Williamsburg | 434 Humboldt St. (Jackson St.) | Brooklyn | 718-349-3355

The thoroughly American offerings at this Williamsburg newcomer from a Brooklyn Star alum include all-domestic wines and beers to go with local meats, cheeses and small plates prepared by guest chefs; the space sports an old-school, rock-embedded exterior, while the interior is lined with subway tiles and light woods.

	FOOD	DECOR	SERVICE	COST

Hummus Kitchen *Kosher/Mediterranean*
20 | 12 | 16 | $23

East 80s | 1613 Second Ave. (bet. 83rd & 84th Sts.) | 212-988-0090
Kips Bay | 444 Third Ave. (bet. 30th & 31st Sts.) | 212-696-0055
Midtown | 768 Ninth Ave. (bet. 51st & 52nd Sts.) | 212-333-3009
West 80s | 416 Amsterdam Ave. (80th St.) | 212-799-0003
www.hummuskitchen.com

These "casual" Med standbys whip up "quality" hummus with a "special zing" along with a raft of other vegetarian options; despite "smallish" settings and "disorganized" service, they're an "affordable" "fast-food alternative", especially for those who need it "kosher."

Hummus Place *Israeli/Kosher/Vegetarian*
21 | 10 | 18 | $22

East Village | 109 St. Marks Pl. (bet. Ave. A & 1st Ave.) | 212-529-9198
West 70s | 305 Amsterdam Ave. (bet. 74th & 75th Sts.) | 212-799-3335
West Village | 71 Seventh Ave. S. (bet. Barrow & Bleecker Sts.) |
212-924-2022
www.hummusplace.com

Those who like their hummus "silky" and their pita bread "fresh" and "warm" kvell over the kosher vegetarian offerings at these "popular" Israelis; though decor is nearly "nonexistent", service is "pleasant", the grub "filling" and the tabs "terrific."

Hundred Acres *American*
23 | 23 | 23 | $55

SoHo | 38 MacDougal St. (Prince St.) | 212-475-7500 |
www.hundredacresnyc.com

"Farm-fresh" New American "home cooking" arrives in an appropriately "country-road" setting at this SoHo charmer that's kin to Cookshop and Five Points; its "cult following" commends its "delicious brunch" and "awesome" garden room, only wishing there were "more menu options."

Il Bambino *Italian*
25 | 18 | 20 | $23

Astoria | 34-08 31st Ave. (bet. 34th & 35th Sts.) | Queens |
718-626-0087 | www.ilbambinonyc.com

Panini addicts rave about the "beyond-crispy" bread and "fantastic ingredients" in the "bargain"-priced pressed sandwiches at this "rustic" Astoria Italian; factor in "impeccable service" with "zero pretense" and a "cozy" back garden, and it's a neighborhood "must try."

Il Buco *Italian/Mediterranean*
26 | 23 | 24 | $66

NoHo | 47 Bond St. (bet. Bowery & Lafayette St.) | 212-533-1932 |
www.ilbuco.com

The "wonderful" "rustic" atmosphere belies the "sophisticated cooking" at this "cozy" "farmhouse" facsimile in NoHo, where the "delish" Med-Italian dishes come with "spectacular" wines and "spot-on service"; it's "on the expensive side", but oh so "romantic", particularly in the "marvelous cellar."

Il Buco Alimentari e
Vineria *Italian/Mediterranean*
24 | 20 | 21 | $64

NoHo | 53 Great Jones St. (bet. Bowery & Lafayette St.) | 212-837-2622 |
www.ilbucovineria.com

"More relaxed" but just "as good" as nearby sibling Il Buco, this NoHo restaurant/wine bar/market combo specializes in "amazing" pastas, "strong" house-cured salumi and other Med-Italian fare; the "prices are high", the communal seating "tight" and the din can be "deafening", but that's to be expected at such a "hot spot."

Il Cantinori *Italian*
23 | 23 | 23 | $69

Greenwich Village | 32 E. 10th St. (bet. B'way & University Pl.) | 212-673-6044 | www.ilcantinori.com

"Top-of-the-line" Tuscan cooking is the draw at this "classy" Village "favorite", "still going strong" after more than three decades; it's known as a "celebrity hangout" with a concordant "price factor", but "genuine" hospitality and "gorgeous flowers" make it a "special-occasion" destination for mere mortals.

Il Cortile *Italian*
22 | 19 | 21 | $56

Little Italy | 125 Mulberry St. (bet. Canal & Hester Sts.) | 212-226-6060 | www.ilcortile.com

"*Buongusto* is an understatement" at this "memory-lane" Italian, a "good bet on Mulberry" since 1975 thanks to its "hearty" food served by waiters who have "been there forever"; though it's "a bit pricey" for the area, regulars report a seat in the "delightful" garden atrium is "worth the trip" alone.

Il Gattopardo *Italian*
25 | 21 | 24 | $79

Midtown | 13-15 W. 54th St. (bet. 5th & 6th Aves.) | 212-246-0412 | www.ilgattopardonyc.com

Following a move to new digs down the block, this Midtown Southern Italian still offers "formal dining in the European manner" via a "terrific" menu, "smooth" service and an "inviting" bi-level setting; its atrium is especially "lovely" for a "unique" brunch or lunch, but be prepared for "hold-on-to-your-wallet" tabs.

Il Giglio *Italian*
23 | 17 | 21 | $76

TriBeCa | 81 Warren St. (bet. B'way & Greenwich St.) | 212-571-5555 | www.ilgigliorestaurant.com

An "empty stomach and a full wallet" are necessities at this "longtime" TriBeCa Italian where a meal begins with complimentary antipasti followed by a "luxurious" array of "old-world classics"; "outdated" decor, "tight quarters" and high prices are offset by "attentive" service and "generous portions."

Ilili *Lebanese*
26 | 23 | 23 | $59

Flatiron | 236 Fifth Ave. (bet. 27th & 28th Sts.) | 212-683-2929 | www.ililinyc.com

The "famous" Brussels sprouts are "a must" at this "alluring" Flatiron Lebanese, but "you can't go wrong" with any of the "creative", "beautifully presented" plates paired with a cocktail list that's just as "original and delicious"; a "cavernous" setting with "sleek, modern" furnishings completes this "wonderful experience" that's particularly "great for groups."

Il Laboratorio del Gelato *Ice Cream*
25 | 13 | 17 | $7

Lower East Side | 188 Ludlow St. (Houston St.) | 212-343-9922 | www.laboratoriodelgelato.com

It's the "best thing to come out of a lab since penicillin" say fans of the "silky smooth" artisanal gelato served at this LES gelateria-cum-research facility; with "so many flavors, so little time", routinely "long lines" and upmarket pricing, there's only one sensible strategy: "skip dinner and go right to it."

Il Mulino *Italian*   25 | 19 | 23 | $88

Greenwich Village | 86 W. Third St. (bet. Sullivan & Thompson Sts.) | 212-673-3783 | www.ilmulino.com

Il Mulino Uptown *Italian*

East 60s | 37 E. 60th St. (bet. Madison & Park Aves.) | 212-750-3270 | www.ilmulino.com

Trattoria Il Mulino *Italian*

Flatiron | 36 E. 20th St. (bet. B'way & Park S.) | 212-777-8448 | www.trattoriailmulino.com

At least once, "everyone should experience" this "old-time" Village Italian where "huge portions" of *magnifico* fare (including "a ton of free appetizers") are dispatched by "old-world waiters" in "tight", "crowded" quarters; there's "modern" decor at the UES offshoot and a "casual" vibe at the Flatiron trattoria, but whichever you choose, "bring loads of money."

NEW Il Mulino Prime *Italian/Steak*   – | – | – | E

SoHo | 331 W. Broadway (Grand St.) | 212-226-0020 | www.ilmulino.com
From the Il Mulino team comes this new spin-off of the burgeoning brand, a SoHo steakhouse offering prime beef alongside its signature Italian classics; the striking space eschews standard chop-shop decor with whitewashed walls stenciled with Ernest Hemingway quotes along with white papier-mâché taxidermy.

Il Postino *Italian*   22 | 18 | 21 | $70

East Midtown | 337 E. 49th St. (bet. 1st & 2nd Aves.) | 212-688-0033 | www.ilpostinony.com

Waiters inhale, then recite a "huge list of daily specials" at this "old-world" U.N.-area Italian that will also "cook anything you want"; an "intimate" "opera"-enhanced space further boosts the "wonderful dining experience", but value-seekers avoid the "reliably expensive" tabs by going for the lunchtime prix fixe.

Il Tinello *Italian*   23 | 20 | 23 | $88

Midtown | 16 W. 56th St. (bet. 5th & 6th Aves.) | 212-245-4388 | www.iltinellony.com

"Serenity" reigns at this Midtown "grande dame" exuding "senior appeal" and patrolled by "conscientious" waiters in "black tie"; everyone agrees that the Northern Italian cooking is "superb", but given the "corporate-checkbook" tabs, many save it for "special occasions."

Il Vagabondo *Italian*   20 | 17 | 20 | $51

East 60s | 351 E. 62nd St. (bet. 1st & 2nd Aves.) | 212-832-9221 | www.ilvagabondo.com

"Old-school" Italian fans find "all the favorites" at this 1965-vintage Upper Eastsider, where the food "sticks to your ribs" and the waiters have "been there for centuries"; the decor may be "nothing to write home about", but the "unique" indoor bocce court is.

	FOOD	DECOR	SERVICE	COST

Inakaya *Japanese*
22 | 21 | 20 | $54

Midtown | NY Times Bldg. | 231 W. 40th St. (bet. 7th & 8th Aves.) | 212-354-2195 | www.inakayany.com

It's always "showtime" at this "high-drama" Japanese robatayaki specialist in the NY Times building, where "friendly" staffers dish out "grilled delights" (plus "swanky sushi") while engaging in ritualized "yelling and screaming"; however, all the "fun" – which is most intense at the robata counter – can add up to "big bucks."

Indochine *French/Vietnamese*
21 | 21 | 19 | $62

Greenwich Village | 430 Lafayette St. (bet. Astor Pl. & 4th St.) | 212-505-5111 | www.indochinenyc.com

Ever "sexy" – even "timeless" – this "'80s hot spot" opposite the Public Theater still lures "attractive thin" folk with "on-target" French-Vietnamese fare served in "exotic" digs à la 1930s Saigon; perhaps its "elegance is slightly worn", but the "people-watching" is as stellar as ever.

Indus Valley *Indian*
23 | 16 | 21 | $33

West 90s | 2636 Broadway (100th St.) | 212-222-9222 | www.indusvalleyny.com

Though the ambiance may be "average", the "intensely flavorful" eats at this UWS Indian are "a cut above", ditto the "solicitous" service; pennypinchers find the $15 weekend lunch buffet "awesome", and allow it's "worth the few extra bucks" at dinner.

Ippudo *Japanese/Noodle Shop*
25 | 19 | 19 | $32

Greenwich Village | 65 Fourth Ave. (bet. 9th & 10th Sts.) | 212-388-0088
Midtown | 321 W. 51st St. (bet. 8th & 9th Aves.) | 212-974-2500
www.ippudony.com

"If you can stand the long waits" – somewhere between "20 minutes" to "life-long" – you'll be "rewarded" with "seriously satisfying noodles" and "scrumptious pork buns" at these Japanese ramen spots; the Village original offers "fun" decor, the Midtown branch is "more spacious" and "chic", and both employ staffers who cheer when you arrive.

Isa *Mediterranean*
▽ 22 | 18 | 18 | $53

Williamsburg | 348 Wythe Ave. (S. 2nd St.) | Brooklyn | 347-689-3594 | www.isa.gg

"Quirky" is the mindset at this Williamsburg eatery from restaurateur Taavo Somer (Freemans) where the industrial "log cabin" decor and "psychedelic" menu art nearly overwhelm the "creative" Mediterranean cooking; a "warm atmosphere" and moderate price point make it "worth trying."

Isabella's *American/Mediterranean*
20 | 18 | 19 | $49

West 70s | 359 Columbus Ave. (77th St.) | 212-724-2100 | www.isabellas.com

"Convenient" for a "post–Museum of Natural History" meal, this "UWS staple" delivers "dependable" Mediterranean-American fare for "reasonable" sums; "go early" if you want a seat on the "large" sidewalk patio, because the "light, airy" interior can feel a bit "frantic", especially during brunch.

	FOOD	DECOR	SERVICE	COST

Island Burgers & Shakes *Burgers*
21 | 13 | 18 | $22

Midtown | 766 Ninth Ave. (bet. 51st & 52nd Sts.) | 212-307-7934
West 80s | 422 Amsterdam Ave. (80th St.) | 212-877-7934
www.islandburgersandshakes.com
"Huge burgers" on "big buns" accessorized with "every topping known to man" are the raisons d'être of these "retro" West Side patty palaces that "finally sell fries" too; "spoon-licking shakes" sweeten the sour taste left by "sparse seating and service."

I Sodi *Italian*
25 | 18 | 22 | $66

West Village | 105 Christopher St. (bet. Bleecker & Hudson Sts.) | 212-414-5774 | www.isodinyc.com
Like a "little bit of Florence" in the West Village, this "small" Italian supplies "generously sized" portions of "first-tier" Tuscan fare lubricated by a "substantial wine list" and signature Negronis; "charming" service makes the "tight squeeze" seem delightfully "intimate", even "romantic."

Isola *Italian*
▽ 24 | 27 | 22 | $59

SoHo | Mondrian SoHo Hotel | 9 Crosby St. (bet. Grand & Howard Sts.) | 212-389-0000 | www.isolasoho.com
The "gorgeous", glass-lined greenhouse setting is on par with the "excellent" coastal Italian fare offered at this "classy" spot in the Mondrian SoHo Hotel; the crowd is fittingly "trendy" for such a "high-end" experience, but ultimately it's all about the "hard-to-beat atmosphere."

Italianissimo *Italian*
21 | 17 | 21 | $57

East 80s | 307 E. 84th St. (bet. 1st & 2nd Aves.) | 212-628-8603 | www.italianissimony.net
Its "jewel box" size reflects the neighborhood-"gem" status of this *"bellissimo"* UES Italian where the "just-like-mama" cooking and "brick-walled" setting seem right out of a "Woody Allen" movie; "solicitous" service and an "excellent" $27 early-bird make this one a "great find."

Ithaka *Greek/Seafood*
22 | 17 | 22 | $48

East 80s | 308 E. 86th St. (bet. 1st & 2nd Aves.) | 212-628-9100 | www.ithakarestaurant.com
"Neighborhood tavernas" don't get much more "relaxed" than this "quiet" Yorkville Greek where the "honest" food and "wonderful grilled fish" channel Santorini – or at least "Astoria"; maybe the whitewashed setting could be "spiffed up", but thankfully the tables are "far enough apart" and service is "attentive."

I Trulli *Italian*
23 | 21 | 22 | $63

Kips Bay | 122 E. 27th St. (bet. Lexington & Park Ave. S.) | 212-481-7372 | www.itrulli.com
"Rustic but sophisticated", this Kips Bay Southern Italian purveys a trulli "special" Puglian menu paired with "outstanding" wines via its adjoining enoteca; an "expansive" garden and "roaring" fireplace are seasonal draws, though "helpful" service and "costly" tabs are part of the package year-round.

NEW Ivan Ramen *Japanese/Noodle Shop*
19 | 13 | 17 | $21

Lower East Side | 25 Clinton St. (bet. Houston & Stanton Sts.) | 646-678-3859

continued

NEW Ivan Ramen Slurp Shop *Japanese/Noodle Shop*

Hell's Kitchen | Gotham West Mkt. | 600 11th Ave. (bet. 44th & 45th Sts.) | 212-582-7942
www.ivanramen.com

Ivan Orkin's flagship noodle shop follow-up to his popular counter in the Gotham West Market finally arrives in the LES, offering "creative", "delectable" takes on traditional ramen with "fantastic" broths, as well as izakaya-style small plates; just "be prepared to wait" at both locations, although the Hell's Kitchen outlet allows diners to slurp away at one of the food hall's communal tables.

Jackson Diner *Indian* ⟨21⟩ ⟨12⟩ ⟨16⟩ ⟨$24⟩

Greenwich Village | 72 University Pl. (bet. 10th & 11th Sts.) | 212-466-0820 | www.jacksondinernyc.com
Jackson Heights | 37-47 74th St. (bet. 37th Ave. & 37th Rd.) | Queens | 718-672-1232 | www.jacksondiner.com

Jackson Heights' Little India is home to this 30-plus-year-old subcontinental that also has a "winner" of a Village offshoot; the decor is "pure diner" at both, but the grub is "satisfying", the prices "low" and the service "laid-back" – and regulars say the lunchtime "buffet is the way to go."

Jackson Hole *Burgers* ⟨20⟩ ⟨13⟩ ⟨18⟩ ⟨$24⟩

East 60s | 232 E. 64th St. (bet. 2nd & 3rd Aves.) | 212-371-7187
Murray Hill | 521 Third Ave. (35th St.) | 212-679-3264
West 80s | 517 Columbus Ave. (85th St.) | 212-362-5177
Bayside | 35-01 Bell Blvd. (35th Ave.) | Queens | 718-281-0330
East Elmhurst | 69-35 Astoria Blvd. (70th St.) | Queens | 718-204-7070
www.jacksonholeburgers.com

Whether the burgers at this mini-chain are "quite tasty" or merely "run-of-the-mill", everyone agrees that their "manhole"-cover size makes them "reasonable values"; those who find the "old-time" diner decor "outdated" are relieved that the staff gets them in and out "fast."

Jack the Horse Tavern *American* ⟨21⟩ ⟨20⟩ ⟨20⟩ ⟨$49⟩

Brooklyn Heights | 66 Hicks St. (Cranberry St.) | Brooklyn | 718-852-5084 | www.jackthehorse.com

A "cozy, taverny" vibe, "terrific cocktails" and "upscale" American comfort fare delivered by a "cheerful" crew make a "neighborhood go-to" of this Brooklyn Heights "hideaway"; some find the menu "limited" and "slightly pricey", but all welcome the new next-door Oyster Room dispensing bivalves and small plates.

Jacob's Pickles *Southern* ⟨21⟩ ⟨20⟩ ⟨20⟩ ⟨$34⟩

West 80s | 509 Amsterdam Ave. (bet. 84th & 85th Sts.) | 212-470-5566 | www.jacobspickles.com

An UWS "den of decadence", this "country-meets-city" tavern keeps 'em coming with "fantastic fried chicken" and other well-priced "Southern comfort" faves (including, yes, "divine pickles") dished up in "casual" surrounds; it all goes down well with suds from the "amazing" beer list that helps you forget the "long line" to get in.

	FOOD	DECOR	SERVICE	COST

Jacques *French*
21 | 17 | 18 | $48

East 80s | 206 E. 85th St. (bet. 2nd & 3rd Aves.) | 212-327-2272 |
www.jacquesbrasserie.com
NoLita | 20 Prince St. (bet. Elizabeth & Mott Sts.) | 212-966-8886 |
www.jacques1534.com
The "fabulous" mussels are the standout dish at these "traditional"
French brasseries in NoLita and the Upper East Side; though a few find
the settings "old-fashioned" and "noisy", the "reasonable" pricing is
fine as is.

Jaiya *Thai*
20 | 18 | 18 | $40

East 80s | 1553 Second Ave. (bet. 80th & 81st Sts.) | 212-717-8877
Kips Bay | 396 Third Ave. (28th St.) | 212-889-1330
www.jaiya.com
Whether you prefer "spicy" or "incendiary", these East Side Thais offer
"authentic" Siamese food running the gamut from standard classics to
"challenging, take-no-hostages" dishes; "decent" price points trump the
"noisy" settings and less-than-stellar service.

Jake's Steakhouse *Steak*
23 | 19 | 22 | $69

Fieldston | 6031 Broadway (242nd St.) | Bronx | 718-581-0182 |
www.jakessteakhouse.com
"Scenic views of Van Cortlandt Park" make the "Manhattan-quality"
steaks taste even juicier at this "neighborhood" Fieldston chophouse
where the service is "professional" and the beer selection "vast";
although "expensive", it's "cheaper than the city", and there's "valet
parking" to boot.

James *American*
23 | 23 | 22 | $49

Prospect Heights | 605 Carlton Ave. (St. Marks Ave.) | Brooklyn |
718-942-4255 | www.jamesrestaurantny.com
"Creative", "full-of-flavor" Americana with a "local" focus match with an
"awesome" drink list at this "charming" Prospect Heights haunt, quar-
tered in "welcoming" whitewashed-brick digs; it's "convenient to BAM"
and the Barclays Center, but also a local brunch magnet.

Jane *American*
21 | 18 | 21 | $41

Greenwich Village | 100 W. Houston St. (bet. LaGuardia Pl. & Thompson
St.) | 212-254-7000 | www.janerestaurant.com
"Young" types head to this "upbeat" Village American for "quite tasty"
cooking, with "moderate" tabs, "austere" decor and "generally good
service" on the side; though "insanely busy", the weekend brunch is
the scene to make, provided you can stomach "loud" decibels on top
of your "hangover."

Jean-Georges *French*
28 | 28 | 28 | $166

West 60s | Trump Int'l Hotel | 1 Central Park W. (61st St.) |
212-299-3900 | www.jean-georgesrestaurant.com
"Everything you would expect and more", Jean-Georges Vongerichten's
CPW "icon" packs its "ethereal" New French menu with "sophisticated
surprises", presented with "aplomb" by "meticulous" staffers in a "calming", "elegant" milieu (where "jackets are required"); "excellent wine
pairings" can add to the already "dizzying" tabs, but for such an "extraordinary experience", it's "actually worth the high price."

	FOOD	DECOR	SERVICE	COST

Jean-Georges' Nougatine *French*
27 | 23 | 25 | $71

West 60s | Trump Int'l Hotel | 1 Central Park W. (61st St.) |
212-299-3900 | www.jean-georgesrestaurant.com
"The next best thing to Jean-Georges", this "more relaxed" front room
provides an "attractive" backdrop for savoring "artful" New French
fare and "seamless" service at a cost that's "easier on the pocket";
though open all day, it's known for the "exceptional" $38 prix fixe
lunch ("a steal").

Jeanne & Gaston *French*
24 | 21 | 24 | $53

West Village | 212 W. 14th St. (bet. 7th & 8th Aves.) | 212-675-3773 |
www.jeanneandgaston.com
"Delectable" French fare at "terrific prices" is yours at this "friendly",
somewhat "unknown" West Village bistro offering prix fixes with a "wide
variety of choices", along with à la carte options too; in warm weather,
the "welcoming" interior is augmented by a "lovely" back garden.

Jeepney *Filipino*
∇ 22 | 16 | 19 | $38

East Village | 201 First Ave. (bet. 12th & 13th Sts.) | 212-533-4121 |
www.jeepneynyc.com
The Maharlika team strikes again with this "cool" Filipino gastropub in
the East Village, where the hearty, "adventuresome" dishes are meant for
sharing; it's named after repurposed Jeeps from the WWII era, and the
"kitschy" setting features large pin-up photos and colorful murals.

Jeffrey's Grocery *American*
∇ 23 | 20 | 19 | $53

West Village | 172 Waverly Pl. (Christopher St.) | 646-398-7630 |
www.jeffreysgrocery.com
There's "Wisconsin" in the air at Gabe Stulman's "hip" West Village
American, a "homey", all-day thing where the "tasty" menu is as limited
as the square footage; "divine oysters" and "attention to detail" offset
the "not-Midwestern prices", though a few feel it's "more scene than
place to eat."

Jewel Bako *Japanese*
24 | 20 | 23 | $88

East Village | 239 E. Fifth St. (bet. 2nd & 3rd Aves.) | 212-979-1012 |
www.jewelbakosushi.com
"Casually elegant" and "expensively" priced, this bamboo-lined East
Village Japanese slices a "flawless symphony" of "incredibly fresh fish";
for best results, aficionados "sit at the sushi bar" and go the "omakase"
route, though no matter where you land, owners Jack and Grace Lamb
"really take care of you."

J.G. Melon *Pub Food*
21 | 13 | 16 | $30

East 70s | 1291 Third Ave. (74th St.) | 212-744-0585
"Old-school preppies" and modern-day "bros" catch up over "frosty
mugs", "juicy" burgers and "awesome" cottage fries at this "Upper East
Side institution" that recalls "old-time", circa-1972 NY; it's "always
packed", despite the cash-only policy and "brusque service."

Jing Fong *Chinese*
21 | 13 | 13 | $23

Chinatown | 20 Elizabeth St. (bet. Bayard & Canal Sts.) | 212-964-5256 |
www.jingfongny.com
Set in a "football field–size" hall, this "bustling" C-town Cantonese rolls

out "delectable" dim sum "à la Hong Kong" on "quickly moving carts" propelled by "brusque" staffers; it's "crowded at peak hours", a "hectic madhouse" on weekends and "affordable" all the time.

Jin Ramen *Japanese/Noodle Shop*　▽ 23 | 18 | 22 | $23

Morningside Heights | 3183 Broadway (bet. 125th St. & Tiemann Pl.) | 646-559-2862

"Slurp-alicious" bowls of hand-pulled noodles will "warm you up" at this "inexpensive" Morningside Heights ramen shop where the "limited" menu is dispatched by an "attentive" team; the sleek, wood-lined space is "cute" but "cramped", so diners may have to "wait at peak times."

Joe *Coffee*　21 | 14 | 20 | $9

Chelsea | 405 W. 23rd St. (bet. 9th & 10th Aves.) | 212-206-0669
East 70s | 1045 Lexington Ave. (bet. 74th & 75th Sts.) | 212-988-2500
Greenwich Village | 9 E. 13th St. (bet. 5th Ave. & University Pl.) | 212-924-3300
Midtown | Grand Central | 44 Grand Central Terminal (bet. Lexington & Vanderbilt Aves.) | 212-661-8580
Morningside Heights | 550 W. 120th St. (bet. Amsterdam Ave. & B'way) | 212-851-9101
West 80s | 514 Columbus Ave. (bet. 84th & 85th Sts.) | 212-875-0100
West Village | 141 Waverly Pl. (Gay St.) | 212-924-6750

Joe Pro Shop *Coffee*

Flatiron | 131 W. 21st St. (bet. 6th & 7th Aves.) | 212-924-7400
www.joenewyork.com

"Cheerful" baristas whip up "high-quality" coffee drinks at this growing mini-chain that also serves a "small selection of nice pastries"; the "unassuming" settings are pleasantly "unpretentious", while the Joe Pro Shop in the Flatiron offers classes and the chance to sample "beans from guest roasters."

Joe Allen *American*　18 | 18 | 20 | $46

Midtown | 326 W. 46th St. (bet. 8th & 9th Aves.) | 212-581-6464 | www.joeallenrestaurant.com

Known for its "posters of Broadway bombs" and "serviceable" American grub, this "timeless" Theater District joint is still a magnet for "showbiz" types and those who love them; après-theater "stargazing" – "yes, that's who you think it is in that dark corner" – lends "glamour" to the proceedings.

Joe & Pat's *Italian/Pizza*　25 | 11 | 19 | $25

Castleton Corners | 1758 Victory Blvd. (bet. Manor Rd. & Winthrop Pl.) | Staten Island | 718-981-0887 | www.joeandpatspizzany.com

It's all about the "deliciously thin, crispy" pizzas at this Castleton Corners Italian "staple" that's been dishing up "delicious" family meals for "gen-erations" of Staten Island folks; there's "not much atmosphere" to speak of, but "fast" service and modest tabs go a long way.

Joe's Pizza *Pizza*　24 | 9 | 16 | $9

Greenwich Village | 150 E. 14th St. (bet. Irving Pl. & 3rd Ave.) | 212-388-9474

continued

West Village | 7 Carmine St. (bet. Bleecker St. & 6th Ave.) |
212-366-1182
www.joespizzanyc.com

"Legendary to locals", this "grab-and-go" West Village pizzeria (with
a Greenwich Village offshoot) has been slinging "hot-out-of-the-oven"
slices since 1975; "hole-in-the-wall" looks and "stand-up counter
service" are part of this "quintessential NY" experience, but explain why
some are "not impressed."

Joe's Shanghai *Chinese* ‖ 22 ‖ 10 ‖ 14 ‖ $27 ‖

Chinatown | 9 Pell St. (bet. Bowery & Doyers St.) | 212-233-8888
Midtown | 24 W. 56th St. (bet. 5th & 6th Aves.) | 212-333-3868
Flushing | 136-21 37th Ave. (bet. Main & Union Sts.) | Queens |
718-539-3838
www.joeshanghairestaurants.com

"Delicate, savory and fun to eat", the "signature soup dumplings" at
these Chinese "staples" are "justly famous"; trade-offs include "long
lines", "perfunctory service" and "no atmosphere", yet they're "always
packed for a reason."

John Brown Smokehouse *BBQ* ‖ ∇ 25 ‖ 14 ‖ 17 ‖ $26 ‖

Long Island City | 10-43 44th Dr. (bet. 10th & 11th Sts.) | Queens |
347-617-1120 | www.johnbrownseriousbbq.com

"No-nonsense", "authentic" BBQ (including "awesome burnt ends")
is the specialty of this Kansas City–style joint in Long Island City that
also provides "plentiful sides" and a "great craft beer selection"; it's a
"simple setup", i.e. you "order at the counter and pick up your tray
when it's ready."

John Dory Oyster Bar *Seafood* ‖ 21 ‖ 19 ‖ 17 ‖ $61 ‖

Flatiron | Ace Hotel | 1196 Broadway (29th St.) | 212-792-9000 |
www.thejohndory.com

Berthed in the Flatiron's Ace Hotel, this "airy" seafooder from April
Bloomfield and Ken Friedman offers everything from "succulent oysters"
to "inspired" small plates; "hefty" tabs for "guppy-size portions" are
offset by the "happening vibe", kitschy-"cool" digs and those "sublime"
Parker House rolls.

John's of 12th Street *Italian* ‖ 21 ‖ 14 ‖ 19 ‖ $40 ‖

East Village | 302 E. 12th St. (2nd Ave.) | 212-475-9531 |
www.johnsof12thstreet.com

"Upholding the art of Italian cooking" since 1908, this East Village "institution" endures thanks to "no-nonsense" red-sauce meals (plus some
vegan selections), all at "fair prices"; "no credit cards" and "nothing-
fancy" decor – think "Chianti bottles" and "melted candle wax" – add to
the "time-warp" vibe.

John's Pizzeria *Pizza* ‖ 23 ‖ 15 ‖ 17 ‖ $25 ‖

Midtown | 260 W. 44th St. (bet. 7th & 8th Aves.) | 212-391-7560
West Village | 278 Bleecker St. (Jones St.) | 212-243-1680
www.johnspizzerianyc.com

"True" "NY-style pizza" emerges from the coal-fired brick ovens of these
separately owned "bang-for-the-buck" "institutions"; the West Village

original is "worth the wait in line" ("forget the decor"), while the Theater District outlet is set in a high-ceilinged "old church."

JoJo *French*
24 | 20 | 23 | $75

East 60s | 160 E. 64th St. (bet. Lexington & 3rd Aves.) | 212-223-5656 | www.jojorestaurantnyc.com

The French fare is "delectable" at this UES "jewel" in the Jean-Georges Vongerichten "crown", backed up by an "excellent" wine list and a "lovely townhouse setting", whose "intimate" rooms prompt "romance aplenty"; the feeling of "magic" in the air "makes the prices easier to swallow."

Jones Wood Foundry *British*
21 | 20 | 20 | $48

East 70s | 401 E. 76th St. (bet. 1st & York Aves.) | 212-249-2700 | www.joneswoodfoundry.com

Bringing a bit of "jolly old England" to Yorkville, this wood-paneled British pub dispenses "wonderful fish 'n' chips" and other "simple" classics washed down with an "impressive" suds selection; "ambiance is what sells this place", along with "helpful" service and a "lovely garden."

Jordans Lobster Dock *Seafood*
22 | 8 | 15 | $31

Sheepshead Bay | 3165 Harkness Ave. (Plumb 2nd St.) | Brooklyn | 718-934-6300 | www.jordanslobster.com

Locals "pretend they're in Maine" at this longtime Sheepshead Bay seafooder where live lobsters in "big tanks" make for ultra-"fresh" eating; sure, the "decor's as minimal as the service", but tabs are "dirt-cheap" and an on-site retail market means you can "eat your goodies at home."

Joseph Leonard *American*
24 | 19 | 22 | $53

West Village | 170 Waverly Pl. (Grove St.) | 646-429-8383 | www.josephleonard.com

"Original", "deeply satisfying" takes on New American standards draw "super-cool" folks to Gabe Stulman's West Village "hot spot" that ups the ante with "reasonable" tariffs and open-all-day hours; the "hiply rustic", "lumberjacky" setting is so "tiny" that "crowded" conditions and long "waits" are a given.

Joya *Thai*
24 | 17 | 19 | $23

Cobble Hill | 215 Court St. (bet. Warren & Wyckoff Sts.) | Brooklyn | 718-222-3484

Scenes don't get much more "boisterous" or "fun" than at this Cobble Hill Thai where a mix of "awesome" food, "cheap" tabs and "sleek" design attracts "young, hip" throngs; "dance-club" acoustics send regulars to the "more peaceful" back garden, but there's no sidestepping the "so-so service" and "cash-only" rule.

Jubilee *French*
21 | 17 | 19 | $59

East Midtown | 948 First Ave. (bet. 52nd & 53rd Sts.) | 212-888-3569 | www.jubileeny.net

A "clientele of a certain age" touts this "longtime" Sutton Place–area bistro as a haven of "relaxed sophistication" that's like a "quick trip to Paris"; it's "not noisy" and the seafood-oriented French fare (including "claim-to-fame" moules) is "tasty", so it's no wonder "reservations for dinner" are recommended.

	FOOD	DECOR	SERVICE	COST

Juliana's *Pizza*
26 | 20 | 22 | $26

Dumbo | 19 Old Fulton St. (bet. Front & Water Sts.) | Brooklyn | 718-596-6700 | www.julianaspizza.com

The "founder of Grimaldi's" turns out "incredible" thin-crust, coal-oven-fired pizza with both "classic and innovative" toppings at this "real-deal" parlor under the Brooklyn Bridge; what's more, regulars report that the line is often "half as long" as at some of its competitors – "for now."

Jungsik *Korean*
27 | 26 | 27 | $136

TriBeCa | 2 Harrison St. (Hudson St.) | 212-219-0900 | www.jungsik.kr

"Phenomenal" contemporary Korean food is "tantalizingly presented" by "warm, informed" staffers in a "beautiful" setting at this "special-occasion" TriBeCan; it's "a big splurge" to be sure – especially if you choose the "revelatory tasting menu" – but "worth it" for a "memorable experience."

Juni *American*
27 | 24 | 27 | $100

Midtown | Hotel Chandler | 12 E. 31st St. (bet. 5th & Madison Aves.) | 212-995-8599 | www.juninyc.com

Let "outstanding" Australian chef Shaun Hergatt put your "palate in seventh heaven" with his "ambitious" New American dishes at this "hushed" retreat in Midtown's Hotel Chandler; dinner, featuring a variety of à la carte and tasting-menu options, is on the "expensive" side, but the prix fixe lunches are "great deals."

Junior's *Diner*
19 | 13 | 17 | $29

Midtown | Grand Central | 89 E. 42nd St., Lower Dining Concourse (Vanderbilt Ave.) | 212-983-5257
Midtown | 1515 Broadway (7th Ave.) | 212-302-2000
Downtown Brooklyn | 386 Flatbush Ave. Extension (Dekalb Ave.) | Brooklyn | 718-852-5257
www.juniorscheesecake.com

"World famous" for its "stupendous" cheesecakes, this Downtown Brooklyn "icon" and its Midtown offshoots also sling a "huge menu" of "decent" American diner fare, served in "gigantic portions" by "swift" staffers; sure, the atmosphere's "frenetic" and the decor "bland", but the "fair prices" alone make it "worth a visit."

Junoon *Indian*
24 | 25 | 23 | $69

Flatiron | 27 W. 24th St. (bet. 5th & 6th Aves.) | 212-490-2100 | www.junoonnyc.com

"Out-of-this-world haute Indian" dining in "elegant" environs makes this "classy" Flatiron spot a "destination", whether in the main room with its "well-spaced tables" or in the "dark", "intriguing" front lounge; you can really "rack up a bill", but staffers who "go out of their way to make you feel special" add value.

Juventino *American*
∇ 26 | 22 | 22 | $52

Park Slope | 370 Fifth Ave. (bet. 5th & 6th Sts.) | Brooklyn | 718-360-8469 | www.juventinonyc.com

"Delicious and full of surprises" describes the Latin-inflected New American fare at this Park Slope "original" with "rustic-chic" decor and a garden patio; "be ready to wait" for the "great" weekend brunch, or stop by weekdays when it's reportedly "less crowded."

	FOOD	DECOR	SERVICE	COST

Kafana *E European*
▽ 25 | 21 | 21 | $33

East Village | 116 Ave. C (bet. 7th & 8th Sts.) | 212-353-8000 | www.kafananyc.com

"Traditional, old-school" Serbian cooking that's like a "trip to Belgrade" is the draw at this "unusual" East Village option where the "hedonistic" menu is a "must-try for meat lovers"; the servers are "knowledgeable", and the "warm", brick-lined space is studded with photos reflecting the "Eastern European" mood.

Kajitsu *Japanese/Vegetarian*
▽ 25 | 24 | 26 | $101

Murray Hill | 125 E. 39th St. (bet. Lexington & Park Aves.) | 212-228-4873 | www.kajitsunyc.com

This wood-lined, "Zen"-like Japanese vegetarian in Murray Hill is a "hushed" oasis for ancient Buddhist shojin cuisine, served kaiseki-style at dinner by a "phenomenal" staff (and priced "as if it were Harry Winston jewels"); the more casual first-floor adjunct goes by the name Kokage, and offers non-vegetarian, à la carte dishes for lunch and dinner.

Kanoyama *Japanese*
▽ 24 | 18 | 21 | $58

East Village | 175 Second Ave. (bet. 11th & 12th Sts.) | 212-777-5266 | www.kanoyama.com

"Artfully arranged" sushi, including "varieties you don't often see", is the hook at this East Village Japanese "adventure" that seals the deal with tabs that are "reasonable" vis-à-vis the "high quality"; maybe the place "doesn't look like much", but an adjacent sake/oyster bar allows room to spread out.

Kashkaval Garden *Mediterranean*
▽ 22 | 17 | 19 | $30

Midtown | 852 Ninth Ave. (bet. 55th & 56th Sts.) | 212-245-1758 | www.kashkavalgarden.com

A "good first-date place", this "casual" Midtown Med offers a "wide selection of tapas" (plus some "quality" fondues), all for "reasonable" dough; an "inviting" interior and a small, "under-the-radar" back garden add to its appeal.

Kati Roll Company *Indian*
22 | 8 | 15 | $14

East Midtown | 229 E. 53rd St. (bet. 2nd & 3rd Aves.) | 212-888-1700
Greenwich Village | 99 MacDougal St. (Bleecker St.) | 212-420-6517
Midtown | 49 W. 39th St. (bet. 5th & 6th Aves.) | 212-730-4280
www.thekatirollcompany.com

"Grab-and-go" Indian street food is the concept at these counter-service joints specializing in "mouthwatering" kati wraps stuffed with "fragrant ingredients"; "exceptional value" keeps them as "busy as Bombay" at lunchtime, "no-decor" settings notwithstanding.

Katz's Delicatessen *Deli*
25 | 11 | 14 | $26

Lower East Side | 205 E. Houston St. (Ludlow St.) | 212-254-2246 | www.katzsdelicatessen.com

For a "quintessential taste of Jewish NY", check out this circa-1888 LES "institution" where the "mile-high" pastrami sandwich is the most "legendary" of its "dependably delicious" deli staples; "cafeterialike" looks, a cash-only policy and "sometimes surly service" don't prevent it from being "usually packed with all strata of society", including cinephiles reenacting that "racy scene" from *When Harry Met Sally*.

	FOOD	DECOR	SERVICE	COST

Kaz an Nou *Caribbean/French* ▽ 22 | 16 | 20 | $32

Prospect Heights | 53 Sixth Ave. (bet. Bergen & Dean Sts.) | Brooklyn | 718-938-3235 | www.kazannou.com

"Dim lighting and cozy seating" set an "interesting" stage for French-Caribbean fare "with a twist" at this "small" spot in Prospect Heights; come with cash and wine (it's BYO), and be prepared for a wait – it doesn't accept reservations.

Keens Steakhouse *Steak* 26 | 24 | 24 | $81

Midtown | 72 W. 36th St. (bet. 5th & 6th Aves.) | 212-947-3636 | www.keens.com

A "throwback to the '80s" – the 1880s, that is – this "bucket-list" Midtown steakhouse is renowned for its "legendary mutton chop" and "powerhouse" porterhouse, served in a "Smithsonian"-worthy setting with thousands of "glorious" antique clay pipes hanging from the ceiling; "gracious" service, "top-notch" private rooms and "the Torah" of single-malt scotch lists are further reasons why this one is "up there with the best" in town.

Kefi *Greek* 23 | 17 | 19 | $40

West 80s | 505 Columbus Ave. (bet. 84th & 85th Sts.) | 212-873-0200 | www.kefirestaurant.com

"Finally reopened" following a water main break, Michael Psilakis' "big", "boisterous" UWS taverna is just as "super" as ever offering "confident", "down-home Greek" cooking at tabs that are particularly "easy on the wallet"; even though the decor's "simple" and the acoustics "noisy", everyone's mighty "glad it's back."

Kellari Taverna *Greek/Seafood* 22 | 20 | 21 | $56

Midtown | 19 W. 44th St. (bet. 5th & 6th Aves.) | 212-221-0144 | www.kellariny.com

"Mouthwatering" displays of "fresh fish on ice" beckon at this "sophisticated" Midtown Greek seafooder offering "next-flight-to-Athens" quality cooking; though some menu items are "pricey", the $32 pre-theater prix fixe is a "steal" – and "efficient" staffers "make sure you make your curtain."

Keste Pizza e Vino *Pizza* 23 | 14 | 16 | $30

West Village | 271 Bleecker St. (Morton St.) | 212-243-1500 | www.kestepizzeria.com

"Blow-you-away" Neapolitan pizzas ("oh, that crust!") with "fresh, flavorful toppings" are the draw at this "popular", "no-frills" West Village pizzeria; but while the goods may be "hard to beat", trade-offs include "so-so service", "super-cramped" digs and "indulgence" pricing.

Khe-Yo *Laotian* 24 | 19 | 21 | $59

TriBeCa | 157 Duane St. (bet. Hudson St. & W. B'way) | 212-587-1089 | www.kheyo.com

The "underexposed, underappreciated" cuisine of Laos gets its due at this Marc Forgione–backed TriBeCan where the "helpful" staff guides diners through the "bold", "adventurous" menu; the brick- and wood-lined space exudes "hip" vibrations, and there's a daytime cafe, Khe-Yosk, that serves banh mi sandwiches.

	FOOD	DECOR	SERVICE	COST

Kings' Carriage House *American*
21 | 24 | 22 | $63

East 80s | 251 E. 82nd St. (bet. 2nd & 3rd Aves.) | 212-734-5490 |
www.kingscarriagehouse.com

Best known for its "lovely setting", this Upper East Side "hidden treasure"
is nestled in a "romantic" duplex suggesting an "English country house";
the prix fixe-only New American menu is also "top-drawer", with "gracious" service, "quiet" decibels and "dainty" afternoon tea as bonuses.

NEW Kingside *American*
19 | 21 | 20 | $53

Midtown | Viceroy Hotel New York | 124 W. 57th St. (bet. 6th & 7th
Aves.) | 212-707-8000 | www.kingside-restaurant.com

"Satisfying" American food turns up at this all-day venue set in an "airy",
tile-lined space in Midtown's Viceroy Hotel; though breakfast and brunch
can be "serene", it's a "loud" "scene" at night, with "hip" folks, "pre-
Carnegie Hall" types and "billionaires from the block" guzzling "amazing"
cocktails at the "stylish bar."

Kin Shop *Thai*
22 | 15 | 20 | $56

West Village | 469 Sixth Ave. (bet. 11th & 12th Sts.) | 212-675-4295 |
www.kinshopnyc.com

"Taking Thai in new directions", chef Harold Dieterle's "ambitious" West
Villager "gives your taste buds a workout" via "vibrant", "inventive"
dishes delivered by a "helpful" team; loyalists insist the "unique" flavors
trump the "serene" but somewhat "pedestrian" setting.

Ki Sushi *Japanese*
▽ 26 | 20 | 24 | $50

Cobble Hill | 122 Smith St. (bet. Dean & Pacific Sts.) | Brooklyn |
718-935-0575

This "intimate" Cobble Hill Japanese serves "memorable signature rolls"
made with "high-quality fish" in a "typical", "low-key" setting; it may be
"on the expensive side", but with "extremely nice" service thrown into
the mix, it's "worth every cent."

Kitchenette *Southern*
20 | 15 | 18 | $25

Morningside Heights | 1272 Amsterdam Ave. (bet. 122nd & 123rd Sts.) |
212-531-7600

TriBeCa | 156 Chambers St. (bet. B'way & Greenwich St.) | 212-267-6740
www.kitchenetterestaurant.com

Southern "comfort" cooking is the specialty of these "kitschy" "country
farmhouse"–inspired standbys where both the menus and the portions
are "big"; the "cutesy", "small-town" decor earns mixed response, but all
agree on the "rushed" service and low tabs.

Knickerbocker Bar & Grill *American*
22 | 21 | 21 | $55

Greenwich Village | 33 University Pl. (9th St.) | 212-228-8490 |
www.knickerbockerbarandgrill.com

"Time warps" don't get more "lovable" than this 1977-vintage Villager,
an "old-school" source of "no-surprises" Americana that's "solid" but
"won't knock your socks off"; though the room's a tad "tattered", "warm"
service and "surprisingly good" weekend jazz make this one a keeper.

Koi *Japanese*
24 | 23 | 21 | $68

Hudson Square | Trump SoHo Hotel | 246 Spring St. (bet. 6th Ave. &
Varick St.) | 212-842-4550

| | | FOOD | DECOR | SERVICE | COST |

continued

Midtown | Bryant Park Hotel | 40 W. 40th St. (bet. 5th & 6th Aves.) |
212-921-3330
www.koirestaurant.com

"Fashionistas" and other "trendy" types nibble "Japanese delicacies"
(including "designer" sushi) at these "plush" hotel retreats; the "LA vibe"
and "wonderfully snooty" service are a "bit too Beverly Hills" for some,
but even enthusiasts agree it's best to "avoid getting stuck with the bill."

Ko Sushi *Japanese*   20 | 15 | 19 | $35

East 70s | 1329 Second Ave. (70th St.) | 212-439-1678
East 80s | 1619 York Ave. (85th St.) | 212-772-8838
www.newkosushi.com

These "no-frills", separately owned Japanese Upper Eastsiders furnish
a "neighborhood" following with "tasty" raw fish that's "priced right";
"quick" service makes the "cafeteria"-like settings more palatable,
though aesthetes recommend the "reliable delivery."

Kotobuki *Japanese*   25 | 16 | 16 | $38

Greenwich Village | 56 Third Ave. (bet. 10th & 11th Sts.) |
212-353-5088 | www.kotobukimanhattan.com

A venerated Long Island sushi chainlet takes on Manhattan at this Village
beachhead, where "outstanding" cuts of fish and "innovative" entrees are
ferried by an "attentive" crew in minimalist environs; given its avid fan
base, the no-rez policy is worth bearing in mind when planning a visit.

Kouzan *Japanese*   22 | 20 | 20 | $37

West 90s | 685 Amsterdam Ave. (93rd St.) | 212-280-8099 |
www.kouzanjapanese.com

Starting with its "dim lighting" and "serene" feeling, this "pretty" Upper
West Side Japanese "raises expectations" that are met by "quality"
sushi and cooked items, all delivered by a "bend-over-backwards"
team; throw in tabs geared to the "99%" and no wonder it's such a
"neighborhood asset."

Kristalbelli *Korean*   ∇ 24 | 23 | 23 | $61

Midtown | 8 W. 36th St. (bet. 5th & 6th Aves.) | 212-290-2211 |
www.kristalbelli.com

A "classy" yet "hip" vibe matches the "high-end" Korean cuisine offered
at this "Rolls-Royce"–esque K-town restaurant/lounge where the "refined" dishes include meats that diners barbecue on "cool", smoke-free
crystal grills; "attentive" staffers help distract from the "pricey" tabs.

NEW Krupa Grocery *American*   – | – | – | M

Windsor Terrace | 231 Prospect Park W. (Windsor Pl.) | Brooklyn |
718-709-7098 | www.krupagrocery.com

A local hit from day one, this Windsor Terrace American offers a crowd-
pleasing, three-meal-a-day American menu and an interesting drinks list
(it's from the owners of Windsor Wine across the street); the sleek space
boasts a sizable bar and a picnic table-equipped back garden.

Ktchn *American*   21 | 19 | 19 | $48

Hell's Kitchen | Out Hotel | 508 W. 42nd St. (bet. 10th & 11th Aves.) |
212-868-2999 | www.ktchnnyc.com

"Off the beaten path" in Way West Hell's Kitchen, this straight-friendly eatery in the city's first gay hotel serves no-surprises, "reasonably priced" New Americana shuttled by a flirty, "attentive" crew; the oh-so-"sleek", white-on-white setting is nearly as stylish as the "skinny jean"–clad crowd.

Kuma Inn *Filipino/Thai*

▽ 25 | 12 | 21 | $37

Lower East Side | 113 Ludlow St., 2nd fl. (bet. Delancey & Rivington Sts.) | 212-353-8866 | www.kumainn.com

One of NYC's "best hidden gems", this "obscure" Filipino-Thai accessed up a flight of LES stairs puts out an "avant-garde" small-plates menu "exploding with flavor"; the "hole-in-the-wall" digs are "tight", but the "price is right" and "BYO makes it even better."

Kum Gang San *Korean*

21 | 14 | 17 | $38

Midtown | 49 W. 32nd St. (bet. B'way & 5th Ave.) | 212-967-0909
Flushing | 138-28 Northern Blvd. (bet. Bowne & Union Sts.) | Queens | 718-461-0909
www.kumgangsan.net

These 24/7 "kitsch" palaces sling Korean BBQ in "cavernous" settings equipped with waterfalls and pianos; the "traditional" food is "solid", the decor "age-worn" and the service "rush-rush", but it's still "good for first-timers" and "out-of-towners."

Kunjip *Korean*

22 | 10 | 16 | $29

Midtown | 9 W. 32nd St. (5th Ave.) | 212-216-9487 | www.kunjip.net

Always open and almost "always crowded", this "popular" 24/7 K-town venue plies an "extensive menu" of "traditional Korean cooking" in a "no-frills" atmosphere; while seating's "cramped" and servers "rush you out the door", the "solid" chow largely redeems all.

Kurumazushi *Japanese*

▽ 25 | 16 | 22 | $147

Midtown | 7 E. 47th St., 2nd fl. (bet. 5th & Madison Aves.) | 212-317-2802 | www.kurumazushi.com

The "ethereal, next-level" sushi "couldn't be fresher or more delicious" at chef Toshihiro Uezu's pioneering Midtown eatery, perched in a "peaceful", second-floor space; tabs may be "extravagant", but the prices are "warranted" for a "traditional experience" on par with "high-end places in Japan."

Kyochon Chicken *Chicken*

20 | 15 | 15 | $18

Midtown | 319 Fifth Ave. (bet. 32nd & 33rd Sts.) | 212-725-9292
Flushing | 156-50 Northern Blvd. (bet. 156th & 157th Sts.) | Queens | 718-939-9292
www.kyochonus.com

Fried chicken gets an "oh-so-spicy" Korean spin – and some "soy-garlic" inflections – at these "addictive" Midtown-Flushing satellites of the global poultry chain; "modern" food-court design distracts from the "small portions" and tabs that are "a bit pricey for wings."

Kyo Ya *Japanese*

26 | 22 | 23 | $115

East Village | 94 E. Seventh St., downstairs (1st Ave.) | 212-982-4140

The Kyoto-style fare is "sublime" à la carte, but the multicourse kaiseki dinners are "legendary for good reason" at this "secret gem" in the East Village; the ambiance is "serene", but seating is limited, so be sure to make a reservation – and be prepared to pay top dollar.

	FOOD	DECOR	SERVICE	COST

La Baraka *French*   ▽ 23 | 19 | 25 | $53

Flushing | 255-09 Northern Blvd. (2 blocks east of Little Neck Pkwy.) |
Queens | 718-428-1461 | www.labarakarest.com

Renowned for the "hospitality" of "lovely hostess" Lucette, this long-standing Flushing venue follows through with "terrific" Tunisian-accented French fare; though the decor "needs an update", tabs are "reasonable" and the overall mood definitely "enjoyable."

La Boîte en Bois *French*   22 | 17 | 21 | $62

West 60s | 75 W. 68th St. (bet. Columbus Ave. & CPW) | 212-874-2705 |
www.laboitenyc.com

A longtime "pre-theater favorite" near Lincoln Center, this "tiny" French boîte turns out "classic" bistro dishes in a "congenial" setting overseen by "fast-moving" staffers; "sardine"-can dimensions, "old-fashioned" decor and kinda "pricey" tabs come with the territory.

La Bonne Soupe *French*   20 | 15 | 18 | $34

Midtown | 48 W. 55th St. (bet. 5th & 6th Aves.) | 212-586-7650 |
www.labonnesoupe.com

"Serviceable" enough for a "quick bite", this 40-plus-year-old Midtown "pinch hitter" is best known for its "divine onion soup", though the rest of its French bistro menu is certainly "reliable"; "brusque" service, "crowded" conditions and "no-frills" looks are blunted by good "value."

L'Absinthe *French*   23 | 22 | 21 | $76

East 60s | 227 E. 67th St. (bet. 2nd & 3rd Aves.) | 212-794-4950 |
www.labsinthe.com

"Toulouse-Lautrec" would feel at home in this "classic" UES brasserie where the "fine food", "attentive service" and very Gallic ambiance evoke a "midnight-in-Paris" mood; granted, it's "expensive" to "pretend you're in France", but its "upscale crowd" doesn't seem to care.

La Colombe Torrefaction *Coffee*   24 | 20 | 21 | $7

SoHo | 270 Lafayette St. (Prince St.) | 212-625-1717
TriBeCa | 319 Church St. (Lispenard St.) | 212-343-1515
www.lacolombe.com

"Fantastic coffee" with the power of "rocket fuel" is the draw at these java joints imported from Philly; "yummy pastries" are also on offer, and while there's often a "long line", "knowledgeable" baristas work to ensure it moves quickly.

NEW Ladurée *Bakery/French*   24 | 25 | 23 | $39

SoHo | 398 W. Broadway (bet. Broome & Spring Sts.) | 646-392-7868 |
www.ladureeus.com

"Glorious excess reigns" at this SoHo outpost of the luxury French bakery, with an up-front patisserie showcasing "phenomenal" macarons abetted by a "candy-box" rear dining room offering "quite good" Gallic fare; *bien sûr*, it's "pricey", but payoffs include a knockout back garden.

Lady Mendl's *Teahouse*   22 | 25 | 22 | $49

Gramercy Park | Inn at Irving Pl. | 56 Irving Pl. (bet. 17th & 18th Sts.) |
212-533-4466 | www.ladymendls.com

Ladies live it up à la *Downton Abbey* at this "mahvelous" Gramercy tearoom where "excellent" servers present "tasty" sandwiches and sweets along with "wonderful" brews in an "elegant" Victorian setting;

it's "pricey" whether "your boyfriend" comes or not, but a "pampered afternoon" is the reward.

La Esquina Mexican

23 | 23 | 20 | $52

SoHo | 114 Kenmare St. (bet. Cleveland Pl. & Lafayette St.) | 646-613-7100 | www.esquinanyc.com

Cafe de la Esquina Mexican

Williamsburg | 225 Wythe Ave. (3rd St.) | Brooklyn | 718-393-5500 | www.esquinabk.com

"Straight-up *delicioso*" describes both the food and the scene at this ever-"trendy" SoHo Mexican comprised of a "dive"-like taqueria, casual indoor/outdoor cafe and "ultracool", hard-to-access underground grotto; the Williamsburg spin-off set in a "futuristic retro diner" comes equipped with a moody back room and "huge outdoor patio."

Lafayette French

22 | 24 | 20 | $62

NoHo | 380 Lafayette St. (Great Jones St.) | 212-533-3000 | www.lafayetteny.com

A "gorgeous", "expansive" space with "plenty of room to breathe" lures "beautiful people" to this "bustling" all-day NoHo cafe that's a showcase for Andrew Carmellini's "hearty" French cooking; insiders say it "shines best at breakfast", though the front bakery is a "great pit stop" for "delicious bread" and "delectable" pastries any time.

La Follia Italian

▽ 22 | 20 | 23 | $43

Gramercy Park | 226 Third Ave. (19th St.) | 212-477-4100 | www.lafollianyc.com

Whether you land in the up-front enoteca or the rear dining room, the same "terrific" Italian small plates and pastas are available at this "casual" Gramercy "neighborhood place"; fans like the "sincere" service and "affordable" rates, the "no-reservations policy" not so much.

La Fonda del Sol Spanish

21 | 20 | 21 | $59

East Midtown | 200 Park Ave. (enter on 44th St. & Vanderbilt Ave.) | 212-867-6767 | www.patinagroup.com

Conveniently sited above Grand Central, this reincarnation of a "classic" '60s Spaniard offers both a "lively after-work bar" serving "upscale tapas" and a "soothing", more "sophisticated" back room; it's "a bit high-priced", but at least the service is "professional."

La Grenouille French

28 | 28 | 28 | $126

Midtown | 3 E. 52nd St. (bet. 5th & Madison Aves.) | 212-752-1495 | www.la-grenouille.com

Still *"extraordinaire"* after "so many years", this Midtown "institution" leaves "all your senses satisfied" with "superb" haute French cuisine, "pampering" service and a "soigné" setting festooned with "soaring floral arrangements"; jackets and deep pockets are de rigueur here, but it's "well worth the splurge" for a "memorable" meal at what is surely the "last of its breed"; P.S. the departure of its beloved front-of-house leader, Charles Masson, has loyalists waiting to see what happens next.

La Lanterna di Vittorio Italian

20 | 22 | 20 | $34

Greenwich Village | 129 MacDougal St. (bet. 3rd & 4th Sts.) | 212-529-5945 | www.lalanternacaffe.com

It's all about the "romantic feel" at this Village Italian "slice of heaven" purveying "enjoyable", "affordable" light bites in "quaint" quarters lit by a fireplace and "lantern-filled" garden; "live jazz" in the adjoining bar adds further "first-date" appeal.

	FOOD	DECOR	SERVICE	COST

L'Albero Dei Gelati *American*

23 | 18 | 18 | $18

Park Slope | 341 Fifth Ave. (4th St.) | Brooklyn | 718-788-2288 | www.alberodeigelati.com

A walk-up window for "top-notch" gelato in flavors both "classic" and "unique" ("saffron, blue cheese") lures 'em to this Park Slope offshoot of a Lombardy, Italy, favorite; inside, it's a "delightful" coffee/wine bar with a "sustainable/slow cooking" ethos serving "serious" panini and more — and the "magic" back garden seals the deal.

La Lunchonette *French*

∇ 22 | 14 | 20 | $45

Chelsea | 130 10th Ave. (18th St.) | 212-675-0342

"It hasn't changed much in all these years, and that's a good thing" say supporters of this "low-key", "fair-priced" West Chelsea bistro; its "divey charm" is just the thing post–"High Line" – and on Sunday night there's a "chanteuse/accordionist."

La Mangeoire *French*

23 | 20 | 21 | $60

East Midtown | 1008 Second Ave. (bet. 53rd & 54th Sts.) | 212-759-7086 | www.lamangeoire.com

If you "can't get to Provence", check out this next-best-thing East Midtowner where chef Christian Delouvrier whips up "imaginative takes on traditional country French dishes"; its longevity (since 1975) may be due to the "warm" service and "transporting" South-of-France decor.

La Masseria *Italian*

23 | 20 | 23 | $60

Midtown | 235 W. 48th St. (bet. B'way & 8th Ave.) | 212-582-2111 | www.lamasserianyc.com

Showgoers tout this "quick-pace" Times Square–area Italian for its "hearty" cooking, "sweet farmhouse" setting and "fast" service that "gets you to the theater on time"; "crowded" conditions and "pricey-but-worth-the-money" tabs complete the overall appealing picture.

Lambs Club *American*

22 | 24 | 23 | $78

Midtown | Chatwal Hotel | 132 W. 44th St. (bet. 6th & 7th Aves.) | 212-997-5262 | www.thelambsclub.com

You'll be "looking around for Nick and Nora Charles" given the "red leather" deco decor at Geoffrey Zakarian's "sophisticated" Theater Districter; the New American food is just as "fabulous", ditto the service, and in winter the fireplace is "roaring", but "steep" tabs have some going for cocktails in the upstairs lounge instead.

La Mela *Italian*

21 | 14 | 20 | $35

Little Italy | 167 Mulberry St. (bet. Broome & Grand Sts.) | 212-431-9493 | www.lamelarestaurant.com

"Belly-busting, multicourse" meals are the backbone of this "old-school Little Italy" vet where the "solid" Southern Italian cooking can be ordered either à la carte or in family-style prix fixes; maybe the decor "leaves much to be desired", but "service is "prompt" and the pricing "fair."

L&B Spumoni Gardens *Ice Cream/Pizza* | 23 | 11 | 16 | $26 |

Gravesend | 2725 86th St. (bet. W. 10th & 11th Sts.) | Brooklyn |
718-449-1230 | www.spumonigardens.com

This circa-1939 Gravesend "icon" is beloved for its "twin legends" –
Sicilian square pizza that "rules" and spumoni in portions to feed
"all the families in your building"; there's a "dated" dining room, but
in summer most opt to order at the window and "eat outside" with
the "neighborhood characters."

Landmarc *French* | 20 | 18 | 19 | $52 |

Midtown | Time Warner Ctr. | 10 Columbus Circle, 3rd fl. (60th St. at
B'way) | 212-823-6123
TriBeCa | 179 W. Broadway (bet. Leonard & Worth Sts.) | 212-343-3883
www.landmarc-restaurant.com

"Safe bets" for dining at "pleasing price points", Marc Murphy's
"popular" French bistros offer "hearty" Gallic fare paired with especially
economical wine lists; the TriBeCa original is more of a "neighborhood
destination", while the "big", "loud" TWC offshoot is a "godsend" for
"shoppers" and the "stroller" set.

Landmark Tavern *Pub Food* | 19 | 18 | 20 | $42 |

Hell's Kitchen | 626 11th Ave. (46th St.) | 212-247-2562 |
www.thelandmarktavern.org

Around for 140-plus years, this "off-the-beaten-path" Hell's Kitchen
tavern is deemed "worth the detour" for its "cozy olde NY" atmosphere
alone; grab a pint and some "standard" pub grub delivered by a "caring"
crew – "they don't make 'em like this anymore."

Land Thai Kitchen *Thai* | 22 | 12 | 18 | $31 |

West 80s | 450 Amsterdam Ave. (bet. 81st & 82nd Sts.) |
212-501-8121 | www.landthaikitchen.com

"Big on flavor" but not in decor or size, this UWS "neighborhood Thai"
dispenses "delicious" standards "quick" at "wallet-friendly" rates; since
"waits" are the norm at peak times, many elect for "takeout/delivery."

L & W Oyster Co. *Seafood* | 20 | 19 | 18 | $45 |

Flatiron | 254 Fifth Ave. (bet. 28th & 29th Sts.) | 212-203-7772 |
www.landwoyster.com

A "find" near Madison Square Park, this Flatiron seafooder dispenses "informal beach-style" favorites (fresh oysters, a lobster BLT) in airy, urban-
clam-shack environs; solid service and an overall "fun atmosphere" have
most plotting to "go back again" soon.

La Palapa *Mexican* | 23 | 20 | 21 | $36 |

East Village | 77 St. Marks Pl. (bet. 1st & 2nd Aves.) | 212-777-2537 |
www.lapalapa.com

"High-class Mexican" cuisine "cooked with love" is offered "cheap" and
served with "courtesy" at this East Village cantina; the "luscious margaritas" that pack "plenty of punch" take your mind off "scrunched" seating,
but "bring ear protection" at peak times.

	FOOD	DECOR	SERVICE	COST

L'Apicio *Italian*
23 | 22 | 22 | $63

East Village | 13 E. First St. (bet. Bowery & 2nd Ave.) | 212-533-7400 | www.lapicio.com

An "early hit" with "fashionable" folk, this "wonderful" East Village Italian from the Dell'anima/L'Artusi team offers a "refined", pasta-centric menu in a big, "glam" room; "appreciative" service, an "amazing bar scene" and a "bustling" mood complete the "trendy" picture.

La Pizza Fresca *Italian/Pizza*
▽ 23 | 19 | 22 | $47

Flatiron | 31 E. 20th St. (bet. B'way & Park Ave. S.) | 212-598-0141 | www.lapizzafresca.com

It was a "granddaddy of the artisanal pizza trend", and this Flatiron "favorite" continues to turn out "superior" Neapolitan pies along with "terrific pasta"; "attentive" staffers with "smiles on all faces" help maintain the "relaxed" mood.

La Pulperia *Pan-Latin*
▽ 22 | 16 | 22 | $47

Midtown | 371 W. 46th St. (bet. 8th & 9th Aves.) | 212-956-3055 | www.pulperianyc.com

A "sweet addition to Restaurant Row", this "charming" yearling offers a "delicious" Pan-Latin menu with a seafood focus, plus a raw bar and "inventive" cocktails; its name means 'general store', and the rustic interior is festooned with Mexican floor tiles and shelves brimming with liquor bottles and colorful produce.

La Rivista *Italian*
20 | 16 | 20 | $50

Midtown | 313 W. 46th St. (bet. 8th & 9th Aves.) | 212-245-1707 | www.larivistanyc.com

"Conveniently located on Restaurant Row", this Theater District "standby" offers "reliable" Italian basics at "sensible" tabs for those who "want to be sure to make their curtain"; some say the decor "could use updating", but others like the "old-school" vibe and nightly piano playing.

L'Artusi *Italian*
26 | 23 | 24 | $71

West Village | 228 W. 10th St. (bet. Bleecker & Hudson Sts.) | 212-255-5757 | www.lartusi.com

"Inspired Italian cuisine" prepared with "quality ingredients and flair", "precise" service and a "lovely", "lively" setting explain why it's always so "crowded" at this West Village "scene" that's a "perfect date spot"; sure, it's "pricey", but no one cares after uncorking a bottle from the "serious" wine list.

La Sirène *French*
▽ 25 | 18 | 24 | $59

Hudson Square | 558½ Broome St. (Varick St.) | 212-925-3061 | www.lasirenenyc.com

"Decadent" preparations of "traditional" French cuisine shuttled by "charming" staffers are the lures at this "small" Hudson Square bistro; though seating is "tight", loyalists call it "cozy" and all agree on the "exceptional" service.

Las Ramblas *Spanish*
▽ 23 | 15 | 19 | $48

West Village | 170 W. Fourth St. (bet. Cornelia & Jones Sts.) | 646-415-7924

Like "spending a couple of hours in Barcelona" without the airfare, this "tiny" West Village tapas joint offers "fantastic" tidbits and "delicious sangria" for little dinero; staffers "make sure everyone's happy" despite "noisy", crowded conditions, so just "grab a table and start ordering."

La Superior *Mexican*

▽ | 23 | 12 | 15 | $21

Williamsburg | 295 Berry St. (bet. 2nd & 3rd Sts.) | Brooklyn | 718-388-5988 | www.lasuperiornyc.com

"Fantastic tiny tacos" and offbeat takes on Mexican street food hit the trifecta for "tasty, authentic, cheap" satisfaction at this Williamsburg "standout"; the "cramped", undistinguished setting and cash-only policy don't keep the neighborhood masses from queuing up.

Lattanzi *Italian*

23 | 20 | 22 | $60

Midtown | 361 W. 46th St. (bet. 8th & 9th Aves.) | 212-315-0980 | www.lattanzinyc.com

Something "special" on Restaurant Row, this "better-than-average" Italian separates itself from the pack with an unusual post-theater menu of Roman-Jewish specialties; otherwise, it's a strictly "old-guard" experience with "gracious" service and a "charming" setting featuring lots of "dining nooks and crannies."

Laut *Malaysian/Thai*

20 | 14 | 17 | $30

Union Square | 15 E. 17th St. (bet. B'way & 5th Ave.) | 212-206-8989 | www.lautnyc.com

Southeast Asia's "vast variety of flavors" get their due at this Union Square purveyor of "authentic", "delicious" dishes from Malaysia, Thailand and beyond; there's "no ambiance" to speak of, but "affordable" tabs and "friendly" service keep things copacetic; P.S. a Williamsburg offshoot is in the works.

Lavagna *Italian*

25 | 18 | 21 | $49

East Village | 545 E. Fifth St. (bet. Aves. A & B) | 212-979-1005 | www.lavagnanyc.com

At this "unassuming" yet "polished" Alphabet City "gem", "terrific" Tuscan cooking, "attentive" staffers and "cozy, brick-walled" digs work "romantic" wonders; factor in "affordable" prices, and it's no wonder the "tight" digs are "always crowded."

La Vara *Spanish*

26 | 22 | 25 | $55

Cobble Hill | 268 Clinton St. (bet. Verandah Pl. & Warren St.) | Brooklyn | 718-422-0065 | www.lavarany.com

"Every morsel is delicious" at this "exotic" Cobble Hill Spaniard where tapas featuring "Moorish and Jewish influences" are paired with an "accessible" wine list; "warm, well-trained" servers patrol the "simple, minimalist" setting that's "high energy" to some, "crazy busy" to others.

La Vigna *Italian*

24 | 19 | 22 | $40

Forest Hills | 100-11 Metropolitan Ave. (70th Ave.) | Queens | 718-268-4264 | www.lavignany.com

Merging "local charm" and "big-city quality", this Forest Hills "standout" rolls out "excellent" Italian food conveyed by "nice-to-see-you-again" staffers; the "simple" setting is similarly in keeping with the "down-home" neighborhood feel.

	FOOD	DECOR	SERVICE	COST

La Villa Pizzeria *Pizza*
22 | **18** | **21** | **$29**

Mill Basin | Key Food Plaza | 6610 Ave. U (66th St.) | Brooklyn | 718-251-8030
Park Slope | 261 Fifth Ave. (bet. 1st St. & Garfield Pl.) | Brooklyn | 718-499-9888
Howard Beach | Lindenwood Shopping Ctr. | 8207 153rd Ave. (82nd St.) | Queens | 718-641-8259
www.lavillaparkslope.com

These "basic neighborhood red-sauce" joints dish out "first-rate" pizzas along with a "lengthy" roster of "comfort" Italian items; nondescript settings and "loud" acoustics are offset by "modest" tabs.

Lavo *Italian*
19 | **19** | **18** | **$70**

Midtown | 39 E. 58th St. (bet. Madison & Park Aves.) | 212-750-5588 | www.lavony.com

It's one "crazy" "scene" at this "pricey" Midtown Italian that rivals nearby sibling Tao as a "meet-and-mingle" hub for "Botox-and-high-heels" types and the "expense-account suits" who love them; just bring "earplugs" and an appetite – the "garlicky" fare is "surprisingly good" – and then "go party" in the "thumping" downstairs club.

Lazzara's *Pizza*
▽ **23** | **10** | **14** | **$20**

Midtown | 221 W. 38th St. (bet. 7th & 8th Aves.) | 212-944-7792 | www.lazzaraspizza.com

"Square and superb" sums up the thin-crust pizzas produced by this "under-the-radar" Midtown "staple"; its second-floor "hole-in-the-wall" setting is a "busy" scene at lunch, so plenty procure pies to go.

NEW Lea *Italian/Pizza*
– | **–** | **–** | **M**

Ditmas Park | 1022 Cortelyou Rd. (bet. Coney Island Ave. & Stratford Rd.) | Brooklyn | 718-928-7100 | www.leabrooklyn.com

From the team behind Mimi's Hummus and the Castello Plan, this Ditmas Park Italian delivers a midpriced lineup led by pizzas from a wood-burning oven; with a roomy bar and sidewalk seating, its airy, vibrant quarters fill up fast – particularly at brunch.

Le Bernardin *French/Seafood*
29 | **28** | **29** | **$162**

Midtown | 155 W. 51st St. (bet. 6th & 7th Aves.) | 212-554-1515 | www.le-bernardin.com

"Nothing short of amazing", this "stellar" Midtown stalwart via Maguy Le Coze and chef Eric Ripert showcases an "elaborate" menu of French seafood and "extraordinary wines", served by a "deft" team in "luxuri-ous" environs – no surprise, it's garnered No. 1 Food and Service honors in NYC; though the prix fixe-only dinners are "very expensive" (starting at $135), admirers insist this "magical" experience is "not just a meal", but rather "dining perfection"; P.S. Aldo Sohm, a new nearby wine bar at 151 W. 51st St., offers a well-curated wine list along with small plates, cheese and charcuterie.

Le Bilboquet *French*
21 | **19** | **15** | **$83**

East 60s | 20 E. 60th St. (bet. Madison & Park Aves.) | 212-751-3036
Back after a hiatus in new, "bigger" digs, this UES French bistro serves an "upscale" menu to "power" types, "Euro locals" and "Park Avenue dowagers"; the "attitude is still there", however, so if you're not a regular,

brace yourself for "rude" treatment, though the "outrageous" pricing extends to all.

Le Cirque *French* 24 | 25 | 25 | $101

East Midtown | 151 E. 58th St. (bet. Lexington & 3rd Aves.) | 212-644-0202 | www.lecirque.com

Sirio Maccioni's "sophisticated" East Midtown "classic" lives up to its "stellar reputation" thanks to "dynamite" French fare and "crisp" service; though some folks are "perfectly happy" hitting the "more affordable" cafe, for others only the jacket-required main room – with its "gorgeous", circus-inspired Adam Tihany design and "stratospheric" cost – will do.

L'Ecole *French* 23 | 20 | 22 | $56

SoHo | The International Culinary Ctr. | 462 Broadway (Grand St.) | 212-219-3300 | www.lecolenyc.com

"Eager students" cook for you at this "charming" International Culinary Center trainer French restaurant in SoHo; with "delicious" execution that's "often as good as the pros" and prix fixe menus proffering "excellent value", its "occasional slip-ups" are easy to overlook.

Le Colonial *French/Vietnamese* 23 | 24 | 21 | $63

East Midtown | 149 E. 57th St. (bet. Lexington & 3rd Aves.) | 212-752-0808 | www.lecolonialnyc.com

At this "gorgeous" East Midtowner, you'll be "transported to an exotic place" where the spirit of 1920s "colonial Indochine" is in the air and on the plate in the form of "terrific" French-Vietnamese fare; the "old Saigon" sensibility extends to a "comfortable upstairs lounge", though prices are strictly modern day.

Left Bank *American* 24 | 22 | 23 | $52

West Village | 117 Perry St. (Greenwich St.) | 212-727-1170 | www.leftbanknewyork.com

European-influenced New American fare is "served with care" at this West Villager where the "attractive" space is suitable for conversation; "decent prices" further its status as a solid "neighborhood hangout."

Le Gamin *French* ▽ 21 | 17 | 18 | $29

Greenpoint | 108 Franklin St. (Noble St.) | Brooklyn | 718-770-7918
Prospect Heights | 556 Vanderbilt Ave. (bet. Bergen & Dean Sts.) | Brooklyn | 718-789-5171
www.legamin.com

"If you want to feel like you've stepped out of the bustle of the city and into a quaint cafe in France", check out these "simple" Greenpoint and Prospect Heights bistros known for their signature crêpes; the "comforting" French fare comes at "reasonable" rates, and "sweet" back gardens seal the deal.

Legend *Chinese* 20 | 13 | 15 | $29

Chelsea | 88 Seventh Ave. (bet. 15th & 16th Sts.) | 212-929-1778 | www.legendbarrestaurant.com
West 70s | 127 W. 72nd St. (bet. Amsterdam & Columbus Aves.) | 917-441-4793 | www.legend72.com
West 100s | 258 W. 109th St. (bet. Amsterdam Ave. & B'way) | 212-222-4800 | www.legendupperwest.com

"Your mouth won't feel the same" after sampling the "super-hot", "super-good" Sichuan fare at these affordable Chinese favorites; happy-hour deals at the "A-1 bar" draw a "vibrant crowd", and timid palates should know that the menu also features less fiery dishes.

Le Gigot *French* 24 | 19 | 24 | $61

West Village | 18 Cornelia St. (bet. Bleecker & 4th Sts.) | 212-627-3737 | www.legigotrestaurant.com

"Everything's right" at this "petite" West Village bistro, a "Francophile's dream" where "meticulously prepared" Provençal dishes come via a "superb" staff; granted, the seating's "tight" and the tabs "pricey", but it's hard to beat for a "romantic dinner for two."

Le Grainne Cafe *French* ▽ 22 | 18 | 20 | $32

Chelsea | 183 Ninth Ave. (21st St.) | 646-486-3000 | www.legrainnecafe.com

A "charming breath of France" blows your way at this "cozy" Chelsea French cafe where "delightful vittles" and birdbath-size café au laits supply "simple" comfort; habitués say the "crowded" digs and "occasionally distracted" service are the trade-offs for feeling "transported."

Le Marais *French/Kosher/Steak* 21 | 16 | 17 | $62

Midtown | 150 W. 46th St. (bet. 6th & 7th Aves.) | 212-869-0900 | www.lcmarais.net

"If you're a kosher carnivore", this Theater District French "staple" comes across with "excellent steaks" that pass muster with the highest authority; maybe the service "doesn't match" the food quality and the surrounds are "forgettable", but it's generally "packed" all the same.

The Lemon Ice King of Corona *Ice Cream* 25 | 6 | 18 | $6

Corona | 52-02 108th St. (52nd Ave.) | Queens | 718-699-5133 | www.thelemonicekingofcorona.com

Loyal subjects say this 1940s Corona "legend" is "not to be missed" in the "high heat of summer" 'cause its Italian ices are the "very best" of the breed; after enduring the "long line" and choosing from a "multitude of flavors", complete the "stroll back in time" by "watching the old guys play bocce" in the park nearby.

Leopard at des Artistes *Italian* 22 | 26 | 23 | $84

West 60s | 1 W. 67th St. (bet. Columbus Ave. & CPW) | 212-787-8767 | www.theleopardnyc.com

Dining amid "sumptuous" Howard Chandler Christy murals always lifts the spirits at this "nicely done" Café des Artistes "reincarnation" near Lincoln Center; with a "breathtaking" space, "genuine" Italian fare and "personalized attention", it has a "luxury" that justifies the "bruises to your credit card" say its tony regulars.

Leo's Latticini *Italian/Sandwiches* ▽ 26 | 11 | 22 | $15

Corona | 46-02 104th St. (46th Ave.) | Queens | 718-898-6069

Mama's of Corona

Willets Point | Citi Field | 12301 Roosevelt Ave. (behind the scoreboard) | Queens | no phone

"Nobody makes a sandwich" like this Corona "old-school Italian deli" where the subs are "fit for royalty" and the mozz is among the "best in the boroughs"; its Citi Field stand services Mets fans on game days, but, unfortunately, without those "adorable ladies" behind the counter.

	FOOD	DECOR	SERVICE	COST

Le Pain Quotidien *Bakery/Belgian* | 18 | 15 | 15 | $25 |

Chelsea | 52 Ninth Ave. (bet. 14th & 15th Sts.) | 646-350-4789
East 60s | 833 Lexington Ave. (bet. 63rd & 64th Sts.) | 646-762-2209
NEW East 60s | 1270 First Ave. (bet. 68th & 69th Sts.) | 212-988-5001
East 70s | 252 E. 77th St. (bet. 2nd & 3rd Aves.) | 212-249-8600
East 80s | 1131 Madison Ave. (bet. 84th & 85th Sts.) | 212-327-4900
Flatiron | 931 Broadway (bet. 21st & 22nd Sts.) | 646-395-9926
Greenwich Village | 10 Fifth Ave. (8th St.) | 212-253-2324
Midtown | 922 Seventh Ave. (58th St.) | 212-757-0775
West 60s | 60 W. 65th St. (bet. B'way & CPW) | 212-721-4001
West 70s | 50 W. 72nd St. (bet. Columbus Ave. & CPW) | 212-712-9700
www.lepainquotidien.com
Additional locations throughout the NY area

For an "unfussy" "coffee-shop alternative", try this "quickie" Belgian bakery/cafe chain patronized for its "easy" menus (with "many organic choices") served in "rustic" rooms at "elbow-to-elbow" communal tables; "predictability" and "disorganized" service are a pain, but "inexpensive" tabs and "all-around-town" locations compensate.

Le Paris Bistrot *French* | ∇ 21 | 18 | 21 | $43 |

East 90s | 1312 Madison Ave. (93rd St.) | 212-289-0997 | www.leparisbistrot.com

A "nice whiff of Paris" in Carnegie Hill, this "quiet" French bistro serves a "reliable" menu in a high-ceilinged space that includes an upper dining loft; some find it on the "cramped" side, but the service is "friendly" and the tabs moderate.

Le Parisien *French* | 23 | 17 | 21 | $42 |

Kips Bay | 163 E. 33rd St. (bet. Lexington & 3rd Aves.) | 212-889-5489 | www.leparisiennyc.com

"Teleport" to the "banks of the Seine" via this "cozy" Kips Bay French bistro offering "excellent", "well-priced" renditions of "all the classics"; "charming" staffers compensate for "tiny" dimensions and help seal its standing as a local "winner."

Le Perigord *French* | 24 | 21 | 25 | $83 |

East Midtown | 405 E. 52nd St. (bet. FDR Dr. & 1st Ave.) | 212-755-6244 | www.leperigord.com

"Classic to the core", this circa-1964 exemplar of "the way fine dining used to be" offers "true French haute cuisine" in a "calm" Sutton Place room overseen by "pampering" staffers under the watchful eye of owner Georges Briguet; its "old-money" following calls it "pure pleasure", the ooh-la-la tabs notwithstanding.

Le Pescadeux *Seafood* | 21 | 18 | 22 | $54 |

SoHo | 90 Thompson St. (bet. Prince & Spring Sts.) | 212-966-0021 | www.lepescadeuxnyc.com

A slice of Quebec in SoHo, this "relaxed" French-Canadian seafood specialist offers "delicious" midpriced dishes in pairable half-orders, a "catchy" hook that diversifies your meal; "congenial" hospitality and occasional live music enhance the "inviting" ambiance.

	FOOD	DECOR	SERVICE	COST

Le Philosophe *French*

23 | 17 | 21 | $62

NoHo | 55 Bond St. (bet. Bowery & Lafayette St.) | 212-388-0038 | www.lephilosophe.us

"Delicious", age-old Gallic dishes – think frogs' legs, lobster Thermidor, duck à l'orange – turn up at this NoHo French bistro that's a hit with "locals" despite "tiny" dimensions and "humble" decor; "getting a table can be a challenge", but if you can identify all of the philosophers on the wall mural, your meal's free.

Le Relais de Venise L'Entrecôte *French/Steak*

21 | 18 | 20 | $43

East Midtown | 590 Lexington Ave. (52nd St.) | 212-758-3989 | www.relaisdevenise.com

It's all about "value" at this "unique" East Midtown French brasserie where the "one-trick-pony" menu consists only of steak frites and salad for a $29 fixed price; fans find it "quick and easy", though the no-reservations rule can make for waits at prime times.

Le Rivage *French*

21 | 16 | 21 | $47

Midtown | 340 W. 46th St. (bet. 8th & 9th Aves.) | 212-765-7374 | www.lerivagenyc.com

"Old-school" French dining is alive and well at this circa-1958 Restaurant Row survivor where the "middle-of-the-road" Gallic offerings are "consistent" and the staff "understands curtain time"; the digs may be "dated", but the post-theater $25 prix fixe is quite the "deal."

Les Halles *French/Steak*

20 | 16 | 17 | $50

Financial District | 15 John St. (bet. B'way & Nassau St.) | 212-285-8585
Kips Bay | 411 Park Ave. S. (bet. 28th & 29th Sts.) | 212-679-4111
www.leshalles.net

Ever "popular", these "vibrant" French brasseries are known for their "first-rate" steak frites, "dark" lighting and "noisy" decibels; though the "people-watching" can be "fun", "don't count on seeing" long-gone chef-at-large Anthony Bourdain.

Le Veau d'Or *French*

21 | 17 | 19 | $63

East 60s | 129 E. 60th St. (bet. Lexington & Park Aves.) | 212-838-8133

"Forgotten" French bistro classics work their "throwback" magic on loyal patrons of this circa-1937 Eastsider; though it's "had a full life" – and it shows – here's hoping it'll "continue forever."

Lexington Brass *American*

20 | 19 | 18 | $45

East Midtown | Hyatt 48 Lex Hotel | 517 Lexington Ave. (48th St.) | 212-392-5976 | www.lexingtonbrass.com

A location near Grand Central and a "decent" all-day roster of American comfort faves draw office workers and out-of-towners to this "fun", roomy Midtowner; the bar is appreciated for its "special cocktails" – including "custom Bloody Marys" at brunch – and staff that "keeps 'em flowing."

Le Zie *Italian*

20 | 14 | 19 | $47

Chelsea | 172 Seventh Ave. (bet. 20th & 21st Sts.) | 212-206-8686 | www.lezie.com

"High-end in quality but not in price" sums up the Venetian cuisine at this "lively" Chelsea Italian; regulars suggest the "back room" if quiet dining is preferred, and say "beware" the "daily specials" that sell for "much more" than the regular fare.

The Library at the Public *American*   18 | 21 | 18 | $55

Greenwich Village | Public Theater | 425 Lafayette St. (bet. Astor Pl. & 4th St.) | 212-539-8777 | www.thelibraryatthepublic.com

"Hidden away" upstairs at the Public Theater is this "gem" providing "pricey" American fare from chef Andrew Carmellini in "dark", "clubby" quarters with a "vibrant" bar scene; opinions are mixed on the food ("terrific" vs. "nothing special"), but all agree it "couldn't be easier before the show."

LIC Market *American*   25 | 21 | 23 | $31

Long Island City | 21-52 44th Dr. (23rd St.) | Queens | 718-361-0013 | www.licmarket.com

"One of the highlights of LIC" is this "homey-looking" "charmer" beloved for its "inventive-but-not-fussy" American fare with a "farm-to-table" ethos; with a "caring staff" and "good price point" to seal its "popularity", the "tight" quarters "fill up quickly", especially at brunch – if only "it were twice the size."

Lido *Italian*   24 | 20 | 22 | $46

Harlem | 2168 Frederick Douglass Blvd. (117th St.) | 646-490-8575 | www.lidoharlem.com

Harlem denizens declare you "don't need to go Downtown for first-rate Italian food" thanks to this "solid" Uptown player; its "skillfully prepared" dishes are served in "relaxed" environs by "friendly" staffers, with no letup in "quality" during the popular "bottomless-mimosa" brunch.

Liebman's Delicatessen *Deli/Kosher*   22 | 10 | 18 | $24

Riverdale | 552 W. 235th St. (Johnson Ave.) | Bronx | 347-227-0776 | www.liebmansdeli.com

For a "corned beef on rye, hold the cardiogram", check out this "quint-essential" kosher Jewish deli that's been a "Riverdale landmark" for "delicious", "stacked-high" sandwiches since 1953; it "hasn't changed in years" – as evidenced in the "faded" decor and "slapdash" service – but to fans it "never disappoints."

Lil' Frankie's Pizza *Italian/Pizza*   ∇ 25 | 16 | 19 | $40

East Village | 19 First Ave. (bet. 1st & 2nd Sts.) | 212-420-4900 | www.lilfrankies.com

Really "solid" Italian fare "without frills" at an "affordable price" is the signature of this "casual", cash-only East Villager, a sibling of Frank, Sauce and Supper; it offers "standout" Neapolitan pizzas, late hours and a "garden room", so it's no wonder it gets way-"crowded" at peak times.

Lincoln *Italian*   25 | 26 | 25 | $84

West 60s | Lincoln Ctr. | 142 W. 65th St. (bet. Amsterdam Ave. & B'way) | 212-359-6500 | www.lincolnristorante.com

"One to savor", this "civilized option" on the Lincoln Center campus matches chef Jonathan Benno's "exceptional" modern Italian cuisine with "immaculate" service in a "striking", "glass-walled" setting with an open kitchen; the "first-class" experience "costs an arm and a leg", but "you get what you pay for" pre-performance or on "that special occasion."

The Lion *American*

FOOD	DECOR	SERVICE	COST
24	23	20	$76

Greenwich Village | 62 W. Ninth St. (bet. 5th & 6th Aves.) |
212-353-8400 | www.thelionnyc.com

Chef-owner John DeLucie conjures up "old-school" NY at this "fashionable" Village American where a "huge skylight, eclectic art and photos" provide an apt backdrop for the "handsome, affluent crowd"; the "homey-yet-upscale" fare takes a backseat to the "stimulating" scene, but it's just as "delicious."

NEW Little Collins *Coffee*

FOOD	DECOR	SERVICE	COST
–	–	–	I

East Midtown | 667 Lexington Ave. (bet. 55th & 56th Sts.) |
212-308-1969 | www.littlecollinsnyc.com

Inspired by the coffeehouses of Melbourne, this East Midtowner produces its flat whites and other java drinks using Counter Culture beans and a state-of-the-art under-counter brewing system; there are Australian-accented sandwiches and other light bites, enjoyed on-premises by those lucky enough to nab a table.

NEW Little Lamb *Mongolian*

FOOD	DECOR	SERVICE	COST
–	–	–	M

Flushing | Sky View Ctr. | 40-24 College Point Blvd. (bet. 40th Rd. & Roosevelt Ave.) | Queens | 718-359-1668 | www.littlelambusa.com
Located amid big-box stores in a Flushing mall is this link of a Mongolian hot-pot chain from China, where every table is fitted with an induction cooker; diners select raw veggies and proteins (Australian lamb is the specialty) to drop into bubbling broth, with staffers guiding the uninitiated.

Little Muenster *Sandwiches*

FOOD	DECOR	SERVICE	COST
21	13	17	$15I

NEW Battery Park City | Hudson Eats | 200 Vesey St. (West St.) |
212-786-0186
Lower East Side | 100 Stanton St. (bet. Ludlow & Orchard Sts.) |
212-203-7197
www.littlemuenster.com

"Satisfy your grilled cheese cravings" at this "cute" LES "hole-in-the-wall" (with a counter in Hudson Eats), where fromage fanciers melt over the "awesome" cheese-centric sandwiches made from artisanal ingredients and toasted with "nice technique"; matched with "hearty" tomato soup, they "definitely hit the spot."

Littleneck *Seafood*

FOOD	DECOR	SERVICE	COST
23	21	22	$42

Gowanus | 288 Third Ave. (bet. Carroll & President Sts.) | Brooklyn |
718-522-1921
NEW Littleneck Outpost *Seafood*
Greenpoint | 128 Franklin St. (Milton St.) | Brooklyn | 718-363-3080
www.littleneckbrooklyn.com

"Wonderful" New England–style seafood washes up at this cash-only Gowanus clam shack and its new Greenpoint offshoot, where the "well-priced" roster ranges from "always-fresh" raw bar fare to steamers to rolls; "cozy", marine-themed quarters helps lure "hipster-looking locals" – as do the "great-deal" $1 oysters at happy hour.

| | FOOD | DECOR | SERVICE | COST |

Little Owl *American/Mediterranean*
| | 27 | 21 | 24 | $62 |

West Village | 90 Bedford St. (Grove St.) | 212-741-4695 |
www.thelittleowlnyc.com

"It's little for sure", but this "charming", "intimate" West Villager makes a sizable impression as "knowledgeable" servers set down chef Joey Campanaro's "terrific" Med–New American plates; "savvy foodies" find it "worth calling a month in advance" to land a "really difficult" reservation.

Little Poland *Diner/Polish*
| | 21 | 7 | 15 | $20 |

East Village | 200 Second Ave. (bet. 12th & 13th Sts.) | 212-777-9728
"Heaping portions" of "filling" Polish "diner food" comes "cheap as can be" at this "old-time" East Village "greasy spoon"; "drab" the interior may be, but wait till you taste those "perfect pierogi" – you couldn't do better in Gdansk.

NEW Little Prince *French*
| | ▽ 23 | 19 | 20 | $59 |

SoHo | 199 Prince St. (bet. MacDougal & Sullivan Sts.) | 212-335-0566 |
www.littleprincesoho.com

"Take a Francophile" to this "charming" SoHo bistro, where the "well-executed takes" on Gallic classics "pack a punch" – especially the "acclaimed French Onion Soup Burger"; the "cool crowd", "playful staff" and banquette-lined digs "straight out of the Left Bank" complete the "memorable" rendezvous.

Lobster Joint *New England/Seafood*
| | 22 | 16 | 18 | $31 |

NEW Lower East Side | 201 E. Houston St. (bet. Ludlow & Orchard Sts.) | 646-896-1110

Greenpoint | 1073 Manhattan Ave. (bet. Dupont & Eagle Sts.) | Brooklyn | 718-389-8990
www.lobsterjoint.com

"Lobster fresher than a Brooklyn waiter" is the lure at this "laid-back" Greenpoint seafood shack (with a "raffish" LES spin-off) that furnishes "quality" New England–style fare and "no-nonsense" cocktails "without cleaning out your wallet"; come summer, a "picnic-table backyard" expands the "simple" setup.

Locale *Italian*
| | ▽ 21 | 22 | 22 | $41 |

Astoria | 33-02 34th Ave. (33rd St.) | Queens | 718-729-9080 |
www.localeastoria.com

Set in a "residential" corner of Astoria, this midpriced "neighborhood gem" offers "cut-above-normal" Italian fare in a "pleasant", "SoHo"-like space; its "friendly" staff, enticing bar and weekend brunch are additional reasons it's "worth a try."

Locanda Verde *Italian*
| | 24 | 22 | 20 | $64 |

TriBeCa | Greenwich Hotel | 377 Greenwich St. (N. Moore St.) |
212-925-3797 | www.locandaverdenyc.com

Andrew Carmellini's "still-hot-as-a-pistol" TriBeCa Italian draws a "masters-of-the-universe" crowd (especially at "power breakfast") with an irresistible mix of "heavenly" cooking and "hip" vibrations; it's "bustling, loud and tight" at prime times, but the fact that reservations remain "hard to come by" speaks for itself.

	FOOD	DECOR	SERVICE	COST

Locanda Vini & Olii *Italian*
25 | 24 | 22 | $56

Clinton Hill | 129 Gates Ave. (bet. Cambridge Pl. & Grand Ave.) |
Brooklyn | 718-622-9202 | www.locandavinieolii.com

"Cool ex-pharmacy digs" with the "original cabinetry intact" are the
backdrop for "wonderful", "rustic" Northern Italian cooking at this
"idiosyncratic" Clinton Hill "hideaway"; staffers who "know exactly how
to make you feel welcome" are one more reason it's "always a treat."

Lodge *American*
∇ 22 | 21 | 19 | $31

Williamsburg | 318 Grand St. (Havemeyer St.) | Brooklyn |
718-486-9400 | www.lodgenyc.com

"Cure last night's hangover" at this Williamsburg brunch "favorite", a
"Saturday afternoon staple" for "inventive" midpriced American fare with
"plenty of vegetarian and vegan options"; set on a "relatively hopping"
corner, its rustic "cabin" space (antler chandeliers, tree-trunk tables)
includes outdoor seating and a take-out adjunct, General Store.

Lombardi's *Pizza*
24 | 14 | 16 | $25

NoLita | 32 Spring St. (bet. Mott & Mulberry Sts.) | 212-941-7994 |
www.firstpizza.com

This NoLita pizza "shrine", which claims to have been America's first pizzeria, still draws throngs with its "real-deal" coal-fired, thin-crust, "never-
miss" pies; it doesn't take plastic or reservations, and you may have to
"tussle with the tourists to get a table", but it's a true "slice of NY" – even
though it "doesn't do slices."

Lomzynianka *Polish*
∇ 25 | 14 | 20 | $21

Greenpoint | 646 Manhattan Ave. (bet. Nassau & Norman Aves.) |
Brooklyn | 718-389-9439 | www.lomzynianka.com

It's "classic Greenpoint" all the way at this local "treasure" with a "family-
owned feel" dishing up "wonderful" Polish home cooking that rises above
the "modest" decor; a BYO policy and "super-cheap" prices mean "you
can't go wrong" here – except when you try to pronounce the name.

London Lennie's *Seafood*
24 | 19 | 22 | $46

Middle Village | 63-88 Woodhaven Blvd. (bet. Fleet Ct. & Penelope
Ave.) | Queens | 718-894-8084 | www.londonlennies.com

It's been in operation since 1959 and this Middle Village seafooder
"hasn't lost its touch", putting forth a "wide selection" of "fresh", "unfussy" shore fare in "big", "nothing-fancy" digs; "fast" service and "fair
prices" are two more reasons it's "always crowded."

NEW Los Americanos *Pan-Latin*
– | – | – | M

TriBeCa | 305 Church St. (bet. Lispenard & Walker Sts.) | 212-680-0101 |
www.losamericanos.com

Unfussy Pan-Latin dishes from chef Ryan Skeen (ex Allen & Delancey)
and cocktails to match are the specialty of this all-day TriBeCa eatery;
the trim, wood-paneled space looks like a gussied-up diner, with seating
in booths and at the counter/bar.

NEW Los Tacos *Mexican*
– | – | – | I

Chelsea | Chelsea Mkt. | 75 Ninth Ave. (bet. 15th & 16th Sts.) |
212-256-0343 | www.lostacos1.com

Fans willing to brave chaotic Chelsea Market are rewarded by comida
from this Mexican stand vending a short roster of simple quesadillas

and tacos (natch); big glass jars on the counter hold aguas frescas, plus there's an array of condiments to customize your budget-priced grub. hed."

Lot 2 *American*
▽ 24 | 20 | 23 | $36

Park Slope | 687 Sixth Ave. (bet. 19th & 20th Sts.) | Brooklyn | 718-499-5623 | www.lot2restaurant.com

Locals find a lot to like at this "friendly" standby on the Park Slope/ Greenwood Heights border, from "reliably delicious", locavore-oriented American fare (including an "honest" grass-fed burger) to "inventive" pours from the bar's "cocktail mavens"; a "cozy" vibe and menu that "changes regularly" make it "easy to go often."

Lotus Blue *Chinese*
▽ 23 | 18 | 19 | $41

TriBeCa | 110 Reade St. (W. B'way) | 212-267-3777 | www.lotusbluebar.com

"Not your typical" Chinese joint, this "upscale", scarlet-walled TriBeCa find is a "fantastic" source of "authentic, well-prepared" cuisine with roots in the southwest's Yunnan Province; the bar's creative cocktails ensure the mood's anything but blue.

Loukoumi Taverna *Greek*
▽ 25 | 20 | 21 | $35

Astoria | 45-07 Ditmars Blvd. (bet. 45th & 46th Sts.) | Queens | 718-626-3200 | www.loukoumitaverna.com

"Excellent", "authentic" taverna fare leads the charge at this "warm, inviting" Astoria Greek; it's located "a bit away" from the main neighborhood action, but "affordable" tabs and a back garden clinch the "good-on-all-counts" endorsement.

Louro *American/Portuguese*
26 | 23 | 26 | $62

West Village | 142 W. 10th St. (bet. Greenwich Ave. & Waverly Pl.) | 212-206-0606 | www.louronyc.com

"Innovative" chef David Santos' "passion shows through" in his "fantastic", Portuguese-influenced American cuisine at this "memorable" West Villager that also boasts "standout service" and an "inviting", "unstuffy" feel; on Monday nights it morphs into the Nossa Mesa Supper Club, presenting intriguingly themed tasting menus that "always impress."

Lucali *Pizza*
27 | 20 | 21 | $29

Carroll Gardens | 575 Henry St. (bet. Carroll St. & 1st Pl.) | Brooklyn | 718-858-4086 | www.lucali.com

Wood-fired-oven pies to "dream about" plus "ethereal" calzones ensure this "rustic", cash-only Carroll Gardens standout more than "holds its own" as a pizza-lover's "must"; yes, its "small" dimensions and no-reservations policy make it an "ordeal" to get in, but that "hellishly long" wait "isn't for nothing" – and "it's BYO to boot."

Luce *Italian*
20 | 16 | 19 | $48

West 60s | 2014 Broadway (bet. 68th & 69th Sts.) | 212-724-1400 | www.lucenyc.com

Proximity to Lincoln Center is the "primary draw" at this "convenient" Italian serving "tasty, varied" traditional dishes via "timely" servers; its "no-frills" interior can get "crowded" and "noisy" at peak times, but the sidewalk tables are ideal for "watching the passersby."

Lucien *French*

▽ 23 | 14 | 20 | $53

East Village | 14 First Ave. (1st St.) | 212-260-6481 | www.luciennyc.com
"Charming" owner Lucien Bahaj's East Village French "favorite" presents "first-rate bistro" classics in "convivial" quarters that will "take you to Paris in a flash"; ok, it's on the "cramped" side, but tell that to its regulars who "leave with a smile every time."

NEW Lucky Luna *Chinese/Mexican*

– | – | – | I

Greenpoint | 167 Nassau Ave. (Diamond St.) | Brooklyn | 718-383-6038 | www.luckyluna-ny.com
Mexican and Taiwanese flavors mingle at this casual Greenpoint eatery exploring the street foods of both cultures with its ethically sourced meats and local ingredients tucked into tacos and steamed bao; the simple space's arty feel matches the bar's playful cocktails.

Luke's Lobster *Seafood*

24 | 12 | 17 | $25

NEW East Midtown | 685 Third Ave. (bet. 43rd & 44th Sts.) | 646-657-0066
East 80s | 242 E. 81st St. (bet. 2nd & 3rd Aves.) | 212-249-4241
East Village | 93 E. Seventh St. (bet. Ave. A & 1st Ave.) | 212-387-8487
Financial District | 26 S. William St. (bet. Beaver & Broad Sts.) | 212-747-1700
Midtown | Plaza Food Hall | 1 W. 59th St. (5th Ave.) | 646-755-3227
West 80s | 426 Amsterdam Ave. (bet. 80th & 81st Sts.) | 212-877-8800
Dumbo | 11 Water St. (bet. New Dock & Old Fulton Sts.) | Brooklyn | 917-882-7516
www.lukeslobster.com
"Like a crack addiction" for "lobster-roll aficionados", these "go-to" seafood shacks supply an "incredibly fresh" version "loaded" with "succulent chunks" of meat and "no filler"; expect to spend a few clams, and be ready for "bare-bones" settings that mean takeout may be a "better idea."

Luksus *American*

▽ 23 | 22 | 24 | $124

Greenpoint | 615 Manhattan Ave. (bet. Driggs & Nassau Aves.) | Brooklyn | 718-389-6034 | www.luksusnyc.com
Scandinavian flavors and a "creative" spark enliven the "brilliant" New American tasting menus at this Greenpoint hideaway tucked in Tørst's back room; the striking light-wood space with an open kitchen is "full of beautiful Brooklyn people" who say the $95 set price (plus an "amazing" beer pairing option) is "worth every penny."

Lulu & Po *American*

▽ 25 | 20 | 22 | $43

Fort Greene | 154 Carlton Ave. (bet. Myrtle & Willoughby Aves.) | Brooklyn | 917-435-3745 | www.luluandpo.com
Fort Greene denizens "adore" this "tiny" neighborhood "secret" and its "inventive, consistently delicious" New American small plates; the "top-notch" team manning the funky space also furnishes "fantastic cocktails", and the tabs won't put you in the po-house.

Lupa *Italian*

24 | 18 | 22 | $63

Greenwich Village | 170 Thompson St. (bet. Bleecker & Houston Sts.) | 212-982-5089 | www.luparestaurant.com
Just "like home" – but "with incredible food" – this "informal" Villager is a showcase for Mario Batali's "simple" yet "flavorful" Roman dishes and

"terrific wines" dispatched in "rustic" digs by a "good-humored" crew; "reasonable prices" offset the "seating squeeze" and "boisterous" decibels ("lunch is quieter"), and regulars report that "advance reservations" are a must.

Lure Fishbar *Seafood*
24 | 23 | 21 | $64

SoHo | 142 Mercer St. (Prince St.) | 212-431-7676 | www.lurefishbar.com

It's "quite the scene" at this "packed" SoHo cellar seafooder where the "fresh" catch is "perfectly cooked" and on par with the "classy", "cruise-ship" decor; though tabs are steep and the "ebullient", "mixed-age" crowd can kick up a racket, most consider it an "all-around winner."

Lusardi's *Italian*
25 | 20 | 24 | $68

East 70s | 1494 Second Ave. (bet. 77th & 78th Sts.) | 212-249-2020 | www.lusardis.com

"Friendly" owner Mario Lusardi oversees the "vintage poster"–lined room at this longtime UES "institution" where the Tuscan food is as "terrific" as the "gracious" service and "old-fashioned style"; its "adult", "high-end crowd" doesn't mind the "expensive" checks, given that it has "maintained its quality over the years."

Luzzo's *Pizza*
25 | 15 | 20 | $29

East Village | 211 First Ave. (bet. 12th & 13th Sts.) | 212-473-7447
NEW **Brooklyn Heights** | 145 Atlantic Ave. (bet. Clinton & Henry Sts.) | Brooklyn | 718-855-6400
www.luzzospizza.com

Fans "thank the pizza gods" for these "no-frills" joints, where "superior" Neapolitan-style pies emerge from coal-fired ovens with enough "authenticity" to "make an Italian grandma proud"; they're kinda "dumpy" and often "jammed", but the Brooklyn Heights follow-up to the East Village original boasts a back patio.

Lychee House *Chinese*
∇ 23 | 16 | 20 | $47

East Midtown | 141 E. 55th St. (bet. Lexington & 3rd Aves.) | 212-753-3900 | www.lycheehouse.com

Ranking a "notch above most", this East Midtown Chinese offers a "wide variety" of "well-prepared", midpriced "fine Shanghainese and Malaysian" dishes, plus "inventive dim sum", backed by libations from a full bar; aside from "waiters in tuxes", ambiance ain't the focus here.

Mable's Smokehouse *BBQ*
∇ 23 | 15 | 18 | $32

Williamsburg | 44 Berry St. (11th St.) | Brooklyn | 718-218-6655 | www.mablessmokehouse.com

Get your "BBQ fix" at this "spacious", "laid-back" Williamsburg joint where the "plentiful" ribs, brisket and pulled pork pack "bold and robust flavors" and are "priced just right"; "cafeteria-style ordering" and "shared tables" bolster the "transports-you-to-Tennessee" vibe.

Macao Trading Co. *Chinese/Portuguese*
∇ 21 | 23 | 21 | $51

TriBeCa | 311 Church St. (bet. Lispenard & Walker Sts.) | 212-431-8750 | www.macaonyc.com

Channeling a 1940s "Macao gambling parlor", this "dazzling", bi-level TriBeCan offers plentiful "eye candy" to go with its Chinese-Portuguese chow; late-night, it turns "club"-like – "loud and crowded" with uneven service – but most are having too much "fun" to care.

	FOOD	DECOR	SERVICE	COST

Macelleria *Italian/Steak*
24 | 21 | 20 | $70

Meatpacking District | 48 Gansevoort St. (bet. Greenwich & Washington Sts.) | 212-741-2555 | www.macelleria.com

"When you want some pasta with your steak", try this "buzzy" Meatpacking Italian chophouse whose "unadorned" fare "doesn't disappoint" but also "doesn't come cheap"; it boasts a "witty butcher theme" indoors, while alfresco seats afford prime "MPD crowd"–watching.

Machiavelli *Italian*
23 | 24 | 21 | $49

West 80s | 519 Columbus Ave. (85th St.) | 212-724-2658 | www.machiavellinyc.com

"Dine like a prince" at this "elegant", three-meal-a-day UWS Italian, where plush upholstered chairs, candelabras and "gorgeous" "Renaissance"-inspired murals – not to mention live classical music most nights – set the "romantic" tone; the "pricey", "carefully prepared" Northern Italian fare is somewhat more down to earth (pastas, pizzas).

Macondo *Pan-Latin*
▽ 23 | 21 | 21 | $44

Lower East Side | 157 E. Houston St. (bet. Allen & Eldridge Sts.) | 212-473-9900 | www.macondonyc.com

This "friendly", "lively" Lower Eastsider "transports you to urban Latin America" with its "clever" decor and "flavor-packed", "street food"–inspired small plates washed down with "strong" "tropical" cocktails; it hosts a *muy* "happening bar scene", so be ready for "crowds and noise."

Madangsui *Korean*
▽ 23 | 14 | 18 | $40

Midtown | 35 W. 35th St. (bet. 5th & 6th Aves.) | 212-564-9333 | www.madangsui.com

Koreatown cognoscenti "head straight for the BBQ" at this "authentic" Seoul-fooder where the meat hits the grill at your table and an "efficient" crew keeps the proceedings on track; there's "not much" in the way of decor, but then the "long waits" on weekends aren't for the scenery.

Madiba *S African*
▽ 24 | 21 | 20 | $42

Fort Greene | 195 DeKalb Ave. (bet. Adelphi St. & Carlton Ave.) | Brooklyn | 718-855-9190 | www.madibarestaurant.com

For a "real taste of South Africa", hit this "unassuming, relaxed" Fort Greene "hangout" that feels "like a vacation" thanks to its "cool" eclectic look, "comforting", "affordable" fare and "warm" service (just "don't be in a rush"); regulars note it's "the place to watch futbol/ World Cup games."

Madison Bistro *French*
23 | 19 | 21 | $52

Midtown | 238 Madison Ave. (bet. 37th & 38th Sts.) | 212-447-1919 | www.madisonbistro.com

"Every neighborhood should have a local bistro" like this Midtown "sleeper" that's appreciated for its "quality" French classics and prix fixe deals; "well-behaved" locals are drawn to its "friendly" vibe and "relaxing" (if "generic") room that's "conducive to conversation."

Madison's *Italian*
▽ 21 | 16 | 21 | $42

Riverdale | 5686 Riverdale Ave. (bet. 258th & 259th Sts.) | Bronx | 718-543-3850

"One of the more upscale" options on Riverdale's "main drag", this "popular" Italian fallback features "fresh, well-prepared" fare delivered by an "attentive" crew; those who "don't want to go" to Manhattan call it a "safe" bet.

Maharlika *Filipino*

∇ 21 | 17 | 19 | $42

East Village | 111 First Ave. (bet. 6th & 7th Sts.) | 646-392-7880 | www.maharlikanyc.com

Filipino food gets "redefined" at this "hip" East Villager that jump-starts the "not-mainstream" cuisine with some modern "twists" (Spam fries, anyone?); its "enthusiastic audience" happily overlooks the kinda "tight" conditions given the overall "cozy" mood, "warm" service and bargain tabs.

Maialino *Italian*

25 | 23 | 24 | $68

Gramercy Park | Gramercy Park Hotel | 2 Lexington Ave. (21st St.) | 212-777-2410 | www.maialinonyc.com

"Another triumph for Danny Meyer", this "top-shelf" take on a Roman trattoria facing Gramercy Park features "exceptional" Italian fare – notably the "mouthwatering roast suckling pig" – from a "warm", "efficient" staff; with a "convivial" crowd filling its "simple but tasteful" space, the "only downside" is it's "hard to score a reservation."

Maison Harlem *French*

21 | 21 | 18 | $38

Manhattanville | 341 St. Nicholas Ave. (127th St.) | 212-222-9224 | www.maisonharlem.com

Like a little "chunk of Paris" transported to NYC, this all-day bistro "gem" on the Harlem/Manhattanville border supplies "solid" French classics in "super-cozy" quarters with a "vintage" vibe (boosted by live jazz on Monday nights); it's a "bustling scene" that expands out onto the sidewalk in warmer months.

Maison Kayser *Bakery/French*

22 | 17 | 17 | $31

East 70s | 1294 Third Ave. (74th St.) | 212-744-3100
NEW **East 80s** | 1535 Third Ave. (74th St.) | 212-744-3100
NEW **Flatiron** | 921 Broadway (21st St.) | 212-979-1600
NEW **Midtown** | 8 W. 40th St. (bet. 5th & 6th Aves.) | 212-354-2300
Midtown | 1800 Broadway (bet. CPS & 58th St.) | 212-245-4100
www.maisonkayserusa.com

Beloved for their "heavenly" French pastries and breads, these all-day outposts of a Parisian patisserie/cafe chain are "favorites" for "glorious breakfasts" and "light lunches" in "plain but modern" settings; they're "slightly pricey" and "frenetic" at prime times, but the "elegant clientele" keeps jamming in "cheek-by-jowl."

Malatesta Trattoria *Italian*

24 | 18 | 21 | $49

West Village | 649 Washington St. (Christopher St.) | 212-741-1207 | www.malatestatrattoria.com

"Wonderful" trattoria staples at "reasonable", cash-only rates mean for most this "friendly", "popular" way West Village Italian is well "worth" the "long waits" at prime times; the "simple" interior gets "crowded and noisy", but in summer "sidewalk dining" offers a bit more elbow room.

Malecon *Dominican*

20 | 10 | 16 | $22

Washington Heights | 4141 Broadway (175th St.) | 212-927-3812
West 90s | 764 Amsterdam Ave. (bet. 97th & 98th Sts.) | 212-864-5648

continued

Kingsbridge | 5592 Broadway (231st St.) | Bronx | 718-432-5155
www.maleconrestaurants.com

"If you're looking for a fix" of "super-good" "traditional" Dominican fare, it's "hard to beat" these "favorites" known especially for their "mmm" rotisserie chicken slathered in "garlicky goodness"; "huge portions" at "bargain" prices mean most don't mind if the settings are on the "tacky" side.

Maloney & Porcelli *Steak*   25 | 22 | 24 | $77

Midtown | 37 E. 50th St. (bet. Madison & Park Aves.) | 212-750-2233 | www.maloneyandporcelli.com

"Expense accounts" were made for Alan Stillman's Midtown chop-house, a "class operation all the way" where the steaks are "prepared to perfection" – and the "one-of-a-kind" pork shank "may be even better"; "clubby" decor and "friendly" service keep regulars regular, while the nightly wine dinner is an "exceptional value" ("stagger home carefully").

Mamoun's *Mideastern*   23 | 8 | 18 | $10

East Village | 22 St. Marks Pl. (bet. 2nd & 3rd Aves.) | 212-387-7747
Greenwich Village | 119 MacDougal St. (bet. Minetta Ln. & W. 3rd St.) | 212-674-8685
www.mamouns.com

"Tasty and hasty" sums up these cross-Village Middle Eastern "favorites", whose "awesome" falafel and shawarma "can't be beat for cheap, filling eats" served into "the wee hours"; "bare-bones" digs with a serious "space crunch" don't keep them from "bustling."

Mandoo Bar *Korean*   23 | 12 | 18 | $22

Midtown | 2 W. 32nd St. (bet. B'way & 5th Ave.) | 212-279-3075 | www.mandoobarnyc.com

"Man oh mandoo" – the "freshest", "fast and fab" dumplings made right in front of you are the main event at this "reliable" Garment District Korean; its "no-decor" digs are "small" and "often crowded", but "cheap" prices compensate.

Manducatis *Italian*   22 | 16 | 22 | $44

Long Island City | 13-27 Jackson Ave. (47th Ave.) | Queens | 718-729-4602 | www.manducatis.com

Manducatis Rustica *Ice Cream/Pizza*

Long Island City | 46-33 Vernon Blvd. (bet. 46th & 47th Sts.) | Queens | 718-937-1312 | www.manducatisrustica.com

"You expect Tony Bennett to arrive" any minute at this "warm", "family-run" LIC Italian supplying "wonderful" "homestyle" fare and wines from a "deep" list (plus there's the "scaled-down" Rustica offshoot focusing on pizza and gelato); yes, the look may be "dated", but loyalists say that only "adds to the charm."

Manetta's *Italian*   ∇ 24 | 18 | 22 | $37

Long Island City | 10-76 Jackson Ave. (11th St.) | Queens | 718-786-6171

"Delish" Italiana "straight out of nonna's kitchen" – including "fantastic" wood-fired pizza – and service that's "all smiles" have locals calling this

LIC "mainstay" the "perfect neighborhood restaurant"; "family-run" and kid-friendly, it "exudes comfort", especially in winter before the fireplace.

Manzo *Italian/Steak*
▽ 24 | 19 | 22 | $70

Flatiron | Eataly | 200 Fifth Ave. (bet. 23rd & 24th Sts.) | 212-229-2180 | www.eataly.com

The sole "white-tablecloth" option within Eataly, the Batali-Bastianich team's Flatiron "foodie mecca", this "carnivore heaven" presents a "*delizioso*" beef-centric Italian menu that also features "wonderful fresh pastas"; being located in a "bustling", "noisy" market is "not the sexiest", and "you pay for the privilege" – but to most it's "worth every hard-earned penny."

Má Pêche *American*
23 | 18 | 21 | $68

Midtown | Chambers Hotel | 15 W. 56th St. (bet. 5th & 6th Aves.) | 212-757-5878 | www.momofuku.com

With the "welcome" addition of "dim sum–style" plates to complement its "delightful" shared dishes, David Chang's "upbeat" Midtown New American maintains its rep for "creativity"; distractions from decor that "could be cozier" include large-format spreads for groups and "the best" sweets from Milk Bar upstairs.

Marc Forgione *American*
25 | 23 | 23 | $83

TriBeCa | 134 Reade St. (bet. Greenwich & Hudson Sts.) | 212-941-9401 | www.marcforgione.com

Iron Chef Marc Forgione "takes comfort food to a new level" at this "candlelit, characterful" TriBeCa New American declared "a winner all around" thanks to its "lovely" "upscale lodge" decor and "wonderful" "pro" service; it's a "perfect date" place – just book far ahead and plan on a "pricey" tab.

Marcony *Italian*
25 | 22 | 23 | $72

Kips Bay | 184 Lexington Ave. (bet. 31st & 32nd Sts.) | 646-837-6020 | www.marconyusa.com

When an "Italian vacation" isn't in the cards, there's always this Kips Bay "standout" whose "fantastic" classic dishes with "service to match" arrive in "Capri-comes-to-NY" digs (including "sidewalk seating"); given the "all-around wonderful" experience, fans don't blink at the "pricey" tab and "out-of-the-way" locale.

Marco Polo *Italian*
▽ 23 | 21 | 21 | $54

Carroll Gardens | 345 Court St. (Union St.) | Brooklyn | 718-852-5015 | www.marcopoloristorante.com

"Old-school Italian in every respect", this Carroll Gardens vet presents "upscale red-sauce" fare in a "warm" space complete with fireplace and murals; "treat-you-like-family" service and an "amazing happy hour" are two more reasons locals keep coming.

NEW Marco's *Italian*
24 | 20 | 22 | $64

Prospect Heights | 295 Flatbush Ave. (bet. Prospect Pl. & St. Marks Ave.) | Brooklyn | 718-230-0427 | www.marcosbrooklyn.com

If "Italy and Alice Waters had a love child" it would be this upscale Prospect Heights "Franny's sibling", where chef Danny Amend spotlights pristine seasonal ingredients in his "deceptively simple" pastas and wood-grill dishes that pack "extraordinary flavor"; the "cozy" setup includes a front bar pouring standout cocktails and wines, and there's also a back garden.

Marea *Italian/Seafood* | 27 | 26 | 26 | $117 |

Midtown | 240 Central Park S. (bet. B'way & 7th Ave.) | 212-582-5100 | www.marea-nyc.com

"Prepare to be thrilled" at this "all-star" Italian on Central Park South, which presents chef Michael White's "brilliantly executed" seafood and housemade pastas in "lovely", "refined" surroundings tended by a staff that's "gracious and on-cue"; just "dress pretty" and "bring your bank manager" since "they're not shy with the pricing" – though lunch is a "more affordable" option.

NEW Margaux *French/Mediterranean* ▽ | 17 | 21 | 19 | $50 |

Greenwich Village | Marlton Hotel | 5 W. Eighth St. (bet. 5th & 6th Aves.) | 212-321-0111 | www.margauxnyc.com

A seriously "hip" refuge from morning till late-night, this cafe in the Village's Marlton Hotel proffers seasonally driven French-Med fare; while some say the kitchen's still working out the kinks, the "charming" setup complete with "vibrant bar" oozes Parisian élan.

Mario's *Italian* | 22 | 16 | 21 | $41 |

Arthur Avenue/Belmont | 2342 Arthur Ave. (bet. Crescent Ave. & 184th St.) | Bronx | 718-584-1188 | www.mariosrestarthurave.com

A Neapolitan "home away from home" on the Arthur Avenue "tourist strip", this "iconic red-sauce" joint is nearly a century old and still "never steers you wrong"; "old-time waiters" working the "bustling", "no-pretense" digs ensure regulars remain in their "comfort zone."

Mari Vanna *Russian* | 20 | 24 | 20 | $53 |

Flatiron | 41 E. 20th St. (bet. B'way & Park Ave. S.) | 212-777-1955 | www.marivanna.ru

Like "stepping into your grandmother's house in Moscow" – but with a "party" vibe fueled by "flowing vodka" – this "fabulous" Flatiron magnet for "expats" and "beautiful young things" serves up "hearty" Russian staples; "attentive" service and a "unique-in-NY" experience help justify the "pricey" tab.

The Mark *American* | 23 | 24 | 22 | $85 |

East 70s | Mark Hotel | 25 E. 77th St. (bet. 5th & Madison Aves.) | 212-744-4300 | www.themarkhotel.com

"Another dining coup" by Jean-Georges Vongerichten, this "very UES" enclave is "always on the mark" with "top-notch" New American fare and "deferential" service at predictably "high prices"; since the "lovely" dining room is usually on the "quiet" side, go-getters head for the "vibrant bar."

Market Table *American* | 24 | 18 | 21 | $63 |

West Village | 54 Carmine St. (Bedford St.) | 212-255-2100 | www.markettablenyc.com

A "solid farm-to-table" approach makes for "engaging dishes" at this West Village New American, a corner outfit with "big picture windows", "warm" service and an "unpretentious" vibe; it "continues to amaze" a wide following, meaning it's on the "crowded" and "loud" side at prime times.

	FOOD	DECOR	SERVICE	COST

MarkJoseph Steakhouse *Steak*

24 | 18 | 23 | $72

South Street Seaport | 261 Water St. (bet. Dover St. & Peck Slip) | 212-277-0020 | www.markjosephsteakhouse.com

Pack a "huuuge appetite" and a "corporate card" to best enjoy this chop shop "on the fringe of the Financial District", where "lunch is a better value"; "no-frills", "standard steakhouse" digs put the focus on the "outstanding" beef (and "even better" bacon appetizer) delivered by "friendly pro" staffers.

Marlow & Sons *American*

▽ 24 | 19 | 21 | $49

Williamsburg | 81 Broadway (Berry St.) | Brooklyn | 718-384-1441 | www.marlowandsons.com

"Pitch-perfect", "farm-fresh" New American fare from a "limited", "daily changing" lineup (including oysters from the raw bar) is the lure at this all-day Williamsburg pioneer that still packs plenty of "hipster" cred; the "dark, quirky", micro-size confines can be "cramped", so many angle to "sit outside."

The Marrow *German/Italian*

22 | 19 | 22 | $64

West Village | 99 Bank St. (Greenwich St.) | 212-428-6000 | www.themarrownyc.com

Fans of Harold Dieterle (Perilla) are "pleased" with this West Villager whose upscale German-Italian menu "reflecting the chef's heritage" packs "lots of meat" and "tons of flavor"; the "creative wine list" is a boon, as is the "quiet, spacious" corner space.

Marseille *French/Mediterranean*

21 | 20 | 20 | $51

Midtown | 630 Ninth Ave. (44th St.) | 212-333-2323 | www.marseillenyc.com

"Like being in Paris – but with better service" – this Theater District French-Med brasserie serves a "well-priced", "quality" menu in a rather "hectic" room that suggests "Casablanca"; its trump card is "convenience" to Broadway shows, and they know how to "get you out in time for your curtain."

NEW The Marshal *American*

24 | 18 | 22 | $47

Hell's Kitchen | 628 10th Ave. (bet. 44th & 45th Sts.) | 212-582-6300 | www.the-marshal.com

The "farm-to-table philosophy" comes to Hell's Kitchen via this "brilliant" arrival, whose ever-evolving menu of "terrific" New American fare is matched with a "thoughtful" list of "NY beers and wines"; its "tiny" space can get "cramped and loud", but "friendly" staffers help keep the feel "relaxed."

NEW Marta *Italian/Pizza*

─ | ─ | ─ | M

Flatiron | Martha Washington Hotel | 29 E. 29th St. (bet. Madison & Park Aves.) | 212-651-3800 | www.chelseahotels.com

Danny Meyer and Maialino chef Nick Anderer have teamed up on this Italian arrival inside the Flatiron's newly revamped Martha Washington Hotel, where cracker-thin Roman-style pizzas are joined by classic dishes cooked *alla brace* (over embers); the airy, rustic-yet-polished space features a small copper bar and an open kitchen boasting two wood-burning ovens and an imposing open-fire grill.

	FOOD	DECOR	SERVICE	COST

Martha *American*
▽ 22 | 18 | 21 | $47

Fort Greene | 184 Dekalb Ave. (bet. Carlton Ave. & Cumberland St.) | Brooklyn | 718-596-4147 | www.marthabrooklyn.com

"An adventure that's not fussy", this "upbeat" Fort Greene entry offers a carefully sourced menu of "inventive", Asian-influenced New American plates that feel "exciting and comforting at the same time"; it's no surprise the "inviting", subway-tiled space gets "lively."

Maruzzella *Italian*
21 | 15 | 20 | $47

East 70s | 1483 First Ave. (bet. 77th & 78th Sts.) | 212-988-8877 | www.maruzzellanyc.com

There's "nothing fancy" about this UES "quintessential neighborhood Italian", just "surprisingly good" cooking brought to table by "old-school" servers; "friendly owners" on the scene and "reasonable"-for-the-zip-code rates make the "modest" decor easy to overlook.

Mary's Fish Camp *Seafood*
25 | 16 | 20 | $52

West Village | 64 Charles St. (4th St.) | 646-486-2185 | www.marysfishcamp.com

"Like a visit to Cape Cod", this "funky" West Village seafood shack is famed for its "kicking lobster rolls" served in a "primitive" room by a "heavily tattooed" crew; sinkers include "cramped" seats and a "no-reservations" rule that leads to "long waits", but ultimately the "hard-to-beat" catch triumphs.

Masa *Japanese*
25 | 24 | 25 | $585

Midtown | Time Warner Ctr. | 10 Columbus Circle, 4th fl. (60th St. at B'way) | 212-823-9800

Bar Masa *Japanese*

Midtown | Time Warner Ctr. | 10 Columbus Circle, 4th fl. (60th St. at B'way) | 212-823-9800
www.masanyc.com

Ever an "ethereal experience", this Time Warner Center Japanese stunner showcases chef Masayoshi Takayama's "sublime" sushi via a $450-and-up omakase considered "worth skipping the mortgage payment for" ("it's a bucket list thing"); meanwhile, the à la carte menu in the "comfortable" neighboring bar maintains "superb quality" at a somewhat "more reasonable" cost.

Mas (Farmhouse) *American*
27 | 24 | 26 | $103

West Village | 39 Downing St. (Bedford St.) | 212-255-1790 | www.masfarmhouse.com

"Mas is more!" cheer champions of this West Village "culinary wonder", where chef Galen Zamarra works "magic" crafting "delectable", "emphatically seasonal" American cuisine; with "tasteful decor" and a "first-rate" staff to ensure "elevated" dining "on all fronts", it's a "splurge" – but "when you're looking to impress, it doesn't disappoint."

Max Caffe *Italian*
▽ 22 | 19 | 19 | $26

Morningside Heights | 1262 Amsterdam Ave. (bet. 122nd & 123rd Sts.) | 212-531-1210

continued

Max SoHa *Italian*

Morningside Heights | 1274 Amsterdam Ave. (123rd St.) |
212-531-2221
www.maxsoha.com

"Popular with the Columbia crowd", these "friendly", low-cost Upper
Westsiders have two distinct personalities: cash-only Soha offers "rustic"
Italian staples in a "cozy" space with the option to "eat outside", while
the Caffe features "comfy couches and chairs for relaxing and eating."

Maya *Mexican* 22 | 20 | 20 | $52

East 60s | 1191 First Ave. (bet. 64th & 65th Sts.) | 212-585-1818 |
www.richardsandoval.com

"Not your usual Mexican" cucina, this "elevated" Upper Eastsider supplies "exciting" cooking with "full flavor in every bite" via a "solicitous"
staff; the "smart setting" (with a "vibrant" tequileria attached) "tends to
get loud" and it runs "a little pricey", "but hey, you get what you pay for."

Mayfield *American* 24 | 20 | 21 | $39

Crown Heights | 688 Franklin Ave. (Prospect Pl.) | Brooklyn |
347-318-3643 | www.mayfieldbk.com

"A real find" in Crown Heights, this "comfortable" New American offers a
"wonderful" lineup of "Southern-influenced" plates in charmingly "rough-
and-tumble" digs; staffers who "know what they're doing" suit the happening neighborhood, but the "price point is vintage Brooklyn."

NEW Mayhem & Stout *Sandwiches* – | – | – | I

Murray Hill | 711 Second Ave. (bet. 38th & 39th Sts.) | 212-986-1600 |
www.mayhemandstout.yolasite.com

A favorite vendor at food markets around town, this specialist in braised
meat sandwiches and locavore-oriented condiments has put down roots
in Murray Hill; its simple storefront houses a handful of tables, while its
made-to-order approach and slew of options threaten ordering mayhem
at the counter.

Maysville *American* 21 | 19 | 19 | $63

Flatiron | 17 W. 26th St. (bet. B'way & 6th Ave.) | 646-490-8240 |
www.maysvillenyc.com

"Cool" New American fare with "a touch of Southern influence" and an
"energetic" scene fueled by a "literal wall" of whiskeys define this Flatiron
follow-up to Brooklyn's Char No. 4; just "bring your earplugs" for crowds
"as loud as the Kentucky Derby on the home stretch."

Maze *French* 19 | 20 | 19 | $76

Midtown | London NYC Hotel | 151 W. 54th St. (bet. 6th & 7th Aves.) |
212-468-8889 | www.gordonramsay.com

This New French eatery proffers "simple, elegant" small plates in a "bustling" space off the lobby of Midtown's London NYC Hotel; those who
find it "too noisy" and "pricey" at dinner note it's "terrific" for a quieter
lunch, when there's a "wonderful" four-course prix fixe for $30.

Maz Mezcal *Mexican* 21 | 19 | 20 | $41

East 80s | 316 E. 86th St. (bet. 1st & 2nd Aves.) | 212-472-1599 |
www.mazmezcal.com

"Hits all the right spots" say Yorkville locals of this "family-owned"

Mexican "standby" where a "lively neighborhood crowd" assembles for "tasty" classics; "reasonable prices" and "friendly" service are two more reasons it's "still packed after all these years."

NEW Meadowsweet *American/Mediterranean* — | — | — | M

Williamsburg | 149 Broadway (bet. Bedford & Driggs Aves.) | Brooklyn | 718-384-0673 | www.meadowsweetnyc.com

Housed in the former Dressler digs and opened by one of its ex-chefs, this upscale Williamsburg arrival specializes in Med-tinged New American fare and craft cocktails; with banquettes and a wraparound bar, its airy space features retro touches like antique wallpaper and a 1900s-era tile floor.

Meatball Shop *Sandwiches* 22 | 16 | 18 | $26

Chelsea | 200 Ninth Ave. (bet. 22nd & 23rd Sts.) | 212-257-4363
East 70s | 1462 Second Ave. (bet. 76th & 77th Sts.) | 212-257-6121
Lower East Side | 84 Stanton St. (bet. Allen & Orchard Sts.) | 212-982-8895
NEW West 80s | 447 Amsterdam Ave. (81st St.) | 212-422-1752
West Village | 64 Greenwich Ave. (11th St.) | 212-982-7815
Williamsburg | 170 Bedford Ave. (bet. N. 7th & 8th Sts.) | Brooklyn | 718-551-0520
www.themeatballshop.com

"Typical and not-so-typical combos" mean there's a meatball "for everyone" at these "cool" sandwich shops also beloved for their "scrumptious" cocktails (at some locations) and "to-die-for ice cream sandwiches"; factor in "economical" pricing, and it's no wonder they're often "packed" with "young" types who don't blink at the "brutal lines."

Meat Hook Sandwich Shop *Sandwiches* — | — | — | I

Williamsburg | 459 Lorimer St. (bet. Grand & Powers Sts.) | Brooklyn | 718-302-4665 | www.the-meathook.com

Williamsburg denizens wrap their hooks around hefty sandwiches at this adjunct of locavore butcher The Meat Hook, the snout-to-tail purists whose pastured beef, pork and lamb are stars of the menu board; there's beer to wash it all down, though given the knife-thin space (just 12 seats) many take the goods on the hoof.

Megu *Japanese* 23 | 25 | 23 | $96

TriBeCa | 62 Thomas St. (bet. B'way & Church St.) | 212-964-7777
Megu Midtown *Japanese*
East Midtown | 845 United Nations Plaza (bet. 47th & 48th Sts.) | 212-964-7777
www.megurestaurants.com

"Impressive", "over-the-top" decor centered around a "giant Buddha" ice sculpture sets the stage for "delectable" modern Japanese "fine dining" at these TriBeCa–East Midtown "stunners", where "meticulous" service takes the edge off "steep" tabs; they're perfect for a "power meal", "date" or any time "someone else is paying."

Mehtaphor *Eclectic* 26 | 25 | 25 | $59

TriBeCa | Duane Street Hotel | 130 Duane St. (Church St.) | 212-542-9440 | www.mehtaphornyc.com

"Get your taste buds tingling" with "amazing" Eclectic small plates from "singular chef" Jehangir Mehta (Graffiti) at this "quiet, little" "oasis" in

TriBeCa's Duane Street Hotel; the ultracompact quarters are understated, but it stands out as something "wonderfully different."

Melba's American/Southern | 24 | 20 | 21 | $38 |

Harlem | 300 W. 114th St. (8th Ave.) | 212-864-7777 |
www.melbasrestaurant.com

"Divine chicken 'n' waffles" and other "Southern"-accented American comfort classics "done right" are the thing at this "warm" Harlem retreat; its "small" setting is "chill and homey" by day, "hopping and grooving" come evening (especially on Tuesdays when there's live music).

Melt Shop Sandwiches | 19 | 11 | 14 | $14 |

East Midtown | 601 Lexington Ave. (bet. 53rd & 54th Sts.) |
212-759-6358
NEW Financial District | 111 Fulton St. (bet. Nassau & William Sts.) |
646-741-7910
Flatiron | 55 W. 26th St. (bet. B'way & 6th Ave.) | 212-447-6358
NEW Midtown | 135 W. 50th St. (bet. 6th & 7th Aves.) | 212-447-6358
www.meltshop.com

"Gooey yumminess" is the hallmark of these sandwich shops, which turn out "indulgent" toasted creations that "aren't your mama's grilled cheese"; the counter-service format is low on frills, but they're "quick and comforting" even if you're dining "at your desk."

Mémé Mediterranean/Moroccan | 23 | 16 | 22 | $52 |

West Village | 581 Hudson St. (Bank St.) | 646-692-8450 |
www.memeonhudson.com

It's the "Mediterranean on Hudson Street" at this "affordable" West Villager dispensing "wonderful" small plates and entrees with "Moroccan flair"; "friendly" service and an appealing "bohemian" vibe will "keep you returning", unless the "tight-packed tables" make you feel like you're "flying coach."

Mercadito Mexican | 22 | 15 | 18 | $35 |

East Village | 179 Ave. B (bet. 11th & 12th Sts.) | 212-529-6490
www.mercaditorestaurants.com

To "quench taco cravings", hit this Alphabet City Mexican "favorite" for "fair-priced", "authentic tastes"; yes, the "tiny", "rustic" space is "tight" (especially at brunch), but a "pleasant" staff that's "quick to refill your perfectly crafted margarita" helps keep the vibe "fun."

Mercato Italian | ∇ 22 | 16 | 16 | $44 |

Midtown | 352 W. 39th St. (bet. 8th & 9th Aves.) | 212-643-2000 |
www.mercatonyc.com

A "pleasant surprise" in the restaurant-"barren" zone near Port Authority, this "well-kept secret" slings "genuine homestyle" Italian food in a "cozy", "rustic" setting; factor in "reasonable" rates and to most it's "worth seeking out" if you're in the area.

Mercer Kitchen American/French | 21 | 21 | 19 | $59 |

SoHo | Mercer Hotel | 99 Prince St. (Mercer St.) | 212-966-5454 |
www.themercerkitchen.com

Ever "chic", Jean-Georges Vongerichten's "still buzzy" SoHo vet in the Mercer Hotel is touted for "enjoyable" Franco-American cooking offered

	FOOD	DECOR	SERVICE	COST

in "dimly lit" subterranean digs; given the "social" atmosphere and servers who "don't rush you", it's "easy to talk and linger" here.

Mermaid Inn *Seafood*   22 | 18 | 20 | $48

East Village | 96 Second Ave. (bet. 5th & 6th Sts.) | 212-674-5870
West 80s | 568 Amsterdam Ave. (bet. 87th & 88th Sts.) | 212-799-7400

Mermaid Oyster Bar *Seafood*

Greenwich Village | 79 MacDougal St. (bet. Bleecker & Houston Sts.) |
212-260-0100
www.themermaidnyc.com

"Like being in Nantucket", these "neighborly" seafooders provide "well-seasoned" catch (including a "lovely" lobster roll) in funky nautical settings; "jolly" vibes, "good-humored" service and "bargain" oysters at the "happy hour-and-a-half" are further reasons it's often "packed to the gills."

Mesa Coyoacan *Mexican*   25 | 22 | 24 | $36

Williamsburg | 372 Graham Ave. (bet. Conselyea St. & Skillman Ave.) |
Brooklyn | 718-782-8171 | www.mesacoyoacan.com

There's "always something to discover" at this "upbeat" Williamsburg Mexican, a dispenser of "sensational" Mexico City–style cuisine and "absolutely killer margaritas" at an "affordable" cost; a "very cool" staff and "creative" decor help keep the mood "warm" and "inviting."

Meson Sevilla *Spanish*   ∇ 22 | 17 | 20 | $39

Midtown | 344 W. 46th St. (bet. 8th & 9th Aves.) | 212-262-5890 |
www.mesonsevilla.com

Broadway ticket–holders seeking a paella fix turn to this "popular" Restaurant Row Spaniard (with Italian dishes too) for "pleasant" provender and sangria; the room's "a bit tatty" and gets "elbow-to-elbow" precurtain, but it's hard to beat the "convenience" or the "value."

Mezetto *Mediterranean*   ∇ 23 | 23 | 24 | $44

Lower East Side | 161 E. Houston St. (Allen St.) | 212-933-4587 |
www.mezetto.com

Meze with "flair" is the signature of this "wonderful little" Lower Eastsider, where an "excellent" array of Mediterranean small plates pairs with wines and cocktails; those drawn to the "refined yet laid-back" style (and "reasonable" tabs) "look forward to" a repeat.

Michael Jordan's   21 | 20 | 19 | $64
The Steak House NYC *Steak*

Midtown | Grand Central | 23 Vanderbilt Ave. (42nd St.) | 212-655-2300 |
www.michaeljordansnyc.com

It's the "unusual location" – a balcony overlooking the "scurrying" masses in Grand Central's Main Concourse – that's the hook at this "reliable" chophouse, where the beef is "aged" and the prices "high"; critics find "nothing original" going on here, but to fans the "spectacular setting" alone makes it a "slam dunk."

Michael's *Californian*   22 | 21 | 22 | $76

Midtown | 24 W. 55th St. (bet. 5th & 6th Aves.) | 212-767-0555 |
www.michaelsnewyork.com

"Media titans" ("did Diane really just say that?") collect at this "classy" Midtowner that's known more for its breakfast and lunch "power" scenes than its "fresh", "premium-priced" Californian fare and "pro" service; "relaxed" dinner comes "without the hot crowd", but the food's "very good" and there's always the "lovely" room's "fresh flowers and art" to look at.

Mighty Quinn's Barbecue *BBQ* 26 | 14 | 17 | $26

NEW **Battery Park City** | Hudson Eats | 200 Vesey St. (West St.) | 212-417-7000

East Village | 103 Second Ave. (6th St.) | 212-677-3733

NEW **West Village** | 75 Greenwich Ave. (bet. Bank & 11th Sts.) | 646-524-7889

NEW **Crown Heights** | Berg'n | 899 Bergen St. (bet. Classon & Franklin Aves.) | Brooklyn | 718-857-2337

www.mightyquinnsbbq.com

'Cue connoisseurs "salivate just thinking about" the "smoky goodness" of the "top-tier" (but "wallet-friendly") Texas and Carolina-style BBQ at these "quintessential" pit stops; the original East Village cafeteria is known for its "ravenous hordes" and "substantial" lines, but the West Village sequel and counters inside Hudson Eats and Berg'n are new alternatives.

Mihoko's 21 Grams *French/Japanese* ▽ 22 | 25 | 21 | $99

Flatiron | 16 W. 22nd St. (bet. 5th & 6th Aves.) | 212-741-0021 | www.mihokos21grams.com

"A unique establishment" from culture-savvy Mihoko Kiyokawa, this Flatiron Franco-Japanese presents high-end prix fixe and omakase menus in a "stunning", Versailles-like setting that recalls "an art gallery"; service borders on "stuffy", but "it works" for a "fancy night out."

Mike's Bistro *American* 25 | — | 24 | $72

East Midtown | 127 E. 54th St. (bet. Lexington & Park Aves.) | 212-799-3911 | www.mikesbistro.com

Recently relocated to expansive East Midtown digs, this upscale standby continues to deliver the eponymous chef-owner's "delicious", "imaginative" New American dishes; yes, "you pay", but "wonderful service" and "Mike going from table to table" add value – "his mother must be kvelling."

Mile End *Deli* 22 | 13 | 17 | $24

Boerum Hill | 97 Hoyt St. (bet. Atlantic Ave. & Pacific St.) | Brooklyn | 718-852-7510

Mile End Sandwich Shop *Sandwiches*

NoHo | 53 Bond St. (bet. Bowery & Lafayette St.) | 212-529-2990 www.mileenddeli.com

Prepare for "a different kind" of "fress" at these "finds" where the Montreal-style Jewish deli eats highlight "*incroyable*" house-smoked meats; the "tiny" spaces get "a little smushed", but even purists "gotta admit" they give the old guard "a run for their money."

NEW Milk River *Asian/Caribbean* ▽ 22 | 25 | 18 | $41

Prospect Heights | 960 Atlantic Ave. (bet. Grand & Washington Aves.) | Brooklyn | 718-636-8600 | www.milkriverbrooklyn.com

Prospect Heights locals "truly love" this spacious bar and eatery thanks to its "welcoming" atmosphere and "excellent" roster of Caribbean-Asian chow; after dark, revelers "can't go wrong" as the upstairs lounge hosts DJs and reggae-tinged live music.

	FOOD	DECOR	SERVICE	COST

Mill Basin Deli *Deli/Kosher*

| 24 | 19 | 21 | $27 |

Flatlands | 5823 Ave. T (bet. 58th & 59th Sts.) | Brooklyn |
718-241-4910 | www.millbasindeli.com

"Memories of delis past come alive" when noshing on a "what-could-be-better pastrami on rye" at this circa-1972 Mill Basin vet; given such "rich Jewish delicacies" and a setting dressed up with "gallery"-worthy fine art, mavens tolerate the no-frills service and "Manhattan prices."

Millesime *French*

| ▽ 21 | 23 | 21 | $68 |

Flatiron | Carlton Hotel | 92 Madison Ave. (29th St.) | 212-889-7100 |
www.millesimenyc.com

"Tucked away" in the Carlton Hotel is this French "gem" that's appreciated as much for its "authentic bistro" looks and "enchanting" stained-glass skylight as for its "very good" fare (with "like-in-Paris prices" attached); it's a "quiet oasis" by day that "comes alive" after dark, especially when there's live jazz in the "terrific" salon.

Milos *Greek/Seafood*

| 27 | 23 | 24 | $93 |

Midtown | 125 W. 55th St. (bet. 6th & 7th Aves.) | 212-245-7400 |
www.milos.ca

"Seafood for the gods" is the signature of this "high-end" Midtown Greek, which also boasts "expert service", a "beautiful" "whitewashed" space and plenty of "buzz"; the by-the-pound pricing runs "steep" enough that you may "need a second job", but "bargain" lunch and pre-theater prix fixes "save a lot of drachmas."

NEW Mimi Cheng's Dumplings *Taiwanese*

East Village | 179 Second Ave. (12th St.) | no phone |
www.mimichengs.com

Two sisters have opened this tiny Taiwanese dumpling slinger in the East Village, where the chalkboard menu features just four variations – chicken, pork, veggie and a dessert version – made from local, sustainable ingredients and paired with zingy housemade sauces.

Mimi's Hummus *Mideastern*

| ▽ 25 | 18 | 21 | $21 |

Ditmas Park | 1209 Cortelyou Rd. (bet. Argyle & Westminster Rds.) |
Brooklyn | 718-284-4444 | www.mimishummus.com

"Hummus-fueled nirvana" that's "hard to come by without a passport" is on tap at this "cute" Ditmas Park nook where the "killer" namesake (paired with "tender pita") is joined by other "really terrific" Middle Eastern fare; the "heady" flavors are easy on the wallet, but "matchbox"-size digs mean many do "takeout."

Minca *Japanese/Noodle Shop*

| ▽ 23 | 11 | 14 | $19 |

East Village | 536 E. Fifth St. (bet. Aves. A & B) | 212-505-8001 |
www.newyorkramen.com

There are "no pretenses" at this "traditional-style" Japanese noodle shop in the East Village, just the "charming simplicity" of "oishii" ("delicious") ramen featuring "rich", "slurp-worthy" broth, plus gyoza "just like in Tokyo"; its "tiny", "basic" space is "perpetually packed", but "fast", "friendly" servers keep things on track.

	FOOD	DECOR	SERVICE	COST

Minetta Tavern *French* | 24 | 21 | 22 | $68 |

Greenwich Village | 113 MacDougal St. (Minetta Ln.) | 212-475-3850 |
www.minettatavernny.com

Channeling "long-gone better times", Keith McNally's "retro" remodel
of a classic 1937 Village tavern is still "sceney" thanks to French cooking
that's as "delicious" as the "Madonna-Gwyneth-Sting" celeb sightings;
the "back room" is the place to sit and the "epic" Black Label burger the
thing to order, provided you can snag a "difficult reservation."

Mira Sushi & Izakaya *Japanese* | ∇ 23 | 19 | 21 | $47 |

Flatiron | 46 W. 22nd (bet. 5th & 6th Aves.) | 212-989-7889 |
www.mirasushi.com

"The only problem is trying to choose" among the "flavorful" options
at this Flatiron "hidden gem", where sushi meets "unique" Asian street
food–inspired small plates; hip yet "tasteful" decor and "down-to-earth"
service help keep locals coming "on a regular basis."

Miriam *Israeli/Mediterranean* | ∇ 23 | 18 | 21 | $33 |

Park Slope | 79 Fifth Ave. (Prospect Pl.) | Brooklyn | 718-622-2250 |
www.miriamrestaurant.com

"Dinner is a pleasure" but "brunch is the meal" that has Park Slopers
flocking to this "affordable" Israeli-Med, whose narrow space is a "mob
scene" on weekends, but happily service remains "prompt"; "go at off
times" for a calmer taste of its "tasty" fare.

NEW Mission Cantina *Mexican* | 20 | 14 | 17 | $30 |

Lower East Side | 172 Orchard St. (Stanton St.) | 212-254-2233 |
www.missioncantinanyc.com

With chef Danny Bowien's Mission Chinese on hiatus, his "cheery,
casual" LES Mexican steps into the void with "creative takes" on tacos
that never stray from "approachability", plus "interesting drinks"; even
those who find the eating "underwhelming" grant it's "popular", peso-
friendly and "fun."

Miss Korea BBQ *Korean* | 20 | 14 | 19 | $38 |

Midtown | 10 W. 32nd St. (bet. B'way & 5th Ave.) | 212-736-3232 |
www.misskoreabbq.com

"Don't miss" this "second-floor" Korean BBQ specialist, a "popular" pick
for "delicious" classics; with its "spacious", Zen-like space, it feels somewhat "higher-end" compared to others in K-town "without being more
expensive" – no wonder it's "always packed."

Miss Lily's *Jamaican* | 20 | 19 | 17 | $39 |

Greenwich Village | 132 W. Houston St. (Sullivan St.) | 646-588-5375
NEW Miss Lily's 7A Cafe *Jamaican*
East Village | 109 Ave. A (7th St.) | 212-812-1482
www.misslilysnyc.com

Serge Becker's "sexy" Village Jamaican (with a new Alphabet City
offshoot) features a clever "diner"-like interior pulsing with "hip" island
tunes and overseen by an "utterly beautiful" staff; the well-priced Caribbean eats are "delicious" – plus there's next-door Melvin's Juice Box for
"fresh, green, tasty" juices and snacks.

	FOOD	DECOR	SERVICE	COST

Miss Mamie's *Soul Food/Southern* | 21 | 12 | 17 | $28 |

West 100s | 366 W. 110th St. (Columbus Ave.) | 212-865-6744

Miss Maude's *Soul Food/Southern*

Harlem | 547 Lenox Ave. (bet. 137th & 138th Sts.) | 212-690-3100
www.spoonbreadinc.com

"Real Southern comfort food" in "tremendous portions" keeps the
crowds coming to these Harlem/Upper UWS soul fooders; ok, the decor
is "kind of plain" and the "friendly" servers "can be slow", but no one
minds given the "tasty" eats and "fair prices."

The Modern *American/French* | 26 | 26 | 25 | $127 |

Midtown | Museum of Modern Art | 9 W. 53rd St. (bet. 5th & 6th Aves.) |
212-333-1220 | www.themodernnyc.com

"Modern in every respect" – from the "gastronomically exciting",
"beautifully presented" French–New American cuisine to the "spare,
elegant" setting with "wonderful sculpture garden views" – this "Danny
Meyer gem" inside MoMA draws a "well-dressed", "arty" clientele;
to dodge the main dining room's "costly" prix fixe-only tabs, go for
"lower-priced" small plates in the "lively" front bar, where you'll "still feel
pampered and privileged."

Moim *Korean* | ▽ 23 | 21 | 19 | $42 |

Park Slope | 206 Garfield Pl. (7th Ave.) | Brooklyn | 718-499-8092 |
www.moimrestaurant.com

"Nouveau Korean" is the specialty of this Park Sloper that's also appreciated for its "modern" decor and "lovely" garden; it's "not the big new
thing" anymore – it's even something of a "hidden secret" – meaning "no
more ridiculous waits" for a table.

Móle *Mexican* | 20 | 17 | 19 | $38 |

East 80s | 1735 Second Ave. (bet. 89th & 90th Sts.) | 212-289-8226
West Village | 57 Jane St. (Hudson St.) | 212-206-7559
Williamsburg | 178 Kent Ave. (4th Pl.) | Brooklyn | 347-384-2300
www.molenyc.com

"Tasty", "authentic" Mexican food turns up at this "everyday" mini-chain
that seals the deal with "even better" margaritas; "tight" confines,
"loud music" and "hurried" service are trumped by fair prices and a
"good happy hour."

Molyvos *Greek* | 23 | 20 | 21 | $63 |

Midtown | Wellington Hotel | 871 Seventh Ave. (bet. 55th & 56th Sts.) |
212-582-7500 | www.molyvos.com

An "oh-so-convenient location" to Carnegie Hall and City Center is
one of the draws at this "perennial favorite" that follows through with
"delicious" Greek grub and "amiable" service; "nice decor", "bearable"
acoustics and a "spacious-by-Manhattan-standards" setting complete
the "solid" picture.

Momofuku Ko *American* | 27 | 19 | 25 | $163 |

East Village | 163 First Ave. (bet. 10th & 11th Sts.) | 212-500-0831 |
www.momofuku.com

David Chang's famed East Village "gastronomic theater" provides a
"one-of-a-kind" "epicurean adventure" via its Asian-inflected American
tasting menus served at the chef's counter with "perfect pacing and flaw-

less execution"; yep, the $125 set price is "steep", but there's a reason the web-only reservations fill "in minutes"; P.S. a move to roomier digs at 8 Extra Place is in the works.

Momofuku Noodle Bar *American*
23 | 17 | 20 | $39

East Village | 171 First Ave. (bet. 10th & 11th Sts.) | 212-777-7773 | www.momofuku.com

"Thank you, David Chang!" cheer countless fans of this "high-energy" East Village American's famously "mind-blowing ramen" and "mouthwatering" pork buns; the "tight space" with "elbow-to-elbow" seating and "waits to get in" is "not for the lingering diner", but at least "the price is right."

Momofuku Ssäm Bar *American*
25 | 18 | 21 | $53

East Village | 207 Second Ave. (13th St.) | 212-254-3500 | www.momofuku.com

"Not your ssäm old" scene, David Chang's "East Village hot spot" reliably "hits the mark" with "inventive", Asian-inspired American fare, including the "spectacular" bo ssäm pork shoulder "large-format meal"; as ever, the streamlined space is "justifiably crowded", but "fantastic cocktails" help the "wait" pass quickly.

Momo Sushi Shack *Japanese*
∇ 26 | 21 | 23 | $55

Bushwick | 43 Bogart St. (Moore St.) | Brooklyn | 718-418-6666 | www.momosushishack.com

Understated but "definitely not a shack", this cash-only Bushwick Japanese "go-to" serves "interesting, delicious" small plates and "unconventional-in-NY" sushi (including lots of veggie options); its wooden communal tables "fill up fast" at prime times, so "get there early."

Momoya *Japanese*
22 | 18 | 19 | $50

Chelsea | 185 Seventh Ave. (21st St.) | 212-989-4466
West 80s | 427 Amsterdam Ave. (bet. 80th & 81st Sts.) | 212-580-0007
www.momoyanyc.com

Sushiphiles head to these "unassuming" Chelsea-UWS Japanese eateries for "generous portions" of "amazingly fresh" fish, plus "top-notch" cooked dishes, at "won't-break-the-bank" prices; "modern" decor and "helpful" service are other reasons they're "always bustling."

NEW Monarch Room *American*
– | – | – | E

Chelsea | 408 W. 15th St. (bet. 9th & 10th Aves.) | 646-790-7070 | www.nymonarch.com

The swanky, dramatic digs with a retro cruise ship–industrial vibe – not to mention the roaring bar scene – threaten to outshine the farm-to-table fare (and raw bar) at this West Chelsea American, but its dressed-to-impress crowd doesn't seem to mind.

Monkey Bar *American*
18 | 21 | 19 | $69

Midtown | Elysée Hotel | 60 E. 54th St. (bet. Madison & Park Aves.) | 212-308-2950 | www.monkeybarnewyork.com

"Jazz-age ambiance" endures at Graydon Carter's Midtown canteen bedecked with now-"legendary" murals of 1920s-era celebs monkeying around; its American grub is "better than it needs to be" and accompanied by "creative" cocktails, so while the "see-and-be-seen" scene has cooled, to most this remains an NYC "must-experience."

	FOOD	DECOR	SERVICE	COST

Mon Petit Cafe *French*
| 20 | 15 | 19 | $48 |

East 60s | 801 Lexington Ave. (62nd St.) | 212-355-2233 |
www.monpetitcafe.com

A "bit of Paris in the shadow of Bloomingdale's", this "tiny" vet offers
"homey French" staples that hit the spot "in the middle of an intense
shopping day"; its tearoom-style space "may not meet the standards of
the Designers Guild", but to fans it has a certain "charm."

NEW Montana's Trail House *Southern*
| – | – | – | M |

Bushwick | 455 Troutman St. (bet. Cypress & Scott Aves.) | Brooklyn |
917-966-1666 | www.montanastrailhouse.com

Updated Southern faves like fried chicken with kale slaw go down well
with craft cocktails at this Appalachian-inspired Bushwick resto-bar
that stays open late; its former-gas-station digs sport rustic touches
(old-timey flags, taxidermy), but the bookcase that spins open to the
outdoors steals the show.

Mont Blanc *Austrian/Swiss*
| 21 | 15 | 22 | $50 |

Midtown | 315 W. 48th St. (bet. 8th & 9th Aves.) | 212-582-9648 |
www.montblancrestaurant.com

Fondue freaks seek out this "cozy" Theater District "time capsule" that's
been serving "delicious" Swiss-Austrian staples since 1982; "gracious"
staffers overseen by a "charming" owner "get you to the show on time",
so it's a "win-win all around" – even if it "could use a face-lift."

Montebello *Italian*
| 22 | 18 | 21 | $65 |

East Midtown | 120 E. 56th St. (bet. Lexington & Park Aves.) |
212-753-1447 | www.montebellonyc.com

One of the "best-kept secrets in Midtown" is this "oasis of peace and
quiet" where "personalized" service and "fantastic" Northern Italian fare
keep a longtime "dedicated clientele" returning; it's "a bit on the expensive side", but hey, at least "you can linger."

Montmartre *French*
| 21 | 19 | 20 | $61 |

Chelsea | 158 Eighth Ave. (18th St.) | 646-596-8838 |
www.montmartrenyc.com

Following change-ups in the kitchen, they've "gotten it right" at Gabe
Stulman's Chelsea outpost, where the familiar French bistro menu nonetheless "reaches beyond" the "conventional clichés"; the snug interior
staffed by a "super-friendly" crew is "comfortable" enough, but fans
especially "love the back garden."

Monument Lane *American*
| 22 | 20 | 21 | $49 |

West Village | 103 Greenwich Ave. (W. 12th St.) | 212-255-0155 |
www.monumentlane.com

Serving "New American food in an old American setting", this West
Village tavern offers "tasty" updates on "comforting" classics in a "sweet,
intimate" space that "evokes NY of yore"; its "friendly", "laid-back" vibe
extends to the sidewalk seating area in summer.

Morandi *Italian*
| 22 | 21 | 20 | $61 |

West Village | 211 Waverly Pl. (bet. Charles St. & 7th Ave. S.) |
212-627-7575 | www.morandiny.com

A somewhat under-the-radar "jewel in Keith McNally's crown", this
all-day West Village trattoria offers an "off-the-hook" Italian menu in

| | FOOD | DECOR | SERVICE | COST |

"rustic", "perennially buzzy" confines; the "energy is contagious" – but if the "noise overwhelms", "sit out on the sidewalk and people-watch."

Morgans BBQ *BBQ*
▽ 22 | 15 | 16 | $30

Prospect Heights | 267 Flatbush Ave. (St. Marks Ave.) | Brooklyn | 718-622-2224 | www.morgansbrooklynbarbecue.com

"Legit Texas BBQ" from a transplanted Austin pitmaster distinguishes this Prospect Heights smokehouse, where the "terrific" choices include brisket, pulled pork, turkey tails and sides like Frito pie; the no-frills interior is joined by a sidewalk seating area in summer, and the adjacent Elbow Room stall supplies the "inventive" mac 'n' cheese.

NEW Morgenstern's Finest Ice Cream *Ice Cream*
– | – | – | I

Lower East Side | 2 Rivington St. (bet. Bowery & Chrystie St.) | 212-209-7684 | www.morgensternsnyc.com

Nick Morgenstern (Goat Town) returns to his pastry-chef roots with this LES scoop shop producing small-batch ice creams and sorbets in novel flavors like Sichuan peppercorn–chocolate and Aperol-grapefruit, plus sundaes, shakes and more; the storefront, a modern take on the classic parlor, has been jammed from day one.

Morimoto *Japanese*
26 | 26 | 24 | $100

Chelsea | 88 10th Ave. (bet. 15th & 16th Sts.) | 212-989-8883 | www.morimotonyc.com

"There's a reason he's an Iron Chef" gush admirers of Masaharu Morimoto's West Chelsea namesake, which "breaks the mold" with "unforgettable" Japanese cuisine (including an "elaborate" omakase) set down by "expert" servers in a "fantasy" setting; it's "everything you'd expect it to be" – not excluding the "high-end" cost.

Morso *Italian*
23 | 22 | 23 | $65

East Midtown | 420 E. 59th St. (bet. 1st Ave. & Sutton Pl.) | 212-759-2706 | www.morso-nyc.com

"Far off the beaten track", this "upscale" East Midtowner from Pino Luongo presents *"bellissimo"* Italian fare in a "tastefully modern" interior showcasing "delightful" Pop Art; in warm weather, the "wonderful terrace" with "magical views" of the Queensboro Bridge and Roosevelt Island trolley further boosts the appeal.

Morton's The Steakhouse *Steak*
24 | 21 | 23 | $82

Financial District | 136 Washington St. (Albany St.) | 212-608-0171
Midtown | 551 Fifth Ave. (45th St.) | 212-972-3315
www.mortons.com

"Go hungry" to these "corporate" chophouses where "huge" steaks with "just the right char" arrive with bountiful sides; it's predictably "expensive" (the "bar bites are the best deal"), but "classy" service and "upmarket" confines keep its "expense-account" crowd content.

NEW Moscow 57 *Russian*
– | – | – | M

Lower East Side | 168½ Delancey St. (bet. Attorney & Clinton Sts.) | 212-260-5775 | www.moscow57.com

The brainchild of Ellen Kaye – whose family owned the Russian Tea Room for decades – this crimson-hued LES boîte presents classic dishes from Russia and Central Asia, washed down with infused vodkas; but what really sets it apart is the diverse live music, offered every night it's open (Wednesday–Sunday).

Moti Mahal Delux *Indian*

FOOD	DECOR	SERVICE	COST
22	16	21	$33

East 60s | 1149 First Ave. (63rd St.) | 212-371-3535 | www.motimahaldelux.us

"Innovative", relatively "high-end" Indian tandoor cooking – including "famous", "to-die-for" signature butter chicken – is the specialty of this Upper Eastsider; it's a link of an "unusual" international chain, but its "simple", "comfortable" setting possesses a "friendly neighborhood vibe" bolstered by "efficient" "pro" service.

Motorino *Pizza*

FOOD	DECOR	SERVICE	COST
24	14	18	$33

East Village | 349 E. 12th St. (bet. 1st & 2nd Aves.) | 212-777-2644
Williamsburg | 139 Broadway (bet. Bedford & Driggs Aves.) | Brooklyn | 718-599-8899
www.motorinopizza.com

The "gold standard" for "artsy" Neapolitan-style pies, these "pizza havens" layer "superb ingredients" on "sublime thin crusts" with a result that may "haunt your dreams" (especially the "out-of-this-world" Brussels sprout–pancetta); while the Williamsburg original now inhabits roomier digs, expect no frills there or in the East Village.

Moustache *Mideastern*

FOOD	DECOR	SERVICE	COST
22	12	16	$27

East Harlem | 1621 Lexington Ave. (102nd St.) | 212-828-0030
East Village | 265 E. 10th St. (bet. Ave. A & 1st Ave.) | 212-228-2022
West Village | 90 Bedford St. (bet. Barrow & Grove Sts.) | 212-229-2220
www.moustachepizza.com

"Straightforward", "delicious" Middle Eastern staples come at a "low price" at these "popular" places; service is "nonchalant" and the "no-decor" setups tilt "tiny and cramped", but the minute that "just-baked pita" arrives, "all is forgiven."

NEW Mozzarella & Vino *Italian*

	FOOD	DECOR	SERVICE	COST
∇	22	19	22	$55

Midtown | 33 W. 54th St. (bet. 5th & 6th Aves.) | 646-692-8849 | www.mozzarellaevino.com

Those "craving authentic" buffalo mozzarella and "decent wines by the glass" can count on the "simple", "tasty" menu at this "casual but stylish" Midtown Italian "across from MOMA"; the "light, cozy" space leads to a rear garden room ("such a nice surprise").

MP Taverna *Greek*

FOOD	DECOR	SERVICE	COST
24	22	23	$44

Astoria | 31-29 Ditmars Blvd. (33rd St.) | Queens | 718-777-2187 | www.michaelpsilakis.com

Chef Michael Psilakis brings "new twists" on Greek eats to "the toughest crowd" and "hits a home run" at this "upbeat" Astoria duplex, where "shockingly good" "modern" cuisine arrives via an "informed" staff; add a "bustling bar" and "affordable" tabs, and "this place will convince you."

Mr. Chow *Chinese*

FOOD	DECOR	SERVICE	COST
23	21	21	$80

East Midtown | 324 E. 57th St. (bet. 1st & 2nd Aves.) | 212-751-9030
Mr. Chow Tribeca *Chinese*
TriBeCa | 121 Hudson St. (Moore St.) | 212-965-9500
www.mrchow.com

"Upper-crust dining" endures at this longtime East Side Chinese (and its younger TriBeCa sibling) offering a "delicious", "classic" menu; voters split on its buzz factor – "still glamorous" vs. "lost its luster" – but there's agreement on the "elegant" settings and "high" price tags.

Mr. K's *Chinese*   23 | 23 | 23 | $63

East Midtown | 570 Lexington Ave. (51st St.) | 212-583-1668 | www.mrksny.com

An "opulent" pink art deco interior is the backdrop for "sumptuous" Chinese dining at this "high-class" East Side "throwback" overseen by a "ritzy, tuxedoed" staff; yes, prices run "high", but there's always the $28 prix fixe lunch.

NEW Mulberry & Vine *American*   ∇ 18 | 18 | 19 | $24

TriBeCa | 73 Warren St. (bet. Greenwich St. & W. B'way) | 212-791-6300 | www.mulberryandvine.com

Locavores and herbivores turn to this TriBeCa American cafe for a "variety of health-conscious", "seasonal" dishes that work for an "innovative" breakfast or lunch; it's "expensive" for the genre, but the convenience is hard to beat whether you eat within its "cute", "spacious" digs or carry out.

Murray's Cheese Bar *American*   23 | 15 | 20 | $38

West Village | 264 Bleecker St. (bet. Leroy & Morton Sts.) | 646-476-8882 | www.murrayscheesebar.com

A "cheese heaven" spun off from the popular down-the-block shop, this West Village American offers a fromage-focused lineup from "amazing" flights and wine pairings to "fabulous" fondue and "heavenly grilled cheese"; barely bigger than a wedge of Wensleydale, it's "busy" and "crowded" at prime times, but to most it's "charming" nonetheless.

Musket Room *New Zealand*   26 | 24 | 25 | $83

NoLita | 265 Elizabeth St. (bet. Houston & Prince Sts.) | 212-219-0764 | www.musketroom.com

"Beautifully composed, interesting and delicious" is the consensus on the "unexpected" New Zealand cooking at this NoLita "gem", also appreciated for its "outstanding" Kiwi wines; the "kind", "knowledgeable" staff and "understated" environs (including verdant herb garden views in the back room) further justify the "expensive" tab.

M. Wells Dinette *Québécois*   24 | 18 | 18 | $47

Long Island City | MoMA PS1 | 22-25 Jackson Ave. (46th Ave.) | Queens | 718-786-1800 | www.magasinwells.com

French-Canadian chef Hugue Dufour and wife Sarah Obraitis deliver an "amazing experience" at this lunch-only, museum-admission-not-required cafeteria inside LIC's MoMA PS1; the "rich, delicious" Québécois fusion fare comes in a former schoolhouse space whose "funky" classroom look is complete with chalkboard menus and cubbyhole desks, and in summer there's a rooftop annex for drinks and snacks.

NEW M. Wells Steakhouse *Steak*   22 | 19 | 21 | $90

Long Island City | 43-15 Crescent St. (bet. 43rd Ave. & 44th Rd.) | Queens | 718-786-9060 | www.magasinwells.com

Located in a LIC "converted auto-body shop", this Québécois-accented take on the classic steakhouse from Hugue Dufour and Sarah Obraitis presents chops "as big as your head" from a "wood-burning grill"

	FOOD	DECOR	SERVICE	COST

in the open kitchen (where there's also a live trout tank); a new patio with its own bar only adds to the "wonderful, unique" – and "pricey" – experience.

Nanni *Italian*

| 22 | 12 | 20 | $61 |

East Midtown | 146 E. 46th St. (bet. Lexington & 3rd Aves.) | 212-697-4161 | www.nanninyc.com

"Loyal regulars" populate this "old-world" Northern Italian near Grand Central, where "excellent" classic dishes "like grandma's" are ferried by beloved, "been-there-forever" waiters; yes, it's "expensive" given the "ancient surroundings", but you'll "not leave disappointed."

Naples 45 *Italian/Pizza*

| 21 | 17 | 19 | $40 |

East Midtown | 200 Park Ave. (45th St.) | 212-972-7001 | www.naples45.com

This "handy", "commuter"-friendly venue near Grand Central knocks out a "solid", if "unspectacular", Southern Italian menu led by "authentic" Neapolitan pizza; relatively "inexpensive" tabs offset the "loud" acoustics and crazy "bustle" at lunchtime, when it fills up with "non-CEO" types; P.S. closed weekends.

NEW Narcissa *American*

| 27 | 25 | 24 | $81 |

East Village | Standard East Village Hotel | 21 Cooper Sq. (bet. 4th & 5th Sts.) | 212-228-3344 | www.narcissarestaurant.com

Chef John Fraser (Dovetail) "doesn't disappoint" at this "hot spot" in the Standard East Village Hotel, where the "complex" New American fare stars "delicious" rotisserie specialties and "amazing vegetables", some from co-owner André Balazs' upstate farm; the "attentive" staff, "sociable" crowd and "lovely", light-filled space seal the "fab" deal.

The National *American*

| 19 | 18 | 17 | $53 |

East Midtown | Benjamin Hotel | 557 Lexington Ave. (50th St.) | 212-715-2400 | www.thenationalnyc.com

"Crazy-busy for lunch, quieter and more relaxed at dinner", Geoffrey Zakarian's "business" nexus in East Midtown's Benjamin Hotel presents a "comfortable" setting for "solid", "simple" American cooking; noise levels are "loud" and the service "spotty", but the crowds keep coming.

Natsumi *Japanese*

| 20 | 16 | 20 | $46 |

Midtown | Amsterdam Court Hotel | 226 W. 50th St. (bet. B'way & 8th Ave.) | 212-258-2988 | www.natsuminyc.com

Amid the Theater District "madness" lies this Japanese "sleeper" that "exceeds expectations" with its "delectable sushi", "helpful" service and "reasonable" rates; other endearments include a "sleek" room "not filled to the brim with tourists" and a "tolerable noise level."

NEW Navy *Seafood*

| – | – | – | M |

SoHo | 137 Sullivan St. (bet. Houston & Prince Sts.) | 212-533-1137 | www.navynyc.com

From the team behind TriBeCa's Smith & Mills, with *Top Chef* alum Camille Becerra in the kitchen, this guppy-size SoHo seafooder presents a daily changing menu starring raw-bar and house-cured selections; hip, breezy maritime decor and bold cocktails complete the happening package.

	FOOD	DECOR	SERVICE	COST

Naya *Lebanese* — 22 | 17 | 20 | $36

East Midtown | 1057 Second Ave. (bet. 55th & 56th Sts.) |
212-319-7777 | www.nayarestaurants.com

Naya Express *Lebanese*

East Midtown | 688 Third Ave. (43rd St.) | 212-557-0007

NEW **Midtown** | 54 W. 56th St. (bet. 5th & 6th Aves.) | 212-944-7777
www.nayaexpress.com

Meze mavens dig into "marvelous" Lebanese dishes at this "classy"
Eastsider where the "staff treats you like family", but the "striking",
"all-white" interior feels more "futuristic railway car" than homey
taverna; meanwhile, the "lunchtime lines" at the counter-service Express
offshoots "say it all."

Negril *Caribbean/Jamaican* — 23 | 20 | 21 | $56

Greenwich Village | 70 W. Third St. (bet. La Guardia Pl. & Thompson
St.) | 212-477-2804 | www.negrilvillage.com

"Hot food, hot crowd" sums up this "modern" Village Jamaican where
the "lively" scene is fueled by "phenomenal" cocktails and "flavorful",
"dressed-up" Caribbean fare; sure, other competitors are "less expensive", but you're paying for the "upscale" milieu here.

Nello *Italian* — 18 | 18 | 17 | $118

East 60s | 696 Madison Ave. (bet. 62nd & 63rd Sts.) | 212-980-9099
Money is no object at this one-of-a-kind UES Italian, famed for serving
"nothing-out-of-this-world" food for "mortgage-the-house" sums;
habitués jockey for the "sidewalk seats" on Madison Avenue ("the place
to be seen"), where a "pretentious" crowd is attended to by staffers who
"think they're celebs."

Nerai *Greek* — ▽ 22 | 23 | 21 | $68

Midtown | 55 E. 54th St. (bet. Madison & Park Aves.) | 212-759-5554 |
www.nerainyc.com

"Elegant and quiet", this "upscale" Midtown Greek caters to "business"
types with "thoughtfully prepared", seafood-focused fare delivered by
an "accommodating" crew in "sleek", breezy digs; though it's not cheap,
there's a prix fixe lunch to "provide value."

Neta *Japanese* — 25 | 19 | 24 | $137

Greenwich Village | 61 W. Eighth St. (6th Ave.) | 212-505-2610 |
www.netanyc.com

"Sublime sushi", "wonderful small plates" and "dazzling" omakase
options net a loyal fan base for this "civilized" Village Japanese; the
"nondescript space" is brightened by "knowledgeable" staffers and
an "entertaining" sushi bar, and though "not cheap", it's "a great way
to spoil yourself."

New Imperial Palace *Chinese* — ▽ 22 | 11 | 15 | $28

Flushing | 136-13 37th Ave. (Main St.) | Queens | 718-939-3501
This Flushing Chinese "treasure" specializes in "mouthwatering"
Cantonese-style seafood dishes, including the "exceptional" signature
Dungeness crab over sticky rice; a "cavernous dining hall"–type place, it
"caters to large families" and often requires a "wait to be seated"
at prime times.

	FOOD	DECOR	SERVICE	COST

New Leaf *American*

22 | 25 | 21 | $48

Inwood | Fort Tryon Park | 1 Margaret Corbin Dr. (190th St.) |
212-568-5323 | www.newleafrestaurant.com

Almost "like a country inn", this "getaway" in "lovely" Fort Tryon Park
provides a "stunning", "surrounded-by-trees" setting for its "farm-to-
table" American fare, especially out on the "magical" terrace; all profits
go to Bette Midler's NY Restoration Project, so few mind if it's on
the "pricey" side.

New Malaysia *Malaysian*

∇ 23 | 15 | 17 | $18

Chinatown | Chinatown Arcade | 46-48 Bowery (Canal St.) |
212-964-0284 | www.newmalaysiarestaurant.com

Despite an "awkward location" in a Chinatown alley ("find it!"), this
Malaysian mainstay has been "packing in the locals" for nearly 40 years;
given its "huge menu" of "delicious", seriously "inexpensive" dishes,
"flavor" junkies happily overlook its nothing-fancy milieu.

New WonJo *Korean*

23 | 14 | 19 | $36

Midtown | 23 W. 32nd St. (bet. B'way & 5th Ave.) | 212-695-5815 |
www.newwonjo.com

"Korean awesomeness" 24/7 is the deal at this K-town vet whose
"crave"-worthy specialties include tableside BBQ; you "gotta love the
charcoal" grills (vs. more typical gas ones) – but "long lines" at peak
hours are also part of the package.

Ngam *Thai*

∇ 23 | 17 | 18 | $35

East Village | 99 Third Ave. (bet. 12th & 13th Sts.) | 212-777-8424 |
www.ngamnyc.com

"Spunky" chef Hong Thaimee is "usually on-site sharing the love"
as she turns out "wonderful", "imaginative" twists on Thai comfort
classics at this East Village "charmer"; "interesting" cocktails and
a "fun" (if "small") rough-hewn space are two more reasons it's an
all-around "favorite."

Nha Trang *Vietnamese*

24 | 9 | 15 | $20

Chinatown | 148 Centre St. (bet. Walker & White Sts.) | 212-941-9292
Chinatown | 87 Baxter St. (bet. Bayard & Canal Sts.) | 212-233-5948
www.nhatrangone.com

"Fantastic" pho and other "authentic" Vietnamese eats trump "institutional decor" and the "rushed service you'd expect" at these "hole-in-
the-wall" Chinatown joints; "incredibly reasonable" prices are one more
reason they're "worth a stop" even if you're not on jury duty.

Nice Green Bo *Chinese*

22 | 5 | 11 | $21

Chinatown | 66 Bayard St. (bet. Elizabeth & Mott Sts.) | 212-625-2359 |
www.nicegreenbo.com

"Hungry hordes" hit this Chinatown "hole-in-the-wall" to nosh on "some
of NY's best soup dumplings" and other "first-rate, bargain-priced"
Shanghai specialties; "dumpy" digs and "grumpy" staffers are just part
of the experience.

Nice Matin *French/Mediterranean*

19 | 17 | 18 | $47

West 70s | 201 W. 79th St. (Amsterdam Ave.) | 212-873-6423 |
www.nicematinnyc.com

"Always running full throttle", this all-day UWS "hive" doles out "reliable"

French-Med eats in a "casual" yet "glamorous" space channeling the "south of France", complete with "sidewalk seating" to "watch the passing scene"; however, given the prime-time "noise" and "crush", regulars say it's "best off-peak."

Nick & Stef's Steakhouse *Steak* | 22 | 20 | 22 | $71 |

Midtown | 9 Penn Plaza (bet. 7th & 8th Aves.) | 212-563-4444 | www.patinagroup.com

"Incredibly convenient to MSG" – diners can even use a private arena entrance – this "comfortable" Penn Plaza steakhouse boasts "perfectly cooked" beef and service that's "past the level of friendly"; even if the style's "sort of a decade ago", it's "a bright spot" in a food-challenged nabe.

Nick & Toni's Cafe *Mediterranean* | 19 | 14 | 19 | $52 |

West 60s | 100 W. 67th St. (bet. B'way & Columbus Ave.) | 212-496-4000 | www.nickandtoniscafe.com

Just a "short walk" from Lincoln Center, this "low-key" offshoot of the "popular" East Hampton standby plies "enjoyable", "straightforward" Mediterranean fare via a "quick" team; "reasonable" rates make it a good bet "pre-movie or -show", with the chance of spotting "journalists from nearby ABC."

Nick's *Pizza* | 23 | 14 | 19 | $26 |

East 90s | 1814 Second Ave. (94th St.) | 212-987-5700 | www.nicksnyc.com

Forest Hills | 108-26 Ascan Ave. (bet. Austin & Burns Sts.) | Queens | 718-263-1126

A "step above your everyday pizza place", these UES–Forest Hills joints specialize in "charred", thin-crust pies with "perfect sauce" and some "gourmet flair"; true, the decor and service are strictly "no-frills", but they fill the bill as "family"-friendly choices with a "neighborhood feel."

Nicola's *Italian* | 22 | 17 | 21 | $71 |

East 80s | 146 E. 84th St. (Lexington Ave.) | 212-249-9850 | www.nicolasnyc.com

"Yes, it's like a private club" and that's fine with the "well-heeled" regulars who seek out this "unhurried" Upper Eastsider for "scrumptious", "old-time" Italian cooking and "warm welcomes"; it's "expensive" and "a wee bit dated", but at least you can "develop membership status" with return visits.

Nicoletta *Italian/Pizza* ∇ | 19 | 16 | 19 | $33 |

East Village | 160 Second Ave. (10th St.) | 212-432-1600 | www.nicolettanyc.com

Sample big-shot chef Michael White's wares "without the usual price tag" at this East Village pizzeria, home to thick-crust pies topped with intriguingly "different combinations"; the results earn a split decision ("amazing" vs. "disappointing"), though most agree it's "sort of a no-frills place."

Nightingale 9 *Vietnamese* ∇ | 23 | — | 21 | $31 |

Carroll Gardens | 345 Smith St. (bet. Carroll & 2nd Sts.) | Brooklyn | 347-689-4699 | www.nightingale9.com

Carroll Gardens locals "keep coming back" for "delicious", "farm-to-table" renditions of Vietnamese street fare at this "friendly", "fair-priced" Carroll Gardens "favorite"; recently relocated to the roomier ex-Seersucker digs, it has added new dishes to its "creative" lineup and now has a full bar.

99 Miles to Philly *Cheesesteaks*

| 20 | 9 | 16 | $14 |

East Midtown | 300 E. 45th St. (2nd Ave.) | 212-297-9500
Greenwich Village | 94 Third Ave. (bet. 12th & 13th Sts.) | 212-253-2700
www.99milestophilly.com

The closest you'll get to Philly that "doesn't involve a Chinatown bus", these Greenwich Village–East Midtown cheesesteak palaces proffer a marquee sandwich that's a "solid", "satisfying", "gooey mess"; late-night availability trumps "grungy" looks and minimal seating, but aesthetes advise "get it to go."

Ninja *Japanese*

| ∇ 13 | 23 | 20 | $57 |

TriBeCa | 25 Hudson St. (bet. Duane & Reade Sts.) | 212-274-8500 | www.ninjanewyork.com

With "jumping ninjas and a roaming magic act", they really "go all out" at this "gimmicky" TriBeCa theme joint done up "like a Japanese village" in feudal times; it's "fun for kids", but grown-ups' opinions vary ("naff" vs. a "blast") – most agree you'll "shell out" for only "so-so" eats.

Nino's *Italian*

| 21 | 19 | 21 | $54 |

East 70s | 1354 First Ave. (bet. 72nd & 73rd Sts.) | 212-988-0002 | www.ninosnyc.com

Nino's Bellissima Pizza *Pizza*

East Midtown | 890 Second Ave. (bet. 47th & 48th Sts.) | 212-355-2355 | www.ninospositano.com

Nino's Positano *Pizza*

East Midtown | 890 Second Ave. (bet. 47th & 48th Sts.) | 212-355-2355 | www.ninospositano.com

Nino's Tuscany Steak House *Italian/Steak*

Midtown | 117 W. 58th St. (bet. 6th & 7th Aves.) | 212-757-8630 | www.ninostuscany.com

"More than a typical neighborhood Italian", these "civilized" standbys exude "old-world charm" from the "comfortable" settings to the "delicious", "traditional" cooking; maybe they're "a little pricey", but "smiling" host Nino always "enhances the experience."

Ninth Street Espresso *Coffee*

| ∇ 23 | 15 | 19 | $6 |

Chelsea | 75 Ninth Ave. (bet. 15th & 16th Sts.) | 212-228-2930
East Midtown | 109 E. 56th St. (bet. Lexington & Park Aves.) | 646-559-4793
East Village | 700 E. 9th St. (Ave. C) | 212-358-9225
East Village | 341 E. 10th St. (Ave. B) | 212-777-3508
www.ninthstreetespresso.com

This pioneering "coffee-lover's coffeehouse" chainlet is a "go-to" for "meticulously prepared", "damn good" java – notably "espresso that packs some punch" – made with beans from Queens' Dallis Bros.; its spaces featuring a "simple aesthetic" are staffed by "serious" yet "mellow" baristas.

	FOOD	DECOR	SERVICE	COST

Nizza *French/Italian*

| | 21 | 15 | 18 | $43 |

Midtown | 630 Ninth Ave. (bet. 44th & 45th Sts.) | 212-956-1800 | www.nizzanyc.com

"Won't-break-the-bank" prices for "solid" classics from the French-Italian Riviera ensure this "casual" Theater District spot is plenty "popular" pre- or post-curtain; the noise level can be "a bit much", but in warm weather there's always the sidewalk seating; P.S. the gluten-free options are "impressive."

Nobu *Japanese*

| | 27 | 23 | 24 | $93 |

TriBeCa | 105 Hudson St. (Franklin St.) | 212-334-4445

Nobu 57 *Japanese*

Midtown | 40 W. 57th St. (bet. 5th & 6th Aves.) | 212-757-3000

Nobu, Next Door *Japanese*

TriBeCa | 105 Hudson St. (Franklin St.) | 212-219-0500
www.noburestaurants.com

Ever "a classic", Nobu Matsuhisa's TriBeCa "masterpiece" upholds its "well-deserved reputation" with "heavenly" Japanese-Peruvian fare and "professional" service in an "iconic" setting by David Rockwell; the "high quality" extends to its "more relaxed" next-door annex and a "vast" Midtown branch that "screams 57th Street", though it "obviously comes at a price."

Nocello *Italian*

| | 22 | 18 | 22 | $55 |

Midtown | 257 W. 55th St. (bet. B'way & 8th Ave.) | 212-713-0224 | www.nocello.net

"Enduring and endearing" – as well as "convenient" if you're bound for Carnegie Hall or City Center – this "cozy" Tuscan turns out "plentiful" platefuls of "fine" "traditional" fare; "charming owners" who "take pride" add "warmth" to the "unassuming" digs.

NoHo Star *American/Asian*

| | 19 | 17 | 20 | $38 |

NoHo | 330 Lafayette St. (Bleecker St.) | 212-925-0070 | www.nohostar.com

The "offbeat" menu "should just say 'everything, plus Chinese'" at this "long-standing" NoHo "favorite" that "cheerfully" offers Asian specialties side by side with "kicked-up" American eats; tabs "priced right" and a "comfy" setting are other reasons this "star keeps shining."

Noir New York City *American*

| | ▽ 24 | 24 | 23 | $60 |

East Midtown | 151 E. 50th St. (bet. Lexington & 3rd Aves.) | 212-753-1144 | www.noir-ny.com

"Sophistication" is the aim at this bi-level East Midtown brasserie, where "superb", lightly tweaked takes on American classics are ferried by a "professional" team; the chandeliered space with a curvy staircase has a "luxurious feel", though it "turns into a club" with DJs as the night advances.

NoMad *American/European*

| | 26 | 26 | 24 | $88 |

Flatiron | NoMad Hotel | 1170 Broadway (28th St.) | 347-472-5660 | www.thenomadhotel.com

"Sublime all around", this "hot scene" in the NoMad Hotel offers Daniel Humm's "irresistible" American-European fare (including the "roast chicken of a lifetime") served by a "smooth" team in several "plush"

	FOOD	DECOR	SERVICE	COST

rooms; regulars say it's a definite addition to your "must-eat list", so long as you're prepared to pay "special-occasion prices."

NEW The NoMad Bar *American*   — | — | — | M

Flatiron | NoMad Hotel | 10 W. 28th St. (B'way) | 347-472-5660 | www.thenomadhotel.com

An offshoot of the NoMad around the corner, this Flatiron boîte specializes in ultra-refined cocktails – including show-stopper 'explosions' served in big spigotted vessels, meant for a crowd – and elevated bar bites (think chicken pot pie with foie gras and truffles); the moody, bi-level space sports banquettes, a fireplace and lots of dark wood.

Nom Wah Tea Parlor *Chinese*   21 | 13 | 14 | $22

Chinatown | 13 Doyers St. (bet. Chatham Sq. & Pell St.) | 212-962-6047 | www.nomwah.com

You may "need Google Maps" to find it, but it's worth seeking out this "quintessential" Chinatown parlor for its "dazzling array" of "real-deal", "made-to-order" dim sum at "bargain" rates; around since 1920 but recently "revitalized", it's a "favorite" – "go early or really late" to avoid a wait.

Noodle Pudding *Italian*   23 | 18 | 21 | $42

Brooklyn Heights | 38 Henry St. (bet. Cranberry & Middagh Sts.) | Brooklyn | 718-625-3737

A "beacon" in Brooklyn Heights, this "boisterous" Italian is usually "hopping by 6:30" thanks to its "loyal local following" that loves the "fantastic", "nonna"-worthy fare and "delightful" staff; cash-only, no-reservations hassles are offset by the "convivial" mood and "more-than-fair" prices.

Nook *Eclectic*   ▽ 23 | 11 | 19 | $34

Midtown | 746 Ninth Ave. (bet. 50th & 51st Sts.) | 212-247-5500

Only "slightly bigger than a walk-in closet", this "aptly named" West Midtown "neighborhood hangout" compensates for its "cramped setting" and "sometimes gruff" service with "well-prepared" Eclectic eats; the cash-only policy hardly matters since "BYO makes it a super bargain."

NEW Norman's Cay *Caribbean/Seafood*   — | — | — | M

Lower East Side | 74 Orchard St. (bet. Broome & Grand Sts.) | 646-481-1229 | www.normanscaynyc.com

A stuffed shark, lots of whitewashed wood and a suspended puddle-jumper plane nod to the islands at this narrow Lower Eastsider specializing in Caribbean seafood; from the Grey Lady team, it features a second-floor lounge where the cocktail list is heavy on rum.

Norma's *American*   24 | 19 | 19 | $47

Midtown | Le Parker Meridien Hotel | 119 W. 56th St. (bet. 6th & 7th Aves.) | 212-708-7460 | www.normasnyc.com

Folks "serious about breakfast" tout this "decadent" Parker Meridien American known for its portions so "huge", you "may never eat again"; yes, the tabs are "crazy expensive" – e.g. the "zillion-dollar lobster frittata" (ok, it's only $1,000) – but the setting is "sleek", the service "pro" and the brunches "quintessential."

Northeast Kingdom *American*

▽ 25 | 22 | 21 | $41

Bushwick | 18 Wyckoff Ave. (Troutman St.) | Brooklyn | 718-386-3864 | www.north-eastkingdom.com

This "cool little" Bushwick "pioneer" is a "solid" bet for real-deal "farm-to-table" American fare, where your meal might even feature foraging finds from the husband-and-wife proprietors; its "warm" and "unassuming" quarters include a fireplace-equipped "den" downstairs serving cocktails and snacks till 1 AM.

North End Grill *American/Seafood*

24 | 23 | 24 | $74

Battery Park City | 104 North End Ave. (bet. Murray & Vesey Sts.) | 646-747-1600 | www.northendgrillnyc.com

Finally, there's "destination dining in Battery Park City" via Danny Meyer's "spacious" American standout serving an "imaginative" seafood-centric menu delivered by a "couldn't-be-nicer" crew; the "airy", "contemporary" room is "reasonably quiet", so lively sorts join the "Wall Street overachievers" at the bar.

Northern Spy Food Co. *American*

22 | 19 | 22 | $39

East Village | 511 E. 12th St. (bet. Aves. A & B) | 212-228-5100 | www.northernspyfoodco.com

This "wonderfully eccentric" East Village "locavore destination" turns out "savory", "farm-to-table" American food at "moderate" rates; "warm and fuzzy" service makes up for the "very small space" that gets "crammed" at prime times.

North Square *American*

25 | 21 | 23 | $52

Greenwich Village | Washington Sq. Hotel | 103 Waverly Pl. (MacDougal St.) | 212-254-1200 | www.northsquareny.com

It's a "favorite" of "NYU profs" and other "Washington Square regulars", but otherwise this "swell little neighborhood place" mostly flies under the radar; "superior" New American cuisine, "civilized" service and a "grown-up", "comfy" setting where you "can talk without going hoarse" keep it a "neighborhood standby."

No. 7 *American*

21 | 13 | 16 | $24

Fort Greene | 7 Greene Ave. (bet. Cumberland & Fulton Sts.) | Brooklyn | 718-522-6370 | www.no7restaurant.com

No. 7 Sub *Sandwiches*

Flatiron | Ace Hotel | 1188 Broadway (bet. 28th & 29th Sts.) | 212-532-1680

Midtown | Plaza Food Hall | 1 W. 59th St., lower level (5th Ave.) | 646-755-3228

Dumbo | 11 Water St. (bet. New Dock & Old Fulton Sts.) | Brooklyn | 917-618-4399

No. 7 North

Greenpoint | 931 Manhattan Ave. (bet. Java & Kent Sts.) | Brooklyn | 718-389-7775

www.no7sub.com

This "cool", BAM-handy Fort Greene number is a "local favorite" for "intriguing" New American innovations "that all work" ("two words: broccoli tacos!"); its counter-serve outlets follow up with "can't-be-beat" sub sandwiches whose "quality ingredients" and "wacky combos" likewise venture "beyond the common herd."

	FOOD	DECOR	SERVICE	COST

Novitá *Italian*
24 | 18 | 22 | $64

Gramercy Park | 102 E. 22nd St. (bet. Lexington Ave. & Park Ave. S.) | 212-677-2222 | www.novitanyc.com

The "definition of 'neighborhood gem'", this Gramercy vet serves Northern Italian fare so "scrumptious" that no one seems to mind the "cheek-to-jowl" seating and "concomitant noise levels"; "highly efficient" service and "modestly priced wines" are other reasons regulars plead "please keep this a secret."

Nucci's *Italian*
23 | 18 | 22 | $34

Tottenville | 4842 Arthur Kill Rd. (S. Bridge St.) | Staten Island | 718-967-3600
West Brighton | 616 Forest Ave. (Oakland Ave.) | Staten Island | 718-815-4882
www.nuccis.net

"Sensational pizza" and other Italian "basics" have locals "dining regularly" at these "reliable" Staten Islanders; "fair prices" and "make-you-feel-like-family" service trump "mediocre" atmospherics, so most consider them decent "neighborhood" fallbacks.

Numero 28 *Pizza*
23 | 14 | 17 | $28

East 70s | 1431 First Ave. (bet. 74th & 75th Sts.) | 212-772-8200
East Village | 176 Second Ave. (bet. 11th & 12th Sts.) | 212-777-1555
West 90s | 660 Amsterdam Ave. (92nd St.) | 212-706-7282
West Village | 28 Carmine St. (bet. Bedford & Bleecker Sts.) | 212-463-9653
www.numero28.com

"In a sea of neighborhood pizza joints", these "homey" outlets produce "remarkable", "crispy" real-deal Neapolitan pies (including a 29-inch "oblong") in "blazing", wood-fired brick ovens; the "unpretentious", cash-only style is more reason to be "pleasantly surprised by the quality."

Num Pang *Cambodian/Sandwiches*
23 | 9 | 14 | $13

NEW **Battery Park City** | Hudson Eats | 200 Vesey St. (West St.) | 212-227-1957
Chelsea | Chelsea Mkt. | 75 Ninth Ave. (bet. 15th & 16th Sts.) | 212-390-8851
Flatiron | 1129 Broadway (bet. 25th & 26th Sts.) | 212-647-8889
Greenwich Village | 28 E. 12th St. (bet. 5th Ave. & University Pl.) | 212-255-3271
NEW **Midtown** | 148 W. 48th St. (bet. 6th & 7th Aves.) | 212-421-0743
Murray Hill | 140 E. 41st St. (bet. Lexington & 3rd Aves.) | 212-867-8889
www.numpangnyc.com

"Cambodia's answer" to the banh mi craze, this local chain dispenses "damn good" sandwiches "worth standing in line for", with "more-than-fair" prices and "speedy service" to sweeten the deal; the setups are "fast food"-style, but most agree "you can't go wrong" here.

Nyonya *Malaysian*
23 | 14 | 17 | $22

Little Italy | 199 Grand St. (bet. Mott & Mulberry Sts.) | 212-334-3669
Bath Beach | 2322 86th St. (Bay 34th St.) | Brooklyn | 718-265-0888
Sunset Park | 5323 Eighth Ave. (54th St.) | Brooklyn | 718-633-0808
www.ilovenyonya.com

When you crave "spice and exotic flavors", these "amazing" Malaysians fill the bill with "generous" servings of "fresh", "delicious" standards at "ridiculously good" rates (just "bring cash"); "assembly-line" service and "packed", "no-frills" quarters only "add to the experience."

NYY Steak *Steak* | 22 | 22 | 22 | $75 |

NEW Midtown | 7 W. 51st St. (bet. 5th & 6th Aves.) | 646-307-7910
Concourse/Downtown | Yankee Stadium | 1 E. 161st St., Gate 6 (River Ave.) | Bronx | 646-977-8325
www.nyysteak.com

There's "no other place like" this ticket holders–only chophouse within Yankee Stadium, where "solid" steaks served in a room "adorned with memorabilia" are a "grand slam" for pinstripe fans who can swing the "high prices"; meanwhile, a sprawling, all-seasons offshoot pinch-hits near Rockefeller Center.

Oaxaca *Mexican* | 21 | 13 | 17 | $15 |

NEW East Village | 125 E. Seventh St. (bet. Ave. A & 1st Ave.) | 212-677-3340
West 80s | 424 Amsterdam Ave. (bet. 80th & 81st Sts.) | 212-580-4888
West Village | 48 Greenwich Ave. (bet. 10th & 11th Sts.) | 212-366-4488
NEW Bedford-Stuyvesant | 1116 Bedford Ave. (Quincy St.) | Brooklyn | 718-230-8111
Gowanus | 250 Fourth Ave. (bet. Carroll & President Sts.) | Brooklyn | 718-222-1122
www.oaxacatacos.com

"Addictive", "legit" tacos keep 'em coming to these "casual" Mexicans where the "cheap prices" also "hit the mark"; "no-frills" settings and "don't-hold-your-breath" service mean most rely on them as "stop-by-on-your-way-home" kinds of places.

Oceana *American/Seafood* | 25 | 23 | 23 | $77 |

Midtown | McGraw Hill Bldg. | 120 W. 49th St. (bet. 6th & 7th Aves.) | 212-759-5941 | www.oceanarestaurant.com

"Business folk" and "pre-theater" people alike gravitate to this "cavernous" Rock Center American seafooder for its "pristine fish", "gorgeous raw bar" and "classy" service; the "upscale" environs complete with outdoor seating help make it a "go-to" despite the "hefty" tab.

Ocean Grill *Seafood* | 23 | 21 | 22 | $60 |

West 70s | 384 Columbus Ave. (bet. 78th & 79th Sts.) | 212-579-2300 | www.oceangrill.com

"Still hopping after all these years", this UWS seafooder lures "big crowds" for "tasty", "simply grilled" marine cuisine dished up in a "white-tablecloth", "Hamptons-esque" setting; when the "noise level gets too high", insiders escape to the "pleasant" sidewalk seats.

OddFellows Ice Cream Company *Ice Cream* | 24 | 19 | 22 | $8 |

NEW East Village | 76 E. Fourth St. (bet. Bowery & 2nd Ave.) | 917-475-1812
Williamsburg | 175 Kent Ave. (N. 3rd St.) | Brooklyn | 347-599-0556
www.oddfellowsnyc.com

"The next big thing for ice cream" may be this "cute" Williamsburg soda fountain and its new East Village spin-off, whose small-batch output entices with "mind-blowing combos" à la maple-bacon pecan; "friendly" counter folk and frequent flavor change-ups mean "there's always a reason to go back."

	FOOD	DECOR	SERVICE	COST

The Odeon *American/French*

| | 20 | 18 | 19 | $52 |

TriBeCa | 145 W. Broadway (bet. Duane & Thomas Sts.) | 212-233-0507 | www.theodeonrestaurant.com

"Historical hipness" clings to this "iconic" '80s-era bistro, once a happening scene and now a "favorite mainstay" for TriBeCa locals seeking "well-prepared" Franco-American meals; the "relaxed vibe" and "great people-watching" mean it's "still fun" for everything from brunch to "late-night" snacking.

Ofrenda *Mexican*

| | ∇ 21 | 17 | 21 | $42 |

West Village | 113 Seventh Ave. S. (bet. 4th & 10th Sts.) | 212-924-2305 | www.ofrendanyc.com

"High-end", "fabuloso" Mexican fare – and "even better margaritas" – delivered by a "terrific" staff makes this "bustling", "bar-esque" West Villager a "go-to for neighborhood foodies"; "fun" outdoor seating and "amazing deals" at happy hour and brunch seal the deal.

Okeanos *Greek*

| | ∇ 22 | 19 | 20 | $41 |

Park Slope | 314 Seventh Ave. (8th St.) | Brooklyn | 347-725-4162 | www.okeanosnyc.com

A "find" for Greek eats "with an emphasis on seafood", this Park Slope sleeper plies all the Hellenic hallmarks, notably the freshest catch "cooked to perfection"; the "neighborhood" space is unremarkable but "peaceful", and regulars report "they don't rush you."

NEW Okonomi/Yuji Ramen *Japanese*

| | – | – | – | I |

Williamsburg | 150 Ainslie St. (bet. Leonard & Lorimer Sts.) | Brooklyn | no phone | www.okonomibk.com

Chef Yuji Haraguchi's two-in-one Williamsburg nook ladles out his popular noodle soups on Mondays and Tuesdays, when it operates as Yuji Ramen, then morphs into Okonomi for the rest of the week, serving Japan's traditional ichiju-sansai set meals (a daily changing breakfast and lunch comprising soup, veggies and seafood); the wood-lined space has but two tables and a tiny bar, so waits are a given.

Old Homestead *Steak*

| | 25 | 19 | 22 | $84 |

Chelsea | 56 Ninth Ave. (bet. 14th & 15th Sts.) | 212-242-9040 | www.theoldhomesteadsteakhouse.com

"Old-style NY" dining doesn't get much more authentic than this steakhouse "original" that's been grilling "perfectly seared" chops in Chelsea since 1868; "huge" tabs don't faze its core crowd of "men spending too much", though "massive" portions leave them as "over-stuffed" as the furniture.

Olea *Mediterranean*

| | ∇ 24 | 21 | 20 | $34 |

Fort Greene | 171 Lafayette Ave. (Adelphi St.) | Brooklyn | 718-643-7003 | www.oleabrooklyn.com

"Delicious", "ambitious" tapas and a "dream"-worthy brunch "bring the Mediterranean" – and "the masses" – to this "inviting" Fort Greene "mainstay"; it boasts a "BAM-convenient" address, "charming" service and "gentle" live music – but just go "off-peak" to avoid a "wait."

Olive's *Sandwiches*

| | ∇ 23 | 17 | 19 | $30 |

NEW Battery Park City | Hudson Eats | 200 Vesey St. (West St.) | 212-858-0111

continued

SoHo | 120 Prince St. (bet. Greene & Wooster Sts.) | 212-941-0111
www.olivesnyc.com

For a "quick bite", this "teeny" SoHo "take-out place" and its new Hudson Eats offshoot fill the bill with "delicious" sandwiches, soups and treats "at the right price"; there are "crazy lines at lunch", but it's hard to beat as a "shopping pit stop."

Olives *Mediterranean*   21 | 20 | 20 | $59

Union Square | W Hotel Union Sq. | 201 Park Ave. S. (17th St.) |
212-353-8345 | www.olivesnewyork.com

"Singles" mingle at this "fun" W Union Square Med plying an "inventive", "pricey" menu spotlighting "marvelous" flatbreads, served up in "modern" environs; though chef Todd English is no longer involved, the scene remains much the same, including lots of "socializing" at the "lively" (and "noisy") adjacent bar.

Omai *Vietnamese*   22 | 13 | 17 | $47

Chelsea | 158 Ninth Ave. (bet. 19th & 20th Sts.) | 212-633-0550 |
www.omainyc.com

A longtime "solid neighborhood" "go-to", this "pleasant", "little" Chelsea Vietnamese serves up "delicious", "delicate" standards; "reasonable prices" and a location "close to the Joyce Theater" are pluses, though the "low-key" space is on the "tight" side.

Omonia Cafe *Coffee/Greek*   22 | 18 | 18 | $24

Astoria | 32-20 Broadway (33rd St.) | Queens | 718-274-6650
Bay Ridge | 7612 Third Ave. (bet. 76th & 77th Sts.) | Brooklyn |
718-491-1435
www.omoniacafe.com

A "mind-boggling array" of "heavenly" sweets awaits at these Greek coffeehouses also serving some savory bites, where "neon lights" and a "disco vibe" suit "teenagers" who "hang out and socialize" late-night; P.S. Astoria's Next Door adjunct dabbles in more experimental pastries (cheesecake baklava, anyone?).

NEW 100 Montaditos *Sandwiches*   20 | 18 | 19 | $16

Greenwich Village | 176 Bleecker St. (bet. MacDougal & Sullivan Sts.) |
646-719-1713
Lower East Side | 177 Ludlow St. (bet. Houston & Stanton Sts.) |
646-666-0993
www.us.100montaditos.com

"Scrumptious mini-sandwiches" with a "plethora of choices" are "ridiculously affordable" at these branches of the Spain-based chain; "quick" counter servers also dispense beer and sangria at this instant "student hangout" that boasts a "bite-sized" backyard.

One if by Land, Two if by Sea *American*   23 | 26 | 25 | $101

West Village | 17 Barrow St. (bet. 7th Ave. S. & W. 4th St.) |
212-255-8649 | www.oneifbyland.com

"Steeped in history" and "romance", this "historic" Village "rendezvous" set in Aaron Burr's former carriage house offers "excellent" American cuisine delivered by staffers who "take their job seriously"; "mood-setting" touches – "candlelit rooms", four fireplaces, a piano bar – distract from the "special occasion"-level, prix fixe–only tabs.

	FOOD	DECOR	SERVICE	COST

101 *American/Italian* — 21 | 21 | 21 | $50

Bay Ridge | 10018 Fourth Ave. (100th St.) | Brooklyn | 718-833-1313 |
www.101bayridge.com

It's "still tough to find a table" on prime nights at this longtime Bay Ridge "local joint" whose "quality" midpriced Italian-American fare, "wonderful location overlooking the Verrazano" and convenient valet parking keep 'em coming; a "busy, loud" atmosphere is part of the package.

107 West *Eclectic* — 20 | 18 | 19 | $46

West 100s | 2787 Broadway (bet. 107th & 108th Sts.) | 212-864-1555 |
www.107west.com

A "longtime haunt" near Columbia, this no-frills "favorite" plies a "wide-ranging" Eclectic menu spanning the gamut from Cajun and Tex-Mex basics to pastas and sushi; maybe it's "nothing too exciting", but "fair prices" and "happy-to-have you" service keep the seats full.

1 or 8 *Japanese* — 24 | 22 | 22 | $58

Williamsburg | 66 S. Second St. (Wythe Ave.) | Brooklyn |
718-384-2152 | www.oneoreightbk.com

"Unique style" permeates this "off-the-beaten-path" Williamsburg sushi standout spinning "unconventional" takes on Japanese fare in a "sleek white" setting that's a "minimalist's" dream; along with the "high-quality" fare, regulars single out the "delightful staff" as key to the "consistently solid" experience.

NEW Onomea *Hawaiian* — — | — | — | M

Williamsburg | 84 Havemeyer St. (Metropolitan Ave.) | Brooklyn |
347-844-9559

Among NYC's only sources for Aloha State specialties, this budget-friendly Williamsburg Hawaiian serves up favorites like poke (marinated raw aki tuna) and Spam musubi (a rice roll starring everyone's favorite canned meat); the wood-lined space's backlit images of the islands boost the exotic mood.

Ootoya *Japanese/Noodle Shop* — 23 | 20 | 19 | $36

Flatiron | 8 W. 18th St. (bet. 5th & 6th Aves.) | 212-255-0018
Midtown | 141 W. 41st St. (bet. B'way & 6th Ave.) | 212-704-0833
www.ootoya.us

Turning out "Japanese comfort food" "at its best", these "nothing-fancy" branches of a Tokyo-based izakaya chain provide a "delicious" lineup of "down-to-earth" favorites like yakitori, soba and soup bowls; given "reasonable" pricing, the only hitch is the occasional "wait."

Oriental Garden *Chinese/Seafood* — 21 | 12 | 16 | $34

Chinatown | 14 Elizabeth St. (bet. Bayard & Canal Sts.) | 212-619-0085 |
www.orientalgardenny.com

"Don't let the drab decor fool you" at this C-town Cantonese vet, because its "wonderful" dim sum and seafood fresh "from the tanks" just might "knock your socks off"; the mood gets "manic" at prime times, but at least the "banquet" comes "without an insane price."

Orsay *French* — 18 | 20 | 18 | $65

East 70s | 1057 Lexington Ave. (75th St.) | 212-517-6400 |
www.orsayrestaurant.com

An UES facsimile of "bygone France" by way of "Balthazar", this French

brasserie offers the "expected" dishes (at "unexpectedly high prices")
to a "boisterous", "multigenerational" crowd; "indifferent" service and a
"lovely" art nouveau setting cement the "classique" feel.

Orso *Italian*

24 | 20 | 23 | $60

Midtown | 322 W. 46th St. (bet. 8th & 9th Aves.) | 212-489-7212 |
www.orsorestaurant.com

A "Theater District standard" for decades, this "crowded-but-convivial"
Restaurant Row Italian still supplies "reliably delicious", "upscale" fare
via a "quick" staff of "would-be actors"; it's on the "plain" side and "reserving way ahead is a must", but to fans it's "worth it" for the "Broadway
star"–gazing alone.

Oslo Coffee Roasters *Coffee*

∇ 23 | 18 | 22 | $7

East 70s | 422 E. 75th St. (bet. 1st & York Aves.) | 718-782-0332
Williamsburg | 133 Roebling St. (4th St.) | Brooklyn | 718-782-0332
Williamsburg | 328 Bedford Ave. (S. 2nd St.) | Brooklyn | 718-782-0332
www.oslocoffee.com

"Reawaken the five senses" with "delicious" brews from roasted-in-house
beans at these "cool" Williamsburg-born coffee bars; "plain-and-simple"
setups staffed by "fun baristas", they're reliable neighborhood stop-ins
when you're "on the go."

Osteria al Doge *Italian*

21 | 18 | 19 | $51

Midtown | 142 W. 44th St. (bet. B'way & 6th Ave.) | 212-944-3643 |
www.osteria-doge.com

Exuding "old-world charm", this Times Square duplex rolls out "tasty"
Venetian standards at a "reasonable-for-Midtown" price; the space is
"cozy" (even if some say it "could use a face-lift"), while the "speedy"
staff "gets you to the theater on time."

Osteria Laguna *Italian*

∇ 20 | 19 | 20 | $49

East Midtown | 209 E. 42nd St. (bet. 2nd & 3rd Aves.) | 212-557-0001 |
www.osteria-laguna.com

Offering a "welcome" "neighborhood feel in a non-neighborhood area",
this "busy" Italian between Grand Central and the U.N. serves "straight-
ahead" Venetian eats at relatively "reasonable" rates; it's a "perfect lunch
spot for on-the-go execs", with a "people-watching" bonus when the
French doors are open.

Osteria Morini *Italian*

25 | 19 | 22 | $60

SoHo | 218 Lafayette St. (bet. Broome & Spring Sts.) | 212-965-8777 |
www.osteriamorini.com

Chef Michael White "goes bohemian" at this "boisterous" SoHo Italian
where the "rustic" Emilia-Romagna menu is highlighted by "sublime pastas"; it's "not cheap", and can feel "crammed" at prime times, but there's
a reason it's "always busy."

Otto *Italian/Pizza*

23 | 19 | 19 | $41

Greenwich Village | 1 Fifth Ave. (8th St.) | 212-995-9559 |
www.ottopizzeria.com

"Energetic" to say the least, this "happening" enoteca/pizzeria from the
Batali-Bastianich crew lures "lots of families" and "NYU students" with
"fantastic" pizzas and pastas, a "huge wine list" and "decent prices"; it's

a perennially "packed", "fun, loud" scene – especially in the "Italian train station"–esque front bar.

	FOOD	DECOR	SERVICE	COST

NEW Otto's Tacos *Mexican* ▽ 22 | 15 | 20 | $13

East Village | 141 Second Ave. (10th St.) | 646-678-4018 |
www.ottostacos.com

Taco buffs otto "try everything" on the "streamlined menu" at this snug East Village taqueria, where the LA-style goods "are packed with flavor" thanks to five "quality" fillings and housemade corn tortillas; the counter staff's "friendly as can be", but "tight seating" argues for "grab and go."

Ouest *American* 22 | 21 | 21 | $72

West 80s | 2315 Broadway (84th St.) | 212-580-8700 |
www.ouestny.com

"Special-night-out" celebrants make for this "civilized" "oasis" from Tom Valenti, calling it "one of the few classy places" on the "Upper Ouest Side"; "wonderful" New American fare and "expert" service in a "comfortable" setting help justify the "expensive" tab – though wallet-watchers say the $34 early-bird is "is the way to go."

Ovelia *Greek* ▽ 21 | 18 | 18 | $33

Astoria | 34-01 30th Ave. (34th St.) | Queens | 718-721-7217 |
www.ovelia-ny.com

A "go-to" for Astorians seeking "Greek chic", this bar/eatery offers "fresh" Hellenic specialties with a "modern twist", including housemade sausages; "hospitable" owners, modest tabs and a "casual", "pleasant" setting with outdoor seating help keep it "popular."

Ovest Pizzoteca *Pizza* ▽ 24 | 18 | 21 | $33

Chelsea | 513 W. 27th St. (bet. 10th & 11th Aves.) | 212-967-4392 |
www.ovestnyc.com

"Fantastic" wood-oven pizza "like Naples says it should be" is the special-ty of this West Chelsea "neighborhood" pie parlor (a cousin of Luzzo's), also offering pastas and panini; "appropriate" tabs and a "relaxed" vibe tempt regulars to "hang out" well into the night.

Oyster Bar *Seafood* 22 | 18 | 18 | $54

Midtown | Grand Central | 89 E. 42nd St., Lower Level (Park Ave.) |
212-490-6650 | www.oysterbarny.com

NEW Oyster Bar Brooklyn *Seafood*

Park Slope | 254 Fifth Ave. (bet. Carroll St. & Garfield Pl.) | Brooklyn |
347-294-0596 | www.oysterbarbrooklyn-hub.com

"Historic" is the word on this 1913-vintage seafood mecca in Grand Central's lower level serving "divine" bivalves and "classic" pan roasts in a "glorious" setting outfitted with arched tile ceilings, long counters and an "old-school" rear saloon; surveyors find the smaller-scale Park Slope replica rather "underwhelming" in comparison, though the menu is as "pricey" as the mother ship.

Pachanga Patterson *Mexican* ▽ 23 | 23 | 23 | $32

Astoria | 33-17 31st Ave. (bet. 33rd & 34th Sts.) | Queens |
718-554-0525 | www.pachangapatterson.com

A "not-so-hidden gem" in Astoria, this "hip" Mexican from the Vesta folks puts a "cool spin" on tacos and other classics – but some say so-phisticated cocktails are its real "strong suit"; "multicolored string lights and candles" enliven its "low-key" interior, while the "sunny" backyard is a warm-weather "find."

Pacificana *Chinese* `24` `18` `18` `$28`

Sunset Park | 813 55th St. (8th Ave.) | Brooklyn | 718-871-2880 | www.sunset-park.com

"Delicious" dim sum draws "throngs" to this 500-seat, "you're-in–Hong Kong" Sunset Park banquet hall, where a well-priced Cantonese menu backs up what's on the "rolling carts"; on weekends it's a "madhouse" packed with "big multigenerational parties", but "be patient" – it's "worth the wait."

NEW Pacifico's Fine Foods *American* `–` `–` `–` `M`

Crown Heights | 798 Franklin Ave. (Lincoln Pl.) | Brooklyn | 917-966-2670 | www.pacificosfinefoods.com

Chef Shanna Pacifico, who made her chops at Peter Hoffman's eateries (Savoy, Back Forty), strikes out on her own with this cozy Crown Heights arrival; offering midpriced, Brazilian-influenced American fare with – natch – a farm-to-table ethos, it has a small bar that stays open late on prime nights.

NEW Pagani *Italian* ▽ `21` `19` `20` `$50`

West Village | 289 Bleecker St. (7th Ave. S.) | 212-488-5800 | www.paganinyc.com

"They know what they're doing" at this "unpretentious" West Village Italian, where "helpful" servers deliver an "interesting array" of "well-thought-out" pastas and small plates; since it's also "reasonably priced", the "biggest issue" is "knowing when to stop ordering."

Palà *Pizza* ▽ `22` `20` `21` `$37`

Lower East Side | 198 Allen St. (bet. Houston & Stanton Sts.) | 212-614-7252 | www.palapizza.com

A "delightful" "surprise", this LES pizzeria "caters to gluten-free and vegan needs" with separate menus that size up as "delicious and interesting" as the traditional pies also on offer; cool industrial digs and "divine" cocktails from the small bar earn extra credit.

The Palm *Steak* `25` `20` `23` `$78`

East Midtown | 837 Second Ave. (45th St.) | 212-687-2953
Midtown | 250 W. 50th St. (bet. B'way & 8th Ave.) | 212-333-7256
TriBeCa | 206 West St. (bet. Chambers & Warren Sts.) | 646-395-6393
Palm Too *Steak*
East Midtown | 840 Second Ave. (bet. 44th & 45th Sts.) | 212-687-2953
www.thepalm.com

"What you want in a steakhouse" is what's on offer at this "quintessential" chain delivering "ginormous" cuts and "huge lobsters" in "nostalgic", caricature-adorned digs; service swings from "caring" to "resentful", but that makes no difference to the "old boys" who say "if I could afford to go every day, I would"; P.S. the 1926 original is at 837 Second Avenue.

Palma *Italian* `25` `24` `23` `$63`

West Village | 28 Cornelia St. (bet. Bleecker & 4th Sts.) | 212-691-2223 | www.palmanyc.com

Sicilian cooking made with "loving care" tastes like "nonna's" at this "charming" West Villager with a "like-you're-in-Italy" vibe; its "lovely garden" is a "summer favorite", the private party–only carriage house is "perfect for a special occasion", and now there's a next-door wine bar, Aperitivo Di Palma.

Palm Court *American*
FOOD	DECOR	SERVICE	COST
18	24	19	$69

Midtown | Plaza Hotel | 768 Fifth Ave. (59th St.) | 212-546-5300 | www.theplazany.com

It doesn't "come much more elegant" than this Plaza Hotel American "icon", where a "gracious" staff glides through the "gilded" palm-lined setting to offer the "royal" treatment at breakfast, lunch and afternoon tea; now overseen by The Lambs Club's Geoffrey Zakarian, it's undergoing a redo that will add a prominent bar.

Palo Santo *Pan-Latin*
FOOD	DECOR	SERVICE	COST
▽ 23	20	21	$40

Park Slope | 652 Union St. (bet. 4th & 5th Aves.) | Brooklyn | 718-636-6311 | www.palosanto.us

A "change from the usual", this Park Slope "favorite" crafts "surprising", "*delicioso*" Pan-Latin dishes from "seasonal" ingredients – some plucked from its rooftop garden – including at the "not-to-be-missed" brunch; other endearments are a "pleasantly dark-and-moody" space with "artistic" decor touches and the "sweetest" staff.

Pampano *Mexican/Seafood*
FOOD	DECOR	SERVICE	COST
23	19	20	$59

East Midtown | 209 E. 49th St., 2nd fl. (bet. 2nd & 3rd Aves.) | 212-751-4545

Pampano Taqueria *Mexican*
East Midtown | Crystal Pavilion | 805 Third Ave. (bet. 49th & 50th Sts.) | 212-751-5257

www.richardsandoval.com

Coastal Mexican cuisine "hits the high notes" at this "upscale", second-floor East Midtown seafooder from chef Richard Sandoval and tenor Plácido Domingo; the more casual, street-level Botaneria dispenses cocktails and "interesting tapas", while the "secret" lunch-only Taqueria, located in an underground food court, sells tacos and guac.

Pam Real Thai Food *Thai*
FOOD	DECOR	SERVICE	COST
22	8	17	$25

Hell's Kitchen | 404 W. 49th St. (bet. 9th & 10th Aves.) | 212-333-7500 | www.pamrealthaifood.com

"Real-deal" Thai, "spiced to your taste", comes via a "speedy" staff at this cash-only Hell's Kitchen "favorite" that makes an "excellent pre-theater" choice; the interior is "kinda dumpy", but to most that's "worth tolerating" given pricing that's among the area's "best values."

Paola's *Italian*
FOOD	DECOR	SERVICE	COST
23	19	21	$67

East 90s | Wales Hotel | 1295 Madison Ave. (92nd St.) | 212-794-1890 | www.paolasrestaurant.com

As a "sophisticated" haunt for "ritzy" Upper Eastsiders, this "attractive" Carnegie Hill Italian wins favor with "*delizioso*" cuisine and "hospitality" via the "gracious" eponymous owner and her "tip-top" staff; wallet-watchers dub it "Payola's" – but it's "thriving" (and "loud") for a reason.

Papaya King *Hot Dogs*
FOOD	DECOR	SERVICE	COST
22	6	16	$9

East 80s | 179 E. 86th St. (3rd Ave.) | 212-369-0648

continued

East Village | 3 St. Marks Pl. (bet. 2nd & 3rd Aves.) | 646-692-8482
www.papayaking.com

"Easier than a trip to Coney Island", these wiener wonderlands supply "happiness in a tube" via "damn fine" hot dogs and papaya drinks on the "cheap" (even for "fast food"); ok, you're "not going for the ambiance", but as an "only-in-NYC-baby" experience, "nothing beats" 'em.

Pappardella *Italian*   20 | 16 | 20 | $49

West 70s | 316 Columbus Ave. (75th St.) | 212-595-7996 |
www.pappardella.com

This "inviting" UWS "neighborhood joint" is "long established" as a "not-too-expensive" fallback for "tasty pastas" and other "solid" Italian standards; whether you "relax" indoors or "sit outside" and take in the Columbus Avenue scene, count on "no pressure."

Paradou *French*   ∇ 20 | 17 | 17 | $59

Meatpacking District | 8 Little W. 12th St. (bet. Greenwich & Washington Sts.) | 212-463-8345 | www.paradounyc.com

Something rather "charming" in the "yuppie theme park" that is the Meatpacking District, this "informal" bistro bats out "solid" French grub for "reasonable" dough; it's best known for its "great" all-seasons garden and "energetic" brunches fueled by "unlimited champagne cocktails."

The Park *Mediterranean*   18 | 23 | 15 | $39

Chelsea | 118 10th Ave. (bet. 17th & 18th Sts.) | 212-352-3313 |
www.theparknyc.com

"Beautiful" multitiered surroundings are the draw at this Chelsea vet that's a "relaxing" stop "before or after the High Line" thanks to its "fantastic" year-round garden "dressed up like Central Park"; the Med fare is just "ok", but it's a "bargain" compared to "higher-priced neighbors."

NEW Park Avenue Spring/   – | – | – | E
Summer/Autumn/Winter *American*

Flatiron | 360 Park Ave. S. (26th St.) | 212-951-7111 |
www.parkavenyc.com

Following a hiatus, a reboot of the former UES New American has opened in the Flatiron, where it seeks to replicate its Uptown success in the cavernous space previously home to Hurricane Club; as before, it's an homage to the four seasons (with the name, menu and AvroKO-designed decor changing quarterly), though this time around it strives to be a lighter, more accessible spot geared toward younger Downtowners.

NEW Parker & Quinn *American*   ∇ 23 | 23 | 21 | $46

Midtown | Refinery Hotel | 64 W. 39th St. (bet. 5th & 6th Aves.) |
212-729-0277 | www.parkerandquinnnyc.com

"Much needed" in the dining-deprived Garment District, the Refinery Hotel's capacious bar/eatery supplies "surprisingly good" American fare that's "satisfying" if "not necessarily inventive"; a "nicely decorated", vintage-style space with "vantage points" from raised booths makes for a "fun" vibe.

	FOOD	DECOR	SERVICE	COST

Park Side *Italian*
| 25 | 20 | 23 | $53 |

Corona | 107-01 Corona Ave. (bet. 51st Ave. & 108th St.) | Queens | 718-271-9321 | www.parksiderestaurantny.com
"Local color" abounds at this "Corona landmark" beloved for its "old-school" Italian cooking and "energetic" following, from "politicians" to "goodfellas"; with "valet parking", "plentiful" portions and "classy" "waiters in tuxes", it "rivals Arthur Avenue – down to the "bocce games in the park across the street."

Parlor Steakhouse *Steak*
| 22 | 20 | 21 | $60 |

East 80s | 1600 Third Ave. (90th St.) | 212-423-5888 | www.parlorsteakhouse.com
"One of the few decent options above 86th Street", this "much-needed" Carnegie Hill steakhouse serves "quality" surf 'n' turf in a "lovely" modern setting; a "hopping bar scene" and convenience to the 92nd Street Y compensate for the "pricey" tabs.

Parm *Italian/Sandwiches*
| 24 | 16 | 19 | $32 |

NoLita | 248 Mulberry St. (bet. Prince & Spring Sts.) | 212-993-7189 | www.parmnyc.com
They elevate chicken, meatball or eggplant parm to "dizzying heights" at this NoLita adjunct of Torrisi, where "high-end heros" lead the "simple menu" of "Americanized Italian food at its best"; its diner-esque space is "tiny", so "come early" to avoid the "wait" and the "squish"; P.S. branches in Williamsburg, the UWS, Park Slope and Hudson Eats are in the works.

Parmys Persian Fusion *Persian*
| – | – | – | M |

East Village | 125 First Ave. (bet. 7th St. & St. Marks Pl.) | 212-335-0207 | www.parmyspersianfusion.com
Despite the name, there's no fusion in evidence at this reasonably priced East Villager dishing up Persian classics including fragrant rice dishes, stews and kebabs; the nothing-fancy space features exposed-brick archways and decorative carpets on the walls.

Pascalou *French*
| 21 | 15 | 19 | $44 |

East 90s | 1308 Madison Ave. (bet. 92nd & 93rd Sts.) | 212-534-7522 | www.pascalou.info
So long as you don't mind sitting "elbow-to-elbow", this UES vet is "dependable" for "authentic" French fare served in the "tiniest" space; a "welcoming" vibe and "cost-conscious" tabs – "especially the early-bird" – are additional bonuses.

Pasha *Turkish*
| 20 | 18 | 20 | $43 |

West 70s | 70 W. 71st St. (bet. Columbus Ave. & CPW) | 212-579-8751 | www.pashanewyork.com
It's a bit like being "magically transported" to the "Bosphorus" at this "sedate" UWS retreat where "fine" Turkish staples are enhanced by "attentive" service and "civilized" surroundings; adherents applaud it as a "fairly priced" fallback "near Lincoln Center."

Pastrami Queen *Deli/Kosher*
| 22 | 8 | 16 | $26 |

East 70s | 1125 Lexington Ave. (78th St.) | 212-734-1500 | www.pastramiqueen.com
"Outstanding pastrami" is the claim to fame of this "terrific" UES deli that's the "real thing" for "overstuffed sandwiches" and other kosher

"basics done right"; seating is "almost an afterthought" in its "cramped, dingy" space, so regulars say "takeout is best."

Patricia's *Italian*   25 | 20 | 22 | $38

Morris Park | 1082 Morris Park Ave. (bet. Haight & Lurting Aves.) | Bronx | 718-409-9069 | www.patriciasnyc.com

Bronx-based boosters of this Morris Park Italian say it "satisfies" any hankering for "solid" "homestyle cooking" and "excellent" wood-fired pizzas; "comfortable, relatively quiet" environs, "friendly" service and good "bang for the buck" round out the "dependable" picture.

Patsy's *Italian*   22 | 18 | 21 | $61

Midtown | 236 W. 56th St. (bet. B'way & 8th Ave.) | 212-247-3491 | www.patsys.com

It "doesn't get more old-school" than this 70-plus-year-old Midtown "throwback", a "favorite of Sinatra's" that still purveys "delicious" Neapolitan cooking and "quality service"; maybe it could use a "refresh", but the "heaping" portions and Theater District proximity are fine as is.

Patsy's Pizzeria *Pizza*   21 | 12 | 16 | $27

Chelsea | 318 W. 23rd St. (bet. 8th & 9th Aves.) | 646-486-7400 | www.patsyspizzeria.us
East Harlem | 2287 First Ave. (bet. 117th & 118th Sts.) | 212-534-9783 | www.thepatsyspizza.com
East Midtown | 801 Second Ave. (43rd St.) | 212-878-9600 | www.patsyspizzeria.us
East 60s | 1279 First Ave. (69th St.) | 212-639-1000 | www.patsyspizzerianewyork.com
East 60s | 206 E. 60th St. (bet. 2nd & 3rd Aves.) | 212-688-9707 | www.patsyspizzerianewyork.com
Greenwich Village | 67 University Pl. (bet. 10th & 11th Sts.) | 212-533-3500 | www.patsyspizzeria.us
West 70s | 61 W. 74th St. (bet. Columbus Ave. & CPW) | 212-579-3000 | www.patsyspizzeria.us

"Long-standing in the NY pizza wars", the circa-1933 East Harlem pie parlor original and its separately owned spin-offs continue to turn out "yummy, thin-crust" beauties at "easy-on-the-wallet" prices; diehard fans say "the original's best", though all locations share "generic" decor and barely "decent service."

Paulie Gee's *Pizza*   27 | 21 | 23 | $29

Greenpoint | 60 Greenpoint Ave. (bet. Franklin & West Sts.) | Brooklyn | 347-987-3747 | www.pauliegee.com

The "destination-worthy" pizza "will leave you speechless" at this Greenpoint purveyor of "outstanding" wood-fired Neapolitan pies flaunting "one-of-a-kind" toppings (vegan varieties included) and a "crispy", charred crust; even with a "packed" house the mood's "fun and funky", not least due to "routine table visits from Paulie himself."

NEW The Pavilion *American*   – | – | – | M

Union Square | 20 Union Sq. W. (17th St.) | 212-677-7818 | www.thepavilionnyc.com

Union Square Park's historic pavilion is finally back in action with the debut of this American eatery, where a locavore-oriented menu is practically required given the Greenmarket proximity; open only in temperate weather, its open-air space features lots of foliage, a bar and outdoor seating.

Peacefood Café *Kosher/Vegan/Vegetarian* | 23 | 17 | 17 | $29 |

Greenwich Village | 41 E. 11th St. (bet. B'way & University Pl.) | 212-979-2288

West 80s | 460 Amsterdam Ave. (82nd St.) | 212-362-2266

www.peacefoodcafe.com

"Fresh, creative" (and kosher) "vegan deliciousness" – including "awesome chickpea fries" and "terrific baked goods" – keeps "health-conscious" types coming to these "relaxed" Village-UWS joints; service can be "spacey", but nonetheless the "guilt-free", "affordable" eating here has most "feeling at peace."

Peaches *Southern* ▽ | 25 | 20 | 21 | $37 |

Bedford-Stuyvesant | 393 Lewis Ave. (MacDonough St.) | Brooklyn | 718-942-4162

Peaches HotHouse *Southern*

Bedford-Stuyvesant | 415 Tompkins Ave. (Hancock St.) | Brooklyn | 718-483-9111

www.bcrestaurantgroup.com

Easier than keeping "granny in the kitchen all day", these Bed-Stuy "local beacons" win "three thumbs up" for their "delicious" Southern staples; whether for "delightful" platters at Peaches or "spicy" fried chicken at The HotHouse, they're "well worth" the frequent wait.

NEW The Peacock *British* ▽ | 22 | 22 | 21 | $67 |

Midtown | William Hotel | 24 E. 39th St. (bet. Madison & Park Aves.) | 646-837-6776 | www.thepeacocknyc.com

"Lovely" "old money"–style decor befits the "proper" "upscale" British fare served at this arrival in Midtown's William Hotel; the "classy", wood-accented space includes two dining rooms, a lounge and a library bar; P.S. for an "old-school pub" experience, head downstairs to The Shakespeare.

Peanut Butter & Co. *Sandwiches* | 20 | 12 | 17 | $15 |

Greenwich Village | 240 Sullivan St. (bet. Bleecker & 3rd Sts.) | 212-677-3995 | www.ilovepeanutbutter.com

"Kitschy and creative", this Village niche "celebrates peanut butter in all its glory" with sandwiches spanning the "classics" to "concoctions you'd never think of" ("the Elvis should be on everyone's bucket list"); it's "fun with the kids", though the "bare-bones" digs can be a "squeeze."

Pearl & Ash *American* | 24 | 21 | 22 | $78 |

NoLita | 220 Bowery (bet. Prince & Spring Sts.) | 212-837-2370 | www.pearlandash.com

Expect a "hot scene" at this Bowery standout where "talented chef" Richard Kuo's New American small plates are "brilliant", but the "spectacular", "never-ending" wine list is the star of the show; with a narrow, "chic" space manned by a "cheerful" staff, it's a "rockin' good" time with the volume set "loud."

Pearl Oyster Bar *New England/Seafood*   27 | 15 | 21 | $53

West Village | 18 Cornelia St. (bet. Bleecker & 4th Sts.) | 212-691-8211 |
www.pearloysterbar.com

"Succulent lobster rolls" to "swoon" over lead the lineup of "primo" New
England seafood at this ever-"popular" West Village "treasure" from
Rebecca Charles; a "small", "informal setting" with no reservations
makes it "hard to get in", so savvier sorts go early "to be in line."

Pearl Room *Seafood*   22 | 20 | 21 | $58

Bay Ridge | 8201 Third Ave. (82nd St.) | Brooklyn | 718-833-6666 |
www.thepearlroom.com

"As fancy as it gets in Bay Ridge", this seafaring "surprise" provides
"excellent preparations" of "fresh" fin fare served by an "attentive" crew;
factor in a setting suitable for "romantic" encounters and "celebrations",
and it's no surprise the tab can be "pretty pricey."

Peasant *Italian*   25 | 22 | 22 | $69

NoLita | 194 Elizabeth St. (bet. Prince & Spring Sts.) | 212-965-9511 |
www.peasantnyc.com

From the "warm, inviting space" to the "fabulous", "wood-fired" cuisine,
this "unforgettable" Italian "outshines" many of its NoLita neighbors; it's
not cheap, but romeos bent on "romance" head for the "civilized" cellar
wine bar for after-dinner drinks.

Peking Duck House *Chinese*   23 | 15 | 18 | $43

Chinatown | 28 Mott St. (bet. Chatham Sq. & Pell St.) | 212-227-1810
East Midtown | 236 E. 53rd St. (bet. 2nd & 3rd Aves.) | 212-759-8260
www.pekingduckhousenyc.com

With its "juicy" meat and "savory, crispy skin", the signature Peking duck
carved tableside is a "real treat" at these "old-fashioned" Chinese eateries; decor and service may be somewhat "lacking", but "wine lovers"
applaud the BYO policy at the Chinatown location.

Pellegrino's *Italian*   21 | 17 | 20 | $44

Little Italy | 138 Mulberry St. (bet. Grand & Hester Sts.) | 212-226-3177 |
www.pellegrinosristorante.com

"High-quality" "red-sauce" cooking and "personal service" from
tuxedoed waiters foster the "happy ambiance" at this Little Italy
"winner"; regulars prefer sitting outside and taking in the only-in-NY
Mulberry Street "scene."

Penelope *American*   22 | 18 | 19 | $26

Kips Bay | 159 Lexington Ave. (30th St.) | 212-481-3800 |
www.penelopenyc.com

Kips Bay locals tout this "adorable" neighborhood "favorite" for "fab",
"comfort"-oriented New American plates served in "country cafe" digs at
a "reasonable cost"; the "amazing brunch" is in "high demand", so bring
"patience" to deal with the inevitable "waits."

The Penrose *American*   20 | 19 | 16 | $30

East 80s | 1590 Second Ave. (bet. 82nd & 83rd Sts.) | 212-203-2751 |
www.penrosebar.com

Almost "too hip for the neighborhood", this "happening" UES gastropub
plies "tasty cocktails" and "solid" American bar food (including a "win-

ner" of a burger); it also stands out thanks to its "homey" vintage decor and "downtown vibe."

Pepolino *Italian*

25 | 18 | 23 | $67

TriBeCa | 281 W. Broadway (bet. Canal & Lispenard Sts.) | 212-966-9983 | www.pepolino.com

"Hiding in plain sight" on the fringes of TriBeCa, this "charming" trattoria delivers a "magic combination" of "savory" Tuscan farm cuisine and "attentive" service amid "rustic" surrounds; the experience is "not cheap", but given the "high quality", insiders still consider it a "deal."

Pera *Mediterranean*

20 | 20 | 18 | $57

Midtown | 303 Madison Ave. (bet. 41st & 42nd Sts.) | 212-878-6301 | www.peranyc.com

SoHo | 54 Thompson St. (bet. Broome & Spring Sts.) | 212-878-6305 | www.soho.peranyc.com

These "attractive" eateries make "civilized" choices for Turkish-accented Mediterranean fare – including a "lovely range" of meze – served in "modern" surrounds; the Midtown original is a "no-brainer for business", while the stylin' SoHo spin-off sports a "stunning outdoor deck."

Perilla *American*

24 | 19 | 23 | $65

West Village | 9 Jones St. (bet. Bleecker & W. 4th Sts.) | 212-929-6868 | www.perillanyc.com

It was Harold Dieterle's first restaurant, and this snug West Villager still "delivers on its star-chef reputation" with "creative" New American standards (witness the "glory that is the spicy duck meatball") served by a "polished" staff; an "intimate" feel and "reasonable" prices "for the quality" make it a "spot-on" choice.

Periyali *Greek*

24 | 21 | 23 | $65

Flatiron | 35 W. 20th St. (bet. 5th & 6th Aves.) | 212-463-7890 | www.periyali.com

"Dependably rewarding" since 1987, this Flatiron "Greek classic" remains a "refined" refuge for "superb fresh fish" and "gracious service" in "soothing", "not-too-loud" surrounds; "upscale" admirers attest the "like-you're-in-Greece" experience is "worth the high price."

Perla *Italian*

25 | 21 | 23 | $68

Greenwich Village | 24 Minetta Ln. (bet. MacDougal St. & 6th Ave.) | 212-933-1824 | www.perlanyc.com

"Righteous" pastas and other "rustic" plates are a "pure delight" at this "cozy" Village Italian from restaurateur Gabe Stulman (Joseph Leonard, Jeffrey's Grocery); "celebrities mixed in with the hoi polloi" make for a "crazy-busy" scene, but with a "charming" crew to boost the "warm feelings", it's "worth the try" to snag a table.

Perry St. *American*

26 | 25 | 24 | $71

West Village | 176 Perry St. (West St.) | 212-352-1900 | www.perrystrestaurant.com

"Another Jean-Georges gem", this "haut de gamme" West Villager sees chef Cedric Vongerichten continue the family legacy ("like father, like son") with "top-notch" New American cuisine served by a "pro" staff in a "chic, sexy", "modern" Richard Meier–designed space "on the Hudson

River"; sure, it's "expensive and a little out of the way", but to most the "memorable" experience is "well worth" it.

Per Se *American/French*

27	28	28	$341

Midtown | Time Warner Ctr. | 10 Columbus Circle (60th St. at B'way) | 212-823-9335 | www.perseny.com

When it comes to Thomas Keller's "off-the-charts" Time Warner Center French–New American, "everything you've heard is true": it's an "unforgettable" experience from the "exhilarating" nine-course tasting menu and "gold-standard" service to the "elegant", jackets-required setting with "spectacular" Central Park views; yes, the $310 set price presumes "bottomless pockets", but there's always the "best-kept-secret" lounge offering relatively "affordable" à la carte small plates.

Persepolis *Persian*

22	17	21	$42

East 70s | 1407 Second Ave. (bet. 73rd & 74th Sts.) | 212-535-1100 | www.persepolisnewyork.com

A "standout" among the "few Persians" in town, this Upper Eastsider offers "interesting", "well-spiced" Iranian dishes (the signature "sourcherry rice is a treat") in an "understated" milieu; given the "personal service" and overall "value", it's "easy to relax and enjoy" here.

Peter Luger Steak House *Steak*

28	16	21	$87

Williamsburg | 178 Broadway (Driggs Ave.) | Brooklyn | 718-387-7400 | www.peterluger.com

"A must for any meat enthusiast", this "legendary" (circa-1887) Williamsburg "shrine" to steak "never gets old" as "crusty" "characters" serve "top-of-the-line" "traditional" cuts like the famed "melt-in-yourmouth" porterhouse; the "vintage" "beer-hall" quarters are "packed for good reason", but "bring a wad" since "you'll pay big" and "they only accept cash."

Petite Abeille *Belgian*

20	16	18	$35

Flatiron | 44 W. 17th St. (bet. 5th & 6th Aves.) | 212-727-2989
Stuyvesant Town/Peter Cooper Village | 401 E. 20th St. (1st Ave.) | 212-727-1505
TriBeCa | 134 W. Broadway (bet. Duane & Thomas Sts.) | 212-791-1360 www.petiteabeille.com

"Fresh, tasty" moules frites and other "hearty" Belgian classics pair with a "vast" beer selection at these "unpretentious" "neighborhood" bistros, which are also "favorite" brunch fallbacks; for a "casual, low-key" meal, "you could do a whole lot worse."

Petite Crevette *French/Seafood*

▽ 23	19	21	$36

Columbia Street Waterfront District | 144 Union St. (Hicks St.) | Brooklyn | 718-855-2632

"Excellent fish the French way" is the lure at this "quirky", cash-only Columbia Street Waterfront pioneer offering an "interesting", everchanging roster of seafood dishes; "closet"-size but packing "lots of character", it has a BYO policy to "make it economical" – plus its "fun" wine bar sibling, the Flying Lobster, is next door.

	FOOD	DECOR	SERVICE	COST

Petrossian *Continental/French*
24 | 23 | 23 | $81

Midtown | 182 W. 58th St. (7th Ave.) | 212-245-2214 |
www.petrossian.com

"Caviar is king" at this "formal" art deco "classic" near Carnegie Hall
where the staff "never rushes you" and the "very expensive" French-
Continental menu includes some "bargain prix fixe" options for the
non-"hedge-fund-guys"; there's also a "little cafe next door" perfect
for a "quick bite."

Philip Marie *American*
19 | 16 | 20 | $48

West Village | 569 Hudson St. (W. 11th St.) | 212-242-6200 |
www.philipmarie.com

A "dependable, neighborhood bistro–type" New American with a "prime
West Village location", this "laid-back" standby does a "solid" job dispensing "homestyle cooking" in "pleasant" environs; "reasonable prices"
in a tony zone help keep 'em coming back "time and time again."

Philippe *Chinese*
23 | 19 | 21 | $76

East 60s | 33 E. 60th St. (bet. Madison & Park Aves.) | 212-644-8885 |
www.philippechow.com

"Low-lit and high-class", this East Side Chinese channels "Mr. Chow"
with "well-crafted" cuisine served to a "glamorous" crowd in digs that
turn "cacophonous" when going full tilt (though the back room's more
"chill"); the $23 prix fixe lunch dodges the "sky-high" tabs – but while you
may "run into Lil' Kim", skeptics shrug the scene's "better than the food."

Pho Bang *Noodle Shop/Vietnamese*
21 | 5 | 13 | $14

Little Italy | 157 Mott St. (bet. Broome & Grand Sts.) | 212-966-3797
Elmhurst | 82-90 Broadway (bet. 45th & Whitney Aves.) | Queens |
718-205-1500
Flushing | 41-07 Kissena Blvd. (bet. Barclay & 41st Aves.) | Queens |
718-939-5520

"Just as the name says", these "no-nonsense" Vietnamese joints cater
to "pho phans" with "delicious" soup bowls and a "big bang for the
buck"; otherwise they're "dingy" setups where the staffers "could be
a little more courteous."

Phoenix Garden *Chinese*
23 | 7 | 15 | $31

Murray Hill | 242 E. 40th St. (bet. 2nd & 3rd Aves.) | 212-983-6666 |
www.phoenixgardennyc.com

"Save-yourself-a-trip-to-Chinatown solid" Cantonese cooking and the
"added benefit" of a BYO policy make this "unassuming" Murray Hill vet
a "real find"; fans overlook the "attitude", "dreary decor" and cash-only
policy because you can't beat the "value."

Pho Viet Huong *Vietnamese*
∇ 24 | 11 | 17 | $21

Chinatown | 73 Mulberry St. (bet. Bayard & Canal Sts.) | 212-233-8988 |
www.phoviethuong.com

"Superb" pho for "very little dough" leads the "bewilderingly broad"
menu of "top-notch" Vietnamese eats at this C-town stalwart; the
decor's "nondescript" and service "can be iffy", but it's "full of jurors"
and "court staff" at lunchtime all the same.

| | FOOD | DECOR | SERVICE | COST |

Piadina *Italian*
▽ 22 | 18 | 21 | $46

Greenwich Village | 57 W. 10th St. (bet. 5th & 6th Aves.) |
212-460-8017 | www.piadinanyc.com

A "rustic" grotto "hideaway" best known to its "local crowd", this
"small", cash-only Villager is appreciated for its "incredible pastas"
and other "real-deal" Italiana ("be sure to try" the namesake flatbread);
fans appreciate that it's "intimate" enough to get amorous, but
"not crazy-priced."

Piccola Venezia *Italian*
25 | 17 | 23 | $64

Astoria | 42-01 28th Ave. (42nd St.) | Queens | 718-721-8470 |
www.piccola-venezia.com

"You name it, they prepare it" at this venerable Astoria "charmer", where
the "menu's only a suggestion" and the "traditional" Italian dishes are
"impeccably" rendered; it's "a little pricey" given the "dated" decor, but
"personalized service" ensures everyone feels "like family."

Piccolo Angolo *Italian*
25 | 14 | 22 | $50

West Village | 621 Hudson St. (Jane St.) | 212-229-9177 |
www.piccoloangolo.com

Beloved, departed owner Renato Migliorini is sorely missed, but this
"family-run" West Village vet carries on with its "wonderful" Northern
Italian fare delivered in "tight" but "homey" and "festive" quarters;
supremely "amiable" service cements its standing as a "neighborhood
favorite" ("reservations are a must").

Piccolo Cafe *Coffee/Italian*
23 | 18 | 20 | $29

Gramercy Park | 157 Third Ave. (bet. 15th & 16th Sts.) | 212-260-1175
Midtown | 274 W. 40th St. (8th Ave.) | 212-302-0143
Midtown | 238 Madison Ave. (37th St.) | 212-447-4399
West 70s | 313 Amsterdam Ave. (bet. 74th & 75th Sts.) | 212-873-0962
www.piccolocafe.us

These "cheerful" cafes are linked to a Italy-based coffee roaster, so count
on espresso from imported beans and "real Italian" bites including "delicious" pastas and panini; just don't expect much seating because, as the
name implies, they're "teensy-weensy."

Picholine *French/Mediterranean*
26 | 25 | 26 | $112

West 60s | 35 W. 64th St. (bet. B'way & CPW) | 212-724-8585 |
www.picholinenyc.com

As a "first-class" destination, Terry Brennan's quietly "gorgeous" Lincoln
Center–area French-Med goes "the whole nine yards" with a "superb"
staff serving "beautifully rendered" cuisine, right up to the famously
"exquisite" cheese-course finale; it's "the lap of luxury" for a "grown-up"
clientele, but be ready to "pay for it."

NEW Pickle Shack *American*
– | – | – | M

Gowanus | 256 Fourth Ave. (Carroll St.) | Brooklyn | 347-763-2127 |
www.pickleshacknyc.com

The picklers of Brooklyn Brine and the brewmasters of Dogfish Head
are behind this Gowanus arrival serving a pickle-centric, all-vegetarian
American menu of sandwiches and bar bites in unassuming, tavernlike
digs; the stellar suds list and big back patio are major draws.

	FOOD	DECOR	SERVICE	COST

Pies-N-Thighs *Southern*
24 | 14 | 18 | $24

Williamsburg | 166 S. Fourth St. (Driggs Ave.) | Brooklyn |
347-529-6090 | www.piesnthighs.com

"Crispy, juicy", "knocks-it-out-of-the-park" fried chicken, "damn good"
pie and other "down-home" Southern favorites make this "funky, fun"
Williamsburg joint "the place to go when you're feeling gluttonous";
maybe its "snug", "packed" space and waits "day and night" are "not so
special", but "bargain" prices compensate.

Pietro's *Italian/Steak*
25 | 15 | 23 | $71

East Midtown | 232 E. 43rd St. (bet. 2nd & 3rd Aves.) | 212-682-9760 |
www.pietrosnyc.com

In the Grand Central area since 1932, this "old-school" holdout rests its
rep on "excellent steaks" and "superior" Italian basics served in "copious
amounts" by a "gracious", "been-there-for-years" staff; the room's "not
glamorous", but "loyal" regulars appreciate the "quiet" vibe – or more
"lively" times at its "great bar."

Pig and Khao *SE Asian*
24 | 17 | 20 | $41

Lower East Side | 68 Clinton St. (bet. Rivington & Stanton Sts.) |
212-920-4485 | www.pigandkhao.com

Chef Leah Cohen's Lower Eastsider aims to be "creative" and "nails it"
with "awesome" Southeast Asian fare featuring Thai and Filipino "home-
cooking elements" and plenty of pork; the space sports a "cute" garden
and a chef's counter, the service is "unpretentiously hip" and it "won't
break the bank, either."

The Pines *American*
▽ 21 | 18 | 18 | $59

Gowanus | 284 Third Ave. (bet. Carroll & President Sts.) | Brooklyn |
718-596-6560 | www.thepinesbrooklyn.com

"Ambitious", sometimes "edgy" New American cuisine and creative
cocktails are the lure at this "hip" Gowanus nook that fires up the
backyard grill on summer weekends; however, a few gripe it's "overpriced
for the location and decor", which is artfully downscale, with reclaimed-
church-pew seating.

NEW Pine Tree Cafe *American*
– | – | – | M

Bronx Park | Leon Levy Visitor Ctr., NY Botanical Garden | 2900 Southern
Blvd. (Bronx Park Rd.) | Bronx | no phone | www.nybg.org

Restaurateur Stephen Starr (Buddakan, Morimoto) is behind this new
counter-serve American cafe in the New York Botanical Garden, nestled
in a grove of century-old pine trees; the menu includes family favorites
like pizza, panini and salads, and the airy, window-lined setting boasts
expansive views of the lush scenery.

Ping's Seafood *Chinese/Seafood*
20 | 12 | 14 | $30

Chinatown | 22 Mott St. (bet. Chatham Sq. & Mosco St.) | 212-602-9988
Elmhurst | 8302 Queens Blvd. (Goldsmith St.) | Queens | 718-396-1238
www.pingsnyc.com

With "first-rate" seafood backed by "varied", "flavorful" dim sum, these
Cantonese contenders stay "ping on target"; despite "simple" settings
and "not-that-welcoming" service, they "pack 'em in", especially for that
"madhouse" Sunday brunch.

	FOOD	DECOR	SERVICE	COST

Pio Pio *Peruvian* | 22 | 15 | 17 | $30 |

East 90s | 1746 First Ave. (bet. 90th & 91st Sts.) | 212-426-5800
Hell's Kitchen | 604 10th Ave. (bet. 43rd & 44th Sts.) | 212-459-2929
Kips Bay | 210 E. 34th St. (bet. 2nd & 3rd Aves.) | 212-481-0034
West 90s | 702 Amsterdam Ave. (94th St.) | 212-665-3000
Mott Haven | 264 Cypress Ave. (bet. 138th & 139th Sts.) | Bronx |
718-401-3300
Jackson Heights | 84-21 Northern Blvd. (85th St.) | Queens |
718-426-1010
Jackson Heights | 84-02 Northern Blvd. (bet. 84th & 85th Sts.) | Queens |
718-426-4900
Middle Village | 62-30 Woodhaven Blvd. (bet. Dry Harbor Rd. & 62nd
Dr.) | Queens | 718-458-0606
www.piopio.com

Dishing out "huge portions" of "juicy" rotisserie chicken with "addicting" green sauce, these "no-frills" Peruvians prove you can indulge in a "satisfying" meal without "breaking the bank"; some warn service might be "rushed" and noise levels "outrageous", but they're "fun with a group" and "family-friendly" to boot.

NEW Piora *American* | 26 | 23 | 25 | $103 |

West Village | 430 Hudson St. (bet. Morton St. & St. Lukes Pl.) |
212-960-3801 | www.pioranyc.com

Greeted as a "real winner on all fronts", this West Villager showcases chef Chris Cipollone's "refined", "creative" New American plates with Korean and Italian influences, including plenty "for vegetable lovers"; "top-notch" service and a "beautiful, understated" space clinch a classy experience that, while "expensive", comes "pretension-free."

Pisticci *Italian* | 24 | 19 | 21 | $40 |

Morningside Heights | 125 La Salle St. (B'way) | 212-932-3500 |
www.pisticcinyc.com

It "doesn't get much better for local Italian" than this "warm, homey" Columbia-area "favorite" for "scrumptious" food at "reasonable prices" and free "jazz on Sundays"; the "no-reservations" rule can be "a drag", yet the "long lines" deter few.

PizzArte *Pizza* | 20 | 17 | 17 | $37 |

Midtown | 69 W. 55th St. (bet. 5th & 6th Aves.) | 212-247-3936 |
www.pizzarteny.com

"True" Neapolitan pizzas and "well-curated" artwork, all for sale, make an "intriguing" combo at this Midtown Italian, also vending pastas and more; its "modern", "bowling-lane-thin" duplex digs can feel "cramped", but there's a "nice bar" and the location's hard to beat "before Carnegie Hall" or City Center.

NEW Pizzetteria Brunetti *Pizza* | ▽ 26 | 21 | 24 | $37 |

West Village | 626 Hudson St. (bet. Horatio & Jane Sts.) |
212-255-5699 | www.pizzetteriabrunetti.com

Run by "pizza savants" Michael and Jason Brunetti, this "warm" West Villager (a Westhampton Beach transplant) puts forth "incredible" Neapolitan pies including a "not-to-be-missed" clam specialty; "reasonable pricing" and "comfortable" digs with a rear patio help ensure "everyone feels at home."

	FOOD	DECOR	SERVICE	COST

P.J. Clarke's *Pub Food* | 19 | 18 | 18 | $43 |

East Midtown | 915 Third Ave. (55th St.) | 212-317-1616

P.J. Clarke's at Lincoln Square *Pub Food*

West 60s | 44 W. 63rd St. (Columbus Ave.) | 212-957-9700

P.J. Clarke's on the Hudson *Pub Food*

Battery Park City | 4 World Financial Ctr. (Vesey St.) | 212-285-1500

Sidecar at P.J. Clarke's *Pub Food*

East Midtown | 205 E. 55th St. (3rd Ave.) | 212-317-2044
www.pjclarkes.com

A bastion of "old NY coolness", this circa-1884 East Midtown saloon is beloved for its "first-rate" burgers and raw bar, "legendary bartenders" and all-around "fun scene"; while the newer spin-offs don't have the original's "historic" "charm", Sidecar upstairs is a "speakeasy"-like "hide-away", Lincoln Center is perfect pre-show and Battery Park City boasts "lovely water views."

The Place *American/Mediterranean* ▽ 23 | 21 | 23 | $56 |

West Village | 310 W. Fourth St. (bet. Bank & W. 12th Sts.) | 212-924-2711 | www.theplaceny.com

"Nestled" below sidewalk level, this "quintessential West Village date spot" is "sure to impress" with its "romantic", fireplace-equipped setting, "decadent" Med–New American cooking and "warm" service; the only quibble is with the "boring name", which fans complain "doesn't do it justice."

Plaza Food Hall *Food Market* | 22 | 20 | 17 | $40 |

Midtown | Plaza Hotel | 1 W. 59th St., lower level (5th Ave.) | 212-986-9260 | www.theplazany.com

A "great way to graze", this "vibrant" "one-stop shop" below The Plaza provides "outstanding" Eclectic options via "varying food stations" issuing sushi, pizza, grill fare and much more; partly run by Todd English, it's plenty "popular" despite "so-so" service and "lunch counter–style" seating.

Pó *Italian* | 25 | 16 | 22 | $58 |

West Village | 31 Cornelia St. (bet. Bleecker & 4th Sts.) | 212-645-2189 | www.porestaurant.com

Pocket-size but "charming", this "longtime" Villager remains an "absolute gem" furnishing "first-quality" Italian fare "without an ounce of pretense"; "repeat customers" confirm the "tight squeeze" is "so worth it" for "amazing" dining that "won't break the bank."

Poke *Japanese* ▽ 26 | 17 | 22 | $43 |

East 80s | 343 E. 85th St. (bet. 1st & 2nd Aves.) | 212-249-0569 | www.pokesushinyc.com

The "finest fish" lures UES sushiphiles to this cash-only Japanese BYO, a modest standby touted for its "creative" rolls and "off-menu" items; "affordable" rates ensure it's "always busy", even if critics take a poke at the "no-reservations policy" and "long lines."

Pok Pok Ny *Thai* | 24 | 14 | 19 | $41 |

Columbia Street Waterfront District | 127 Columbia St. (bet. Degraw & Kane Sts.) | Brooklyn | 718-923-9322 | www.pokpokny.com

"Deep cuts beyond the typical Thai" are the specialty of Andy Ricker's "terrific" Columbia Street Waterfront outpost dishing up "spicy, exciting", "amazeballs" flavors tailor-made for the "adventurous eater"; the no-reservations policy spells "long waits", but there's always across-the-street sib Whiskey Soda Lounge for cocktails and snacks – plus Pok Pok Phat Thai is set to reopen soon in roomy down-the-block digs at 127 Columbia Street.

Pommes Frites Belgian | 24 | 9 | 17 | $12 |

East Village | 123 Second Ave. (7th St.) | 212-674-1234 |
www.pommesfrites.ws

"Crispy outside yet tender inside", the "world-class" Belgian fries arrive with a "crazy array of dipping sauces" at this East Village one-trick pony where there's often "a line out the door" (especially for a "late-night snack"); since the "tiny" digs are usually "packed", most get it "to go."

Pomodoro Rosso Italian | 21 | 16 | 21 | $46 |

West 70s | 229 Columbus Ave. (bet. 70th & 71st Sts.) | 212-721-3009 |
www.pomodororossonyc.com

It's like "mama's in the kitchen" cooking up "hearty" Italian classics at this "quaint" UWS vet near Lincoln Center that's run with "loving care"; the "quintessential neighborhood gem", it's "always busy", so make a reservation to dodge the "wait for a table."

Pongsri Thai Thai | 21 | 12 | 18 | $28 |

Chelsea | 165 W. 23rd St. (bet. 6th & 7th Aves.) | 212-645-8808
Chinatown | 106 Bayard St. (Baxter St.) | 212-349-3132
Midtown | 244 W. 48th St. (bet. B'way & 8th Ave.) | 212-582-3392
www.pongsri.net

"Authentic curries" and other "quality" Thai eats are "delivered with real spice" at these "bargain-priced" veterans; the decor's "not fancy", but "convenient" locations and "fast" service make them a "good choice" when you're "pressed for time."

Ponticello Italian | ▽ 23 | 20 | 23 | $68 |

Astoria | 46-11 Broadway (bet. 46th & 47th Sts.) | Queens |
718-278-4514 | www.ponticelloristorante.com

Ever "reliable" since 1982, this Astoria Northern Italian boasts a "terrific" roster of "classics" served by seasoned waiters who ensure you'll be "well taken care of"; if it seems "slightly overpriced" for the "old-world" ambiance, habitués still "feel completely at home."

Ponty Bistro African/French | 24 | 16 | 22 | $41 |

Gramercy Park | 218 Third Ave. (bet. 18th & 19th Sts.) | 212-777-1616 |
www.pontybistro.com

"Sparking your taste buds", this all-day Gramercy "find" offers "original" French-Senegalese dishes livened up with African spices and "charming" service; it's also "well priced" (notably the $25 early-bird), but word's "getting out" and the "narrow" room fills up fast.

Porchetta Italian/Sandwiches | 21 | 8 | 16 | $18 |

East Village | 110 E. Seventh St. (bet. Ave. A & 1st Ave.) |
212-777-2151 | www.porchettanyc.com

Famed for its "crave-worthy" namesake – "divine" Italian-style roast pork sandwiches and platters – Sara Jenkins' "tiny" East Villager offers a few other options nowadays (even "excellent carnitas tacos" if you're lucky); the setup is "counter service with a few stools", so most do "takeout."

Pork Slope *BBQ*

19 | **16** | **17** | **$29**

Park Slope | 247 Fifth Ave. (bet. Carroll St. & Garfield Pl.) | Brooklyn | 718-768-7675 | www.porkslopebrooklyn.com

"Elevated bar food is the idea" at chef Dale Talde's "laid-back" Park Slope saloon presenting a BBQ-based menu with plenty of "satisfying" porky options; it also pours an "extensive" brown-liquor selection, but "be prepared" – its roadhouselike room "gets crowded" in peak hours.

Porsena *Italian*

23 | **16** | **21** | **$50**

East Village | 21 E. Seventh St. (bet. 2nd & 3rd Aves.) | 212-228-4923 | www.porsena.com

The "knowing hand" of chef-owner Sara Jenkins elevates the "heavenly pastas" and other "delicious, straightforward" Italian staples at this "friendly" East Villager; it works as a "down-to-earth" "date spot", albeit one that's apt to be "busy" and "uninteresting" to look at.

Porter House New York *Steak*

26 | **25** | **24** | **$84**

Midtown | Time Warner Ctr. | 10 Columbus Circle (60th St. at B'way) | 212-823-9500 | www.porterhousenewyork.com

From "exceptional cuts of meat" to "interesting" sides, a "feast awaits" at Michael Lomonaco's TWC "destination steakhouse"; "impeccable" service helps justify the "expensive" tab, as do the "elegant" room's Central Park views that are as "impressive" as the food.

Posto *Pizza*

23 | **13** | **18** | **$28**

Gramercy Park | 310 Second Ave. (18th St.) | 212-716-1200 | www.postothincrust.com

The "thinnest", "winningest" crust is the hallmark of this Gramercy pizzeria, a "local hot spot" cranking out "splendid" pies at "accessible prices"; its "small", "publike" digs are usually "packed and noisy", so the to-go trade stays brisk.

Potlikker *American*

▽ **22** | **21** | **23** | **$38**

Williamsburg | 338 Bedford Ave. (bet. 2nd & 3rd Sts.) | Brooklyn | 718-388-9808 | www.potlikkerbrooklyn.com

Marking the return of chef Liza Queen (Queen's Hideaway), this "adorable" Williamsburg nook furnishes "unique" tweaks on American comfort fare like brick chicken, adding a strong seasonal slant; service is "super-attentive", and the updated-diner digs are a magnet for brunch.

Press 195 *Sandwiches*

23 | **17** | **20** | **$23**

Bayside | 4011 Bell Blvd. (bet. 40th & 41st Aves.) | Queens | 718-281-1950 | www.press195.com

The "hardest part is choosing" from the "extensive list" of "amazing panini" at this "casual" Bayside "favorite", but the "terrific" Belgian fries are a no-brainer; with a full bar, "the best craft beers" and a "fun patio" out back, it's no wonder locals "love this place."

Prime Grill *Kosher/Steak*

24 | **23** | **20** | **$79**

Midtown | 25 W. 56th St. (bet. 5th & 6th Aves.) | 212-692-9292 | www.theprimegrill.primehospitalityny.com

"Buzzing" with a Midtown crowd, this recently relocated "standard bearer" for kosher steak "impresses" with its "top-quality" beef and sushi, as well as its "beautiful" balconied setting; tabs run "expensive", but to most the "client-worthy" experience is "worth the price."

Prime Meats *American/Steak*　24 | 21 | 20 | $54

Carroll Gardens | 465 Court St. (Luquer St.) | Brooklyn | 718-254-0327 | www.frankspm.com

The "name says it" about this carnivore-oriented brother to Frankies Spuntino in Carroll Gardens, where "delicious", "German-inspired" American steakhouse fare arrives via a "whiskered", "über-hip" staff; the "cool, Prohibition-style" digs get "packed" and it "doesn't take reservations", so "arrive early."

Primola *Italian*　23 | 16 | 20 | $69

East 60s | 1226 Second Ave. (bet. 64th & 65th Sts.) | 212-758-1775

No stranger to "Page Six" mentions, this "clubby" Italian satisfies its "moneyed UES" clientele with "dependable" pastas at "steep prices"; count on service "with a smile" if you're a regular, a "celebrity" or "wearing dark glasses", but for first-timers the "attitude" can be "intimidating."

Print *American*　25 | 24 | 24 | $58

Hell's Kitchen | Ink48 Hotel | 653 11th Ave. (bet. 47th & 48th Sts.) | 212-757-2224 | www.printrestaurant.com

Way "out of the way" in West Hell's Kitchen, this "yet-to-be-discovered" New American is "first-rate" for "locavoracious" fare and "smart" service in "stylish" environs; insiders have cocktails after dinner on the "rooftop lounge" with its drop-dead, 360-degree "skyline view."

Prospect *American*　▽ 23 | 20 | 22 | $58

Fort Greene | 773 Fulton St. (bet. Oxford St. & Portland Ave.) | Brooklyn | 718-596-6826 | www.prospectbk.com

This "solid" addition to Fort Greene is appreciated for its "excellent" locavore-oriented New American fare and "fantastic" drinks "served with loving care"; a "relaxed", "inviting" setting "within walking distance of the Barclays Center and BAM" helps justify the "Manhattan"-level pricing.

Prosperity Dumpling *Chinese*　23 | 3 | 14 | $6

Lower East Side | 46 Eldridge St. (bet. Canal & Hester Sts.) | 212-343-0683 | www.prosperitydumpling.com

"Frugal foodies" find "awesome", "meaty dumplings" and other "tasty" items at this cash-only, "bang-for-your-buck" LES Chinese; "long lines" and "haphazard" service in "utterly cramped" surrounds make the case for takeout.

Prune *American*　24 | 15 | 21 | $62

East Village | 54 E. First St. (bet. 1st & 2nd Aves.) | 212-677-6221 | www.prunerestaurant.com

Chef Gabrielle Hamilton's "idiosyncratic" East Village vet remains as "fascinating" as ever thanks to "inspired" New American "food for thought" – and a recently overhauled dinner menu – "graciously" presented in a "tiny", "cheek-by-jowl" space; habitués say "all hail the Prune brunch!" despite the inevitable "long wait."

	FOOD	DECOR	SERVICE	COST

Public *Eclectic* — 25 | 25 | 24 | $74

NoLita | 210 Elizabeth St. (bet. Prince & Spring Sts.) | 212-343-7011 | www.public-nyc.com

"Still hot" after 10-plus years, this NoLita "mainstay" offers a "bold", "inventive" Eclectic menu that riffs on "Aussie and Kiwi cuisine", matched with "well-curated" wines; its "unpretentious yet elegant" AvroKO-designed space and "fresh, fun", "knowledgeable" staff ensure it works for meals from brunches "with friends" to "romantic" dinners.

Pulqueria *Mexican* — ∇ 23 | 26 | 15 | $48

Chinatown | 11 Doyers St., downstairs (bet. Bowery & Pell St.) | 212-227-3099 | www.pulquerianyc.com

"Hidden down an unmarked staircase" off a Chinatown alley is this "speakeasy-style" Mexican "surprise" from the Apothéke folks, turning out "beyond-the-ordinary" tacos and other bites washed down with "interesting" pulque cocktails; the "cool vibe" tilts kinda "crazy late-night", especially when there's "amazing" live music and dancing.

Pure Food & Wine *Vegan/Vegetarian* — 24 | 21 | 22 | $56

Gramercy Park | 54 Irving Pl. (bet. 17th & 18th Sts.) | 212-477-1010 | www.purefoodandwine.com

"Slightly cooked food never tasted so good" rave fans of the "flavorful", "beautifully executed" "raw creations" at this "one-of-a-kind" Gramercy vegan; "laid-back" surrounds with a "lovely" garden enhance the "pricey" experience, as does springing for the tasting menu ("every course is a surprise").

Pure Thai Cookhouse *Thai* — 26 | 15 | 21 | $25

Midtown | 766 Ninth Ave. (bet. 51st & 52nd Sts.) | 212-581-0999 | www.purethaishophouse.com

Reviewers "revel in delicious flavors" at this "cut-above" Midtown Thai serving "spicy", "fair-priced" specialties (many starring "handmade noodles") via an "efficient" crew; you'll be "shoehorned" into "shack"-like digs with plastic-stool seating, but otherwise expect a "first-rate" meal.

Purple Yam *Asian* — ∇ 23 | 17 | 20 | $32

Ditmas Park | 1314 Cortelyou Rd. (bet. Argyle & Rugby Rds.) | Brooklyn | 718-940-8188 | www.purpleyamnyc.com

"Sophisticated" Pan-Asian fare with an "emphasis on Filipino" flavors – as in the "signature chicken adobo" – is the "unusual", "totally approachable" specialty of this "cozy", "welcoming" Ditmas Park "gem"; that it's "inexpensive" for the "upscale" milieu ensures it's generally "packed."

Pylos *Greek* — 26 | 23 | 23 | $54

East Village | 128 E. Seventh St. (bet. Ave. A & 1st Ave.) | 212-473-0220 | www.pylosrestaurant.com

The "refined" Greek menu is "creative in wonderful ways" at this "higher-end" East Village Hellenic tucked into a "warm", "lively" space with clay pots lining the ceiling; "attentive" service "with a smile" makes it all the more "charming."

Qi *Asian/Thai* — 21 | 21 | 17 | $30

Flatiron | 31 W. 14th St. (bet. 5th & 6th Aves.) | 212-929-9917
Midtown | 675 Eighth Ave. (43rd St.) | 212-247-8992

continued

Qi Thai Grill *Thai*
Williamsburg | 176 N. Ninth St. (bet. Bedford & Driggs Aves.) | Brooklyn | 718-302-1499
www.qirestaurant.com
Chef Pichet Ong delivers "well-prepared", "beautifully presented" Asian-Thai dishes at these "trendy" contenders; "reasonable prices" belie their "glittery", "Buddhist temple"–meets-"nightclub" decor, especially at the "hopping", "over-the-top" Theater District "find" done up in "chandeliers and holograms."

Quality Italian *Italian/Steak* | 24 | 23 | 23 | $75 |
Midtown | 57 W. 57th St. (6th Ave.) | 212-390-1111 | www.qualityitalian.com
This "massive", multilevel Midtown followup to nearby Quality Meats rolls out "wonderful steaks and Italian options" with "theatrical flourish", e.g. the chicken parm "marvel" that's sized and served like a "12-inch pizza"; basically "one big party" boasting "fantastic" bars and a "pro" staff, it screams "special occasion" ("romantic or business"), with "high prices" attached.

Quality Meats *American/Steak* | 26 | 24 | 24 | $81 |
Midtown | 57 W. 58th St. (bet. 5th & 6th Aves.) | 212-371-7777 | www.qualitymeatsnyc.com
In a city populated by "classic" chop shops, this "sexy", "modern" Midtowner is a "breath of fresh air", teaming "skilled" service with a "creative" American steakhouse menu that runs the gamut from "fabulous" cuts of beef to "killer ice cream"; sure, it's something of a "splurge", but it certainly "lives up to its name."

Quatorze Bis *French* | 20 | 19 | 20 | $64 |
East 70s | 323 E. 79th St. (bet. 1st & 2nd Aves.) | 212-535-1414
"Steady" and "essential", this "longtime" UES French bistro remains a local "favorite" for its "delicious" "Left Bank menu" and "welcoming" atmosphere; it's "not cheap" and could "use a face-lift", but its "prosperous clientele" deems it a "pleasant experience" all the same.

Queen *Italian* | 23 | 16 | 23 | $57 |
Brooklyn Heights | 84 Court St. (bet. Livingston & Schermerhorn Sts.) | Brooklyn | 718-596-5955 | www.queenrestaurant.com
A circa-1958 "Brooklyn Heights institution" near the courthouses, this "homey" Italian continues its reign as an area "favorite" for "true redsauce" fare minus culinary gimmicks; given the "gracious service" and "reasonable" tabs, most pardon the "dated" decor.

Queen of Sheba *Ethiopian* | ∇ 25 | 17 | 15 | $28 |
Hell's Kitchen | 650 10th Ave. (bet. 45th & 46th Sts.) | 212-397-0610 | www.shebanyc.com
"Hidden" in Hell's Kitchen, this "real-thing" Ethiopian offers "flavorful" fare – "numerous" veggie dishes included – that's eaten with your hands and "a heap of injera" bread; even with "small" quarters and "slow" pacing, it's a "repeater" for the cost-conscious crowd.

	FOOD	DECOR	SERVICE	COST

Queens Comfort *Southern*

▽ **22** | **18** | **21** | **$23**

Astoria | 40-09 30th Ave. (Newtown Rd.) | Queens | 718-728-2350 | www.queenscomfort.com

"Get your comfort on" at this Astoria joint dishing up Southern "pig-out" fare with a "twist" (try the "insanely good" disco fries) in "simple" digs with a "wacky", "chill" vibe; it's "cash-only but cheap and BYO" – no wonder there are "lines on weekends", especially for "brunch with a live DJ."

Queens Kickshaw *Coffee/Sandwiches*

21 | **18** | **20** | **$26**

Astoria | 40-17 Broadway (bet. 41st & Steinway Sts.) | Queens | 718-777-0913 | www.thequeenskickshaw.com

"Divine grilled cheese" taken "to the next level" and other "creative", fromage-focused eats are the specialty of this all-day, "all-vegetarian" Astoria "gem"; its "serious" coffee drinks and craft beers are a "huge plus", as are the "reasonable prices", late-night menu and "hip", "touch-of-Brooklyn" vibe.

🆕 Racines *French*

– | **–** | **–** | **M**

TriBeCa | 94 Chambers St. (bet. B'way & Church St.) | 646-644-6255 | www.racinesny.com

An American cousin to a pair of Paris wine bars, this industrial-chic TriBeCa arrival, backed by the owner of nearby Chambers Street Wines, offers a brief, upscale French menu spotlighting local ingredients; however, it's the impressive list of vintages focusing on small-producer, biodynamic labels that's the real star here.

Radiance Tea House *Teahouse*

▽ **21** | **22** | **21** | **$33**

Midtown | 158 W. 55th St. (bet. 6th & 7th Aves.) | 212-217-0442 | www.radiancetea.com

Radiating "calm" amid the "Midtown madness", this "delightful" teahouse matches a "huge" selection of "exotic" brews with an affordable menu of "light", Chinese-accented bites; the "very Zen" surroundings (which also house a gift shop) lend "spiritual quietude."

🆕 Raizes

– | **–** | **–** | **M**

Churrascaria *Portuguese/Seafood*

Greenpoint | 139 Nassau Ave. (McGuinness Blvd.) | Brooklyn | 718-389-0088

Though influences from Portugal and New England make this Greenpointer a seafood-lover's find, its specialty is rodizio-style grilled meats; look for the yellow car atop its roof (a remnant of the space's body-shop past) as well as a striking steel-beamed ceiling inside.

Ralph's Famous Italian Ices *Ice Cream*

24 | **10** | **20** | **$7**

Kips Bay | 144 E. 24th St. (bet. Lexington & 3rd Aves.) | 212-533-5333
Bayside | 214-13 41st Ave. (Bell Blvd.) | Queens | 718-428-4578
Glen Oaks | 264-21 Union Tpke. (265th St.) | Queens | 718-343-8724
Whitestone | Clintonville Plaza | 12-48 Clintonville St. (12th Rd.) | Queens | 718-746-1456
Arden Heights | 3285 Richmond Ave. (Gurley Ave.) | Staten Island | 718-967-1212
Elm Park | 501 Port Richmond Ave. (Catherine St.) | Staten Island | 718-273-3675
Eltingville | 4212 Hylan Blvd. (bet. Armstrong & Robinson Aves.) | Staten Island | 718-605-5052

continued

New Dorp | 2361 Hylan Blvd. (Otis Ave.) | Staten Island | 718-351-8133
Prince's Bay | 6272 Amboy Rd. (Bloomingdale Rd.) | Staten Island |
718-605-8133
Prince's Bay | 890 Huguenot Ave. (bet. Amboy & Drumgoole Rds.) |
Staten Island | 718-356-8133
www.ralphsices.com
Additional locations throughout the NY area

There's "nothing better on a hot summer day" than the "ah-mazing" Italian ices in a "dizzying" array of flavors at this "beloved" SI-based chain; you've gotta "stand in line" at the circa-1949 Elm Park "original", but it "goes quickly" – fans only wish this "NY highlight" were "open all year."

NEW Ramen. Co *Japanese/Noodle Shop*   — | — | — | I

Financial District | 100 Maiden Ln. (Pearl St.) | 646-490-8456
Chef Keizo Shimamoto's famed ramen burger has made the transition from Smorgasburg to this Financial District joint, where it's served alongside traditional Japanese ramen soups and bento boxes; the bright space has just a few seats, so most get it to go.

Randazzo's *Seafood*   22 | 9 | 18 | $36

Sheepshead Bay | 2017 Emmons Ave. (21st St.) | Brooklyn |
718-615-0010
A "real Brooklyn joint" – "packed" and "boisterous" with lotsa "local color" – this "iconic" Sheepshead Bay clam bar is beloved for its "simple", "fresh" seafood plus random "red-sauce" classics in "ginormous portions"; the "dinerlike" interior is strictly no-frills, but "sitting outside as the boats come in" is hard to beat.

Rao's *Italian*   21 | 17 | 21 | $83

East Harlem | 455 E. 114th St. (Pleasant Ave.) | 212-722-6709 |
www.raos.com
It practically "takes an act of Congress" to score a "coveted table", but if you "get lucky", Frank Pellegrino's East Harlem Italian lives up to the "mystique" with its "terrific" cooking and "central-casting" crowd; short of VIP connections, ordinary folks can visit the "one in Las Vegas" or just "buy the sauce in jars."

Raoul's *French*   24 | 21 | 22 | $74

SoHo | 180 Prince St. (bet. Sullivan & Thompson Sts.) | 212-966-3518 |
www.raouls.com
The "'it' factor" endures at this "classic", circa-1975 SoHo bistro that stays "true to itself" and its arty admirers with "surprisingly serious" French fare served in a "sexy" setting that includes a "beautiful", "lively" bar and "magical" garden accessed through the kitchen; though it can be "noisy and crowded", few rue its "popularity" or high price.

Rare Bar & Grill *Burgers*   21 | 15 | 18 | $35

Chelsea | Hilton NY Fashion District Hotel | 152 W. 26th St. (bet. 6th &
7th Aves.) | 212-807-7273
Murray Hill | Affinia Shelburne Hotel | 303 Lexington Ave. (37th St.) |
212-481-1999
www.rarebarandgrill.com
Given their "top-notch" burgers and french fry samplers, these "mid-scale" patty purveyors are rarely less than "bustling"; if the Murray Hill

| | FOOD | DECOR | SERVICE | COST |

original is too "packed", the Chelsea spin-off has a "ton of space" – and "hoppin'" rooftop bars await at both.

NEW Rasa Malaysian
— | — | — | M

Greenwich Village | 25 W. Eighth St. (bet. 5th & 6th Aves.) | 212-253-9888 | www.rasanyc.com

A former Laut chef has teamed with his sister to open this casual Village nook showcasing dishes from their native Malaysia, plus sushi; exposed-brick walls, painted greenery and attractive plate presentations add splash to the compact space.

Ravagh Persian
23 | 13 | 19 | $35

East 60s | 1237 First Ave. (bet. 66th & 67th Sts.) | 212-861-7900
Midtown | 11 E. 30th St. (bet. 5th & Madison Aves.) | 212-696-0300
www.ravaghpersiangrill.com

Among "NYC's few" options for classic Persian cooking, these Eastsiders dish up "solid", "stick-to-your-ribs" fare including "succulent kebabs" and "delicious" rice dishes; "generous" portions and "value" prices offset the "lacking decor."

Raymi Peruvian
21 | 22 | 21 | $53

Flatiron | 43 W. 24th St. (bet. 5th & 6th Aves.) | 212-929-1200 | www.richardsandoval.com

Richard Sandoval does Peruvian at this Flatiron "gem" whose "tasty, innovative" dishes include "outstanding" ceviche, best accompanied by the bar's "fantastic pisco cocktails"; a "big, buzzy, beautiful" space and "warm service" help justify the "pricey" tab.

Rayuela Pan-Latin
23 | 22 | 21 | $58

Lower East Side | 165 Allen St. (bet. Rivington & Stanton Sts.) | 212-253-8840 | www.rayuelanyc.com

Besides being an eyeful, this "snazzy" Lower Eastsider "wows the palate" with "bold" Pan-Latin tapas served in a "lovely" duplex setting centered around an "amazing" live olive tree; "gracious" staffers oversee a milieu that's "sceney" – and accordingly "pricey."

Recette American
24 | 16 | 20 | $83

West Village | 328 W. 12th St. (Greenwich St.) | 212-414-3000 | www.recettenyc.com

"Inspired", "adventurous" New American small plates (and "exceptional" multicourse tasting menus) keep this "pricey", "unfussy" West Villager "bustling" and "noisy"; some say the "pretty" but "beyond-tiny" room is "too squeezed", but to most it's a "fun", even "rather romantic" scene.

Red Bamboo Pan-Asian/Vegan
22 | 14 | 19 | $23

Greenwich Village | 140 W. Fourth St. (6th Ave.) | 212-260-7049 | www.redbamboo-nyc.com

With an "all-vegan" menu "straddling soul food and Pan-Asian cuisines", this Villager specializes in "clever", "so convincing" mock versions of meat and fish dishes, from "kickin'" Creole chicken to Thai beef curry; the no-frills setting is matched with "affordable" tabs.

	FOOD	DECOR	SERVICE	COST

Red Cat *American/Mediterranean* — 24 | 19 | 22 | $57

Chelsea | 227 10th Ave. (bet. 23rd & 24th Sts.) | 212-242-1122 | www.theredcat.com

The "Chelsea art-world vibe" thrives at this "lively" vet near the High Line that remains a "favorite" for "top-notch" Med-American fare; "solid service" and a "charming" (if "loud") ambiance keep its "gallery-hopping" clientele content despite kinda "pricey" tabs.

Red Egg *Chinese* — 19 | 15 | 15 | $30

Little Italy | 202 Centre St. (Howard St.) | 212-966-1123 | www.redeggnyc.com

"Not nearly as hectic" as the usual dim sum specialists, this "contemporary" Little Italy Chinese dispenses "high-quality" tidbits that are "made to order" and served by a "competent" crew with "no carts" in sight; despite the "lounge"-like setting, prices remain egg-ceptably "low."

Redeye Grill *American/Seafood* — 19 | 19 | 19 | $64

Midtown | 890 Seventh Ave. (56th St.) | 212-541-9000 | www.redeyegrill.com

Steadily "busy" for nearly two decades, Shelly Fireman's "classy" Midtowner puts forth a "dependable" American menu starring "tons of seafood"; "prompt" service, a "dramatic" setting and "pretty-penny" pricing are all part of the "vibrant" experience – and that location directly opposite Carnegie Hall sure is "handy."

RedFarm *Chinese* — 25 | 18 | 21 | $54

NEW **West 70s** | 2170 Broadway (bet. 76th & 77th Sts.) | 212-724-9700

West Village | 529 Hudson St. (bet. Charles & W. 10th Sts.) | 212-792-9700

www.redfarmnyc.com

Ed Schoenfeld and Joe Ng opened a "new chapter" in NYC's Chinese food scene with these locavore standouts known for their "upscale", "creative riffs" on traditional specialties (notably "amazing dim sum"); the new Upper Westsider is "much larger" than the "cramped" West Village original, but both are "frenetic", "noisy and hard to get into" – "if only they took reservations!"

Red Gravy *Italian* — 23 | 20 | 21 | $55

Brooklyn Heights | 151 Atlantic Ave. (bet. Clinton & Henry Sts.) | Brooklyn | 718-855-0051 | www.redgravynyc.com

Saul Bolton "does it again" with this instant "neighborhood favorite" in Brooklyn Heights, whose "slightly different take on Italian" marries "old-country" flavors with a "gifted chef's panache"; factor in "warm", low-key digs and a "gracious" staff, and to most it's worth the slightly "pricey" tab.

The Redhead *Southern* — 23 | 16 | 20 | $41

East Village | 349 E. 13th St. (bet. 1st & 2nd Aves.) | 212-533-6212 | www.theredheadnyc.com

"Justifiably spoken of with adoration", this East Village Southern bar/eatery slings comfort faves like "killer fried chicken" and "fun drinks" at "relatively inexpensive" rates; it's a "bustling", "cramped" "hole-in-the-wall" that doesn't take reservations, but "courteous" service is another reason it's "worth the wait."

Red Hook Lobster Pound *Seafood*   24 | 9 | 17 | $30

NEW **East Village** | 16 Extra Pl. (off 1st St., bet. Bowery & 2nd Ave.) | 212-777-7225
Red Hook | 284 Van Brunt St. (bet. Pioneer & Verona Sts.) | Brooklyn | 718-858-7650
www.redhooklobster.com

Cranking out some of "NYC's best lobster rolls" – bursting with "big, fresh hunks" of Maine crustacean – these "order-at-the-counter" joints deliver "Down East authenticity" in "nothing-fancy", "picnic table"-equipped setups; the East Villager pours beer, while the BYO Red Hook original offers steamed lobster dinners.

Red Rooster *American*   22 | 22 | 21 | $54

Harlem | 310 Lenox Ave. (bet. 125th & 126th Sts.) | 212-792-9001 | www.redroosterharlem.com

"A scene to say the least", Marcus Samuelsson's "jumping Harlem joint" provides "outstanding" Southern-accented American fare and "wow" cocktails with a side of "superb" people-watching; maybe it's "expensive for the neighborhood", but nonetheless it's "always packed"; P.S. there's often live music downstairs at Ginny's Supper Club.

Regency Bar & Grill *American*   ▽ 19 | 23 | 20 | $86

East 60s | Loews Regency Hotel | 540 Park Ave. (61st St.) | 212-759-4100 | www.regencybarandgrill.com

Following a "grand reopening" via the Sant Ambroeus team, this UES "home of the power breakfast" in the Loews Regency Hotel boasts "lovely" new decor; opinions differ on the "high-end" New American fare by chef Dan Silverman (ex Standard Grill, Lever House), but all agree it's "pricey."

Remi *Italian*   23 | 22 | 21 | $66

Midtown | 145 W. 53rd St. (bet. 6th & 7th Aves.) | 212-581-4242 | www.remi-ny.com

"Reliable" "all-around quality" marks this "upscale" Midtown Italian vet, where "outstanding" Venetian specialties are "served with panache" to "pre-theater" and "business" types; the "serene" space with its "impressive" Grand Canal mural is "pretty" enough to help you forget the "expense account"-ready prices.

Republic *Asian*   19 | 15 | 17 | $27

Union Square | 37 Union Sq. W. (bet. 16th & 17th Sts.) | 212-627-7172 | www.thinknoodles.com

Long a "Union Square standby", this Asian "mess hall" still "does the trick" with "filling" bowls of noodles and more at "bargain-basement prices"; the "communal-style" setup is "awkward" and "noisy as all get-out", but its "young" followers eat and exit "in a flash."

NEW Reserve Cut *Kosher/Steak*   ▽ 25 | 24 | 24 | $116

Financial District | The Setai Club & Spa Wall St. | 40 Broad St. (Exchange Pl.) | 212-747-0300 | www.reservecut.com

"Who knew that kosher could taste, look and feel glamorous?" marvel the observant of this "beautiful" Financial District steakhouse's "standout" beef, sushi and French fusion dishes; prices are "expense-account" level, but the staff makes sure you're "happy."

Resto *Belgian* | 20 | 18 | 18 | $46 |

Kips Bay | 111 E. 29th St. (bet. Lexington & Park Aves.) | 212-685-5585 | www.restonyc.com

A "hedonist's delight", this "energetic" Kips Bay "favorite" provides the "refreshing" chance to chow down on "delicious, meat-centric" Belgian eats, backed by a "tremendous beer selection"; regulars report the "sublime hangover pasta" is the thing to get at weekend brunch.

Reynard *American* | 23 | 23 | 21 | $60 |

Williamsburg | Wythe Hotel | 80 Wythe Ave. (11th St.) | Brooklyn | 718-460-8004 | www.reynardsnyc.com

This "vibrant" Williamsburg New American from Andrew Tarlow (Diner, Marlow & Sons) is a "cool trendsetter"–worthy scene that's also "deeply serious" about its "wonderful, creative" seasonal food and drink; factor in a "fabulous" setting in the converted-1901-factory Wythe Hotel, and it's an all-around "wow" – with prices to match.

Ricardo Steak House *Steak*   ▽ | 23 | 20 | 21 | $63 |

East Harlem | 2145 Second Ave. (bet. 110th & 111th Sts.) | 212-289-5895 | www.ricardosteakhouse.com

East Harlem has a "real gem" in this "well-done" steakhouse where "simply delicious" chops are served with "flair" to a crowd with "energy" to spare; its art-lined room and "quiet patio" also draw applause, not to mention the "value" pricing.

Risotteria *Italian* | 21 | 9 | 15 | $27 |

West Village | 270 Bleecker St. (Morton St.) | 212-924-6664 | www.risotteria.com

A "celiac's delight", this West Village Italian works "gluten-free magic" with a "delish" menu showcasing the "art of risotto" plus wheatless pizza; the "tiny", "crammed" space may be "not much to look at", but fans would "squeeze in" for the "fair prices" alone.

NEW Risotteria Melotti *Italian* | – | – | – | M |

East Village | 309 E. Fifth St. (bet. 1st & 2nd Aves.) | 646-755-8939 | www.risotteriamelottinyc.com

A haven for the gluten-free, this midpriced East Villager celebrates risotto, offering some 15 variations of the hearty Italian dish, plus salads and antipasti; it uses rice from the owners' own fields in Italy, bags of which can be purchased within its snug, rustic space.

NEW Ristorante Morini *Italian* | 26 | 23 | 25 | $98 |

East 80s | 1167 Madison Ave. (bet. 85th & 86th Sts.) | 212-249-0444 | www.ristorantemorini.com

"Another winner" from chef Michael White, this "civilized" UES "outpost of the mini-empire" lavishes the "Blue Jasmine" crowd with "unbelievable", "flawlessly executed" regional Italian cuisine; "buzzy bar" notwithstanding, a few find the "impeccable" service and "tasteful" bi-level space "a bit formal", though they're in keeping with the "banker's prices."

River Café *American*

	FOOD	DECOR	SERVICE	COST
	26	27	26	$150

Dumbo | 1 Water St. (bet. Furman & Old Fulton Sts.) | Brooklyn | 718-522-5200 | www.rivercafe.com

"Sensational" views of Lower Manhattan set a "romantic" mood, but fans say you'll also be "swept off your feet" by the New American fare at this Dumbo waterfront "icon"; naturally, the prix fixe–only dinners are "very expensive", but "never-misses-a-beat" service helps make it "memorable for any occasion – or a random Tuesday, for that matter."

Riverpark *American*

	FOOD	DECOR	SERVICE	COST
	25	26	25	$65

Kips Bay | 450 E. 29th St. (1st Ave.) | 212-729-9790 | www.riverparknyc.com

"Hidden" in a Kips Bay office complex, Tom Colicchio's "top-notch" New American dispenses "simple, delicious" seasonal fare using ingredients from its own "urban garden"; an "impressive bar", "airy" interior and patio with "incredible views" complete the "upscale" "getaway" experience that's rated "worth the price tag" and the "trek."

River Styx *American*

	FOOD	DECOR	SERVICE	COST
	—	—	—	M

Greenpoint | 21 Greenpoint Ave. (Water St.) | Brooklyn | 718-383-8833 | www.riverstyxny.com

This stylish Greenpointer from the folks behind Williamsburg's Roebling Tea Room offers moderately priced, seafood-focused New American fare, much of it cooked in a wood-fired brick oven; the space nods to the area's nautical past with wharf-chic decor and whimsically named cocktails.

Robataya *Japanese*

	FOOD	DECOR	SERVICE	COST
	25	23	22	$67

East Village | 231 E. Ninth St. (bet. 2nd Ave. & Stuyvesant St.) | 212-979-9674 | www.robataya-ny.com

"Secure a reservation" at this Japanese East Villager's robata counter and watch as the cooks grill "delicious" meats, seafood and veggies over an open hearth, serving 'em up on long paddles; the bill "adds up quickly", but most don't mind given the overall "fun experience."

Robert *American*

	FOOD	DECOR	SERVICE	COST
	22	27	23	$63

Midtown | Museum of Art and Design | 2 Columbus Circle (bet. B'way & 8th Ave.) | 212-299-7730 | www.robertnyc.com

It's "all about" the "wondrous" Central Park views at this museum "aerie" high above Columbus Circle, though its "pricey" American fare is "fine" too – and nightly live jazz further boosts the "special" mood; insiders say the experience is just as "striking" over cocktails in the lounge, but either way, a window table is "key."

Roberta's *Italian/Pizza*

	FOOD	DECOR	SERVICE	COST
	26	18	20	$38

Bushwick | 261 Moore St. (Bogart St.) | Brooklyn | 718-417-1118 | www.robertaspizza.com

"Killer creativity" and "quality ingredients" (some grown on-site) add up to "masterpiece pizzas" and other "incredible" Italian-accented dishes at this "funky", "beloved" Bushwick pioneer; "crazy lines" are part of the "adventure", so go "off-peak" or "pass the time" at the "tiki tent" back bar.

	FOOD	DECOR	SERVICE	COST

Roberto *Italian*
27 | 19 | 22 | $63

Arthur Avenue/Belmont | 603 Crescent Ave. (Hughes Ave.) | Bronx | 718-733-9503 | www.roberto089.com

For a "true Arthur Avenue experience", fans of "old-world" Italian cooking head to this "busy" Bronx bastion where chef Roberto Paciullo's "pricey" but "unforgettable" dishes are delivered by a "gracious" staff; given the "small" setting and no-reservations policy, just know "you may have to wait" for a table.

Rock Center Café *American*
19 | 22 | 19 | $56

Midtown | Rockefeller Ctr. | 20 W. 50th St. (bet. 5th & 6th Aves.) | 212-332-7620 | www.patinagroup.com

With its "rink-side" view of skaters during the winter and open-air tables in front of the Prometheus statue in summer, this Rock Center American is an "undeniable draw" for "tourists" and "holiday guests"; "only average" food proves that you're paying for "location, location, location."

Rocking Horse Cafe *Mexican*
22 | 16 | 19 | $37

Chelsea | 182 Eighth Ave. (bet. 19th & 20th Sts.) | 212-463-9511 | www.rockinghorsecafe.com

"Handy" in the neighborhood, this "buoyant" Chelsea veteran "rocks on" with "quality" Mexican staples and "fab" margaritas at "value" rates (especially the "best-kept-secret" $16 brunch); the "lively scene" can get "noisy", but in summer there's "terrific", quieter sidewalk seating.

Roebling Tea Room *American*
21 | 21 | 13 | $7

Williamsburg | 143 Roebling St. (Metropolitan Ave.) | Brooklyn | 718-963-0760 | www.roeblingtearoom.com

"Don't let the name fool you" – though this "chill" Williamsburg hang does pour "wonderful teas", it's more about the "inventive", "darn-good" seasonal American fare (including "the best burger") and drinks list; the "super-cute" setting opens to a roomy patio.

Rolf's *German*
16 | 22 | 17 | $41

Gramercy Park | 281 Third Ave. (22nd St.) | 212-473-8718 | www.rolfsnyc.com

Best experienced "around the holidays", this circa-1968 Gramercy German "time warp" is a "sight to see" when the "jaw-droppingly" "gaudy" Oktoberfest and Christmas decorations go up ("bring your sunglasses"); too bad the "run-of-the-mill" food makes a case for just a "drink at the bar."

Roll-n-Roaster *Sandwiches*
22 | 13 | 17 | $15

Sheepshead Bay | 2901 Emmons Ave. (bet. Nostrand Ave. & 29th St.) | Brooklyn | 718-769-6000 | www.rollnroaster.com

"Retro fast-food" fans roll into this "busy" Sheepshead Bay "institution" to chow down on "bangin'" roast beef sandwiches and "must-have" cheese fries served into the wee hours; the aging digs are pretty "beat up", but "there's a reason why they've been in business" since 1970.

Roman's *Italian*
▽ 24 | 18 | 22 | $56

Fort Greene | 243 DeKalb Ave. (bet. Clermont & Vanderbilt Aves.) | Brooklyn | 718-622-5300 | www.romansnyc.com

Its "seasonally" attuned Italian menu "changes every day, but the quality doesn't" at this "hip", snug Fort Greene sibling of Marlow & Sons that's a "memorable" blend of culinary "passion" and "neighborhoody" vibes; no reservations means waits are "standard", providing time to size up the bar's "talented mixologists."

Room Service *Thai*

20 | 22 | 18 | $28

Midtown | 690 Ninth Ave. (bet. 47th & 48th Sts.) | 212-582-0999 | www.roomservicerestaurant.com

"Decked out with mirrors and chandeliers", this "eye-popping" Theater District Thai is a "jazzy" destination for "spot-on" Thai bites at a "fair price"; an "upbeat" vibe, "cool cocktails" and "fun-loving" crowd is all part of the "like-a-nightclub" milieu.

NEW Root & Bone *Southern*

— | — | — | M

East Village | 200 E. Third St. (bet. Aves. A & B) | 646-682-7076 | www.rootnbone.com

Two *Top Chef* alums have teamed up on this tiny East Villager whose elevated takes on Southern staples go down well with the bar's barrel-aged cocktails; rustic and wood-filled, the space features folksy touches (vintage school chairs, old-fashioned floral china) plus a market/take-out area.

Rosa Mexicano *Mexican*

23 | 22 | 22 | $51

East Midtown | 1063 First Ave. (58th St.) | 212-753-7407
Flatiron | 9 E. 18th St. (bet. B'way & 5th Ave.) | 212-533-3350
West 60s | 61 Columbus Ave. (62nd St.) | 212-977-7700
www.rosamexicano.com

From the "terrific" tableside guacamole to the "habit-forming" pomegranate margaritas, the fare's "reliably delicious" at these "enjoyable", "upscale" Mexican cantinas; while tabs can be on the "pricey" side, "attentive" service and "lively" settings make dining here "feel like a party."

Rosanjin *Japanese*

▽ 26 | 24 | 26 | $150

TriBeCa | 141 Duane St. (bet. B'way & Church St.) | 212-346-0664 | www.rosanjintribeca.com

Aesthetically "amazing", this "top-end" TriBeCa Japanese kaiseki specialist showcases the "heavenly" tastes and textures of "traditional", "beautifully presented" set menus; "exquisite" service from a kimono-clad staff and a "petite", "serene" setting make for a "transporting" experience that's (predictably) "expensive."

Rosemary's *Italian*

22 | 22 | 18 | $50

West Village | 18 Greenwich Ave. (10th St.) | 212-647-1818 | www.rosemarysnyc.com

"Fabulously fresh" ingredients – some right from the "roof garden" – go into the "modern takes on simple" Italian fare at this "popular" West Villager; given the "no-reservations" policy, its "inviting" space is a "noisy" "scene" with "long waits" at dinner and brunch, but lunch is "quieter."

Rose Water *American*

25 | 19 | 23 | $51

Park Slope | 787 Union St. (bet. 5th & 6th Aves.) | Brooklyn | 718-783-3800 | www.rosewaterrestaurant.com

Park Slope's original "locavore heaven", this way-"cozy" New American vet remains a "consistently fabulous" source for "inventive", "seasonally driven" fare and service "like a finely oiled machine"; it's a "favorite" for brunch, where the only thorn is "bumping elbows" in the "tight space" (try for the outdoor seats in summer).

Rossini's *Italian*

FOOD	DECOR	SERVICE	COST
22	18	22	$63

Murray Hill | 108 E. 38th St. (bet. Lexington & Park Aves.) | 212-683-0135 | www.rossinisrestaurant.com

The "good old days" endure at this 1978-vintage Murray Hill Italian touted for its "excellent" Tuscan fare and "seamless" service from "tuxedo"-attired staffers; the nightly piano player and live "opera music" on Saturdays help soothe any "sticker shock."

NEW Rotisserie Georgette *French*

24	22	22	$73

East 60s | 14 E. 60th St. (bet. 5th & Madison Aves.) | 212-390-8060 | www.rotisserieg.com

"Hands-on" owner Georgette Farkas ensures "everything's spectacular" at this UES "charmer" devoted to "beautifully prepared" French rotisserie fare from an open kitchen; its "well-heeled" crowd declares the overall experience "as crisp as the skin" on the "sublime" signature poule de luxe – and "totally worth" the "decadent" tab.

Rouge et Blanc *French/Vietnamese*

23	22	22	$58

SoHo | 48 MacDougal St. (bet. Houston & Prince Sts.) | 212-260-5757 | www.rougeetblancnyc.com

This SoHo "sleeper" achieves "subtlety" with a "brilliant" French-Vietnamese lineup that "marries perfectly" with its "wonderful" wine list; a "low-key" space ("think *The Quiet American*") and "never-rushed" service make it a "hidden gem" – at least until the "masses catch on."

Rubirosa *Italian/Pizza*

25	18	21	$41

NoLita | 235 Mulberry St. (bet. Prince & Spring Sts.) | 212-965-0500 | www.rubirosanyc.com

"Perfecto" pizzas and "soulful" pastas offered at a "fair price" keep this tolerably "trendy" NoLita Italian on "solid footing" with its "funky downtown" crowd; it's "friendly enough" and "rocks with energy" at prime times, so expect a "wait" for entrée into its "cramped" quarters.

Ruby Foo's *Asian*

19	20	18	$45

Midtown | 1626 Broadway (49th St.) | 212-489-5600 | www.rubyfoos.com

Theatergoers, tourist "throngs" and "kids galore" pile into this "fun", "cavernous" Times Square Asian serving "better-than-expected" eats with a side of "kitsch"; the "'50s Hollywood Chinese" decor and "spotty" service lead some to sigh that "better choices abound."

Rucola *Italian*

25	22	23	$47

Boerum Hill | 190 Dean St. (Bond St.) | Brooklyn | 718-576-3209 | www.rucolabrooklyn.com

Full of "locally grown goodness", the "superb", "rustic" Italian fare at this Boerum Hill "gem" comes in "warm" digs with an "indie vibe"; it's "tiny" and "doesn't take reservations", so expect "waits" and a "squeeze" – the "hard-working staff" helps keep the mood "happy"; P.S. mornings it dispenses Stumptown brews and pastries.

	FOOD	DECOR	SERVICE	COST

Rue 57 *French*
18 **18** **17** **$51**

Midtown | 60 W. 57th St. (6th Ave.) | 212-307-5656 | www.rue57.com
"Convenience is key" at this veteran brasserie that's "well located" in the heart of Midtown, turning out "reliable" if "not outstanding" French eats plus sushi; despite "uneven" service, "noisy" decibels and a "tourist"-centric crowd, it's usually "bustling" – verging on "hectic."

NEW The Runner *American*
– **–** **–** **M**

Clinton Hill | 458-460 Myrtle Ave. (bet. Washington & Waverly Aves.) | Brooklyn | 718-643-6500 | www.therunnerbk.com
Inspired by early American cookery, this Clinton Hill eatery specializes in roasts and other homey dishes from a wood-burning oven, served in rustic digs with a back patio; its separate barroom is strong on craft beers – chef Andrew Burman co-owns Gowanus' Other Half Brewing Co. – and offers its own brief menu.

Runner & Stone *American/Bakery*
∇ **22** **20** **21** **$41**

Gowanus | 285 Third Ave. (bet. Carroll & President Sts.) | Brooklyn | 718-576-3360 | www.runnerandstone.com
"Outstanding breads" are the star at this "cute" all-day Gowanus bakery/eatery from Smorgasburg vets; some find the simple New American fare a bit "ordinary" compared to the "absolutely amazing" baked goods, but it's an "oasis" for a "quick bite" or drink at the bar.

NEW Russ & Daughters Cafe *Jewish*
– **–** **–** **M**

Lower East Side | 127 Orchard St. (bet. Delancey & Rivington Sts.) | 212-475-4881 | www.russanddaughterscafe.com
After 100 years in business, LES icon Russ & Daughters has begat this around-the-corner cafe, which slings classic Jewish comfort staples – from latkes and knishes to, yes, umpteen smoked fish varieties; with banquettes and display shelves, the cheery luncheonette-esque setting is reminiscent of the original shop.

Russian Samovar *Continental/Russian*
17 **14** **17** **$60**

Midtown | 256 W. 52nd St. (bet. B'way & 8th Ave.) | 212-757-0168 | www.russiansamovar.com
"Home away from home" for "Russian-speakers", this "cheerful" Theater District stalwart serves Russo-Continental staples amid live piano-led "festivity" that gets louder as the night progresses; tasty "infused vodkas" distract from the kinda "cheesy" decor.

Russian Tea Room *Continental/Russian*
19 **25** **21** **$68**

Midtown | 150 W. 57th St. (bet. 6th & 7th Aves.) | 212-581-7100 | www.russiantearoomnyc.com
Its "glamorously ostentatious" decor intact, this "legendary" Russo-Continental stunner by Carnegie Hall still provides a "glitzy" czarist backdrop for "posh" noshing built around caviar and blini; "outrageous" prices for "so-so" food have fans lamenting its "former glory", but it's hard to top as a "theatrical experience" for "out-of-towners."

Ruth's Chris Steak House *Steak*
25 **21** **24** **$75**

Midtown | 148 W. 51st St. (bet. 6th & 7th Aves.) | 212-245-9600 | www.ruthschris.com
A slather of "melted butter" adds some "extra-fab" sizzle to the "big

cuts" of beef at this "first-rate" Theater District link of the New Orleans–based steakhouse chain; likewise, the "personalized" service and
"upscale" woodwork are as "impressive" as the tabs are "high."

Rye *American*

	FOOD	DECOR	SERVICE	COST
	▽ 24	23	21	$47

Williamsburg | 247 S. First St. (bet. Havemeyer & Roebling Sts.) |
Brooklyn | 718-218-8047 | www.ryerestaurant.com

A "speakeasy-style" setting complete with a vintage bar sets the scene
for "fine cocktails" paired with "first-rate" American fare at this Williamsburg "standout"; "low-key" and "charming" with "no airs", it hosts a
happy hour that's among the "best in the 'hood.'"

Sacred Chow *Kosher/Vegan/Vegetarian*

	FOOD	DECOR	SERVICE	COST
	▽ 24	16	21	$21

Greenwich Village | 227 Sullivan St. (bet. Bleecker & 3rd Sts.) |
212-337-0863 | www.sacredchow.com

The "delicious" organic, kosher and vegan offerings (think "exceptional
fake meatballs") at this "cute, quirky" Villager may just make carnivores
"believe"; it's small in size and "popular" with the health-minded, so
"definitely make a reservation."

Sahara *Turkish*

	FOOD	DECOR	SERVICE	COST
	23	17	20	$30

Sheepshead Bay | 2337 Coney Island Ave. (bet. Aves. T & U) | Brooklyn |
718-376-8594 | www.saharanewyork.com

It's "old-school at this point", but this durable Sheepshead Bay Turk is
"hard to beat" for "seriously good" grilled fare ("kebab is king") at the
right price; the "huge" space may be "short on ambiance", but that
doesn't hurt its "popularity" with "groups and families."

Saju Bistro *French*

	FOOD	DECOR	SERVICE	COST
	21	19	21	$45

Midtown | Mela Hotel | 120 W. 44th St. (6th Ave.) | 212-997-7258 |
www.sajubistro.com

A "slice of Paree" in Times Square, this "very French" bistro is "spot-on"
for "traditional Provençal dishes" offered at "fair" prices; it's especially
"convenient" pre-theater with an "engaging" staff to get you in and out.

Sakagura *Japanese*

	FOOD	DECOR	SERVICE	COST
	24	21	21	$66

East Midtown | 211 E. 43rd St. (bet. 2nd & 3rd Aves.) | 212-953-7253 |
www.sakagura.com

"Like Tokyo" but "minus the 14-hour plane ride", this "relaxing" Japanese
izakaya tucked beneath a "nondescript" office building near Grand
Central is the "real deal" for "incredible" small plates matched with
"exceptional" sakes; naturally, its "high quality" comes with a "price
tag to match."

SakaMai *Japanese*

	FOOD	DECOR	SERVICE	COST
	▽ 24	20	22	$56

Lower East Side | 157 Ludlow St. (Stanton St.) | 646-590-0684 |
www.sakamai.com

Fans "can't say enough" about this "hip" yet "peaceful" LES izakaya
where "talented" staffers dispense "genius" Japanese bites (the "egg on
egg on egg" is a "must") with "beautiful" drinks and sake flights; you'll
"definitely drop some change", but the quality "rewards" it.

	FOOD	DECOR	SERVICE	COST

Sake Bar Hagi *Japanese* ▽ 21 | 12 | 17 | $40

Midtown | 152 W. 49th St. (7th Ave.) | 212-764-8549 |
www.sakebarhagi.com

Just off Times Square, this "underground" izakaya "fills up fast" with
folks unwinding over "down-home" Japanese bar food and "plenty of
booze on the cheap" – so get there soon after work or prepare to wait;
there's "no decor" to speak of, but the crowd "lends atmosphere."

Sala One Nine *Spanish* ▽ 23 | 21 | 22 | $39

Flatiron | 35 W. 19th St. (bet. 5th & 6th Aves.) | 212-229-2300 |
www.salaonenine.com

"Excellent" tapas and sangria fuel the "energetic" scene at this "inviting",
"no-attitude" Flatiron Spaniard that works for "hanging out with friends"
or going on a "fun date"; its "fantastic happy-hour" deals spell "crowded"
conditions in the after-work hours.

Salinas *Spanish* 22 | 22 | 21 | $59

Chelsea | 136 Ninth Ave. (bet. 18th & 19th Sts.) | 212-776-1990 |
www.salinasnyc.com

"Charmed" Chelsea dwellers hail this "creative" Spaniard for its "terrific
tapas" and "unusually elegant" space complete with a "retractable roof"
sheltering a "fabulous garden"; sure, it's on the "pricey" side, but this is
"one to reckon with."

Salt & Fat *American/Asian* 25 | 16 | 21 | $38

Sunnyside (Queens) | 41-16 Queens Blvd. (bet. 41st & 42nd Sts.) |
Queens | 718-433-3702 | www.saltandfatny.com
The name shows a "sense of humor", but they "take the food seriously"
at this Sunnyside "rising star" where "inventive" small plates showcase
a "delectable" blend of New American and Asian flavors, offered at
"Queens prices"; "no reservations" and "hole-in-the-wall" dimensions
mean "waits" at prime times.

Salumeria Rosi Parmacotto *Italian* 24 | 17 | 19 | $59

West 70s | 283 Amsterdam Ave. (bet. 73rd & 74th Sts.) | 212-877-4800
Il Ristorante Rosi *Italian*
East 70s | 903 Madison Ave. (bet. 72nd & 73rd Sts.) | 212-517-7700
www.salumeriarosi.com
The "quality shines" at chef Cesare Casella's *"molto Italiano"* UWS
enoteca/salumeria, where the cured meats, Tuscan small plates and
wines seem like a gift from "the mother country"; the roomier Madison
Avenue spin-off serves much of the same in a more upscale, white-
tableclothed room.

Salvation Taco *Mexican* 21 | 20 | 15 | $41

Murray Hill | Pod 39 Hotel | 145 E. 39th St. (bet. Lexington & 3rd Aves.) |
212-865-5800 | www.salvationtaco.com
"Showstopper" creations with an "unusual" bent come courtesy of April
Bloomfield and Ken Friedman (The Breslin, Spotted Pig) at this "sexy"
Murray Hill Mexican where "after-work crowds" congregate for "pricey",
"tiny" but "full-of-flavor" tacos and snacks; "don't miss the rooftop"
for "killer" cocktails.

Sammy's Fishbox *Seafood*

| 21 | 16 | 18 | $62 |

City Island | 41 City Island Ave. (Rochelle St.) | Bronx | 718-885-0920 | www.sammysfishbox.com

"You will not leave hungry" could be the motto of this "huge" City Island vet, which has been churning out "generous" servings of seafood since 1966; though not cheap, it's something of a "tourist" magnet, so count on it being "crowded in summer months."

Sammy's Noodle Shop

| 20 | 8 | 16 | $27 |

& Grill *Chinese/Noodle Shop*

West Village | 453 Sixth Ave. (11th St.) | 212-924-6688

"Bring your appetite" to this "efficient" West Village Chinese that rolls out a "wide menu" of "inexpensive" comfort items, notably noodle soups; seriously "worn-out" digs and service "without a smile" explain why it's mostly a "neighborhood take-out" option.

Sammy's Roumanian *Jewish*

| 21 | 12 | 19 | $55 |

Lower East Side | 157 Chrystie St. (Delancey St.) | 212-673-0330

This LES "heartburn city" brings on "old-fashioned" Jewish staples "covered in schmaltz" and vodka in ice blocks in a "grungy basement" setting where a keyboardist spouts "nonstop shtick"; like being in a "perpetual bar mitzvah", the clamorous "cavorting" could cause "cardiac arrest" – but it's a "great way to go."

Sammy's Shrimp Box *Seafood*

| 23 | 17 | 21 | $51 |

City Island | 64 City Island Ave. (Horton St.) | Bronx | 718-885-3200 | www.shrimpboxrestaurant.com

Docked "at the end of the strip" near its Fish Box forerunner, this "casual" City Islander dispenses "down-to-earth" "fried seafood" and "lots of it" at a "nice price"; it's a standard "hang in the summer", where you should expect "very crowded" conditions.

Samurai Mama *Japanese*

| ▽ 24 | 21 | 21 | $38 |

Williamsburg | 205 Grand St. (bet. Bedford & Driggs Aves.) | Brooklyn | 718-599-6161 | www.samuraimama.com

"Craveable" udon soups, "crazy-good" dumplings and other "vibrant" Japanese classics are on offer at this Williamsburg "staple"; "warm welcomes", "good prices" and a "special" setting evoking an "inn outside of Tokyo" are other reasons it's a "neighborhood" "favorite."

Sandro's *Italian*

| 24 | 14 | 21 | $73 |

East 80s | 306 E. 81st St. (bet. 1st & 2nd Aves.) | 212-288-7374 | www.sandrosnyc.com

Almost "better than a ticket to Rome", this "cozy" Upper Eastsider "rises above the ordinary" with "lovely" Italian cuisine via "mercurial" chef-owner Sandro Fioriti, who sometimes greets diners in his "pajama bottoms"; even if the "high prices" don't match the "simple setting", fans say it's "difficult to beat."

Sanford's *American*

| 24 | 21 | 21 | $30 |

Astoria | 30-13 Broadway (bet. 30th & 31st Sts.) | Queens | 718-932-9569 | www.sanfordsnyc.com

In business since 1922 but recently given a "contemporary" upgrade, this 24/7 Astoria "super-diner" serves "higher-caliber" American comfort food at "reasonable" rates; the formula is "deservedly popular", especially at brunch when the "only drawback is the wait" – good thing an expansion is in the works.

San Matteo *Italian/Pizza*

▽ 25 | 15 | 20 | $32

East 80s | 1739 Second Ave. (90th St.) | 212-426-6943 | www.sanmatteopanuozzo.com

"Close your eyes, bite into your bubbling pizza" just out of the "glowing wood oven" and "you're in Napoli" sigh fans of this UES Italian "find", where the *panuozzi* (sandwiches) and espresso drinks are equally "wonderful"; it's "cheap" and "charming", but also a "tight squeeze" given its "tiny" dimensions.

San Pietro *Italian*

22 | 19 | 22 | $87

Midtown | 18 E. 54th St. (bet. 5th & Madison Aves.) | 212-753-9015 | www.sanpietrorestaurant.us

"Filled with CEOs" and "older sophisticates" at lunch, this "top-notch" Southern Italian is a Midtown "class act" offering "sumptuous" cuisine and "treat-you-like-royalty" service; it's "wildly costly", however, so it helps if "money is no object."

Sant Ambroeus *Italian*

▽ 21 | 19 | 20 | $65

East 70s | 1000 Madison Ave. (bet. 77th & 78th Sts.) | 212-570-2211
NEW **NoLita** | 265 Lafayette St. (bet. Prince & Spring Sts.) | 212-966-2770
West Village | 259 W. Fourth St. (Perry St.) | 212-604-9254

NEW Sant Ambroeus at the Regency *Italian*

East 60s | 540 Park Ave. (61st St.) | 212-229-4050
www.santambroeus.com

"Sophisticated" sorts are drawn to these "Milano-in-NY" cafes where "chichi" Italian nibbles are served in a "civilized" milieu; the crowd runs the gamut from "past-due trophy wives" to "first-rate Eurotrash" who don't mind the "snooty" service and "splurge"-worthy tabs.

Sapphire Indian Cuisine *Indian*

21 | 19 | 18 | $41

West 60s | 1845 Broadway (bet. 60th & 61st Sts.) | 212-245-4444 | www.sapphireindian.com

This "quiet" Indian "retreat" off Columbus Circle is touted for its "reliable" kitchen, "courteous" service, "comfortable" quarters and location "convenient to Lincoln Center"; though it's a tad "more expensive" than some, the $17 buffet lunch is a "bargain."

Sarabeth's *American*

20 | 18 | 19 | $38

East 90s | 1295 Madison Ave. (92nd St.) | 212-410-7335 | www.sarabeth.com
Kips Bay | 381 Park Ave. S. (27th St.) | 212-335-0093 | www.sarabeth.com
Midtown | Lord & Taylor | 424 Fifth Ave., 5th fl. (bet. 38th & 39th Sts.) | 212-827-5068 | www.sarabeth.com
Midtown | 40 Central Park S. (6th Ave.) | 212-826-5959 | www.sarabethscps.com
TriBeCa | 339 Greenwich St. (bet. Harrison & Jay Sts.) | 212-966-0421 | www.sarabeth.com

continued

West 80s | 423 Amsterdam Ave. (bet. 80th & 81st Sts.) | 212-496-6280 | www.sarabeth.com

Longtime "favorites" for breakfast and brunch, these "charming" all-day eateries draw devotees with "hearty" American comfort food and baked goods; though the morning's "festive chaos" can be too "bracing" for some, at night a quieter, "grown-up" vibe prevails.

Saraghina *Pizza*
▽ 25 | 23 | 18 | $51

Bedford-Stuyvesant | 435 Halsey St. (Lewis Ave.) | Brooklyn | 718-574-0010 | www.saraghinabrooklyn.com

A Bed-Stuy "hidden treasure", this all-day "favorite" stands out with "excellent" Neapolitan pizzas and other Italian dishes showcasing "top-quality ingredients" plus "the best" cocktails and coffee; the "rustic" interior and "cool backyard" possess "fantastic ambiance", so the only downsides are cash-only and no-reservations policies ("expect waits at peak times").

Saravanaa Bhavan *Indian/Vegetarian*
23 | 9 | 13 | $27

Kips Bay | 81 Lexington Ave. (26th St.) | 212-679-0204
West 70s | 413 Amsterdam Ave. (80th St.) | 212-721-7755
www.saravanabhavan.com

"Packed" at prime times, these links of an international chain sling "absolutely delicious" South Indian veggie fare, including "crispy, buttery" dosas that are a "must-try"; "brusque" service and interiors that "need an upgrade" are offset by "interesting flavors" and "value" pricing.

Sardi's *Continental*
19 | 22 | 21 | $58

Midtown | 234 W. 44th St. (bet. 7th & 8th Aves.) | 212-221-8440 | www.sardis.com

Sure, it's mainly a "tourist joint", but this circa-1921 "showbiz institution" is still touted as a Theater District "must-experience" famed for its "caricatures of famous actors on the walls" and its "Broadway stargazing"; if its Continental fare and career waiters seem "passionately outdated", fans insist that's part of the "charm."

Sarge's Deli *Deli/Sandwiches*
23 | 15 | 20 | $25

Murray Hill | 548 Third Ave. (bet. 36th & 37th Sts.) | 212-679-0442 | www.sargesdeli.com

"Back and thriving" after a serious fire, this 24/7 Murray Hill deli remains an "old-school" source for "whopping" pastrami sandwiches and other "quintessential" Jewish "fixes" in renovated but "essentially unchanged" diner digs; "decent prices" and the inevitable "food coma" are part of the "classic" experience.

Sasabune *Japanese*
25 | 11 | 21 | $129

East 70s | 401 E. 73rd St. (1st Ave.) | 212-249-8583 | www.sasabunenyc.com

"Trust the chefs" at Kenji Takahashi's "outstanding" UES Japanese offering "unforgettable", omakase-only meals featuring "delicate", "skillfully prepared" sushi; even though the digs are "cramped" and the service "rushed", devotees happily shell out "bank loan"–worthy sums for such a "high-quality" experience.

	FOOD	DECOR	SERVICE	COST

Sauce *Italian*

▽ 23 | 17 | 20 | $48

Lower East Side | 78 Rivington St. (Allen St.) | 212-420-7700 | www.saucerestaurant.com

"Comfortable, homelike and always crowded", this "booming" LES sibling of Lil' Frankie's and Supper provides "fresh, flavorful" Southern Italian eats in nonna's-meets–funky hangout digs (plus sidewalk seating); "too bad it's cash-only", though the BYO policy helps keep the tab "reasonable."

NEW Saul *American*

23 | 20 | 23 | $80

Prospect Heights | Brooklyn Museum | 200 Eastern Pkwy. (bet. Flatbush & Washington Aves.) | Brooklyn | 718-935-9842 | www.saulrestaurant.com

"Settling into its new home inside the Brooklyn Museum", Saul Bolton's "grown-up" fine-dining destination makes a "fantastic addition" to the borough's "cultural heart", providing "work-of-art" New American cuisine via an "accommodating" staff; if a few find the setup "institutional", to most it's suitably "elegant" – and there's also The Counter for casual lunching and brunching.

Saxon & Parole *American*

24 | 24 | 23 | $63

NoHo | 316 Bowery (Bleecker St.) | 212-254-0350 | www.saxonandparole.com

"Energetic" and "happening", this "stylish" NoHo "scene" from the AvroKO team "oozes cool", drawing deep-pocketed "beautiful people" into its equestrian-themed, "Ralph Lauren"-worthy digs; the "sophisticated" meat-centric American menu is matched with "eye-opening cocktails."

Sazon *Puerto Rican*

23 | 21 | 22 | $50

TriBeCa | 105 Reade St. (bet. B'way & Church St.) | 212-406-1900 | www.sazonnyc.com

"High-class" Puerto Rican fare draws both "down-home and beautiful" types to this "sexy" TriBeCa spot, where the popular pernil is "as good as your abuela's"; "upbeat" music and sangria with the "right amount of flair" ratchet up the "fun", "noisy" vibe.

Scaletta *Italian*

22 | 20 | 23 | $60

West 70s | 50 W. 77th St. (bet. Columbus Ave. & CPW) | 212-769-9191 | www.scalettaristorante.com

Inventive it's not, but this "dependable" UWS "favorite" has been serving "solid", "old-style" Northern Italiana with "simple elegance" for more than a quarter century; the "spacious seating" and "blissful quiet" make conversation here a "pleasure", and "no one pushes you out the door."

Scalinatella *Italian*

24 | 18 | 21 | $102

East 60s | 201 E. 61st St., downstairs (3rd Ave.) | 212-207-8280

"Exceptional" Capri-style dishes draw a moneyed crowd to this "private club"-like UES Italian, situated downstairs in an "intimate" grotto; service is as "impressive" as the "fabulous" food, but if your server steers you toward the specials, brace yourself for "sticker shock."

Scalini Fedeli *Italian*

26 | 24 | 26 | $100

TriBeCa | 165 Duane St. (bet. Hudson & Staple Sts.) | 212-528-0400 | www.scalinifedeli.com

"Well beyond fantastic" rave fans of Michael Cetrulo's TriBeCa "favorite" and its "superlative", "pricey" Italian fare (prix fixe–only options start at $70) that's "rivaled only by the amazing service"; the "old-time glamorous" setting strikes upstarts as "a bit stodgy", but to most it's "top of the line" for "special occasions."

Scalino *Italian*   ▽ 23 | 15 | 21 | $43

NEW Greenpoint | 659 Manhattan Ave. (bet. Nassau & Norman Aves.) | Brooklyn | 718-389-8606
Park Slope | 347 Seventh Ave. (10th St.) | Brooklyn | 718-840-5738
It's "endearing" to be "treated like a regular" at these "small" but "proud" neighborhood Italians in Park Slope and Greenpoint serving "generous" plates of "simple", "earthy" pastas and other staples; "comfortable" and "no-frills", they deliver "value" – and naturally "fill up fast."

Scarlatto *Italian*   21 | 18 | 20 | $48

Midtown | 250 W. 47th St. (bet. B'way & 8th Ave.) | 212-730-4535 | www.scarlattonyc.com
Expect "no gimmicks" at this "pleasant" Italian standby "in the middle of the Theater District", just "tasty" standards delivered by a "prompt" crew; "reasonable"-for-the-neighborhood prices get even more so if you order the "bargain" prix fixe.

Scarpetta *Italian*   25 | 22 | 23 | $86

Chelsea | 355 W. 14th St. (bet. 8th & 9th Aves.) | 212-691-0555 | www.scarpettanyc.com
Fans say it's all about the "rightfully hyped" spaghetti at this "sleek" 14th Street Italian, where the "modern" bill of fare consists of "elegantly simple" dishes; sure, you'll "pay dearly" for the privilege, but "top-notch" service and a "beautiful" setting are compensations; P.S. founding chef Scott Conant is no longer involved.

Schiller's *Eclectic*   17 | 19 | 17 | $38

Lower East Side | 131 Rivington St. (Norfolk St.) | 212-260-4555 | www.schillersny.com
Balthazar's younger, "lower-priced" cousin, this "cool" LES bistro from Keith McNally is an ever-"packed" nexus for "solid" Eclectic fare delivered by a "well-meaning" team; even though the "noisy" room is "a place to be seen, not heard", it remains a perennial Downtown "favorite."

Schnipper's Quality Kitchen *American*   20 | 13 | 16 | $17

NEW East Midtown | 570 Lexington Ave. (51st St.) | 212-826-8100
Flatiron | 23 E. 23rd St. (bet. Madison & Park Ave. S.) | 212-233-1025
Midtown | 620 Eighth Ave. (41st St.) | 212-921-2400
www.schnippers.com
These "upscale fast-food joints" vend "tasty", "fair-priced" American staples – burgers and sandwiches, salads, "thick" shakes – in "cafeteria"-style settings; "place your order at the counter" and staffers deliver it to your table "quick", even when the scene's "hustle-bustle."

NEW Schnitz *Sandwiches*   – | – | – | I

East Village | 177 First Ave. (11th St.) | 646-861-3923 | www.schnitznyc.com
Modern takes on the schnitzel sandwich (e.g. the Mrs. Child, with chicken, greens and celery root rémoulade), a few sides and tap beer and

wine make up the brief menu at this East Villager from the popular Smorgasburg vendor; the basic, counter-service setup includes a few tables.

Scottadito Osteria Toscana *Italian*   22 | 20 | 21 | $34

Park Slope | 788 Union St. (bet. 6th & 7th Aves.) | Brooklyn | 718-636-4800 | www.scottadito.com

Whether for the "lunch deal", an "intimate dinner" or the "best brunch", this Park Sloper "steals hearts" with its "delicious" Northern Italian fare and "Tuscan farmhouse" setting ("sit by the fireplace"); "warm" service and a well-priced wine list complete the picture.

SD26 *Italian*   25 | 24 | 24 | $75

Flatiron | 19 E. 26th St. (bet. 5th & Madison Aves.) | 212-265-5959 | www.sd26ny.com

From "dynamic" father-daughter duo Tony and Marisa May, this "chic" Madison Square Park "destination" rolls out "exceptional" Italian fare in a "glamorous", "soaring" setting; "deep pockets" come in handy here, but further payoffs include "gracious" service and a "killer" wine list (which can also be explored at the "cool" front bar/lounge).

Sea *Thai*   23 | 24 | 20 | $33

Williamsburg | 114 N. Sixth St. (Berry St.) | Brooklyn | 718-384-8850 | www.seathainyc.com

It's all about the "awe-inspiring interior" at this "nightclub"-like Williamsburg Thai resembling a "dreamy temple" complete with a "huge Buddha"; "party" people swaying to the "techno" soundtrack report that the "served-fast" chow is as "delicious" as the "bargain" tab.

Sea Fire Grill *Seafood*   28 | 26 | 27 | $83

East Midtown | 158 E. 48th St. (bet. Lexington & 3rd Aves.) | 212-935-3785 | www.theseafiregrill.com

At this "elite" East Midtown sibling to Benjamin Steak House, "off-the-boat-delicious" seafood is offered alongside "scrumptious" beef (natch) and an "extensive wine list"; it's "not cheap", but factor in "impeccable service" and a "tasteful", "romantic" setting "complete with fireplace" and "gorgeous bar", and fans "love this place" all the same.

Sea Grill *Seafood*   24 | 25 | 24 | $75

Midtown | Rockefeller Ctr. | 19 W. 49th St. (bet. 5th & 6th Aves.) | 212-332-7610 | www.theseagrillnyc.com

With a "prime setting" overlooking the skating rink and holiday Christmas tree, this "iconic" Rock Center seafooder is a "treat" that's "not just for tourists"; sure, the pricing is "special-occasion" level, but the "quality" fare and "exceptional" service are "worth the occasional splurge."

Seäsonal *Austrian*   24 | 19 | 23 | $72

Midtown | 132 W. 58th St. (bet. 6th & 7th Aves.) | 212-957-5550 | www.seasonalnyc.com

"Classic" Austrian cuisine gets "playful", "seasonal" spins at this "refined" Midtowner also appreciated for its "wonderful wines"; some wonder "why it's not more beloved" given its "convenience" to Carnegie Hall and City Center – "expensive" tabs may be a clue (though the prix fixe lunch is an "amazing deal").

	FOOD	DECOR	SERVICE	COST

2nd Ave Deli Deli/Kosher
23 | 13 | 18 | $29

East 70s | 1442 First Ave. (75th St.) | 212-737-1700
Kips Bay | 162 E. 33rd St. (bet. Lexington & 3rd Aves.) | 212-689-9000
www.2ndavedeli.com

Folks with a yen for a "cholesterol blast" indulge in "sky-high" sandwiches and other "comforting" noshes at these "legit" kosher delis; still, the "happy heartburn" "doesn't come cheap", especially given the sometimes "curt" service, "generic" decor and a "claustrophobic" setup in Kips Bay (the UES outpost is "a tad roomier").

Serafina Italian
18 | 16 | 16 | $45

East 60s | 33 E. 61st St. (bet. Madison & Park Aves.) | 212-702-9898
East 70s | 1022 Madison Ave., 2nd fl. (79th St.) | 212-734-2676
Meatpacking District | 7 Ninth Ave. (Little W. 12th St.) | 646-964-4494
Midtown | 38 E. 58th St. (bet. Madison & Park Aves.) | 212-832-8888
Midtown | Dream Hotel | 210 W. 55th St. (bet. B'way & 7th Ave.) | 212-315-1700
Midtown | Time Hotel | 224 W. 49th St. (bet. B'way & 8th Ave.) | 212-247-1000
West 70s | NYLO Hotel | 2178 Broadway (77th St.) | 212-595-0092
www.sarafinarestaurant.com

Everyone from "families" to "fashionistas" turns up at this "easy" Italian mini-chain that's renowned for its "super" thin-crust pizzas, backed up with "satisfying" if "basic" pastas and salads; expect a "hectic" scene and "rushed" service, but also a "good buy for your buck."

Serendipity 3 Dessert
19 | 20 | 16 | $35

East 60s | 225 E. 60th St. (bet. 2nd & 3rd Aves.) | 212-838-3531 | www.serendipity3.com

"Must-try" frozen hot chocolate is the signature (the rest of the "good" American comfort offerings are a mere "prelude") at this "whimsical", circa-1954 East Side sweets 'n' gifts "institution"; despite "high prices", "sassy" service and "crazy crowds", it's a magnet for "tourists" and "grandchildren" alike.

Sette Mezzo Italian
22 | 16 | 19 | $79

East 70s | 969 Lexington Ave. (bet. 70th & 71st Sts.) | 212-472-0400
The "simple" Italian fare is "excellent" but almost beside the point at this UES "cognoscenti" clubhouse, where "upscale" regulars get "house accounts" and "personable" service, but for everyone else it's cash only and "snark, snark, snark"; either way, expect "tight tables" and a "steep" tab.

Seva Indian Cuisine Indian
∇ 25 | 17 | 23 | $22

Astoria | 30-07 34th St. (30th Ave.) | Queens | 718-626-4440 | www.sevaindianrestaurant.com

Not your average curry house, this "small but cozy" Astoria standout spotlights "flavorful" Northern Indian cuisine that can be made "as spicy as you want"; everyone leaves "happily full", and the prix fixes and all-you-can-eat weekend brunch supply amazing "bang for the buck."

evilla Spanish
24 | 16 | 21 | $45

st Village | 62 Charles St. (W. 4th St.) | 212-929-3189 | v.sevillarestaurantandbar.com

know what they're doing" at this 1941-vintage West Village "garlic haven" delivering "fabulous paellas" and other low-cost Spanish classics via "efficient" staffers; maybe the decor's getting "worn", but patrons downing "out-of-this-world sangria" are having too much "fun" to notice.

Sfoglia *Italian*
25 | 19 | 23 | $69

East 90s | 1402 Lexington Ave. (92nd St.) | 212-831-1402 | www.sfogliarestaurant.com

Widely praised for "authentic" Italian cooking, "knowledgeable" servers and "romantic" faux farmhouse digs, this Carnegie Hill standby near the 92nd Street Y is an "oasis of class"; though "pricey", most agree it's "worth the money" – "getting a table" is the real problem.

Shabu-Shabu 70 *Japanese*
∇ 23 | 15 | 21 | $44

East 70s | 314 E. 70th St. (bet. 1st & 2nd Aves.) | 212-861-5635 | www.shabushabu70.com

"Fun" shabu-shabu cooked at the table, plus "very good" sushi, are the draws at this "simple", "casual" UES "neighborhood" Japanese; affordable rates and "congenial" service are two more reasons it's been around for more than three decades.

Shabu-Tatsu *Japanese*
∇ 26 | 19 | 25 | $39

East Village | 216 E. 10th St. (bet. 1st & 2nd Aves.) | 212-477-2972 | www.shabutatsu.com

If "cook-your-own" is what you seek, this "authentic", moderately priced Japanese East Villager lets you simmer "super-tasty" shabu-shabu and sukiyaki in hot pots at your table; service is efficient enough, but diminutive dimensions spell "difficulties in getting a table."

Shake Shack *Burgers*
21 | 12 | 15 | $16

Battery Park City | 215 Murray St. (bet. North End Ave. & West St.) | 646-545-4600

NEW **East Midtown** | Grand Central | 87 E. 42nd St. (bet. Lexington & Vanderbilt Aves.) | 646-517-5804

East 80s | 154 E. 86th St. (bet. Lexington & 3rd Aves.) | 646-237-5035

Flatiron | Madison Square Park | 23rd St. (bet. B'way & Madison Ave.) | 212-889-6600

Midtown | InterContinental Hotel Times Sq. | 691 Eighth Ave. (bet. 43rd & 44th Sts.) | 646-435-0135

West 70s | 366 Columbus Ave. (77th St.) | 646-747-8770

Downtown Brooklyn | Fulton Street Mall | 409 Fulton St. (Adams St.) | Brooklyn | 718-307-7590

NEW **Dumbo** | 1 Old Fulton St. (Water St.) | Brooklyn | 718-307-7590

NEW **Park Slope** | 170 Flatbush Ave. (Pacific St.) | Brooklyn | 347-442-7711

Willets Point | Citi Field | 12301 Roosevelt Ave. (126th St.) | Queens | no phone
www.shakeshack.com

"Prodigiously expanding", Danny Meyer's "elevated-fast-food" chain "may be in every city" soon thanks to its "juicy, flavorful burgers", "thick shakes" and other "fairly priced", "made-to-order" delights; it draws "Disney ride"-worthy lines at some locations, notably the "charming" Madison Square Park original (slated to close soon for renovations).

NEW Shalom Japan *Japanese/Jewish* ▽ 25 | 20 | 23 | $63

Williamsburg | 310 S. Fourth St. (Rodney St.) | Brooklyn | 718-388-4012 |
www.shalomjapannyc.com

If you think Jewish-Japanese food is a "strange concept", the "terrific",
"exciting" "marriage of cuisines" by "newlywed" chefs at this cozy
South Williamsburg standout may "change your mind"; converts advise:
reserve ahead, check out the chalkboard menu and "splurge" a little.

Sheep Station *Australian* ▽ 22 | 18 | 23 | $26

Park Slope | 149 Fourth Ave. (Douglass St.) | Brooklyn | 718-857-4337 |
www.sheepstation.net

Down Under suds and burgers prepared "Southern Hemisphere–style"
fill out the "hearty" Australian menu at this "cheeky" Park Slope "neighborhood" hang; though there's "plenty of space", it gets packed on "big
sports days", especially for "cricket and rugby."

Shi *Asian* ▽ 22 | 24 | 22 | $41

Long Island City | 4720 Center Blvd. (Vernon Blvd.) | Queens |
347-242-2450 | www.shilic.com

"Fantastic views of the NYC skyline" combine with "delicious" Pan-Asian
cuisine, "amazing cocktails" and a "lovely staff" for a winning overall
experience at this "upscale" LIC high-rise dweller; since it's "stronger
than most in the area", insiders advise reserving in advance.

NEW Shinobi Ramen *Japanese/Noodle Shop* – | – | – | I

Bushwick | 53 Morgan Ave. (Grattan St.) | Brooklyn | no phone |
www.shinobinoodle.blogspot.com

Ramen, that of-the-moment specialty, arrives in the neighborhood of
the moment, Bushwick, via this cash-only, BYO nook whose chalkboard
menu lists some half-dozen noodle soups daily, plus Japanese snacks;
the slim space has just one communal table plus a few seats along
the window.

Shorty's *Cheesesteaks* 21 | 12 | 16 | $20

Financial District | 62 Pearl St. (bet. Broad St. & Coenties Slip) |
212-480-3900
Flatiron | 66 Madison Ave. (bet. 27th & 28th Sts.) | 212-725-3900
Midtown | 576 Ninth Ave. (bet. 41st & 42nd Sts.) | 212-967-3055
www.shortysnyc.com

When "homesick for Philly", these "specialty" joints come in handy for
"darn good impersonations of classic cheesesteaks" washed down with
craft suds; just be aware they're "basically bars" that are particularly
"earsplitting" when Eagles games are on the tube.

Shula's Steak House *Steak* 21 | 18 | 21 | $67

Midtown | Westin New York Times Square Hotel | 270 W. 43rd St. (bet.
B'way & 8th Ave.) | 212-201-2776 | www.westinny.com

Not surprisingly, a "football" theme prevails at this Times Square outlet
of gridiron coach Don Shula's steakhouse chain; it scores with "tasty"
beef and "efficient" service, but while its memorabilia may appeal to
"Dolphins fans", for Jets and Giants supporters "nothing's remarkable"
enough to come "running back."

	FOOD	DECOR	SERVICE	COST

Shun Lee Palace *Chinese*   24 | 20 | 22 | $59

East Midtown | 155 E. 55th St. (bet. Lexington & 3rd Aves.) |
212-371-8844 | www.shunleepalace.net
Michael Tong's "venerable" circa-1971 Eastsider remains a "grande
dame" of "fine Chinese dining", delivering "exceptional" dishes via
"outstanding" staffers in "elegant" environs; just bring a "fat wallet" –
it's among the "classiest" of its kind, and priced accordingly.

Shun Lee West *Chinese*   22 | 20 | 21 | $55

West 60s | 43 W. 65th St. (bet. Columbus Ave. & CPW) | 212-769-3888 |
www.shunleewest.com
At Michael Tong's UWS exemplar of "upscale" dining, "fancy" Chinese
food is dispatched by a "top-drawer" team in an "exotic", black-
lacquered space festooned with gilded dragons; sure, it's "high priced"
and a bit "old-fashioned", but there's a reason why it's been a neighborhood "cornerstone" since the '80s.

Siggy's Good Food *Mediterranean*   23 | 17 | 20 | $25

NoHo | 292 Elizabeth St. (bet. Bleecker & Houston Sts.) | 212-226-5775
Brooklyn Heights | 76 Henry St. (bet. Orange & Pineapple Sts.) |
Brooklyn | 718-237-3199
www.siggysgoodfood.com
"They're doing things right" at these "busy" "neighborhood cafes" in
Brooklyn Heights and NoHo serving "delicious" Med-accented fare
featuring "organic" meats and veggies; "courteous" service and "cool
crowd-watching" are pluses, not to mention the sidewalk tables at
the Brooklyn location.

Sik Gaek *Korean*   ▽ 22 | 14 | 18 | $42

Flushing | 161-29 Crocheron Ave. (162nd St.) | Queens | 718-321-7770
Sunnyside (Queens) | 49-11 Roosevelt Ave. (50th St.) | Queens |
718-205-4555
www.sikgaekusa.com
Lovers of "super-fresh" Korean seafood crowd these "high-energy",
low-budget Queens standbys dishing up "authentic" specialties to the
tune of "blaring hip-hop"; though the sight of ocean critters "still wrig-
gling in the pot" can be "off-putting", it's "fun" for "big groups" and high
on "exotic excitement."

NEW The Simone *French*   ▽ 25 | 21 | 25 | $83

East 80s | 151 E. 82nd St. (bet. Lexington & 3rd Aves.) | 212-772-8861
"Expect good things" from this white-tablecloth Upper Eastsider whose
"elegant", "well-executed" French dishes and "excellent" wines come
via a "skillful, charming" staff; fans fret they "won't be able to land
reservations" soon given its already-"stellar" rep and tables that don't
number even a dozen.

Sinigual *Mexican*   21 | 20 | 19 | $45

Murray Hill | 640 Third Ave. (41st St.) | 212-286-0250 |
www.sinigualrestaurants.com
"Delicious" Mexican standards and "potent margaritas" get a "modern
spin" at this "convivial" contender near Grand Central; the "cavernous"
space can get "noisy" (especially after work at the bar), but the "tableside guac" alone justifies the "price of admission."

	FOOD	DECOR	SERVICE	COST

Sip Sak *Turkish*
| | 22 | 16 | 18 | $43 |

East Midtown | 928 Second Ave. (bet. 49th & 50th Sts.) | 212-583-1900 |
www.sip-sak.com
"Fresh, deliciously spiced" Turkish specialties come at "fair" rates at
this U.N.-area "standby"; the "Montparnasse-meets-the-Dardanelles"
decor is considered "just ok", but the food and service shore up an
overall "satisfying" experience.

Sirio *Italian*
| | 22 | 22 | 23 | $92 |

East 60s | Pierre Hotel | 795 Fifth Ave. (61st St.) | 212-940-8195 |
www.siriony.com
Legendary restaurateur Sirio Maccioni (Le Cirque) brings his brand
of old-school sophistication to the UES's Pierre Hotel via this import
from Las Vegas; targeted to mature movers and shakers, it delivers
"expensive", "delicious" Tuscan fare served in "elegant" Adam
Tihany–designed confines.

Sistina *Italian*
| | 23 | 19 | 21 | $86 |

East 80s | 1555 Second Ave. (bet. 80th & 81st Sts.) | 212-861-7660 |
www.sistinany.com
A "mature clientele" favors this "civilized" UES "white-tablecloth" Italian,
where "inspired" cuisine is matched with an "outstanding" wine list;
"impeccable" service and attractive, "old-world" decor make the "mind-
blowing" pricing easier to swallow.

606 R&D *American*
| | 23 | 21 | 22 | $47 |

Prospect Heights | 606 Vanderbilt Ave. (bet. Prospect Pl. & St. Marks
Ave.) | Brooklyn | 718-230-0125 | www.606vanderbiltbklyn.com
A "popular" pick along "Vanderbilt Avenue's growing Restaurant Row",
this "mellow" Prospect Heights spot plies "delectable" American "farm-
to-table" fare within a "bright", narrow space augmented with a roomy
backyard; locals love watching them crank up the resident machine to
make the "amazing donuts" on weekend mornings, and the prix fixe
Sunday supper is a "steal."

67 Burger *Burgers*
| | 22 | 16 | 19 | $18 |

Fort Greene | 67 Lafayette Ave. (bet. Elliott Pl. & Fulton St.) | Brooklyn |
718-797-7150
Park Slope | 234 Flatbush Ave. (bet. Bergen St. & 6th Ave.) | Brooklyn |
718-399-6767
www.67burger.com
"Quick" and "affordable", these "low-key" Brooklynites purvey "fab"
burgers grilled to your specs with an "intriguing" array of toppings; the
over-the-counter setups are "nothing fancy", but they're an "easy" option
"before a Barclays event" or BAM.

NEW Skal *Icelandic*
| | ∇ 22 | 20 | 21 | $54 |

Lower East Side | 37 Canal St. (Ludlow St.) | 212-777-7518 |
www.skalnyc.com
"First-class, always-interesting" Icelandic cuisine is the focus of this
"friendly" "little" Lower Eastsider with an out-of-the-way address and
slightly "pricey" menu; its "light, airy" corner space is open till the wee
hours and features a "cool bar" mixing Nordic-accented cocktails.

S'MAC *American*

23	10	14	$16

East Village | 345 E. 12th St. (bet. 1st & 2nd Aves.) | 212-358-7917
Kips Bay | 157 E. 33rd St. (bet. Lexington & 3rd Aves.) | 212-683-3900
www.smacnyc.com

"Fancy", "delicious" mac 'n' cheese is the specialty of these "affordable" "pleasure palaces" that offer vegan, gluten-free and customized variants in addition to the "ooey-gooey/crusty" classic; given "minimal seating" and kinda "cheesy" decor, many opt for the "take-and-bake" option.

The Smile *Mediterranean*

22	19	17	$28

NoHo | 26 Bond St., downstairs (bet. Bowery & Lafayette St.) | 646-329-5836 | www.thesmilenyc.com

Smile to Go *Mediterranean*

SoHo | 22 Howard St. (bet. Crosby & Lafayette Sts.) | 646-863-3893 | www.smiletogonyc.com

"Hidden beneath a NoHo side street", this "inviting" all-day cafe (with a SoHo take-out adjunct) "caters to the quietly fashionable set" with its "lovely, vegetable-forward" Med dishes, "solid" coffee and "refreshing" drinks; service is "just ok", but the moderate prices leave customers "pleased."

The Smith *American*

19	16	17	$44

East Midtown | 956 Second Ave. (bet. 50th & 51st Sts.) | 212-644-2700
East Village | 55 Third Ave. (bet. 10th & 11th Sts.) | 212-420-9800
West 60s | 1900 Broadway (63rd St.) | 212-496-5700
www.thesmithnyc.com

"Don't expect an intimate conversation" at this "million-decibel" mini-chain that supplies "basic" but "appealing" American grub to "under-35" throngs out to "eat and be merry"; "especially popular for brunch", they're routinely "bustling" thanks to "good value" and "upbeat" vibes.

Smith & Wollensky *Steak*

25	20	22	$80

East Midtown | 797 Third Ave. (49th St.) | 212-753-1530 | www.smithandwollenskynyc.com

"Get your year's quota" of "superior" beef at this "classic" East Midtown steakhouse where "enormous", "juicy" cuts and "powerful" libations arrive in a "boys'-club" setting packed with "chummy" suits "bonding over business"; staffers "straight out of the '50s" run the show, delivering checks best settled by "expense account."

Smoke Joint *BBQ*

23	14	17	$26

Fort Greene | 87 S. Elliott Pl. (bet. Fulton St. & Lafayette Ave.) | Brooklyn | 718-797-1011 | www.thesmokejoint.com

"Get your BBQ fix" at this "funky" Fort Greene standby for "outstanding", "smoky" pit meats and "top-shelf bourbons to match"; maybe it's "rough around the edges", but factor in "budget" prices and most will happily "eat while standing" – "'cuz it's so packed" (especially "pre-BAM and Barclays events").

Smorgasburg *Food Market*

25	17	17	$20

Dumbo | Brooklyn Bridge Park | 30 Water St. (bet. New Dock & Old Fulton Sts.) | Brooklyn | no phone

continued

Williamsburg | East River Waterfront (bet. 6th & 7th Sts.) | Brooklyn |
no phone
www.smorgasburg.com

"Eat yourself silly sampling everything" at these "open-air" "waterfront" markets (Saturdays in Williamsburg, Sundays in Dumbo) whose "passionate vendors" represent the "best of Brooklyn's artisanal food scene"; "insane crowds" and "long lines" are part of the "fun" experience – as are "amazing views of Manhattan."

Smorgas Chef *Scandinavian*   21 | 18 | 20 | $42

Financial District | 53 Stone St. (William St.) | 212-422-3500
Midtown | Scandinavia House | 58 Park Ave. (bet. 37th & 38th Sts.) |
212-847-9745
www.smorgas.com

Fans would return "just for the meatballs", but these "low-key" Scandinavians also offer other "terrific" classics – many based on ingredients from the owners' "own upstate farm" – at prices that won't "break the bank"; the FiDi original is kinda "spare", but the Midtowner "in the middle of Scandinavia House" is downright "elegant."

Snack *Greek*   23 | 16 | 21 | $46

SoHo | 105 Thompson St. (bet. Prince & Spring Sts.) | 212-925-1040 |
www.snacksoho.com

NEW Snack EOS *Greek*
Midtown | 522 Ninth Ave. (39th St.) | 646-964-4964 |
www.snackeos.com

Snack Taverna *Greek*
West Village | 63 Bedford St. (Morton St.) | 212-929-3499 |
www.snacktaverna.com

SoHo's "teeny" longtime "favorite" for "fresh, simple" Greek staples has begot spin-offs that are more of "a step up"; the 12-seat original's ideal for "grabbing lunch" ("eaten in or on the go"), while the all-day West Villager and "delightful" Midtown "find" offer modern, "inventive" takes on Hellenic cuisine with a "farm-to-table" spin.

sNice *Sandwiches/Vegetarian*   ∇ 21 | 16 | 17 | $16

Park Slope | 315 Fifth Ave. (3rd St.) | Brooklyn | 718-788-2121
This "chill" Park Slope sandwich spot proves that vegetarian fare can be both "delicious" and "healthy"; everyone from "moms-to-be" to "laptop" users finds the "diverse" menu and "friendly community spirit" soNice.

Soba Koh *Japanese/Noodle Shop*   ∇ 25 | 20 | 21 | $41

East Village | 309 E. Fifth St. (bet. 1st & 2nd Aves.) | 212-254-2244 |
www.sobakoh-nyc.com

"Refined", "artisanal soba", as well as "interesting specials" and "small dishes", keep business brisk at this "refined" East Village noodle shop run by a "friendly" crew; the "austere" but "genuine" setting includes a "tiny glass room" where the buckwheat noodles are made "by hand" – no wonder it's considered a "cut above" the crowd.

	FOOD	DECOR	SERVICE	COST

Soba Nippon *Japanese/Noodle Shop*   ∇ 22 | 19 | 21 | $47

Midtown | 19 W. 52nd St. (bet. 5th & 6th Aves.) | 212-489-2525 |
www.sobanippon.com

They "grow their own buckwheat" to make the "fresh, tasty" noodles at
this Midtown Japanese soba standout, whose "personal" service and
"calm" atmosphere make it "perfect for stressed-out afternoons"; if the
"simple" decor looks a bit "worn", no one seems to mind much.

Soba Totto *Japanese/Noodle Shop*   24 | 18 | 19 | $48

East Midtown | 211 E. 43rd St. (bet. 2nd & 3rd Aves.) | 212-557-8200 |
www.sobatotto.com

"Stunning" housemade soba and "fresh" yakitori (but no sushi) beckon
Grand Central commuters to this "dimly lit" Midtown Japanese; the
prices may be a bit "expensive" for the genre, but it's a pleasure to "sit at
the bar and watch the charcoal pros work their magic."

Soba-ya *Japanese/Noodle Shop*   22 | 17 | 20 | $33

East Village | 229 E. Ninth St. (bet. 2nd & 3rd Aves.) | 212-533-6966 |
www.sobaya-nyc.com

At this "low-key" East Village Japanese, the "perfectly made" soba
features "refreshing broths" and "delicious noodles"; the no-reservations
policy can cause "weekend waits", but "affordable" price tags and "pleasant" environs more than compensate.

Socarrat Paella Bar *Spanish*   22 | 17 | 20 | $49

Chelsea | 259 W. 19th St. (bet. 7th & 8th Aves.) | 347-491-4236
East Midtown | 953 Second Ave. (bet. 50th & 51st Sts.) | 212-759-0101
NoLita | 284 Mulberry St. (bet. Houston & Prince Sts.) | 212-219-0101
www.socarratnyc.com

These "low-key" Spaniards dish up some of the best paella "this side
of Valencia", along with "hard-to-resist" tapas and "fantastic" sangria
choices; the Chelsea original is on the "cramped" side, but there's more
elbow room at the East Midtown and NoLita spin-offs.

Sofrito *Puerto Rican*   24 | 21 | 22 | $52

East Midtown | 400 E. 57th St. (bet. 1st Ave. & Sutton Pl.) |
212-754-5999 | www.sofritony.com

"To-die-for" mofongo and pernil get washed down with "fruity vacation
drinks" at this "clubby" Sutton Place Puerto Rican, where "loud Latin music" booms and someone's always "celebrating something"; the "enormous" repasts are "surprisingly affordable", but "bring your earplugs."

Soigne *American*   22 | 19 | 22 | $47

Park Slope | 486 Sixth Ave. (12th St.) | Brooklyn | 718-369-4814 |
www.soignebrooklyn.com

A "young, sharp couple" runs this "hidden Park Slope gem" that
shines with "delicious" American fare, a serious wine list and "warm"
service; "pricey-for-the-nabe" tabs have some going only on "special
occasions", but to others it's a "go-to" for brunch, date night or drinks
at the "solid" bar.

Sojourn *American*   25 | 21 | 22 | $53

East 70s | 244 E. 79th St. (bet. 2nd & 3rd Aves.) | 212-537-7745 |
www.sojournrestaurant.com

This "sexy" Upper Eastsider dispenses a "wide range" of "creative"

American small plates and "unusual beers" to an "attractive clientele"; the "dimly lit" setting exudes a "downtown" vibe and the staff is "knowledgeable", but "order carefully" or the bill may be a "shock."

Solera *Spanish* ∇ 23 | 18 | 22 | $60

East Midtown | 216 E. 53rd St. (bet. 2nd & 3rd Aves.) | 212-644-1166 | www.soleryny.com

"Civilized" is the word for this longtime East Midtown Spaniard where "terrific" tapas, "plenty of paella" and Iberian wines are dispensed by a "friendly" crew; prices are on the "high" side, but the payoff is a "comfortable" setting where "it's possible to converse."

NEW Somtum Der *Thai* ∇ 22 | 15 | 18 | $29

East Village | 85 Ave. A (bet. 4th & 6th Sts.) | 212-260-8570 | www.somtumder.com

Presenting "nuanced" Thai flavors – "subtle" to "bold" to "knock-your-socks-off-spicy" – this "terrific" East Village offshoot of a Bangkok eatery specializes in "authentic" dishes from the Isan region; with "reasonable" prices and a "lively", "modern" interior, it's perfect for groups and "sharing lots of plates."

Song *Thai* ∇ 22 | 18 | 17 | $24

Park Slope | 295 Fifth Ave. (bet. 1st & 2nd Sts.) | Brooklyn | 718-965-1108

Park Slopers sing the praises of this "family-friendly" Joya sibling, where the "fantastic" Thai dishes are both "inexpensive" and "generously portioned"; if the high "volume of music and chatter" inside rankles, there's always the "rear garden."

Soto *Japanese* 26 | 19 | 20 | $104

West Village | 357 Sixth Ave. (bet. Washington Pl. & W. 4th St.) | 212-414-3088

Sushiphiles rate the uni and other "exquisite" delicacies the "ultimate" at chef Sotohiro Kosugi's West Village "oasis of Zen"; the decor is "simple", the service "standard" and there's "nothing crazy" when it comes to the à la carte and omakase dinners – just "refined-as-possible" cuts of fish, priced "accordingly."

South Fin Grill *Seafood* ∇ 19 | 22 | 19 | $56

South Beach | 300 Father Capodanno Blvd. (Sand Ln.) | Staten Island | 718-447-7679 | www.southfingrill.com

"Outstanding views of the ocean" from the "spacious", "special occasion"-worthy interior or outside tables "right on South Beach" are the key attraction at this "pricey" SI seafooder; the food and service are rated just "decent", but the "great bar with huge drinks" compensates.

South Gate *American* ∇ 20 | 21 | 20 | $73

Midtown | JW Marriott Essex House | 154 Central Park S. (bet. 6th & 7th Aves.) | 212-484-5120 | www.southgaterestaurantnyc.com

Somewhat "under the radar" despite an "unbeatable" Essex House location, this "quiet CPS find" offers Kerry Heffernan's "delightful" New Americana in "glam" quarters; ok, maybe "you'd expect better service" given the "stiff price", but most just focus on the "view of Central Park."

Sparks Steak House *Steak*

FOOD	DECOR	SERVICE	COST
25	21	23	$93

East Midtown | 210 E. 46th St. (bet. 2nd & 3rd Aves.) | 212-687-4855 |
www.sparkssteakhouse.com

"Carnivores with expense accounts" descend on this circa-1966 East Midtown chophouse for "succulent" steaks and an "endless" wine list proffered by "career waiters" in "clubby" surrounds; maybe the vibe's "anachronistic", but tradition is "what they're selling" here, and regulars think it's "worth every penny."

Speedy Romeo *Italian/Pizza*

	FOOD	DECOR	SERVICE	COST
▽	23	21	20	$36

Clinton Hill | 376 Classon Ave. (Greene Ave.) | Brooklyn | 718-230-0061 |
www.speedyromeo.com

Housed in a former body shop, this "high-quality" Clinton Hill Italian specializes in "top-notch" wood-fired pizzas topped with "housemade mozz" and other "fresh" ingredients, but it also serves grill dishes; the "casual", brick-lined space centered around an open kitchen is done up in old-school Brooklyn style.

Spice *Thai*

FOOD	DECOR	SERVICE	COST
21	15	17	$26

Chelsea | 199 Eighth Ave. (bet. 20th & 21st Sts.) | 212-989-1116
Chelsea | 236 Eighth Ave. (22nd St.) | 212-620-4585
East 70s | 1479 First Ave. (77th St.) | 212-744-6374
East Village | 104 Second Ave. (6th St.) | 212-533-8900
Greenwich Village | 77 E. 10th St. (4th Ave.) | 212-388-9006
Greenwich Village | 39 E. 13th St. (bet. B'way & University Pl.) |
212-982-3758
West 80s | 435 Amsterdam Ave. (81st St.) | 212-362-5861
NEW **Boerum Hill** | 193 Smith St. (Warren St.) | Brooklyn |
718-722-7871
Park Slope | 61 Seventh Ave. (Lincoln Pl.) | Brooklyn | 718-622-6353
Long Island City | 47-45 Vernon Blvd. (48th Ave.) | Queens |
718-392-7888
www.spicethainyc.com

"Generous" helpings of "straightforward" Thai fare offered "cheap" keep this chain "popular" among "college" types and others "on a budget"; "lively" but "noisy" environs and "unenthusiastic" service are part of the package, but there's always "reliable" delivery.

Spice Market *SE Asian*

FOOD	DECOR	SERVICE	COST
24	27	22	$67

Meatpacking District | 403 W. 13th St. (9th Ave.) | 212-675-2322 |
www.spicemarketnewyork.com

"Still going strong" after more than a decade in the Meatpacking District, this "club"-like "favorite" from Jean-Georges Vongerichten "delights the senses" with its "delectable", "gussied-up" Southeast Asian street food, "exotic drinks" and "dreamy" decor; though "noisy" and "not cheap", it's "fun for groups" and private parties downstairs.

Spicy & Tasty *Chinese*

	FOOD	DECOR	SERVICE	COST
▽	24	12	19	$24

Flushing | 39-07 Prince St. (Roosevelt Ave.) | Queens | 718-359-1601 |
www.spicyandtasty.com

The "name says it all" about this cash-only Flushing Chinese where the "hot, hot, hot" Sichuan cooking will "open your sinuses" but won't scorch your wallet; overlook the "nonexistent" decor, no-reservations rule and any "communication problems" with the staff – it's "all about the food" here.

	FOOD	DECOR	SERVICE	COST

Spiga *Italian*
22 | 18 | 21 | $62

West 80s | 200 W. 84th St. (bet. Amsterdam Ave. & B'way) | 212-362-5506 | www.spiganyc.com

Among the "best-kept secrets on the UWS", this "off-the-beaten-path" trattoria is a "tiny sanctuary" of "rich", "refined" Italian cooking; ok, the "romantic" setting skews "tight" and the tabs may be "a little pricey", but "gracious" service helps make up for it.

Spigolo *Italian*
21 | 14 | 20 | $62

East 80s | 1561 Second Ave. (81st St.) | 212-744-1100 | www.spigolonyc.com

Now in "roomier" digs not far from its original UES space, this trattoria remains a favorite for "fantastic" (if "pricey") Italian classics delivered by a "congenial" crew; snagging a reservation can be "tough", but first come, first served outside seating eases the process in summer.

Spina *Italian*
∇ 24 | 17 | 21 | $48

East Village | 175 Ave. B (11th St.) | 212-253-2250 | www.spinarestaurant.com

"Fresh pastas like nonna makes" are the draw at this "cute", midpriced East Village Italian where the noodles are "made right in front of you"; a "relaxing" ambiance and "gracious" service help cement its reputation as an "inviting" neighborhood nexus.

Spotted Pig *European*
24 | 19 | 19 | $54

West Village | 314 W. 11th St. (Greenwich St.) | 212-620-0393 | www.thespottedpig.com

More than a decade on, this West Village gastropub is a "still-hip" "favorite" where April Bloomfield's "terrific" Modern European fare (including a "damn-good burger") draws a "celeb"-studded crowd; the "gritty"-"glam" environs get "crazy-crowded", but at least they finally started taking reservations.

S Prime Steakhouse *Steak*
∇ 23 | 22 | 22 | $72

Astoria | 35-15 36th St. (bet. 35th & 36th Aves.) | Queens | 718-707-0660 | www.sprimenyc.com

"Surprised to see this high-end steakhouse in Astoria", locals praise its "mouthwatering" dry-aged beef and extensive raw-bar offerings expertly served in "modern" digs with an "impressive wine cellar on display"; charging "city prices", it's still somewhat "undiscovered" and on the "quieter" side.

Spring Street Natural *Health Food*
21 | 17 | 19 | $35

SoHo | 62 Spring St. (Lafayette St.) | 212-966-0290 | www.springstreetnatural.com

Spring Natural Kitchen *Health Food*

West 80s | 474 Columbus Ave (83rd St.) | 646-596-7434 | www.springnaturalkitchen.com

"Not just for the granola crowd", this "affordable" SoHo longtimer and its Upper West Side offshoot sling "wholesome" dishes featuring veggies, fish and fowl that suit everyone from "vegans to carnivores"; given the "relaxing" "hippie" ambiance, "you can sit forever and won't be bothered."

More on zagat.com

	FOOD	DECOR	SERVICE	COST

Spunto *Pizza*
▽ 22 | 13 | 18 | $23

West Village | 65 Carmine St. (7th Ave. S.) | 212-242-1200 |
www.spuntothincrust.com
"Gorgeous thin-crust pizzas" crowned with "departure-from-the-usual"
toppings are the calling card of this West Village member of the Gruppo/
Posto/Vezzo family; the "relaxed" digs are small, so many try for the
patio seating – or choose "speedy" delivery.

Sripraphai *Thai*
27 | 14 | 18 | $26

Woodside | 64-13 39th Ave. (bet. 64th & 65th Sts.) | Queens |
718-899-9599 | www.sripraphairestaurant.com
"Trek out on the 7 train" to this Woodside "holy grail of Thai food"
offering an "enormous choice" of "memorable" dishes at varied heat
levels ("make sure you really mean it if you ask for 'very spicy'"); "cash-
only" with "perfunctory" service and decor, it's also "super-cheap" and
"out-of-this-world."

Stamatis *Greek*
24 | 16 | 20 | $39

Astoria | 29-09 23rd Ave. (bet. 29th & 31st Sts.) | Queens |
718-932-8596
"If you can't get to Greece", this "well-established", "family-oriented"
Astoria taverna provides an "authentic" alternative with its "reliable"
Hellenic cooking; maybe the "stark" decor is less transporting, but
"reasonable prices" take the edge off.

Standard Grill *American*
22 | 22 | 20 | $60

Meatpacking District | Standard Hotel | 848 Washington St. (bet. Little
W. 12th & 13th Sts.) | 212-645-4100 | www.thestandardgrill.com
A "happening" crowd collects at this "festive" scene in the Meatpacking's
Standard Hotel, drawn by its "reliably good" American bites, "fun people-
watching" and front cafe "pickup scene"; still, "deafening" decibels and
"shoulder-to-shoulder" crowds lead some to dub it a "place more to be
seen than fed."

St. Anselm *American/Steak*
28 | 20 | 21 | $51

Williamsburg | 355 Metropolitan Ave. (4th St.) | Brooklyn |
718-384-5054
At this "cool" but "not pretentious" Williamsburg steakhouse, you can
"watch the chefs at the flaming grill" as they "wrestle with giant slabs" of
impeccably sourced, "indulgently delicious" meat, matched with "interesting sides and starters"; the barlike digs are tiny, prices "reasonable"
and reservations not taken, so "crazy-long waits" are the norm – but for
some of "the city's best" beef, it's "so worth it" ("have a drink next door
at Spuyten Duyvil" to pass the time).

Stanton Social *Eclectic*
24 | 21 | 20 | $58

Lower East Side | 99 Stanton St. (Ludlow St.) | 212-995-0099 |
www.thestantonsocial.com
"Young" things flock to this "energetic" Lower Eastsider to graze on
"delicious" Eclectic share plates and "yummy" cocktails in a "chic"
duplex setting; given the "extreme decibels" and "ridiculous waits", its
"bachelorette"-heavy crowd calls it "quite the scene", even if cynics yawn
it's "played out."

	FOOD	DECOR	SERVICE	COST

NEW Stella 34 *Italian*
23 | 22 | 21 | $47

Midtown | Macy's | 151 W. 34th St. (bet. B'way & 7th Ave.) |
212-967-9251 | www.stella34.com

"You forget you're in Macy's" while dining at this "stylish" Midtown "respite" from the Patina Group offering "shockingly good" pastas, pizzas and other upscale Italian fare (including "don't-miss" gelato) via a dedicated "express elevator"; "gorgeous" panoramic views of Herald Square "add to the charm."

STK *Steak*
23 | 23 | 20 | $79

Meatpacking District | 26 Little W. 12th St. (bet. 9th Ave. & Washington St.) | 646-624-2444
Midtown | 1114 Sixth Ave. (bet. 42nd & 43rd Sts.) | 646-624-2455
www.stkhouse.com

Rolling a steakhouse and a nightclub into one "trendy" package, these Midtown-Meatpacking "scenes" serve "very good" beef in "glamorous", "thumping", "lounge"-like environs full of "beautiful people"; pricing is "steep", so "bring the black card" and remember "you're paying for the vibe."

Stonehome Wine Bar *American*
∇ 21 | 18 | 21 | $44

Fort Greene | 87 Lafayette Ave. (Portland Ave.) | Brooklyn |
718-624-9443 | www.stonehomewinebar.com

"Unpretentious" but "romantic", this "cozy" Fort Greene wine bar boasts a 200-strong selection of "fairly priced" vintages matched with an "ever-changing" menu of "solid" New American fare; equipped with a "pretty back garden", it's perfectly located "if you're going to BAM."

Stone Park Café *American*
24 | 20 | 23 | $49

Park Slope | 324 Fifth Ave. (3rd St.) | Brooklyn | 718-369-0082 |
www.stoneparkcafe.com

"Inventive" seasonal New American cooking in a "moderately upscale" milieu earns "neighborhood favorite" status for this Park Sloper; a "wonderful" staff, outdoor tables and a "fantastic brunch" are further enticements, so if tabs are "a bit pricey", to most it's worth the "splurge."

Strip House *Steak*
25 | 22 | 23 | $89

Greenwich Village | 13 E. 12th St. (bet. 5th Ave. & University Pl.) |
212-328-0000
Midtown | 15 W. 44th St. (bet. 5th & 6th Aves.) | 212-336-5454
www.striphouse.com

Strip House Next Door *Steak*

Greenwich Village | 11 E. 12th St., downstairs (bet. 5th Ave. & University Pl.) | 212-838-9197 | www.striphousegrill.com

Loyalists "love" the crimson "boudoir decor" to match the "red meat" at these "energetic" chophouses, where "gracious" staffers serve up "magnificent" steaks, "high-quality" sides and "brilliant" cocktails; it's a "special night out" with an accordingly "expensive" price tag.

Stumptown Coffee Roasters *Coffee*
23 | 19 | 18 | $10

Flatiron | Ace Hotel | 18 W. 29th St. (B'way) | 347-414-7805
Greenwich Village | 30 W. Eighth St. (MacDougal St.) | 347-414-7802
www.stumptowncoffee.com

Experience the "best" of "third-wave West Coast coffee" at these

Portland outposts brewing "sublime" java from "meticulously selected", "freshly roasted" beans; there can be "endless crowds" both in the "fabulous" Ace Hotel and the Village, but "talented" "hipster baristas" keep the "line moving fast."

Sugiyama *Japanese* ▽ 27 | 19 | 24 | $105

Midtown | 251 W. 55th St. (bet. B'way & 8th Ave.) | 212-956-0670 | www.sugiyama-nyc.com

"You'd swear you were in Tokyo" at this "serene" Japanese Midtowner where "skillful" chef Nao Sugiyama's "outstanding" kaiseki meals are ferried by "warm", "wonderful" servers; the "unforgettable experience" comes at a "steep" prix fixe–only tab, but the pre-theater deal packs "value."

Sunshine Co. *American* ▽ 22 | 22 | 18 | $31

Prospect Heights | 780 Washington Ave. (Sterling Pl.) | Brooklyn | 347-750-5275 | www.sunshinecobk.com

"Sunny" at weekend brunch and "cozy for dinner" too, this standout from the Milk Bar team is a "wonderful addition" to Prospect Heights; "doing it right" with "delicious", "creative" American cooking, it features a casually "gorgeous" room and a bar mixing expert drinks.

Superfine *Mediterranean* ▽ 19 | 17 | 16 | $38

Dumbo | 126 Front St. (bet. Jay & Pearl Sts.) | Brooklyn | 718-243-9005

Despite its "neighborhood bar" vibe, this "funky" Dumbo hideaway supplies "surprisingly good", locavore-friendly Med fare to soak up the cocktails; an antique pool table within its "high-ceilinged", ex-warehouse space is a "fun" touch, as is the "live bluegrass" at Sunday brunch.

Supper *Italian* ▽ 24 | 17 | 20 | $46

East Village | 156 E. Second St. (bet. Aves. A & B) | 212-477-7600 | www.supperrestaurant.com

This "low-key" East Villager from the Frank crew is a perennial "favorite" thanks to its "wonderful", "simple" Italian fare offered at "low prices"; despite "tight" communal tables, "long waits" and a cash-only policy, the "rustic" digs are "always bustling."

SushiAnn *Japanese* ▽ 23 | 16 | 21 | $78

Midtown | 38 E. 51st St. (bet. Madison & Park Aves.) | 212-755-1780 | www.sushiann.com

"Business-oriented" types converge on this "consistently excellent" Japanese Midtowner for "simple", "high-quality" sushi; the traditionally decorated digs have "no pretensions" and the prices are "steep", but its "CEOs-in-training" crowd doesn't seem to mind.

Sushi Azabu *Japanese* ▽ 25 | 16 | 25 | $129

TriBeCa | 428 Greenwich St. (bet. Laight & Vestry Sts.) | 212-274-0428

Among TriBeCa's "best-kept secrets" is this "intimate" basement sushi "bunker", a "refined" temple of Japanese dining where "serious" chefs craft "buttery" bites from "extremely fresh" fish; such "attention to detail" comes at a "high price" (especially for the "superb omakase") but to most it's worth "shelling out the clams."

	FOOD	DECOR	SERVICE	COST

Sushi Damo *Japanese*   24 | 19 | 20 | $46

Midtown | 330 W. 58th St. (bet. 8th & 9th Aves.) | 212-707-8609 |
www.sushidamo.com

With "quality" sushi, "prompt" service and "median" prices, this "under-
the-radar" Japanese standby near the Time Warner Center "ticks off
all the boxes"; maybe the rather "stark" digs "could use an update", but
ultimately it's "reliable" enough for an "easy" meal.

Sushiden *Japanese*   23 | 18 | 22 | $75

Midtown | 123 W. 49th St. (bet. 6th & 7th Aves.) | 212-398-2800
Midtown | 19 E. 49th St. (bet. 5th & Madison Aves.) | 212-758-2700
www.sushiden.com

"Catering to the Japanese businessman crowd", these "no-frills"
Midtown vets vend "exquisite" sushi and sashimi in "serene" settings;
"attentive" service compensates for the "wallet-capturing" tabs, though
they're decidedly cheaper than "going to Tokyo."

Sushi Dojo *Japanese*   ▽ 24 | 18 | 21 | $85

East Village | 110 First Ave. (bet. 6th & 7th Sts.) | 646-692-9398 |
www.sushidojonyc.com

"Clean and simple with just a subtle twist here and there", the "expertly
prepared" omakase is an "awesome value" at this "sleek" East Villager
from a Morimoto alum; given its "laid-back" vibe, it's "fun" to sit at the
sushi bar and watch the chefs (but be sure to reserve ahead).

NEW Sushi Katsuei *Japanese*   — | — | — | M

Park Slope | 210 Seventh Ave. (3rd St.) | Brooklyn | 718-788-5338 |
www.sushikatsuei.com

Though this Park Slope Japanese offers a standard lineup of appetizers
and sushi, it's the sophisticated omakase (options start at $45) that sets
it apart from the pack; the bright, no-frills interior housing a lengthy sushi
bar and a few tables is augmented with patio seating in summer.

NEW Sushi Nakazawa *Japanese*   27 | 23 | 26 | $196

West Village | 23 Commerce St. (bet. Bedford St. & 7th Ave. S.) |
212-924-2212 | www.sushinakazawa.com

"Maestro" Daisuke Nakazawa, protégé of the renowned Jiro Ono, is
"diligent, humorous" and "proud of each masterpiece" served at this
West Village Japanese "temple" of sushi; whether at the "entertaining"
marble bar or in the back room, it's a "transcendent" experience – but be
ready to "upset your wallet" (the omakase-only options start at $120)
and reserve "at midnight a month ahead, or you'll miss out."

Sushi Seki *Japanese*   25 | 13 | 21 | $84

NEW Chelsea | 208 W. 23rd St. (bet. 7th & 8th Aves.) | 212-255-5988
East 60s | 1143 First Ave. (bet. 62nd & 63rd Sts.) | 212-371-0238 |
www.sushisekinyc.com

"The freshness of the fish shines through" in the "artful" omakase preparations by chef Seki at this "wow" Japanese Eastsider and its Chelsea
offshoot; though they're "pricey" with "not the best decor", "careful"
service and "innovative" output keep the crowd "happy."

	FOOD	DECOR	SERVICE	COST

Sushi Sen-nin *Japanese* ▽ 26 | 18 | 21 | $60

Midtown | 30 E. 33rd St. (bet. Madison & Park Aves.) | 212-889-2208 | www.sushisennin.com

Though it's a "neighborhood favorite", this Midtown Japanese remains an "under-the-radar" source for "some of the freshest sushi" around at prices "accessible" enough for "semi-regular" dining; "friendly" service is another plus, so never mind if the atmosphere is "less than impressive."

Sushi Yasuda *Japanese* 28 | 23 | 25 | $102

East Midtown | 204 E. 43rd St. (bet. 2nd & 3rd Aves.) | 212-972-1001 | www.sushiyasuda.com

Though "Mr. Yasuda has left the building", his "legacy lives on" at this East Midtown destination for "sublime" sushi crafted by "chefs who've devoted their lives to the art"; the space is "light and crisp", the service "unparalleled" (there's no tipping) and, despite the "hit to your wallet", ordering omakase at the bar delivers the "full experience."

Sushi Zen *Japanese* 25 | 21 | 23 | $73

Midtown | 108 W. 44th St. (bet. B'way & 6th Ave.) | 212-302-0707 | www.sushizen-ny.com

It's "less touted" than some, but supporters say this Japanese "island of calm" is "one of the Theater District's best" given its "pristine", "beautifully presented" sushi; "excellent" service and "small" but "Zen"-like digs help justify the "expensive" tabs.

Sweet Chick *Southern* ▽ 21 | 17 | 20 | $31

NEW **Lower East Side** | 178 Ludlow St. (Houston St.) | 646-657-0233
Williamsburg | 164 Bedford Ave. (N. 8th St.) | Brooklyn | 347-725-4793
www.sweetchicknyc.com

"Refined", "quirky", "delectable" takes on Southern staples – think "creative chicken 'n' waffle combos" – and "seasonal" cocktails make this "informal" Williamsburg eatery (with a new LES spin-off) an "excellent place to indulge"; it gets "jam-packed" at prime times, but "friendly" staffers help keep the feel "fun."

Sweetleaf *Coffee* ▽ 22 | 19 | 21 | $8

Williamsburg | 135 Kent Ave. (5th St.) | Brooklyn | 347-725-4862
Long Island City | 10-93 Jackson Ave. (11th St.) | Queens | 917-832-6726
www.sweetleaflic.com

A "mecca" for "local" javaphiles, this LIC gourmet coffeehouse is touted for its "amazing" premium pours and "friendly", "living room"-like vibe complete with working turntable for customer use; the word on the foosball-equipped Williamsburg spin-off: "just as good as the original."

Sweet Revenge *Dessert* ▽ 22 | 15 | 21 | $16

West Village | 62 Carmine St. (Bedford St.) | 212-242-2240 | www.sweetrevengenyc.com

All "delicious things on the planet unite" at this "cozy" West Village dessert-and-wine bar where "amazing cupcakes" are matched, pairings-style, with "spot-on" beers and wines; it's "perfect" for a date or "chilling with friends", with a few savory items on offer for non-sweet tooths.

	FOOD	DECOR	SERVICE	COST

Swifty's *American*
∇ 16 | 17 | 19 | $76

East 70s | 1007 Lexington Ave. (bet. 72nd & 73rd Sts.) | 212-535-6000 |
www.swiftysnyc.com

"If you don't own a house in the Hamptons", you probably "won't feel
at home" at this UES "neighborhood club" where "the elite meet for
meatloaf" and other "flatline" American standards; outsiders are exiled
to the front of the house, but the choicest "social x-ray" people-watching
is in the back room.

Swine *American*
∇ 20 | 18 | 19 | $51

West Village | 531 Hudson St. (bet. Charles & 10th Sts.) |
212-255-7675 | www.swinenyc.com

While the surprisingly "upscale", "limited" menu beckons "pork-lovers",
it may be the "bone marrow–and-brisket burger" that's most "addictive"
at this bi-level West Villager; "friendly" and "loud" with a "pub feel",
it's right for "hanging with your buds" over some beers or even a
"bacon-infused cocktail."

Sylvia's *Soul Food/Southern*
18 | 14 | 19 | $35

Harlem | 328 Lenox Ave. (bet. 126th & 127th Sts.) | 212-996-0660 |
www.sylviasrestaurant.com

A "true icon of Harlem", this circa-1962 soul-food "mainstay" warms
hearts with "generous" helpings of Southern classics and a "fun" Sunday
gospel brunch; old-timers opine it's "not what it used to be" but allow it's
still "worth a visit", as the "tour buses out front" suggest.

Szechuan Gourmet *Chinese*
23 | 12 | 17 | $28

Midtown | 21 W. 39th St. (bet. 5th & 6th Aves.) | 212-921-0233 |
www.szechuan-gourmet.com
Midtown | 242 W. 56th St. (bet. B'way & 8th Ave.) | 212-265-2226 |
www.szechuangourmet56nyc.com
NEW **West 100s** | 239 W. 105th St. (B'way) | 212-865-8808
Flushing | 135-15 37th Ave. (bet. Main & Prince Sts.) | Queens |
718-888-9388 | www.szechuangourmetnyc.com

"If you can take the heat", head for these "real Sichuans" where the
"fiery" cuisine "beats the wontons off" typical Chinese joints; although
the "brusque" service and "dumpy" decor aren't nearly as sizzling, "low
prices" compensate.

NEW Tablao *Spanish*
─ | ─ | ─ | M

TriBeCa | 361 Greenwich St. (bet. Franklin & Harrison Sts.) |
212-334-4043 | www.tablaonyc.com

Live flamenco shows are among the many things to ogle at this lavish
TriBeCa tapas bar helmed by son-and-father team Frank and Francisco
Castro (the latter ex Toledo); rustic brick meets chandeliers and mirrors
within its glitzy digs, where sangria is prepared tableside.

Table d'Hôte *American/French*
23 | 16 | 22 | $55

East 90s | 44 E. 92nd St. (bet. Madison & Park Aves.) | 212-348-8125 |
www.tabledhote.info

If you're "unable to take that trip to Paris", check out this Carnegie Hill
"tradition" (since 1978) plying "delicious" French-American fare in
"neighborly" confines; given the *très* "petite" dimensions, however, you
might consider packing a "shoehorn."

	FOOD	DECOR	SERVICE	COST

Taboon *Mediterranean/Mideastern* | 24 | 20 | 21 | $55 |

Hell's Kitchen | 773 10th Ave. (52nd St.) | 212-713-0271 |
www.taboononline.com

Taboonette *Sandwiches*

Greenwich Village | 30 E. 13th St. (bet. 5th Ave. & University Pl.) |
212-510-7881 | www.taboonette.com

"Different and delightful", this slightly "pricey" Hell's Kitchen "gem"
delivers "knockout" Med–Middle Eastern dishes accompanied by
"amazing" bread and "unique" cocktails in a "charming", "bustling"
room; meanwhile, the "quick" Village outpost vending "excellent pita
sandwiches" is "a real boon to the neighborhood."

Taci's Beyti *Turkish* | 24 | 15 | 20 | $31 |

Sheepshead Bay | 1955 Coney Island Ave (bet. Ave. P & Quentin Rd.) |
Brooklyn | 718-627-5750 | www.tacisbeyti.com

In a refreshingly "hipster-free corner of Brooklyn", this long-standing
BYO Turk is a Sheepshead Bay "favorite" for "huge portions" of
"delicious" classic dishes, including "juicy" kebabs; the staff "couldn't
be nicer", ditto the prices, so never mind if the atmosphere is
"nothing special."

Tacombi at Fonda Nolita *Mexican* | ∇ 25 | 25 | 21 | $26 |

NoLita | 267 Elizabeth St. (bet. Houston & Prince Sts.) | 917-727-0179 |
www.tacombi.com

"It feels like a beach stand" at this "laid-back" NoLita Mexican where
"small", "delicious" tacos are served from a vintage VW van parked in a
"big garage" space; "cool, funky" and easy on the wallet, it's "perfect for
large groups" or even "date" night.

NEW Taco Santo *Mexican* | – | – | – | I |

Park Slope | 669 Union St. (bet. 4th & 5th Aves.) | Brooklyn |
347-227-7777 | www.tacosanto.us

From the Palo Santo folks, this nearby Park Slope Mexican offers a
brief, low-cost menu starring tacos built with housemade tortillas and
premium ingredients like heritage pork and lobster, washed down with
craft beers and cocktails; there are a few tables plus bar seating in its
tiny, rustic interior, but come summer the picnic tables out front are the
place to be.

Taïm *Israeli/Vegetarian* | 25 | 11 | 17 | $15 |

NoLita | 45 Spring St. (Mulberry St.) | 212-219-0600
West Village | 222 Waverly Pl. (bet. 11th & Perry Sts.) | 212-691-1287
www.taimfalafel.com

The "falafel to end all falafel" – plus "fresh, well-seasoned" salads and
sides – is the claim to fame of these "modern" vegetarian Israelis from
chef Einat Admony (Balaboosta); both are hard to beat for a "reasonably
priced" "quick bite", but the West Village original is mostly "grab-and-
go" given its "tiny" size.

Takahachi *Japanese* | 24 | 16 | 21 | $43 |

East Village | 85 Ave. A (bet. 4th & 6th Sts.) | 212-505-6524
TriBeCa | 145 Duane St. (bet. B'way & Church St.) | 212-571-1830
www.takahachi.net

"Creative sushi" and "tasty" Japanese home-cooking basics at a favorable "quality-to-price ratio" earn these TriBeCa–East Village twins "favorite-in-the-'hood" status; a "helpful" staff adds warmth to the "nothing-fancy" setups, which "bustle" at prime times.

Takashi *Japanese*

27 | 20 | 24 | $78

West Village | 456 Hudson St. (bet. Barrow & Morton Sts.) | 212-414-2929 | www.takashinyc.com

"Give your taste buds a thrill" at this West Village "beef-lover's paradise" devoted to yakiniku (DIY Japanese BBQ), from "expensive" "succulent cuts" to more "obscure" parts, e.g. the "must-try testicargot"; "picnic benches" and "swift" service boost the "terrific" mood – and it's worth reserving for the "late-night ramen" too.

Talde *Asian*

25 | 21 | 22 | $49

Park Slope | 369 Seventh Ave. (bet. 30th & 31st Sts.) | Brooklyn | 347-916-0031 | www.taldebrooklyn.com

Chef Dale Talde oversees this "high-energy" Park Slope Pan-Asian where the "creative", pork and seafood–heavy menu is rated a "triumph", likewise the bar's "tasty cocktails" and beers; it takes no reservations and the "tavern"-like digs are usually "jammed" – good thing the staff's so "patient and helpful."

Tamarind *Indian*

26 | 26 | 25 | $69

TriBeCa | 99 Hudson St. (bet. Franklin & Harrison Sts.) | 212-775-9000 | www.tamarind22.com

"On par with the best in London or Mumbai", this TriBeCa Indian is a "revelation" for "sophisticated", "delicately spiced", "brightly flavored" fare; factor in "hospitable" service and "beautiful", "modern" surrounds, and it's "well worth" the "high price tag" – though the $25 lunch prix fixe is a "deal."

Tang Pavilion *Chinese*

23 | 19 | 23 | $41

Midtown | 65 W. 55th St. (bet. 5th & 6th Aves.) | 212-956-6888 | www.tangpavilionnyc.com

"Terrific" traditional Shanghai cooking makes this "sophisticated" Midtown Chinese a "top choice" near City Center and Carnegie Hall; some aesthetes note its once-"classy" decor is "getting a little frayed", but the service remains "polished" as ever, and "reasonable prices" are the crowning touch.

Tanoreen *Mediterranean/Mideastern*

27 | 20 | 24 | $42

Bay Ridge | 7523 Third Ave. (76th St.) | Brooklyn | 718-748-5600 | www.tanoreen.com

"Wake up, Manhattan" – this Bay Ridge standout boasts a "marvelous", "always-changing", "modestly priced" menu of "superb", "aromatic" Med–Middle Eastern fare by chef Rawia Bishara, who "welcomes all her guests in person"; "comfortable" and "unassuming", it's "worth the trip from just about anywhere."

Tanoshi Sushi *Japanese*

26 | 11 | 21 | $74

East 70s | 1372 York Ave. (bet. 73rd & 74th Sts.) | 646-727-9056 | www.tanoshisushinyc.com

continued

Tanoshi Bento *Japanese*

East 70s | 1372 York Ave. (bet. 73rd & 74th Sts.) | 917-265-8254 | www.tanoshibento.com

"Exquisite omakase sushi" for a "comfortable price" (around $50) is the draw at this "small", "cramped" Yorkville Japanese without "any fancy veneer", just "no-nonsense cool" (plus "flavorful" bento boxes and soba next door); it's "hard to get a reservation", but the "value" makes it "worth the hassle."

Tao *Asian*

23 | 27 | 22 | $72

Midtown | 42 E. 58th St. (bet. Madison & Park Aves.) | 212-888-2288 | www.taorestaurant.com

NEW **Tao Downtown** *Asian*

Chelsea | Maritime Hotel | 92 Ninth Ave. (bet. 16th & 17th Sts.) | 212-888-2724 | www.taodowntown.com

It's still "quite a scene" at this "soaring" Midtown Pan-Asian and its newer Chelsea spin-off, where a "giant", "serene Buddha" overlooks the "lush, exotic" confines and all the "action"; "flirty" service, "tasty" food and "creative" drinks complete the "expensive", "party"-friendly package.

Tarallucci e Vino *Italian*

20 | 17 | 18 | $37

East Village | 163 First Ave. (10th St.) | 212-388-1190
Flatiron | 15 E. 18th St. (bet. B'way & 5th Ave.) | 212-228-5400
West 80s | 475 Columbus Ave. (83rd St.) | 212-362-5454
www.tarallucievino.net

When you seek a "drop-in spot for a glass of wine" and a "step-up-from-your-standard-Italian" bite, these "cute", "relaxed" fallbacks are a "safe" bet; "quality" espresso and pastries (the mainstays of the East Village original) make them morning "favorites" as well.

Taro Sushi *Japanese*

▽ 24 | 18 | 20 | $52

Park Slope | 244 Flatbush Ave. (St. Marks Ave.) | Brooklyn | 718-398-5240 | www.tarosushibrooklyn.com

Regulars call this Park Slope "hidden treasure" the "real thing" for sushi with "special fish from Japan" and "seasoned-just-right" rice; "low-key", "moderately priced" and "consistent", it's "very loved" and thus "always packed."

Tartine *French*

22 | 15 | 17 | $35

West Village | 253 W. 11th St. (4th St.) | 212-229-2611 | www.tartinecafenyc.com

At this cash-only West Village bistro, "delectable" French basics and a "could-be-in-Paris" vibe come at an "affordable" price, helped along by the BYO policy; the "tiny" space can be "tight", and "long waits" are a given, so regulars try for one of the sidewalk tables.

Tartinery *French/Sandwiches*

23 | 20 | 19 | $31

NEW **Battery Park City** | Hudson Eats | 200 Vesey St. (West St.) | 212-417-7000
Midtown | Plaza Food Hall | 1 W. 59th St. (5th Ave.) | 646-755-3231

continued

NoLita | 209 Mulberry St. (bet. Kenmare & Spring Sts.) | 212-300-5838 |
www.tartinery.com
The namesake open-faced French sandwiches are "amazing" and the
look "modern" at this NoLita cafe (with Plaza Food Hall and Hudson Eats
offshoots), where "cool Parisian meets cool NYC"; factor in "friendly"
service, and it even works as a casual "date place."

Tasty Hand-Pulled Noodles *Noodle Shop*   ▽ 22 | 4 | 14 | $13
Chinatown | 1 Doyers St. (Bowery) | 212-791-1817 |
www.tastyhandpullednoodlesnyc.com
Soups brimming with "springy, chewy" noodles and "excellent" dumplings are the stars at this tiny Chinatown "hole-in-the-wall"; "quick"
service and "cheap" tabs – plus a view of the chefs at work "slamming
and pulling" dough – help distract from the seriously "sketchy" decor.

Tatiana *Russian*   ▽ 18 | 18 | 15 | $52
Brighton Beach | 3152 Brighton Sixth St. (Brightwater Ct.) | Brooklyn |
718-891-5151 | www.tatianarestaurant.com
The "vodka flows like the Volga" at this 20-plus-year-old Brighton Beach
nightclub offering "surprisingly good" Russian grub that takes a backseat
to the "over-the-top" "Vegas-style" floor show; alfresco fans prefer the
"beautiful" Atlantic Ocean scenery from a boardwalk table.

Taverna Kyclades *Greek/Seafood*   26 | 13 | 19 | $38
East Village | 228 First Ave. (bet. 13th & 14th Sts.) | 212-432-0010
Astoria | 33-07 Ditmars Blvd. (33rd St.) | Queens | 718-545-8666 |
www.tavernakyclades.com
"Super-fresh" seafood worthy of the "Greek gods" draws droves to this
Astoria Hellenic (with a new East Village offshoot), where "can't-go-
wrong" prices offset the "tight, noisy" setting; the real rub is the no-
reservations policy and attendant "horrendous lines" – be sure to
"get there early."

NEW Tavern on the Green *American*   – | – | – | M
Central Park | Central Park W. (bet. 66th & 67th Sts.) | 212-877-8684 |
www.tavernonthegreen.com
After a massive renovation, this Central Park icon is finally back in
business, now with a creative, something-for-everyone American menu;
the richly appointed, 700-seat space includes a bar and sprawling courtyard and garden areas, as well as, of course, floor-to-ceiling windows
looking out on the park.

T-Bar Steak & Lounge *Steak*   22 | 20 | 21 | $61
East 70s | 1278 Third Ave. (73rd St.) | 212-772-0404 | www.tbarnyc.com
"Lively" and "welcoming" with "well-prepared" beef at "serious but acceptable prices", this "tony" steakhouse (by Tony Fortuna) is "the place
to go" for a drink or a bite on the UES; just prepare for some "noise" and
a "crazy middle-aged-single crowd" at the bar.

Tea & Sympathy *Teahouse*   21 | 19 | 19 | $30
West Village | 108 Greenwich Ave. (Jane St.) | 212-989-9735 |
www.teaandsympathynewyork.com
"Anglophiles and expat Brits" make a beeline for this "tiny" West Village
teahouse where English comfort food arrives on "charmingly varied

china"; "helpful"-but-"cheeky" service is a "hallmark", ditto the "long wait", but satisfied sippers say it's the "perfect place for afternoon tea."

Telepan *American* | 26 | 22 | 25 | $76

West 60s | 72 W. 69th St. (Columbus Ave.) | 212-580-4300 | www.telepan-ny.com

"A class act", Bill Telepan's UWS "destination" was "early to the farm-to-table party" and continues to offer "outstanding", "beautifully presented" New American fare in a "civilized" setting near Lincoln Center; such "excellence without the pretense" still comes with a "high" price tag – though the $28 lunch prix fixe is a "bargain."

NEW Telepan Local *American* | 23 | 20 | 22 | $60

TriBeCa | 329 Greenwich St. (bet. Duane & Jay Sts.) | 212-966-9255 | www.telepanlocal.com

This TriBeCa sequel to Telepan is "much cooler in clientele and price", offering "sassy" American small plates and mains that make "wildly creative use" of "high-quality" local ingredients; the "energetic", wood-paneled space "with an Aspen vibe" is on the "small" side, but "lovely" service adds warmth.

Telly's Taverna *Greek/Seafood* | 22 | 16 | 19 | $40

Astoria | 28-13 23rd Ave. (bet. 28th & 29th Sts.) | Queens | 718-728-9056 | www.tellystaverna.com

"Simple perfection" via the "freshest" grilled fish is yours at this "old-time" Astoria Greek taverna, where the nothing-fancy digs are "large", "relaxing" and overseen by a "friendly, never-rushed" staff; factor in "fair prices", and no wonder it's a local "favorite."

Tenzan *Japanese* | 20 | 15 | 18 | $36

East Midtown | 988 Second Ave. (bet. 52nd & 53rd Sts.) | 212-980-5900 | www.tenzanrestaurants.com
East 80s | 1714 Second Ave. (89th St.) | 212-369-3600 | www.tenzansushi89.com
West 70s | 285 Columbus Ave. (73rd St.) | 212-580-7300 | www.tenzanrestaurants.com
Bensonhurst | 7119 18th Ave. (71st St.) | Brooklyn | 718-621-3238 | www.tenzanrestaurants.com

These "neighborhood staples" turn out "solid sushi" and other "basic but tasty" Japanese fare at a "bang-for-your-buck" price point; since their decor's "nothing to write home about", it's no wonder that they do a brisk "take-out and delivery" business.

NEW Terra Tribeca *Italian* | ∇ 21 | 21 | 20 | $41

TriBeCa | 222 W. Broadway (Franklin St.) | 212-625-0900

This "cozy" TriBeCa wine bar run by a husband-and-wife team offers some 25 by-the-glass Italian vintages matched with a "nice variety" of cicchetti (small plates); the "lovely" space features one long center communal table and bottles lining the brick walls.

Terroir *Italian* | 20 | 18 | 21 | $39

East Village | 413 E. 12th St. (bet. Ave. A & 1st Ave.) | 646-602-1300 |
Kips Bay | 439 Third Ave. (bet. 30th & 31st Sts.) | 212-481-1920 |
TriBeCa | 24 Harrison St. (bet. Greenwich & Hudson Sts.) | 212-625-9463

continued

Terroir on the Porch *Italian*

Chelsea | High Line at 15th St. (10th Ave.) | no phone
www.wineisterroir.com

These "unstuffy" enotecas offer "enormous" wine lists and "tasty" Italian small plates via a "well-versed" staff; they're perfect for those who are "into wine, but not into hoity-toity" – though wallet-watchers say those "tasty bites" can "add up"; P.S. the seasonal High Line location boasts "Hudson River views."

Tertulia *Spanish*

24 | 19 | 20 | $60

West Village | 359 Sixth Ave. (Washington Pl.) | 646-559-9909 | www.tertulianyc.com

"Northern Spain" comes to "Nuevo York" via this West Villager from chef Seamus Mullen, dispensing "fabulous" tapas in "rustic", stone-walled digs; it's a "muy caliente" scene with "high prices" and "waits" at prime times, but fans insist it's "worth it."

Tessa *Mediterranean*

– | – | – | M

West 70s | 349 Amsterdam Ave. (bet. 76th & 77th Sts.) | 212-390-1974 | www.tessanyc.com

This Upper West Side arrival puts forth a midpriced menu of modern Mediterranean small plates and grill dishes; exposed brick and steel gate-lined ceilings make for an industrial-cool vibe in its first-floor bar and spacious upstairs dining room.

NEW Texas de Brazil *Brazilian/Steak*

▽ 24 | 23 | 23 | $69

East 60s | 1011 Third Ave. (bet. 60th & 61st Sts.) | 212-537-0060 | www.texasdebrazil.com

"Meat, meat, meat!" is the focus at this UES branch of the national Brazilian churrascaria chain, where the "fun, different experience" features an endless set-price parade of grilled viands carved tableside by gaucho waiters, plus a bountiful salad bar; with a "gorgeous" bi-level space, it's "great for groups."

Thai Market *Thai*

23 | 17 | 19 | $25

West 100s | 960 Amsterdam Ave. (bet. 107th & 108th Sts.) | 212-280-4575 | www.thaimarketny.net

"Authentic" dishes that go way "beyond pad Thai" mean this "no-frills" Upper Westsider "fills up quick" at prime times; the "funky" decor evokes "street carts in Bangkok", as do the "reasonable" prices – no surprise, it's a hit with the "college crowd."

Thalassa *Greek/Seafood*

24 | 24 | 23 | $77

TriBeCa | 179 Franklin St. (bet. Greenwich & Hudson Sts.) | 212-941-7661 | www.thalassanyc.com

"Elegant" Greek seafood is the specialty of this "high-end" TriBeCa "special-occasion" option; of course, such "fine" fish comes at a price ("you help pay its airfare"), but "first-rate" service and an "expansive", "Santorini"-esque setting soften any sticker shock.

	FOOD	DECOR	SERVICE	COST

Thalia *American* — 20 | 20 | 20 | $47

Midtown | 828 Eighth Ave. (50th St.) | 212-399-4444 |
www.restaurantthalia.com

A "pre-show standby", this "reliable" Theater District vet plies "solid",
"well-priced" American fare ferried by "pleasant" staffers who ensure
that you'll "make your show"; its "lively crowd" can kick up some "noise",
but that's all part of the "open, friendly atmosphere."

Third Rail Coffee *Coffee* — ∇ 22 | 8 | 15 | $14

East Village | 159 Second Ave. (10th St.) | 646-580-1240
Greenwich Village | 240 Sullivan St. (3rd St.) | 646-580-1240
www.thirdrailcoffee.com

"They take coffee seriously" at these "high-end" Village java shops that
"pack in the people" with "robust" brews "perfectly prepared" by "well-
trained" baristas who "care deeply about your cup" of joe; they're "tight"
on space but still manage a "relaxing, inviting" vibe.

Thistle Hill Tavern *American* — 21 | 18 | 19 | $41

Park Slope | 441 Seventh Ave (15th St.) | Brooklyn | 347-599-1262 |
www.thistlehillbrooklyn.com

Already a "neighborhood stalwart", this midpriced Park Slope American
rolls out "reliable" gastropub fare in "bustling" corner tavern digs; alright,
it can feel a tad "tight" at prime times, but the "accommodating" staff
and "well-done cocktails" keep things "comfortable."

Tía Pol *Spanish* — 23 | 15 | 20 | $54

Chelsea | 205 10th Ave. (bet. 22nd & 23rd Sts.) | 212-675-8805 |
www.tiapol.com

More than a decade on, this West Chelsea Spaniard is "still amazing"
– and still "perpetually packed" – thanks to "delectable" tapas and "well-
chosen" Iberian wines served in a beyond-"cozy" space; most take the
"cramped" quarters in stride because it stays "crowded for good reason."

Tiella *Italian* — 25 | 16 | 22 | $59

East 60s | 1109 First Ave. (bet. 60th & 61st Sts.) | 212-588-0100 |
www.tiellanyc.com

"Marvelous" little namesake pizzas, "housemade pastas" and other
"delectable" Neapolitan dishes lure Eastsiders to this "informal", pricey
Italian; it's "about the size and shape of a Pullman dining car", but "caring" service makes it feel more "charming" than "crowded."

Tiny's *American* — 21 | 17 | 18 | $45

TriBeCa | 135 W. Broadway (bet. Duane & Thomas Sts.) | 212-374-1135 |
www.tinysnyc.com

This "cool" TriBeCan from nightlife czar Matt Abramcyk is indeed "tiny",
but its "rustic, bohemian" interior tilts more "cute" than "cramped";
its equally compact American menu stars a "to-die-for kale salad",
while upstairs the "energetic, loud, dark bar" dispenses "fun"
cocktails and nibbles.

Tipsy Parson *Southern* — 22 | 21 | 21 | $41

Chelsea | 156 Ninth Ave. (bet. 19th & 20th Sts.) | 212-620-4545 |
www.tipsyparson.com

"Too cute for words", this midpriced Chelsea "standout" near the High
Line dishes up "decadent" Southern standards "with a slightly modern

twist", backed by "delish cocktails"; "easy-with-a-smile" service helps keep the mood "happy."

Toby's Estate Coffee *Coffee*   ▽ 22 | 22 | 19 | $7

NEW **Flatiron** | 160 Fifth Ave. (bet. 20th & 21st Sts.) | 646-559-0161
Williamsburg | 125 N. Sixth St. (bet. Bedford Ave. & Berry St.) | Brooklyn | 347-457-6160
www.tobysestate.com

"Top-notch" single-origin, house-roasted beans make for "excellent" coffee (including the "best flat whites") at these Aussie imports that also vend "fresh pastries" and light savories; the "huge", "lovely" Williamsburg "favorite" is a "happening scene", while the Flatiron outpost is more of a grab-and-go nook.

Toby's Public House *Pizza*   ▽ 24 | 18 | 21 | $30

NoLita | 86 Kenmare St. (Mulberry St.) | 212-274-8629
Greenwood Heights | 686 Sixth Ave. (21st St.) | Brooklyn | 718-788-1186
www.tobyspublichouse.com

"Amazing gourmet brick-oven pizzas" are the stars at these "terrific" "neighborhood joints" in Greenwood Heights and NoLita, where there are also "lots of salads", appetizers and "tasty beers on tap"; they're "often filled to the brim", so "come early or prepare for a wait."

Tocqueville *American/French*   27 | 26 | 27 | $95

Flatiron | 1 E. 15th St. (bet. 5th Ave. & Union Sq.) | 212-647-1515 | www.tocquevillerestaurant.com

A "jewel" of the Flatiron, this "world-class experience" pairs chef Marco Moreira's "remarkable", seasonal French–New American cuisine with "wonderful" wines in "serenely elegant" environs (perfect for "civilized conversation"); the $29 lunch prix fixe is an "incredible value", but the dinner "splurge" is declared "worth every penny and more" – especially given such "stellar service."

Tolani *Eclectic*   ▽ 21 | 20 | 21 | $56

West 70s | 410 Amsterdam Ave. (bet. 79th & 80th Sts.) | 212-873-6252 | www.tolaninyc.com

"Well-prepared" Eclectic bites are served tapas-style along with "diverse" wines at this "charming" UWS "hideaway" that works for a "light snack or full meal"; a "dark, relaxing", "romantic" vibe and "friendly" service help cement its "neighborhood favorite" status.

Toloache *Mexican*   23 | 17 | 20 | $48

East 80s | 166 E. 82nd St. (bet. Lexington & 3rd Aves.) | 212-861-4505
NEW **Greenwich Village** | 205 Thompson St. (bet. Bleecker & W. 3rd Sts.) | 212-420-0600
Midtown | 251 W. 50th St. (bet. B'way & 8th Ave.) | 212-581-1818
Toloache Taqueria *Mexican*
Financial District | 83 Maiden Ln. (bet. Gold & William Sts.) | 212-809-9800
www.toloachenyc.com

It's "worth fighting the crowds" at this mini-chain for "terrifically inventive", "high-class" Mexican fare, including "soft tacos with genius fillings"; "colorful" settings, "creative" margaritas and "deafening dins" are part of the package (except for the FiDi Taqueria, a counter-serve "storefront").

Tommaso *Italian*

23 | 19 | 22 | $51

Bath Beach | 1464 86th St. (bet. Bay 8th St. & 15th Ave.) | Brooklyn | 718-236-9883 | www.tommasoinbrooklyn.com

Although touted for its "old-world" red-sauce favorites the "way you remember them", the real draw at this 40-plus-year-old Italian on the border of Bath Beach and Dyker Heights is the "opera floor show" on certain nights; beyond the "festive" vibe and "loving" service, it also boasts an "amazing" wine cellar.

Tomoe Sushi *Japanese*

25 | 9 | 16 | $51

Greenwich Village | 172 Thompson St. (bet. Bleecker & Houston Sts.) | 212-777-9346 | www.tomoesushi.com

"Go early" or be prepared for "lines out the door" at this "tiny" Village Japanese where the lure is "entertainingly big" slabs of "wonderful" sushi at "value" tabs; "tight" digs, "nonexistent" decor and so-so service are the trade-offs, but no one cares given the "quality-for-the-dollar" ratio.

Tom's *Diner*

17 | 15 | 19 | $19

Prospect Heights | 782 Washington Ave. (Sterling Pl.) | Brooklyn | 718-636-9738 | www.tomsbrooklyn.com

Tom's Coney Island *Diner*

Coney Island | 1229 Boardwalk W. (Stillwell Ave.) | Brooklyn | 718-942-4200

Lines wrap "around the block" on weekend mornings at this circa-1936 Prospect Heights diner beloved as much for its "sweet" service and "old-school vibe" as for its "to-die-for" pancakes and "good prices"; it slings breakfast and lunch only, but the Coney Island spin-off stays open later.

Tony's Di Napoli *Italian*

22 | 17 | 21 | $44

East 60s | 1081 Third Ave. (bet. 63rd & 64th Sts.) | 212-888-6333
Midtown | Casablanca Hotel | 147 W. 43rd St. (bet. 6th & 7th Aves.)
212-221-0100
www.tonysnyc.com

Made for "large groups", these "welcoming" Italians take a page from the "Carmine's" playbook, purveying "heaping" portions" of "reliable" red-sauce standards at "affordable" prices; "tons of people" turn up to kick up a "din" and leave "completely satiated."

Topaz *Thai*

23 | 16 | 20 | $30

Midtown | 127 W. 56th St. (bet. 6th & 7th Aves.) | 212-957-8020

Near Carnegie Hall and City Center, this "simple" Thai slings "flavorful" classics priced way "low" for the zip code; "drab" digs with "no elbow room" and variable service offset the "bargain" tabs, but still it's "always packed."

Torishin *Japanese*

▽ 25 | 19 | 21 | $66

East 60s | 1193 First Ave. (bet. 64th & 65th Sts.) | 212-988-8408 | www.torishinny.com

It's "chicken heaven" at this "super-authentic", "packed" UES yakitori joint whose "top-notch" skewers showcase poultry in its every permutation; "sit at the bar and watch the chefs" for the full experience – it's expensive, but cheaper than the "plane ride" to Tokyo.

	FOOD	DECOR	SERVICE	COST

NEW Toro *Spanish*
25 | 24 | 22 | $73

Chelsea | 85 10th Ave. (bet. 15th & 16th Sts.) | 212-691-2360 |
www.toro-nyc.com

"Come with an adventurous mind and stomach" to this big, "buzzy" West
Chelsea "scene", a Boston import bringing an "ambitious approach to
tapas" and other Spanish dishes; it gets "crazy and loud" at prime times,
with a "pretty crowd to match the elaborate setting" – which includes a
separate speakeasy-style lounge, Backbar.

Torrisi Italian Specialties *Italian*
25 | 18 | 23 | $130

NoLita | 250 Mulberry St. (bet. Prince & Spring Sts.) | 212-965-0955 |
www.torrisinyc.com

"Each time is a new adventure" at this NoLita destination where the
"excellent modern takes" on Italian-American favorites reflect "what's in
season"; it's "tiny" ("feels like you're in someone's home dining room")
and the prix fixe–only price is $100, but "you get what you pay for" – it's
"worth fighting for a reservation."

Tortilleria Nixtamal *Mexican*
▽ 25 | 15 | 20 | $22

Corona | 104-05 47th Ave. (bet. 104th & 108th Sts.) | Queens |
718-699-2434 | www.tortillerianixtamal.com

It's "all about the masa" ground in-house at this Corona Mexican
renowned for the freshest tortillas "this side of the Rio Grande", as
well as "authentic" tacos and "melt-in-your-mouth" tamales; sure,
it's a "hole-in-the-wall", but compensations include "friendly" service
and "Queens prices."

Totonno's Pizzeria Napolitano *Pizza*
26 | 13 | 16 | $21

Coney Island | 1524 Neptune Ave. (bet. 15th & 16th Sts.) | Brooklyn |
718-372-8606

It's "worth the trek to Coney Island" – not to mention the "wait for a
table", cash-only policy and "sass"-tinged service – for this 90-plus-year-
old pizzeria's "fabulous" coal-oven pies; the photo-lined space is strictly
"no-frills", but that's just part of the "experience you won't soon forget."

Totto Ramen *Japanese/Noodle Shop*
25 | 11 | 16 | $21

NEW **Hell's Kitchen** | 464 W. 51st St. (bet. 9th & 10th Aves.) |
646-596-9056

Midtown | 366 W. 52nd St. (bet. 8th & 9th Aves.) | 212-582-0052 |
www.tottoramen.com

"Be prepared for a 'totto' day of waiting" for a seat at these much-
"hyped", "no-frills" West Midtown/Hell's Kitchen ramen shops – you'll
be "rewarded" with "outstanding", "slurpilicious bowls of steaming goodness"; the 52nd Street original has the look and feel of a "subterranean
hallway", while the 51st Street offshoot has a bit more elbow room.

Tournesol *French*
23 | 17 | 21 | $45

Long Island City | 50-12 Vernon Blvd. (bet. 50th & 51st Aves.) | Queens |
718-472-4355 | www.tournesolnyc.com

Just like finding "Paris in Queens", this "convivial" LIC bistro offers
"magnifique" French fare at "easy-on-the-pocketbook" rates; yes, the
"cramped space" means "you really have to like your neighbor", but the
"warm welcome" from a "most pleasant" staff compensates.

	FOOD	DECOR	SERVICE	COST

Tra Di Noi *Italian*

▽ **25** | **15** | **23** | **$43**

Arthur Avenue/Belmont | 622 E. 187th St. (bet. Belmont & Hughes Sts.) | Bronx | 718-295-1784

"Like a meal at grandma's house", this family-run "jewel" off Arthur Avenue might offer "not much decor" but it's warmed by "truly accommodating" service; still, it's the "fresh", "cooked-just-right" Italian classics that make it "worth the trip."

Traif *Eclectic*

26 | **19** | **22** | **$50**

Williamsburg | 229 S. Fourth St. (bet. Havemeyer & Roebling Sts.) | Brooklyn | 347-844-9578 | www.traifny.com

The name alone (which roughly translates as 'non-kosher') is a "surefire way to attract buzz" in the Hasidic Williamsburg vicinity, and this "pork-lover's paradise" delivers an array of "dynamite" Eclectic small plates at a "reasonable" price; "helpful" service and snug quarters with an all-seasons patio round out this "great find."

Trattoria Dell'Arte *Italian*

22 | **20** | **22** | **$61**

Midtown | 900 Seventh Ave. (bet. 56th & 57th Sts.) | 212-245-9800 | www.trattoriadellarte.com

A "perennial favorite" opposite Carnegie Hall, this "bustling" Tuscan is ever a "safe bet" with its "terrific" pizza, "requisite" antipasti bar and "amusing" body-parts decor; it's "convenient" for a work lunch or "pre-theater", but just "bring your appetite – and your credit card."

Trattoria L'incontro *Italian*

26 | **20** | **25** | **$61**

Astoria | 21-76 31st St. (Ditmars Blvd.) | Queens | 718-721-3532 | www.trattorialincontro.com

"It's all about the specials" at this "warm", "classy" Astoria Italian where the "encyclopedic" daily list is "impressively recited by heart" by "extremely attentive" staffers; even if you order off the "huge" menu, you'll still get chef-owner Rocco Sacramone's "incredible cooking", featuring "both traditional and inventive" dishes.

Trattoria Pesce & Pasta *Italian/Seafood*

20 | **15** | **20** | **$41**

East 80s | 1562 Third Ave. (bet. 87th & 88th Sts.) | 212-987-4696
West 90s | 625 Columbus Ave. (bet. 90th & 91st Sts.) | 212-579-7970
West Village | 262 Bleecker St. (Leroy St.) | 212-645-2993
www.trattoriapescepastanyc.com

"Simple, well-done" seafood and pastas at a "fair price" is the "satisfying" formula at these "cozy, old-fashioned" neighborhood Italians; they're "not night-out-on-the-town" picks, but they fill the bill when you "don't want a fuss."

Trattoria Romana *Italian*

24 | **18** | **21** | **$51**

Dongan Hills | 1476 Hylan Blvd. (Benton Ave.) | Staten Island | 718-980-3113

"First-rate", "cooked-to-perfection" Italian cuisine makes this "welcoming" Dongan Hills "mainstay" a "worthwhile" Staten Island destination; "attentive" service, "reasonable" prices and a chef-owner who "treats his guests like family" help explain the "throngs" waiting in line.

	FOOD	DECOR	SERVICE	COST

Trattoria Trecolori *Italian*

21	19	22	$47

Midtown | 254 W. 47th St. (B'way) | 212-997-4540 |
www.trattoriatrecolori.com

The staff "makes everyone feel at home" at this "inviting" Theater District Italian, a "red-sauce" mainstay that earns ovations for its "value" pricing and "lively" atmosphere; it "gets packed" pre- and post-curtain, meaning reservations are "a must."

Tre Dici *Italian*

22	19	22	$54

Flatiron | 128 W. 26th St. (bet. 6th & 7th Aves.) | 212-243-8183

Tre Dici Steak *Steak*

Flatiron | 128 W. 26th St., upstairs (bet. 6th & 7th Aves.) | 212-243-2085
www.tredicinyc.com

"Delicious" Italian fare prepared with "hip flair" is the draw at this "genial" Flatiron standby with a "modern" look; upstairs, a steakhouse with a "mysterious entryway" serves "tasty" beef in "seductive" crimson red digs that look one part "speakeasy", one part "bordello."

Tres Carnes *Tex-Mex*

22	14	18	$16

NEW **East Midtown** | 954 Third Ave. (bet. 57th & 58th Sts.) |
212-989-8737

Financial District | 101 Maiden Ln. (Pearl St.) | 212-989-8737
NEW **Flatiron** | 688 Sixth Ave. (22nd St.) | 212-989-8737
www.trescarnes.com

"Tasty", "smoky" meats star at these Tex-Mex quick stops, but the tacos, burritos and bowls are also available with "a plethora of veggie choices"; counter-serve setups have many saying "best to take out" – either way it'll only run "a few pesos."

Trestle on Tenth *American*

20	16	19	$51

Chelsea | 242 10th Ave. (24th St.) | 212-645-5659 |
www.trestleontenth.com

"Rustic" New American cuisine with Swiss inflections and an "intelligent" wine list appeal to gallery-goers and High Line hoofers alike at this "exposed-brick" Chelsea "oasis"; a "lovely" garden out back and "accommodating" staffers take the edge off of the slightly "pricey" tabs.

Tribeca Grill *American*

22	21	22	$66

TriBeCa | 375 Greenwich St. (Franklin St.) | 212-941-3900 |
www.myriadrestaurantgroup.com

"Still a winner", Drew Nieporent and Robert De Niro's "iconic", 20-plus-year-old TriBeCan maintains its "high standards" with "delicious" New American fare and a "masterfully chosen", 2,000-strong wine list; the "focused" service and "airy", "upbeat" milieu help keep it "popular", while the $25 prix fixe lunch dodges otherwise "pricey tabs."

Triomphe *French*

24	22	24	$74

Midtown | Iroquois Hotel | 49 W. 44th St. (6th Ave.) | 212-453-4233 |
www.triomphe-newyork.com

A "real find" in the Theater District, this all-day French "jewel box" in the Iroquois Hotel turns out "excellent" cuisine in "pleasing-to-the-eye" presentations; its "tiny", "quiet" quarters and "superb service" help take the sting out of "expensive" prices.

	FOOD	DECOR	SERVICE	COST

Tulsi *Indian*
24 | 22 | 23 | $57

East Midtown | 211 E. 46th St. (bet. 2nd & 3rd Aves.) | 212-888-0820 | www.tulsinyc.com

Chef Hemant Mathur's "refined", "exquisite" "contemporary Indian cooking" includes "some unusual" specialties at this "classy" standout near Grand Central; opinions vary on whether it's "pricey" or "reasonable", but most agree on the "excellent" service and "lovely" setting with "quaint netting between tables."

Turkish Cuisine *Turkish*
23 | 17 | 22 | $36

Hell's Kitchen | 631 Ninth Ave. (bet. 44th & 45th Sts.) | 212-397-9650 | www.turkishcuisinenyc.com

"Consistent", "tasty" Turkish fare at "reasonable" rates make this Theater District veteran a "delightful" choice "pre-curtain"; fans focus on the "pleasant" service rather than the "down-to-earth" decor, or head for the back garden.

Turkish Kitchen *Turkish*
23 | 18 | 21 | $42

Kips Bay | 386 Third Ave. (bet. 27th & 28th Sts.) | 212-679-6633 | www.turkishkitchen.com

"As real as it gets", this "tried-and-true" Kips Bay Turk earns "undying loyalty" with "high-quality" traditional eats at "modest" prices; "courteous" staffers oversee the "comfortable" setting, and the "lavish" Sunday brunch "defeats all efforts at self-control."

Tuscany Grill *Italian*
25 | 20 | 22 | $47

Bay Ridge | 8620 Third Ave. (bet. 86th & 87th Sts.) | Brooklyn | 718-921-5633 | www.tuscanygrillbrooklyn.com

Beloved in Bay Ridge for its "excellent" contemporary Tuscan food at midrange prices, this "quiet", "cozy little neighborhood" Italian caters to a "mature, upscale" crowd; valet parking and "welcoming" service are further reasons it's "been around for years."

12th Street Bar & Grill *American*
21 | 19 | 20 | $39

Park Slope | 1123 Eighth Ave. (12th St.) | Brooklyn | 718-965-9526 | www.12thstreetbarandgrill.com

A locals' "go-to", this South Sloper is an "old reliable" for "well-prepared" yet "affordable" New Americana delivered by an "accommodating" crew; the "pretty" main dining room is fit for a casual "date", while the round-the-corner pub offers the same menu with "sports on the telly."

12 Chairs *American/Mideastern*
22 | 17 | 20 | $30

SoHo | 56 MacDougal St. (bet. Houston & Prince Sts.) | 212-254-8640 | www.12chairscafe.com

The kind of "nice cheapie" that "high-rent" SoHo "could use more of", this "chill" cafe dishes up "value"-priced, "lovingly made" American-Mideastern noshes in "cozy, familial" digs (though it does have "more than 12 chairs"); with so many "basic pleasures", most "can't wait to go back."

21 Club *American*
23 | 25 | 25 | $81

Midtown | 21 W. 52nd St. (bet. 5th & 6th Aves.) | 212-582-7200 | www.21club.com

The "legacy lives on" at this 1929-vintage "Midtown institution", a former speakeasy and current "bastion" of "true NY" that "retains its cachet" with "playfully elegant" looks (i.e. the barroom's famed "hanging decorations") and "smooth" staffers delivering "classic" American plates; the experience includes upstairs private rooms, a jackets-required policy and a "big price tag", though the $49 pre-theater prix fixe is a veritable "bargain."

26 Seats *French*   23 | 19 | 21 | $48

East Village | 168 Ave. B (bet. 10th & 11th Sts.) | 212-677-4787 | www.26seatsbistro.com

A "date night" to remember kicks into gear at this "romantic" Alphabet City option, a "cozy" French bistro featuring "delightful" classics, "lovely" service and endearingly "mismatched decor"; yes, it's as "minuscule" as the name implies, but skimpy square footage aside, "great value" abounds.

Two Boots *Pizza*   19 | 10 | 15 | $14

East 80s | 1617 Second Ave. (84th St.) | 212-734-0317
East Village | 42 Ave. A (bet. 3rd & 4th Sts.) | 212-254-1919
Hell's Kitchen | 625 Ninth Ave. (bet. 44th & 45th Sts.) | 212-956-2668
Midtown | Grand Central Station | 89 E. 42nd St., Lower Dining Concourse (Vanderbilt Ave.) | 212-557-7992
NoHo | 74 Bleecker St. (B'way) | 212-777-1033
West 90s | 2547 Broadway (bet. 95th & 96th Sts.) | 212-280-2668
West Village | 201 W. 11th St. (7th Ave. S.) | 212-633-9096
www.twoboots.com

"Nontraditional" is the word for these "Cajun-inspired" pizzerias where a "crunchy" cornmeal crust, "yummy" toppings and "provocative" names add some "N'Awlins" flavor; the settings and service are "casual" and tailor-made "for kids."

NEW 2 Duck Goose *Chinese*   — | — | — | M

Gowanus | 400 Fourth Ave. (6th St.) | Brooklyn | 347-987-4808 | www.2duckgoose.com

Refined, modern takes on Cantonese classics are the specialty of this Hong Kong–inspired arrival to Park Slope, whose compact menu stars a show-stopper whole duck 'feast'; its modest, brick-lined space is along the burgeoning Fourth Avenue strip.

2 West *American*   22 | 21 | 22 | $57

Battery Park City | Ritz-Carlton Battery Park | 2 West St. (Battery Pl.) | 917-790-2525 | www.ritzcarlton.com

This Battery Park New American may be "low-key" for a Ritz-Carlton resident, but business types value its "peaceful" vibe, not to mention its "delicious" food and "excellent" service; a "beautiful" Hudson River panorama is part of the package, as is an "expensive" tab.

Txikito *Spanish*   26 | 19 | 24 | $53

Chelsea | 240 Ninth Ave. (bet. 24th & 25th Sts.) | 212-242-4730 | www.txikitonyc.com

Those "dreaming of San Sebastián" make for this "lively", "casual" Chelsea Spaniard serving a "fascinating", ever-evolving array of "real-deal" Basque tapas via "warm, smart" staffers; with "so many wonderful choices", it "can get expensive in a hurry", but at least the "terrific" wine selection is "moderately priced."

	FOOD	DECOR	SERVICE	COST

Umami Burger *Burgers*

23 15 18 $27

NEW **Battery Park City** | Hudson Eats | 200 Vesey St. (West St.) |
917-728-4400
Greenwich Village | 432 Sixth Ave. (bet. 9th & 10th Sts.) | 212-677-8626
www.umami.com

"Living up to much of the hype", this popular LA-based patty purveyor
brings NYC its "juicy", "upscale" burgers packing "strong", umami-rich
flavors like Parmesan ("dreamy") and truffle ("a must"); the sleek Villager has table service and a full bar – not to mention "waits" at prime
times – while the Hudson Eats branch is just a counter.

Uncle Boons *Thai*

25 18 21 $54

NoLita | / Spring St. (bet. Bowery & Elizabeth St.) | 646-370-6650 |
www.uncleboons.com

A pair of Per Se vets is "making fireworks" at this NoLita standout where
the "inventive" Thai fare "like you've never had" packs "complex flavor
profiles", some "scorchingly" "spicy"; a "relaxed" staff oversees the
"cozy", kitsch-filled setting, which includes a bar mixing "strong drinks."

Uncle Jack's Steakhouse *Steak*

24 22 24 $82

Midtown | 440 Ninth Ave. (bet. 34th & 35th Sts.) | 212-244-0005
Midtown | 44 W. 56th St. (bet. 5th & 6th Aves.) | 212-245-1550
Bayside | 39-40 Bell Blvd. (40th Ave.) | Queens | 718-229-1100
www.unclejacks.com

"Perfectly seasoned and cooked" beef served in "tremendous" portions
is the stock-in-trade of these steakhouses with "pleasing" "old-school"
decor and "high" but "worth-every-penny" prices; best of all may
be the "excellent" staff that treats everyone like "Uncle Jack's favorite
niece or nephew."

Uncle Nick's *Greek*

20 12 17 $37

Chelsea | 382 Eighth Ave. (29th St.) | 212-609-0500
Hell's Kitchen | 747 Ninth Ave. (bet. 50th & 51st Sts.) | 212-245-7992
www.unclenicksgreekrestaurant.com

Fan say there's "no need to venture to Astoria" given the "tasty", "stick-
to-your-ribs" chow and "affordable" tabs at these "casual" Greek tavernas known for their "wonderful flaming cheese" dish; sure, the settings
are on the "shabby" side, but they stay "busy" all the same.

Union Square Cafe *American*

27 23 26 $76

Union Square | 21 E. 16th St. (bet. 5th Ave. & Union Sq.) |
212-243-4020 | www.unionsquarecafe.com

"The appeal never dims" at this Union Square "flagship of the Danny
Meyer empire" that remains "excellent in all areas", from the "incredible"
New American fare to the "elegant but comfortable", "conversation-
friendly" room and "impeccable" service; "getting a reservation is still
hard" – especially since it announced plans to close and relocate in 2015
– so "if you can only get a seat at the bar, go for it."

Upstate *Seafood*

▽ 25 18 23 $44

East Village | 95 First Ave. (bet. 5th & 6th Sts.) | 917-408-3395 |
www.upstatenyc.com

"Superb" oysters and "super" craft beers are among the lures at this
"affordable" East Villager offering "simple, expertly executed seafood

dishes" via a "knowledgeable" crew; just know that no reservations and "small" dimensions make it "tough to get a table."

	FOOD	DECOR	SERVICE	COST

NEW Urbo *Eclectic*
| — | — | — | M |

Midtown | 11 Times Sq. (at 42nd St. & 8th Ave.) | 212-542-8950 | www.urbonyc.com

A fitting arrival to larger-than-life Times Square, this gargantuan, tri-level showpiece from a Russian restaurateur emphasizes local ingredients on its various Eclectic menus; the all-day options range from food carts and a casual cafe to an extravagant, still-in-the-works dining venue, plus there are coffee and cocktail bars.

Ushiwakamaru *Japanese*
| 27 | 18 | 24 | $100 |

Greenwich Village | 136 W. Houston St. (bet. MacDougal & Sullivan Sts.) | 212-228-4181 | www.ushiwakamarunyc.com

For a "super-deluxe", "like-in-Tokyo" experience, sit at the sushi bar at this "small", "traditional" Village Japanese, order the "amazing omakase" and let the "friendly chefs" "do their thing"; it "doesn't come cheap", but to connoisseurs the cost is "reasonable" since with "undeniable quality" it rivals "the most expensive places in town."

Uskudar *Turkish*
| 24 | 14 | 21 | $37 |

East 70s | 1405 Second Ave. (bet. 73rd & 74th Sts.) | 212-988-4046 | www.uskudarnyc.com

Although "narrow" with "just a handful of tables", this "welcoming, well-run" UES "hole-in-the-wall" does a brisk business thanks to its "excellent", "straightforward" Turkish cuisine and "wonderful", "personal" service; "easy-on-the-wallet" prices seal the deal.

Utsav *Indian*
| 22 | 20 | 20 | $43 |

Midtown | 1185 Sixth Ave. (bet. 46th & 47th Aves.) | 212-575-2525 | www.utsavny.com

Although somewhat "difficult to find", this Theater District Indian delivers "above-average" classics in "civilized" modern digs manned by a "gracious" crew; if prices seem a "little high", the daily lunch buffet and $35 pre-theater prix fixe are a relative "bargain."

Uva *Italian*
| 23 | 21 | 20 | $45 |

East 70s | 1486 Second Ave. (bet. 77th & 78th Sts.) | 212-472-4552 | www.uvawinebar.com

"Beautiful food" and "beautiful people" collide at this "bustling", "noisy" UES "date destination" tradiing in "delicious" Italian dishes and "wonderful wines"; an "enchanting" back garden, "decent" prices and "attentive" service secure its standing as a "neighborhood favorite."

Valbella *Italian*
| 24 | 24 | 24 | $91 |

Meatpacking District | 421 W. 13th St. (bet. 9th Ave. & Washington St.) | 212-645-7777 | www.valbellanyc.com
Midtown | 11 E. 53rd St. (bet. 5th & Madison Aves.) | 212-888-8955 | www.valbellamidtown.com

Thanks to "excellent" Italian cuisine, "terrific" wines, "lavish" settings and "solicitous" service, these "classy" destinations draw a "mix of ages" in the mood to "celebrate"; just "bring an appetite" and your "expense account" – and keep their "unbelievable private rooms" in mind for "special occasions."

	FOOD	DECOR	SERVICE	COST

The Vanderbilt *American* | 21 | 21 | 19 | $44 |

Prospect Heights | 570 Vanderbilt Ave. (Bergen St.) | Brooklyn |
718-623-0570 | www.thevanderbiltnyc.com

"Now an old standby" on Prospect Heights' happening Vanderbilt Avenue strip, Saul Bolton's "stylish", midpriced American gastropub trades in "delightful", "strictly in-season" small plates washed down with "delicious cocktails"; locals rate it a "friendly", "no-hassles" experience.

Vanessa's Dumpling House *Chinese* | 19 | 5 | 12 | $11 |

East Village | 220 E. 14th St. (bet. 2nd & 3rd Aves.) | 212-529-1329
Lower East Side | 118 Eldridge St. (bet. Broome & Grand Sts.) |
212-625-8008
Williamsburg | 310 Bedford Ave. (bet. 1st & 2nd Sts.) | Brooklyn |
718-218-8809
www.vanessas.com

Just a few dollars fund a "pig out" at these "always-busy" dumpling dispensers whose "amazing" namesake specialty is fried or steamed "while you wait"; the setups with minimal seating are "utilitarian" and service is "insouciant" at best, but for a "cheap, fast, filling" nosh, you "can't beat" 'em.

Van Leeuwen
Artisan Ice Cream *Coffee/Ice Cream* | 24 | 16 | 18 | $7 |

East Village | 48 E. Seventh St. (2nd Ave.) | 718-715-0758
Boerum Hill | 81 Bergen St. (Smith St.) | Brooklyn | 347-763-2979
Greenpoint | 632 Manhattan Ave. (bet. Nassau & Norman Aves.) |
Brooklyn | 718-701-1630
www.vanleeuwenicecream.com

"Fantastic" small-batch ice cream in "unusual flavors" ("subtle" Earl Grey to "overpowering" ginger) plus "amazing" vegan varieties is the kinda "expensive" specialty of these locavore scoop joints; their small storefronts double as coffee bars, dispensing "stellar" java from Toby's Estate as well as pastries.

Veselka *Ukrainian* | 21 | 12 | 17 | $23 |

East Village | 144 Second Ave. (9th St.) | 212-228-9682 |
www.veselka.com

The "all-encompassing menu" of "hearty", "fair-priced" Ukrainian staples ("handmade pierogi", "terrific borscht") at this 24/7 East Village "institution" draws everyone from "families" to the "post-party crowd"; maybe there's "no decor" to speak of, but it's got "old-time atmosphere" to spare.

Vesta *Italian* | ▽ 25 | 20 | 22 | $39 |

Astoria | 21-02 30th Ave. (21st St.) | Queens | 718-545-5550 |
www.vestavino.com

Among the "besta" in its "residential" corner of Astoria, this local "favorite" serves a "limited menu" of pizzas and other "simple" Italian dishes with a "sustainable", "seasonal" bent at "remarkably fair" prices; the unpretentious digs can be "cramped" at peak hours, but an "engaging" staff keeps things simpatico.

	FOOD	DECOR	SERVICE	COST

Vesuvio *Italian*

22 | 15 | 20 | $32

Bay Ridge | 7305 Third Ave. (bet. 73rd & 74th Sts.) | Brooklyn |
718-745-0222 | www.vesuviobayridge.com

It may "not have the name recognition" of other Brooklyn pizza stalwarts, but this "comfortable" neighborhood Italian in Bay Ridge has been slinging "delicious" pies since 1953, along with an "abundance" of pastas; "friendly" staffers, "fair" tabs and "never a long wait" keep regulars regular.

Vezzo *Pizza*

23 | 16 | 16 | $24

Kips Bay | 178 Lexington Ave. (31st St.) | 212-839-8300 |
www.vezzothincrust.com

"Paper-thin", "crispy"-crusted pies with "toppings to suit any taste" are the specialty of this "busy", "bargain-priced" Kips Bay pizzeria; the digs are "tight" and service can be "slooow", but all's forgiven after a bite of that "outstanding" Shroomtown pie.

Via Brasil *Brazilian/Steak*

▽ 20 | 16 | 18 | $50

Midtown | 34 W. 46th St. (bet. 5th & 6th Aves.) | 212-997-1158 |
www.viabrasilrestaurant.com

A "mainstay" of 46th Street's "Little Brazil" strip, this circa-1978 stalwart turns out "traditional" meat-centric Brazilian fare chased with "strong drinks"; if the "dark" surroundings are on the "charmless" side, "personable" staffers and "reasonable-for-Midtown" tabs compensate.

Via Emilia *Italian*

22 | 16 | 21 | $41

Flatiron | 47 E. 21st St. (bet. B'way & Park Ave. S.) | 212-505-3072 |
www.viaemilianyc.net

Known for its "delectable" Emilia-Romagnan food paired with "excellent wines from the region" (including "the best Lambruscos"), this "friendly" Flatiron Italian is also appreciated for its "reasonable prices"; the "bright" setting may be on the "stark" side, but at least there's "elbow room" between tables.

Via Quadronno *Italian*

21 | 14 | 17 | $40

East 70s | 25 E. 73rd St. (bet. 5th & Madison Aves.) | 212-650-9880
Midtown | GM Bldg. | 767 Fifth Ave. (59th St.) | 212-421-5300
www.viaquadronno.com

"Rub elbows" with "all the chic Euro moms" over panini and espresso at this "seriously clubby" UES rendition of a Milanese bar (with a counter-service spin-off in the GM building); it's "pricey" and the "cozy" digs get "tight", but it's perfect "before shopping or the museums."

ViceVersa *Italian*

23 | 22 | 23 | $58

Midtown | 325 W. 51st St. (bet. 8th & 9th Aves.) | 212-399-9291 |
www.viceversanyc.com

At this "vibrant" Theater District staple, the "top-notch" Italian cooking garners as much praise as the "attentive" staffers who will "get you out in time" for your curtain; factor in a "sleek" interior augmented with a "delightful" back patio, and it's an all-around "pleasant" dining experience.

Victor's Cafe *Cuban*

24 | 22 | 23 | $55

Midtown | 236 W. 52nd St. (bet. B'way & 8th Ave.) | 212-586-7714 |
www.victorscafe.com

Around since 1963, this Theater District Cuban "doesn't rest on its laurels", supplying "solid" food and "fantastic" mojitos in "energetic" environs exuding classic "Havana style – ceiling fans and all"; "old-world" service and live music enhance this "welcome respite", but be prepared for "noise" and "tourists."

The View *American*

17	24	20	$109

Midtown | Marriott Marquis Hotel | 1535 Broadway (bet. 45th & 46th Sts.) | 212-704-8900 | www.theviewny.com

"As the name implies", it's all about the "second-to-none" 360-degree views of Manhattan at this "revolving" Times Square hotel eatery; just "be prepared to spend" to dine on "so-so" American grub with "lots of tourists", though even jaded natives admit it can be a "fun experience."

Villa Berulia *Italian*

25	20	25	$55

Murray Hill | 107 E. 34th St. (bet. Lexington & Park Aves.) | 212-689-1970 | www.villaberulia.com

"Warm hospitality" is the hallmark of this longtime Murray Hill "fallback" that "strives for perfection" with "excellent" Italian fare served by a "top-notch" crew; if the room's a bit "old-fashioned", to "mature" patrons it feels "like coming home."

Villa Mosconi *Italian*

23	17	23	$49

Greenwich Village | 69 MacDougal St. (bet. Bleecker & Houston Sts.) | 212-674-0320 | www.villamosconi.com

Red-sauce fanciers endorse this "old-school" Village Italian "throwback" (since 1976) for its "generous portions" of "smack-your-lips-good" classics delivered by "delightful" staffers; maybe the "old-world" digs could "use updating", but "decent prices" please its "longtime" regulars.

Vincent's *Italian*

21	14	18	$41

Little Italy | 119 Mott St. (Hester St.) | 212-226-8133 | www.02de1be.netsolhost.com

A Little Italy fixture since "before you were born", this 1904-vintage Italian is renowned for its "incredible" hot marinara sauce that "makes the dishes sing"; "quick" service, comfy "old-school" digs and "price-is-right" tabs cement its "standby" status.

Vinegar Hill House *American*

24	21	20	$54

Vinegar Hill | 72 Hudson Ave. (bet. Front & Water Sts.) | Brooklyn | 718-522-1018 | www.vinegarhillhouse.com

"Brooklyn to its core", this "hipster magnet" in "middle-of-nowhere" Vinegar Hill is "worth seeking out" for "incredibly crafted" New American "market cooking" served in "funky", "cozy" digs complete with the "most romantic garden"; the only rubs are "cramped" conditions and "long waits" (reservations are recommended).

Virgil's Real Barbecue *BBQ*

20	15	17	$38

Midtown | 152 W. 44th St. (bet. B'way & 6th Ave.) | 212-921-9494 | www.virgilsbbq.com

"Decent" BBQ turns up in Times Square at this 20-year-old "crowd-pleaser" that rolls out "huge portions" of "greasy" grub in "massive" digs; ok, it's "not Texas" and the setup's "nothing memorable", but you'd never know it from the hordes of "tourists" crowding in.

	FOOD	DECOR	SERVICE	COST

Vitae *American*

▽ 24 | 22 | 22 | $71

Midtown | 4 E. 46th St. (bet. 5th & Madison Aves.) | 212-682-3562 | www.vitaenyc.com

A "beautiful", "modern" bi-level space and "even better" seasonal American cooking have fans calling this upscale Midtowner a Grand Central-area "gem"; a roomy front bar offering lots of by-the-glass wines, a "quieter", "romantic" upstairs with a "view of the scene below" and "personable" service help justify the "expensive" bill.

v{iv} Bar & Restaurant *Thai*

▽ 21 | 22 | 21 | $28

Hell's Kitchen | 717 Ninth Ave. (49th St.) | 212-581-5999 | www.vivnyc.com

Standing out from the Ninth Avenue pack with its "modern", "neon-lit" design and "nightclub atmosphere", this Hell's Kitchen Thai offers "delicious" renditions of the "typical" dishes; "reasonable prices" and a "fun" front bar seal the deal.

V-Note *Vegan*

23 | 19 | 20 | $42

East 70s | 1522 First Ave. (bet. 79th & 80th Sts.) | 212-249-5009 | www.v-notenyc.com

"Who could imagine that vegan food could become addictive?" marvel those "hooked" on this Upper Eastsider's "artfully prepared", "delicious", comfort-oriented dishes; a "refined", often "quiet" setting, "organic wines" and "reasonable prices" complete the "pleasant surprise."

Volare *Italian*

23 | 17 | 23 | $50

Greenwich Village | 147 W. Fourth St. (6th Ave.) | 212-777-2849 | www.volarenyc.com

Step back into "old-school NYC" at this Village Italian that's been plying "solid" "red-sauce" staples since the 1970s; given "reasonable prices" and "warm" staffers who "make you feel at home", no one minds much if the quarters could use "freshening up."

Wa Jeal *Chinese*

24 | 13 | 16 | $34

East 80s | 1588 Second Ave. (bet. 82nd & 83rd Sts.) | 212-396-3339 | www.wajealrestaurant.com

For a "10-alarm fire" of the taste buds, diners turn to this "excellent" UES Chinese praised for "incendiary" but "amazingly nuanced" Sichuan cooking (there are also milder dishes for tender palates); factor in "quick service" and "comfortable prices", and never mind if the decor's not much.

Wallsé *Austrian*

25 | 22 | 24 | $88

West Village | 344 W. 11th St. (Washington St.) | 212-352-2300 | www.kg-ny.com

"Top-notch" Modern Austrian fare keeps "schnitzel fans" coming to Kurt Gutenbrunner's "welcoming" "Vienna-in-NYC" West Villager that's hung with "Julian Schnabel artwork"; "impeccable" service ensures that the "sophisticated" experience measures up to the steep tab.

Walter Foods *American*

▽ 22 | 19 | 20 | $42

Williamsburg | 253 Grand St. (Roebling St.) | Brooklyn | 718-387-8783

continued

Walter's *American*

Fort Greene | 166 DeKalb Ave. (Cumberland St.) | Brooklyn |
718-488-7800
www.walterfoods.com

Embodying Brooklyn's "Socratic ideal of a neighborhood place" are these
"pub-ish" providers of spiffed-up American comfort dishes and "killer"
cocktails in Williamsburg and Fort Greene; "reasonable" prices and
"comfortable" interiors seal the deal – they "care about the details
and it shows."

NEW Wasabi *Japanese*

— | — | — | I

Midtown | 561 Seventh Ave. (bet. 40th & 41st Sts.) | 212-575-1410 |
www.wasabi.us.com

This 3,400-sq.-ft. Times Square link of a London chain offers sushi both
individually wrapped and in mixed sets, plus bento boxes, noodle soups
and more; its bright, mod space has a big seating area plus a counter
running along the windows.

Water Club *American*

22 | 25 | 24 | $76

Kips Bay | East River & 30th St. (enter on 23rd St.) | 212-545-1155 |
www.thewaterclub.com

"Inspiring water views" from a barge docked on the East River lend a
"romantic" aura to this "charming" vet, where a "pro" staff serves "excellent" American fare (including at the "terrific" Sunday brunch); sure, it's
"geared toward tourists" and best enjoyed "when your rich uncle is in
town", but it's hard to top for "special-occasion" dining.

Water's Edge *American/Seafood*

22 | 25 | 23 | $69

Long Island City | East River & 44th Dr. (Vernon Blvd.) | Queens |
718-482-0033 | www.watersedgenyc.com

"Romantic" is the word for this Long Island City "special-occasion" favorite where the "magnificent" Manhattan skyline views induce swoons; the
"well-prepared" American seafood may be "expensive for what you get",
but not when you factor in the "exceptional ambiance."

NEW The Water Table *New England*

— | — | — | E

Kips Bay | India St. Pier (at FDR Dr. & 23rd St.) | 917-499-5727 |
www.thewatertablenyc.com

This dinner boat sailing from Skyport Marina in Kips Bay serves locavore-
oriented New England fare in a $75 three-course prix fixe, plus cocktails
and East Coast beers and wines; the WWII-era vessel, outfitted with
wooden tables and benches, boasts a rollicking, rock 'n' roll vibe.

Watty & Meg *American*

20 | 19 | 20 | $44

Cobble Hill | 248 Court St. (Kane St.) | Brooklyn | 718-643-0007 |
www.wattyandmeg.com

"Flavor abounds" in the "interesting" "market-to-table" New American dishes at this "welcoming" Cobble Hill "neighborhood place"; the
"comfortable", "spacious" interior and "quaint" sidewalk seating are all
"kid-friendly", yet the noise level usually "isn't too bad", meaning "proper
conversation is possible."

	FOOD	DECOR	SERVICE	COST

Waverly Inn *American* | 22 | 22 | 20 | $74

West Village | 16 Bank St. (Waverly Pl.) | 917-828-1154 |
www.waverlynyc.com

Maybe the "celebrity buzz has slowed", but Graydon Carter's "clubby"
West Villager still offers "high-end" spins on American "home-cooking"
favorites in "cozy" confines (complete with Edward Sorel murals); in
winter, regulars say a "cozy booth by the fireplace" is "where it's at."

NEW **The Wayfarer** *American/Seafood* ∇ 18 | 17 | 16 | $61

Midtown | Quin Hotel | 101 W. 57th St. (bet. 6th & 7th Aves.) |
212-691-0030 | www.thewayfarernyc.com

In Midtown's Quin Hotel, this seafood-focused modern American
features curved banquettes and large windows to "watch the activity
outside", plus a bar and upstairs lounge; though the enterprise is
obviously in "rookie season", optimists say it's a "new kid on the
block worth watching."

West Bank Cafe *American* | 19 | 17 | 21 | $46

Hell's Kitchen | 407 W. 42nd St. (bet. 9th & 10th Aves.) | 212-695-6909 |
www.westbankcafe.com

Convenient to 42nd Street's Theater Row, this pre-curtain "standby"
keeps its audience coming back with "satisfying" American chow served
in "congenial" environs; the menu "may not be the most exciting", but
the prices are "fair" and they get you "out on time" for your show.

Westville *American* | 23 | 14 | 18 | $28

Chelsea | 246 W. 18th St. (8th Ave.) | 212-924-2223
East Village | 173 Ave. A (11th St.) | 212-677-2033
Hudson Square | 333 Hudson St. (bet. Charlton & Vandam Sts.) |
212-776-1404
West Village | 210 W. 10th St. (Bleecker St.) | 212-741-7971
www.westvillenyc.com

These "homey" standbys maintain a loyal fan base with "wonderful",
market-oriented American fare that includes many "interesting vegetable
dishes" at "super-value" tabs; overseen by a "courteous" crew, they're
predictably "busy", but the waits are "well worth it."

Wheated *Pizza* ∇ 21 | 18 | 20 | $23

Ditmas Park | 905 Church Ave. (bet. Coney Island Ave. & Stratford Rd.) |
Brooklyn | 347-240-2813 | www.wheatedbrooklyn.com

"Delicious" "artisanal" pizzas – built on sourdough crusts and named for
Brooklyn neighborhoods – are "what set apart" this "welcoming" Ditmas
Park pie place; small and "pleasant" with an "energetic" bar dispensing
"great whiskeys" and cocktails, it's a "nice option for the neighborhood."

Whitehall *British* ∇ 21 | 19 | 19 | $48

West Village | 19 Greenwich Ave. (W. 10th St.) | 212-675-7261 |
www.whitehall-nyc.com

This "cool" West Villager provides a "convivial" backdrop for its "brilliant" brown spirits–and–British eats lineup; diners choose between the
"buzzy", tile-lined front barroom and rear dining room serving a meat-
heavy menu of small plates and mains.

	FOOD	DECOR	SERVICE	COST

NEW **White Street** *American* | – | – | – | E

TriBeCa | 221 W. Broadway (bet. Franklin & White Sts.) | 212-944-8378 |
www.whitestreetnyc.com

Ex–North End Grill chef Floyd Cardoz does upscale New American with a
global spin at this splashy TriBeCa arrival; its high-ceilinged, brick-walled
space has an old-school vibe (leather banquettes, white tablecloths,
chandeliers, Venetian mirrors) and includes a roomy bar/lounge and a
private dining room.

'Wichcraft *Sandwiches* | 19 | 13 | 16 | $16

Chelsea | 601 W. 26th St. (bet. 11th & 12th Aves.) | 212-780-0577
Chelsea | 269 11th Ave. (bet. 27th & 28th Sts.) | 212-780-0577
East Midtown | 245 Park Ave. (47th St.) | 212-780-0577
Flatiron | 11 E. 20th St. (B'way) | 212-780-0577
Greenwich Village | 60 E. Eighth St. (Mercer St.) | 212-780-0577
Midtown | 555 Fifth Ave. (46th St.) | 212-780-0577
Midtown | 11 W. 40th St. (6th Ave.) | 212-780-0577
Midtown | Rockefeller Ctr. | 1 Rockefeller Plaza (bet. 5th & 6th Aves.) |
212-780-0577
TriBeCa | 397 Greenwich St. (Beach St.) | 212-780-0577
West 60s | David Rubenstein Atrium at Lincoln Ctr. | 61 W. 62nd St.
(Columbus Ave.) | 212-780-0577
www.wichcraftnyc.com
Additional locations throughout the NY area

"Original" sandwiches and "on-the-go" snacks made from "quality"
ingredients justify the "premium" price tags at this ever-expanding chain
from *Top Chef*'s Tom Colicchio; "no-frills" setups and "inconsistent"
service don't deter the lunchtime "masses."

Wild *American/Pizza* | – | – | – | M

West Village | 535 Hudson St. (bet. Charles & Perry Sts.) | 212-929-2920
Williamsburg | 340 Bedford Ave. (bet. S. 2nd & 3rd Sts.) | Brooklyn |
347-599-0699
www.eatdrinkwild.com

Farm-to-table is the focus of these green-leaning Americans whose
seasonal, veggie-heavy menus star gluten-free pizzas and regional wines
and beers; they're casual and barn-chic, with sidewalk seating in the
West Village and a glassed-in greenhouse room in Williamsburg.

Wild Ginger *Asian/Vegan* | 22 | 18 | 20 | $28

Cobble Hill | 112 Smith St. (bet. Dean & Pacific Sts.) | Brooklyn |
718-858-3880 | www.wildgingeronline.com
Little Italy | 380 Broome St. (bet. Mott & Mulberry Sts.) | 212-966-1883 |
www.wildgingeronline.com
Williamsburg | 212 Bedford Ave. (bet. 5th & 6th Sts.) | Brooklyn |
718-218-8828 | www.wildgingerny.com

For a "healthy change of pace", find "vegan paradise" at these separately
owned standbys where the "creative", "flavorful" Pan-Asian dishes
feature "mock meat" that "even carnivores can enjoy"; "cheap" prices
complete the "wholesome" picture.

Willow Road *American* | ∇ 22 | 21 | 18 | $57

Chelsea | 85 10th Ave. (15th St.) | 646-484-6566 |
www.willowroadnyc.com

Ideal after "walking the High Line", this 'gastro-bar' facing Chelsea

| | FOOD | DECOR | SERVICE | COST |

Market offers "better-than-expected" New American fare and cocktails in "cool", airy, industrial-chic digs; despite kinda "pricey" tabs, its maintains a "fun" following that kicks up a "crowded and loud" scene at prime times.

NEW Wilma Jean *Southern* — | — | — | M

Carroll Gardens | 345 Smith St. (Carroll St.) | Brooklyn | 718-422-0444
A lower-priced Southerner from the couple behind Carroll Gardens' erstwhile Seersucker, this Smith Street arrival reprises a few favorites from the old place (hello, fried chicken and cheese grits) on its brief, down-home menu; inhabiting the lightly redone original Nightingale 9 digs, it has a casual vibe.

NEW The Winslow *American/British* — | — | — | M

Gramercy Park | 243 E. 14th St. (bet. 2nd & 3rd Aves.) | 212-777-7717 | www.thewinslownyc.com
Plenty of elbow room and a laid-back vibe endear this new Gramercy Park spot to the neighborhood, as do its British-American pub grub and gin-focused cocktails; its wood-paneled room features seating at a marble bar and at large wooden tables tucked in the back.

Wo Hop *Chinese* 21 | 6 | 15 | $20

Chinatown | 17 Mott St. (bet. Mosco & Worth Sts.) | 212-962-8617 | www.wohopnyc.com
"Old-school" is an understatement when it comes to this 1938-vintage Chinatown double-decker known for "tried-and-true" Cantonese cooking at "rock-bottom", cash-only rates; despite "abrupt" service and "dingy" digs decorated with a "zillion photos", "long lines" are the norm – especially "late-night."

Wolfgang's Steakhouse *Steak* 25 | 20 | 22 | $90

East Midtown | 200 E. 54th St. (3rd Ave.) | 212-588-9653
Midtown | NY Times Bldg. | 250 W. 41st St. (bet. 7th & 8th Aves.) | 212-921-3720
Midtown | 4 Park Ave. (33rd St.) | 212-889-3369
TriBeCa | 409 Greenwich St. (bet. Beach & Hubert Sts.) | 212-925-0350
www.wolfgangssteakhouse.net
"Spectacular steak" and "over-the-top sides" reign at this "manly" local meatery chain, each location of which sports a "different feel"; you may have to "not eat for a week to pay off the bill", but then again, you might not need to because the portions are so "huge."

Wollensky's Grill *Steak* 24 | 18 | 21 | $63

East Midtown | 201 E. 49th St. (3rd Ave.) | 212-753-0444 | www.smithandwollenskynyc.com
"Less highfalutin" and somewhat "cheaper" than its next-door big brother, Smith & Wollensky, this "casual" East Midtowner serves "dynamite" steaks and burgers in "high-energy" environs; it's especially beloved for its "late-dining" hours (open nightly till 2 AM).

Wondee Siam *Thai* 21 | 9 | 17 | $26

Hell's Kitchen | 813 Ninth Ave. (bet. 53rd & 54th Sts.) | 917-286-1726
Midtown | 792 Ninth Ave. (bet. 52nd & 53rd Sts.) | 212-459-9057

continued

West 100s | 969 Amsterdam Ave. (bet. 107th & 108th Sts.) | 212-531-1788

"Consistently delicious" Thai fare brings back "memories of Bangkok" at these "hole-in-the-wall" Westsiders; ok, they're "not fancy" and "seating is limited", but service is "fast" and regulars say the "rock-bottom prices" are the key to their enduring "popularity."

NEW Writing Room *American*   22 | 22 | 22 | $59

East 80s | 1703 Second Ave. (bet. 88th & 89th Sts.) | 212-335-0075 | www.thewritingroomnyc.com

"Something wonderful has taken the place of Elaine's" – namely, this Upper Eastsider boasting "friendly" service and "hearty" American "gourmet comfort food"; photos of its predecessor's "famous patrons" line the walls in front, while their literary works enjoy pride of place in the "beautiful, inviting" rear library room.

Wu Liang Ye *Chinese*   25 | 12 | 14 | $37

Midtown | 36 W. 48th St. (bet. 5th & 6th Aves.) | 212-398-2308 | www.wuliangyenyc.com

Just off Rock Center and "one of the best Chinese restaurants north of C-town" is this source for "real-deal", "tingly" Sichuan cooking ("bring tissues to deal with your runny nose"); "bargain prices" outweigh the "glum" digs and "rushed" service.

Xi'an Famous Foods *Chinese/Noodle Shop*   23 | 8 | 14 | $14

Chinatown | 67 Bayard St. (bet. Bowery & Mott St.) | 718-885-7788
East Village | 81 St. Marks Pl. (1st Ave.) | 212-786-2068
Midtown | 24 W. 45th St. (bet. 5th & 6th Aves.) | 212-786-2068
NEW West 100s | 2675 Broadway (bet. 101st & 102nd Sts.) | 212-786-2068
Williamsburg | 86 Beadel St. (bet. Morgan & Vandervoort Aves.) | Brooklyn | 212-786-2068
Flushing | Golden Shopping Mall | 41-28 Main St. (41st Rd.) | Queens | 718-888-7713
www.xianfoods.com

"Freakin' awesome" hand-pulled noodles and "famous" cumin-lamb burgers are menu "standouts" at these "seriously no-frills" purveyors of "spicy" Western Chinese food; seats are "lacking" and service is "pretty much nonexistent", but "low, low prices" keep them "popular."

Xixa *Mexican*   ∇ 25 | 23 | 25 | $60

Williamsburg | 241 S. Fourth St. (Havemeyer St.) | Brooklyn | 718-388-8860 | www.xixany.com

"Much like" its sibling, Traif, this "cool" Williamsburg standout presents a "unique experience" featuring "innovative, tasty" takes on Mexican fare, best sampled via the "mind-blowing", "reasonably priced" tasting menu; equally "inventive" drinks and a snazzy setting are other reasons it's rated a "must."

Yakitori Totto *Japanese*   25 | 14 | 18 | $52

Midtown | 251 W. 55th St. (bet. B'way & 8th Ave.) | 212-245-4555 | www.tottonyc.com

"If it can be put on a skewer, they'll do it" at this "small", "popular" Midtown yakitori den where "heavenly" meats, veggies and "chicken parts you never knew existed" are grilled on sticks; it's a real "excursion to Tokyo" complete with "cramped", "noisy" digs, "long waits" and tabs that can "add up quickly."

Yama *Japanese*

	FOOD	DECOR	SERVICE	COST
	24	14	20	$42

East Midtown | 308 E. 49th St. (bet. 1st & 2nd Aves.) | 212-355-3370
Gramercy Park | 122 E. 17th St. (Irving Pl.) | 212-475-0969 |
www.yamasushinyc.com

"Bigger is better" declare sushiphiles of these East Side Japanese "go-tos" for "monster-size" slabs of the "freshest fish", offered at a "decent price"; the price of popularity: their "drab" setups are generally "crowded" with "long waits" at prime times.

Yefsi Estiatorio *Greek*

	FOOD	DECOR	SERVICE	COST
	23	17	21	$58

East 70s | 1481 York Ave. (bet. 78th & 79th Sts.) | 212-535-0293 |
www.yefsiestiatorio.com

It's "Greek food at its finest" at this "upscale", "real-deal" Yorkville "favorite" where "wonderful" mezes are the focus, and the service is "warm and friendly"; the "rustic", "like-in-Athens" setting "can get noisy", but in summer there's always the "charming garden."

Yerba Buena *Pan-Latin*

	FOOD	DECOR	SERVICE	COST
	22	17	20	$52

East Village | 23 Ave. A (bet. 1st & 2nd Sts.) | 212-529-2919
West Village | 1 Perry St. (Greenwich Ave.) | 212-620-0808
www.ybnyc.com

Chef Julian Medina delivers "delectable", "inventive" Pan-Latin fare matched with "creative drinks" at these "stylish" crosstown siblings manned by a "helpful" crew; just be aware that the space is "tight" and the "noise level rises a few decibels" as the night wears on.

Yuba *Japanese*

	FOOD	DECOR	SERVICE	COST
	∇ 24	15	21	$49

Greenwich Village | 105 E. Ninth St. (bet. 3rd & 4th Aves.) |
212-777-8188 | www.yubarestaurant.com

"Small" and "easily overlooked", this Japanese is worth seeking out when in the Village given its "outstanding", "unusual" sushi and cooked items; though the setting is "nondescript", fans focus on its "warm" vibe and favorable "quality-to-price ratio."

Yuca Bar *Pan-Latin*

	FOOD	DECOR	SERVICE	COST
	21	13	16	$34

East Village | 111 Ave. A (7th St.) | 212-982-9533 |
www.yucabarnyc.com

"Upbeat" and "crowded" with "good-looking" types, this "colorful" East Villager mixes "better-than-average", well-priced Pan-Latin fare with "killer" drinks; it gets "loud" and service can lag, but for "people-watching" by the open doors and windows, it's hard to beat.

Yunnan Kitchen *Chinese*

	FOOD	DECOR	SERVICE	COST
	∇ 23	18	19	$36

Lower East Side | 79 Clinton St. (Rivington St.) | 212-253-2527 |
www.yunnankitchen.com

Offering a "fun take on Modern Chinese" cooking, this Lower Eastsider's market-driven fare focuses on the "powerfully flavored" cuisine of the eponymous province; a "trendy" but "cramped" space and "loud" acoustics come with the territory.

	FOOD	DECOR	SERVICE	COST

Yura on Madison *Sandwiches*

20 | **13** | **13** | **$22**

East 90s | 1292 Madison Ave. (92nd St.) | 212-860-1707 |
www.yuraonmadison.com

A "perfect pre-museum stop", this "pricey" Carnegie Hill cafe vending "consistently delicious" sandwiches, salads and baked goods is also a "hangout" for local "prep school girls" and their "Madison Avenue moms"; it "needs more seating", so many go the "take-out" route.

Zabb Elee *Thai*

22 | **12** | **17** | **$27**

East Village | 75 Second Ave. (bet. 4th & 5th Sts.) | 212-505-9533
Elmhurst | 71-28 Roosevelt Ave. (72nd St.) | Queens | 718-426-7992
www.zabbelee.com

"Complex flavors" – some of them "blistering hot" – distinguish these "affordable" Thais in the East Village and Elmhurst, purveyors of "delicious", "unusual" Northeastern Isan cooking; "friendly" staffers add warmth to the otherwise kinda "sterile" environs.

Zaytoons *Mideastern*

21 | **15** | **19** | **$22**

Carroll Gardens | 283 Smith St. (Sackett St.) | Brooklyn | 718-875-1880
Clinton Hill | 472 Myrtle Ave. (bet. Hall St. & Washington Ave.) | Brooklyn | 718-623-5522
Prospect Heights | 594 Vanderbilt Ave. (St. Marks Ave.) | Brooklyn | 718-230-3200
www.zaytoons.com

For "tasty", "reliable" Middle Eastern fare, stay tooned to these nothing-fancy Brooklyn standbys where "tables are close" but the prices are "terrific"; Carroll Gardens and Clinton Hill are BYO, while Prospect Heights boasts a "pleasant garden."

Ze Café *French/Italian*

20 | **21** | **19** | **$58**

East Midtown | 398 E. 52nd St. (1st Ave.) | 212-758-1944 |
www.zecafe.com

You almost "feel like you're in a flower shop" at this Sutton Place "jewel box" – no surprise given that it's run by Zezé, one of NYC's top florists; the "tasty" French-Italian light bites are perfect for "lunch with the ladies" ("dah-ling!"), so no one seems to mind the "steep" pricing.

Zengo *Pan-Latin*

20 | **21** | **20** | **$56**

Murray Hill | 622 Third Ave. (40th St.) | 212-808-8110 |
www.richardsandoval.com

A "beautiful" tri-level space designed by AvroKO sets the stage for a "special" experience at this Grand Central–area Pan-Latin presenting Richard Sandoval's "imaginative" Asian-accented cuisine; "pricey" tabs and "tiny portions" can vex, but "welcoming" service and a "cool" downstairs tequila lounge tip the balance.

Zenkichi *Japanese*

27 | **27** | **26** | **$68**

Williamsburg | 77 N. Sixth St. (Wythe Ave.) | Brooklyn | 718-388-8985 |
www.zenkichi.com

With "dark warrens" and booths "separated by privacy screens", the "intimate" atmosphere is a key appeal of this "hidden, unique" Williamsburg Japanese izakaya that's "perfect for romantic dates"; however, the "expensive", small plates–centric fare is just as "exquisite", and it's delivered by "pro" staffers who are always just a button-push away.

	FOOD	DECOR	SERVICE	COST

Zen Palate *Asian/Vegetarian* | 20 | 14 | 17 | $29 |

Hell's Kitchen | 663 Ninth Ave. (46th St.) | 212-582-1669
Murray Hill | 516 Third Ave. (34th St.) | 212-685-6888
www.zenpalate.com

It's "amazing what they do with tofu" at these Asian-influenced vegetarian standbys featuring a variety of "fake-meat" dishes that "even a carnivore can love"; foes pronounce them "stereotypical", but at least the "fair pricing" outweighs the "harried" service and "dingy" decor.

Zero Otto Nove *Italian/Pizza* | 23 | 20 | 22 | $45 |

Flatiron | 15 W. 21st St. (bet. 5th & 6th Aves.) | 212-242-0899
Arthur Avenue/Belmont | 2357 Arthur Ave. (186th St.) | Bronx |
718-220-1027
www.roberto089.com

"Fabulous pizzas and pastas" top the list of "hearty" Southern Italian speciaties at these "reliable" "favorites"; the Arthur Avenue original (done up like an "old-fashioned" courtyard) doesn't take reservations, so "be prepared to wait" – or check out the "large" Flatiron offshoot.

Zibetto Espresso Bar *Coffee*   ▽ | 24 | 16 | 22 | $13 |

Midtown | 1385 Sixth Ave. (56th St.) | 646-707-0505 |
www.zibettoespresso.com

It "feels like Italy" at this "simple", "standing-only" sliver of a Midtown espresso bar, where nattily attired baristas pull "delizioso" shots behind a marble counter; its prime location makes it a good choice for caffeinating "before heading to MoMA."

Zio Ristorante *Italian*   ▽ | 22 | 22 | 21 | $54 |

Flatiron | 17 W. 19th St. (bet. 5th & 6th Aves.) | 212-352-1700 |
www.zio-nyc.com

A "spacious" former-dance-club space is the backdrop for "delicious", sometimes "inventive" Italian dishes at this Flatiron "find"; its "pretty", "quiet" dining room offers "space between tables and a sense of privacy", while the "sharp" front bar/lounge hosts more of a "busy" scene.

Zizi Limona *Mediterranean/Mideastern*   ▽ | 24 | 21 | 18 | $43 |

Williamsburg | 129 Havemeyer St. (1st St.) | Brooklyn | 347-763-1463 |
www.zizilimona.com

"Super yum" flavors from the Middle East and the Mediterranean are the lure at this "bustling" Williamsburg "gem" overseen by a "friendly" staff; a "decent price point" and "warm" interior in which shelves of for-sale comestibles "serve as decor" are further reasons it's "not to be missed."

NEW Zona Rosa *Mexican*   ▽ | 23 | 24 | 22 | $36 |

Williamsburg | 571 Lorimer St. (Metropolitan Ave.) | Brooklyn |
917-324-7423 | www.zonarosabrooklyn.com

"Fabulous, quirky design" – complete with a "sublime rooftop deck" and kitchen "built inside an Airstream trailer" – meets a "greatest-party-in-Brooklyn" vibe at this Williamsburg Mexican; fueling the fiesta are "delicious" dishes and "incredible margaritas."

Zum Schneider *German* | 22 | 19 | 20 | $35 |

East Village | 107 Ave. C (7th St.) | 212-598-1098 |
www.nyc.zumschneider.com

It's all about the "humongous" Bavarian steins of beer and German brats at this affordable East Village "slice of Munich" that's a "boisterous" "haus away from home" where "every day's a party"; hit the ATM first since it's "cash only", and prepare to wait during Oktoberfest.

Zum Stammtisch *German*   23 | 19 | 21 | $40
Glendale | 69-46 Myrtle Ave. (bet. 69th Pl. & 70th St.) | Queens | 718-386-3014 | www.zumstammtisch.com
"Go with an appetite" to this Glendale German whose "hearty" classics come in "you-won't-leave-hungry" portions; "pleasant frauleins in Alpine costume" toting steins of "frosty beer" bolster the kitschy "hofbrauhaus-in-Bavaria" vibe, while affordable prices ensure it won't "bring out the wurst in you."

Zutto *Japanese/Noodle Shop*   ▽ 23 | 20 | 20 | $56
TriBeCa | 77 Hudson St. (Harrison St.) | 212-233-3287 | www.zuttonyc.com
"They do ramen, and everything else, right" at this TriBeCa Japanese whose menu also includes "high-quality" sushi, buns and more; with "laid-back ambiance", service that "makes you feel at home" and "easy-going" prices, "no wonder it's been here forever."

ZZ's Clam Bar *Seafood*   ▽ 24 | 21 | 21 | $98
Greenwich Village | 169 Thompson St. (bet. Bleecker & Houston Sts.) | 212-254-3000 | www.zzsclambar.com
The "Torrisi guys" do it again with this "tiny" Village boîte whose "elevated raw-bar" fare and fancy libations come via a sharp-dressed, "friendly" staff; "wallet-emptying" prices have some going just "for cocktails and apps" – but with only 12 seats, "good luck getting in."

INDEXES

Special Features

Listings cover the best in each category and include names, locations and Food ratings. Multi-location restaurants' features may vary by branch.

BAR/SINGLES SCENES

NEW All'onda | **G Vill**	23
Arlington Club | **E 70s**	21
Atlantic Grill | **E 70s**	22
NEW Bacchanal | **L Italy**	—
Bagatelle | **Meatpacking**	21
Beauty & Essex | **LES**	23
NEW Berg'n | **Crown Hts**	—
Blue Ribbon | **multi.**	24
Blue Water | **Union Sq**	24
Bobo | **W Vill**	24
NEW Bodega Negra | **Chelsea**	23
NEW Bo's | **Flatiron**	20
Breslin | **Flatiron**	24
Brother Jimmy's | **multi.**	17
Bryant Pk Grill/Cafe | **Midtown**	18
Buddakan | **Chelsea**	25
Cabana | **multi.**	22
Cafe Noir | **TriBeCa**	—
Catch | **Meatpacking**	23
Citrus B&G | **W 70s**	20
Crave Fishbar | **E Midtown**	24
DBGB | **E Vill**	22
Del Frisco's | **Midtown**	25
NEW Dirty French | **LES**	—
Dos Caminos | **multi.**	20
Dutch | **SoHo**	23
NEW East Pole | **E 60s**	22
El Toro Blanco | **W Vill**	22
Freemans | **LES**	23
NEW Gato | **NoHo**	24
General | **LES**	22
Harlow | **E Midtown**	20
Hillstone | **multi.**	22
Hudson Clearwater | **W Vill**	22
NEW Humboldt/Jackson | **W'burg**	—
Joya | **Cobble Hill**	24
NEW Kingside | **Midtown**	19
Koi | **Midtown**	24
La Esquina | **SoHo**	23
Lafayette | **NoHo**	22
Lavo | **Midtown**	19
Lure Fishbar | **SoHo**	24
Macao Trading | **TriBeCa**	21
NEW Margaux | **G Vill**	17

Maysville | **Flatiron**	21
Miss Lily's | **G Vill**	20
NEW Monarch Rm. | **Chelsea**	—
Otto | **G Vill**	23
NEW Park Avenue | **Flatiron**	—
Penrose | **E 80s**	20
Perla | **G Vill**	25
Pulqueria | **Chinatown**	23
NEW Rist. Morini | **E 80s**	26
Rosemary's | **W Vill**	22
Salvation Taco | **Murray Hill**	21
Saxon & Parole | **NoHo**	24
Smith | **multi.**	19
Spice Market | **Meatpacking**	24
Standard Grill | **Meatpacking**	22
Stanton Social | **LES**	24
STK | **Meatpacking**	23
Tao | **multi.**	23
NEW Toro | **Chelsea**	25
Willow Road | **Chelsea**	22

BEER STANDOUTS

Alchemy | **Park Slope**	20
B&B Winepub | **SoHo**	21
B. Café | **W 80s**	21
NEW Berg'n | **Crown Hts**	—
Birreria | **Flatiron**	20
Blue Smoke | **multi.**	21
Breslin | **Flatiron**	24
Café d'Alsace | **E 80s**	22
Cannibal | **Hell's Kit**	21
Cleveland | **NoLita**	22
Colicchio/Sons | **Chelsea**	26
DBGB | **E Vill**	22
Dinosaur BBQ | **multi.**	23
Eleven Madison | **Flatiron**	28
Fette Sau | **W'burg**	26
5 Napkin Burger | **multi.**	20
Flex Mussels | **multi.**	24
Fraunces Tav. | **Financial**	17
NEW Gander | **Flatiron**	—
Gramercy Tavern | **Flatiron**	28
Heidelberg | **E 80s**	21
Jacob's Pickles | **W 80s**	21
Jake's Steakhse. | **Fieldston**	23
John Brown Smokehse. | **LIC**	25
Luksus | **Greenpt**	23

Petite Abeille | **multi.**	20
NEW Pickle Shack | **Gowanus**	–
Press 195 | **Bayside**	23
Queens Kickshaw | **Astoria**	21
Resto | **Kips Bay**	20
NEW Runner | **Clinton Hill**	–
Spotted Pig | **W Vill**	24
Toby's Public | **multi.**	24
Upstate | **E Vill**	25
Zum Schneider | **E Vill**	22

BREAKFAST

Balthazar | **SoHo**	24
Bakehse. Bistro | **Meatpacking**	21
Barney Greengrass | **W 80s**	24
NEW Baz Bagel | **L Italy**	–
Brasserie | **E Midtown**	21
Breslin | **Flatiron**	24
Bubby's | **multi.**	19
Butter | **Midtown**	22
Buvette | **W Vill**	24
Cafe Luxembourg | **W 70s**	21
Cafe Gitane | **multi.**	22
Cafe Mogador | **E Vill**	24
NEW Café Paulette | **Ft Greene**	–
Café Sabarsky/Fledermaus | **E 80s**	22
NEW Cafe Standard | **E Vill**	20
Carnegie Deli | **Midtown**	23
Casa Lever | **Midtown**	23
City Bakery | **Flatiron**	22
Clinton St. Baking | **LES**	24
Community | **Morningside Hts**	21
Cookshop | **Chelsea**	23
Coppelia | **Chelsea**	20
E.A.T. | **E 80s**	20
Egg | **W'burg**	23
Five Leaves | **Greenpt**	24
Forty Four | **Midtown**	21
Friedman's Lunch | **multi.**	21
NEW Hamilton's Soda | **W Vill**	–
Hudson Clearwater | **W Vill**	22
NEW Hudson Eats | **Battery Pk**	–
Jean-Georges | **W 60s**	28
Jean-Georges' Noug. | **W 60s**	27
Jeffrey's Grocery | **W Vill**	23
Joseph Leonard | **W Vill**	24
Katz's Deli | **LES**	25
NEW Kingside | **Midtown**	19
Kitchenette | **multi.**	20
NEW Krupa | **Windsor Terr.**	–

NEW Ladurée | **SoHo**	24
Lafayette | **NoHo**	22
Lambs Club | **Midtown**	22
Landmarc | **W 60s**	20
Le Pain Q. | **multi.**	18
Locanda Verde | **TriBeCa**	24
Machiavelli | **W 80s**	23
Maialino | **Gramercy**	25
Maison Kayser | **multi.**	22
NEW Margaux | **G Vill**	17
Marlow/Sons | **W'burg**	24
Michael's | **Midtown**	22
Morandi | **W Vill**	22
NEW Mulberry/Vine | **TriBeCa**	18
Nice Matin | **W 70s**	19
NoHo Star | **NoHo**	19
Norma's | **Midtown**	24
Okonomi | **W'burg**	–
Palm Court | **Midtown**	18
NEW Parker/Quinn | **Midtown**	23
Penelope | **Kips Bay**	22
Regency B&G | **E 60s**	19
Reynard | **W'burg**	20
Rosemary's | **W Vill**	22
Sant Ambroeus | **multi.**	21
Sarabeth's | **multi.**	20
Standard Grill | **Meatpacking**	22
Tartine | **W Vill**	22
Tom's | **Prospect Hts**	17
Veselka | **E Vill**	21
NEW Wayfarer | **Midtown**	18

BRUNCH

ABC Kitchen | **Flatiron**	25
Almond | **Flatiron**	21
Amy Ruth's | **Harlem**	22
Applewood | **Park Slope**	24
Aquagrill | **SoHo**	27
Artisanal | **Midtown**	23
Atlantic Grill | **multi.**	22
A Voce | **Midtown**	23
Back Forty | **E Vill**	22
Bagatelle | **Meatpacking**	21
Balaboosta | **NoLita**	23
Balthazar | **SoHo**	24
Bar Americain | **Midtown**	23
Barbounia | **Flatiron**	23
Bar Tabac | **Cobble Hill**	20
NEW Baz Bagel | **L Italy**	–
Black Whale | **City Is**	23
Blue Ribbon Bakery | **W Vill**	23

Blue Water | **Union Sq**	24
Bocca Lupo | **Cobble Hill**	22
Brasserie 8½ | **Midtown**	22
Bubby's | **multi.**	19
Buttermilk | **Carroll Gdns**	25
Cafe Cluny | **W Vill**	21
Café d'Alsace | **E 80s**	22
Cafe Loup | **W Vill**	19
Cafe Luluc | **Cobble Hill**	22
Cafe Luxembourg | **W 70s**	21
Cafe Mogador | **E Vill**	24
Carlyle | **E 70s**	23
Cebu | **Bay Ridge**	20
NEW Cecil | **Harlem**	23
Celeste | **W 80s**	24
Char No. 4 | **Cobble Hill**	22
NEW Cheri | **Harlem**	—
NEW Clam | **W Vill**	23
Cleveland | **NoLita**	22
Clinton St. Baking | **LES**	24
Colicchio/Sons | **Chelsea**	26
NEW Colonia Verde | **Ft Greene**	—
Colonie | **Bklyn Hts**	24
Community | **Morningside Hts**	21
Cookshop | **Chelsea**	23
Cornelia St. | **W Vill**	20
Craftbar | **Flatiron**	23
db Bistro Moderne | **Midtown**	24
DBGB | **E Vill**	22
Dell'anima | **W Vill**	25
Diner | **W'burg**	23
Dino | **Ft Greene**	20
Dutch | **SoHo**	23
NEW East Pole | **E 60s**	22
Edi & The Wolf | **E Vill**	19
Egg | **W'burg**	23
NEW Élan | **Flatiron**	—
El Quinto Pino | **Chelsea**	25
NEW Emily | **Clinton Hill**	—
Empellón | **W Vill**	23
NEW Empire Diner | **Chelsea**	21
Extra Virgin | **W Vill**	23
Fat Radish | **LES**	21
Five Leaves | **Greenpt**	24
Five Points | **NoHo**	21
Flatbush Farm | **Park Slope**	21
44 & X/44½ | **Hell's Kit**	22
Fourth | **G Vill**	20
NEW French Louie | **Boerum Hill**	26
Friend/Farmer | **Gramercy**	20

NEW Gander | **Flatiron**	—
Good | **W Vill**	22
Great Jones Cafe | **NoHo**	23
Hearth | **E Vill**	25
Hope & Anchor | **Red Hook**	21
Hundred Acres | **SoHo**	23
Il Gattopardo | **Midtown**	25
Ilili | **Flatiron**	26
Isabella's | **W 70s**	20
Jack the Horse | **Bklyn Hts**	21
James | **Prospect Hts**	23
Jane | **G Vill**	21
JoJo | **E 60s**	24
Joseph Leonard | **W Vill**	24
Juventino | **Park Slope**	26
Kin Shop | **W Vill**	22
Kitchenette | **multi.**	20
NEW Ladurée | **SoHo**	24
Lafayette | **NoHo**	22
Lambs Club | **Midtown**	22
L'Apicio | **E Vill**	23
Lavo | **Midtown**	19
Le Gigot | **W Vill**	24
Leopard/des Artistes | **W 60s**	22
Le Philosophe | **NoHo**	23
Lexington Brass | **E Midtown**	20
LIC Market | **LIC**	25
Lido | **Harlem**	24
Lion | **G Vill**	24
NEW Little Prince | **SoHo**	23
Locale | **Astoria**	21
Locanda Verde | **TriBeCa**	24
Lodge | **W'burg**	22
Maialino | **Gramercy**	25
Má Pêche | **Midtown**	23
NEW Marco's | **Prospect Hts**	24
Mark | **E 70s**	23
Marrow | **W Vill**	22
NEW Marshal | **Hell's Kit**	24
NEW Meadowsweet | **W'burg**	—
Mercadito | **E Vill**	22
Mile End | **Boerum Hill**	22
Minetta Tavern | **G Vill**	24
Miriam | **Park Slope**	23
Miss Lily's | **multi.**	20
Miss Mamie/Maude | **Harlem**	21
Mon Petit Cafe | **E 60s**	20
Montmartre | **Chelsea**	21
Murray's Cheese Bar | **W Vill**	23
NEW Narcissa | **E Vill**	27

Nice Matin	**W 70s**	19
Norma's	**Midtown**	24
Northern Spy	**E Vill**	22
Ocean Grill	**W 70s**	23
Odeon	**TriBeCa**	20
Ofrenda	**W Vill**	21
Olea	**Ft Greene**	24
Ouest	**W 80s**	22
Palm Court	**Midtown**	18
Palo Santo	**Park Slope**	23
Paradou	**Meatpacking**	20
Penelope	**Kips Bay**	22
Perilla	**W Vill**	24
Petrossian	**Midtown**	24
Potlikker	**W'burg**	22
Prune	**E Vill**	24
Public	**NoLita**	25
Queens Comfort	**Astoria**	22
Red Rooster	**Harlem**	22
Resto	**Kips Bay**	20
NEW Rist. Morini	**E 80s**	26
River Café	**Dumbo**	26
Riverpark	**Kips Bay**	25
River Styx	**Greenpt**	—
Rocking Horse	**Chelsea**	22
NEW Root & Bone	**E Vill**	—
Rosemary's	**W Vill**	22
Rose Water	**Park Slope**	25
Runner & Stone	**Gowanus**	22
Sanford's	**Astoria**	24
Sarabeth's	**multi.**	20
Saxon & Parole	**NoHo**	24
Scottadito	**Park Slope**	22
Seva Indian	**Astoria**	25
NEW Shalom Japan	**W'burg**	25
606 R&D	**Prospect Hts**	23
NEW Skal	**LES**	22
Spotted Pig	**W Vill**	24
Stanton Social	**LES**	24
NEW Stella 34	**Midtown**	23
Stone Park	**Park Slope**	24
Sunshine Co.	**Prospect Hts**	22
Superfine	**Dumbo**	19
Sylvia's	**Harlem**	18
NEW Tablao	**TriBeCa**	—
Tartine	**W Vill**	22
NEW Tavern/Green	**Central Pk**	—
Telepan	**W 60s**	26
NEW Telepan Local	**TriBeCa**	23
Tertulia	**W Vill**	24

Tipsy Parson	**Chelsea**	22
Tom's	**Prospect Hts**	17
Tribeca Grill	**TriBeCa**	22
Turkish Kitchen	**Kips Bay**	23
Union Sq. Cafe	**Union Sq**	27
Vanderbilt	**Prospect Hts**	21
Water Club	**Kips Bay**	22
Waverly Inn	**W Vill**	22
Willow Road	**Chelsea**	22
NEW Winslow	**Gramercy**	—
NEW Writing Room	**E 80s**	22

BUFFET

(Check availability)

Benares	**multi.**	21
Bombay Palace	**Midtown**	21
Bukhara Grill	**E Midtown**	25
Chola	**E Midtown**	23
Churrascaria	**Midtown**	24
Darbar	**multi.**	23
Dhaba	**Kips Bay**	24
NEW Fogo de Chão	**Midtown**	24
Indus Valley	**W 90s**	23
Jackson Diner	**multi.**	21
Sapphire Indian	**W 60s**	21
Seva Indian	**Astoria**	25
NEW Texas de Brazil	**E 60s**	24
Utsav	**Midtown**	22
View	**Midtown**	17

BYO

A Cafe/Wine Rm.	**W 100s**	24
Afghan Kebab	**multi.**	20
Azuri Cafe	**Hell's Kit**	25
Buddha Bodai	**Chinatown**	22
Butcher Bar	**Astoria**	21
Di Fara	**Midwood**	25
Gazala's	**Hell's Kit**	22
Kaz an Nou	**Prospect Hts**	22
Kuma Inn	**LES**	25
Little Poland	**E Vill**	21
Lomzynianka	**Greenpt**	25
Lucali	**Carroll Gdns**	27
Nook	**Midtown**	23
Oaxaca	**multi.**	21
Peking Duck	**Chinatown**	23
Petite Crevette	**Columbia St.**	23
Pho Bang	**L Italy**	21
Phoenix Gdn.	**Murray Hill**	23
Poke	**E 80s**	26
Qi	**W'burg**	21

Queens Comfort | **Astoria**	22
Red Hook Lobster | **Red Hook**	24
Sauce | **LES**	23
Taci's Beyti | **Sheepshead**	24
Tanoshi | **E 70s**	26
Tartine | **W Vill**	22
Tea & Sympathy | **W Vill**	21
Wondee Siam | **Hell's Kit**	21
Zaytoons | **multi.**	21

CELEBRITY CHEFS

Einat Admony	
Balaboosta | **NoLita**	23
NEW Bar Bolonat | **W Vill**	—
Taïm | **multi.**	25
Nick Anderer	
NEW Marta | **Flatiron**	—
Michael Anthony	
Gramercy Tavern | **Flatiron**	28
Julieta Ballesteros	
Crema | **Flatiron**	22
Dan Barber	
Blue Hill | **G Vill**	26
Lidia Bastianich	
Felidia | **E Midtown**	25
Mario Batali	
Babbo | **G Vill**	26
Casa Mono | **Gramercy**	24
Del Posto | **Chelsea**	26
Eataly | **Flatiron**	23
Esca | **Hell's Kit**	25
Lupa | **G Vill**	24
Manzo | **Flatiron**	24
Otto | **G Vill**	23
Jonathan Benno	
Lincoln | **W 60s**	25
April Bloomfield	
Breslin | **Flatiron**	24
John Dory Oyster | **Flatiron**	21
Salvation Taco | **Murray Hill**	21
Spotted Pig | **W Vill**	24
Saul Bolton	
Red Gravy | **Bklyn Hts**	23
NEW Saul | **Prospect Hts**	23
Vanderbilt | **Prospect Hts**	21
David Bouley	
Bouley | **TriBeCa**	29
Brushstroke/Ichimura | **TriBeCa**	26
Daniel Boulud	
Bar Boulud | **W 60s**	24
Boulud Sud | **W 60s**	25
Café Boulud | **E 70s**	26
Daniel | **E 60s**	28
db Bistro Moderne | **Midtown**	24
DBGB | **E Vill**	22
Danny Bowien	
NEW Mission Cantina | **LES**	20
Jimmy Bradley	
Harrison | **TriBeCa**	22
Red Cat | **Chelsea**	24
Terrance Brennan	
Artisanal | **Midtown**	23
Picholine | **W 60s**	26
David Burke	
David Burke/Bloom. | **E Midtown**	20
NEW David Burke Fab. | **Midtown**	—
David Burke Fishtail | **E 60s**	24
David Burke Kitchen | **SoHo**	25
Joey Campanaro	
Little Owl | **W Vill**	27
Marco Canora	
Hearth | **E Vill**	25
Terroir | **multi.**	20
Floyd Cardoz	
NEW White Street | **TriBeCa**	—
Andrew Carmellini	
NEW Bar Primi | **E Vill**	—
Dutch | **SoHo**	23
Lafayette | **NoHo**	22
Library/Public | **G Vill**	18
Locanda Verde | **TriBeCa**	24
Michael Cetrulo	
Scalini Fedeli | **TriBeCa**	26
David Chang	
Má Pêche | **Midtown**	23
Momofuku Ko | **E Vill**	27
Momofuku Noodle | **E Vill**	23
Momofuku Ssäm Bar | **E Vill**	25
Rebecca Charles	
Pearl Oyster | **W Vill**	27
Tom Colicchio	
Colicchio/Sons | **Chelsea**	26
Craft | **Flatiron**	26
Craftbar | **Flatiron**	23
Riverpark | **Kips Bay**	25
'Wichcraft | **multi.**	19
Christian Delouvrier	
La Mangeoire | **E Midtown**	23
John DeLucie	
Bill's Food/Drink | **Midtown**	18
Crown | **E 80s**	23
Lion | **G Vill**	24
Alain Ducasse	
Benoit | **Midtown**	23

More on zagat.com

Wylie Dufresne	
Alder | **E Vill**	22
Todd English	
Ça Va | **Midtown**	22
Plaza Food Hall | **Midtown**	22
Sandro Fioriti	
Sandro's | **E 80s**	24
Bobby Flay	
Bar Americain | **Midtown**	23
NEW Gato | **NoHo**	24
Marc Forgione	
NEW American Cut | **TriBeCa**	24
Khe-Yo | **TriBeCa**	24
Marc Forgione | **TriBeCa**	25
John Fraser	
Dovetail | **W 70s**	27
NEW Narcissa | **E Vill**	27
Amanda Freitag	
NEW Empire Diner | **Chelsea**	21
Alex Garcia	
A.G. Kitchen | **W 70s**	18
Alex Guarnaschelli	
Butter | **Midtown**	23
Kurt Gutenbrunner	
Blaue Gans | **TriBeCa**	22
Café Sabarsky/Fledermaus | **E 80s**	22
Wallsé | **W Vill**	25
Ilan Hall	
NEW Gorbals | **W'burg**	—
Gabrielle Hamilton	
Prune | **E Vill**	24
Peter Hoffman	
Back Forty | **multi.**	22
Daniel Humm	
Eleven Madison | **Flatiron**	28
NoMad | **Flatiron**	26
NEW NoMad Bar | **Flatiron**	—
Hung Huynh	
Catch | **Meatpacking**	23
General | **LES**	22
Eiji Ichimura	
Brushstroke/Ichimura | **TriBeCa**	26
Sara Jenkins	
Porchetta | **E Vill**	21
Porsena | **E Vill**	23
Thomas Keller	
Bouchon Bakery | **Midtown**	23
Per Se | **Midtown**	27
Mark Ladner	
Del Posto | **Chelsea**	26
Paul Liebrandt	
Elm | **W'burg**	25

Anita Lo	
Annisa | **W Vill**	28
Michael Lomonaco	
Porter House | **Midtown**	26
Nobu Matsuhisa	
Nobu | **multi.**	27
Jehangir Mehta	
Graffiti | **E Vill**	28
Mehtaphor | **TriBeCa**	26
Carlo Mirarchi	
Blanca | **Bushwick**	24
Roberta's | **Bushwick**	26
Marco Moreira	
NEW Botequim | **G Vill**	—
15 East | **Union Sq**	26
Tocqueville | **Flatiron**	27
Masaharu Morimoto	
Morimoto | **Chelsea**	26
Seamus Mullen	
NEW El Colmado | **Hell's Kit**	—
Tertulia | **W Vill**	24
Marc Murphy	
NEW Kingside | **Midtown**	19
Landmarc | **multi.**	20
Daisuke Nakazawa	
NEW Sushi Nakazawa | **W Vill**	27
Ivan Orkin	
NEW Ivan Ramen | **multi.**	19
Charlie Palmer	
Aureole | **Midtown**	26
NEW Charlie Palmer | **Midtown**	—
David Pasternack	
NEW Barchetta | **Chelsea**	—
Esca | **Hell's Kit**	25
Alfred Portale	
Gotham B&G | **G Vill**	28
Michael Psilakis	
FishTag | **W 70s**	23
MP Taverna | **Astoria**	24
Cesar Ramirez	
Chef's/Brooklyn Fare | **Downtown Bklyn**	28
Mary Redding	
Mary's Fish | **W Vill**	25
Mads Refslund	
Acme | **NoHo**	21
Andy Ricker	
Pok Pok Ny | **Columbia St.**	24
Eric Ripert	
Le Bernardin | **Midtown**	29
Marcus Samuelsson	
Red Rooster | **Harlem**	22

Richard Sandoval
Maya | E 60s — 22
Pampano | E Midtown — 23
Zengo | Murray Hill — 20

Alex Stupak
Empellón | multi. — 23

Gari Sugio
Gari | multi. — 26

Nao Sugiyama
Sugiyama | Midtown — 27

Masayoshi Takayama
Masa/Bar Masa | Midtown — 25

Dale Talde
Pork Slope | Park Slope — 19
Talde | Park Slope — 25

Bill Telepan
Telepan | W 60s — 26
NEW Telepan Local | TriBeCa — 23

Laurent Tourondel
Arlington Club | E 70s — 21

Tom Valenti
Ouest | W 80s — 22

Jean-Georges Vongerichten
ABC Cocina | Flatiron — 24
ABC Kitchen | Flatiron — 25
Jean-Georges | W 60s — 28
JoJo | E 60s — 24
Mark | E 70s — 23
Mercer Kitchen | SoHo — 21
Perry St. | W Vill — 26
Spice Market | Meatpacking — 24

David Waltuck
NEW Élan | Flatiron — —

Jonathan Waxman
Barbuto | W Vill — 26

Michael White
Ai Fiori | Midtown — 26
Butterfly | TriBeCa — 19
Costata | SoHo — 25
Marea | Midtown — 27
Nicoletta | E Vill — 19
Osteria Morini | SoHo — 25
NEW Rist. Morini | E 80s — 26

Jody Williams
Buvette | W Vill — 24

Geoffrey Zakarian
Lambs Club | Midtown — 22
National | E Midtown — 19
Palm Court | Midtown — 18

Galen Zamarra
Mas | W Vill — 27

CHILD-FRIENDLY

(* children's menu available)

Alice's Tea* | multi. — 20
Allswell | W'burg — 22
Amorina* | Prospect Hts — 23
Ample Hills | multi. — 27
Amy Ruth's | Harlem — 22
Arirang Hibachi* | multi. — 23
Artie's* | City Is — 22
Atlantic Grill* | multi. — 22
Bamonte's | W'burg — 23
BareBurger* | multi. — 21
Bark | Park Slope — 20
Barney Greengrass | W 80s — 24
NEW Baz Bagel | L Italy — —
BLT Burger* | G Vill — 22
Blue Ribbon* | multi. — 24
Blue Smoke* | Kips Bay — 22
Blue Water* | Union Sq — 24
Boathouse* | Central Pk — 17
Bocca Lupo | Cobble Hill — 22
Brasserie Cognac* | multi. — 19
Brennan | Sheepshead — 23
Brooklyn Crab | Red Hook — 20
Brooklyn Farmacy | Carroll Gdns — 22
Brother Jimmy's* | multi. — 17
Bubby's* | multi. — 19
Buttermilk* | Carroll Gdns — 25
Café Habana/Outpost | Ft Greene — 21
Calexico | multi. — 22
Carmine's* | Midtown — 21
ChipShop* | multi. — 20
Cowgirl* | W Vill — 18
Crema* | Flatiron — 22
DBGB* | E Vill — 22
Dinosaur BBQ* | multi. — 23
Eddie's Sweet Shop | Forest Hills — 24
NEW El Vez | Battery Pk — —
NEW Emily | Clinton Hill — —
Farm/Adderley* | Ditmas Pk — 23
5 Napkin Burger* | multi. — 20
Flatbush Farm | Park Slope — 21
NEW Fogo de Chão | Midtown — 24
Franny's | Park Slope — 25
Friend/Farmer* | Gramercy — 20
Ganso | Downtown Bklyn — 23
Gargiulo's | Coney Is — 22
Gigino* | multi. — 20
Good Enough* | W 80s — 20

Grey Dog* | **multi.**	22
NEW Hamilton's Soda | **W Vill**	—
Hill Country | **Flatiron**	23
Hill Country Chicken | **multi.**	20
NEW Hometown | **Red Hook**	—
Isabella's* | **W 70s**	20
Jackson Hole* | **multi.**	20
Jack the Horse | **Bklyn Hts**	21
Joe & Pat's | **Castelton Cnrs**	25
Junior's* | **multi.**	19
L&B Spumoni* | **Gravesend**	23
L'Albero/Gelati* | **Park Slope**	23
Landmarc* | **multi.**	20
La Villa Pizzeria | **multi.**	22
Le Pain Q.* | **multi.**	18
Legend* | **multi.**	20
Little Muenster | **multi.**	21
London Lennie's* | **Middle Vill**	24
Mable's Smokehse. | **W'burg**	23
Max* | **TriBeCa**	18
Melt Shop | **multi.**	19
Mermaid* | **multi.**	22
Miss Mamie/Maude | **Harlem**	21
Nick's | **multi.**	23
Ninja | **TriBeCa**	13
Noodle Pudding | **Bklyn Hts**	23
Otto | **G Vill**	23
Palm* | **TriBeCa**	25
Peanut Butter Co. | **G Vill**	20
Pera* | **Midtown**	20
Riverview* | **LIC**	22
Rock Center Café* | **Midtown**	19
Rosa Mexicano* | **multi.**	23
Ruby Foo's* | **Midtown**	19
Sammy's Fishbox* | **City Is**	21
Sammy's Shrimp* | **City Is**	23
Sarabeth's | **multi.**	20
Schiller's* | **LES**	17
Sea Grill* | **Midtown**	24
2nd Ave Deli | **multi.**	23
Serendipity 3 | **E 60s**	19
Shabu-Shabu 70 | **E 70s**	23
Shake Shack* | **multi.**	21
S'MAC | **multi.**	23
Smorgas Chef* | **Midtown**	21
Sylvia's* | **Harlem**	18
NEW Texas de Brazil | **E 60s**	24
Tony's Di Napoli | **Midtown**	22
Two Boots* | **multi.**	19
Veselka | **E Vill**	21

View* | **Midtown**	17
Virgil's* | **Midtown**	20
Zero Otto | **Arthur Ave./Belmont**	23
Zum Stammtisch | **Glendale**	23

COCKTAIL STARS

Alder | **E Vill**	22
Atera | **TriBeCa**	26
NEW Bacchanal | **L Italy**	—
NEW Bar Chuko | **Prospect Hts**	—
NEW Bar Primi | **E Vill**	—
Beatrice Inn | **W Vill**	20
NEW Beautique | **Midtown**	—
Beauty & Essex | **LES**	23
NEW Bergen Hill | **Carroll Gdns**	—
Betony | **Midtown**	25
NEW Black Ant | **E Vill**	—
Char No. 4 | **Cobble Hill**	22
Crif Dogs | **E Vill**	23
NEW Decoy | **W Vill**	—
Distilled | **TriBeCa**	23
Dutch | **SoHo**	23
Eleven Madison | **Flatiron**	28
Elm | **W'burg**	25
Empellón | **E Vill**	23
Estela | **NoLita**	25
Fort Defiance | **Red Hook**	23
Franny's | **Park Slope**	25
NEW French Louie | **Boerum Hill**	26
NEW Fung Tu | **LES**	23
Hudson Clearwater | **W Vill**	22
Macao Trading | **TriBeCa**	21
NEW Marco's | **Prospect Hts**	24
Maysville | **Flatiron**	21
Minetta Tavern | **G Vill**	24
Momofuku Ssäm Bar | **E Vill**	25
Monkey Bar | **Midtown**	18
NEW M. Wells Steakhse. | **LIC**	22
NEW Navy | **SoHo**	—
NEW NoMad Bar | **Flatiron**	—
Pachanga Patterson | **Astoria**	23
Perla | **G Vill**	25
NEW Piora | **W Vill**	26
P.J. Clarke's | **multi.**	19
Prime Meats | **Carroll Gdns**	24
Prospect | **Ft Greene**	23
Red Rooster | **Harlem**	22
River Styx | **Greenpt**	—
NEW Root & Bone | **E Vill**	—
Rye | **W'burg**	24
SakaMai | **LES**	24

Salvation Taco | **Murray Hill**	21
Saxon & Parole | **NoHo**	24
NEW Skal | **LES**	22
Tiny's | **TriBeCa**	21
NEW Toro | **Chelsea**	25
NEW Winslow | **Gramercy**	—
Yerba Buena | **multi.**	22
ZZ's Clam Bar | **G Vill**	24

COLLEGE-CENTRIC

Columbia
Community | **Morningside Hts**	21
Ellington | **W 100s**	16
Kitchenette | **Morningside Hts**	20
Maoz | **E 90s**	21
Max Caffe/SoHa | **Morningside Hts**	22
Miss Mamie/Maude | **Harlem**	21
107 West | **W 100s**	20
Pisticci | **Morningside Hts**	24
Thai Market | **W 100s**	23

NYU
Angelica Kit. | **E Vill**	23
Artichoke Basille | **E Vill**	22
BaoHaus | **E Vill**	20
Blue 9 Burger | **G Vill**	20
Café Habana/Outpost | **NoLita**	21
Caracas | **E Vill**	26
Crif Dogs | **E Vill**	23
Dos Toros | **G Vill**	20
NEW Emmett's | **SoHo**	21
Gyu-Kaku | **G Vill**	22
Ippudo | **G Vill**	25
John's/12th St. | **E Vill**	21
La Esquina | **SoHo**	23
Mamoun's | **multi.**	23
99 Miles/Philly | **G Vill**	20
Num Pang | **G Vill**	23
NEW 100 Montaditos | **G Vill**	20
Otto | **G Vill**	23
Republic | **Union Sq**	19
S'MAC | **E Vill**	23
Smith | **E Vill**	19
Spice | **G Vill**	21
Vanessa's Dumpling | **E Vill**	25
Veselka | **E Vill**	21

COMMUTER OASIS

Grand Central
Ammos | **Midtown**	21
Aretsky's Patroon | **E Midtown**	25
Benjamin Steak | **Midtown**	27
Bobby Van's | **Midtown**	23
Cafe Centro | **E Midtown**	21

Café Grumpy | **Midtown**	21
Capital Grille | **E Midtown**	24
Docks Oyster | **Murray Hill**	20
Hatsuhana | **Midtown**	25
Joe | **Midtown**	21
Junior's | **Midtown**	19
La Fonda/Sol | **E Midtown**	21
Lexington Brass | **E Midtown**	20
Luke's Lobster | **E Midtown**	24
Michael Jordan | **Midtown**	21
Morton's | **Midtown**	24
Nanni | **E Midtown**	22
Naples 45 | **E Midtown**	21
Naya | **E Midtown**	22
Num Pang | **Murray Hill**	23
Osteria Laguna | **E Midtown**	20
Oyster Bar | **Midtown**	22
Palm | **E Midtown**	25
Pera | **SoHo**	20
Pietro's | **E Midtown**	25
Sakagura | **E Midtown**	24
Shake Shack | **Midtown**	21
Sinigual | **Murray Hill**	21
Soba Totto | **E Midtown**	24
Sparks | **E Midtown**	25
Sushi Yasuda | **E Midtown**	28
Tulsi | **E Midtown**	24
Two Boots | **Midtown**	19
Zengo | **Murray Hill**	20

Penn Station
Arno | **Midtown**	21
Brother Jimmy's | **Midtown**	17
Casa Nonna | **Midtown**	22
NEW David Burke Fab. | **Midtown**	—
Delmonico's | **Midtown**	23
Frankie & Johnnie's | **Midtown**	23
Gaonnuri | **Midtown**	20
Keens | **Midtown**	26
Lazzara's | **Midtown**	23
Nick & Stef's | **Midtown**	22
NEW Parker/Quinn | **Midtown**	23
Uncle Jack's | **Midtown**	24
Uncle Nick's | **Chelsea**	20

Port Authority
Ça Va | **Midtown**	22
Chez Josephine | **Hell's Kit**	21
Chimichurri Grill | **Hell's Kit**	21
Esca | **Hell's Kit**	25
Etc. Etc. | **Midtown**	23
5 Napkin Burger | **Midtown**	21
Hakkasan | **Midtown**	23
Inakaya | **Midtown**	22

John's Pizzeria | **Midtown**	23
Ktchn | **Hell's Kit**	21
Marseille | **Midtown**	21
Mercato | **Midtown**	22
Qi | **Midtown**	21
Schnipper's | **Midtown**	20
Shake Shack | **Midtown**	21
Shorty's | **Midtown**	21
Shula's | **Midtown**	21
NEW Urbo | **Midtown**	—
West Bank | **Hell's Kit**	19
Wolfgang's | **Midtown**	25

FIREPLACES

A Casa Fox | **LES**	24
Alberto | **Forest Hills**	25
Alta | **G Vill**	25
Antica Pesa | **W'burg**	23
Applewood | **Park Slope**	24
Asellina | **Flatiron**	20
Battery Gdns. | **BPC**	19
Beatrice Inn | **W Vill**	20
Benjamin Steak | **Midtown**	27
Boathouse | **Central Pk**	17
Bouley | **TriBeCa**	29
Blossom | **W Vill**	22
Ça Va | **Midtown**	22
Cebu | **Bay Ridge**	20
NEW Cheri | **Harlem**	—
Christos | **Astoria**	22
Club A Steak | **E Midtown**	23
Cornelia St. | **W Vill**	20
Donovan's | **Bayside**	21
Dutch | **SoHo**	23
F & J Pine | **Van Nest**	23
Forty Four | **Midtown**	21
Friend/Farmer | **Gramercy**	20
Giorgione | **Hudston Sq**	24
Glass House | **Midtown**	20
House | **Gramercy**	23
I Trulli | **Kips Bay**	23
JoJo | **E 60s**	24
Keens | **Midtown**	26
Lady Mendl's | **Gramercy**	22
La Lanterna | **G Vill**	20
Lambs Club | **Midtown**	22
Manetta's | **LIC**	24
Marco Polo | **Carroll Gdns**	23
NoMad | **Flatiron**	26
NEW NoMad Bar | **Flatiron**	—
Northeast Kingdom | **Bushwick**	25

One if by Land | **W Vill**	23
Per Se | **Midtown**	27
Place | **W Vill**	23
Public | **NoLita**	25
Quality Meats | **Midtown**	26
SakaMai | **LES**	24
Salinas | **Chelsea**	22
Scottadito | **Park Slope**	22
Sea Fire Grill | **E Midtown**	28
Telly's Taverna | **Astoria**	22
Tiny's | **TriBeCa**	21
Triomphe | **Midtown**	24
21 Club | **Midtown**	23
Vinegar Hill Hse. | **Vinegar Hill**	24
Water Club | **Kips Bay**	22
Waverly Inn | **W Vill**	22
NEW Writing Room | **E 80s**	22

FOOD MARKETS

NEW Berg'n | **Crown Hts**	—
Eataly | **Flatiron**	23
NEW Gotham West | **Hell's Kit**	25
NEW Hudson Eats | **Battery Pk**	—
Plaza Food Hall | **Midtown**	22
Smorgasburg | **multi.**	25

GLUTEN-FREE OPTIONS

(Call to discuss specific needs)

Alta | **G Vill**	25
Amali | **E 60s**	24
Angelica Kit. | **E Vill**	23
BareBurger | **multi.**	21
Betony | **Midtown**	25
Bistango | **multi.**	22
Blue Smoke | **multi.**	21
Bocca/Bacco | **multi.**	20
Candle 79 | **E 70s**	24
Caracas | **multi.**	26
China Grill | **Midtown**	23
Del Posto | **Chelsea**	26
Don Antonio | **Midtown**	22
NEW Dosa Royale | **Carroll Gdns**	24
Etc. Etc. | **Midtown**	23
5 Napkin Burger | **multi.**	21
Friedman's Lunch | **multi.**	21
Hill Country | **Flatiron**	23
Hummus Pl. | **multi.**	21
Keste Pizza | **W Vill**	23
Lexington Brass | **E Midtown**	20
Nice Matin | **W 70s**	19
Nizza | **Midtown**	21

Nom Wah Tea | **Chinatown**	21
Palà | **LES**	22
Palm Court | **Midtown**	18
Pappardella | **W 70s**	20
Peacefood Café | **multi.**	23
Risotteria | **W Vill**	21
NEW Risotteria Melotti | **E Vill**	—
Rosa Mexicano | **multi.**	23
Rubirosa | **NoLita**	25
Ruby Foo's | **Midtown**	19
S'MAC | **multi.**	23
Smith | **multi.**	19
Tao | **multi.**	23
V-Note | **E 70s**	23
Wild | **multi.**	—
Zengo | **Murray Hill**	20

GREEN/LOCAL/ ORGANIC

Brucie | **Cobble Hill**	20
ABC Cocina | **Flatiron**	24
ABC Kitchen | **Flatiron**	25
Aita | **Clinton Hill**	25
Aldea | **Flatiron**	24
NEW All'onda | **G Vill**	23
Amali | **E 60s**	24
Ample Hills | **multi.**	27
Angelica Kit. | **E Vill**	23
Applewood | **Park Slope**	24
Aroma Kitchen | **NoHo**	23
Aureole | **Midtown**	26
Aurora | **multi.**	24
Babbo | **G Vill**	26
Back Forty | **E Vill**	22
Bar Boulud | **W 60s**	24
Barbuto | **W Vill**	26
NEW Barchetta | **Chelsea**	—
BareBurger | **multi.**	21
Bark | **Park Slope**	20
Battersby | **Boerum Hill**	27
Bell Book/Candle | **W Vill**	23
Betony | **Midtown**	25
Blossom | **Chelsea**	22
Blue Hill | **G Vill**	26
Blue Marble | **multi.**	21
Brooklyn Farmacy | **Carroll Gdns**	22
Buttermilk | **Carroll Gdns**	25
Café Habana/Outpost | **Ft Greene**	21
Candle Cafe | **E 70s**	23
Candle 79 | **E 70s**	24
Caravan/Dreams | **E Vill**	23

City Bakery | **Flatiron**	22
Clinton St. Baking | **LES**	24
Colicchio/Sons | **Chelsea**	26
Colonie | **Bklyn Hts**	24
Community | **Morningside Hts**	21
NEW Contra | **LES**	25
Cookshop | **Chelsea**	23
Craft | **Flatiron**	26
Dell'anima | **W Vill**	25
Del Posto | **Chelsea**	26
Diner | **W'burg**	23
NEW Dover | **Carroll Gdns**	27
NEW East Pole | **E 60s**	22
Egg | **W'burg**	23
Eleven Madison | **Flatiron**	28
NEW Emily | **Clinton Hill**	—
Esca | **Hell's Kit**	25
Farm/Adderley | **Ditmas Pk**	23
Fat Radish | **LES**	21
Fette Sau | **W'burg**	26
Five Points | **NoHo**	21
Flatbush Farm | **Park Slope**	21
Fletcher's | **Gowanus**	20
Frankies | **multi.**	23
Franny's | **Park Slope**	25
NEW French Louie | **Boerum Hill**	26
General Greene | **Ft Greene**	20
NEW Glasserie | **Greenpt**	24
Good Fork | **Red Hook**	23
Gotham B&G | **G Vill**	28
Gramercy Tavern | **Flatiron**	28
Grocery | **Carroll Gdns**	27
Hearth | **E Vill**	25
NEW Humboldt/Jackson | **W'burg**	—
Hundred Acres | **SoHo**	23
Il Buco | **NoHo**	26
Juventino | **Park Slope**	26
Kin Shop | **W Vill**	22
L'Artusi | **W Vill**	26
La Vara | **Cobble Hill**	26
Le Pain Q. | **Flatiron**	18
Lincoln | **W 60s**	25
Locanda Verde | **TriBeCa**	24
Lot 2 | **Park Slope**	24
NEW Lucky Luna | **Greenpt**	—
Lupa | **G Vill**	24
Marc Forgione | **TriBeCa**	25
NEW Marco's | **Prospect Hts**	24
Market Table | **W Vill**	24

Marlow/Sons | **W'burg**	24
Marrow | **W Vill**	22
NEW Marshal | **Hell's Kit**	24
Mas | **W Vill**	27
NEW Mayhem & Stout | **Murray Hill**	—
NEW Meadowsweet | **W'burg**	—
Meat Hook Sandwich | **W'burg**	—
NEW Mimi Cheng's | **E Vill**	—
Momofuku Ko | **E Vill**	27
Momofuku Noodle | **E Vill**	23
Momofuku Ssäm Bar | **E Vill**	25
NEW Mulberry/Vine | **TriBeCa**	18
NEW Narcissa | **E Vill**	27
NEW Navy | **SoHo**	—
New Leaf | **Inwood**	22
Nightingale 9 | **Carroll Gdns**	23
NoMad | **Flatiron**	26
Northern Spy | **E Vill**	22
Palo Santo | **Park Slope**	23
Paulie Gee's | **Greenpt**	27
NEW Pavilion | **Union Sq**	—
Peaches | **Bed-Stuy**	25
Pearl Oyster | **W Vill**	27
Per Se | **Midtown**	27
Prime Meats | **Carroll Gdns**	24
Print | **Hell's Kit**	25
Prune | **E Vill**	24
Pure Food/Wine | **Gramercy**	24
Redhead | **E Vill**	23
Riverpark | **Kips Bay**	25
Roberta's | **Bushwick**	26
Roman's | **Ft Greene**	24
NEW Root & Bone | **E Vill**	—
Rosemary's | **W Vill**	22
Rose Water | **Park Slope**	25
Rucola | **Boerum Hill**	25
NEW Saul | **Prospect Hts**	23
Sfoglia | **E 90s**	25
606 R&D | **Prospect Hts**	23
Smoke Joint | **Ft Greene**	23
Smorgas Chef | **multi.**	21
Snack | **multi.**	23
Stone Park | **Park Slope**	24
Telepan | **W 60s**	26
NEW Telepan Local | **TriBeCa**	23
Tía Pol | **Chelsea**	23
Tocqueville | **Flatiron**	27
Tortilleria Nixtamal | **Corona**	25
Trestle on 10th | **Chelsea**	20

Txikito | **Chelsea**	26
Union Sq. Cafe | **Union Sq**	27
Upstate | **E Vill**	25
NEW Urbo | **Midtown**	—
Vanderbilt | **Prospect Hts**	21
Van Leeuwen | **multi.**	24
Veselka | **E Vill**	21
Vesta | **Astoria**	25
NEW Wilma Jean | **Carroll Gdns**	—

GROUP DINING

Almayass | **Flatiron**	23
Almond | **Flatiron**	21
Alta | **G Vill**	25
Arirang Hibachi | **multi.**	23
Artisanal | **Midtown**	23
Atlantic Grill | **multi.**	22
Back Forty | **SoHo**	22
Balthazar | **SoHo**	24
Bar Americain | **Midtown**	23
Beauty & Essex | **LES**	23
Becco | **Midtown**	23
Blaue Gans | **TriBeCa**	22
BLT Prime | **Gramercy**	25
BLT Steak | **E Midtown**	24
Blue Fin | **Midtown**	23
Blue Smoke | **multi.**	22
Blue Water | **Union Sq**	24
Boathouse | **Central Pk**	17
Bond 45 | **Midtown**	19
Buddakan | **Chelsea**	25
Cabana | **multi.**	22
Calle Ocho | **W 80s**	20
Carmine's | **multi.**	21
Casa Nonna | **Midtown**	22
China Grill | **Midtown**	23
Churrascaria | **Midtown**	24
Colicchio/Sons | **Chelsea**	26
Congee | **LES**	20
Crispo | **W Vill**	24
DBGB | **E Vill**	22
NEW Decoy | **W Vill**	—
Del Frisco's | **multi.**	25
Dinosaur BBQ | **multi.**	23
Dominick's | **Arthur Ave./Belmont**	23
Don Peppe | **S Ozone Pk**	25
Dos Caminos | **multi.**	20
NEW El Vez | **Battery Pk**	—
F & J Pine | **Van Nest**	23
Fette Sau | **W'burg**	26
Fig & Olive | **multi.**	21

NEW Fogo de Chão | **Midtown**	24
Golden Unicorn | **Chinatown**	22
Gyu-Kaku | **multi.**	22
Havana Central | **Midtown**	19
Hill Country | **Flatiron**	23
Ilili | **Flatiron**	26
Jing Fong | **Chinatown**	21
Kuma Inn | **LES**	25
Kum Gang San | **multi.**	21
Landmarc | **Midtown**	20
Má Pêche | **Midtown**	23
Momofuku Ssäm Bar | **E Vill**	25
Morimoto | **Chelsea**	26
Ninja | **TriBeCa**	13
NEW NoMad Bar | **Flatiron**	—
Otto | **G Vill**	23
Oyster Bar | **Midtown**	22
Pacificana | **Sunset Pk**	24
NEW Park Avenue | **Flatiron**	—
Peking Duck | **multi.**	23
Peter Luger | **W'burg**	28
Public | **NoLita**	25
Quality Meats | **Midtown**	26
Redeye Grill | **Midtown**	19
Red Rooster | **Harlem**	22
Rosa Mexicano | **multi.**	23
Ruby Foo's | **Midtown**	19
Sahara | **Sheepshead**	23
Sammy's Roumanian | **LES**	21
Sik Gaek | **multi.**	22
Spice Market | **Meatpacking**	24
Standard Grill | **Meatpacking**	22
Stanton Social | **LES**	24
NEW Stella 34 | **Midtown**	23
Tamarind | **TriBeCa**	26
Tanoreen | **Bay Ridge**	27
Tao | **multi.**	23
NEW Tavern/Green | **Central Pk**	—
NEW Texas de Brazil | **E 60s**	24
Tony's Di Napoli | **Midtown**	22
Tribeca Grill | **TriBeCa**	22
NEW 2 Duck Goose | **Gowanus**	—
Victor's Cafe | **Midtown**	24
Yerba Buena | **E Vill**	22
Zengo | **Murray Hill**	20

HAPPY HOURS

Allswell | **W'burg**	22
Atrium Dumbo | **Dumbo**	23
A Voce | **Midtown**	23
Back Forty | **multi.**	22

Bell Book/Candle | **W Vill**	23
Brooklyn Star | **W'burg**	24
Costata | **SoHo**	25
Crave Fishbar | **E Midtown**	24
Cull & Pistol | **Chelsea**	24
Distilled | **TriBeCa**	23
Docks Oyster | **Murray Hill**	20
Ed's Chowder | **W 60s**	20
Elm | **W'burg**	25
Emporio | **NoLita**	24
FishTag | **W 70s**	23
Five Points | **NoHo**	21
Flex Mussels | **multi.**	24
Fonda | **multi.**	24
Fritzl's Lunch | **Bushwick**	—
Gyu-Kaku | **multi.**	22
Haru | **multi.**	21
Jacques | **multi.**	21
John Dory Oyster | **Flatiron**	21
Keens | **Midtown**	26
Littleneck | **multi.**	23
Lobster Joint | **multi.**	22
Maialino | **Gramercy**	25
Marco Polo | **Carroll Gdns**	23
Mermaid | **multi.**	22
Millesime | **Flatiron**	21
Móle | **multi.**	20
NEW Monarch Rm. | **Chelsea**	—
MP Taverna | **Astoria**	24
Ofrenda | **W Vill**	21
Oyster Bar | **Midtown**	22
Red Rooster | **Harlem**	22
Rosa Mexicano | **multi.**	23
Rye | **W'burg**	24
Sala One Nine | **Flatiron**	23
Sea Fire Grill | **E Midtown**	28
Terroir | **multi.**	20
Thalia | **Midtown**	20
Penrose | **E 80s**	20
Upstate | **E Vill**	25

HISTORIC PLACES

(Year opened; * building)

1763 | Fraunces Tav.* | **Financial**	17
1787 | One if by Land* | **W Vill**	23
1863 | City Hall* | **TriBeCa**	22
1868 | Landmark Tav.* | Hell's Kit	19
1870 | Kings' Carriage* | **E 80s**	21
1884 | P.J. Clarke's | **E Midtown**	19
1885 | Keens | **Midtown**	26

More on zagat.com

1887 | Peter Luger | **W'burg**	28
1888 | Katz's Deli | **LES**	25
1892 | Ferrara | **L Italy**	23
1896 | Rao's | **E Harlem**	21
1900 | Bamonte's | **W'burg**	23
1902 | Angelo's/Mulberry | **L Italy**	23
1904 | Vincent's | **L Italy**	21
1905 | Morgan* | **Murray Hill**	19
1906 | Barbetta | **Midtown**	22
1907 | Gargiulo's | **Coney Is**	22
1908 | Barney Greengrass | **W 80s**	24
1908 | John's/12th St. | **E Vill**	21
1910 | Wolfgang's* | **Midtown**	25
1911 | Commerce* | **W Vill**	23
1913 | Oyster Bar | **Midtown**	22
1917 | Leopard/des Artistes* | **W 60s**	22
1919 | Mario's | **Arthur Ave./Belmont**	22
1920 | Leo's Latticini/Corona | **Corona**	26
1920 | Nom Wah Tea | **Chinatown**	21
1920 | Waverly Inn | **W Vill**	22
1921 | Sardi's | **Midtown**	19
1922 | Sanford's | **Astoria**	24
1924 | Totonno Pizza | **Coney Is**	26
1926 | Frankie & Johnnie's | **Midtown**	23
1926 | Palm | **E Midtown**	25
1927 | Ann & Tony's | **Arthur Ave./Belmont**	21
1927 | Russian Tea | **Midtown**	19
1929 | Eisenberg's | **Flatiron**	17
1929 | Empire Diner | **Chelsea**	21
1929 | John's Pizzeria | **W Vill**	23
1929 | 21 Club | **Midtown**	23
1930 | Carlyle | **E 70s**	23
1930 | El Quijote | **Chelsea**	22
1932 | Papaya King | **E 80s**	22
1932 | Pietro's | **E Midtown**	25
1933 | Patsy's | **E Harlem**	21
1934 | Tavern/Green | **Central Pk**	–
1936 | Heidelberg | **E 80s**	21
1936 | Monkey Bar* | **Midtown**	18
1936 | Tom's | **Prospect Hts**	17
1937 | Carnegie Deli | **Midtown**	23
1937 | Denino's | **Elm Pk**	26
1937 | Le Veau d'Or | **E 60s**	21

1937 | Minetta Tavern* | **G Vill**	24
1938 | Wo Hop | **Chinatown**	21
1939 | Spumoni Gdn. | **Gravesend**	23
1941 | Sevilla | **W Vill**	24
1942 | B & H Dairy | **E Vill**	24
1944 | Patsy's | **Midtown**	21
1945 | Ben's Best | **Rego Pk**	24
1950 | Junior's | **Downtown Bklyn**	19
1953 | Liebman's | **Riverdale**	22
1953 | Vesuvio | **Bay Ridge**	22
1954 | Serendipity 3 | **E 60s**	19
1954 | Veselka | **E Vill**	21
1957 | Arturo's | **G Vill**	23
1958 | Queen | **Bklyn Hts**	23
1959 | Brasserie | **E Midtown**	21
1959 | El Parador | **Murray Hill**	22
1959 | Four Seasons | **E Midtown**	26
1959 | London Lennie's | **Middle Vill**	24
1960 | Bull & Bear | **E Midtown**	23
1960 | Chez Napoléon | **Midtown**	22
1960 | Joe & Pat's | **Castelton Cnrs**	25
1961 | Corner Bistro | **W Vill**	22
1962 | La Grenouille | **Midtown**	28
1962 | Sylvia's | **Harlem**	18
1963 | Joe Allen | **Midtown**	18
1963 | Victor's Cafe | **Midtown**	24
1964 | Di Fara | **Midwood**	25
1964 | Le Perigord | **E Midtown**	24

HOTEL DINING

6 Columbus Hotel Blue Ribbon Sushi | **SoHo**	25
Ace Hotel Breslin | **Flatiron**	24
John Dory Oyster | **Flatiron**	21
No. 7 | **Flatiron**	21
Stumptown | **Flatiron**	23
Affinia Shelburne Hotel Rare B&G | **Murray Hill**	21
Amsterdam Court Hotel Natsumi | **Midtown**	20
Archer Hotel NEW David Burke Fab. | **Midtown**	–
Benjamin Hotel National | **E Midtown**	19
Blakely Hotel Abboccato | **Midtown**	20

Bowery Hotel
  Gemma | **E Vill** — 23

Bryant Park Hotel
  Koi | **Midtown** — 24

Carlton Hotel
  Millesime | **Flatiron** — 21

Carlyle Hotel
  Carlyle | **E 70s** — 23

Casablanca Hotel
  Tony's Di Napoli | **Midtown** — 22

Cassa Hotel
  Butter | **Midtown** — 23

Chambers Hotel
  Má Pêche | **Midtown** — 23

Chandler Hotel
  Juni | **Midtown** — 27

Chatwal Hotel
  Lambs Club | **Midtown** — 22

City Club Hotel
  db Bistro Moderne | **Midtown** — 24

Crosby Street Hotel
  Crosby Bar | **SoHo** — 22

Dream Downtown Hotel
  NEW Bodega Negra | **Chelsea** — 23
  Cherry | **Chelsea** — 22

Dream Hotel
  Serafina | **Midtown** — 18

Duane Street Hotel
  Mehtaphor | **TriBeCa** — 26

Dylan Hotel
  Benjamin Steak | **Midtown** — 27

Elysée Hotel
  Monkey Bar | **Midtown** — 18

Empire Hotel
  Ed's Chowder | **W 60s** — 20

Excelsior Hotel
  Calle Ocho | **W 80s** — 20

Gansevoort Meatpacking
  NEW Chester | **Meatpacking** — —

Gansevoort Park Ave. Hotel
  Asellina | **Flatiron** — 20

Gramercy Park Hotel
  Maialino | **Gramercy** — 25

Greenwich Hotel
  Locanda Verde | **TriBeCa** — 24

Hilton NY Fashion District Hotel
  Rare B&G | **Chelsea** — 21

Hyatt 48 Lex Hotel
  Lexington Brass | **E Midtown** — 20

Hyatt Union Sq. Hotel
  NEW Botequim | **G Vill** — —
  Fourth | **G Vill** — 20

Ink48 Hotel
  Print | **Hell's Kit** — 25

Inn at Irving Pl.
  Lady Mendl's | **Gramercy** — 22

InterContinental Hotel Times Sq.
  Ça Va | **Midtown** — 22
  Shake Shack | **Midtown** — 21

Iroquois Hotel
  Triomphe | **Midtown** — 24

James Hotel
  David Burke Kitchen | **SoHo** — 25

Jane Hotel
  Cafe Gitane | **W Vill** — 23

JW Marriott Essex House
  South Gate | **Midtown** — 20

Langham Place Fifth Ave. Hotel
  Ai Fiori | **Midtown** — 26

Le Parker Meridien
  Burger Joint | **Midtown** — 23
  Norma's | **Midtown** — 24

Lombardy Hotel
  Harlow | **E Midtown** — 20

London NYC Hotel
  Gordon Ramsay | **Midtown** — 22
  Maze | **Midtown** — 19

Ludlow Hotel
  NEW Dirty French | **LES** — —

Mandarin Oriental Hotel
  Asiate | **Midtown** — 26

Maritime Hotel
  Tao | **Chelsea** — 23

Mark Hotel
  Mark | **E 70s** — 23

Marlton Hotel
  NEW Margaux | **G Vill** — 17

Marriott Marquis Hotel
  View | **Midtown** — 17

Martha Washington Hotel
  NEW Marta | **Flatiron** — —

McCarren Hotel
  Elm | **W'burg** — 25

Mela Hotel
  Saju Bistro | **Midtown** — 21

Mercer Hotel
  Mercer Kitchen | **SoHo** — 21

Mondrian SoHo Hotel
  Isola | **SoHo** — 24

NoMad Hotel
  NoMad | **Flatiron** — 26

NYLO Hotel
  Serafina | **W 70s** — 18

Pierre Hotel
  Sirio | **E 60s** — 22

SPECIAL FEATURES

NoMad | **Flatiron**	26
NEW NoMad Bar | **Flatiron**	—
NEW Okonomi | **W'burg**	—
Pearl & Ash | **NoLita**	24
Perla | **G Vill**	25
Pok Pok Ny | **Columbia St.**	24
Pulqueria | **Chinatown**	23
Red Rooster | **Harlem**	22
Reynard | **W'burg**	23
NEW Rist. Morini | **E 80s**	26
River Styx | **Greenpt**	—
NEW Root & Bone | **E Vill**	—
Rosemary's | **W Vill**	22
NEW Runner | **Clinton Hill**	—
Saxon & Parole | **NoHo**	24
Standard Grill | **Meatpacking**	22
NEW Sushi Nakazawa | **W Vill**	27
NEW Toro | **Chelsea**	25
Willow Road | **Chelsea**	22

JACKET REQUIRED

Carlyle | **E 70s**	23
Daniel | **E 60s**	28
Four Seasons | **E Midtown**	26
Jean-Georges | **W 60s**	28
La Grenouille | **Midtown**	28
Le Bernardin | **Midtown**	29
Le Cirque | **E Midtown**	24
Per Se | **Midtown**	27
River Café | **Dumbo**	26
21 Club | **Midtown**	23

MEET FOR A DRINK

Acme | **NoHo**	21
NEW All'onda | **G Vill**	23
NEW American Cut | **TriBeCa**	24
Aretsky's Patroon | **E Midtown**	25
Artisanal | **Midtown**	23
Astor Room | **Astoria**	20
Atlantic Grill | **multi.**	22
Atrium Dumbo | **Dumbo**	23
Aurora | **W'burg**	24
Back Forty | **SoHo**	22
Bar Boulud | **W 60s**	24
Barbounia | **Flatiron**	23
NEW Barchetta | **Chelsea**	—
Betony | **Midtown**	25
Bill's Food/Drink | **Midtown**	18
Blue Fin | **Midtown**	23
Blue Water | **Union Sq**	24
NEW Bodega Negra | **Chelsea**	23

Bond St | **NoHo**	25
Boqueria | **Flatiron**	23
NEW Bo's | **Flatiron**	20
Bryant Pk Grill/Cafe | **Midtown**	18
Buddakan | **Chelsea**	25
Butterfly | **TriBeCa**	19
NEW Cafe El Pres. | **Flatiron**	—
Cafe Luxembourg | **W 70s**	21
Casa Lever | **Midtown**	23
Catch | **Meatpacking**	23
NEW Chalk Point | **SoHo**	—
Char No. 4 | **Cobble Hill**	22
City Hall | **TriBeCa**	22
Colicchio/Sons | **Chelsea**	26
Daniel | **E 60s**	28
DBGB | **E Vill**	22
Del Frisco's | **Midtown**	25
NEW Dinner on Ludlow | **LES**	21
Dos Caminos | **multi.**	20
Dutch | **SoHo**	23
NEW Eddy | **E Vill**	—
NEW Élan | **Flatiron**	—
El Toro Blanco | **W Vill**	22
NEW El Vez | **Battery Pk**	—
Flatbush Farm | **Park Slope**	21
Four Seasons | **E Midtown**	26
Freemans | **LES**	23
NEW French Louie | **Boerum Hill**	26
Glass House | **Midtown**	20
Gotham B&G | **G Vill**	28
Gramercy Tavern | **Flatiron**	28
Gran Electrica | **Dumbo**	22
Hakkasan | **Midtown**	23
Harlow | **E Midtown**	20
Harry's Cafe | **Financial**	22
Hillstone | **multi.**	22
Jack the Horse | **Bklyn Hts**	21
Jean-Georges | **W 60s**	28
J.G. Melon | **E 70s**	21
Keens | **Midtown**	26
Kellari Taverna | **Midtown**	22
NEW Kingside | **Midtown**	19
Koi | **Midtown**	24
Lafayette | **NoHo**	22
La Fonda/Sol | **E Midtown**	21
Lambs Club | **Midtown**	22
Landmarc | **Midtown**	20
Lavo | **Midtown**	19
Le Bernardin | **Midtown**	29
Le Cirque | **E Midtown**	24

Le Colonial | **E Midtown** 23
Library/Public | **G Vill** 18
Lincoln | **W 60s** 25
Lotus Blue | **TriBeCa** 23
Louro | **W Vill** 26
Macao Trading | **TriBeCa** 21
Maialino | **Gramercy** 25
Mari Vanna | **Flatiron** 20
Mark | **E 70s** 23
Masa/Bar Masa | **Midtown** 25
Maysville | **Flatiron** 21
Michael Jordan | **Midtown** 21
Minetta Tavern | **G Vill** 24
Modern | **Midtown** 26
NEW Monarch Rm. | **Chelsea** —
Monkey Bar | **Midtown** 18
National | **E Midtown** 19
Natsumi | **Midtown** 20
Nobu | **Midtown** 27
NoMad | **Flatiron** 26
NEW Norman's Cay | **LES** —
Northeast Kingdom | **Bushwick** 25
North End Grill | **Battery Pk** 24
Odeon | **TriBeCa** 20
Orsay | **E 70s** 18
Ouest | **W 80s** 22
Park | **Chelsea** 18
Penrose | **E 80s** 20
Pies-N-Thighs | **W'burg** 24
P.J. Clarke's | **multi.** 19
Pulqueria | **Chinatown** 23
Quality Italian | **Midtown** 24
Raoul's | **SoHo** 24
Rayuela | **LES** 23
Red Rooster | **Harlem** 22
Reynard | **W'burg** 23
Roberta's | **Bushwick** 26
Roebling Tea Room | **W'burg** 21
Roman's | **Ft Greene** 24
Salvation Taco | **Murray Hill** 21
Saxon & Parole | **NoHo** 24
SD26 | **Flatiron** 25
NEW Skal | **LES** 22
Spice Market | **Meatpacking** 24
Standard Grill | **Meatpacking** 22
Stanton Social | **LES** 24
STK | **Meatpacking** 23
Stone Park | **Park Slope** 24
Talde | **Park Slope** 25
Tao | **multi.** 23

NEW Tavern/Green | **Central Pk** —
NEW Telepan Local | **TriBeCa** 23
NEW Toro | **Chelsea** 25
21 Club | **Midtown** 23
NEW Urbo | **Midtown** —
Willow Road | **Chelsea** 22
Wollensky's | **E Midtown** 24
Zengo | **Murray Hill** 20

MUSIC/LIVE ENTERTAINMENT

(Call for types and times of performances)

Blue Smoke | **Kips Bay** 22
Blue Water | **Union Sq** 24
Cávo | **Astoria** 22
Chez Josephine | **Hell's Kit** 21
Cornelia St. | **W Vill** 20
Delta Grill | **Midtown** 20
General | **LES** 22
Knickerbocker | **G Vill** 22
La Lanterna | **G Vill** 20
Moscow 57 | **LES** —
River Café | **Dumbo** 26
Sofrito | **E Midtown** 24
Sylvia's | **Harlem** 18
Tommaso | **Bath Bch** 23

NEWCOMERS

Alfredo 100 | **Midtown** —
All'onda | **G Vill** 23
American Cut | **TriBeCa** 24
Antonioni's | **LES** —
Bacchanal | **L Italy** —
Barawine | **Harlem** 20
BarBacon | **Midtown** 22
Bar Bolonat | **W Vill** —
Barchetta | **Chelsea** —
Bar Chuko | **Prospect Hts** —
Bar Primi | **E Vill** —
Bassanova | **Chinatown** 21
Bâtard | **TriBeCa** —
Baz Bagel | **L Italy** —
Beautique | **Midtown** —
Bergen Hill | **Carroll Gdns** —
Berg'n | **Crown Hts** —
Black Ant | **E Vill** —
Bodega Negra | **Chelsea** 23
Bo's | **Flatiron** 20
Botequim | **G Vill** —
Bunna Cafe | **Bushwick** —
Butterfish | **Midtown** —

Restaurant	Rating
Cafe Cambodge | **E Vill**	—
Cafe El Pres. | **Flatiron**	—
Café Paulette | **Ft Greene**	—
Cafe Standard | **E Vill**	20
Cagen | **E Vill**	—
Cecil | **Harlem**	23
Cerveceria | **W'burg**	—
Chalk Point | **SoHo**	—
Charlie Palmer | **Midtown**	—
Cherche Midi | **NoLita**	—
Cheri | **Harlem**	—
Cherry Izakaya | **W'burg**	—
Chester | **Meatpacking**	—
China Blue | **TriBeCa**	18
Clam | **W Vill**	23
Claudette | **G Vill**	—
Colonia Verde | **Ft Greene**	—
Contra | **LES**	25
David Burke Fab. | **Midtown**	—
Decoy | **W Vill**	—
Dinner on Ludlow | **LES**	21
Dirty French | **LES**	—
Dosa Royale | **Carroll Gdns**	24
Dover | **Carroll Gdns**	27
Dutch Kills Centraal | **LIC**	21
East & West | **Hell's Kit**	—
East Pole | **E 60s**	22
East 12th | **E Vill**	25
Eddy | **E Vill**	—
Élan | **Flatiron**	—
El Colmado | **Hell's Kit**	—
El Vez | **Battery Pk**	—
Emily | **Clinton Hill**	—
Emmett's | **SoHo**	21
Empire Diner | **Chelsea**	21
Flinders Lane | **E Vill**	—
Fogo de Chão | **Midtown**	24
French Louie | **Boerum Hill**	26
Fung Tu | **LES**	23
Gander | **Flatiron**	—
Gato | **NoHo**	24
Glady's | **Crown Hts**	—
Glasserie | **Greenpt**	24
Gorbals | **W'burg**	—
Gotham West | **Hell's Kit**	25
The Greek | **TriBeCa**	21
Greenpt Fish | **Greenpt**	—
Grindhaus | **Red Hook**	—
Hamilton's Soda | **W Vill**	—
Han Dynasty | **G Vill**	23
Hirohisa | **SoHo**	—
Hometown | **Red Hook**	—
Hudson Eats | **Battery Pk**	—
Humboldt/Jackson | **W'burg**	—
Il Mulino Prime | **SoHo**	—
Ivan Ramen | **Hell's Kit**	19
Kingside | **Midtown**	19
Krupa | **Windsor Terr.**	—
Ladurée | **SoHo**	24
Lea | **Ditmas Pk**	—
Little Collins | **E Midtown**	—
Little Lamb | **Flushing**	—
Little Prince | **SoHo**	23
Los Americanos | **TriBeCa**	—
Los Tacos | **Chelsea**	—
Lucky Luna | **Greenpt**	—
Marco's | **Prospect Hts**	24
Margaux | **G Vill**	17
Marshal | **Hell's Kit**	24
Marta | **Flatiron**	—
Mayhem & Stout | **Murray Hill**	—
Meadowsweet | **W'burg**	—
Milk River | **Prospect Hts**	22
Mimi Cheng's | **E Vill**	—
Mission Cantina | **LES**	20
Monarch Rm. | **Chelsea**	—
Montana's Trail | **Bushwick**	—
Morgenstern's | **LES**	—
Moscow 57 | **LES**	—
Mozzarella & Vino | **Midtown**	22
Mulberry/Vine | **TriBeCa**	18
M. Wells Steakhse. | **LIC**	22
Narcissa | **E Vill**	27
Navy | **SoHo**	—
NoMad Bar | **Flatiron**	—
Norman's Cay | **LES**	—
100 Montaditos | **multi.**	20
Onomea | **W'burg**	—
Otto's Tacos | **E Vill**	22
Pacifico's | **Crown Hts**	—
Pagani | **W Vill**	21
Park Avenue | **Flatiron**	—
Parker/Quinn | **Midtown**	23
Pavilion | **Union Sq**	—
Peacock | **Midtown**	22
Pickle Shack | **Gowanus**	—
Pine Tree Cafe | **Bronx Pk**	—
Piora | **W Vill**	26
Pizzetteria Brunetti | **W Vill**	26
Racines | **TriBeCa**	—

Rothmann's
Rouge Tomate
Sambuca
Seersucker
Sen
Sezz Medi'
Shalezeh
Solo
Son Cubano
Sorella
Steak Frites
Sueños
Super Linda
Sweet Melissa
Trattoria Toscana
Tre Otto
Veatery
Veritas
Whym
Wildwood Barbeque
Wong

OUTDOOR DINING

Agnanti | **Astoria**	23
Alma | **Columbia St.**	20
A.O.C. | **multi.**	20
Aquagrill | **SoHo**	27
Aurora | **W'burg**	24
Avra | **E Midtown**	25
Bacchus | **Downtown Bklyn**	21
Back Forty | **E Vill**	22
Barbetta | **Midtown**	22
Bar Corvo | **Prospect Hts**	24
Battery Gdns. | **BPC**	19
NEW Berg'n | **Crown Hts**	—
Blue Water | **Union Sq**	24
Boathouse | **Central Pk**	17
Bobo | **W Vill**	24
Bogota | **Park Slope**	24
Bottega | **E 70s**	20
Brass. Ruhlmann | **Midtown**	19
Bryant Pk Grill/Cafe | **Midtown**	18
Cacio e Pepe | **E Vill**	20
Cafe Asean | **W Vill**	22
Cafe Centro | **E Midtown**	21
Cafe Mogador | **W'burg**	24
Cávo | **Astoria**	22
NEW Cheri | **Harlem**	—
Cleveland | **NoLita**	22
Cole's Dock Side | **Great Kills**	23
Conviv. Osteria | **Park Slope**	26

Crosby Bar | **SoHo**	22
Da Nico | **L Italy**	21
Dinosaur BBQ | **multi.**	23
Edi & The Wolf | **E Vill**	19
NEW Empire Diner | **Chelsea**	21
Esca | **Hell's Kit**	25
Farm/Adderley | **Ditmas Pk**	23
Flatbush Farm | **Park Slope**	21
44 & X/44½ | **Hell's Kit**	22
Frankies | **Carroll Gdns**	23
NEW French Louie | **Boerum Hill**	26
Gigino | **Battery Pk**	20
Gnocco | **E Vill**	23
Good Fork | **Red Hook**	23
Gran Electrica | **Dumbo**	22
Grocery | **Carroll Gdns**	27
NEW Hudson Eats | **Battery Pk**	—
Isabella's | **W 70s**	20
I Trulli | **Kips Bay**	23
NEW Ivan Ramen | **LES**	19
Jeanne & Gaston | **W Vill**	24
Juventino | **Park Slope**	26
NEW Ladurée | **SoHo**	24
La Esquina | **W'burg**	23
La Lanterna | **G Vill**	20
La Mangeoire | **E Midtown**	23
L&B Spumoni | **Gravesend**	23
NEW Marco's | **Prospect Hts**	24
Montmartre | **Chelsea**	21
M. Wells Dinette | **LIC**	24
NEW M. Wells Steakhse. | **LIC**	22
New Leaf | **Inwood**	22
Pachanga Patterson | **Astoria**	23
Palma | **W Vill**	25
NEW Pavilion | **Union Sq**	—
Pera | **SoHo**	20
Pines | **Gowanus**	21
NEW Pizzetteria Brunetti | **W Vill**	26
Pure Food/Wine | **Gramercy**	24
Riverpark | **Kips Bay**	25
Roberta's | **Bushwick**	26
Roebling Tea Room | **W'burg**	21
NEW Runner | **Clinton Hill**	—
Salinas | **Chelsea**	22
San Pietro | **Midtown**	22
Sripraphai | **Woodside**	27
Stonehome | **Ft Greene**	21
NEW Taco Santo | **Park Slope**	—
Tartine | **W Vill**	22

NEW Tavern/Green | **Central Pk**	—
Terroir | **Chelsea**	20
Trestle on 10th | **Chelsea**	20
ViceVersa | **Midtown**	23
Vinegar Hill Hse. | **Vinegar Hill**	24
Water Club | **Kips Bay**	22
Water's Edge | **LIC**	22
Traif | **W'burg**	26
NEW Zona Rosa | **W'burg**	23

PEOPLE-WATCHING

Acme | **NoHo**	21
Amaranth | **E 60s**	21
Antica Pesa | **W'burg**	23
Bagatelle | **Meatpacking**	21
Balthazar | **SoHo**	24
NEW Beautique | **Midtown**	—
Beatrice Inn | **W Vill**	20
Breslin | **Flatiron**	24
Café Boulud | **E 70s**	26
Cafe Gitane | **NoLita**	23
Carnegie Deli | **Midtown**	23
Casa Lever | **Midtown**	23
NEW Cherche Midi | **NoLita**	—
Cipriani D'twn | **SoHo**	24
Da Silvano | **G Vill**	21
Elio's | **E 80s**	24
Four Seasons | **E Midtown**	26
Fred's at Barneys | **E 60s**	22
Harlow | **E Midtown**	20
Harry Cipriani | **Midtown**	23
Indochine | **G Vill**	21
Joe Allen | **Midtown**	18
Katz's Deli | **LES**	25
Lavo | **Midtown**	19
Le Bilboquet | **E 60s**	21
Le Cirque | **E Midtown**	24
Leopard/des Artistes | **W 60s**	22
Lion | **G Vill**	24
Marea | **Midtown**	27
NEW Margaux | **G Vill**	17
Michael's | **Midtown**	22
Minetta Tavern | **G Vill**	24
NEW Monarch Rm. | **Chelsea**	—
Nello | **E 60s**	18
Nicola's | **E 80s**	22
NoMad | **Flatiron**	26
Orsay | **E 70s**	18
Orso | **Midtown**	24
Philippe | **E 60s**	23
Rao's | **E Harlem**	21

Red Rooster | **Harlem**	22
Reynard | **W'burg**	23
Roberta's | **Bushwick**	26
Rosemary's | **W Vill**	22
Sant Ambroeus | **multi.**	21
Sette Mezzo | **E 70s**	22
Sparks | **E Midtown**	25
Spice Market | **Meatpacking**	24
Spotted Pig | **W Vill**	24
Standard Grill | **Meatpacking**	22
Swifty's | **E 70s**	16
21 Club | **Midtown**	23
Via Quadronno | **E 70s**	21
Ze Café | **E Midtown**	20

POWER SCENES

ABC Kitchen | **Flatiron**	24
Ai Fiori | **Midtown**	26
Aretsky's Patroon | **E Midtown**	25
Balthazar | **SoHo**	24
Bar Americain | **Midtown**	23
NEW Beautique | **Midtown**	—
Betony | **Midtown**	25
BLT Prime | **Gramercy**	25
BLT Steak | **E Midtown**	24
Bobby Van's | **E Midtown**	23
Bull & Bear | **E Midtown**	23
Carlyle | **E 70s**	23
Casa Lever | **Midtown**	23
China Grill | **Midtown**	23
Cipriani Club 55 | **Financial**	23
City Hall | **TriBeCa**	22
Daniel | **E 60s**	28
Del Frisco's | **Midtown**	25
Del Posto | **Chelsea**	26
Elio's | **E 80s**	24
Forty Four | **Midtown**	21
Four Seasons | **E Midtown**	26
Fresco | **Midtown**	22
Gotham B&G | **G Vill**	28
Harry's Cafe | **Financial**	22
Jean-Georges | **W 60s**	28
Keens | **Midtown**	26
La Grenouille | **Midtown**	28
Lambs Club | **Midtown**	22
Le Bernardin | **Midtown**	29
Le Cirque | **E Midtown**	24
Lion | **G Vill**	24
Marea | **Midtown**	27
Megu | **multi.**	23
Michael's | **Midtown**	22

Modern | **Midtown**	26
Morton's | **Midtown**	24
Nobu | **multi.**	27
NoMad | **Flatiron**	26
Norma's | **Midtown**	24
North End Grill | **Battery Pk**	24
Peter Luger | **W'burg**	28
Rao's | **E Harlem**	21
Regency B&G | **E 60s**	19
Russian Tea | **Midtown**	19
San Pietro | **Midtown**	22
Sant Ambroeus | **multi.**	21
Sirio | **E 60s**	22
Smith/Wollensky | **E Midtown**	25
Sparks | **E Midtown**	25
21 Club | **Midtown**	23

PRIVATE ROOMS/ PARTIES

Acme | **NoHo**	21
Ai Fiori | **Midtown**	26
Aldea | **Flatiron**	21
Alta | **G Vill**	25
Ample Hills | **Gowanus**	27
Aquavit | **Midtown**	26
Aretsky's Patroon | **E Midtown**	25
Aroma Kitchen | **NoHo**	23
Astor Room | **Astoria**	20
Aureole | **Midtown**	26
A Voce | **Midtown**	23
Bacaro | **LES**	24
Bar Americain | **Midtown**	23
Barbetta | **Midtown**	22
Bar Boulud | **W 60s**	24
Barraca | **W Vill**	21
Battery Gdns. | **BPC**	19
Beauty & Essex | **LES**	23
Benoit | **Midtown**	23
Betony | **Midtown**	25
BLT Fish | **Flatiron**	25
BLT Prime | **Gramercy**	25
BLT Steak | **E Midtown**	24
Blue Hill | **G Vill**	26
Blue Smoke | **Kips Bay**	22
Blue Water | **Union Sq**	24
Bocca/Bacco | **multi.**	20
NEW Bodega Negra | **Chelsea**	23
Bond St | **NoHo**	25
Bottega del Vino | **Midtown**	22
Bouley | **TriBeCa**	29

Breslin | **Flatiron**	24
Buddakan | **Chelsea**	25
Café Boulud | **E 70s**	26
Capital Grille | **E Midtown**	24
Casa Lever | **Midtown**	23
Casa Nonna | **Midtown**	22
Catch | **Meatpacking**	23
Ça Va | **Midtown**	22
Cellini | **Midtown**	22
NEW Chester | **Meatpacking**	—
City Hall | **TriBeCa**	22
Colicchio/Sons | **Chelsea**	26
Conviv. Osteria | **Park Slope**	26
Craft | **Flatiron**	26
Crown | **E 80s**	23
Daniel | **E 60s**	28
David Burke Kitchen | **SoHo**	25
db Bistro Moderne | **Midtown**	24
Del Frisco's | **Midtown**	25
Delmonico's | **Financial**	23
Del Posto | **Chelsea**	26
Dévi | **Flatiron**	23
Dinosaur BBQ | **Morningside Hts**	23
Docks Oyster | **Murray Hill**	20
Eleven Madison | **Flatiron**	28
EN Japanese | **W Vill**	25
Felidia | **E Midtown**	25
Fig & Olive | **Meatpacking**	21
Four Seasons | **E Midtown**	26
Fourth | **G Vill**	20
Frankies | **Carroll Gdns**	23
Fraunces Tav. | **Financial**	17
Freemans | **LES**	23
Fresco | **Midtown**	22
Gabriel's | **W 60s**	22
NEW Gander | **Flatiron**	—
General | **LES**	22
Gramercy Tavern | **Flatiron**	28
Hakkasan | **Midtown**	23
Harry's Cafe | **Financial**	22
Hecho en Dumbo | **NoHo**	23
Hudson Clearwater | **W Vill**	22
Il Buco | **NoHo**	26
Il Buco Alimentari | **NoHo**	24
Il Cortile | **L Italy**	22
Ilili | **Flatiron**	26
Jean-Georges | **W 60s**	28
Jungsik | **TriBeCa**	27
Keens | **Midtown**	26
Lafayette | **NoHo**	22

La Grenouille | **Midtown**	28
Landmark Tav. | **Hell's Kit**	19
Le Bernardin | **Midtown**	29
Le Cirque | **E Midtown**	24
Le Perigord | **E Midtown**	24
Le Zie | **Chelsea**	20
Lincoln | **W 60s**	25
Locanda Verde | **TriBeCa**	24
Lupa | **G Vill**	24
Lure Fishbar | **SoHo**	24
Macelleria | **Meatpacking**	24
Maialino | **Gramercy**	25
Maloney & Porcelli | **Midtown**	25
Marcony | **Kips Bay**	25
Marea | **Midtown**	27
Mas | **W Vill**	27
Megu | **TriBeCa**	23
Michael's | **Midtown**	22
Millesime | **Flatiron**	21
Milos | **Midtown**	27
Modern | **Midtown**	26
NEW Monarch Rm. | **Chelsea**	—
Mr. Chow | **E Midtown**	23
Mr. K's | **E Midtown**	23
National | **E Midtown**	19
Nerai | **Midtown**	22
Nobu | **multi.**	27
NoMad | **Flatiron**	26
Oceana | **Midtown**	25
Palma | **W Vill**	25
Park | **Chelsea**	18
Parlor Steakhse. | **E 80s**	22
Pera | **Midtown**	20
Periyali | **Flatiron**	24
Perry St | **W Vill**	26
Per Se | **Midtown**	27
Picholine | **W 60s**	26
Print | **Hell's Kit**	25
Public | **NoLita**	25
Quality Meats | **Midtown**	26
Raoul's | **SoHo**	24
Redeye Grill | **Midtown**	19
Remi | **Midtown**	23
River Café | **Dumbo**	26
Rock Center Café | **Midtown**	19
NEW Rotisserie Georgette | **E 60s**	24
Russian Tea | **Midtown**	19
Salinas | **Chelsea**	22
Saxon & Parole | **NoHo**	24

Scarpetta | **Chelsea**	25
Scottadito | **Park Slope**	22
SD26 | **Flatiron**	25
Sea Fire Grill | **E Midtown**	28
Sea Grill | **Midtown**	24
Sheep Station | **Park Slope**	22
Shun Lee Palace | **E Midtown**	24
Sparks | **E Midtown**	25
Spice Market | **Meatpacking**	24
Stanton Social | **LES**	24
Stone Park | **Park Slope**	24
NEW Tablao | **TriBeCa**	—
Tamarind | **TriBeCa**	26
Tao | **multi.**	23
Tarallucci | **Flatiron**	20
NEW Tavern/Green | **Central Pk**	—
NEW Telepan Local | **TriBeCa**	23
Thalassa | **TriBeCa**	24
NEW Toro | **Chelsea**	25
Tratt. L'incontro | **Astoria**	26
Tocqueville | **Flatiron**	27
Tribeca Grill | **TriBeCa**	22
21 Club | **Midtown**	23
Uncle Jack's | **multi.**	24
Uva | **E 70s**	23
Valbella | **Meatpacking**	24
Victor's Cafe | **Midtown**	24
Vitae | **Midtown**	24
Water Club | **Kips Bay**	22
NEW Wayfarer | **Midtown**	18
Yerba Buena | **E Vill**	22
Zengo | **Murray Hill**	20
Zizi Limona | **W'burg**	24

QUICK BITES

Arepas Café | **Astoria**	23
A Salt & Battery | **W Vill**	22
Azuri Cafe | **Hell's Kit**	25
BaoHaus | **E Vill**	20
Bark | **Park Slope**	20
NEW Baz Bagel | **L Italy**	—
Blossom du Jour | **multi.**	22
Blue Ribbon Fried | **E Vill**	19
Bouchon Bakery | **Midtown**	23
NEW Cafe El Pres. | **Flatiron**	—
Calexico | **multi.**	22
Caracas | **multi.**	26
NEW Cerveceria | **W'burg**	—
Chick P | **Prospect Hts**	—
City Bakery | **Flatiron**	22
Counter | **Midtown**	21

Creperie | multi.	21
Crif Dogs | multi.	23
Daisy May's | Hell's Kit	22
David Burke/Bloom. | E Midtown	20
NEW Dosa Royale | Carroll Gdns	24
Dos Toros | multi.	20
Empanada Mama | Hell's Kit	23
Fresco | Midtown	22
NEW Gotham West | Hell's Kit	25
Gray's Papaya | W 70s	20
Harlem Shake | Harlem	20
NEW Hudson Eats | Battery Pk	—
Hummus Kit. | multi.	20
Hummus Pl. | multi.	21
Island Burgers | multi.	21
Joe's Pizza | G Vill	24
Kati Roll | multi.	22
La Bonne Soupe | Midtown	20
La Esquina | SoHo	23
NEW Little Collins | E Midtown	—
NEW Los Tacos | Chelsea	—
Little Muenster | multi.	21
Luke's Lobster | multi.	24
Mamoun's | multi.	23
NEW Mayhem & Stout | Murray Hill	—
Meatball Shop | multi.	22
Melt Shop | multi.	19
NEW Mimi Cheng's | E Vill	—
Miss Lily's | multi.	20
NEW Mulberry/Vine | TriBeCa	18
Naya Express | multi.	22
Nice Green Bo | Chinatown	22
99 Miles/Philly | G Vill	20
Oaxaca | multi.	21
NEW 100 Montaditos | multi.	20
NEW Otto's Tacos | E Vill	22
Papaya King | E 80s	22
Plaza Food Hall | Midtown	22
Pommes Frites | E Vill	24
Porchetta | E Vill	21
Prosperity Dumpling | LES	23
Schnipper's | multi.	20
NEW Schnitz | E Vill	—
Shake Shack | multi.	21
Shorty's | multi.	21
Smile to Go | SoHo	22
Taboonette | G Vill	24
NEW Taco Santo | Park Slope	—
Taïm | multi.	25

Toby's Estate | W'burg	22
Toloache | Financial	23
Tres Carnes | multi.	22
Two Boots | multi.	19
Vanessa's Dumpling | multi.	25
Via Quadronno | Midtown	21
NEW Wasabi | Midtown	—

QUIET CONVERSATION

Ammos | Midtown	21
Annisa | W Vill	28
Aroma Kitchen | NoHo	23
Asiate | Midtown	26
Aureole | Midtown	26
Basso56 | Midtown	24
Blue Hill | G Vill	26
Bombay Palace | Midtown	21
Bosie Tea Parlor | W Vill	23
Brasserie 8½ | Midtown	22
Cellini | Midtown	22
Chef's/Brooklyn Fare | Downtown Bklyn	28
NEW China Blue | TriBeCa	18
Circus | E 60s	21
Da Umberto | Flatiron	25
Dawat | E Midtown	23
EN Japanese | W Vill	25
Giovanni | E 80s	22
Il Tinello | Midtown	23
Jean-Georges | W 60s	28
Jungsik | TriBeCa	27
Kings' Carriage | E 80s	21
La Grenouille | Midtown	28
Le Bernardin | Midtown	29
Left Bank | W Vill	24
Le Paris Bistrot | E 90s	21
Madison Bistro | Midtown	23
Marea | Midtown	27
Mas | W Vill	27
Masa/Bar Masa | Midtown	25
Millesime | Flatiron	21
Montebello | E Midtown	22
Mr. K's | E Midtown	23
Nerai | Midtown	22
North Sq. | G Vill	25
Palm Court | Midtown	18
Periyali | Flatiron	24
Perry St. | W Vill	26
Per Se | Midtown	27
Petrossian | Midtown	24
Picholine | W 60s	26

Pietro's | **E Midtown** 25
Radiance Tea | **Midtown** 21
Remi | **Midtown** 23
Rosanjin | **TriBeCa** 26
Sapphire Indian | **W 60s** 21
Scaletta | **W 70s** 22
Sfoglia | **E 90s** 25
Sirio | **E 60s** 22
Solera | **E Midtown** 23
South Gate | **Midtown** 20
Tocqueville | **Flatiron** 27
Triomphe | **Midtown** 24
12 Chairs | **SoHo** 22
Villa Berulia | **Murray Hill** 25
Ze Café | **E Midtown** 20
Zenkichi | **W'burg** 27

RAW BARS

Ammos | **Midtown** 21
Anassa Taverna | **E 60s** 21
Aquagrill | **SoHo** 27
Atlantic Grill | **multi.** 22
Balthazar | **SoHo** 24
Bar Americain | **Midtown** 23
BLT Fish | **Flatiron** 25
Blue Fin | **Midtown** 23
Blue Ribbon | **SoHo** 24
Blue Water | **Union Sq** 24
Brooklyn Crab | **Red Hook** 20
Catch | **Meatpacking** 23
City Hall | **TriBeCa** 22
City Lobster/Steak | **Midtown** 21
NEW Clam | **W Vill** 23
Crave Fishbar | **E Midtown** 24
Cull & Pistol | **Chelsea** 24
David Burke Fishtail | **E 60s** 24
Docks Oyster | **Murray Hill** 20
Dutch | **SoHo** 23
Ed's Chowder | **W 60s** 20
Ed's Lobster Bar | **SoHo** 24
Esca | **Hell's Kit** 25
Fish | **W Vill** 23
Flex Mussels | **multi.** 24
NEW Greenpt Fish | **Greenpt** —
Jack the Horse | **Bklyn Hts** 21
Jeffrey's Grocery | **W Vill** 23
John Dory Oyster | **Flatiron** 21
Jordans Lobster | **Sheepshead** 22
Kanoyama | **E Vill** 24
NEW Kingside | **Midtown** 19
L & W Oyster | **Flatiron** 20

La Pulperia | **Midtown** 22
Littleneck | **multi.** 23
London Lennie's | **Middle Vill** 24
Lure Fishbar | **SoHo** 24
Mark | **E 70s** 23
Marlow/Sons | **W'burg** 24
Mercer Kitchen | **SoHo** 21
Mermaid | **multi.** 22
Millesime | **Flatiron** 21
NEW Monarch Rm. | **Chelsea** —
NEW M. Wells Steakhse. | **LIC** 22
NEW Navy | **SoHo** —
Oceana | **Midtown** 25
Ocean Grill | **W 70s** 23
Oyster Bar | **multi.** 22
Parlor Steakhse. | **E 80s** 22
Pearl Oyster | **W Vill** 27
Pearl Room | **Bay Ridge** 22
P.J. Clarke's | **multi.** 19
Plaza Food Hall | **Midtown** 22
Randazzo's | **Sheepshead Bay** 22
South Fin | **South Bch** 19
Standard Grill | **Meatpacking** 22
Thalia | **Midtown** 20
21 Club | **Midtown** 23
Uncle Jack's | **Midtown** 24
Upstate | **E Vill** 25
Walter | **multi.** 22
ZZ's Clam Bar | **G Vill** 24

ROMANTIC PLACES

ABC Kitchen | **Flatiron** 25
Al Di La | **Park Slope** 26
Alta | **G Vill** 25
Annisa | **W Vill** 28
Antica Pesa | **W'burg** 23
Asiate | **Midtown** 26
Aurora | **multi.** 24
Bacaro | **LES** 24
Barbetta | **Midtown** 22
Blue Hill | **G Vill** 26
Boathouse | **Central Pk** 17
Bobo | **W Vill** 24
Bottino | **Chelsea** 21
Bouley | **TriBeCa** 29
Caviar Russe | **Midtown** 21
Cherry | **Chelsea** 22
Conviv. Osteria | **Park Slope** 26
Crema | **Flatiron** 22
Daniel | **E 60s** 28
Del Posto | **Chelsea** 26

Eleven Madison | **Flatiron**	28
El Quinto Pino | **Chelsea**	25
Erminia | **E 80s**	23
Firenze | **E 80s**	23
Four Seasons | **E Midtown**	26
Gemma | **E Vill**	23
Good Fork | **Red Hook**	23
Gramercy Tavern | **Flatiron**	28
House | **Gramercy**	23
Il Buco | **NoHo**	26
I Sodi | **W Vill**	25
I Trulli | **Kips Bay**	23
JoJo | **E 60s**	24
Kings' Carriage | **E 80s**	21
L'Absinthe | **E 60s**	23
La Grenouille | **Midtown**	28
La Lanterna | **G Vill**	20
La Mangeoire | **E Midtown**	23
Lambs Club | **Midtown**	22
L'Artusi | **W Vill**	26
La Vara | **Cobble Hill**	26
Le Gigot | **W Vill**	24
Little Owl | **W Vill**	27
Locale | **Astoria**	21
Mas | **W Vill**	27
Morimoto | **Chelsea**	26
Mr. K's | **E Midtown**	23
NEW Navy | **SoHo**	–
NoMad | **Flatiron**	26
Olea | **Ft Greene**	24
One if by Land | **W Vill**	23
Ovelia | **Astoria**	21
Palma | **W Vill**	25
Paola's | **E 90s**	23
NEW Pavilion | **Union Sq**	–
Peasant | **NoLita**	25
Piadina | **G Vill**	22
Place | **W Vill**	23
Raoul's | **SoHo**	24
Recette | **W Vill**	24
River Café | **Dumbo**	26
Rouge et Blanc | **SoHo**	23
Rye | **W'burg**	24
Salinas | **Chelsea**	22
Scalini Fedeli | **TriBeCa**	26
Scarpetta | **Chelsea**	25
Sistina | **E 80s**	23
Spice Market | **Meatpacking**	24
Spiga | **W 80s**	22
Tocqueville | **Flatiron**	27

Uva | **E 70s**	23
View | **Midtown**	17
Vinegar Hill Hse. | **Vinegar Hill**	24
Wallsé | **W Vill**	25
Water Club | **Kips Bay**	22
Water's Edge | **LIC**	22
Zenkichi | **W'burg**	27
ZZ's Clam Bar | **G Vill**	24

SENIOR APPEAL

Artie's | **City Is**	22
Aureole | **Midtown**	26
Bamonte's | **W'burg**	23
Barbetta | **Midtown**	22
Barney Greengrass | **W 80s**	24
Benoit | **Midtown**	23
Bistro Vendôme | **E Midtown**	22
Chez Napoléon | **Midtown**	22
Club A Steak | **E Midtown**	23
Dawat | **E Midtown**	23
DeGrezia | **E Midtown**	25
Delmonico's | **Financial**	23
Del Posto | **Chelsea**	26
Due | **E 70s**	22
Embers | **Bay Ridge**	23
Felidia | **E Midtown**	25
Gabriel's | **W 60s**	22
Giovanni | **E 80s**	22
Il Gattopardo | **Midtown**	25
Il Tinello | **Midtown**	23
Ithaka | **E 80s**	22
Jubilee | **E Midtown**	21
Kings' Carriage | **E 80s**	21
La Bonne Soupe | **Midtown**	20
La Grenouille | **Midtown**	28
La Mangeoire | **E Midtown**	23
Lattanzi | **Midtown**	23
Le Cirque | **E Midtown**	24
Leopard/des Artistes | **W 60s**	22
Le Perigord | **E Midtown**	24
Lusardi's | **E 70s**	25
Mark | **E 70s**	23
Mr. K's | **E Midtown**	23
Nerai | **Midtown**	22
Nicola's | **E 80s**	22
Soba Nippon | **Midtown**	22
Palm Court | **Midtown**	18
Piccolo Angolo | **W Vill**	25
Pietro's | **E Midtown**	25
Ponticello | **Astoria**	23
Primola | **E 60s**	23

Quatorze Bis	**E 70s**	20
Remi	**Midtown**	23
NEW Rist. Morini	**E 80s**	26
Rossini's	**Murray Hill**	22
NEW Rotisserie Georgette	**E 60s**	24
Russian Tea	**Midtown**	19
San Pietro	**Midtown**	22
Sardi's	**Midtown**	19
Scaletta	**W 70s**	22
Shun Lee West	**W 60s**	22
Sirio	**E 60s**	22
Sistina	**E 80s**	23
Triomphe	**Midtown**	24
Tuscany Grill	**Bay Ridge**	25
Villa Berulia	**Murray Hill**	25
Ze Café	**E Midtown**	20

STARGAZING

Antica Pesa	**W'burg**	23
Balthazar	**SoHo**	24
Bar Pitti	**G Vill**	23
Beatrice Inn	**W Vill**	20
Bill's Food/Drink	**Midtown**	18
Bond St	**NoHo**	25
Cafe Luxembourg	**W 70s**	21
Carbone	**G Vill**	24
Catch	**Meatpacking**	23
Da Silvano	**G Vill**	21
Elio's	**E 80s**	24
Il Cantinori	**G Vill**	23
Joe Allen	**Midtown**	18
Le Bilboquet	**E 60s**	21
Leopard/des Artistes	**W 60s**	22
Lion	**G Vill**	24
Marea	**Midtown**	27
Michael's	**Midtown**	22
Minetta Tavern	**G Vill**	24
NoMad	**Flatiron**	26
Orso	**Midtown**	24
Philippe	**E 60s**	23
Primola	**E 60s**	23
Rao's	**E Harlem**	21
Red Rooster	**Harlem**	22
Spotted Pig	**W Vill**	24
Standard Grill	**Meatpacking**	22
Waverly Inn	**W Vill**	22

TOUGH TICKETS

ABC Kitchen	**Flatiron**	25
Babbo	**G Vill**	26

Blanca	**Bushwick**	24
Carbone	**G Vill**	24
Chef's/Brooklyn Fare	**Downtown Bklyn**	28
NEW Cherche Midi	**NoLita**	–
NEW Clam	**W Vill**	23
NEW Dirty French	**LES**	–
NEW Gato	**NoHo**	24
Luksus	**Greenpt**	23
Minetta Tavern	**G Vill**	24
Momofuku Ko	**E Vill**	27
NoMad	**Flatiron**	26
Rao's	**E Harlem**	21
NEW Sushi Nakazawa	**W Vill**	27
ZZ's Clam Bar	**G Vill**	24

TRANSPORTING EXPERIENCES

Asiate	**Midtown**	26
Balthazar	**SoHo**	24
Beauty & Essex	**LES**	23
Boathouse	**Central Pk**	17
Buddakan	**Chelsea**	25
Cafe China	**Midtown**	23
Il Buco	**NoHo**	26
Ilili	**Flatiron**	26
Keens	**Midtown**	26
La Grenouille	**Midtown**	28
Lambs Club	**Midtown**	22
Le Colonial	**E Midtown**	23
Library/Public	**G Vill**	18
Masa/Bar Masa	**Midtown**	25
Megu	**TriBeCa**	23
Monkey Bar	**Midtown**	18
Ninja	**TriBeCa**	13
NEW Pavilion	**Union Sq**	–
Per Se	**Midtown**	27
Qi	**Flatiron**	21
Rao's	**E Harlem**	21
Spice Market	**Meatpacking**	24
Tao	**multi.**	23
NEW Urbo	**Midtown**	–
NEW Tavern/Green	**Central Pk**	–
Water's Edge	**LIC**	22
NEW Water Table	**Kips Bay**	–
Waverly Inn	**W Vill**	22

24-HOUR DINING

NEW BCD Tofu	**Midtown**	22
Bubby's	**TriBeCa**	19
Cafeteria	**Chelsea**	20

Coppelia	Chelsea	20
Empanada Mama	Hell's Kit	24
Gahm Mi Oak	Midtown	22
Gray's Papaya	W 70s	20
Kum Gang San	multi.	21
Kunjip	Midtown	22
New WonJo	Midtown	23
Sanford's	Astoria	24
Sarge's Deli	Murray Hill	23
Veselka	E Vill	21

VIEWS

Alma	Columbia St.	20
Angelina's	Tottenville	23
Asiate	Midtown	26
A Voce	Midtown	23
Bakehse. Bistro	Meatpacking	21
Battery Gdns.	BPC	19
Birreria	Flatiron	20
Boathouse	Central Pk	17
Brooklyn Crab	Red Hook	20
Bryant Pk Grill/Cafe	Midtown	18
City Is. Lobster	City Is	22
Gaonnuri	Midtown	20
Gigino	Battery Pk	20
NEW Hudson Eats	Battery Pk	—
Jake's Steakhse.	Fieldston	23
Lincoln	W 60s	25
Michael Jordan	Midtown	21
Modern	Midtown	26
Morso	E Midtown	23
Per Se	Midtown	27
NEW Pine Tree Cafe	Bronx Pk	—
P.J. Clarke's	Battery Pk	19
Porter House	Midtown	26
Randazzo's	Sheepshead Bay	22
Rare B&G	multi.	21
River Café	Dumbo	26
Riverpark	Kips Bay	25
Robert	Midtown	22
Rock Center Café	Midtown	19
Sea Grill	Midtown	24
Shi	LIC	22
South Fin Grill	South Bch	19
South Gate	Midtown	20
NEW Stella 34	Midtown	23
View	Midtown	17
Water Club	Kips Bay	22
Water's Edge	LIC	22

VISITORS ON EXPENSE ACCOUNT

Ai Fiori	Midtown	26
NEW American Cut	TriBeCa	24
Aureole	Midtown	26
Babbo	G Vill	26
Bouley	TriBeCa	29
Café Boulud	E 70s	26
Carbone	G Vill	24
Colicchio/Sons	Chelsea	26
Craft	Flatiron	26
Daniel	E 60s	28
Del Frisco's	Midtown	25
Del Posto	Chelsea	26
Eleven Madison	Flatiron	28
Four Seasons	E Midtown	26
Gari	Midtown	26
Gramercy Tavern	Flatiron	28
Hakkasan	Midtown	23
Il Mulino	G Vill	25
Jean-Georges	W 60s	28
Keens	Midtown	26
Kurumazushi	Midtown	25
La Grenouille	Midtown	28
Lambs Club	Midtown	22
Le Bernardin	Midtown	29
Le Cirque	E Midtown	24
Marea	Midtown	27
Masa/Bar Masa	Midtown	25
Milos	Midtown	27
Modern	Midtown	26
Nobu	multi.	27
Palm	multi.	25
Per Se	Midtown	27
Peter Luger	W'burg	28
Picholine	W 60s	26
NEW Rist. Morini	E 80s	26
River Café	Dumbo	26
Scarpetta	Chelsea	25
Spice Market	Meatpacking	24
NEW Sushi Nakazawa	W Vill	27
Sushi Yasuda	E Midtown	28
Union Sq. Cafe	Union Sq	27

WINE BARS

Alta	G Vill	25
Aroma Kitchen	NoHo	23
Bacaro	LES	24
Bacchus	Downtown Bklyn	21
Balkanika	Hell's Kit	21
NEW Barawine	Harlem	20

Bar Boulud | **W 60s**	24
Bar Jamón | **Gramercy**	22
Bocca/Bacco | **multi.**	20
Bocca Lupo | **Cobble Hill**	22
Bottega Del Vino | **Midtown**	22
Casellula | **Hell's Kit**	25
Corkbuzz | **multi.**	21
Danny Brown | **Forest Hills**	26
El Quinto Pino | **Chelsea**	25
Felice | **E 60s**	21
Il Buco Alimentari | **NoHo**	24
I Trulli | **Kips Bay**	23
L'Albero/Gelati | **Park Slope**	23
Le Bernardin | **Midtown**	29
Mozzarella & Vino | **Midtown**	22
Murray's Cheese Bar | **W Vill**	23
Otto | **G Vill**	23
Palma | **W Vill**	25
Peasant | **NoLita**	25
NEW Racines | **TriBeCa**	—
Salumeria/Rist. Rosi | **W 70s**	24
SD26 | **Flatiron**	25
Stonehome | **Ft Greene**	21
Sweet Revenge | **W Vill**	22
Tarallucci | **multi.**	20
NEW Terra Tribeca | **TriBeCa**	21
Terroir | **multi.**	20
Tolani | **W 70s**	21
Uva | **E 70s**	23
Vesta | **Astoria**	25

WINNING WINE LISTS

ABC Cocina | **Flatiron**	24
ABC Kitchen | **Flatiron**	25
Aldea | **Flatiron**	24
NEW All'onda | **G Vill**	23
Alta | **G Vill**	25
Amali | **E 60s**	24
Annisa | **W Vill**	28
Asiate | **Midtown**	26
Aureole | **Midtown**	26
A Voce | **multi.**	23
Babbo | **G Vill**	26
NEW Bacchanal | **L Italy**	—
Balthazar | **SoHo**	24
Barbetta | **Midtown**	22
Bar Boulud | **W 60s**	24
NEW Bâtard | **TriBeCa**	—
Becco | **Midtown**	23
Betony | **Midtown**	25
BLT Fish | **Flatiron**	25

BLT Prime | **Gramercy**	25
BLT Steak | **E Midtown**	24
Blue Fin | **Midtown**	23
Blue Hill | **G Vill**	26
Bobby Van's | **multi.**	23
Bottega Del Vino | **Midtown**	22
Bouley | **TriBeCa**	29
Brushstroke/Ichimura | **TriBeCa**	26
Café Boulud | **E 70s**	26
Cafe Katja | **LES**	25
Capital Grille | **E Midtown**	24
Carbone | **G Vill**	24
Casa Mono | **Gramercy**	24
'Cesca | **W 70s**	24
Charlie Bird | **SoHo**	25
Chef's/Brooklyn Fare | **Downtown Bklyn**	28
City Hall | **TriBeCa**	22
NEW Claudette | **G Vill**	—
Cocotte | **SoHo**	23
Costata | **SoHo**	25
Craft | **Flatiron**	26
Crown | **E 80s**	23
Daniel | **E 60s**	28
db Bistro Moderne | **Midtown**	24
Del Frisco's | **Midtown**	25
Dell'anima | **W Vill**	25
Del Posto | **Chelsea**	26
NEW Élan | **Flatiron**	—
Eleven Madison | **Flatiron**	28
Esca | **Hell's Kit**	25
Estela | **NoLita**	25
Felidia | **E Midtown**	25
Frankies | **multi.**	23
Franny's | **Park Slope**	25
NEW Gander | **Flatiron**	—
NEW Gato | **NoHo**	24
Gotham B&G | **G Vill**	28
Gramercy Tavern | **Flatiron**	28
Harry's Cafe | **Financial**	22
Hearth | **E Vill**	25
Il Buco | **NoHo**	26
I Trulli | **Kips Bay**	23
Jean-Georges | **W 60s**	28
Junoon | **Flatiron**	24
Lafayette | **NoHo**	22
Lambs Club | **Midtown**	22
Landmarc | **multi.**	20
La Pizza Fresca | **Flatiron**	23
La Vara | **Cobble Hill**	26

Restaurant		Score
Le Bernardin	**Midtown**	29
Le Cirque	**E Midtown**	24
Lupa	**G Vill**	24
Maialino	**Gramercy**	25
Marc Forgione	**TriBeCa**	25
NEW Marco's	**Prospect Hts**	24
Marea	**Midtown**	27
Mas	**W Vill**	27
Megu	**TriBeCa**	23
Michael's	**Midtown**	22
Milos	**Midtown**	27
Minetta Tavern	**G Vill**	24
Modern	**Midtown**	26
Musket Room	**NoLita**	26
NEW M. Wells Steakhse.	**LIC**	22
NEW Narcissa	**E Vill**	27
Nice Matin	**W 70s**	19
NoMad	**Flatiron**	26
Oceana	**Midtown**	25
Osteria Morini	**SoHo**	25
Otto	**G Vill**	23
Ouest	**W 80s**	22
Pearl & Ash	**NoLita**	24
Per Se	**Midtown**	27
Picholine	**W 60s**	26
Porter House	**Midtown**	26
Pure Food/Wine	**Gramercy**	24
NEW Racines	**TriBeCa**	—
Raoul's	**SoHo**	24
Reynard	**W'burg**	23
NEW Rist. Morini	**E 80s**	26
River Café	**Dumbo**	26
NEW Rotisserie Georgette	**E 60s**	24
Rouge et Blanc	**SoHo**	23
San Pietro	**Midtown**	22
Scalini Fedeli	**TriBeCa**	26
Scarpetta	**Chelsea**	25
SD26	**Flatiron**	25
Seäsonal	**Midtown**	24
NEW Simone	**E 80s**	25
Sirio	**E 60s**	22
Sistina	**E 80s**	23
Smith/Wollensky	**E Midtown**	25
Solera	**E Midtown**	23
Sparks	**E Midtown**	25
Thalassa	**TriBeCa**	24
Tía Pol	**Chelsea**	23
Tommaso	**Bath Bch**	23
Tocqueville	**Flatiron**	27
Trestle on 10th	**Chelsea**	20
Tribeca Grill	**TriBeCa**	22
21 Club	**Midtown**	23
Txikito	**Chelsea**	26
Union Sq. Cafe	**Union Sq**	27
Valbella	**Meatpacking**	24
Via Emilia	**Flatiron**	22
Vinegar Hill Hse.	**Vinegar Hill**	24
Wallsé	**W Vill**	25
Water's Edge	**LIC**	22

Cuisines

Includes names, locations and Food ratings.

AFGHAN

Afghan Kebab	**multi.**	20

AFRICAN

Ponty Bistro	**Gramercy**	24

AMERICAN

ABC Kitchen	**Flatiron**	25
Acme	**NoHo**	21
Alchemy	**Park Slope**	20
Alder	**E Vill**	22
Alice's Tea	**multi.**	20
Allswell	**W'burg**	22
Alobar	**LIC**	22
Annisa	**W Vill**	28
Applewood	**Park Slope**	24
Aretsky's Patroon	**E Midtown**	25
Asiate	**Midtown**	26
Astor Room	**Astoria**	20
Atera	**TriBeCa**	26
Atrium Dumbo	**Dumbo**	23
Aureole	**Midtown**	26
NEW Bacchanal	**L Italy**	—
Back Forty	**multi.**	22
B&B Winepub	**SoHo**	21
Bar Americain	**Midtown**	23
NEW Barawine	**Harlem**	20
NEW BarBacon	**Midtown**	22
NEW Bâtard	**TriBeCa**	—
Battersby	**Boerum Hill**	27
Battery Gdns.	**BPC**	19
Beatrice Inn	**W Vill**	20
NEW Beautique	**Midtown**	—
Beauty & Essex	**LES**	23
Beecher's Cellar	**Flatiron**	21
Bell Book/Candle	**W Vill**	23
Benchmark	**Park Slope**	21
Betony	**Midtown**	25
Bill's Food/Drink	**Midtown**	18
Black Whale	**City Is**	23
Blanca	**Bushwick**	24
BLT B&G	**Financial**	22
Blue Hill	**G Vill**	26
Blue Ribbon	**multi.**	24
Blue Ribbon Bakery	**W Vill**	23
Blue Ribbon Fried	**E Vill**	19

Boathouse	**Central Pk**	17
Boulton & Watt	**E Vill**	22
Brindle Room	**E Vill**	20
Bryant Pk Grill/Cafe	**Midtown**	18
Bubby's	**multi.**	19
Butter	**Midtown**	23
Butterfly	**TriBeCa**	19
Buttermilk	**Carroll Gdns**	25
Cafe Cluny	**W Vill**	21
NEW Cafe Standard	**E Vill**	20
Cafeteria	**Chelsea**	20
Camaje	**G Vill**	20
Casellula	**Hell's Kit**	25
Caviar Russe	**Midtown**	21
NEW Cecil	**Harlem**	23
Chadwick's	**Bay Ridge**	23
NEW Chalk Point	**SoHo**	—
Charlie Bird	**SoHo**	25
NEW Chester	**Meatpacking**	—
Cibo	**Murray Hill**	22
Cleveland	**NoLita**	22
Clinton St. Baking	**LES**	24
Colicchio/Sons	**Chelsea**	26
Colonie	**Bklyn Hts**	24
Commerce	**W Vill**	23
Community	**Morningside Hts**	21
NEW Contra	**LES**	25
Cookshop	**Chelsea**	23
Cornelia St.	**W Vill**	20
Craft	**Flatiron**	26
Craftbar	**Flatiron**	23
Crown	**E 80s**	23
David Burke/Bloom.	**E Midtown**	20
NEW David Burke Fab.	**Midtown**	—
David Burke Kitchen	**SoHo**	25
Diner	**W'burg**	23
NEW Dinner on Ludlow	**LES**	21
Distilled	**TriBeCa**	23
Donovan's	**multi.**	21
NEW Dover	**Carroll Gdns**	27
Dovetail	**W 70s**	27
Dutch	**SoHo**	23

NEW Dutch Kills Centraal	**LIC**	21
Dylan Prime	**TriBeCa**	18
NEW East & West	**Hell's Kit**	—
NEW East Pole	**E 60s**	22
East End Kitchen	**E 80s**	21
E.A.T.	**E 80s**	20
NEW Eddy	**E Vill**	—
NEW Élan	**Flatiron**	—
Eleven Madison	**Flatiron**	28
Estela	**NoLita**	25
Fat Radish	**LES**	21
Farm/Adderley	**Ditmas Pk**	23
Fedora	**W Vill**	22
5 & Diamond	**Harlem**	21
Five Leaves	**Greenpt**	24
Five Points	**NoHo**	21
Flatbush Farm	**Park Slope**	21
Fort Defiance	**Red Hook**	23
Forty Four	**Midtown**	21
44 & X/44½	**Hell's Kit**	22
Four Seasons	**E Midtown**	26
Fourth	**G Vill**	20
Fred's at Barneys	**E 60s**	22
Freemans	**LES**	23
NEW French Louie	**Boerum Hill**	26
Friedman's Lunch	**Chelsea**	21
Friend/Farmer	**Gramercy**	20
Fritzl's Lunch	**Bushwick**	—
NEW Gander	**Flatiron**	—
Garden Café	**Inwood**	20
General Greene	**Ft Greene**	20
Ginny's Supper Club	**Harlem**	21
Giorgio's	**Flatiron**	23
Glass House	**Midtown**	20
Good	**W Vill**	22
Good Enough/Eat	**W 80s**	20
Gotham B&G	**G Vill**	28
Gramercy Tavern	**Flatiron**	28
Green Table	**Chelsea**	24
Grey Dog	**multi.**	22
NEW Grindhaus	**Red Hook**	—
Grocery	**Carroll Gdns**	27
Harrison	**TriBeCa**	22
Hearth	**E Vill**	25
Henry's End	**Bklyn Hts**	24
Hillstone	**multi.**	22
House	**Gramercy**	23
Hudson Clearwater	**W Vill**	22

NEW Humboldt/Jackson	**W'burg**	—
Hundred Acres	**SoHo**	23
Isabella's	**W 70s**	20
Jack the Horse	**Bklyn Hts**	21
Jacob's Pickles	**W 80s**	21
James	**Prospect Hts**	23
Jane	**G Vill**	21
Jeffrey's Grocery	**W Vill**	23
Joe Allen	**Midtown**	18
Joseph Leonard	**W Vill**	24
Juni	**Midtown**	27
Juventino	**Park Slope**	26
Kings' Carriage	**E 80s**	21
NEW Kingside	**Midtown**	19
Knickerbocker	**G Vill**	22
NEW Krupa	**Windsor Terr.**	—
Ktchn	**Hell's Kit**	21
Lambs Club	**Midtown**	22
Left Bank	**W Vill**	24
Lexington Brass	**E Midtown**	20
Library/Public	**G Vill**	18
LIC Market	**LIC**	25
Lion	**G Vill**	24
Little Owl	**W Vill**	27
Lodge	**W'burg**	22
Lot 2	**Park Slope**	24
Louro	**W Vill**	26
Luksus	**Greenpt**	23
Lulu & Po	**Ft Greene**	25
Má Pêche	**Midtown**	23
Marc Forgione	**TriBeCa**	25
Mark	**E 70s**	23
Market Table	**W Vill**	24
Marlow/Sons	**W'burg**	24
NEW Marshal	**Hell's Kit**	24
Martha	**Ft Greene**	22
Mas	**W Vill**	27
Mayfield	**Crown Hts**	24
Maysville	**Flatiron**	21
NEW Meadowsweet	**W'burg**	—
Melba's	**Harlem**	24
Mercer Kitchen	**SoHo**	21
Mike's Bistro	**E Midtown**	25
Modern	**Midtown**	26
Momofuku Ko	**E Vill**	27
Momofuku Noodle	**E Vill**	23
Momofuku Ssäm Bar	**E Vill**	25

Restaurant	Location	Score
NEW Monarch Rm.	Chelsea	—
Monkey Bar	Midtown	18
Monument Lane	W Vill	22
NEW Mulberry/Vine	TriBeCa	18
Murray's Cheese Bar	W Vill	23
NEW Narcissa	E Vill	27
National	E Midtown	19
New Leaf	Inwood	22
NoHo Star	NoHo	19
Noir	E Midtown	24
NoMad	Flatiron	26
NEW NoMad Bar	Flatiron	—
Norma's	Midtown	24
Northeast Kingdom	Bushwick	25
North End Grill	Battery Pk	24
Northern Spy	E Vill	22
North Sq.	G Vill	25
No. 7	multi.	21
Oceana	Midtown	25
Odeon	TriBeCa	20
One if by Land	W Vill	23
101	Bay Ridge	21
Ouest	W 80s	22
NEW Pacifico's	Crown Hts	—
Palm Court	Midtown	18
NEW Park Avenue	Flatiron	—
NEW Parker/Quinn	Midtown	23
NEW Pavilion	Union Sq	—
Pearl & Ash	NoLita	24
Penelope	Kips Bay	22
Penrose	E 80s	20
Perilla	W Vill	24
Perry St.	W Vill	26
Per Se	Midtown	27
Philip Marie	W Vill	19
NEW Pickle Shack	Gowanus	—
Pines	Gowanus	21
NEW Pine Tree Cafe	Bronx Pk	—
NEW Piora	W Vill	26
Place	W Vill	23
Potlikker	W'burg	22
Prime Meats	Carroll Gdns	24
Print	Hell's Kit	25
Prospect	Ft Greene	23
Prune	E Vill	24
Quality Meats	Midtown	26
Recette	W Vill	24
Red Cat	Chelsea	24
Redeye Grill	Midtown	19
Red Rooster	Harlem	22
Regency B&G	E 60s	19
Reynard	W'burg	23
River Café	Dumbo	26
Riverpark	Kips Bay	25
River Styx	Greenpt	—
Robert	Midtown	22
Rock Center Café	Midtown	19
Roebling Tea Room	W'burg	21
Rose Water	Park Slope	25
NEW Runner	Clinton Hill	—
Runner & Stone	Gowanus	22
Rye	W'burg	24
Salt & Fat	Sunnyside	25
Sanford's	Astoria	24
Sarabeth's	multi.	20
NEW Saul	Prospect Hts	23
Saxon & Parole	NoHo	24
Schnipper's	multi.	20
Serendipity 3	E 60s	19
606 R&D	Prospect Hts	23
S'MAC	multi.	23
Smith	multi.	19
Soigne	Park Slope	22
Sojourn	E 70s	25
South Gate	Midtown	20
Standard Grill	Meatpacking	22
St. Anselm	W'burg	28
Stonehome	Ft Greene	21
Stone Park	Park Slope	24
Sunshine Co.	Prospect Hts	22
Swifty's	E 70s	16
Swine	W Vill	20
Table d'Hôte	E 90s	23
NEW Tavern/Green	Central Pk	—
Telepan	W 60s	26
NEW Telepan Local	TriBeCa	23
Thalia	Midtown	20
Thistle Hill	Park Slope	21
Tiny's	TriBeCa	21
Tocqueville	Flatiron	27
Trestle on 10th	Chelsea	20
Tribeca Grill	TriBeCa	22
12th St. B&G	Park Slope	21
12 Chairs	SoHo	22
21 Club	Midtown	23
2 West	Battery Pk	22

CUISINES

Union Sq. Cafe | **Union Sq**	27
Vanderbilt | **Prospect Hts**	21
View | **Midtown**	17
Vinegar Hill Hse. | **Vinegar Hill**	24
Vitae | **Midtown**	24
Walter | **multi.**	22
Water Club | **Kips Bay**	22
Water's Edge | **LIC**	22
Watty & Meg | **Cobble Hill**	20
Waverly Inn | **W Vill**	22
NEW Wayfarer | **Midtown**	18
West Bank | **Hell's Kit**	19
Westville | **multi.**	23
NEW White Street | **TriBeCa**	—
Wild | **multi.**	—
Willow Road | **Chelsea**	22
NEW Winslow | **Gramercy**	—
NEW Writing Room | **E 80s**	22

ARGENTINEAN

Buenos Aires | **E Vill**	22
Chimichurri Grill | **Hell's Kit**	21

ARMENIAN

Almayass | **Flatiron**	23

ASIAN

Asiate | **Midtown**	26
Buddakan | **Chelsea**	25
Cafe Asean | **W Vill**	22
China Grill | **Midtown**	23
Citrus B&G | **W 70s**	20
NEW East & West | **Hell's Kit**	—
East Pacific | **multi.**	24
Fatty Fish | **E 60s**	21
General | **LES**	22
NEW Milk River | **Prospect Hts**	22
Pig and Khao | **LES**	24
Purple Yam | **Ditmas Pk**	23
Qi | **multi.**	21
Red Bamboo | **G Vill**	22
Ruby Foo's | **Midtown**	19
Salt & Fat | **Sunnyside**	25
Shi | **LIC**	22
Spice Market | **Meatpacking**	24
Talde | **Park Slope**	25
Tao | **multi.**	23
Wild Ginger | **multi.**	22
Zengo | **Murray Hill**	20
Zen Palate | **Murray Hill**	20

AUSTRALIAN

NEW Flinders Lane | **E Vill**	—
Sheep Station | **Park Slope**	22

AUSTRIAN

Blaue Gans | **TriBeCa**	22
Cafe Katja | **LES**	25
Café Sabarsky/Fledermaus | **E 80s**	22
Edi & The Wolf | **E Vill**	19
Mont Blanc | **Midtown**	21
Seäsonal | **Midtown**	24
Wallsé | **W Vill**	25

BAKERIES

Balthazar | **SoHo**	24
NEW Baz Bagel | **L Italy**	—
Bouchon Bakery | **multi.**	23
ChikaLicious | **E Vill**	23
City Bakery | **Flatiron**	22
Clinton St. Baking | **LES**	24
Ferrara | **L Italy**	23
NEW Ladurée | **SoHo**	24
Lafayette | **NoHo**	22
Le Pain Q. | **multi.**	18
Maison Kayser | **multi.**	22
Runner & Stone | **Gowanus**	22

BARBECUE

Blue Smoke | **multi.**	22
BrisketTown | **W'burg**	24
Brother Jimmy's | **multi.**	17
Butcher Bar | **Astoria**	21
Daisy May's | **Hell's Kit**	22
Dinosaur BBQ | **multi.**	23
Fette Sau | **W'burg**	26
Fletcher's | **Gowanus**	20
Hill Country | **multi.**	23
NEW Hometown | **Red Hook**	—
John Brown Smokehse. | **LIC**	25
Mable's Smokehse. | **W'burg**	23
Mighty Quinn's | **multi.**	26
Morgans BBQ | **Prospect Hts**	22
Pork Slope | **Park Slope**	19
Smoke Joint | **Ft Greene**	23
Virgil's | **Midtown**	20

BELGIAN

B. Café | **multi.**	21
Cannibal | **Hell's Kit**	21
Le Pain Q. | **multi.**	18

Petite Abeille	**multi.**	20
Pommes Frites	**E Vill**	24
Resto	**Kips Bay**	20

BRAZILIAN

NEW Botequim	G Vill	—
Churrascaria	**Midtown**	24
Circus	**E 60s**	21
NEW Fogo de Chão	**Midtown**	24
NEW Pacifico's	**Crown Hts**	—
NEW Texas de Brazil	**E 60s**	24
Via Brasil	**Midtown**	20

BRITISH

A Salt & Battery	**W Vill**	22
Breslin	**Flatiron**	24
ChipShop	**multi.**	20
NEW East Pole	**E 60s**	22
Jones Wood Foundry	**E 70s**	21
NEW Peacock	**Midtown**	22
Tea & Sympathy	**W Vill**	21
Whitehall	**W Vill**	21
NEW Winslow	**Gramercy**	—

BURGERS

Back Forty	**multi.**	22
B&B Winepub	**SoHo**	21
BareBurger	**multi.**	21
Black Iron Burger	**E Vill**	23
Blue 9 Burger	**multi.**	20
Bonnie's Grill	**Park Slope**	22
Brgr	**multi.**	20
Burger Bistro	**multi.**	21
Burger Joint	**multi.**	23
Corner Bistro	**multi.**	22
Counter	**Midtown**	21
db Bistro Moderne	**Midtown**	24
Donovan's	**Bayside**	21
DuMont Burger	**W'burg**	21
5 Napkin Burger	**multi.**	20
Harlem Shake	**Harlem**	20
Island Burgers	**multi.**	21
Jackson Hole	**multi.**	20
J.G. Melon	**E 70s**	21
Keens	**Midtown**	26
NEW Little Prince	**SoHo**	23
Minetta Tavern	**G Vill**	24
Peter Luger	**W'burg**	28
P.J. Clarke's	**multi.**	19
Pork Slope	**Park Slope**	19

NEW Ramen. Co	**Financial**	—
Rare B&G	**multi.**	21
Schnipper's	**multi.**	20
Shake Shack	**multi.**	21
67 Burger	**multi.**	22
Spotted Pig	**W Vill**	24
21 Club	**Midtown**	23
Umami Burger	**G Vill**	23

CAJUN/CREOLE

Bayou	**Rosebank**	24
NEW Bo's	**Flatiron**	20
Delta Grill	**Midtown**	20
Great Jones Cafe	**NoHo**	23

CALIFORNIAN

Michael's	**Midtown**	22

CAMBODIAN

NEW Cafe Cambodge	**E Vill**	—
Num Pang	**multi.**	23

CARIBBEAN

A Cafe/Wine Rm.	**W 100s**	24
Ali's Roti	**multi.**	24
NEW Glady's	**Crown Hts**	—
Kaz an Nou	**Prospect Hts**	22
NEW Milk River	**Prospect Hts**	22
Negril	**G Vill**	23
NEW Norman's Cay	**LES**	—

CAVIAR

Caviar Russe	**Midtown**	21
Petrossian	**Midtown**	24
Russian Tea	**Midtown**	19

CHEESE SPECIALISTS

Artisanal	**Midtown**	23
Beecher's Cellar	**Flatiron**	21
Casellula	**Hell's Kit**	25
Murray's Cheese Bar	**W Vill**	23
Picholine	**W 60s**	26

CHEESESTEAKS

Shorty's	**multi.**	21
99 Miles/Philly	**multi.**	20

CHICKEN

Blue Ribbon Fried	**E Vill**	19
BonChon	**multi.**	21
Coco Roco	**multi.**	21
Hill Country Chicken	**multi.**	20
Kyochon	**multi.**	20

Malecon | **multi.**	20
Pies-N-Thighs | **W'burg**	24
Pio Pio | **multi.**	22
Torishin | **E 60s**	25
Yakitori Totto | **Midtown**	25

CHINESE
(* dim sum specialist)

BaoHaus | **E Vill**	20
Biang! | **Flushing**	25
Big Wong | **Chinatown**	21
Bo-Ky | **multi.**	21
Buddha Bodai* | **Chinatown**	22
Cafe China | **Midtown**	23
Cafe Evergreen* | **E 70s**	22
Chef Ho's | **E 80s**	22
NEW China Blue* | **TriBeCa**	18
Chin Chin | **E Midtown**	22
Congee | **LES**	20
NEW Decoy | **W Vill**	—
Dim Sum Go Go* | **Chinatown**	21
Excellent Dumpling* | **Chinatown**	24
Flor/Mayo | **multi.**	21
456 Shanghai | **Chinatown**	22
NEW Fung Tu | **LES**	23
Golden Unicorn* | **Chinatown**	22
Grand Sichuan | **multi.**	19
Great NY Noodle | **Chinatown**	23
Hakkasan | **Midtown**	23
NEW Han Dynasty | **G Vill**	23
Hop Kee | **Chinatown**	21
Jing Fong* | **Chinatown**	21
Joe's Shanghai | **multi.**	22
Legend | **multi.**	20
Lotus Blue | **TriBeCa**	23
NEW Lucky Luna | **Greenpt**	—
Lychee House* | **E Midtown**	23
Macao Trading | **TriBeCa**	21
Mr. Chow | **multi.**	23
Mr. K's | **E Midtown**	23
New Imperial Palace | **Flushing**	22
Nice Green Bo | **Chinatown**	22
NoHo Star | **NoHo**	19
Nom Wah Tea* | **Chinatown**	21
Oriental Gdn.* | **Chinatown**	21
Pacificana | **Sunset Pk**	24
Peking Duck | **multi.**	23
Philippe | **E 60s**	23

Phoenix Gdn. | **Murray Hill**	23
Ping's Seafood* | **multi.**	20
Prosperity Dumpling | **LES**	23
Red Egg | **L Italy**	19
RedFarm* | **W Vill**	25
Sammy's Noodle Shop | **W Vill**	20
Shun Lee Palace | **E Midtown**	24
Shun Lee West | **W 60s**	22
Spicy & Tasty | **Flushing**	24
Szechuan Gourmet | **multi.**	23
Tang Pavilion | **Midtown**	23
Tasty Hand-Pulled | **Chinatown**	22
NEW 2 Duck Goose | **Gowanus**	—
Vanessa's Dumpling | **multi.**	19
Wa Jeal | **E 80s**	24
Wo Hop | **Chinatown**	21
Wu Liang Ye | **Midtown**	25
Xi'an | **multi.**	23
Yunnan Kitchen | **LES**	23

COFFEE

Abraço Espresso | **E Vill**	26
Blue Bottle | **multi.**	23
Café Grumpy | **multi.**	21
Cafe Lalo | **W 80s**	20
Café Sabarsky/Fledermaus | **E 80s**	22
East End Kitchen | **E 80s**	21
Fika | **multi.**	21
Five Leaves | **Greenpt**	24
Gimme Coffee | **multi.**	23
Grey Dog | **multi.**	22
Joe | **multi.**	21
La Colombe | **multi.**	24
L'Albero/Gelati | **Park Slope**	23
Le Pain Q. | **multi.**	18
NEW Little Collins | **E Midtown**	—
NEW Margaux | **G Vill**	17
Ninth St Espresso | **multi.**	23
Omonia | **multi.**	22
Oslo Coffee | **multi.**	23
Piccolo | **multi.**	23
Queens Kickshaw | **Astoria**	21
Rucola | **Boerum Hill**	25
San Matteo | **E 80s**	25
Sant Ambroeus | **multi.**	21
Saraghina | **Bed–Stuy**	25
Smile | **multi.**	22
Stumptown | **multi.**	23

Sweetleaf | **multi.**	22
Tarallucci | **multi.**	20
Third Rail | **multi.**	22
Toby's Estate | **multi.**	22
NEW Urbo | **Midtown**	–
Van Leeuwen | **multi.**	24
Via Quadronno | **E 70s**	21
Zibetto | **Midtown**	24

CONTINENTAL

Battery Gdns. | **BPC**	19
Cebu | **Bay Ridge**	20
Petrossian | **Midtown**	24
Russian Samovar | **Midtown**	17
Russian Tea | **Midtown**	19
Sardi's | **Midtown**	19

CRÊPES

Creperie | **multi.**	21
Le Gamin | **multi.**	21

CUBAN

Amor Cubano | **E Harlem**	23
Cafe Con Leche | **W 80s**	20
Café Habana/Outpost | **multi.**	21
Cuba | **G Vill**	24
Guantanamera | **Midtown**	22
Havana Alma | **W Vill**	22
Havana Central | **Midtown**	21
Victor's Cafe | **Midtown**	24

DANISH

Copenhagen | **TriBeCa**	19

DELIS

(See also Sandwiches)

B & H Dairy | **E Vill**	24
Barney Greengrass | **W 80s**	24
Ben's Best | **Rego Pk**	24
Ben's Kosher | **multi.**	20
Carnegie Deli | **Midtown**	23
Katz's Deli | **LES**	25
Leo's Latticini/Corona | **multi.**	26
Liebman's | **Riverdale**	22
Mile End | **Boerum Hill**	22
Mill Basin Deli | **Flatlands**	24
Pastrami Queen | **E 70s**	22
Sarge's Deli | **Murray Hill**	23
2nd Ave Deli | **multi.**	23

DESSERT

(See also Ice Cream)

Bouchon Bakery | **multi.**	23
Brooklyn Farmacy | **Carroll Gdns**	22
Cafe Lalo | **W 80s**	20
Café Sabarsky/Fledermaus | **E 80s**	22
ChikaLicious | **E Vill**	23
Chocolate Room | **Cobble Hill**	24
City Bakery | **Flatiron**	22
Ferrara | **L Italy**	23
Junior's | **multi.**	19
Lady Mendl's | **Gramercy**	22
L&B Spumoni | **Gravesend**	23
Omonia | **multi.**	22
Sant Ambroeus | **multi.**	21
Serendipity 3 | **E 60s**	19
Sweet Revenge | **W Vill**	22
Tarallucci | **multi.**	20

DINER

Brooklyn Farmacy | **Carroll Gdns**	22
Coppelia | **Chelsea**	20
NEW Empire Diner | **Chelsea**	21
NEW Hamilton's Soda | **W Vill**	–
Hope & Anchor | **Red Hook**	21
Junior's | **multi.**	19
Little Poland | **E Vill**	21
Schnipper's | **multi.**	20
Tom's | **Coney Is**	17

DOMINICAN

Cafe Con Leche | **W 80s**	20
Malecon | **multi.**	20

EASTERN EUROPEAN

Kafana | **E Vill**	25
Sammy's Roumanian | **LES**	21

ECLECTIC

Abigael's | **Midtown**	23
NEW Berg'n | **Crown Hts**	–
Carol's Cafe | **Todt Hill**	24
NEW Cecil | **Harlem**	23
Corkbuzz | **multi.**	21
Crosby Bar | **SoHo**	22
Do or Dine | **Bed-Stuy**	23
Good Fork | **Red Hook**	23
NEW Gorbals | **W'burg**	–
Graffiti | **E Vill**	28
Juventino | **Park Slope**	26

CUISINES

Mehtaphor | **TriBeCa**	26
Nook | **Midtown**	23
107 West | **W 100s**	20
Public | **NoLita**	25
Schiller's | **LES**	17
Stanton Social | **LES**	24
Tolani | **W 70s**	21
Traif | **W'burg**	26
NEW Urbo | **Midtown**	—

ETHIOPIAN

Awash | **multi.**	21
NEW Bunna Cafe | **Bushwick**	—
Queen of Sheba | **Hell's Kit**	25

EUROPEAN

NEW Bâtard | **TriBeCa**	—
Danny Brown | **Forest Hills**	26
Fushimi | **multi.**	23
NoMad | **Flatiron**	26
Spotted Pig | **W Vill**	24

FILIPINO

Jeepney | **E Vill**	22
Kuma Inn | **LES**	25
Maharlika | **E Vill**	21

FONDUE

Artisanal | **Midtown**	23
Chocolate Room | **Cobble Hill**	24
Kashkaval | **Midtown**	22
Mont Blanc | **Midtown**	21
Murray's Cheese Bar | **W Vill**	23

FRENCH

A Cafe/Wine Rm. | **W 100s**	24
Bagatelle | **Meatpacking**	21
Barbès | **Midtown**	21
Bobo | **W Vill**	24
Bouchon Bakery | **multi.**	23
Bouley | **TriBeCa**	29
Breeze | **Hell's Kit**	21
Buvette | **W Vill**	24
Café Boulud | **E 70s**	26
NEW Cafe Cambodge | **E Vill**	—
Cafe Centro | **E Midtown**	21
Cafe Gitane | **multi.**	23
Café Henri | **LIC**	22
Carlyle | **E 70s**	23
Chef's/Brooklyn Fare | **Downtown Bklyn**	28

NEW Cheri | **Harlem**	—
Creperie | **multi.**	21
Daniel | **E 60s**	28
DBGB | **E Vill**	22
Degustation | **E Vill**	26
NEW Dirty French | **LES**	—
Elm | **W'burg**	25
Fedora | **W Vill**	22
NEW French Louie | **Boerum Hill**	26
Gordon Ramsay | **Midtown**	22
Indochine | **G Vill**	21
Jean-Georges | **W 60s**	28
Jean-Georges' Noug. | **W 60s**	27
Kaz an Nou | **Prospect Hts**	22
La Baraka | **Flushing**	23
La Boîte en Bois | **W 60s**	22
NEW Ladurée | **SoHo**	24
Lafayette | **NoHo**	22
La Grenouille | **Midtown**	28
La Mangeoire | **E Midtown**	23
Le Bernardin | **Midtown**	29
Le Cirque | **E Midtown**	24
L'Ecole | **SoHo**	23
Le Colonial | **E Midtown**	23
Le Gigot | **W Vill**	24
Le Grainne Cafe | **Chelsea**	22
Le Marais | **Midtown**	21
Le Perigord | **E Midtown**	24
Le Pescadeux | **SoHo**	21
Le Rivage | **Midtown**	21
Maison Kayser | **multi.**	22
NEW Margaux | **G Vill**	17
Marseille | **Midtown**	21
Maze | **Midtown**	19
Mercer Kitchen | **SoHo**	22
Mihoko's 21 Grams | **Flatiron**	21
Minetta Tavern | **G Vill**	24
Modern | **Midtown**	26
Nizza | **Midtown**	21
Odeon | **TriBeCa**	20
Pascalou | **E 90s**	21
Per Se | **Midtown**	27
Petite Crevette | **Columbia St.**	23
Petrossian | **Midtown**	24
Picholine | **W 60s**	26
Ponty Bistro | **Gramercy**	24
NEW Racines | **TriBeCa**	—

NEW Rotisserie Georgette | E 60s | 24

Rouge et Blanc | SoHo | 23
NEW Simone | E 80s | 25
Tartinery | multi. | 23
Tocqueville | Flatiron | 27
Triomphe | Midtown | 24
Ze Café | E Midtown | 20

FRENCH (BISTRO)

Almond | Flatiron | 21
A.O.C. | multi. | 20
Bacchus | Downtown Bklyn | 21
Bakehse. Bistro | Meatpacking | 21
Bar Boulud | W 60s | 24
Bar Tabac | Cobble Hill | 20
Benoit | Midtown | 23
Bistro Cassis | W 70s | 20
Bistro Chat Noir | E 60s | 20
Bistro Vendôme | E Midtown | 22
Cafe Cluny | W Vill | 21
Cafe Loup | W Vill | 19
Cafe Luluc | Cobble Hill | 22
Cafe Luxembourg | W 70s | 21
NEW Café Paulette | Ft Greene | —
Camaje | G Vill | 20
NEW Cherche Midi | NoLita | —
Chez Jacqueline | G Vill | 20
Chez Josephine | Hell's Kit | 21
Chez Lucienne | Harlem | 21
Chez Napoléon | Midtown | 22
NEW Claudette | G Vill | —
Cocotte | SoHo | 23
Cornelia St. | W Vill | 20
db Bistro Moderne | Midtown | 24
Jeanne & Gaston | W Vill | 24
JoJo | E 60s | 24
Jubilee | E Midtown | 21
La Bonne Soupe | Midtown | 20
La Lunchonette | Chelsea | 22
Landmarc | multi. | 20
La Sirène | Hudson Sq | 25
Le Bilboquet | E 60s | 21
Le Gamin | multi. | 21
Le Paris Bistrot | E 90s | 21
Le Parisien | Kips Bay | 23
Le Philosophe | NoHo | 23
Le Veau d'Or | E 60s | 21
NEW Little Prince | SoHo | 23

Lucien | E Vill | 23
Madison Bistro | Midtown | 23
Maison Harlem | Manhattanville | 21
Millesime | Flatiron | 21
Mon Petit Cafe | E 60s | 20
Montmartre | Chelsea | 21
Nice Matin | W 70s | 19
Paradou | Meatpacking | 20
Quatorze Bis | E 70s | 20
Raoul's | SoHo | 24
Saju Bistro | Midtown | 21
Table d'Hôte | E 90s | 23
Tartine | W Vill | 22
Tournesol | LIC | 23
26 Seats | E Vill | 23

FRENCH (BRASSERIE)

Artisanal | Midtown | 23
Balthazar | SoHo | 24
Brasserie | E Midtown | 21
Brasserie Cognac | multi. | 19
Brasserie 8½ | Midtown | 22
Brass. Ruhlmann | Midtown | 19
Café d'Alsace | E 80s | 22
Ça Va | Midtown | 22
Jacques | multi. | 21
L'Absinthe | E 60s | 23
Le Relais | E Midtown | 21
Les Halles | multi. | 20
Marseille | Midtown | 21
Orsay | E 70s | 18
Rue 57 | Midtown | 18

GASTROPUB

Alchemy | Amer. | Park Slope | 20
B&B Winepub | Amer. | SoHo | 21
NEW BarBacon | Amer. | Midtown | 22
Boulton & Watt | Amer. | E Vill | 22
Cannibal | Belgian | Hell's Kit | 21
DBGB | Amer. | E Vill | 22
NEW Dutch Kills Centraal | Amer. | LIC | 21
Penrose | Amer. | E 80s | 20
Resto | Belgian | Kips Bay | 20
Spotted Pig | Euro. | W Vill | 24
Thistle Hill | Amer. | Park Slope | 21
Vanderbilt | Amer. | Prospect Hts | 21

GERMAN

Berlyn | **Ft Greene**	22
Blaue Gans | **TriBeCa**	22
Heidelberg | **E 80s**	21
Marrow | **W Vill**	22
Rolf's | **Gramercy**	16
Seäsonal | **Midtown**	24
Zum Schneider | **E Vill**	22
Zum Stammtisch | **Glendale**	23

GREEK

Agnanti | **Astoria**	23
Ammos | **Midtown**	21
Anassa Taverna | **E 60s**	21
Avra | **E Midtown**	25
Bahari Estiatorio | **Astoria**	26
Cávo | **Astoria**	22
Eliá | **Bay Ridge**	26
Elias Corner | **Astoria**	26
Ethos | **multi.**	22
FishTag | **W 70s**	23
NEW The Greek | **TriBeCa**	21
Greek Kitchen | **Hell's Kit**	21
Ithaka | **E 80s**	22
Kefi | **W 80s**	23
Kellari Taverna | **Midtown**	22
Loukoumi | **Astoria**	25
Milos | **Midtown**	27
Molyvos | **Midtown**	23
MP Taverna | **Astoria**	24
Nerai | **Midtown**	22
Okeanos | **Park Slope**	22
Omonia | **multi.**	22
Ovelia | **Astoria**	21
Periyali | **Flatiron**	24
Pylos | **E Vill**	26
Snack | **multi.**	23
Stamatis | **Astoria**	24
Taverna Kyclades | **Astoria**	26
Telly's Taverna | **Astoria**	22
Thalassa | **TriBeCa**	24
Uncle Nick's | **multi.**	20
Yefsi Estiatorio | **E 70s**	23

HAWAIIAN

NEW Onomea | **W'burg**	—

HEALTH FOOD
(See also Vegetarian)

Community | **Morningside Hts**	21
Spring/Natural | **multi.**	21

HOT DOGS

Bark | **Park Slope**	20
Cannibal | **Hell's Kit**	21
Crif Dogs | **multi.**	23
Gray's Papaya | **W 70s**	22
Katz's Deli | **LES**	25
Mile End | **Boerum Hill**	22
Papaya King | **multil.**	22
Shake Shack | **multi.**	21
Smoke Joint | **Ft Greene**	23
Westville | **multi.**	23

ICE CREAM

Amorino | **multi.**	25
Ample Hills | **multi.**	27
Big Gay Ice Cream | **multi.**	23
Blue Marble | **multi.**	21
Brooklyn Farmacy | **Carroll Gdns**	22
Brooklyn Ice Cream | **multi.**	24
Chinatown Ice Cream | **Chinatown**	24
Cones | **W Vill**	24
Eddie's Sweet Shop | **Forest Hills**	24
Grom | **Midtown**	25
Il Laboratorio | **LES**	25
Khe-Yo | **TriBeCa**	24
L'Albero/Gelati | **Park Slope**	23
L&B Spumoni | **Gravesend**	23
Lemon Ice King | **Corona**	25
Manducatis Rustica | **LIC**	22
NEW Morgenstern's | **LES**	—
OddFellows | **E Vill**	24
Ralph's Famous | **multi.**	24
Serendipity 3 | **E 60s**	19
NEW Stella 34 | **Midtown**	23
Van Leeuwen | **multi.**	24

ICELANDIC

NEW Skal | **LES**	22

INDIAN

Amma | **E Midtown**	25
Baluchi's | **multi.**	20
Benares | **multi.**	21
Bombay Palace | **Midtown**	21

Brick Ln. Curry	multi.	21
Bukhara Grill	E Midtown	25
Chola	E Midtown	23
Darbar	multi.	23
Dawat	E Midtown	23
Dévi	Flatiron	23
Dhaba	Kips Bay	24
NEW Dosa Royale	Carroll Gdns	24
Haveli	E Vill	21
Indus Valley	W 90s	23
Jackson Diner	multi.	21
Junoon	Flatiron	24
Kati Roll	multi.	22
Moti Mahal	E 60s	22
Sapphire Indian	W 60s	21
Saravanaa Bhavan	multi.	23
Seva Indian	Astoria	25
Tamarind	TriBeCa	26
Tulsi	E Midtown	24
Utsav	Midtown	22

ISRAELI

Azuri Cafe	Hell's Kit	25
NEW Bar Bolonat	W Vill	—
Chick P	Prospect Hts	—
Hummus Pl.	multl.	21
Miriam	Park Slope	23
Taïm	multi.	25

ITALIAN
(N=Northern; S=Southern)

Abboccato	Midtown	20
Acappella	N	TriBeCa	22
Acqua at Peck Slip	Seaport	21
Acqua Santa	W'burg	22
Ai Fiori	Midtown	26
Aita	Clinton Hill	25
Alberto	N	Forest Hills	25
Al Di La	N	Park Slope	26
NEW Alfredo 100	S	Midtown	—
NEW All'onda	N	G Vill	23
Alloro	E 70s	23
Amorina	Prospect Hts	23
Angelina's	Tottenville	23
Angelo's/Mulberry	S	L Italy	23
Angelo's Pizzeria	multi.	20
Ann & Tony's	Arthur Ave./Belmont	21
Antica Pesa	W'burg	23

NEW Antonioni's	LES	—
Antonucci	E 80s	23
Ápizz	LES	23
Areo	Bay Ridge	24
Armani Rist.	N	Midtown	24
Arno	N	Midtown	21
Aroma Kitchen	NoHo	23
Arturo's	G Vill	23
Asellina	Flatiron	20
Aurora	multi.	24
A Voce	multi.	23
Babbo	G Vill	26
Bacaro	N	LES	24
Bamonte's	W'burg	23
Barbetta	N	Midtown	22
Barbone	E Vill	24
Barbuto	W Vill	26
NEW Barchetta	Chelsea	—
Bar Corvo	N	Prospect Hts	24
Bar Eolo	S	Chelsea	23
Bar Italia	E 60s	23
Barosa	Rego Pk	23
Bar Pitti	G Vill	23
NEW Bar Primi	E Vill	—
Bar Toto	Park Slope	21
Basso56	S	Midtown	24
Basta Pasta	Flatiron	24
Becco	Midtown	23
Beccofino	Riverdale	24
Bella Blu	N	E 70s	22
Bella Via	LIC	22
Best Pizza	W'burg	24
Bianca	N	NoHo	21
Birreria	Flatiron	20
Bistango	multi.	22
Bistro Milano	N	Midtown	20
Bocca	S	Flatiron	22
Bocca/Bacco	multi.	21
Bocca Lupo	Cobble Hill	22
Bocelli	Old Town	25
Bond 45	Midtown	19
Bottega	E 70s	20
Bottega Del Vino	Midtown	22
Bottino	N	Chelsea	21
Bread To Go	W Vill	20
Bricco	Midtown	20
Brucie	Cobble Hill	20
Cacio e Pepe	S	E Vill	20

Cafe Fiorello | **W 60s**	20
Caffe e Vino | **Ft Greene**	22
Caffe Storico | N | **W 70s**	22
Campagnola | **E 70s**	23
Cara Mia | **Midtown**	20
Caravaggio | **E 70s**	25
Carbone | **G Vill**	24
Carmine's | S | **multi.**	21
Casa Lever | N | **Midtown**	23
Casa Nonna | **Midtown**	22
Celeste | S | **W 80s**	24
Cellini | **Midtown**	22
'Cesca | S | **W 70s**	24
Cibo | N | **Murray Hill**	22
Ciccio | N | **SoHo**	—
Cipriani Club 55 | **Financial**	23
Cipriani D'twn | **SoHo**	24
Circo | N | **Midtown**	23
Coppola's | **multi.**	21
Corsino | **Meatpacking**	21
Costata | **SoHo**	25
Cotta | **W 80s**	22
Covo | **Hamilton Hts**	23
Crispo | N | **W Vill**	24
Da Andrea | **G Vill**	23
Da Nico | **L Italy**	21
Da Noi | N | **multi.**	25
Da Silvano | N | **G Vill**	21
Da Tommaso | N | **Midtown**	21
Da Umberto | N | **Flatiron**	25
Defonte's | **Red Hook**	24
DeGrezia | **E Midtown**	25
Dell'anima | **W Vill**	25
Del Posto | **Chelsea**	26
Dino | **Ft Greene**	20
Dominick's | **Arthur Ave./Belmont**	23
Don Antonio | S | **Midtown**	22
Don Peppe | **S Ozone Pk**	25
Due | N | **E 70s**	22
NEW East 12th | N | **E Vill**	25
Eataly | **Flatiron**	23
Ecco | **TriBeCa**	21
Elio's | **E 80s**	24
Emilia's | **Arthur Ave./Belmont**	23
Emilio's Ballato | **NoLita**	24
Emporio | **NoLita**	24
Enzo's | **multi.**	25
Erminia | S | **E 80s**	23

Esca | S | **Hell's Kit**	25
Etc. Etc. | **Midtown**	23
F & J Pine | **Van Nest**	23
Felice | **multi.**	21
Felidia | **E Midtown**	25
57 Napoli | **E Midtown**	21
Fiorentino's | S | **Gravesend**	23
Firenze | N | **E 80s**	23
Forcella | S | **multi.**	21
Fornino | **multi.**	23
Fragole | **Carroll Gdns**	22
Frank | **E Vill**	21
Frankies | N | **multi.**	23
Franny's | **Park Slope**	25
Fred's at Barneys | N | **E 60s**	22
Fresco | N | **Midtown**	22
Gabriel's | N | **W 60s**	22
Gargiulo's | S | **Coney Is**	22
Gemma | N | **E Vill**	23
Gennaro | **W 90s**	26
Gigino | N | **multi.**	20
Gino's | **Bay Ridge**	23
Giorgione | **Hudston Sq**	24
Giorgio's | **Flatiron**	23
Giovanni | N | **E 80s**	22
Gnocco | **E Vill**	23
Gradisca | **W Vill**	23
Harry Cipriani | N | **Midtown**	23
Harry's Italian | N | **multi.**	21
Hearth | N | **E Vill**	25
Il Bambino | **Astoria**	25
Il Buco | **NoHo**	26
Il Buco Alimentari | **NoHo**	24
Il Cantinori | N | **G Vill**	23
Il Cortile | **L Italy**	22
Il Gattopardo | S | **Midtown**	25
Il Giglio | N | **TriBeCa**	23
Il Mulino | S | **multi.**	25
NEW Il Mulino Prime | **SoHo**	—
Il Postino | **E Midtown**	22
Il Tinello | N | **Midtown**	23
Il Vagabondo | **E 60s**	20
I Sodi | N | **W Vill**	25
Isola | **SoHo**	24
Italianissimo | **E 80s**	21
I Trulli | S | **Kips Bay**	23
Joe & Pat's | **Castelton Cnrs**	25
John's/12th St. | **E Vill**	21

La Follia	**Gramercy**	22
La Lanterna	**G Vill**	20
La Masseria	**Midtown**	23
La Mela	S	**L Italy**	21
L&B Spumoni	**Gravesend**	23
L'Apicio	**E Vill**	23
La Pizza Fresca	**Flatiron**	23
La Rivista	**Midtown**	20
L'Artusi	**W Vill**	26
Lattanzi	S	**Midtown**	23
Lavagna	N	**E Vill**	25
La Vigna	**Forest Hills**	24
La Villa Pizzeria	**multi.**	22
Lavo	**Midtown**	19
NEW Lea	**Ditmas Pk**	–
Leopard/des Artistes	S	**W 60s**	22
Leo's Latticini/Corona	**multi.**	26
Le Zie	N	**Chelsea**	20
Lido	N	**Harlem**	24
Lil' Frankie	**E Vill**	25
Lincoln	**W 60s**	25
Locale	**Astoria**	21
Locanda Verde	**TriBeCa**	24
Locanda Vini	N	**Clinton Hill**	25
Luce	**W 60s**	20
Lupa	**G Vill**	24
Lusardi's	N	**E 70s**	25
Luzzo's	S	**E Vill**	25
Macelleria	N	**Meatpacking**	24
Machiavelli	N	**W 80s**	23
Madison's	**Riverdale**	21
Maialino	**Gramercy**	25
Malatesta	N	**W Vill**	24
Manducatis	S	**LIC**	22
Manetta's	**LIC**	24
Manzo	**Flatiron**	24
Marcony	**Kips Bay**	25
Marco Polo	**Carroll Gdns**	23
NEW Marco's	**Prospect Hts**	24
Marea	**Midtown**	27
Mario's	S	**Arthur Ave./Belmont**	22
Marrow	**W Vill**	22
NEW Marta	S	**Flatiron**	–
Maruzzella	**E 70s**	21
Max SoHa/Caffe	**multi.**	22
Mercato	**Midtown**	22

Montebello	N	**E Midtown**	22
Morandi	**W Vill**	22
Morso	**E Midtown**	23
NEW Mozzarella & Vino	**Midtown**	22
Nanni	N	**E Midtown**	22
Naples 45	S	**E Midtown**	21
Nello	N	**E 60s**	18
Nicola's	N	**E 80s**	22
Nicoletta	**E Vill**	19
Nino's	**multi.**	21
Nizza	**Midtown**	21
Nocello	N	**Midtown**	22
Noodle Pudding	**Bklyn Hts**	23
Novitá	N	**Gramercy**	24
Nucci's	**multi.**	23
Numero 28	**multi.**	23
101	**Bay Ridge**	21
Orso	N	**Midtown**	24
Osteria al Doge	N	**Midtown**	21
Osteria Laguna	N	**E Midtown**	20
Osteria Morini	N	**SoHo**	25
Otto	**G Vill**	23
NEW Pagani	**W Vill**	21
Palma	S	**W Vill**	25
Paola's	**E 90s**	23
Pappardella	**W 70s**	20
Park Side	**Corona**	25
Parm	S	**NoLita**	24
Patricia's	**Morris Pk**	25
Patsy's	**multi.**	21
Patsy's	S	**Midtown**	22
Peasant	**NoLita**	25
Pellegrino's	**L Italy**	21
Pepolino	N	**TriBeCa**	25
Perla	**G Vill**	25
Piadina	**G Vill**	22
Piccola Venezia	**Astoria**	25
Piccolo Angolo	**W Vill**	25
Piccolo Cafe	**multi.**	23
Pietro's	**E Midtown**	25
Pisticci	S	**Morningside Hts**	24
PizzArte	S	**Midtown**	20
Pó	**W Vill**	25
Pomodoro Rosso	**W 70s**	21
Ponticello	N	**Astoria**	23
Porchetta	**E Vill**	21
Porsena	**E Vill**	23

Primola | **E 60s**	23
Quality Italian | **Midtown**	24
Queen | **Bklyn Hts**	23
Rao's | S | **E Harlem**	21
Red Gravy | **Bklyn Hts**	23
Remi | N | **Midtown**	23
Risotteria | **W Vill**	21
NEW Risotteria Melotti | **E Vill**	—
NEW Rist. Morini | **E 80s**	26
Roberta's | **Bushwick**	26
Roberto | **Arthur Ave./Belmont**	27
Roman's | **Ft Greene**	24
Rosemary's | **W Vill**	22
Rossini's | N | **Murray Hill**	22
Rubirosa | **NoLita**	25
Rucola | N | **Boerum Hill**	25
Salumeria/Rist. Rosi | N | **multi.**	24
Sandro's | **E 80s**	24
San Matteo | **E 80s**	25
San Pietro | S | **Midtown**	22
Sant Ambroeus | **multi.**	21
Sauce | S | **LES**	23
Scaletta | N | **W 70s**	22
Scalinatella | **E 60s**	24
Scalini Fedeli | N | **TriBeCa**	26
Scalino | **multi.**	23
Scarlatto | **Midtown**	21
Scarpetta | **Chelsea**	25
Scottadito | N | **Park Slope**	22
SD26 | **Flatiron**	25
Serafina | **multi.**	18
Sette Mezzo | **E 70s**	22
Sfoglia | N | **E 90s**	25
Sirio | N | **E 60s**	22
Sistina | N | **E 80s**	—
Speedy Romeo | **Clinton Hill**	23
Spiga | **W 80s**	22
Spigolo | **E 80s**	—
Spina | **E Vill**	24
NEW Stella 34 | **Midtown**	23
Supper | N | **E Vill**	24
Tarallucci | **multi.**	20
NEW Terra Tribeca | **TriBeCa**	21
Terroir | **multi.**	20
Tiella | S | **E 60s**	25
Tommaso | **Bath Bch**	23
Tony's Di Napoli | S | **multi.**	22
Torrisi | **NoLita**	25

Tra Di Noi | **Arthur Ave./Belmont**	25
Trattoria Dell'Arte | N | **Midtown**	22
Tratt. L'incontro | **Astoria**	26
Tratt. Pesce | **multi.**	20
Tratt. Romana | **Dongan Hills**	24
Trattoria Trecolori | **Midtown**	21
Tre Dici | **Flatiron**	22
Tuscany Grill | N | **Bay Ridge**	25
Uva | **E 70s**	23
Valbella | N | **multi.**	24
Vesta | **Astoria**	25
Vesuvio | **Bay Ridge**	22
Vezzo | **Kips Bay**	23
Via Emilia | N | **Flatiron**	22
Via Quadronno | N | **E 70s**	21
ViceVersa | **Midtown**	23
Villa Berulia | N | **Murray Hill**	25
Villa Mosconi | **G Vill**	23
Vincent's | **L Italy**	21
Volare | **G Vill**	23
Ze Café | **E Midtown**	20
Zero Otto | S | **multi.**	23
Zio Ristorante | **Flatiron**	22

JAMAICAN

Miss Lily's | **multi.**	20
Negril | **G Vill**	23

JAPANESE
(* sushi specialist)

Aburiya Kinnosuke | **E Midtown**	24
Aji Sushi* | **Murray Hill**	21
Arirang Hibachi | **multi.**	23
NEW Bar Chuko | **Prospect Hts**	—
NEW Bassanova | **Chinatown**	21
Blue Fin* | **Midtown**	23
Blue Ribbon Sushi* | **multi.**	25
Blue Ribbon Sushi B&G* | **Midtown**	25
Blue Ribbon/Izakaya | **LES**	22
Bohemian | **NoHo**	25
Bond St* | **NoHo**	25
Brushstroke/Ichimura | **TriBeCa**	26
NEW Butterfish* | **Midtown**	—
NEW Cagen* | **E Vill**	—
Cha An | **E Vill**	22
Cherry* | **Chelsea**	22
NEW Cherry Izakaya | **W'burg**	—
Chuko | **Prospect Hts**	27

EN Japanese | **W Vill**	25
15 East* | **Union Sq**	26
Fushimi* | **multi.**	23
Ganso | **Downtown Bklyn**	23
Gari* | **multi.**	26
Gyu-Kaku | **multi.**	22
Hakata Tonton | **W Vill**	23
Haru* | **multi.**	21
Hasaki* | **E Vill**	23
Hatsuhana* | **Midtown**	25
Hibino* | **multi.**	25
Hide-Chan | **E Midtown**	23
NEW Hirohisa* | **SoHo**	—
Inakaya | **Midtown**	22
Ippudo | **multi.**	25
NEW Ivan Ramen | **multi.**	19
Jewel Bako* | **E Vill**	24
Jin Ramen | **Morningside Hts**	23
Kajitsu | **Murray Hill**	25
Kanoyama* | **E Vill**	24
Ki Sushi* | **Cobble Hill**	26
Koi* | **multi.**	24
Ko Sushi* | **multi.**	20
Kotobuki* | **G Vill**	25
Kouzan* | **W 90s**	22
Kurumazushi* | **Midtown**	25
Kyo Ya | **E Vill**	26
Masa/Bar Masa* | **Midtown**	25
Megu | **multi.**	23
Mihoko's 21 Grams | **Flatiron**	22
Minca | **E Vill**	23
Mira Sushi* | **Flatiron**	23
Momo Sushi Shack* | **Bushwick**	26
Momoya* | **multi.**	22
Morimoto | **Chelsea**	26
Natsumi* | **Midtown**	20
Neta* | **G Vill**	25
Ninja* | **TriBeCa**	13
Nobu | **multi.**	27
NEW Okonomi | **W'burg**	—
1 or 8* | **W'burg**	24
Ootoya | **multi.**	23
Poke* | **E 80s**	26
NEW Ramen. Co | **Financial**	—
Robataya | **E Vill**	25
Rosanjin | **TriBeCa**	26
Sakagura* | **E Midtown**	24
SakaMai | **LES**	24

Sake Bar Hagi | **Midtown**	21
Samurai Mama | **W'burg**	24
Sasabune* | **E 70s**	25
Shabu-Shabu 70* | **E 70s**	23
Shabu-Tatsu | **E Vill**	26
NEW Shalom Japan | **W'burg**	25
NEW Shinobi | **Bushwick**	—
Soba Koh | **E Vill**	25
Soba Nippon* | **Midtown**	22
Soba Totto | **E Midtown**	24
Soba-ya | **E Vill**	22
Soto* | **W Vill**	26
Sugiyama | **Midtown**	27
SushiAnn* | **Midtown**	23
Sushi Azabu* | **TriBeCa**	25
Sushi Damo* | **Midtown**	24
Sushiden* | **Midtown**	23
Sushi Dojo* | **E Vill**	24
NEW Sushi Katsuei* | **Park Slope**	—
NEW Sushi Nakazawa* | **W Vill**	27
Sushi Seki* | **E 60s**	25
Sushi Sen-nin* | **Midtown**	26
Sushi Yasuda* | **E Midtown**	28
Sushi Zen* | **Midtown**	25
Takahachi* | **multi.**	24
Takashi | **W Vill**	27
Tanoshi | **E 70s**	26
Taro Sushi* | **Park Slope**	24
Tenzan* | **multi.**	20
Tomoe Sushi* | **G Vill**	25
Torishin | **E 60s**	25
Totto Ramen | **Hell's Kit**	25
Ushiwakamaru* | **G Vill**	27
NEW Wasabi* | **Midtown**	—
Yakitori Totto | **Midtown**	25
Yama* | **multi.**	24
Yuba* | **G Vill**	24
Zenkichi | **W'burg**	27
Zutto* | **TriBeCa**	23

JEWISH

B & H Dairy | **E Vill**	24
Barney Greengrass | **W 80s**	24
NEW Baz Bagel | **L Italy**	—
Ben's Best | **Rego Pk**	24
Ben's Kosher | **multi.**	20
Carnegie Deli | **Midtown**	23
Katz's Deli | **LES**	25

Lattanzi | **Midtown**	23
Liebman's Deli | **Riverdale**	22
Mile End | **Boerum Hill**	22
Mill Basin Deli | **Flatlands**	24
NEW Russ/Daughters Cafe | **LES**	–
Sammy's Roumanian | **LES**	21
NEW Shalom Japan | **W'burg**	25

KOREAN
(* barbecue specialist)

Arirang Korean | **Midtown**	22
Bann | **Midtown**	24
BCD Tofu | **Midtown**	22
BonChon | **multi.**	21
Cho Dang Gol | **Midtown**	24
Danji | **Midtown**	25
Do Hwa* | **W Vill**	22
Don's Bogam* | **Midtown**	24
Franchia | **Midtown**	25
Gahm Mi Oak | **Midtown**	22
Gaonnuri* | **Midtown**	20
Hangawi | **Midtown**	26
Hanjan | **Flatiron**	23
Jungsik | **TriBeCa**	27
Kristalbelli* | **Midtown**	24
Kum Gang San* | **multi.**	21
Kunjip* | **Midtown**	22
Kyochon | **multi.**	20
Madangsui* | **Midtown**	23
Mandoo Bar | **Midtown**	23
Miss Korea* | **Midtown**	20
Moim | **Park Slope**	23
New WonJo* | **Midtown**	23
Sik Gaek | **multi.**	22

KOSHER/KOSHER-STYLE

Abigael's | **Midtown**	23
Azuri Cafe | **Hell's Kit**	25
Ben's Best | **Rego Pk**	24
Ben's Kosher | **multi.**	20
Buddha Bodai | **Chinatown**	22
NEW Butterfish | **Midtown**	–
Caravan/Dreams | **E Vill**	23
Colbeh | **Midtown**	21
Hummus Kit. | **multi.**	20
Hummus Pl. | **multi.**	21
Le Marais | **Midtown**	21
Liebman's | **Riverdale**	22

Mill Basin Deli | **Flatlands**	24
Pastrami Queen | **E 70s**	22
Peacefood Café | **multi.**	23
Prime Grill | **Midtown**	24
NEW Reserve Cut | **Financial**	25
Sacred Chow | **G Vill**	24
2nd Ave Deli | **multi.**	23

LAOTIAN

Khe-Yo | **TriBeCa**	24

LATIN AMERICAN

NEW Colonia Verde | **Ft Greene**	–
Cómodo | **SoHo**	25

LEBANESE

Al Bustan | **E Midtown**	21
Almayass | **Flatiron**	23
Balade | **E Vill**	24
Ilili | **Flatiron**	26
Naya | **multi.**	22

MALAYSIAN

Fatty Crab | **Meatpacking**	22
Laut | **Union Sq**	20
New Malaysia | **Chinatown**	23
Nyonya | **multi.**	23
NEW Rasa | **G Vill**	–

MEDITERRANEAN

Aldea | **Flatiron**	24
Alta | **G Vill**	25
Amali | **E 60s**	24
Amaranth | **E 60s**	21
Balaboosta | **NoLita**	23
Balkanika | **Hell's Kit**	21
Barbounia | **Flatiron**	23
Bodrum | **W 80s**	20
Boulud Sud | **W 60s**	25
Bustan | **W 80s**	25
Cafe Centro | **E Midtown**	21
Conviv. Osteria | **Park Slope**	26
Dee's | **Forest Hills**	23
Estela | **NoLita**	25
Extra Virgin | **W Vill**	23
Fig & Olive | **multi.**	21
Five Points | **NoHo**	21
NEW Gato | **NoHo**	24
NEW Glasserie | **Greenpt**	24
Hummus Kit. | **multi.**	20
Il Buco | **NoHo**	26

Il Buco Alimentari	**NoHo**	24	Fonda	**multi.**	24
Isa	**W'burg**	22	Gran Electrica	**Dumbo**	22
Isabella's	**W 70s**	20	Hecho en Dumbo	**NoHo**	23
Kashkaval	**Midtown**	22	Hell's Kitchen	**Hell's Kit**	20
Little Owl	**W Vill**	27	La Esquina	**multi.**	23
NEW Margaux	**G Vill**	17	La Palapa	**E Vill**	23
Marseille	**Midtown**	21	La Superior	**W'burg**	23
NEW Meadowsweet	**W'burg**	—	NEW Los Tacos	**Chelsea**	—
Mémé	**W Vill**	23	NEW Lucky Luna	**Greenpt**	—
Mezetto	**LES**	23	Maya	**E 60s**	22
Miriam	**Park Slope**	23	Maz Mezcal	**E 80s**	21
Nice Matin	**W 70s**	19	Mercadito	**E Vill**	22
Nick & Toni	**W 60s**	19	Mesa Coyoacan	**W'burg**	25
Olea	**Ft Greene**	24	NEW Mission Cantina	**LES**	20
Olives	**Union Sq**	21	Móle	**multi.**	20
Park	**Chelsea**	18	Oaxaca	**multi.**	21
Pera	**multi.**	20	Ofrenda	**W Vill**	21
Picholine	**W 60s**	26	NEW Otto's Tacos	**E Vill**	22
Place	**W Vill**	23	Pachanga Patterson	**Astoria**	23
Red Cat	**Chelsea**	24	Pampano	**E Midtown**	23
Siggy's	**multi.**	23	Pulqueria	**Chinatown**	23
Smile	**multi.**	22	Rocking Horse	**Chelsea**	22
Superfine	**Dumbo**	19	Rosa Mexicano	**multi.**	23
Taboon	**multi.**	24	Salvation Taco	**Murray Hill**	21
Tanoreen	**Bay Ridge**	27	Sinigual	**Murray Hill**	21
Tessa	**W 70s**	—	Tacombi/Fonda Nolita	**NoLita**	25
Zizi Limona	**W'burg**	24	NEW Taco Santo	**Park Slope**	—

MEXICAN

Alma	**Columbia St.**	20	Toloache	**multi.**	23
Barrio Chino	**LES**	22	Tortilleria Nixtamal	**Corona**	25
NEW Black Ant	**E Vill**	—	Xixa	**W'burg**	25
NEW Bodega Negra	**Chelsea**	23	NEW Zona Rosa	**W'burg**	23

MIDDLE EASTERN

NEW Cafe El Pres.	**Flatiron**	—	Balaboosta	**NoLita**	23
Café Habana/Outpost	**multi.**	21	NEW Bar Bolonat	**W Vill**	—
Calexico	**multi.**	22	Gazala's	**multi.**	22
Casa Enrique	**LIC**	24	Mamoun's	**multi.**	23
Cascabel Taqueria	**multi.**	19	Mimi's Hummus	**Ditmas Pk**	25
NEW Cerveceria	**W'burg**	—	Moustache	**multi.**	22
Chavela's	**Crown Hts**	24	Taboon	**multi.**	24
Crema	**Flatiron**	22	Tanoreen	**Bay Ridge**	27
Dos Caminos	**multi.**	20	12 Chairs	**SoHo**	22
Dos Toros	**multi.**	20	Zaytoons	**multi.**	21
El Centro	**Midtown**	21	Zizi Limona	**W'burg**	24
El Parador	**Murray Hill**	22		

MONGOLIAN

El Paso	**multi.**	22	NEW Little Lamb	**Flushing**	—
El Toro Blanco	**W Vill**	22		

MOROCCAN

NEW El Vez	**Battery Pk**	—	Barbès	**Midtown**	21
Empellón	**multi.**	23		

Cafe Gitane	multi.	23
Cafe Mogador	multi.	24
Cafe Noir	TriBeCa	—
Mémé	W Vill	23

NEW ENGLAND

Littleneck	multi.	23
Lobster Joint	multi.	22
Luke's Lobster	multi.	24
Mermaid	multi.	22
Pearl Oyster	W Vill	27
NEW Water Table	Kips Bay	—

NEW ZEALAND

Musket Room	NoLita	26

NOODLE SHOPS

Arirang Korean	Midtown	22
NEW Bassanova	Chinatown	21
Biang!	Flushing	25
Bo-Ky	multi.	21
Chuko	Prospect Hts	27
Ganso	Downtown Bklyn	23
Great NY Noodle	Chinatown	23
Hide-Chan	E Midtown	23
Ippudo	multi.	25
NEW Ivan Ramen	multi.	19
Jin Ramen	Morningside Hts	23
Minca	E Vill	23
Momofuku Noodle	E Vill	23
Nightingale 9	Carroll Gdns	23
Ootoya	multi.	23
Pho Bang	multi.	21
NEW Ramen. Co	Financial	—
Republic	Union Sq	19
Sammy's Noodle Shop	W Vill	20
NEW Shinobi	Bushwick	—
Soba Koh	E Vill	25
Soba Nippon	Midtown	22
Soba Totto	E Midtown	24
Soba-ya	E Vill	22
Tasty Hand-Pulled	Chinatown	22
Totto Ramen	Hell's Kit	25
Xi'an	multi.	23
Zutto	TriBeCa	23

NUEVO LATINO

Cabana	multi.	22
Calle Ocho	W 80s	20
Citrus B&G	W 70s	20
Coppelia	Chelsea	20

PAN-LATIN

ABC Cocina	Flatiron	24
A Casa Fox	LES	24
Bogota	Park Slope	24
Coppelia	Chelsea	20
La Pulperia	Midtown	22
NEW Los Americanos	TriBeCa	—
Macondo	LES	23
Palo Santo	Park Slope	23
Rayuela	LES	23
Yerba Buena	multi.	22
Yuca Bar	E Vill	21
Zengo	Murray Hill	20

PERSIAN

Colbeh	Midtown	21
Parmys Persian Fusion	E Vill	—
Persepolis	E 70s	22
Ravagh	multi.	23

PERUVIAN

Coco Roco	multi.	21
Flor/Mayo	multi.	21
Pio Pio	multi.	22
Raymi	Flatiron	21

PIZZA

Adrienne's	Financial	24
Amorina	Prospect Hts	23
Angelo's Pizzeria	multi.	20
Aperitivo Pizza	E Midtown	22
Ápizz	LES	23
Artichoke Basille	multi.	22
Arturo's	G Vill	23
Bella Blu	E 70s	22
Bella Via	LIC	22
Best Pizza	W'burg	24
Bricco	Midtown	20
Co.	Chelsea	22
Covo	Hamilton Hts	23
Dee's	Forest Hills	23
Denino's	Elm Pk	26
Di Fara	Midwood	25
Don Antonio	Midtown	22
NEW Emily	Clinton Hill	—
NEW Emmett's	SoHo	21
57 Napoli	E Midtown	21
Forcella	multi.	21
Fornino	multi.	23
Franny's	Park Slope	25

Gigino | **multi.**	20
Grimaldi's | **multi.**	22
Harry's Italian | **multi.**	21
Joe & Pat's | **Castelton Cnrs**	25
Joe's Pizza | **multi.**	24
John's/12th St. | **E Vill**	21
John's Pizzeria | **multi.**	23
Juliana's | **Dumbo**	26
Keste Pizza | **W Vill**	23
L&B Spumoni | **Gravesend**	23
La Pizza Fresca | **Flatiron**	23
La Villa Pizzeria | **multi.**	22
Lazzara's | **Midtown**	23
NEW Lea | **Ditmas Pk**	—
Lil' Frankie | **E Vill**	25
Lombardi's | **NoLita**	24
Lucali | **Carroll Gdns**	27
Luzzo's | **E Vill**	25
Manducatis Rustica | **LIC**	22
NEW Marta | **Flatiron**	—
Motorino | **multi.**	24
Naples 45 | **E Midtown**	21
Nick's | **multi.**	23
Nicoletta | **E Vill**	19
Nino's | **E Midtown**	21
Numero 28 | **multi.**	23
Otto | **G Vill**	23
Ovest | **Chelsea**	24
Palà | **LES**	22
Patsy's | **multi.**	21
Paulie Gee's | **Greenpt**	27
PizzArte | **Midtown**	20
NEW Pizzetteria Brunetti | **W Vill**	26
Posto | **Gramercy**	23
Roberta's | **Bushwick**	26
Rubirosa | **NoLita**	25
San Matteo | **E 80s**	25
Saraghina | **Bed-Stuy**	25
Speedy Romeo | **Clinton Hill**	23
Spunto | **W Vill**	22
Toby's Public | **multi.**	24
Totonno Pizza | **Coney Is**	26
Two Boots | **multi.**	19
Vesta | **Astoria**	25
Vesuvio | **Bay Ridge**	22
Vezzo | **Kips Bay**	23
Wheated | **Ditmas Pk**	21

Wild | **multi.**	—
Zero Otto | **multi.**	23

POLISH

Little Poland | **E Vill**	21
Lomzynianka | **Greenpt**	25

PORTUGUESE

Louro | **W Vill**	26
Macao Trading | **TriBeCa**	21
NEW Raizes Churrascaria | **Greenpt**	—

PUB FOOD

B&B Winepub | **SoHo**	21
Donovan's | **multi.**	21
Ellington | **W 100s**	16
Fraunces Tav. | **Financial**	17
J.G. Melon | **E 70s**	21
Landmark Tav. | **Hell's Kit**	19
P.J. Clarke's | **multi.**	19

PUERTO RICAN

Sazon | **TriBeCa**	23
Sofrito | **E Midtown**	24

QUÉBÉCOIS

Le Pescadeux | **SoHo**	21
M. Wells Dinette | **LIC**	24

RUSSIAN

Mari Vanna | **Flatiron**	20
NEW Moscow 57 | **LES**	—
Russian Samovar | **Midtown**	17
Russian Tea | **Midtown**	19
Tatiana | **Brighton Bch**	18

SANDWICHES
(See also Delis)

Banh Mi Saigon | **L Italy**	25
Beecher's Cellar | **Flatiron**	21
Best Pizza | **W'burg**	24
Bonnie's Grill | **Park Slope**	22
Bread | **NoLita**	20
Brennan | **Sheepshead**	23
Chick P | **Prospect Hts**	—
Copenhagen | **TriBeCa**	19
Defonte's | **Red Hook**	24
E.A.T. | **E 80s**	20
Eisenberg's | **Flatiron**	17
Friedman's Lunch | **Chelsea**	21
Fritzl's Lunch | **Bushwick**	—
Hanco's | **multi.**	21

CUISINES

Il Bambino | **Astoria**	25
L'Albero/Gelati | **Park Slope**	23
Leo's Latticini/Corona | **multi.**	26
Little Muenster | **multi.**	21
NEW Mayhem & Stout | **Murray Hill**	—
Meatball Shop | **multi.**	22
Meat Hook Sandwich | **W'burg**	—
Melt Shop | **multi.**	19
Mile End | **NoHo**	22
99 Miles/Philly | **multi.**	20
No. 7 | **multi.**	21
Num Pang | **multi.**	23
Olive's | **multi.**	23
NEW 100 Montaditos | **multi.**	20
Parm | **NoLita**	24
Peanut Butter Co. | **G Vill**	20
Porchetta | **E Vill**	21
Press 195 | **Bayside**	23
Queens Kickshaw | **Astoria**	21
Roll-n-Roaster | **Sheepshead**	22
San Matteo | **E 80s**	25
Sarge's Deli | **Murray Hill**	23
NEW Schnitz | **E Vill**	—
Shorty's | **multi.**	21
Smile | **SoHo**	22
sNice | **Park Slope**	21
Taboon | **G Vill**	24
Tartinery | **multi.**	23
Via Quadronno | **E 70s**	21
'Wichcraft | **multi.**	19
Yura on Madison | **E 90s**	20

SCANDINAVIAN

Aquavit | **Midtown**	26
Smorgas Chef | **multi.**	21

SEAFOOD

Ammos | **Midtown**	21
Aquagrill | **SoHo**	27
Artie's | **City Is**	22
Atlantic Grill | **multi.**	22
Avra | **E Midtown**	25
NEW Barchetta | **Chelsea**	—
NEW Bergen Hill | **Carroll Gdns**	—
BLT Fish | **Flatiron**	25
Blue Fin | **Midtown**	23
Blue Water | **Union Sq**	24
Bocelli | **Old Town**	25
Boil | **LES**	23

Brooklyn Crab | **Red Hook**	20
Catch | **Meatpacking**	23
City Hall | **TriBeCa**	22
City Is. Lobster | **City Is**	22
City Lobster/Steak | **Midtown**	21
NEW Clam | **W Vill**	23
Cole's Dock Side | **Great Kills**	23
Cowgirl | **Seaport**	18
Crave Fishbar | **E Midtown**	24
Cull & Pistol | **Chelsea**	24
David Burke Fishtail | **E 60s**	24
Docks Oyster | **Murray Hill**	20
Ed's Chowder | **W 60s**	20
Ed's Lobster Bar | **SoHo**	24
Elias Corner | **Astoria**	26
El Toro Blanco | **W Vill**	22
Esca | **Hell's Kit**	25
Ethos | **multi.**	22
Fish | **W Vill**	23
FishTag | **W 70s**	23
Flex Mussels | **multi.**	24
Francisco's | **Chelsea**	23
NEW Greenpt Fish | **Greenpt**	—
Harlow | **E Midtown**	20
Ithaka | **E 80s**	22
John Dory Oyster | **Flatiron**	21
Jordans Lobster | **Sheepshead**	22
Jubilee | **E Midtown**	21
Kellari Taverna | **Midtown**	22
L & W Oyster | **Flatiron**	20
Le Bernardin | **Midtown**	29
Le Pescadeux | **SoHo**	21
Littleneck | **multi.**	23
Lobster Joint | **multi.**	22
London Lennie's | **Middle Vill**	24
Luke's Lobster | **multi.**	24
Lure Fishbar | **SoHo**	24
Marea | **Midtown**	27
Mary's Fish | **W Vill**	25
Mermaid | **multi.**	22
Millesime | **Flatiron**	21
Milos | **Midtown**	27
NEW Navy | **SoHo**	—
New Imperial Palace | **Flushing**	22
NEW Norman's Cay | **LES**	—
North End Grill | **Battery Pk**	24
Oceana | **Midtown**	25
Ocean Grill | **W 70s**	23

More on zagat.com

Okeanos	**Park Slope**	22
Oriental Gdn.	**Chinatown**	21
Oyster Bar	**Midtown**	22
Pampano	**E Midtown**	23
Pearl Oyster	**W Vill**	27
Pearl Room	**Bay Ridge**	22
Periyali	**Flatiron**	24
Petite Crevette	**Columbia St.**	23
Ping's Seafood	**multi.**	20
NEW Raizes Churrascaria	**Greenpt**	—
Randazzo's	**Sheepshead**	22
Redeye Grill	**Midtown**	19
Red Hook Lobster	**multi.**	24
River Styx	**Greenpt**	—
Sammy's Fishbox	**City Is**	21
Sammy's Shrimp	**City Is**	23
Sea Fire Grill	**E Midtown**	28
Sea Grill	**Midtown**	24
Shula's	**Midtown**	21
Sik Gaek	**multi.**	22
South Fin Grill	**South Bch**	19
Strip House	**multi.**	25
Taverna Kyclades	**Astoria**	26
Telly's Taverna	**Astoria**	22
Thalassa	**TriBeCa**	24
Tratt. Pesce	**multi.**	20
Upstate	**E Vill**	25
Water's Edge	**LIC**	22
NEW Wayfarer	**Midtown**	18
ZZ's Clam Bar	**G Vill**	24

SMALL PLATES
(See also Spanish tapas specialist)

Almayass	Armenian/Lebanese	**Flatiron**	23
Alta	Med.	**G Vill**	25
Beauty & Essex	Amer.	**LES**	23
NEW Bar Chuko	Japanese	**Prospect Hts**	—
NEW Bar Primi	Italian	**E Vill**	—
NEW Bergen Hill	Seafood	**Carroll Gdns**	—
Beyoglu	Turkish	**E 80s**	22
Bocca Lupo	Italian	**Cobble Hill**	22
Buvette	French	**W Vill**	24
Cafe Noir	African/Med.	**TriBeCa**	—
Caffe Storico	Italian	**W 70s**	22

Cannibal	Belgian	**Hell's Kit**	21
Cocotte	French	**SoHo**	23
Corsino	Italian	**Meatpacking**	21
Danji	Korean	**Midtown**	25
NEW David Burke Fab.	Amer.	**Midtown**	—
Degustation	French/Spanish	**E Vill**	26
Empelión	Mex.	**E Vill**	23
EN Japanese	Japanese	**W Vill**	25
Estela	Amer./Med.	**NoLita**	25
Felice	Italian	**multi.**	21
Forty Four	Amer.	**Midtown**	21
Graffiti	Eclectic	**E Vill**	28
Hanjan	Korean	**Flatiron**	23
NEW Humboldt/Jackson	Amer.	**W'burg**	—
Kashkaval	Med.	**Midtown**	22
Lulu & Po	Amer.	**Ft Greene**	25
Lunetta	Italian	**Boerum Hill**	21
Macondo	Pan-Latin	**LES**	23
Má Pêche	Amer.	**Midtown**	23
Maze	French	**Midtown**	19
Mehtaphor	Eclectic	**TriBeCa**	26
Mercadito	Mex.	**E Vill**	22
Mezetto	Med.	**LES**	23
Rayuela	Pan-Latin	**LES**	23
Recette	Amer.	**W Vill**	24
Robataya	Japanese	**E Vill**	25
Sakagura	Japanese	**E Midtown**	24
Salt & Fat	Amer./Asian	**Sunnyside**	25
Salumeria/Rist. Rosi	Italian	**multi.**	24
Sojourn	Amer.	**E 70s**	25
NEW Telepan Local	Amer.	**TriBeCa**	23
NEW Terra Tribeca	Italian	**TriBeCa**	21
Terroir	Italian	**multi.**	20
Traif	Eclectic	**W'burg**	26
Uva	Italian	**E 70s**	23
Vanderbilt	Amer.	**Prospect Hts**	21
Zenkichi	Japanese	**W'burg**	27

SOUL FOOD

Amy Ruth's	**Harlem**	22
Cheryl's Global	**Prospect Hts**	23
Miss Mamie/Maude	**Harlem**	21
Sylvia's	**Harlem**	18

CUISINES

SOUTH AFRICAN

Braai | **Midtown**	20
Madiba | **Ft Greene**	24

SOUTH AMERICAN

Empanada Mama | **Hell's Kit**	24

SOUTHERN

Amy Ruth's | **Harlem**	22
NEW Bo's | **Flatiron**	20
Brooklyn Star | **W'burg**	24
Char No. 4 | **Cobble Hill**	22
Egg | **W'burg**	23
Hill Country Chicken | **multi.**	20
Jacob's Pickles | **W 80s**	21
Kitchenette | **multi.**	20
Melba's | **Harlem**	24
Miss Mamie/Maude | **Harlem**	21
NEW Montana's Trail | **Bushwick**	—
Peaches | **Bed-Stuy**	25
Pies-N-Thighs | **W'burg**	24
Queens Comfort | **Astoria**	22
Redhead | **E Vill**	23
NEW Root & Bone | **E Vill**	—
Sweet Chick | **multi.**	21
Sylvia's | **Harlem**	18
Tipsy Parson | **Chelsea**	22
NEW Wilma Jean | **Carroll Gdns**	—

SOUTHWESTERN

Cowgirl | **multi.**	18

SPANISH
(* tapas specialist)

Andanada 141* | **W 60s**	20
Bar Jamón* | **Gramercy**	22
Barraca | **W Vill**	21
Beso | **St. George**	25
Boqueria* | **multi.**	23
Cafe Espanol | **multi.**	21
Casa Mono* | **Gramercy**	24
Cata | **LES**	22
Degustation | **E Vill**	26
El Charro Espanol* | **W Vill**	23
NEW El Colmado* | **Hell's Kit**	—
El Porrón * | **E 60s**	20
El Pote | **Murray Hill**	23
El Quijote | **Chelsea**	22
El Quinto Pino* | **Chelsea**	25
Francisco's | **Chelsea**	23
La Fonda/Sol | **E Midtown**	21

Las Ramblas* | **W Vill**	23
La Vara* | **Cobble Hill**	26
Meson Sevilla | **Midtown**	22
Sala One Nine* | **Flatiron**	23
Salinas* | **Chelsea**	22
Sevilla | **W Vill**	24
Socarrat* | **multi.**	22
Solera* | **E Midtown**	23
NEW Tablao* | **TriBeCa**	—
Tertulia* | **W Vill**	24
Tía Pol* | **Chelsea**	23
NEW Toro* | **Chelsea**	25
Txikito* | **Chelsea**	26

STEAKHOUSES

NEW American Cut | **TriBeCa**	24
Arirang Hibachi | **multi.**	23
Arlington Club | **E 70s**	21
Artie's | **City Is**	22
Ben & Jack's | **Flatiron**	24
Benchmark | **Park Slope**	21
Benjamin Steak | **Midtown**	27
Bill's Food/Drink | **Midtown**	18
BLT Prime | **Gramercy**	25
BLT Steak | **E Midtown**	24
Bobby Van's | **multi.**	23
Bond 45 | **Midtown**	19
Buenos Aires | **E Vill**	22
Bull & Bear | **E Midtown**	23
Capital Grille | **multi.**	24
NEW Charlie Palmer | **Midtown**	—
Chimichurri Grill | **Hell's Kit**	21
Christos | **Astoria**	22
Churrascaria | **Midtown**	24
Circus | **E 60s**	21
City Hall | **TriBeCa**	22
City Lobster/Steak | **Midtown**	21
Club A Steak | **E Midtown**	23
Costata | **SoHo**	25
Del Frisco's | **multi.**	25
Delmonico's | **multi.**	23
Embers | **Bay Ridge**	23
Empire Steak | **Midtown**	22
Frankie & Johnnie's | **Midtown**	23
Gallaghers | **Midtown**	22
Harry's Cafe | **Financial**	22
NEW Il Mulino Prime | **SoHo**	—
Jake's Steakhse. | **Fieldston**	23
Keens | **Midtown**	26

Le Marais | **Midtown**	21
Le Relais | **E Midtown**	21
Les Halles | **multi.**	20
Macelleria | **Meatpacking**	24
Maloney & Porcelli | **Midtown**	25
Manzo | **Flatiron**	24
MarkJoseph | **Seaport**	24
Michael Jordan | **Midtown**	21
Morton's | **multi.**	24
NEW M. Wells Steakhse. | **LIC**	22
Nick & Stef's | **Midtown**	22
Nino's | **Midtown**	21
NYY Steak | **Concourse/Dntwn**	22
Old Homestead | **Chelsea**	25
Palm | **multi.**	25
Parlor Steakhse. | **E 80s**	22
Peter Luger | **W'burg**	28
Pietro's | **E Midtown**	25
Porter House | **Midtown**	26
Prime Grill | **Midtown**	24
Prime Meats | **Carroll Gdns**	24
Quality Italian | **Midtown**	24
Quality Meats | **Midtown**	26
NEW Reserve Cut | **Financial**	25
Ricardo | **E Harlem**	23
Ruth's Chris | **Midtown**	25
Shula's | **Midtown**	21
Smith/Wollensky | **E Midtown**	25
Sparks | **E Midtown**	25
S Prime | **Astoria**	23
St. Anselm | **W'burg**	28
STK | **multi.**	23
Strip House | **multi.**	25
T-Bar Steak | **E 70s**	22
NEW Texas de Brazil | **E 60s**	24
Tre Dici | **Flatiron**	22
Uncle Jack's | **multi.**	24
Via Brasil | **Midtown**	20
Wolfgang's | **multi.**	25
Wollensky's | **E Midtown**	24

SWISS

Mont Blanc | **Midtown**	21
Trestle on 10th | **Chelsea**	20

TAIWANESE

BaoHaus | **E Vill**	20
NEW Lucky Luna | **Greenpt**	—
NEW Mimi Cheng's | **E Vill**	—

TEAHOUSES

Alice's Tea | **multi.**	20
Bosie Tea Parlor | **W Vill**	23
Cha An | **E Vill**	22
Lady Mendl's | **Gramercy**	22
Radiance Tea | **Midtown**	21
Tea & Sympathy | **W Vill**	21

TEX-MEX

Tres Carnes | **multi.**	22

THAI

Am Thai | **multi.**	23
Ayada | **Elmhurst**	25
Breeze | **Hell's Kit**	21
Chai Home | **multi.**	22
Erawan | **Bayside**	22
Jaiya | **multi.**	20
Joya | **Cobble Hill**	24
Kin Shop | **W Vill**	22
Kuma Inn | **LES**	25
Land Thai | **W 80s**	22
Laut | **Union Sq**	20
Ngam | **E Vill**	23
Pam Real Thai | **Hell's Kit**	22
Pok Pok Ny | **Columbia St.**	24
Pongsri Thai | **multi.**	21
Pure Thai | **Midtown**	26
Qi | **multi.**	21
Room Service | **Midtown**	20
Sea | **W'burg**	23
NEW Somtum Der | **E Vill**	22
Song | **Park Slope**	22
Spice | **multi.**	21
Sripraphai | **Woodside**	27
Thai Market | **W 100s**	23
Topaz | **Midtown**	23
Uncle Boons | **NoLita**	25
v{iv} | **Hell's Kit**	21
Wondee Siam | **multi.**	21
Zabb Elee | **multi.**	22

TURKISH

Akdeniz | **Midtown**	22
A La Turka | **E 70s**	20
Ali Baba | **multi.**	21
Beyoglu | **E 80s**	22
Bodrum | **W 80s**	20
Hanci Turkish | **Hell's Kit**	21
Pasha | **W 70s**	20

CUISINES

Pera	**SoHo**	20	Omai	**Chelsea**	22
Sahara	**Sheepshead**	23	Pho Bang	**multi.**	21
Sip Sak	**E Midtown**	22	Pho Viet Huong	**Chinatown**	24
Taci's Beyti	**Sheepshead**	24	Rouge et Blanc	**SoHo**	23
Turkish Cuisine	**Hell's Kit**	23		
Turkish Kitchen	**Kips Bay**	23		
Uskudar	**E 70s**	24		

UKRAINIAN

Veselka	**E Vill**	21

VEGETARIAN
(* vegan)

Angelica Kit.*	**E Vill**	23
B & H Dairy	**E Vill**	24
Blossom*	**multi.**	22
NEW Bunna Cafe*	**Bushwick**	—
Butcher's Daughter*	**NoLita**	22
Candle Cafe*	**multi.**	23
Candle 79*	**E 70s**	24
Chick P	**Prospect Hts**	—
Gobo*	**W Vill**	22
Hangawi	**Midtown**	26
Hummus Pl.	**multi.**	21
Kajitsu	**Murray Hill**	25
Peacefood Café*	**multi.**	23
NEW Pickle Shack	**Gowanus**	—
Pure Food/Wine*	**Gramercy**	24
Queens Kickshaw	**Astoria**	21
Red Bamboo*	**G Vill**	22
Sacred Chow	**G Vill**	24
Saravanaa Bhavan	**multi.**	23
sNice	**Park Slope**	21
Taïm	**multi.**	25
V-Note*	**E 70s**	23
Wild Ginger*	**multi.**	22
Zen Palate*	**Murray Hill**	20

VENEZUELAN

Arepas	**Astoria**	23
Caracas	**multi.**	26

VIETNAMESE

Banh Mi Saigon	**L Italy**	25
Bo-Ky	**multi.**	21
Bunker Viet.	**Ridgewood**	25
Hanco's	**multi.**	21
Indochine	**G Vill**	21
Le Colonial	**E Midtown**	23
Nha Trang	**Chinatown**	24
Nightingale 9	**Carroll Gdns**	23

Locations

Includes names, cuisines and Food ratings.

Manhattan

BATTERY PARK CITY

(Chambers St. to Battery Pl., west of West St.)

Battery Gdns.	*Amer./Cont.*	19
Blue Ribbon Sushi	*Japanese*	25
Blue Smoke	*BBQ*	21
Dos Toros	*Mex.*	20
El Vez	*Mex.*	—
Gigino	*Italian*	20
Harry's Italian	*Italian*	21
NEW Hudson Eats	*Food Mkt.*	—
Little Muenster	*Sandwiches*	21
Mighty Quinn's	*BBQ*	26
North End Grill	*Amer./Seafood*	24
Num Pang	*Cam./Sandwiches*	23
Olive's	*Sandwiches*	23
P.J. Clarke's	*Pub*	19
Shake Shack	*Burgers*	21
Tartinery	*French/Sandwiches*	23
2 West	*Amer.*	22
Umami Burger	*Burgers*	23

CENTRAL PARK

Boathouse	*Amer.*	17
NEW Tavern/Green	*Amer.*	—

CHELSEA

(30th to 34th Sts., west of 9th Ave.; 14th to 30th Sts., west of 7th Ave.)

Amorino	*Ice Cream*	25
Artichoke Basille	*Pizza*	22
NEW Barchetta	*Italian/Seafood*	—
BareBurger	*Burgers*	21
Bar Eolo	*Italian*	23
Blossom	*Vegan/Veg.*	22
Blue Bottle	*Coffee*	23
Bocca/Bacco	*Italian*	20
NEW Bodega Negra	*Mex.*	23
Bottino	*Italian*	21
Bottino	*Italian*	21
Brgr	*Burgers*	20
Buddakan	*Asian*	25
Café Grumpy	*Coffee*	21
Cafeteria	*Amer.*	20
Cherry	*Japanese*	22

Co.	*Pizza*	22
Colicchio/Sons	*Amer.*	26
Cookshop	*Amer.*	23
Coppelia	*Diner/Pan-Latin*	20
Corkbuzz	*Eclectic*	21
Cull & Pistol	*Seafood*	24
Del Posto	*Italian*	26
El Quijote	*Spanish*	22
El Quinto Pino	*Spanish*	25
NEW Empire Diner	*Diner*	21
Fonda	*Mex.*	24
Francisco's	*Seafood/Spanish*	23
Friedman's Lunch	*Amer.*	21
Grand Sichuan	*Chinese*	19
Green Table	*Amer.*	24
Grey Dog	*Amer.*	22
Joe	*Coffee*	21
La Lunchonette	*French*	22
Legend	*Chinese*	20
Le Grainne Cafe	*French*	22
Le Pain Q.	*Bakery/Belgian*	18
Le Zie	*Italian*	20
NEW Los Tacos	*Mex.*	—
Meatball Shop	*Sandwiches*	22
Momoya	*Japanese*	22
NEW Monarch Rm.	*Amer.*	—
Montmartre	*French*	21
Morimoto	*Japanese*	26
Ninth St Espresso	*Coffee*	23
Num Pang	*Cam./Sandwiches*	23
Old Homestead	*Steak*	25
Omai	*Veg.*	22
Ovest	*Pizza*	24
Park	*Med.*	18
Patsy's	*Pizza*	21
Pongsri Thai	*Thai*	21
Rare B&G	*Burgers*	21
Red Cat	*Amer./Med.*	24
Rocking Horse	*Mex.*	22
Salinas	*Spanish*	22
Scarpetta	*Italian*	25
Socarrat	*Spanish*	22
Spice	*Thai*	21
Sushi Seki	*Japanese*	25
Tao	*Asian*	23

L O C A T I O N S

Terroir | *Italian*	20
Tía Pol | *Spanish*	23
Tipsy Parson | *Southern*	22
NEW Toro | *Spanish*	25
Trestle on 10th | *Amer.*	20
Txikito | *Spanish*	26
Uncle Nick's | *Greek*	20
Westville | *Amer.*	23
'Wichcraft | *Sandwiches*	19
Willow Road | *Amer.*	22

CHINATOWN

(Canal to Pearl Sts., east of B'way)

NEW Bassanova | *Japanese/Noodle Shop*	21
Big Wong | *Chinese*	21
Bo-Ky | *Noodle Shop*	21
Buddha Bodai | *Chinese/Kosher*	22
Chinatown Ice Cream | *Ice Cream*	24
Dim Sum Go Go | *Chinese*	21
Excellent Dumpling | *Chinese*	24
456 Shanghai | *Chinese*	22
Golden Unicorn | *Chinese*	22
Great NY Noodle | *Noodle Shop*	23
Hop Kee | *Chinese*	21
Jing Fong | *Chinese*	21
Joe's Shanghai | *Chinese*	22
New Malaysia | *Malaysian*	23
Nha Trang | *Veg.*	24
Nice Green Bo | *Chinese*	22
Nom Wah Tea | *Chinese*	21
Oriental Gdn. | *Chinese/Seafood*	21
Peking Duck | *Chinese*	23
Pho Viet Huong | *Viet.*	24
Ping's Seafood | *Chinese/Seafood*	20
Pongsri Thai | *Thai*	21
Pulqueria | *Mex.*	23
Tasty Hand-Pulled | *Noodle Shop*	22
Wo Hop | *Chinese*	21
Xi'an | *Chinese/Noodle Shop*	23

EAST HARLEM

(100th to 135th Sts., east of 5th Ave.)

Amor Cubano | *Cuban*	23
El Paso | *Mex.*	22
Moustache | *Mideast.*	22
Patsy's | *Pizza*	21
Rao's | *Italian*	21
Ricardo | *Steak*	23

EAST MIDTOWN

40s

Aburiya Kinnosuke | *Japanese*	24
Ali Baba | *Turkish*	21
Aperitivo Pizza | *Pizza*	22
Aretsky's Patroon | *Amer.*	25
Avra | *Greek/Seafood*	25
Bobby Van's | *Steak*	23
Bukhara Grill | *Indian*	25
Bull & Bear | *Steak*	23
Cafe Centro | *French/Med.*	21
Café Grumpy | *Coffee*	21
Capital Grille | *Steak*	24
Chin Chin | *Chinese*	22
Da Noi | *Italian*	25
Darbar | *Indian*	23
Gyu-Kaku | *Japanese*	22
Il Postino | *Italian*	22
La Fonda/Sol | *Spanish*	21
Lexington Brass | *Amer.*	20
Luke's Lobster | *Seafood*	24
Megu | *Japanese*	23
Nanni | *Italian*	22
Naples 45 | *Italian/Pizza*	21
Naya | *Lebanese*	22
99 Miles/Philly | *Cheestks.*	20
Nino's | *Pizza*	21
Osteria Laguna | *Italian*	20
Palm | *Steak*	25
Pampano | *Mex./Seafood*	23
Patsy's | *Pizza*	21
Pietro's | *Italian/Steak*	25
Sakagura | *Japanese*	24
Sea Fire Grill | *Seafood*	28
Shake Shack | *Burgers*	21
Sip Sak | *Turkish*	22
Smith/Wollensky | *Steak*	25
Soba Totto | *Japanese/Noodle Shop*	24
Sparks | *Steak*	25
Sushi Yasuda | *Japanese*	28
Tulsi | *Indian*	24
'Wichcraft | *Sandwiches*	19
Wollensky's | *Steak*	24
Yama | *Japanese*	24

50s

Al Bustan | *Lebanese*	21
Amma | *Indian*	25
Angelo's Pizzeria | *Pizza*	20
Bistango | *multi.*	22

Bistro Vendôme	*French*	22
BLT Steak	*Steak*	24
Bobby Van's	*Steak*	23
Brasserie	*French*	21
Brick Ln. Curry	*Indian*	21
Chola	*Indian*	23
Club A Steak	*Steak*	23
Crave Fishbar	*Seafood*	24
Darbar	*Indian*	23
David Burke/Bloom.	*Amer.*	20
Dawat	*Indian*	23
DeGrezia	*Italian*	25
Dos Caminos	*Mex.*	20
Ethos	*Greek/Seafood*	22
Felidia	*Italian*	25
57 Napoli	*Pizza*	21
Fika	*Coffee*	21
Four Seasons	*Amer.*	26
Grand Sichuan	*Chinese*	19
Harlow	*Seafood*	20
Hide-Chan	*Japanese/Noodle Shop*	23
Hillstone	*Amer.*	22
Jubilee	*French*	21
Kati Roll	*Indian*	22
La Mangeoire	*French*	23
Le Cirque	*French*	24
Le Colonial	*French/Viet.*	23
Le Perigord	*French*	24
Le Relais	*French/Steak*	21
NEW Little Collins	*Coffee*	—
Lychee House	*Chinese*	23
Melt Shop	*Sandwiches*	19
Mike's Bistro	*Amer.*	25
Montebello	*Italian*	22
Morso	*Italian*	23
Mr. Chow	*Chinese*	23
Mr. K's	*Chinese*	23
National	*Amer.*	19
Naya	*Lebanese*	22
Ninth St Espresso	*Coffee*	23
Noir	*Amer.*	24
Peking Duck	*Chinese*	23
P.J. Clarke's	*Pub*	19
Rosa Mexicano	*Mex.*	23
Schnipper's	*Amer.*	20
Shun Lee Palace	*Chinese*	24
Smith	*Amer.*	19
Socarrat	*Spanish*	22
Sofrito	*Puerto Rican*	24
Solera	*Spanish*	23
Tenzan	*Japanese*	20
Tres Carnes	*Tex-Mex*	22
Wolfgang's	*Steak*	25
Ze Café	*French/Italian*	20

EAST 60s

Alice's Tea	*Teahse.*	20
Amali	*Med.*	24
Amaranth	*Med.*	21
Anassa Taverna	*Greek*	21
Bar Italia	*Italian*	23
Bistro Chat Noir	*French*	20
Brgr	*Burgers*	20
Cabana	*Nuevo Latino*	22
Circus	*Brazilian/Steak*	21
Daniel	*French*	28
David Burke Fishtail	*Seafood*	24
NEW East Pole	*British*	22
El Porrón	*Spanish*	20
Fatty Fish	*Asian*	21
Felice	*Italian*	21
Fig & Olive	*Med.*	21
Fred's at Barneys	*Amer./Italian*	22
Il Mulino	*Italian*	25
Il Vagabondo	*Italian*	20
Jackson Hole	*Burgers*	20
JoJo	*French*	24
L'Absinthe	*French*	23
Le Bilboquet	*French*	21
Le Pain Q.	*Bakery/Belgian*	18
Le Veau d'Or	*French*	21
Maya	*Mex.*	22
Mon Petit Cafe	*French*	20
Moti Mahal	*Indian*	22
Nello	*Italian*	18
Patsy's	*Pizza*	21
Philippe	*Chinese*	23
Primola	*Italian*	23
Ravagh	*Persian*	23
Regency B&G	*Amer.*	19
NEW Rotisserie Georgette	*French*	24
Sant Ambroeus	*Italian*	21
Scalinatella	*Italian*	24
Serafina	*Italian*	18
Serendipity 3	*Dessert*	19
Sirio	*Italian*	22
Sushi Seki	*Japanese*	25
NEW Texas de Brazil	*Brazilian/Steak*	24

Tiella	*Italian*	25
Tony's Di Napoli	*Italian*	22
Torishin	*Japanese*	25

EAST 70s

Afghan Kebab	*Afghan*	20
A La Turka	*Turkish*	20
Alloro	*Italian*	23
Arlington Club	*Steak*	21
Atlantic Grill	*Seafood*	22
BareBurger	*Burgers*	21
B. Café	*Belgian*	21
Bella Blu	*Italian*	22
Blue 9 Burger	*Burgers*	20
Bottega	*Italian*	20
Brasserie Cognac	*French*	19
Brother Jimmy's	*BBQ*	17
Café Boulud	*French*	26
Cafe Evergreen	*Chinese*	22
Campagnola	*Italian*	23
Candle Cafe	*Vegan/Veg.*	23
Candle 79	*Vegan/Veg.*	24
Caravaggio	*Italian*	25
Carlyle	*French*	23
Dos Toros	*Mex.*	20
Due	*Italian*	22
Gari	*Japanese*	26
Haru	*Japanese*	21
J.G. Melon	*Pub*	21
Joe	*Coffee*	21
Jones Wood Foundry	*British*	21
Ko Sushi	*Japanese*	20
Le Pain Q.	*Bakery/Belgian*	18
Lusardi's	*Italian*	25
Maison Kayser	*Bakery/French*	22
Mark	*Amer.*	23
Maruzzella	*Italian*	21
Meatball Shop	*Sandwiches*	22
Nino's	*Italian*	21
Numero 28	*Pizza*	23
Orsay	*French*	18
Oslo Coffee	*Coffee*	23
Pastrami Queen	*Deli/Kosher*	22
Persepolis	*Persian*	22
Quatorze Bis	*French*	20
Salumeria/Rist. Rosi	*Italian*	24
Sant Ambroeus	*Italian*	21
Sasabune	*Japanese*	25
2nd Ave Deli	*Deli/Kosher*	23
Serafina	*Italian*	18
Sette Mezzo	*Italian*	22

Shabu-Shabu 70	*Japanese*	23
Sojourn	*Amer.*	25
Spice	*Thai*	21
Swifty's	*Amer.*	16
Szechuan Gourmet	*Chinese*	23
Tanoshi	*Japanese*	26
T-Bar Steak	*Steak*	22
Uskudar	*Turkish*	24
Uva	*Italian*	23
Via Quadronno	*Italian*	21
V-Note	*Vegan*	23
Yefsi Estiatorio	*Greek*	23

EAST 80s

Alice's Tea	*Teahse.*	20
Antonucci	*Italian*	23
Baluchi's	*Indian*	20
Beyoglu	*Turkish*	22
Burger Bistro	*Burgers*	21
Café d'Alsace	*French*	22
Café Sabarsky/Fledermaus	*Austrian*	22
Cascabel Taqueria	*Mex.*	19
Chef Ho's	*Chinese*	22
Crown	*Amer.*	23
East End Kitchen	*Amer.*	21
E.A.T.	*Amer.*	20
Elio's	*Italian*	24
Erminia	*Italian*	23
Felice	*Italian*	21
Firenze	*Italian*	23
Flex Mussels	*Seafood*	24
Giovanni	*Italian*	22
Gobo	*Vegan/Veg.*	22
Heidelberg	*German*	21
Hummus Kit.	*Kosher/Med.*	20
Italianissimo	*Italian*	21
Ithaka	*Greek/Seafood*	22
Jacques	*French*	21
Jaiya	*Thai*	20
Kings' Carriage	*Amer.*	21
Ko Sushi	*Japanese*	20
Le Pain Q.	*Bakery/Belgian*	18
Luke's Lobster	*Seafood*	24
Maison Kayser	*Bakery/French*	22
Maz Mezcal	*Mex.*	21
Móle	*Mex.*	20
Nicola's	*Italian*	22
Papaya King	*Hot Dogs*	22
Parlor Steakhse.	*Steak*	22
Penrose	*Amer.*	20

Poke | *Japanese*	26
NEW Rist. Morini | *Italian*	26
Sandro's | *Italian*	24
San Matteo | *Italian/Pizza*	25
Shake Shack | *Burgers*	21
NEW Simone | *French*	25
Sistina | *Italian*	23
Spigolo | *Italian*	21
Tenzan | *Japanese*	20
Toloache | *Mex.*	23
Tratt. Pesce | *Italian/Seafood*	20
Two Boots | *Pizza*	19
Wa Jeal | *Chinese*	24
NEW Writing Room | *Amer.*	22

EAST 90s

Brick Ln. Curry | *Indian*	21
El Paso | *Mex.*	22
Le Paris Bistrot | *French*	21
Nick's | *Pizza*	23
Paola's | *Italian*	23
Pascalou | *French*	21
Pio Pio | *Peruvian*	22
Sarabeth's | *Amer.*	20
Sfoglia | *Italian*	25
Table d'Hôte | *Amer./French*	23
Yura on Madison | *Sandwiches*	20

EAST VILLAGE

(14th to Houston Sts., east of
3rd Ave.)

Abraço Espresso | *Coffee*	26
Alder | *American*	22
Angelica Kit. | *Vegan/Veg.*	23
Artichoke Basille | *Pizza*	22
Awash | *Ethiopian*	21
Back Forty | *Amer.*	22
Balade | *Lebanese*	24
B & H Dairy | *Deli/Veg.*	24
BaoHaus | *Taiwanese*	20
Barbone | *Italian*	24
BareBurger | *Burgers*	21
NEW Bar Primi | *Italian*	—
Big Gay Ice Cream | *Ice Cream*	23
NEW Black Ant | *Mex.*	—
Black Iron Burger | *Burgers*	23
Blue Ribbon Fried | *Chicken*	19
Boulton & Watt | *Amer.*	22
Brick Ln. Curry | *Indian*	21
Brindle Room | *Amer.*	20
Buenos Aires | *Argent./Steak*	22

Cacio e Pepe | *Italian*	20
NEW Cafe Cambodge | *Cambodian/French*	—
Cafe Mogador | *Moroccan*	24
NEW Cafe Standard | *Amer.*	20
NEW Cagen | *Japanese*	—
Caracas | *Veg.*	26
Caravan/Dreams | *Kosher/Vegan*	23
Cha An | *Japanese/Teahse.*	22
ChikaLicious | *Dessert*	23
Crif Dogs | *Hot Dogs*	23
DBGB | *French*	22
Degustation | *French/Spanish*	26
NEW East 12th | *Italian*	25
NEW Eddy | *Amer.*	—
Edi & The Wolf | *Austrian*	19
Empellón | *Mex.*	23
NEW Flinders Lane | *Australian*	—
Fonda | *Mex.*	24
Frank | *Italian*	21
Gemma | *Italian*	23
Gnocco | *Italian*	23
Graffiti | *Eclectic*	28
Grand Sichuan | *Chinese*	19
Hasaki | *Japanese*	23
Haveli | *Indian*	21
Hearth | *Amer./Italian*	25
Hummus Pl. | *Israeli/Kosher/Veg.*	21
Jeepney | *Filipino*	22
Jewel Bako | *Japanese*	24
John's/12th St. | *Italian*	21
Kafana | *E Euro.*	25
Kanoyama | *Japanese*	24
Kyo Ya | *Japanese*	26
La Palapa | *Mex.*	23
L'Apicio | *Italian*	23
Lavagna | *Italian*	25
Lil' Frankie | *Italian/Pizza*	25
Little Poland | *Diner/Polish*	21
Lucien | *French*	23
Luke's Lobster | *Seafood*	24
Luzzo's | *Pizza*	25
Maharlika | *Filipino*	21
Mamoun's | *Mideast.*	23
Mercadito | *Mex.*	22
Mermaid | *Seafood*	22
Mighty Quinn's | *BBQ*	26
NEW Mimi Cheng's | *Taiwanese*	—
Minca | *Japanese/Noodle Shop*	23
Miss Lily's | *Jamaican*	20

Momofuku Ko | *Amer.*	27
Momofuku Noodle | *Amer.*	23
Momofuku Ssäm Bar | *Amer.*	25
Motorino | *Pizza*	24
Moustache | *Mideast.*	22
NEW Narcissa | *Amer.*	27
Ngam | *Thai*	23
Nicoletta | *Italian/Pizza*	19
Ninth St Espresso | *Coffee*	23
Northern Spy | *Amer.*	22
Numero 28 | *Pizza*	23
Oaxaca | *Mex.*	21
OddFellows | *Ice Cream*	24
NEW Otto's Tacos | *Mex.*	22
Papaya King | *Hot Dogs*	22
Parmys Persian Fusion | *Persian*	—
Pommes Frites | *Belgian*	24
Porchetta | *Italian/Sandwiches*	21
Porsena | *Italian*	23
Prune | *Amer.*	24
Pylos | *Greek*	26
Redhead | *Southern*	23
Red Hook Lobster | *Seafood*	24
NEW Risotteria Melotti | *Italian*	—
Robataya | *Japanese*	25
NEW Root & Bone | *Southern*	—
NEW Schnitz | *Sandwiches*	—
Shabu-Tatsu | *Japanese*	26
S'MAC | *Amer.*	23
Smith | *Amer.*	19
Soba Koh | *Japanese/Noodle Shop*	25
Soba-ya | *Japanese/Noodle Shop*	22
NEW Somtum Der | *Thai*	22
Spice | *Thai*	21
Spina | *Italian*	24
Supper | *Italian*	24
Sushi Dojo | *Japanese*	24
Takahachi | *Japanese*	24
Tarallucci | *Italian*	20
Taverna Kyclades | *Greek/ Seafood*	26
Terroir | *Italian*	20
Third Rail | *Coffee*	22
26 Seats | *French*	23
Two Boots | *Pizza*	19
Upstate | *Seafood*	25
Vanessa's Dumpling | *Seafood*	25
Van Leeuwen | *Coffee/Ice Cream*	24
Veselka | *Ukrainian*	21
Westville | *Amer.*	23

Xi'an | *Chinese/Noodle Shop*	23
Yerba Buena | *Pan-Latin*	22
Yuca Bar | *Pan-Latin*	21
Zabb Elee | *Thai*	22
Zum Schneider | *German*	22

FINANCIAL DISTRICT

(South of Civic Center, excluding
South St. Seaport)

Adrienne's | *Pizza*	24
BLT B&G | *Amer.*	22
Bobby Van's | *Steak*	23
BonChon | *Chicken*	21
Capital Grille | *Steak*	24
Cipriani Club 55 | *Italian*	23
Delmonico's | *Steak*	23
Felice | *Italian*	21
Fika | *Coffee*	21
Fraunces Tav. | *Pub*	17
Harry's Cafe | *Steak*	22
Harry's Italian | *Italian*	21
Haru | *Japanese*	21
Les Halles | *French/Steak*	20
Luke's Lobster | *Seafood*	24
Melt Shop | *Sandwiches*	19
Morton's | *Steak*	24
NEW Ramen. Co | *Japanese/ Noodle Shop*	—
NEW Reserve Cut | *Kosher/Steak*	25
Shorty's | *Cheestks.*	21
Smorgas Chef | *Scan.*	21
Toloache | *Mex.*	23
Tres Carnes | *Tex-Mex*	22

FLATIRON

(14th to 30th Sts., 7th Ave. to Park
Ave. So., excluding Union Sq.)

ABC Cocina | *Pan-Latin*	24
ABC Kitchen | *Amer.*	25
Aldea | *Med.*	24
Almayass | *Armenian/Lebanese*	23
Almond | *French*	21
Asellina | *Italian*	20
A Voce | *Italian*	23
Barbounia | *Med.*	23
Basta Pasta | *Italian*	24
Beecher's Cellar | *Amer.*	21
Ben & Jack's | *Steak*	24
Birreria | *Italian*	20
BLT Fish | *Seafood*	25
Bocca | *Italian*	22
Boqueria | *Spanish*	23

NEW Bo's	Creole/Southern	20
Breslin	British	24
NEW Cafe El Pres.	Mex.	–
City Bakery	Bakery	22
Craft	Amer.	26
Craftbar	Amer.	23
Crema	Mex.	22
Da Umberto	Italian	25
Dévi	Indian	23
Eataly	Food Mkt./Italian	23
Eisenberg's	Sandwiches	17
NEW Élan	Amer.	–
Eleven Madison	Amer.	28
NEW Gander	Amer.	–
Giorgio's	Amer./Italian	23
Gramercy Tavern	Amer.	28
Grimaldi's	Pizza	22
Hanjan	Korean	23
Hill Country	BBQ	23
Hill Country Chicken	Southern	20
Hillstone	Amer.	22
Ilili	Lebanese	26
Trattoria Il Mulino	Italian	25
Joe	Coffee	21
John Dory Oyster	Seafood	21
Junoon	Indian	24
L & W Oyster	Seafood	20
La Pizza Fresca	Italian/Pizza	23
Le Pain Q.	Bakery/Belgian	18
Maison Kayser	Bakery/French	22
Manzo	Italian/Steak	24
Mari Vanna	Russian	20
NEW Marta	Italian/Pizza	–
Maysville	Amer.	21
Melt Shop	Sandwiches	19
Mihoko's 21 Grams	French/Japanese	22
Millesime	French	21
Mira Sushi	Japanese	23
NoMad	Amer./Euro.	26
NEW NoMad Bar	Amer.	–
No. 7	Sandwiches	21
Num Pang	Cam./Sandwiches	23
Ootoya	Japanese/Noodle Shop	23
NEW Park Avenue	Amer.	–
Periyali	Greek	24
Petite Abeille	Belgian	20
Qi	Asian/Thai	21
Raymi	Peruvian	21
Rosa Mexicano	Mex.	23
Sala One Nine	Spanish	23

Schnipper's	Amer.	20
SD26	Italian	25
Shake Shack	Burgers	21
Shorty's	Cheestks.	21
Stumptown	Coffee	23
Tarallucci	Italian	20
Toby's Estate	Coffee	22
Tocqueville	Amer./French	27
Tre Dici	Italian/Steak	22
Tres Carnes	Tex-Mex	22
Via Emilia	Italian	22
'Wichcraft	Sandwiches	19
Zero Otto	Italian/Pizza	23
Zio Ristorante	Italian	22

GRAMERCY PARK

(14th to 23rd Sts., 1st Ave. to Park Ave. So., excluding Union Sq.)

Bar Jamón	Spanish	22
BLT Prime	Steak	25
Brother Jimmy's	BBQ	17
Casa Mono	Spanish	24
Friend/Farmer	Amer.	20
House	Amer.	23
Lady Mendl's	Teahse.	22
La Follia	Italian	22
Maialino	Italian	25
Novitá	Italian	24
Piccolo Cafe	Coffee/Italian	23
Ponty Bistro	African/French	24
Posto	Pizza	23
Pure Food/Wine	Vegan/Veg.	24
Rolf's	German	16
NEW Winslow	Amer./British	–
Yama	Japanese	24

GREENWICH VILLAGE

(Houston to 14th Sts., 3rd to 6th Aves., excluding NoHo)

NEW All'onda	Italian	23
Alta	Med.	25
Amorino	Ice Cream	25
Artichoke Basille	Pizza	22
Arturo's	Pizza	23
Babbo	Italian	26
BareBurger	Burgers	21
Bar Pitti	Italian	23
Blue Hill	Amer.	26
Blue 9 Burger	Burgers	20
NEW Botequim	Brazilian	–
Burger Joint	Burgers	23
Cafe Espanol	Spanish	21

LOCATIONS

Camaje | *Amer./French*	20
Carbone | *Italian*	24
Chez Jacqueline | *French*	20
NEW Claudette | *French*	—
Corkbuzz | *Eclectic*	21
Creperie | *French*	21
Crif Dogs | *Hot Dogs*	23
Cuba | *Cuban*	24
Da Andrea | *Italian*	23
Da Silvano | *Italian*	21
Dos Toros | *Mex.*	20
5 Napkin Burger | *Burgers*	20
Fourth | *Amer.*	20
Gotham B&G | *Amer.*	28
Grey Dog | *Amer.*	22
Gyu-Kaku | *Japanese*	22
NEW Han Dynasty | *Chinese*	23
Il Cantinori | *Italian*	23
Il Mulino | *Italian*	25
Indochine | *French/Viet.*	21
Ippudo | *Japanese/Noodle Shop*	25
Jackson Diner | *Indian*	21
Jane | *Amer.*	21
Joe | *Coffee*	21
Joe's Pizza | *Pizza*	24
Kati Roll | *Indian*	22
Knickerbocker | *Amer.*	22
Kotobuki | *Japanese*	25
La Lanterna | *Italian*	20
Le Pain Q. | *Bakery/Belgian*	18
Library/Public | *Amer.*	18
Lion | *Amer.*	24
Lupa | *Italian*	24
Mamoun's | *Mideast.*	23
NEW Margaux | *French/Med.*	17
Mermaid | *Seafood*	22
Minetta Tavern | *French*	24
Miss Lily's | *Jamaican*	20
Negril | *Carib./Jamaican*	23
Neta | *Japanese*	25
99 Miles/Philly | *Cheestks.*	20
North Sq. | *Amer.*	25
Num Pang | *Cam./Sandwiches*	23
NEW 100 Montaditos | *Sandwiches*	20
Otto | *Italian/Pizza*	23
Patsy's | *Pizza*	21
Peacefood Café | *Kosher/Vegan/Veg.*	23
Peanut Butter Co. | *Sandwiches*	20
Perla | *Italian*	25

Piadina | *Italian*	22
NEW Rasa | *Malaysian*	—
Red Bamboo | *Pan-Asian/Vegan*	22
Sacred Chow | *Kosher/Vegan/Veg.*	24
Spice | *Thai*	21
Strip House | *Steak*	25
Stumptown | *Coffee*	23
Taboon | *Sandwiches*	24
Third Rail | *Coffee*	22
Toloache | *Mex.*	23
Tomoe Sushi | *Japanese*	25
Umami Burger | *Burgers*	23
Ushiwakamaru | *Japanese*	27
Villa Mosconi | *Italian*	23
Volare | *Italian*	23
'Wichcraft | *Sandwiches*	19
Yuba | *Japanese*	24
ZZ's Clam Bar | *Seafood*	24

HAMILTON HEIGHTS

Covo | *Italian*	23

HARLEM

(110th to 155th Sts., 5th to St. Nicholas Aves.)

Amy Ruth's | *Soul Food*	22
NEW Barawine | *Amer.*	20
NEW Cecil | *Amer./Eclectic*	23
NEW Cheri | *French*	—
Chez Lucienne | *French*	21
5 & Diamond | *Amer.*	21
Ginny's Supper Club | *Amer.*	21
Harlem Shake | *Burgers*	20
Lido | *Italian*	24
Melba's | *Amer./Southern*	24
Miss Mamie/Maude | *Soul Food/Southern*	21
Red Rooster | *Amer.*	22
Sylvia's | *Soul Food/Southern*	18

HELL'S KITCHEN

(34th to 59th Sts., west of 9th Ave.)

Azuri Cafe | *Israeli/Kosher*	25
Balkanika | *Med.*	21
Blossom | *Vegan/Veg.*	22
Blue Bottle | *Coffee*	23
Bocca/Bacco | *Italian*	20
Breeze | *French/Thai*	21
Cannibal | *Belgian*	21
Casellula | *Amer.*	25
Chez Josephine | *French*	21
Chimichurri Grill | *Argent./Steak*	21

Daisy May's	*BBQ*	22
NEW East & West	*Amer./Asian*	—
NEW El Colmado	*Spanish*	—
Empanada Mama	*S Amer.*	24
Esca	*Italian/Seafood*	25
Fika	*Coffee*	21
44 & X/44½	*Amer.*	22
Gazala's	*Mideast.*	22
NEW Gotham West	*Food Mkt.*	25
Greek Kitchen	*Greek*	21
Hanci Turkish	*Turkish*	21
Hell's Kitchen	*Mex.*	20
NEW Ivan Ramen	*Japanese/ Noodle Shop*	19
Ktchn	*Amer.*	21
Landmark Tav.	*Pub*	19
NEW Marshal	*Amer.*	24
Pam Real Thai	*Thai*	22
Pio Pio	*Peruvian*	22
Print	*Amer.*	25
Queen of Sheba	*Ethiopian*	25
Taboon	*Med./Mideast.*	24
Totto Ramen	*Japanese/ Noodle Shop*	25
Turkish Cuisine	*Turkish*	23
Two Boots	*Pizza*	19
Uncle Nick's	*Greek*	20
v{iv}	*Thai*	21
West Bank	*Amer.*	19
Wondee Siam	*Thai*	21
Zen Palate	*Asian/Veg.*	20

HUDSON SQUARE

(Canal to Houston Sts., west of 6th Ave.)

Giorgione	*Italian*	24
Koi	*Japanese*	24
La Sirène	*French*	25
Westville	*Amer.*	23

INWOOD

Garden Café	*Amer.*	20
New Leaf	*Amer.*	22

KIPS BAY

(23rd to 34th Sts., east of Park Ave. So.)

Ali Baba	*Turkish*	21
Baluchi's	*Indian*	20
Bistango	*Italian*	22
Blue Smoke	*BBQ*	21

Brother Jimmy's	*BBQ*	17
Cannibal	*Belgian*	21
Coppola's	*Italian*	21
Dhaba	*Indian*	24
Dos Caminos	*Mex.*	20
East Pacific	*Asian*	24
Ethos	*Greek*	22
Fika	*Coffee*	21
Forcella	*Pizza*	21
Hummus Kit.	*Kosher/Med.*	20
I Trulli	*Italian*	23
Jaiya	*Thai*	20
Le Parisien	*French*	23
Les Halles	*French/Steak*	20
Marcony	*Italian*	25
Penelope	*Amer.*	22
Pio Pio	*Peruvian*	22
Ralph's Famous	*Ice Cream*	24
Resto	*Belgian*	20
Riverpark	*Amer.*	25
Sarabeth's	*Amer.*	20
Saravanaa Bhavan	*Indian/Veg.*	23
2nd Ave Deli	*Deli/Kosher*	23
S'MAC	*Amer.*	23
Terroir	*Italian*	20
Turkish Kitchen	*Turkish*	23
Vezzo	*Pizza*	23
Water Club	*Amer.*	22
NEW Water Table	*New Eng.*	—

LITTLE ITALY

(Broome to Canal Sts., Bowery to Centre St.)

Angelo's/Mulberry	*Italian*	23
NEW Bacchanal	*Amer.*	—
Banh Mi Saigon	*Sandwiches/Vietnamese*	25
NEW Baz Bagel	*Bakery/Jewish*	—
Bo-Ky	*Noodle Shop*	21
Da Nico	*Italian*	21
Ferrara	*Bakery*	23
Il Cortile	*Italian*	22
La Mela	*Italian*	21
Nyonya	*Malaysian*	23
Pellegrino's	*Italian*	21
Pho Bang	*Noodle Shop/Viet.*	21
Red Egg	*Chinese*	19
Vincent's	*Italian*	21
Wild Ginger	*Asian/Vegan*	22

LOWER EAST SIDE

(South of Houston St., east of Bowery & Pike St.)

A Casa Fox	*Pan-Latin*	24
NEW Antonioni's	*Italian*	—
Ápizz	*Italian*	23
Bacaro	*Italian*	24
Barrio Chino	*Mex.*	22
Beauty & Essex	*Amer.*	23
Blue Ribbon/Izakaya	*Japanese*	22
Boil	*Seafood*	23
Café Grumpy	*Coffee*	21
Cafe Katja	*Austrian*	25
Calexico	*Mex.*	22
Cata	*Spanish*	22
Clinton St. Baking	*Amer.*	24
Congee	*Chinese*	20
NEW Contra	*Amer.*	25
Creperie	*French*	21
NEW Dinner on Ludlow	*Amer.*	21
NEW Dirty French	*French*	—
Fat Radish	*British*	21
Freemans	*Amer.*	23
NEW Fung Tu	*Amer./Chinese*	23
General	*Asian*	22
Il Laboratorio	*Ice Cream*	25
NEW Ivan Ramen	*Japanese/Noodle Shop*	19
Katz's Deli	*Deli*	25
Kuma Inn	*Filipino/Thai*	25
Little Muenster	*Sandwiches*	21
Lobster Joint	*New Eng./Seafood*	22
Macondo	*Pan-Latin*	23
Meatball Shop	*Sandwiches*	22
Mezetto	*Med.*	23
NEW Mission Cantina	*Mex.*	20
Móle	*Mex.*	20
NEW Morgenstern's	*Ice Cream*	—
NEW Moscow 57	*Russian*	—
NEW Norman's Cay	*Carib./Seafood*	—
NEW 100 Montaditos	*Sandwiches*	20
Pàlà	*Pizza*	22
Pig and Khao	*SE Asian*	24
Prosperity Dumpling	*Chinese*	23
Rayuela	*Pan-Latin*	23
NEW Russ/Daughters Cafe	*Jewish*	—
SakaMai	*Japanese*	24
Sammy's Roumanian	*Jewish*	21
Sauce	*Italian*	23
Schiller's	*Eclectic*	17
NEW Skal	*Icelandic*	22
Stanton Social	*Eclectic*	24
Sweet Chick	*Southern*	21
Vanessa's Dumpling	*Chinese*	19
Yunnan Kitchen	*Chinese*	23

MANHATTANVILLE

Maison Harlem	*French*	21

MEATPACKING

(14th to Horatio Sts., west of Hudson St.)

Bagatelle	*French*	21
Bakehse. Bistro	*French*	21
Bubby's	*Amer.*	19
Catch	*Seafood*	23
NEW Chester	*Amer.*	—
Corsino	*Italian*	21
Dos Caminos	*Mex.*	20
Fatty Crab	*Malaysian*	22
Fig & Olive	*Med.*	21
Macelleria	*Italian/Steak*	24
Paradou	*French*	20
Serafina	*Italian*	18
Spice Market	*SE Asian*	24
Standard Grill	*Amer.*	22
STK	*Steak*	23
Valbella	*Italian*	24

MIDTOWN

30s

Abigael's	*Eclectic/Kosher*	23
Ai Fiori	*Italian*	26
Arirang Korean	*Korean/Noodle Shop*	22
Arno	*Italian*	21
Artisanal	*French*	23
Barbès	*French/Moroccan*	21
BCD Tofu	*Korean*	22
Ben's Kosher	*Deli/Kosher*	20
BonChon	*Chicken*	21
Brother Jimmy's	*BBQ*	17
Cafe China	*Chinese*	23
Café Grumpy	*Coffee*	21
Casa Nonna	*Italian*	22
Cho Dang Gol	*Korean*	24
Colbeh	*Kosher/Persian*	21
NEW David Burke Fab.	*Amer.*	—
Delmonico's	*Steak*	23
Don's Bogam	*Korean*	24

Franchia	*Korean*	25	Ça Va	*French*	22
Frankie & Johnnie's	*Steak*	23	Churrascaria	*Brazilian/Steak*	24
Friedman's Lunch	*Amer.*	21	City Lobster/Steak	*Seafood/*	21
Gahm Mi Oak	*Korean*	22		*Steak*	
Gaonnuri	*Korean*	20	Counter	*Burgers*	21
Hangawi	*Korean/Veg.*	26	db Bistro Moderne	*French*	24
Juni	*Amer.*	27	Del Frisco's	*Steak*	25
Kati Roll	*Indian*	22	Delta Grill	*Cajun/Creole*	20
Keens	*Steak*	26	Etc. Etc.	*Italian*	23
Kristalbelli	*Korean*	24	Fika	*Amer.*	21
Kum Gang San	*Korean*	21	5 Napkin Burger	*Burgers*	20
Kunjip	*Korean*	22	Forty Four	*Amer.*	21
Kyochon	*Chicken*	20	Frankie & Johnnie's	*Steak*	23
Lazzara's	*Pizza*	23	Gari	*Japanese*	26
Madangsui	*Korean*	23	Glass House	*Amer.*	20
Madison Bistro	*French*	23	Grand Sichuan	*Chinese*	19
Mandoo Bar	*Korean*	23	Gyu-Kaku	*Japanese*	22
Mercato	*Italian*	22	Hakkasan	*Chinese*	23
Miss Korea	*Korean*	20	Harry's Italian	*Italian*	21
New WonJo	*Korean*	23	Haru	*Japanese*	21
Nick & Stef's	*Steak*	22	Hatsuhana	*Japanese*	25
NEW Parker/Quinn	*Amer.*	23	Havana Central	*Cuban*	21
NEW Peacock	*British*	22	Inakaya	*Japanese*	22
Piccolo Cafe	*Coffee/Italian*	23	Joe	*Coffee*	21
Ravagh	*Persian*	23	Joe Allen	*Amer.*	18
Sarabeth's	*Amer.*	20	John's Pizzeria	*Pizza*	23
Smorgas Chef	*Scan.*	21	Junior's	*Diner*	19
Snack	*Greek*	23	Kellari Taverna	*Greek/*	22
NEW Stella 34	*Italian*	23		*Seafood*	
Sushi Sen-nin	*Japanese*	26	Koi	*Japanese*	24
Szechuan Gourmet	*Chinese*	23	Kurumazushi	*Japanese*	25
Uncle Jack's	*Steak*	24	La Masseria	*Italian*	23
Wolfgang's	*Steak*	25	Lambs Club	*Amer.*	22

40s

			La Pulperia	*Pan-Latin*	22
Akdeniz	*Turkish*	22	La Rivista	*Italian*	20
Ammos	*Greek/Seafood*	21	Lattanzi	*Italian*	23
Aureole	*Amer.*	26	Le Marais	*French/Kosher/Steak*	21
Barbetta	*Italian*	22	Le Rivage	*French*	21
Becco	*Italian*	23	Maison Kayser	*Bakery/French*	22
Benjamin Steak	*Steak*	27	Marseille	*French/Med.*	21
Blue Bottle	*Coffee*	23	Meson Sevilla	*Spanish*	22
Blue Fin	*Seafood*	23	Michael Jordan	*Steak*	21
Bobby Van's	*Steak*	23	Mont Blanc	*Austrian/Swiss*	21
Bond 45	*Italian/Steak*	19	Morton's	*Steak*	24
Bouchon Bakery	*Amer./*	23	Nizza	*French/Italian*	21
	French		Num Pang	*Cam./Sandwiches*	23
Bryant Pk Grill/Cafe	*Amer.*	18	Oceana	*Amer./Seafood*	25
Butter	*Amer.*	22	Ootoya	*Japanese/*	23
Cara Mia	*Italian*	20		*Noodle Shop*	
Carmine's	*Italian*	21	Orso	*Italian*	24
			Osteria al Doge	*Italian*	21

LOCATIONS

Oyster Bar	*Seafood*	22
Pera	*Med.*	20
Piccolo Cafe	*Coffee/Italian*	23
Pongsri Thai	*Thai*	21
Qi	*Asian/Thai*	21
Room Service	*Thai*	20
Ruby Foo's	*Asian*	19
Saju Bistro	*French*	21
Sake Bar Hagi	*Japanese*	21
Sardi's	*Continental*	19
Scarlatto	*Italian*	21
Schnipper's	*Amer.*	20
Sea Grill	*Seafood*	24
Serafina	*Italian*	18
Shake Shack	*Burgers*	21
Shorty's	*Cheestks.*	21
Shula's	*Steak*	21
STK	*Steak*	23
Strip House	*Steak*	25
Sushiden	*Japanese*	23
Sushi Zen	*Japanese*	25
Tony's Di Napoli	*Italian*	22
Trattoria Trecolori	*Italian*	21
Triomphe	*French*	24
Two Boots	*Pizza*	19
NEW Urbo	*Eclectic*	—
Utsav	*Indian*	22
Via Brasil	*Brazilian/Steak*	20
View	*Amer.*	17
Virgil's	*BBQ*	20
Vitae	*Amer.*	24
NEW Wasabi	*Japanese*	—
'Wichcraft	*Sandwiches*	19
Wolfgang's	*Steak*	25
Wu Liang Ye	*Chinese*	25
Xi'an	*Chinese/Noodle Shop*	23

50s

Abboccato	*Italian*	20
Afghan Kebab	*Afghan*	20
NEW Alfredo 100	*Italian*	—
Angelo's Pizzeria	*Pizza*	20
Aquavit	*Scan.*	26
Armani Rist.	*Italian*	24
Asiate	*Amer./Asian*	26
A Voce	*Italian*	23
Bann	*Korean*	24
Bar Americain	*Amer.*	23
NEW BarBacon	*Amer.*	22
Basso56	*Italian*	24
NEW Beautique	*Amer./*	—

French	
Benares	*Indian*	21
Benoit	*French*	23
Betony	*Amer.*	25
Bill's Food/Drink	*Amer./ Steak*	18
Bistro Milano	*Italian*	20
Blue Ribbon Sushi B&G	*Japanese*	25
Bobby Van's	*Steak*	23
Bocca/Bacco	*Italian*	20
Bombay Palace	*Indian*	21
Bottega Del Vino	*Italian*	22
Bouchon Bakery	*Amer./ French*	23
Braai	*S African*	20
Brasserie Cognac	*French*	19
Brasserie 8½	*French*	22
Brass. Ruhlmann	*French*	19
Bricco	*Italian*	20
Burger Joint	*Burgers*	23
NEW Butterfish	*Japanese/ Kosher*	—
Capital Grille	*Steak*	24
Carnegie Deli	*Deli*	23
Casa Lever	*Italian*	23
Caviar Russe	*Amer.*	21
Cellini	*Italian*	22
Chai Home	*Thai*	22
NEW Charlie Palmer	*Steak*	—
Chez Napoléon	*French*	22
China Grill	*Asian*	23
Circo	*Italian*	23
Danji	*Korean*	25
Da Tommaso	*Italian*	21
Del Frisco's	*Steak*	25
Don Antonio	*Pizza*	22
El Centro	*Mex.*	21
Empire Steak	*Steak*	22
Fig & Olive	*Med.*	21
Fika	*Coffee*	21
NEW Fogo de Chão	*Brazilian*	24
Fresco	*Italian*	22
Gallaghers	*Steak*	22
Gordon Ramsay	*French*	22
Grom	*Ice Cream*	25
Guantanamera	*Cuban*	22
Harry Cipriani	*Italian*	23
Hummus Kit.	*Kosher/Med.*	20
Il Gattopardo	*Italian*	25
Il Tinello	*Italian*	23

Ippudo | *Japanese/ Noodle Shop*	25
Island Burgers | *Burgers*	21
Joe's Shanghai | *Chinese*	22
Kashkaval | *Med.*	22
NEW Kingside | *Amer.*	19
La Bonne Soupe | *French*	20
La Grenouille | *French*	28
Landmarc | *French*	20
Lavo | *Italian*	19
Le Bernardin | *French/Seafood*	29
Le Pain Q. | *Bakery/Belgian*	18
Luke's Lobster | *Seafood*	24
Maison Kayser | *Bakery/ French*	22
Maloney & Porcelli | *Steak*	25
Má Pêche | *Amer.*	23
Marea | *Italian/Seafood*	27
Masa/Bar Masa | *Japanese*	25
Maze | *French*	19
Melt Shop | *Sandwiches*	19
Michael's | *Cal.*	22
Milos | *Greek/Seafood*	27
Modern | *Amer./French*	26
Molyvos | *Greek*	23
Monkey Bar | *Amer.*	18
NEW Mozzarella & Vino | *Italian*	22
Natsumi | *Japanese*	20
Naya | *Lebanese*	22
Nerai | *Greek*	22
Nino's | *Italian/Steak*	21
Nobu | *Japanese*	27
Nocello | *Italian*	22
Nook | *Eclectic*	23
Norma's | *Amer.*	24
No. 7 | *Sandwiches*	21
NYY Steak | *Steak*	22
Palm | *Steak*	25
Palm Court | *Amer.*	18
Patsy's | *Italian*	22
Per Se | *Amer./French*	27
Petrossian | *Cont./French*	24
PizzArte | *Pizza*	20
Plaza Food Hall | *Food Mkt.*	22
Porter House | *Steak*	26
Prime Grill | *Kosher/Steak*	24
Pure Thai | *Thai*	26
Quality Italian | *Italian/Steak*	24
Quality Meats | *Amer./Steak*	26
Radiance Tea | *Teahse.*	21
Redeye Grill | *Amer./Seafood*	19

Remi | *Italian*	23
Robert | *Amer.*	22
Rock Center Café | *Amer.*	19
Rue 57 | *French*	18
Russian Samovar | *Cont./Russian*	17
Russian Tea | *Cont./Russian*	19
Ruth's Chris | *Steak*	25
San Pietro | *Italian*	22
Seäsonal | *Austrian*	24
Serafina | *Italian*	18
Soba Nippon | *Japanese/ Noodle Shop*	22
South Gate | *Amer.*	20
Sugiyama | *Japanese*	27
SushiAnn | *Japanese*	23
Sushi Damo | *Japanese*	24
Szechuan Gourmet | *Chinese*	23
Tang Pavilion | *Chinese*	23
Tao | *Asian*	23
Tartinery | *French/Sandwiches*	23
Thalia | *Amer.*	20
Toloache | *Mex.*	23
Topaz | *Thai*	23
Totto Ramen | *Japanese/ Noodle Shop*	25
Trattoria Dell'Arte | *Italian*	22
21 Club | *Amer.*	23
Uncle Jack's | *Steak*	24
Valbella | *Italian*	24
Via Quadronno | *Italian*	21
ViceVersa | *Italian*	23
Victor's Cafe | *Cuban*	24
NEW Wayfarer | *Amer./Seafood*	18
Wondee Siam | *Thai*	21
Yakitori Totto | *Japanese*	25
Zibetto | *Coffee*	24

MORNINGSIDE HEIGHTS

Community | *Amer.*	21
Dinosaur BBQ | *BBQ*	23
Jin Ramen | *Japanese/Noodle Shop*	23
Joe | *Coffee*	21
Kitchenette | *Southern*	20
Max Caffe/SoHa | *Italian*	22
Pisticci | *Italian*	24

MURRAY HILL

(34th to 42nd Sts., east of Park Ave.)

Aji Sushi | *Japanese*	21
BareBurger | *Burgers*	21
Cibo | *Amer./Italian*	22
Docks Oyster | *Seafood*	20

LOCATIONS

El Parador	*Mex.*	22
El Pote	*Spanish*	23
Fika	*Coffee*	21
Jackson Hole	*Burgers*	20
Kajitsu	*Japanese/Veg.*	25
NEW Mayhem & Stout	*Sandwiches*	—
Num Pang	*Cam./Sandwiches*	23
Phoenix Gdn.	*Chinese*	23
Rare B&G	*Burgers*	21
Rossini's	*Italian*	22
Salvation Taco	*Mex.*	21
Sarge's Deli	*Deli/Sandwiches*	23
Sinigual	*Mex.*	21
Villa Berulia	*Italian*	25
Zengo	*Pan-Latin*	20
Zen Palate	*Asian/Veg.*	20

NOHO

(Houston to 4th Sts., Bowery to B'way)

Acme	*Amer.*	21
Aroma Kitchen	*Italian*	23
Bianca	*Italian*	21
Bohemian	*Japanese*	25
Bond St	*Japanese*	25
Five Points	*Amer./Med.*	21
Forcella	*Pizza*	21
NEW Gato	*Med.*	24
Great Jones Cafe	*Cajun*	23
Hecho en Dumbo	*Mex.*	23
Il Buco	*Italian/Med.*	26
Il Buco Alimentari	*Italian/Med.*	24
Lafayette	*French*	22
Le Philosophe	*French*	23
Mile End	*Sandwiches*	22
NoHo Star	*Amer./Asian*	19
Saxon & Parole	*Amer.*	24
Siggy's	*Med.*	23
Smile	*Med.*	22
Two Boots	*Pizza*	19

NOLITA

(Houston to Kenmare Sts., Bowery to Lafayette St.)

Balaboosta	*Med./Mideast.*	23
Bread	*Italian/Sandwiches*	20
Butcher's Daughter	*Vegan*	22
Cafe Gitane	*French/Moroccan*	23
Café Habana/Outpost	*Cuban/Mex.*	21
NEW Cherche Midi	*French*	—

Cleveland	*Amer.*	22
Emilio's Ballato	*Italian*	24
Emporio	*Italian*	24
Estela	*Amer./Med.*	25
Gimme Coffee	*Coffee*	23
Grey Dog	*Amer.*	22
Jacques	*French*	21
Lombardi's	*Pizza*	24
Musket Room	*New Zealand*	26
Parm	*Italian/Sandwiches*	24
Pearl & Ash	*Amer.*	24
Peasant	*Italian*	25
Public	*Eclectic*	25
Rubirosa	*Italian/Pizza*	25
Sant Ambroeus	*Italian*	21
Socarrat	*Spanish*	22
Tacombi/Fonda Nolita	*Mex.*	25
Taïm	*Israeli/Veg.*	25
Tartinery	*French/Sandwiches*	23
Toby's Public	*Pizza*	24
Torrisi	*Italian*	25
Uncle Boons	*Thai*	25

SOHO

(Canal to Houston Sts., 6th Ave. to Lafayette St.)

Aquagrill	*Seafood*	27
Aurora	*Italian*	24
Back Forty	*Amer.*	22
Balthazar	*French*	24
B&B Winepub	*Pub*	21
Bistro Les Amis	*French*	20
Blue Ribbon	*Amer.*	24
Blue Ribbon Sushi	*Japanese*	25
Boqueria	*Spanish*	23
NEW Chalk Point	*Amer.*	—
Charlie Bird	*Amer.*	25
Ciccio	*Italian*	—
Cipriani D'twn	*Italian*	24
Cocotte	*French*	23
Cómodo	*Latin Amer.*	25
Costata	*Italian/Steak*	25
Crosby Bar	*Eclectic*	22
David Burke Kitchen	*Amer.*	25
Dos Caminos	*Mex.*	20
Dutch	*Amer.*	23
Ed's Lobster Bar	*Seafood*	24
NEW Emmett's	*Pizza*	21
NEW Hirohisa	*Japanese*	—
Hundred Acres	*Amer.*	23
NEW Il Mulino Prime	*Italian/*	—

Steak

Isola	*Italian*	24
La Colombe	*Coffee*	24
NEW Ladurée	*Bakery/French*	24
La Esquina	*Mex.*	23
L'Ecole	*French*	23
Le Pescadeux	*Seafood*	21
NEW Little Prince	*French*	23
Lure Fishbar	*Seafood*	24
Mercer Kitchen	*Amer./French*	21
NEW Navy	*Seafood*	—
Olive's	*Sandwiches*	23
Osteria Morini	*Italian*	25
Pera	*Med.*	20
Raoul's	*French*	24
Rouge et Blanc	*French/Viet.*	23
Smile	*Med.*	22
Snack	*Greek*	23
Spring/Natural	*Health*	21
12 Chairs	*Amer./Mideast.*	22

SOUTH STREET SEAPORT

Acqua at Peck Slip	*Italian*	21
Cowgirl	*SW*	18
MarkJoseph	*Steak*	24

STUYVESANT TOWN/ PETER COOPER VILLAGE

Petite Abeille	*Belgian*	20

TRIBECA

(Barclay to Canal Sts., west of B'way)

Acappella	*Italian*	22
NEW American Cut	*Steak*	24
Atera	*Amer.*	26
Baluchi's	*Indian*	20
NEW Bâtard	*Amer./Euro.*	—
Benares	*Indian*	21
Blaue Gans	*Austrian/German*	22
Bouley	*French*	29
Brushstroke/Ichimura	*Japanese*	26
Bubby's	*Amer.*	19
Butterfly	*Amer.*	19
Cafe Noir	*African/Med.*	—
NEW China Blue	*Chinese*	18
City Hall	*Soul Food*	22
Copenhagen	*Danish/Sandwiches*	19
Distilled	*Amer.*	23
Dylan Prime	*Amer.*	18
Ecco	*Italian*	21

Fika	*Coffee*	21
Gari	*Japanese*	26
Gigino	*Italian*	20
NEW The Greek	*Greek*	21
Harrison	*Amer.*	22
Il Giglio	*Italian*	23
Jungsik	*Korean*	27
Khe-Yo	*Laotian*	24
Kitchenette	*Southern*	20
La Colombe	*Coffee*	24
Landmarc	*French*	20
Locanda Verde	*Italian*	24
NEW Los Americanos	*Pan-Latin*	—
Lotus Blue	*Chinese*	23
Macao Trading	*Chinese/Portug.*	21
Marc Forgione	*Amer.*	25
Megu	*Japanese*	23
Mehtaphor	*Eclectic*	26
Mr. Chow	*Chinese*	23
NEW Mulberry/Vine	*Amer.*	18
Ninja	*Japanese*	13
Nobu	*Japanese*	27
Odeon	*Amer./French*	20
Palm	*Steak*	25
Pepolino	*Italian*	25
Petite Abeille	*Belgian*	20
NEW Racines	*French*	—
Rosanjin	*Japanese*	26
Sarabeth's	*Amer.*	20
Sazon	*Puerto Rican*	23
Scalini Fedeli	*Italian*	26
Sushi Azabu	*Japanese*	25
NEW Tablao	*Spanish*	—
Takahachi	*Japanese*	24
Tamarind	*Indian*	26
NEW Telepan Local	*Amer.*	23
NEW Terra Tribeca	*Italian*	21
Terroir	*Italian*	20
Thalassa	*Greek/Seafood*	24
Tiny's	*Amer.*	21
Tribeca Grill	*Amer.*	22
NEW White Street	*Amer.*	—
'Wichcraft	*Sandwiches*	19
Wolfgang's	*Steak*	25
Zutto	*Japanese/Noodle Shop*	23

UNION SQUARE

(14th to 18th Sts., 5th Ave. to Irving Pl.)

Blue Water	*Seafood*	24

15 East	*Japanese*	26
Haru	*Japanese*	21
Laut	*Malaysian/Thai*	20
Olives	*Med.*	21
NEW Pavilion	*Amer.*	—
Republic	*Asian*	19
Union Sq. Cafe	*Amer.*	27

WEST 60s

Andanada 141	*Spanish*	20
Atlantic Grill	*Seafood*	22
Bar Boulud	*French*	24
Blossom	*Vegan/Veg.*	22
Boulud Sud	*Med.*	25
Cafe Fiorello	*Italian*	20
Ed's Chowder	*Seafood*	20
Gabriel's	*Italian*	22
Jean-Georges	*French*	28
Jean-Georges' Noug.	*French*	27
La Boîte en Bois	*French*	22
Leopard/des Artistes	*Italian*	22
Le Pain Q.	*Bakery/Belgian*	18
Lincoln	*Italian*	25
Luce	*Italian*	20
Nick & Toni	*Med.*	19
Picholine	*French/Med.*	26
P.J. Clarke's	*Pub*	19
Rosa Mexicano	*Mex.*	23
Sapphire Indian	*Indian*	21
Shun Lee West	*Chinese*	22
Smith	*Amer.*	19
Telepan	*Amer.*	26
'Wichcraft	*Sandwiches*	19

WEST 70s

Alice's Tea	*Teahse.*	20
Bistro Cassis	*French*	20
Brgr	*Burgers*	20
Cafe Luxembourg	*French*	21
Caffe Storico	*Italian*	22
'Cesca	*Italian*	24
Citrus B&G	*Asian/Nuevo Latino*	20
Coppola's	*Italian*	21
Dovetail	*Amer.*	27
Fika	*Coffee*	21
FishTag	*Greek/Seafood*	23
Gari	*Japanese*	26
Gazala's	*Mideast.*	22
Grand Sichuan	*Chinese*	19
Gray's Papaya	*Hot Dogs*	22
Hummus Pl.	*Israeli/Kosher/Veg.*	21

Isabella's	*Amer./Med.*	20
Legend	*Chinese*	20
Le Pain Q.	*Bakery/Belgian*	18
Nice Matin	*French/Med.*	19
Ocean Grill	*Seafood*	23
Pappardella	*Italian*	20
Pasha	*Turkish*	20
Patsy's	*Pizza*	21
Piccolo Cafe	*Coffee/Italian*	23
Pomodoro Rosso	*Italian*	21
Salumeria/Rist. Rosi	*Italian*	24
Saravanaa Bhavan	*Indian/Veg.*	23
Scaletta	*Italian*	22
Serafina	*Italian*	18
Shake Shack	*Burgers*	21
Tenzan	*Japanese*	20
Tessa	*Med.*	—
Tolani	*Eclectic*	21

WEST 80s

Barney Greengrass	*Deli*	24
B. Café	*Belgian*	21
Bodrum	*Med./Turkish*	20
Brother Jimmy's	*BBQ*	17
Bustan	*Med.*	25
Cafe Con Leche	*Cuban/Domin.*	20
Cafe Lalo	*Coffee/Dessert*	20
Calle Ocho	*Nuevo Latino*	20
Candle Cafe	*Vegan/Veg.*	23
Celeste	*Italian*	24
Cotta	*Italian*	22
5 Napkin Burger	*Burgers*	20
Flor/Mayo	*Chinese/Peruvian*	21
Good Enough/Eat	*Amer.*	20
Haru	*Japanese*	21
Hummus Kit.	*Kosher/Med.*	20
Island Burgers	*Burgers*	21
Jackson Hole	*Burgers*	20
Jacob's Pickles	*Southern*	21
Joe	*Coffee*	21
Kefi	*Greek*	23
Land Thai	*Thai*	22
Luke's Lobster	*Seafood*	24
Machiavelli	*Italian*	23
Meatball Shop	*Sandwiches*	22
Mermaid	*Seafood*	22
Momoya	*Japanese*	22
Oaxaca	*Mex.*	21
Ouest	*Amer.*	22
Peacefood Café	*Kosher/ Vegan/Veg.*	23

Sarabeth's | *Amer.*	20
Spice | *Thai*	21
Spiga | *Italian*	22
Spring/Natural | *Health*	21
Tarallucci | *Italian*	20

WEST 90s

Carmine's | *Italian*	21
Gennaro | *Italian*	26
Indus Valley | *Indian*	23
Kouzan | *Japanese*	22
Malecon | *Dominican*	20
Numero 28 | *Pizza*	23
Pio Pio | *Peruvian*	22
Tratt. Pesce | *Italian/Seafood*	20
Two Boots | *Pizza*	19

WEST 100s

A Cafe/Wine Rm. | *Carib./French*	24
Awash | *Ethiopian*	21
Cascabel Taqueria | *Mex.*	19
Ellington | *Pub*	16
Flor/Mayo | *Chinese/Peruvian*	21
Legend | *Chinese*	20
Miss Mamie/Maude | *Soul Food/Southern*	21
107 West | *Eclectic*	20
Szechuan Gourmet | *Chinese*	23
Thai Market | *Thai*	23
Wondee Siam | *Thai*	21
Xi'an | *Chinese/Noodle Shop*	23

WEST VILLAGE

(14th to Houston Sts., west of 6th Ave., excluding Meatpacking)

Annisa | *Amer.*	28
A.O.C. | *French*	20
A Salt & Battery | *British*	22
NEW Bar Bolonat | *Israeli/Mideast.*	—
Barbuto | *Italian*	26
Barraca | *Spanish*	21
Beatrice Inn | *Amer.*	20
Bell Book/Candle | *Amer.*	23
Big Gay Ice Cream | *Ice Cream*	23
Blossom | *Vegan/Veg.*	22
Blue Ribbon Bakery | *Amer.*	23
Bobo | *French*	24
Bosie Tea Parlor | *Teahse.*	23
Bread To Go | *Italian/Sandwiches*	20
Buvette | *French*	24
Cafe Asean | *SE Asian*	22

Cafe Cluny | *Amer./French*	21
Cafe Espanol | *Spanish*	21
Cafe Gitane | *French/Moroccan*	23
Cafe Loup | *French*	19
NEW Clam | *Seafood*	23
Commerce | *Amer.*	23
Cones | *Ice Cream*	24
Cornelia St. | *Amer./French*	20
Corner Bistro | *Burgers*	22
Cowgirl | *SW*	18
Crispo | *Italian*	24
NEW Decoy | *Chinese*	—
Dell'anima | *Italian*	25
Do Hwa | *Korean*	22
Dos Toros | *Mex.*	20
El Charro Espanol | *Spanish*	23
El Toro Blanco | *Mex./Seafood*	22
Empellón | *Mex.*	23
EN Japanese | *Japanese*	25
Extra Virgin | *Med.*	23
Fedora | *Amer./French*	22
Fish | *Seafood*	23
Flex Mussels | *Seafood*	24
Frankies | *Italian*	23
Gobo | *Vegan/Veg.*	22
Good | *Amer.*	22
Gradisca | *Italian*	23
Grand Sichuan | *Chinese*	19
Grey Dog | *Amer.*	22
Hakata Tonton | *Japanese*	23
NEW Hamilton's Soda | *Diner*	—
Havana Alma | *Cuban*	22
Hudson Clearwater | *Amer.*	22
Hummus Pl. | *Israeli/Kosher/Veg.*	21
I Sodi | *Italian*	25
Jeanne & Gaston | *French*	24
Jeffrey's Grocery | *Amer.*	23
Joe | *Coffee*	21
Joe's Pizza | *Pizza*	24
John's Pizzeria | *Pizza*	23
Joseph Leonard | *Amer.*	24
Keste Pizza | *Pizza*	23
Kin Shop | *Thai*	22
L'Artusi | *Italian*	26
Las Ramblas | *Spanish*	23
Left Bank | *Amer.*	24
Le Gigot | *French*	24
Little Owl | *Amer./Med.*	27
Louro | *Amer./Portug.*	26
Malatesta | *Italian*	24

Market Table	*Amer.*	24	Wallsé	*Austrian*	25
Marrow	*German/Italian*	22	Waverly Inn	*Amer.*	22
Mary's Fish	*Seafood*	25	Westville	*Amer.*	23
Mas	*Amer.*	27	Whitehall	*British*	21
Meatball Shop	*Sandwiches*	22	Wild	*Amer./Pizza*	–
Mémé	*Med./Moroccan*	23	Yerba Buena	*Pan-Latin*	22
Mercadito	*Mex.*	22		

Bronx

Mighty Quinn's	*BBQ*	26
Móle	*Mex.*	20

ARTHUR AVENUE/ BELMONT

Monument Lane	*Amer.*	22
Morandi	*Italian*	22
Moustache	*Mideast.*	22
Murray's Cheese Bar	*Amer.*	23

Ann & Tony's	*Italian*	21
Dominick's	*Italian*	23
Emilia's	*Italian*	23
Enzo's	*Italian*	25
Mario's	*Italian*	22
Roberto	*Italian*	27
Tra Di Noi	*Italian*	25
Zero Otto	*Italian/Pizza*	23

Numero 28	*Pizza*	23
Oaxaca	*Mex.*	21
Ofrenda	*Mex.*	21
One if by Land	*Amer.*	23
NEW Pagani	*Italian*	21
Palma	*Italian*	25
Pearl Oyster	*New Eng./Seafood*	27
Perilla	*Amer.*	24

BRONX PARK

NEW Pine Tree Cafe	*Amer.*	–

CITY ISLAND

Artie's	*Seafood/Steak*	22
Black Whale	*Amer.*	23
City Is. Lobster	*Seafood*	22
Sammy's Fishbox	*Seafood*	21
Sammy's Shrimp	*Seafood*	23

Perry St.	*Amer.*	26
Philip Marie	*Amer.*	19
Piccolo Angolo	*Italian*	25
NEW Piora	*Amer.*	26
NEW Pizzetteria Brunetti	*Pizza*	26

CONCOURSE/DOWNTOWN

NYY Steak	*Steak*	22

FIELDSTON

Jake's Steakhse.	*Steak*	23

Place	*Amer./Med.*	23
Pó	*Italian*	25
Recette	*Amer.*	24
RedFarm	*Chinese*	25
Risotteria	*Italian*	21
Rosemary's	*Italian*	22
Sammy's Noodle Shop	*Chinese/ Noodle Shop*	20

KINGSBRIDGE

Malecon	*Dominican*	20

MORRIS PARK

Enzo's	*Italian*	25
Patricia's	*Italian*	25

Sant Ambroeus	*Italian*	21
Sevilla	*Spanish*	24
Snack	*Greek*	23
Soto	*Japanese*	26
Spotted Pig	*Euro.*	24
Spunto	*Pizza*	22
NEW Sushi Nakazawa	*Japanese*	27

MOTT HAVEN

Pio Pio	*Peruvian*	22

RIVERDALE

Beccofino	*Italian*	24
Liebman's	*Deli/Kosher*	22
Madison's	*Italian*	21

Sweet Revenge	*Dessert*	22
Swine	*Amer.*	20
Taïm	*Israeli/Veg.*	25
Takashi	*Japanese*	27
Tartine	*French*	22
Tea & Sympathy	*Teahse.*	21
Tertulia	*Spanish*	24
Tratt. Pesce	*Italian/Seafood*	20
Two Boots	*Pizza*	19

VAN NEST

F & J Pine	*Italian*	23

WAKEFIELD

Ali's Roti	*Carib.*	24

More on zagat.com

Brooklyn

BATH BEACH

Nyonya | *Malaysian* — 23
Tommaso | *Italian* — 23

BAY RIDGE

Areo | *Italian* — 24
Arirang Hibachi | *Japanese* — 23
Burger Bistro | *Burgers* — 21
Cebu | *Continental* — 20
Chadwick's | *Amer.* — 23
Eliá | *Greek* — 26
Embers | *Steak* — 23
Fushimi | *Japanese* — 23
Gino's | *Itallan* — 23
Omonia | *Coffee/Greek* — 22
101 | *Amer./Italian* — 21
Pearl Room | *Seafood* — 22
Tanoreen | *Med./Mideast.* — 27
Tuscany Grill | *Italian* — 25
Vesuvio | *Italian* — 22

BEDFORD-STUYVESANT

Ali's Roti | *Carib.* — 24
Do or Dine | *Eclectic* — 23
Oaxaca | *Mex.* — 21
Peaches | *Southern* — 25
Saraghina | *Pizza* — 25

BENSONHURST

Tenzan | *Japanese* — 20

BOERUM HILL

Battersby | *Amer.* — 27
Blue Bottle | *Coffee* — 23
Coco Roco | *Peruvian* — 21
NEW French Louie | *Amer./French* — 26
Mile End | *Deli* — 22
Rucola | *Italian* — 25
Spice | *Thai* — 21
Van Leeuwen | *Coffee/Ice Cream* — 24

BRIGHTON BEACH

Tatiana | *Russian* — 18

BROOKLYN HEIGHTS

Ample Hills | *Ice Cream* — 27
ChipShop | *British* — 20
Colonie | *Amer.* — 24
Fornino | *Pizza* — 23
Hanco's | *Veg.* — 21
Henry's End | *Amer.* — 24

Jack the Horse | *Amer.* — 21
Luzzo's | *Pizza* — 25
Noodle Pudding | *Italian* — 23
Queen | *Italian* — 23
Red Gravy | *Italian* — 23
Siggy's | *Med.* — 23

BUSHWICK

Blanca | *Amer.* — 24
NEW Bunna Cafe | *Ethiopian/ Vegan* — —
Fritzl's Lunch | *Amer.* — —
Momo Sushi Shack | *Japanese* — 26
NEW Montana's Trail | *Southern* — —
Northeast Kingdom | *Amer.* — 25
Roberta's | *Italian/Pizza* — 26
NEW Shinobi | *Japanese/ Noodle Shop* — —

CARROLL GARDENS

Bergen Hill | *Seafood* — —
Brooklyn Farmacy | *Ice Cream* — 22
Buttermilk | *Amer.* — 25
NEW Dosa Royale | *Indian* — 24
NEW Dover | *Amer.* — 27
Fragole | *Italian* — 22
Frankies | *Italian* — 23
Grocery | *Amer.* — 27
Lucali | *Pizza* — 27
Marco Polo | *Italian* — 23
Nightingale 9 | *Veg.* — 23
Prime Meats | *Amer./Steak* — 24
NEW Wilma Jean | *Southern* — —
Zaytoons | *Mideast.* — 21

CLINTON HILL

Aita | *Italian* — 25
NEW Emily | *Pizza* — —
Locanda Vini | *Italian* — 25
NEW Runner | *Amer.* — —
Speedy Romeo | *Italian/Pizza* — 23
Zaytoons | *Mideast.* — 21

COBBLE HILL

Awash | *Ethiopian* — 21
Bar Tabac | *French* — 20
Blue Marble | *Ice Cream* — 21
Bocca Lupo | *Italian* — 22
Brucie | *Italian* — 20
Cafe Luluc | *French* — 22
Char No. 4 | *Southern* — 22
Chocolate Room | *Dessert* — 24
Hanco's | *Veg.* — 21

Hibino	Japanese	25
Joya	Thai	24
Ki Sushi	Japanese	26
La Vara	Spanish	26
Watty & Meg	Amer.	20
Wild Ginger	Asian/Vegan	22

COLUMBIA STREET WATERFRONT DISTRICT

Alma	Mex.	20
Calexico	Mex.	22
Petite Crevette	French/Seafood	23
Pok Pok Ny	Thai	24

CONEY ISLAND

Gargiulo's	Italian	22
Grimaldi's	Pizza	22
Tom's	Diner	17
Totonno Pizza	Pizza	26

CROWN HEIGHTS

Ali's Roti	Carib.	24
NEW Berg'n	Food Mkt.	—
Chavela's	Mex.	24
NEW Glady's	Carib.	—
Mayfield	Amer.	24
Mighty Quinn's	BBQ	26
NEW Pacifico's	Amer.	—

DITMAS PARK

Am Thai	Thai	23
Farm/Adderley	Amer.	23
NEW Lea	Italian/Pizza	—
Mimi's Hummus	Mideast.	25
Purple Yam	Asian	23
Wheated	Pizza	21

DOWNTOWN BROOKLYN

Bacchus	French	21
Chef's/Brooklyn Fare	French	28
Ganso	Japanese/Noodle Shop	23
Hill Country	BBQ	23
Hill Country Chicken	Southern	20
Junior's	Diner	19
Shake Shack	Burgers	21

DUMBO

Atrium Dumbo	Amer.	23
Brooklyn Ice Cream	Ice Cream	24
Gran Electrica	Mex.	22
Grimaldi's	Pizza	22
Juliana's	Pizza	26
Luke's Lobster	Seafood	24

No. 7	Sandwiches	21
River Café	Amer.	26
Shake Shack	Burgers	21
Smorgasburg	Food Mkt.	25
Superfine	Med.	19

FLATLANDS

| Mill Basin Deli | Deli/Kosher | 24 |

FORT GREENE

Berlyn	German	22
Café Habana/Outpost	Cuban/Mex.	21
NEW Café Paulette	French	—
Caffe e Vino	Italian	22
NEW Colonia Verde	Latin Amer.	—
Dino	Italian	20
General Greene	Amer.	20
Lulu & Po	Amer.	25
Madiba	S African	24
Martha	Amer.	22
No. 7	Amer.	21
Olea	Med.	24
Prospect	Amer.	23
Roman's	Italian	24
67 Burger	Burgers	22
Smoke Joint	BBQ	23
Stonehome	Amer.	21
Walter	Amer.	22

GOWANUS

Ample Hills	Ice Cream	27
Dinosaur BBQ	BBQ	23
Fletcher's	BBQ	20
Littleneck	Seafood	23
Oaxaca	Mex.	21
NEW Pickle Shack	Amer.	—
Pines	Amer.	21
Runner & Stone	Amer./Bakery	22
NEW 2 Duck Goose	Chinese	—

GRAVESEND

| Fiorentino's | Italian | 23 |
| Spumoni Gdn. | Ice Cream/Pizza | 23 |

GREENPOINT

Brooklyn Ice Cream	Ice Cream	24
Café Grumpy	Coffee	21
Calexico	Mex.	22
Five Leaves	Amer.	24
Fornino	Pizza	23
NEW Glasserie	Med.	24
NEW Greenpt Fish	Seafood	—

Le Gamin | *French*	21
Littleneck | *Seafood*	23
Lobster Joint | *New Eng./Seafood*	22
Lomzynianka | *Polish*	25
NEW Lucky Luna | *Chinese/Mex.*	—
Luksus | *Amer.*	23
No. 7 | *Sandwiches*	21
Paulie Gee's | *Pizza*	27
NEW Raizes Churrascaria | *Portug./Seafood*	—
River Styx | *Amer.*	—
Scalino | *Italian*	23
Van Leeuwen | *Coffee/Ice Cream*	24

GREENWOOD HEIGHTS

Toby's Public | *Pizza*	24

KENSINGTON

Am Thai | *Thai*	23

MIDWOOD

Di Fara | *Pizza*	25

MILL BASIN

La Villa Pizzeria | *Pizza*	22

PARK SLOPE

Alchemy | *Amer.*	20
Al Di La | *Italian*	26
A.O.C. | *French*	20
Applewood | *Amer.*	24
Baluchi's | *Indian*	20
BareBurger | *Burgers*	21
Bark | *Hot Dogs*	20
Bar Toto | *Italian*	21
Benchmark | *Amer./Steak*	21
Blue Ribbon | *Amer.*	24
Bogota | *Pan-Latin*	24
Bonnie's Grill | *Burgers*	22
Burger Bistro | *Burgers*	21
Café Grumpy | *Coffee*	21
Calexico | *Mex.*	22
ChipShop | *British*	20
Coco Roco | *Peruvian*	21
Conviv. Osteria | *Med.*	26
Flatbush Farm | *Amer.*	21
Fonda | *Mex.*	24
Franny's | *Italian/Pizza*	25
Hanco's | *Veg.*	21
Juventino | *Amer.*	26
L'Albero/Gelati | *Ice Cream*	23
La Villa Pizzeria | *Pizza*	22
Lot 2 | *Amer.*	24

Miriam | *Israeli/Med.*	23
Moim | *Korean*	23
Okeanos | *Greek*	22
Oyster Bar | *Seafood*	22
Palo Santo | *Pan-Latin*	23
Pork Slope | *BBQ*	19
Rose Water | *Amer.*	25
Scalino | *Italian*	23
Scottadito | *Italian*	22
Shake Shack | *Burgers*	21
Sheep Station | *Australian*	22
67 Burger | *Burgers*	22
sNice | *Sandwiches/Veg.*	21
Soigne | *Amer.*	22
Song | *Thai*	22
Spice | *Thai*	21
Stone Park | *Amer.*	24
NEW Sushi Katsuei | *Japanese*	—
NEW Taco Santo | *Mex.*	—
Talde | *Asian*	25
Taro Sushi | *Japanese*	24
Thistle Hill | *Amer.*	21
12th St. B&G | *Amer.*	21

PROSPECT HEIGHTS

Amorina | *Italian/Pizza*	23
Ample Hills | *Ice Cream*	27
NEW Bar Chuko | *Japanese*	—
Bar Corvo | *Italian*	24
Blue Marble | *Ice Cream*	21
Cheryl's Global | *Soul Food*	23
Chick P | *Israeli/Sandwiches*	—
Chuko | *Japanese/Noodle Shop*	27
James | *Amer.*	23
Kaz an Nou | *Caribb./French*	22
Le Gamin | *French*	21
NEW Marco's | *Italian*	24
NEW Milk River | *Asian/Carib.*	22
Morgans BBQ | *BBQ*	22
PeteZaaz | *Pizza*	25
NEW Saul | *Amer.*	23
606 R&D | *Amer.*	23
Sunshine Co. | *Amer.*	22
Tom's | *Diner*	17
Vanderbilt | *Amer.*	21
Zaytoons | *Mideast.*	21

PROSPECT LEFFERTS GARDENS

Ali's Roti | *Carib.*	24

LOCATIONS

RED HOOK

Brooklyn Crab	*Seafood*	20
Defonte's	*Sandwiches*	24
Fort Defiance	*Amer.*	23
Good Fork	*Eclectic*	23
NEW Grindhaus	*Amer.*	—
NEW Hometown	*BBQ*	—
Hope & Anchor	*Diner*	21
Red Hook Lobster	*Seafood*	24

SHEEPSHEAD BAY

Brennan	*Sandwiches*	23
Jordans Lobster	*Seafood*	22
Randazzo's	*Seafood*	22
Roll-n-Roaster	*Sandwiches*	22
Sahara	*Turkish*	23
Taci's Beyti	*Turkish*	24

SUNSET PARK

Nyonya	*Malaysian*	23
Pacificana	*Chinese*	24

VINEGAR HILL

Vinegar Hill Hse.	*Amer.*	24

WILLIAMSBURG

Acqua Santa	*Italian*	22
Allswell	*Amer.*	22
Antica Pesa	*Italian*	23
Aurora	*Italian*	24
Bamonte's	*Italian*	23
Best Pizza	*Pizza*	24
Blue Bottle	*Coffee*	23
BrisketTown	*BBQ*	24
Brooklyn Star	*Southern*	24
Cafe Mogador	*Moroccan*	24
Caracas	*Veg.*	26
NEW Cerveceria	*Mex.*	—
Chai Home	*Thai*	22
NEW Cherry Izakaya	*Japanese*	—
Crif Dogs	*Hot Dogs*	23
Diner	*Amer.*	23
Dos Toros	*Mex.*	20
DuMont Burger	*Burgers*	21
Egg	*Southern*	23
Elm	*French*	25
Fette Sau	*BBQ*	26
Forcella	*Pizza*	21
Fornino	*Pizza*	23
Fushimi	*Japanese*	23
Gimme Coffee	*Coffee*	23

NEW Gorbals	*Eclectic*	—
NEW Humboldt/Jackson	*Amer.*	—
Isa	*Med.*	22
La Esquina	*Mex.*	23
La Superior	*Mex.*	23
Lodge	*Amer.*	22
Mable's Smokehse.	*BBQ*	23
Marlow/Sons	*Amer.*	24
NEW Meadowsweet	*Amer./ Med.*	—
Meatball Shop	*Sandwiches*	22
Meat Hook Sandwich	*Sandwiches*	—
Mesa Coyoacan	*Mex.*	25
Móle	*Mex.*	20
Motorino	*Pizza*	24
1 or 8	*Japanese*	24
NEW Okonomi	*Japanese*	—
NEW Onomea	*Hawaiian*	—
Oslo Coffee	*Coffee*	23
Oslo Coffee	*Coffee*	23
Peter Luger	*Steak*	28
Pies-N-Thighs	*Southern*	24
Potlikker	*Amer.*	22
Qi	*Asian/Thai*	21
Reynard	*Amer.*	23
Roebling Tea Room	*Amer.*	21
Rye	*Amer.*	24
Samurai Mama	*Japanese*	24
Sea	*Thai*	23
NEW Shalom Japan	*Japanese/ Jewish*	25
Smorgasburg	*Food Mkt.*	25
St. Anselm	*Amer./Steak*	28
Sweet Chick	*Southern*	21
Sweetleaf	*Coffee*	22
Toby's Estate	*Coffee*	22
Traif	*Eclectic*	26
Vanessa's Dumpling	*Chinese*	19
Walter	*Amer.*	22
Wild	*Amer./Pizza*	—
Wild Ginger	*Asian/Vegan*	22
Xi'an	*Chinese/Noodle Shop*	23
Xixa	*Mex.*	25
Zenkichi	*Japanese*	27
Zizi Limona	*Med./Mideast.*	24
NEW Zona Rosa	*Mex.*	23

WINDSOR TERRACE

NEW Krupa	*Amer.*	—

Queens

ASTORIA

Agnanti	*Greek*	23
Arepas	*Veg.*	23
Astor Room	*Amer.*	20
Bahari Estiatorio	*Greek*	26
BareBurger	*Burgers*	21
Butcher Bar	*BBQ*	21
Cávo	*Greek*	22
Christos	*Steak*	22
Elias Corner	*Greek/Seafood*	26
Il Bambino	*Italian*	25
Locale	*Italian*	21
Loukoumi	*Greek*	25
MP Taverna	*Greek*	24
Omonia	*Coffee/Greek*	22
Ovelia	*Greek*	21
Pachanga Patterson	*Mex.*	23
Piccola Venezia	*Italian*	25
Ponticello	*Italian*	23
Queens Comfort	*Southern*	22
Queens Kickshaw	*Coffee/ Sandwiches*	21
Sanford's	*Amer.*	24
Seva Indian	*Indian*	25
S Prime	*Steak*	23
Stamatis	*Greek*	24
Taverna Kyclades	*Greek/ Seafood*	26
Telly's Taverna	*Greek/Seafood*	22
Tratt. L'incontro	*Italian*	26
Vesta	*Italian*	25

BAYSIDE

BareBurger	*Burgers*	21
Ben's Kosher	*Deli/Kosher*	20
BonChon	*Chicken*	21
Donovan's	*Amer.*	21
Erawan	*Thai*	22
Jackson Hole	*Burgers*	20
Press 195	*Sandwiches*	23
Ralph's Famous	*Ice Cream*	24
Uncle Jack's	*Steak*	24

CORONA

Lemon Ice King	*Ice Cream*	25
Leo's Latticini/Corona	*Italian/ Sandwiches*	26
Park Side	*Italian*	25
Tortilleria Nixtamal	*Mex.*	25

DOUGLASTON

Grimaldi's	*Pizza*	22

EAST ELMHURST

Jackson Hole	*Burgers*	20

ELMHURST

Ayada	*Thai*	25
Pho Bang	*Noodle Shop/Viet.*	21
Ping's Seafood	*Chinese/Seafood*	20
Zabb Elee	*Thai*	22

FLUSHING

Biang!	*Chinese/Noodle Shop*	25
Joe's Shanghai	*Chinese*	22
Kum Gang San	*Korean*	21
Kyochon	*Chicken*	20
La Baraka	*French*	23
NEW Little Lamb	*Mongolian*	–
New Imperial Palace	*Chinese*	22
Pho Bang	*Noodle Shop/Viet.*	21
Sik Gaek	*Korean*	22
Spicy & Tasty	*Chinese*	24
Szechuan Gourmet	*Chinese*	23
Xi'an	*Chinese/Noodle Shop*	23

FOREST HILLS

Alberto	*Italian*	25
Baluchi's	*Indian*	20
BareBurger	*Burgers*	21
Cabana	*Nuevo Latino*	22
Danny Brown	*Euro.*	26
Dee's	*Med./Pizza*	23
Eddie's Sweet Shop	*Ice Cream*	24
Grand Sichuan	*Chinese*	19
La Vigna	*Italian*	24
Nick's	*Pizza*	23

GLEN OAKS

Ralph's Famous	*Ice Cream*	24

GLENDALE

Zum Stammtisch	*German*	23

HOWARD BEACH

La Villa Pizzeria	*Pizza*	22

JACKSON HEIGHTS

Jackson Diner	*Indian*	21
Pio Pio	*Peruvian*	22

LONG ISLAND CITY

Alobar	*Amer.*	22
Bella Via	*Italian*	22

Café Henri | *French* 22
Casa Enrique | *Mex.* 24
Corner Bistro | *Burgers* 22
NEW Dutch Kills Centraal | *Amer.* 21
Hibino | *Japanese* 25
John Brown Smokehse. | *BBQ* 25
LIC Market | *Amer.* 25
Manducatis | *Italian* 22
Manetta's | *Italian* 24
M. Wells Dinette | *Québécois* 24
NEW M. Wells Steakhse. | *Steak* 22
Shi | *Asian* 22
Spice | *Thai* 21
Sweetleaf | *Coffee* 22
Tournesol | *French* 23
Water's Edge | *Amer./Seafood* 22

MIDDLE VILLAGE

London Lennie's | *Seafood* 24
Pio Pio | *Peruvian* 22

REGO PARK

Barosa | *Italian* 23
Ben's Best | *Deli/Kosher* 24

RIDGEWOOD

Bunker Viet. | *Veg.* 25

ROCKAWAY BEACH

Caracas | *Veg.* 26

SOUTH OZONE PARK

Don Peppe | *Italian* 25

SUNNYSIDE

Salt & Fat | *Amer./Asian* 25
Sik Gaek | *Korean* 22

WHITESTONE

Ralph's Famous | *Ice Cream* 24

WILLETS POINT

Leo's Latticini/Corona | *Italian/* 26
Sandwiches
Shake Shack | *Burgers* 21

WOODSIDE

Donovan's | *Amer.* 21
Sripraphai | *Thai* 27

Staten Island

ARDEN HEIGHTS

Ralph's Famous | *Ice Cream* 24

CASTLETON CORNERS

Joe & Pat's | *Italian/Pizza* 25

DONGAN HILLS

Tratt. Romana | *Italian* 24

ELM PARK

Denino's | *Pizza* 26
Ralph's Famous | *Ice Cream* 24

ELTINGVILLE

Ralph's Famous | *Ice Cream* 24

GRANT CITY

Fushimi | *Japanese* 23

GREAT KILLS

Arirang Hibachi | *Japanese* 23
Cole's Dock Side | *Seafood* 23

NEW DORP

Ralph's Famous | *Ice Cream* 24

NEW SPRINGVILLE

East Pacific | *Asian* 24

OLD TOWN

Bocelli | *Italian/Seafood* 25

PRINCE'S BAY

Ralph's Famous | *Ice Cream* 24

ROSEBANK

Bayou | *Cajun* 24

SHORE ACRES

Da Noi | *Italian* 25

SOUTH BEACH

South Fin Grill | *Seafood* 19

ST. GEORGE

Beso | *Spanish* 25

TODT HILL

Carol's Cafe | *Eclectic* 24

TOTTENVILLE

Angelina's | *Italian* 23
Da Nico | *Italian* 21
Nucci's | *Italian* 23

TRAVIS-CHELSEA

Da Noi | *Italian* 25

WEST BRIGHTON

Nucci's | *Italian* 23

ZAGAT
2015

New York City Map

Most Popular Restaurants

Map coordinates follow each name.

1 Gramercy Tavern (F-4)

2 Le Bernardin (D-3)

3 5 Napkin Burger (A-2, E-2, G-4)

4 Shake Shack† (A-4, B-2, F-4)

5 Peter Luger (H-7)

6 Union Square Cafe (G-4)

7 ABC Kitchen (G-4)

8 Gotham Bar & Grill (G-4)

9 Jean-Georges (C-2)

10 Bouley (I-3)

11 Daniel (C-4)

12 Rosa Mexicano (C-2, C-5, G-4)

13 21 Club (D-3)

14 2nd Ave Deli (B-5, E-4)

15 Atlantic Grill (B-4, C-2)

16 Marea (C-3)

17 Babbo (H-3)

18 Katz's Deli (H-5)

19 Capital Grille (D-3, E-4, J-4)

20 The Palm (D-3, E-4, J-3)

21 La Grenouille (D-4)

22 Balthazar (H-4)

23 Eleven Madison Park (F-4)

24 Del Posto (G-2)

25 Becco (D-2)

26 Carmine's (A-2, E-3)

27 Del Frisco's (D-3)

28 Per Se (C-2)

29 Jean-Georges' Nougatine (C-2)

30 Telepan (C-2)

31 BareBurger† (B-5, E-4, G-2)

32 Eataly (F-3)

33 Four Seasons (D-4)

34 The Modern* (D-3)

35 Blue Water Grill (G-4)

36 Café Boulud (B-4)

37 Nobu (D-3, I-3)

38 Aquagrill (H-3)

39 Bar Boulud* (C-2)

40 Il Mulino (C-4, H-3, H-4)

41 A Voce (C-2, F-4)

42 Boulud Sud (C-2)

43 Ai Fiori (E-3)

44 Fig & Olive (C-4, D-4, G-2)

45 Carnegie Deli (D-3)

46 Keens (E-3)

47 Wolfgang's (D-4, E-3, E-4, I-3)

48 Bobby Van's† (D-4, E-3, J-4)

49 Lincoln (C-2)

50 Dinosaur Bar-B-Que (A-1, K-6)

---

*Indicates tie with above   † Additional branches not plotted